D1200918

The Discovery of Freedom in Ancient Greece

The Discovery of Freedom in Ancient Greece

KURT RAAFLAUB

FIRST ENGLISH EDITION,
REVISED AND UPDATED FROM THE GERMAN

TRANSLATION BY RENATE FRANCISCONO
Revised by the Author

The University of Chicago Press
Chicago and London

Kurt Raaflaub is professor of classics and history at Brown University. He is the co-editor of *Between Republic and Empire, City-States in Classical Antiquity and Medieval Italy,* and *Democracy, Empire, and the Arts in Fifth-Century Athens.*

The University of Chicago Press, Chicago 60637
The University of Chicago Press, Ltd., London
© 2004 by The University of Chicago
All rights reserved. Published 2004
Printed in the United States of America
13 12 11 10 09 08 07 06 05 04   5 4 3 2 1

ISBN (cloth): 0-226-70101-8

Originally published as *Die Entdeckung der Freiheit: Zur historischen Semantik und Gesellschaftsgeschichte eines politischen Grundbegriffes der Griechen,* © C. H. Beck'sche Verlagsbuchhandlung (Oscar Beck), München 1985.

Library of Congress Cataloging-in-Publication Data

Raaflaub, Kurt A.
    [Entdeckung der Freiheit. English]
    The discovery of freedom in ancient Greece / Kurt Raaflaub—1st English ed.,
rev. and updated from the German / translation by Renate Franciscono ; revised
by the author.
        p.   cm.
    "Originally published as Die Entdeckung der Freiheit: zur historischen
Semantik und Gesellschaftsgeschichte eines politischen Grundbegriffes der
Griechen, © C. H. Beck'sche Verlagsbuchhandlung (Oscar Beck), München
1985"—Verso t.p.
    Includes bibliographical references and index.
    ISBN 0-226-70101-8 (cloth : alk. paper)
    1. Liberty—History.   2. Political science—Greece—History.   I. Title.
JC599.G73 R3313   2004
323.44'0938—dc21

                                                      2003012786

⊚ The paper used in this publication meets the minimum requirements of the
American National Standard for Information Sciences—Permanence of Paper for
Printed Library Materials, ANSI Z39.48-1992.

To Debby

Contents

Preface

The first edition of this book (*Die Entdeckung der Freiheit: Zur historischen Semantik und Gesellschaftsgeschichte eines politischen Grundbegriffs der Griechen*), published in 1985, was a revised version of my *Habilitationsschrift*, defended at the Freie Universität in Berlin in 1979. I began thinking of this project even much earlier, while teaching at a secondary school and holding a part-time position as an assistant at the Institute for Ancient History at the University of Basel. Christian Meier, who had been my dissertation advisor, urged me to pursue it. From him I learned much about the methodology I adopted in this study. My debt to him will be visible throughout, and my gratitude for his advice, encouragement, and friendship cannot be expressed in a few words. The other scholar whose work, especially on Greek social terminology, helped shape my views, is M. I. Finley. His positive reaction to some of my publications was most gratifying.

In Berlin, then a divided city, the topic was especially meaningful. In completing the first draft of the book, discussions with my colleagues in the Institute for Ancient History at the Freie Universität were especially helpful. I single out two names. Jürgen Deininger's lively interest in my ideas and his pointed questions forced me to persist in "digging deeper" than I might have done otherwise; together with Alexander Demandt and Hartmut Galsterer, he served as a referee for my *Habilitation*. Daily conversations with Walter Eder, with whom I shared an office for five years, and his detailed criticism of several chapters helped advance my understanding of many issues.

The book was revised for publication at Brown University in Providence, where I moved in 1978, and was completed in the fall of 1983, twenty years ago. Earlier, in 1976–77, a Junior Fellowship at the Center for Hellenic Studies in Washington, D.C., had offered me the leisure to complete a preliminary study, published in 1981, and to embark on a book-length treatment of the subject. In 1992, my wife, Deborah Boedeker, and I returned to the Center as its directors, where we served in that capacity until 2000. Toward the end of this period, I began the task of revising and updating the book for a new edition, in English, which many friends and colleagues had urged me to prepare. Renate Franciscono's translation served as a useful foundation. I thank her and apologize that my urge to reformulate and rethink compelled me to change so much of her text. I am grateful to the Kommission für Alte Geschichte und Epigraphik of the German Archaeological Institute for accepting the first edition for its monograph series, Vestigia, to the University of Chicago Press for acquiring the rights for an English edition, to Susan Bielstein, the Press's classics editor, for her patience and encouragement, and to Lawrence Tritle for critically reading a first draft of this new version.

I believe that my analysis utilizes all the ancient sources that are relevant for the topic. Given the multitude of historical problems that needed to be discussed or at least touched upon, it was impossible to aim even at near-completeness in references to modern bibliography. In the first edition, I tried to include all the work that I found helpful and essential. Since 1982, the bibliography on archaic and classical Greek history has grown at a frightening pace. I fear that my efforts to incorporate all relevant discussions have been only partly successful. The book is much revised throughout, although I have tried mostly to strengthen my arguments and have seen little reason to change my views. Except where I have indicated otherwise, I have used the translations of the Loeb Classical Library and the Penguin Classics series. Cross-references within the book point not to pages but to specific notes or to the text at a specific note (e.g., "see chap. 6.1, n. 17," or "see chap. 6.1 at n. 17").

Finally, I dedicated the first edition to Debby and to our friends in the western and eastern sectors of Berlin. By now, their city is no longer encircled by the Iron Curtain and divided by the Berlin Wall and thus no longer a symbol of freedom in the midst of an enslaved world. I think with gratitude of the five years of my life that I shared with them. The friendships formed then have stood the test of time. The debt of gratitude I owe to Debby, however, is immeasurably larger and deeper. Without her love, patience, support, and intelligence, I would not be what I am, both as a person and as a scholar. To her I dedicate this new edition as well.

Introduction

1.1. OBJECTIVES AND STATE OF RESEARCH

In a groundbreaking essay, more than forty years ago, Moses Finley emphasized an elementary historical fact:

> To a Greek in the age of Pericles or a Roman in Cicero's day, "freedom" had become a definable concept, and the antinomy, slave-free, a sharp, meaningful distinction. We are their heirs, and also their victims; . . . the simple slave-free antinomy . . . has been . . . harmful as a tool of analysis when applied to some of the most interesting and seminal periods of our history. "Freedom" is no less complex a concept than "servitude" or "bondage"; it is a concept which had no meaning and no existence for most of human history; it had to be invented finally, and that invention was possible only under very special conditions.[1]

These remarks succinctly define the starting point of the present study and the question it is intended to answer. That a historical investigation of the emergence in Greece of a political concept of freedom should still be a genuine desideratum may seem surprising. Freedom is so obviously a central and attractive topic in social, political, and intellectual history and in the history of ideas and political concepts that one would naturally expect the discussion of Greek and Roman ideas of freedom, which began at the end of the eighteenth and in the nineteenth century, to have continued without interruption.[2] In fact, this was hardly the case until about the mid–twentieth century. Since then, however, publications with "Greek freedom" in their titles have appeared in substantial numbers. This makes it necessary to define more precisely the gap that exists even now. A survey of the history of research on this topic in the last two hundred years or so would be informative and valuable but would exceed by far the limits of what is possible here. Nor will I attempt to repeat efforts, undertaken recently by others, to compare ancient and modern concepts of freedom.[3] The purpose of this book is to lay solid foundations for such broader investigations.

When I worked on the first edition of this book in the decade before its publication in 1985, there existed several kinds of publications dealing with the issue of Greek freedom: essays written for general audiences, books interested in philosophy and theology, and a few articles with a specifically historical and political focus. Essays of the first type, usually based on public lectures and often prompted by concerns about threats in our time to all kinds of freedom, generally discuss rather briefly and summarily the different notions of freedom in ancient Greece and their significance both at the time and for later periods. Titles like "What Did the Greeks Mean by Liberty?" or "Freedom—Ideal and Reality" abound. Whether explicitly or not, almost all of these essays are concerned with the definition and assessment of an ideal (apparently lost in our time): "Freedom is one of the great ideals, perhaps the greatest, that have inspired mankind—'La Liberté' as Delacroix painted it on the barricades, 'die Freiheit' for which Beethoven wrote Fidelio. It was the Greeks who invented the word and ideal."[4]

This approach, focusing on phenomena and ideas, finds its justification in part in historical interest and in part in the great importance the concept of freedom enjoyed in philosophy and ethics from the end of the fifth century.[5] It is not by chance, therefore, that encyclopedias of religion and philosophy included "freedom" among their entries long before others did, and that two of the few scholarly books published on the topic in the half-century preceding this one are devoted specifically to this aspect.[6] For both these studies the investigation of conceptual developments to the end of the fifth century serves primarily an introductory purpose and is not seen as a subject with its own intrinsic value. Max Pohlenz's Freedom in Greek Life and Thought (German ed. 1955, English ed. 1966) is intended to be "purely historical" but in the sense of the "history of an ideal" (thus the subtitle) and "a contribution to the fuller understanding of Greek man."[7] As is to be expected of this author, the book is above all an essay in Geistesgeschichte, even in the sections dealing with political aspects; its focus lies in Socratic and post-Socratic ethics and philosophy. Despite its wealth of material and ideas, to the historian it remains largely unprofitable.[8] The same is true of Dieter Nestle's Eleutheria (1967), which investigates "the nature of freedom among the Greeks and in the New Testament." As this subtitle indicates, Nestle, a theologian, intends chiefly to provide a foundation for understanding the use of the Greek word *eleutheros* in the New Testament. His methods are those of textual exegesis, focusing narrowly on one word family and attempting to understand its meaning through the interpretation of exemplary texts. Paying insufficient attention to the social and political context, the book is able to achieve at best an explanation of the use of "freedom" by individual authors. This it does well, especially in the areas of ethics and philosophy. Otherwise, its judgments tend to be undifferentiated and sweeping, and essential political questions are largely ignored.[9]

Many scholars had looked at the concept of freedom as it appears either in a particular author (especially in Herodotus or Thucydides) or in a specific historical situation (the Persian Wars or confrontations of the Hellenistic East with Rome) or in the concerns of specific groups of persons (such as the freedom of the citizen, the intellectual, or the individual); often dealing with social or political issues, these serve as valuable preliminary studies for my present attempt at a comprehensive and systematic synthesis.[10] Few, however, had gone beyond this selective approach to investigate essential elements of the political concept of freedom within an expanded chronological and thematic framework. Examples include Christian Meier's necessarily brief entry in the lexicon *Geschichtliche Grundbegriffe* and seminal essays by Alfred Heuss and Hans Schäfer. The former focuses on the complementarity of power or rule and freedom and throws light on a constitutive aspect, in which freedom not only appears as the opposite of nonfreedom but involves the control of power. The latter discusses freedom in three major forms in which it manifested itself in Greek history—as a concept upholding the aristocratic order, as a possession of all citizens in democracy, and as the emancipated individual's claim in the fourth century—each linked with a specific interpretation of law, customs, and tradition, and representing one of the great periods in Greek history.[11]

Of course, many works contributing important insight on the history of Greek freedom do not mention freedom or *eleutheria* in their titles; these include studies of related terminology and concepts or of social and political structures and behavioral patterns.[12] Nevertheless, when I started my investigation, the lack of pertinent work focusing broadly on the political aspects of freedom was obvious. Significantly, by then far more had been written on Roman *libertas* as a political concept, in part perhaps because of the obvious continuity in terminology, in part because the Roman concept, lacking the Greek emphasis on democracy, had more affinities with modern analogues, and in part because, lacking an independent philosophical tradition, the Romans placed much more emphasis on the social, political, and

legal aspects of freedom than on those pertaining to ethical and philosophical ideals.[13] In Hellenic studies, the history of political concepts was still
considered mainly the domain of philologists or philosophers rather than
historians.[14] Not accidentally—and in sharp contrast to modern political
lexica—articles on freedom and most other crucial concepts were well represented in historical encyclopedias of philosophy and religion but lacking
in those of classical studies, except for brief entries on the cults related to
eleutheria and *libertas.*[15]

Nevertheless, in the 1970s and 1980s a process of rethinking had already
begun, stimulated especially by the works of Finley and Meier. General
awareness had increased that the history of political concepts, including that
of freedom, was a significant part of social and political history and that it
was well worth investigating the complex, and in some respects unique, conditions that enabled the—or some—Greek communities at a certain stage
of their evolution to discover and formulate the value of freedom. The first
edition of the present book reflected such change in awareness and contributed to its further advancement. Several recent publications focus on the
political aspects of this concept, and recent new editions of major classical
encyclopedias include an article on freedom. Moreover, Orlando Patterson's
magisterial book *Freedom in the Making of Western Culture* (1991) contains
a large section on Greece and the ancient world in general.[16]

The present study thus presupposes a readiness to take the Greek concept of freedom seriously as a phenomenon, not primarily of the history of
philosophy and ideas, but of social and political history. My aim is first of
all to determine the period and circumstances in which a political concept
of freedom emerged in Greece. This is all the more important since this
apparently happened in Greece for the first time in world history. Neither
Egypt and the Near Eastern civilizations that preceded the Greek or were
contemporary with it nor China seem to have needed and created such a *political* concept, and our question is precisely why the Greeks did. In other
words, what this study tries to achieve is to understand the leap from hatred
of the slave condition (which is attested in other ancient societies as well and
probably linked to an appreciation of personal freedom at least among the
affected classes) to a society's adoption of a high valuation of freedom and
thus the creation of a concept of political freedom (which is not attested anywhere in antiquity except for Greece).[17] Second, I shall attempt to identify
the social and political conditions that even in Greece initially prevented the
creation of such a concept or made it unnecessary and those that eventually
made it possible or even demanded it. For this purpose it will be necessary

to clarify the relationship between political and social or collective and individual aspects of freedom. Third, I shall examine how and for what reasons the political concept of freedom, once it had arisen, continued to develop, changed its content, became more differentiated, and extended into new areas. At that point of the investigation, the individual or personal components of the concept will be considered part of the social background. As Meier puts it, "With respect to social status, 'freedom' was . . . never more than a term. All thought concerning this concept focused on the freedom of the free citizens in the polis—before philosophy transcended these boundaries."[18] In short, the goal of this study is to understand the emergence and evolution of the Greek concept of freedom as one of the "basic categories of political and social life" in its intimate connection with developments and changes in social and political structures and attitudes.[19]

1.2. HISTORY OF CONCEPTS: APPROACHES AND METHODOLOGY

Methodologically, this study is based on the premise that the history of social and political concepts can be analyzed properly only in constant and close connection with the social and political history of the period in question and by applying a great variety of perspectives and approaches. Although theory postulates for conceptual history an intermediate position between the history of words and ideas and that of facts and events, I understand it firmly "as part, and not only reflection, of a history of reality."[20]

A theory of the history of sociopolitical concepts (*Begriffsgeschichte*) was developed in Germany in the late 1960s and early 1970s by Reinhart Koselleck and other editors of the lexicon *Geschichtliche Grundbegriffe* (GG). As Melvin Richter summarizes it, this work aims at

understanding how those experiencing the historical formation of the modern world in German-speaking Europe conceptualized those great changes, incorporated them within their respective political and social theories, and acted upon these contested understandings. . . . [It] seeks to correlate political and social concepts with the continuity or discontinuity of political, social, and economic structures. But the history thus provided goes beyond social and economic history. Because those who lived through the unprecedented rapid changes of modern history did not all experience, understand, and conceptualize structural transformations in the same way, their prognoses differed sharply, as did their consequent actions as members of different social formations and political groups. The range of alternatives depended upon the concepts available. What these concepts were, how they were contested, and the extent to which they remained constant, were altered, or created *de novo* are the integrating themes of the GG's project. In order to treat them, the GG has utilized both the history of concepts (begriffsgeschichte) and structural social history. Its program is anti-reductionist, positing the mutual interdependence of both types of history. . . . Thus, as formulated by . . . Koselleck, begriffsgeschichte simultaneously refuses to regard concept-formation and language as epiphenomenal, that is, as determined by the external forces of "real history"; while, at the same time, he rejects the theory that political and social languages are autonomous and discrete "discourses" unaffected by anything extra-linguistic.[21]

Much of this program is determined by the lexicon's specific historical intent and thus not immediately applicable to other historical periods. Its primary purpose, after all, is to investigate how during a crucial period of transformation (the so-called *Sattelzeit,* ca. 1750–1850), the dissolution of the old world and the emergence of the modern are reflected in a greatly accelerated and profound transformation of the sociopolitical vocabulary. These conceptual developments, interacting with deep and rapid changes in society, can be characterized by the categories of "temporalization, democratization, ideologization, and politicization." As a result of such rapid transformation, the terminology of previous periods, even if semantically identical or related, is no longer understandable without interpretation and explanation.[22]

All this is decidedly oriented toward the present and its dealing with the past. The investigation of ancient concepts naturally has to proceed from other assumptions and set other goals. Yet an underlying observation seems generally significant: at such "epochal thresholds," "the horizon of experience is made elastic by suddenly erupting but ultimately persistent changes." Since "the entire terminology, and especially its relevant concepts, relates to this horizon of experience reactively and provocatively," a comprehensive and rapid change takes place in the meaning of basic political and social concepts. As a "heuristic principle" this can be used to examine terminological changes in other fast-moving epochs as well. Meier has demonstrated this for fifth-century Greece.[23]

The goals and methods of *Begriffsgeschichte* as a specific historical subdiscipline can be useful as well for the study of premodern histories. Based as it is on the tension between changes in the meaning of words and changes in the sociopolitical context, its purpose is to analyze and interpret historical development as it is reflected in conceptual development. Since concepts always have multiple meanings and incorporate a variety of historical experiences, *Begriffsgeschichte* makes the interrelationship among many concepts visible and explores overlappings, shifts, and new combinations, both synchronically and diachronically. *Begriffsgeschichte* focuses on the function of concepts, discusses sociological aspects, such as class-related perspectives, partisan interests, and social positions that may be reflected in conceptual usage, and tries to uncover possible manipulation and intentional deformation.[24]

Although Koselleck's explanation of the difference between "word" and "concept" (*Begriff*) has not remained uncontested,[25] I will nevertheless use his pragmatically gained understanding of "concept." "A word becomes . . . a concept when the full sociopolitical context of meaning in which—and for which—a word is used enters in its totality into that one word. . . . Concepts are . . . concentrates of many meanings. . . . In overstated formulation: meanings of words can be determined exactly through definitions; concepts can only be interpreted."[26]

Begriffsgeschichte thus is the historical-critical investigation and reconstruction of the process by which a word becomes a concept and a concept changes into its final shape (at the terminal point envisaged in a specific study). A concept includes within itself a variety of historical experiences, factual references, and meanings. Reconstructing its history thus involves several synchronic and diachronic investigations. On the one hand, we dissect the concept into its components and analyze their evolution and eventual fusion. On the other hand, we study the meaning and function of individual components and of the total concept separately in various periods. Since, moreover, the evolution and transformation of concepts reflects, directly and indirectly, changes in social, political, and intellectual experiences and in turn influences such experiences, we can understand the development of concepts only by constantly taking these experiences into account. Conversely, this interactive relationship permits us to use conceptual changes as indicators of how contemporaries experienced and reacted to ongoing changes.[27] Such interdependence probably was more directly effective in early periods, when concepts were not yet readily available, transferable, and alterable, and when changed realities needed to be recognized, understood, and formulated in new ways, all for the first time.

The Greek concept of freedom, too, needs to be examined from such a variety of perspectives. I have done this in two steps. The first consisted of collecting, categorizing, and interpreting synchronically and diachronically the entire range of meanings and uses of *eleutheria,* the principal term for freedom, and other words formed from the same stem (*eleuth-*). The results, including a preliminary sketch of the conceptual development of *eleutheria*, were published in 1981 in a multiauthored work on Greek social terminology and its *Nachleben* in modern languages.[28] The present study focuses on the word's political components and complements this "semasiological" analysis with an "onomasiological" analysis that examines all terms used for a given phenomenon. It draws up and analyzes systematically the resulting "conceptual field or space," by integrating parallel and counter-concepts, by differentiating between general and particular concepts, and by considering linkages and overlappings. All this makes it possible to determine the function and value of a concept in its broader social and political context.[29]

Hence, I include in my investigation all terms projecting into the conceptual space of *eleutheria*, even if only peripherally or on occasion, terms with parallel or partially overlapping meanings, terms that, representing initially dominant concepts, delayed or restricted the development of *eleutheria*, and others that evolved within the latter's range of meanings and eventually became independent. Such terms include *sōtēria* (deliverance, survival), *eunomia* (good order), *isonomia* (political equality), *isēgoria* (equality of speech), *autonomia, autarkeia* (self-sufficiency), *parrhēsia* (freedom of speech), and *dēmokratia*, that is, terms designating above all relations between freedom and self-preservation, order, equality, self-determination, and participation in politics and government. Important preliminary work has been done on most of these terms, but a systematic examination of all these relationships has not been undertaken so far. Although the present study cannot claim to be complete in this respect either, all these terms will be considered carefully at their crucial points of contact with freedom.

If, in this way, the conceptual field of freedom will be filled in, its limits must be demarcated by examining two further categories: contrasting and complementary concepts. The primary contrasting concept obviously is that of nonfreedom (slavery or dependency). Its social component, represented by numerous terms designating an individual's partial or complete nonfreedom, has, for obvious reasons, long been the focus of intensive research.[30] Its political analogue, however, is much less clearly defined; it seems to have been regarded generally as a "mere metaphor" and therefore as unproblematic. Yet the development of a political concept of servitude will afford valuable insights into the conditions that both limited and prompted the emergence of its opposite. The most important complementary concept is that of power or rule (*Herrschaft*), which will help bring into sharp profile some of the central characteristics of the Greek concept of freedom particularly in the fifth century.[31]

Finally, in order to determine the role and relative value of freedom in the political vocabulary of a particular period, we need to extend our view beyond the conceptual field of freedom to the main political concepts encountered in that period. This will help us understand why, for instance, during periods of severe crisis in the archaic age the term "freedom" was either completely ignored or used only with narrow limitations even in contexts where in later times its use would have been self-evident. We thus need to determine to what other sociopolitical values freedom was subordinated or attached, when and under what circumstances it emancipated itself to become an independent value, and what significance and function it then assumed alongside other concepts. Again, the order in which word forms appear becomes fully informative only in a conceptual and comparative context. The fact that in the case of *eleutheria* the word appears first as an adjective (free), then as a nominal (the free), and only much later as an abstract noun (freedom) attains its full significance if we investigate the time, circumstances, and causes of such terminological developments and compare the results with corresponding changes in the formulation of other value concepts. We can then properly appreciate the fact, which surely is important, that the word "free" (*eleutheros*) was substantivized (*eleutheria*) and thus became a political ideal and catchword long after, for example, "good order" (*eunomia*), "justice" (*dikē*), or "equality" (*isonomia, isēgoria*).[32]

1.3. EVIDENCE: VALUE AND LIMITATIONS

In our attempts to shed light on the history of freedom in Greece we need to be aware of some basic difficulties. First of all, most of the concepts used by all later periods in the Western tradition are based to some extent on the terminology developed in antiquity, largely by the Greeks. Accordingly, the freedom concepts of all post-Greek periods are influenced at least in part by the Greek concept and include at least some of its meanings. However they reacted to such influences, later peoples profited from help in formulating and shaping their own concepts.[33] The Greeks, by contrast, could rely neither on such preexisting terminology nor on a corresponding intellectual tradition. Moreover, they formulated their concepts on the basis of thought and behavior patterns, values, and ideas that differed profoundly from those of modern times. This forces us to take little for granted and to begin our examination of the meaning, content, and function of such a concept on a rather elementary level.[34]

This problem is aggravated by the long-term effect of modern ideas and modes of thought on the interpretation of ancient texts and concepts. Jochen Bleicken has drawn attention in particular to the strong influence that the late eighteenth century and the age of liberalism exerted on the discipline of history emerging gradually at the beginning of the nineteenth century and, through it, on our understanding and definition of the Roman concept of freedom—an influence that is still visible in recent scholarship.[35] For similar reasons, great caution must be used in drawing analogies between related Roman concepts and their Greek counterparts. Nor, again, should we assume uncritically that definitions and meanings common in fourth-century Greek works of political theory or philosophy can be used to illuminate conceptual developments in preceding centuries.

Alfred Heuss, for example, comments on the entirely different semantic development in Greece and Rome of terms originally similar in meaning— a difference that can be explained plausibly by divergent social and political developments.[36] Although the terms for "free," *eleutheros* and *liber,* probably go back to the same Indo-European root and are therefore likely to have had the same meaning, the lack of suitable evidence from early Rome prevents us from perceiving what may initially have been a parallel conceptual development under comparable sociopolitical conditions. By the time the extant sources illuminate the Roman concept of freedom—in the late republic—the original similarities are largely obscured by marked differences that separate Rome, the aristocratically ruled head of a world empire, from the Greek poleis of the classical period. We cannot therefore expect that analysis of *libertas* will shed light on specific questions concerning *eleutheria* in the archaic or classical period. Conversely, a "negative comparison" that focuses precisely on differences and contrasts can contribute greatly to illuminating the specific characteristics of the Greek concept of freedom.[37]

To be sure, Greek political philosophy, rhetoric, and historiography of the fourth century bring us to within a couple of centuries of the decisive period in the development of the concept of freedom. But even here caution is advised. Fourth-century historical depictions of events and conditions of the first half of the fifth century, let alone the archaic period, are often based on sources of doubtful historical value and reconstructed from the point of view (and written with the vocabulary) of the authors' own time. This applies to Aristotle as well. Despite his great interest in history, many acute observations, and undeniable merits in preserving invaluable information, his concept of freedom is in all essential respects the product of experiences and political realities of the fourth century. This is even more true of the orators, whose understanding of (or interest in) historical change was minimal.[38] To take their concepts of freedom as representative even of the classical period as a whole would be a serious error and obstruct rather than illuminate our understanding of early conceptual developments and the conditions on which these were based.

Every period analyzes and describes the events of earlier times not only from a perspective informed by its own experiences and problems but also with its own ideological instruments and terminology. This principle holds as well for the historians. Herodotus is a typical example, and for our purposes an especially important one. Although he seems skeptical of the new rational tendencies of his time and pays little overt attention to the profound political changes occurring around him, his account nevertheless is deeply influenced by contemporary intellectual trends and marked by his conscious and constant interaction with the political present of his own troubled time.[39] As a consequence, unless confirmed by independent evidence that is at least nearly contemporary with the events in question, his interpretation of the Persian Wars or of the history of the sixth century (and especially the political and "ideological" terminology he uses) must be taken a priori as evidence for the perception and representation of the time in which he wrote.[40] Since Herodotus is often our only or at least our most important informant, this has considerable methodological consequences. True, in many cases he must have found in his sources (whether oral or written) the historical interpretations he offers and the terms he uses. But we can rarely be certain whether or not this was really the case and to what extent an older conceptual usage was later expanded or given some special emphasis or was reinterpreted propagandistically or ideologically in or shortly before Herodotus's time. When considering Herodotus's terminology, we need to keep all this in mind.[41]

I draw the following methodological conclusions. The use of political concepts needs to be investigated separately for each period of Greek history, primarily on the basis of evidence surviving from that period. We should view with skepticism and caution whatever is not attested in the period itself and avoid inferences drawn from later sources, unless they can be justified convincingly with source-critical or other substantive arguments. Hence, despite—or, rather, precisely because of—the limitations imposed on us by the extant evidence, the present study takes this evidence seriously, including its gaps and silences. The resulting problems represent challenges that need to be accepted as such and resolved by careful evaluation in each case.

The earliest extant "political texts" (the anonymous *Constitution of the Athenians* transmitted among Xenophon's works and the historical works of Herodotus and especially Thucydides) were written in the last third of the fifth century. Although earlier literary genres (epic, lyric, elegy, and drama) were not specifically political in nature, these texts were sung and performed in polis societies that were in many ways intensely competitive and political. Moreover, for centuries poetry served as the primary medium for public and formal expression even of political ideas, criticism, and programs. Archaic and classical poetry from Homer and Hesiod to Aeschylus and Euripides, from Alcaeus and Solon to Pindar, therefore often exhibits a marked political engagement.[42]

For all these reasons, and although only a fraction of the rich literary production of these centuries survives, I believe that it is methodologically justified to make specific use of the argument from silence. If, therefore, political themes (and words related to them) are not touched upon in the sources of a particular period, even though demonstrably these sources would have had reasons to do so, I will assume that such themes and terms did not in fact play a significant role in that period. To put it positively, I shall work with the assumption that the principal political concepts of a period *were* reflected in the literature of their time and thus would have left traces in suitable contexts of the preserved record. As a consequence, I will deliberately avoid using loss of texts to explain lack of evidence for specific meanings or contents. We first need to exhaust every possibility of understanding such gaps on the basis of the extant texts and their social, political, intellectual, and conceptual background. In view of the specific conditions of, and the lack of precedents in, the evolution of Greek political concepts, what seems self-evident to us (and seemed obvious already to the Greeks of later centuries) must not be taken for granted.

Another problem is the extent to which early sources are capable of supplying sufficiently precise and substantive answers to our modern questions about conceptual developments. It has often been lamented that Greek terminology does not reach the level of precision historians or political scientists consider indispensable. The only sensible reaction here is to refrain from applying false standards to the extant material. Rather, contemporary consciousness and precision in the use of terminology must themselves become objects of our investigation. In the process, we should pay close attention not only to context but, for example, to interchangeability of terms or the difference between incidental and emphatic use. After all, our categories for determining the precision of a concept may differ from those of the Greeks, and what we deem insufficient may have been perfectly sufficient for their needs.[43]

Especially for the archaic period, the available evidence will not permit us to form a complete picture. We have to reconcile ourselves to long steps and chronological gaps, summary statements, and a roughly drawn reconstruction, crossing a river, as it were, by jumping from stone to stone rather than on a solid bridge. Often we will have to be content with suggesting plausible possibilities rather than postulating certainty, and various alternatives rather than one fact.[44] Within these limits, however, we can find satisfactory answers if we ask the right questions—that is, questions that are unbiased and appropriate to the sources and historical circumstances. What we are looking for may not be mentioned expressly in the sources, but this is no reason not to look for it.[45] It is, for example, precisely the question of why archaic Greek aristocracies failed to appreciate political freedom that helps us gain important insights into the conditions that finally made the emergence of such a concept possible.

Most of all, we need to be willing to approach the problems broadly and from many angles; to accept as evidence and to problematize not only positive but also negative findings; to go beyond the words by examining the behavior and thought patterns and the sociopolitical structures underlying them; and finally to examine carefully every piece of evidence uncovered in this way for its possible function within the conceptual framework that forms the basis of the present study. Emphasizing the need to establish such a "conceptual framework," Chester Starr quotes Iris Murdoch: "There are certain areas of scholarship, early Greek history is one and Roman law is another, where the scantiness of evidence sets a special challenge to the disciplined mind. It is a game with very few pieces, where the skill of the player lies in complicating the rules. The isolated and uneloquent fact must be exhibited within a tissue of hypothesis subtle enough to make it speak."[46]

1.4. A "GREEK" CONCEPT OF FREEDOM?

The extant evidence imposes on us yet another restriction. From at least the early fifth century, Athenian sources predominate so markedly in the surviving material that we can trace the conceptual development of freedom almost only on the basis of Athenian experiences and perspectives. At the same time, political changes in Athens and the role this city played in Greece after the Persian Wars decisively influenced this concept especially. Moreover, Athens's development in this period was atypical in many respects. Hence, we should not assume as a matter of course that Athenian experiences, behavior, and perceptions can be generalized.[47] It is possible, therefore, that we are not able at all to reconstruct in this period the history of the Greek (rather than the Athenian) concept of freedom. Different conceptions of the nature and limits of political freedom, for example, are attested for Sparta, as we learn from discussions of Athenian democracy by authors of the late fifth and fourth centuries. Other local variants might also have existed.

On the other hand, what happened in Athens intellectually and ideologically affected the entire Greek world. Moreover, orators, historians, and philosophers of the late fifth and fourth centuries who were Athenians or worked predominantly in Athens and absorbed or reacted to the Athenian views of freedom shaped this concept in turn, developed it further, and passed it on as a common Greek heritage first to the Hellenistic world and then to Rome and the later cultural tradition of the Western world. For posterity there was no difference between the "Athenian" and the "Greek" concept of freedom.[48]

1.5. PLURALITY OF STATUSES AND THE VALUE OF FREEDOM

The question of the possible value of freedom in a given sociopolitical context needs to take into account a characteristic trait of all ancient societies. They did not simply separate the free from the unfree but distinguished a variety of statuses "between freedom and slavery," exhibiting a richly differentiated spectrum that varied according to time and place.[49] At the lower end was the slave in the full sense of the word ("chattel slave," *esclave-marchandise*), hardly distinguished from an object; at the upper end was the member of the class(es) currently in power, in full possession of his personal and political freedom and rights. Below the dividing line between free and nonfree, which was itself blurred by numerous overlappings, were several categories of basically unfree persons whose particular status was determined by possession or lack of a variety of rights and elements of freedom. Correspondingly, above that line were other clearly distinguishable groups whose undisputed freedom was diminished by various restrictions and elements of nonfreedom. This applies particularly to archaic societies. It is much less true for classical Athens and Rome: in the context of the ancient world as a whole they represent rare exceptions.

In fifth- and fourth-century Athens the intermediate stages in the sphere of nonfreedom were virtually eliminated. But in that of freedom three groups were sharply separated by rights or privileges, duties or restrictions: citizens, metics (resident aliens), and freedmen.[50] Moreover, the clear distinction made in Athens between citizens and noncitizens seems to have been less strictly valid in other societies. In Sparta, at any rate, only the Spartiates had full citizen rights, but there were other categories of persons with various degrees of partial citizenship and, in addition, large groups of members of the Lacedaemonian state (the *perioikoi*), who possessed local citizenship in dependent communities.[51] The Law Code of Gortyn distinguishes between *eleutheroi* (full citizens) and *apetairoi* (freemen not integrated into the civic organization), who in turn were apparently divided into several categories.[52] A relic of such differentiation survived even in Athens. The inhabitants of the village of Eleutherai near the Boeotian border, which was incorporated into Attica in the sixth century, were Athenian citizens but lacked full citizen rights. Since they were not assigned to any tribe (*phulē*), they did not possess the special rights connected with membership in such civic subdivisions and thus in the Athenian demos as a whole. Fritz Gschnitzer suggests that their status was perhaps comparable to that of Roman "half-citizens" (*cives sine suffragio*).[53]

Such plurality of statuses even among the free could not but affect the value of freedom as a sociopolitical concept. Various groups of free persons in a community shared their free status (in the sense of having control over their persons and work),[54] but they were clearly distinguished from one another by other, group-specific criteria. In Greek societies these criteria tended to be stronger than those which cut across groups. Group-internal identification was therefore primary. Hence, other factors were more important for the position of a group in the overall sociopolitical structure than the personal freedom of its members.

In fifth-century Athens, for instance, a freedman's status was determined only by the criterion of personal freedom. For a citizen, in contrast, the dominant criterion was full citizenship with attendant rights and privileges. Personal freedom was only one of the qualifications required for full citizenship and, in comparison to citizen descent, was secondary for group identification.[55] This distinction applies generally to all classes of citizens, even those whose social standing was scarcely distinguishable from that of freedmen. Nor is it inconsistent with the fact that in both political theory and Athenian self-understanding full citizen rights in democracy depended exclusively on free status. The implication here was that, unlike aristocracy (noble birth) and oligarchy (wealth), democracy did not require additional qualifications. Especially in Athens, therefore, personal freedom was highly valued, but enhanced as it was by a crucial political dimension, the citizen's freeman status was no longer comparable qualitatively with that of a freedman or metic.[56]

To differentiate between the valuation of political and personal freedom is essential for clarifying a number of issues. For instance, the extraordinarily high political value placed on the citizen's personal freedom may have been a means of compensating for the low value accorded the same status in social contexts. This would further help explain the virtually complete absence of commonality among all the free in a community and the pervasive tendency to exclusiveness among the full citizens.[57] The specific institutions characteristic of the Spartiates in Sparta and the *eleutheroi* in Gortyn, and the Athenian citizenship law of 451/450, all united a narrowly defined class of citizens and separated them sharply from all other freemen.

Such considerations are essential throughout our investigation. When trying to determine the possible significance of freedom within a given societal framework, we thus need to take various aspects into account. What kind of freedom, and how much? For what classes in society was it of primary importance, for which secondary and why? Was freedom uniformly and permanently important, or was it significant only under certain conditions or in certain situations (for example, prompted by specific problems)? If in some situations, why not in others? If conditions changed radically or an acute problem was resolved, did the high valuation of freedom disappear along with the factors that had triggered it, or could it be maintained (and if so, under what conditions and with what kinds of adjustments)? Finally, what was the relationship between the value of freedom and that of other concepts, and to what extent did differences exist in this respect between various social groups or classes?

We may certainly assume that where nonfreedom existed there was also a certain awareness of the value of freedom. But other factors could substantially reduce the social impact of such awareness and the valuation of liberty itself, restricting them, for example, to certain categories of persons, to a certain sphere of life, or to certain forms of experience.[58] What might be very important for individual feelings could seem virtually meaningless in a broader social, let alone political, context. Hence, even the existence of clear terminological distinctions between persons of free and unfree status does not necessarily tell us much about the value attached to freedom.[59] We can determine this value and the significance of the consciousness of freedom only if we distinguish between aspects that were essential to individuals in the private sphere and those important to them (and to the community as whole) in the public sphere, and if we analyze each individual phenomenon in its broad social and political context.[60]

1.6. THEMATIC AND CHRONOLOGICAL LIMITS

Conceptual history, as described above, requires broad and differentiated approaches. Freedom played a significant role in many spheres of life, almost all genres of literature, and the most important political events. The task of reconstructing the history of this concept is thus complex. It forces us to take a position on numerous much debated historical and literary problems of the archaic and classical periods. All this has influenced the choice of limits for the present study. As pointed out earlier, its purpose is to trace the evolution of the political use of freedom from its very emergence to the point at which the process of its differentiation in content and function was essentially completed. The investigation focuses primarily on the two predominant categories of external and internal freedom, or better, of freedom of the community and freedom within the community. The results achieved in this study will enable us to address broader and more general questions, to examine individual features and components diachronically, and to compare the Greek concept of freedom with that of other periods and peoples.[61] Some of these aspects will be mentioned at least briefly in the concluding chapter.

As for chronological limits, I will start my investigation with the Homeric epics, which mark the beginning of Greek literature in the late eighth or early seventh century. The Greek Bronze Age ("Mycenaean") civilization will essentially be left out of consideration. Its social and political structures seem closely related to those of the Near Eastern states of the second millennium, in which, apparently, freedom was no significant value. To analyze these civilizations in detail would transcend my professional competence.[62] Greek Bronze Age society does, however, deserve some attention because some Linear B tablets contain the words that later designated free and slave (*eleutheros, doulos*). Their meaning and significance will be discussed briefly in the final section of this chapter.

It might seem natural to terminate my investigation with the end of the

classical and the beginning of the Hellenistic period. The history of freedom did not, of course, stop there, but the imposition of Macedonian rule
marked a deep hiatus—although one in preparation for decades—in the
Greek awareness and realization of freedom.[63] Still, I have chosen an even
earlier chronological boundary: the conclusion of the Peloponnesian War at
the end of the fifth century. The collapse of Athens in 404 ended an epoch
and caused changes that touched all areas of life, marking a turning point
that ranked close to the Persian Wars in its significance for Greek political
and intellectual life and that came to be rooted firmly in the consciousness
of contemporaries and posterity alike.[64]

By that time, the spectrum of meanings and functions of freedom in
both the individual-private and the public-political spheres was, with few
exceptions, fully developed.[65] The politicization and ideologization of freedom had reached a climax both within Greek communities (most of all,
Athens) and in their mutual relations. Freedom figured constantly in the
politicians' rhetorical arsenal and served as a readily available propaganda
slogan. Freedom and autonomy were fixed items in interstate diplomacy
and the language of treaties. The interdependence of freedom and democracy, and the social and institutional foundations on which the citizens'
freedom rested, were general knowledge, used and abused by advocates and
opponents of democracy. In many decades of discussions and confrontations, the Greeks had discovered, experienced, and learned to understand
and formulate the significance, the potential and limitations, and the promises and illusions of freedom in every sphere of politics.

Even in the areas of educational theory, theoretical speculation, and political and moral philosophy, the Pre-Socratic philosophers, the Sophists,
and Socrates himself had laid the foundations for a deeper understanding of
the nature, possibilities, and limits of individual and collective freedom and
the chances to secure and improve it. The thinkers of the fourth century
built on these foundations. How much they owed to their predecessors is
clear in part from sources that survive from the late fifth century and in part
from works written in the early fourth by Xenophon, the older Attic orators,
Plato, and Isocrates. Naturally, these works need to be interpreted with appropriate historical and critical caution, but their authors lived in late-fifth-
century Athens during their formative years and wrote on the basis of the
experiences and knowledge they acquired during that time. These texts also
afford insight into the nature and content of literary genres (especially various types of oratory) that played a central role in political life already in

the late fifth century but survive from that period only in the most meager fragments.

All in all, then, it seems reasonable to maintain that the decisive phases in the development of the concept of political freedom occurred before the end of the fifth century. The inclusion of the fourth century would complete and enrich the picture but would have little impact on the results of this study.[66]

1.7. *DOULOS* AND *ELEUTHEROS* IN GREEK BRONZE AGE SOCIETY

The occurrence of *doulos* and *eleutheros* on Linear B tablets has prompted Fritz Gschnitzer, among others, to argue with great confidence that the corresponding social dichotomy was also important in Mycenaean society.[67] From the same evidence, others have drawn far-reaching conclusions about the social and political structure of the Mycenaean states, including a marked contrast between local autonomy and central power that supposedly became crucially significant in subsequent developments.[68] The latter may well have been the case, but it seems hazardous to link it to terminological clues that, as we shall see, are uncertain themselves. Only three questions are important for our present purposes: What were the content and significance of the terms corresponding to *eleutheros* and *doulos*? What was the function in Mycenaean society of the antithesis free-unfree? And did this terminology and/or function continue unchanged, or was it transformed, during the "Dark Ages"? On these issues I offer a few brief observations.

First, the word *doero* (*doelos/doulos*) appears in social and religious contexts, where it apparently designates forms of dependence as well as function. It is applied, in the formula *teojo doero/-a* (*theou douloi/-ai*, "servants of the god"), to individuals many of whom are also listed as beneficiaries of land allotments. This may mean that, although dependent on the palace, they held important positions in the social hierarchy and therefore were perhaps even counted among the free. In this case, *doulos* in their designation should probably be understood metaphorically—a phenomenon not unknown from later societies. If, however, they were, at least originally, slaves in the strict sense of the word, their status as recorded on the tablets was privileged.[69]

The number of persons designated as *douloi/-ai* is relatively small, and the absence of the word in the very contexts where one would most expect to find it causes problems. For example, one group of tablets lists several hundred women, children, and juveniles who receive rations of food, apparently from the palace administration. In this sense they depend on the palace, but are they slaves? Yvon Garlan thinks that their status, whatever its cause, was so obvious that it did not need to be mentioned. This is possible, but we simply do not know. As Cynthia Shelmerdine observes, "some of these Pylian workers are identified by ethnic adjectives: Milesians, Knidians, Lemnians, Lydians and so on. Were these women in fact acquired from Anatolia and neighboring islands, through trade or warfare?" In sum, although there is little doubt that some of the *doero/-a* were really slaves, the variety of categories of persons designated (or not designated) by this word precludes a unified and simple use of the term.[70] From his examination of the evidence, Alexander Uchitel draws the following conclusions:

1. Mycenaean *do-e-ro,* unlike classical *doulos,* seems to denote some social group independent economically (land- and cattle-owners), but dependent in some uncertain way on private persons (if they are not representatives of the central authority), gods (named and unspecified *theos* in the expression *te-o-jo do-e-ro*), and *da-mo.*

2. The members of this group of the population were subject to conscription in order to work in teams, and the same components of the "*do-e-ro* class" are found *both* as landholders and members of work-teams.[71]

The word *ereutero* (*eleutheros*) has so far been found only in connection with economic or fiscal matters. It designates the exemption by the palace administration of particular groups of persons or categories of specialists from specific quotas of product deliveries.[72] In these contexts, *eleutheros* does not characterize a social status and is far removed from political usage.[73]

Second, the term's specific meaning was obviously connected with the Mycenaean palace economy. The nature and purpose of the extant documents explains why only this meaning has been preserved. It is, of course, possible that *eleutheros* more generally also designated the opposite of *doulos,* in analogy to archaic and classical word usage, but we are not entitled simply to assume this.[74] Even if this was the case, it would by itself say little about the social, let alone political, functions the word pair might have served in this particular society. Since *doulos,* however, seems to have covered a variety of statuses between slavery and freedom, the word did not "represent the polar opposite to liberty," and it is a priori likely that "free" would also have covered a variety of statuses. Given the nature and organization of these particular states and societies, it is even more likely that other contrasts and oppositions were more important than this one. As Garlan concludes, "the opposition between slaves and nonslaves does not appear to have played a major role in the structuring and differentiation of this type of society. What does appear to have constituted a determining factor is the situation of individuals vis-à-vis the palace."[75]

The existence, confirmed by textual and archaeological evidence, of regional settlement centers and perhaps relatively independent village communities has led some scholars to postulate that these were administered by local aristocracies and organs of self-government. This in turn might have caused tensions between central power and local autonomy.[76] Even if so, it is clear that in some significant respects the Mycenaean states corresponded to Near Eastern forms of state organization, though on a considerably more modest level.[77] For our present purposes this has important implications. In Mesopotamia, legally unfree persons are attested in various status categories and substantial numbers. Yet (in contrast to those immediately affected by slavery) society as a whole and especially those in power apparently accorded low value to free status (which essentially means that other values were much more important), and the notion of political freedom is entirely absent.[78] This is perhaps best explained by the towering position of the godlike king. In comparison to him, all members of the state, even the highest dignitaries, must have viewed themselves as slaves and were treated and occasionally described as such. Late reflections of these relations are evident in the Persian Empire of the sixth and fifth centuries and at that time made a deep impression on the Greeks.[79] Thorkild Jacobsen expresses well what is at issue here:

In a civilization which sees the whole universe as a state, obedience must necessarily stand out as a prime virtue. For a state is built on obedience, on the unquestioned acceptance of authority. It can cause no wonder, therefore, to find that in Mesopotamia the "good life" was the "obedient life." The individual stood at the center of ever wider circles of authority which delimited his freedom of action.[80]

However such relations might have been realized under the rather different geopolitical conditions of Greece and Crete, some essential analogies certainly existed.[81] They should warn us not to ascribe too much social, let alone political, significance to the status opposition between *eleutheros* and *doulos*.

Third, the problem of continuity versus discontinuity from the Mycenaean to the archaic period continues to be much debated. The fact that the

Linear B documents contain not only names but also numerous words and titles that are also attested in archaic sources has encouraged proponents of broad continuity.[82] Archaeological evidence suggests that continuity was stronger in some areas than in others. Overall, it seems clear that in many spheres of life and culture, lines of development—clearly recognizable, although rarely straight and undisturbed—lead from the Bronze Age through the turbulent Dark Ages to the archaic period. This applies much less, however, to social and political structures, functions and statuses, and least of all to those elements that were integral to the central political authority and economy of the palaces, existed and had meaning only in connection with them, and necessarily disappeared when they were destroyed.[83]

This is true as well for the specialized meaning of *eleutheros,* the only meaning documented for Bronze Age Greece. To be sure, in the fifth and fourth centuries *eleutheros* could signify "free of debt," and in the early sixth century Solon hailed the removal of debt markers as the "liberation" of Mother Earth. Whatever the terminological continuity from the Bronze Age, such usage is directly linked to laws of debt and obligations and the specific status of the ruined debtor in the periods involved.[84] A better argument for at least partial continuity of meaning can be made in the case of *doulos.* Yet the fact that the most important term for personal dependency and non-freedom in the Homeric epics is not *doulos* but *dmōs* should give us pause.[85] On currently available evidence it is altogether unclear how much the archaic *douloi* had in common with their like-termed Mycenaean predecessors.

In sum, in those respects that are important for the present study, an unbroken continuity is highly questionable. We have no way of ascertaining what value the Bronze Age Greeks placed on freedom in social life. That it was a political value is most unlikely. Hence, although some strands of development in the individual and private spheres of life and in religion, crafts, and other areas may have originated in Mycenaean times, the history of the concept of political freedom begins after the destruction of the Bronze Age civilization and the Dark Ages, in the archaic and classical periods.

Awareness of Freedom in Archaic Greek Society

2.1. *ELEUTHEROS* AND *DOULOS* IN THE ARCHAIC PERIOD

In the extant archaic literature, the words *eleutheros* and *doulos,* later of great importance to Greek social and political life, are notably rare. This is significant and needs explaining. I begin by summarizing the available evidence, grouped in four basic categories.[1]

The Evidence

Personal freedom. This aspect receives much attention already in Homer. While the stem *doul-* appears in both epics as an adjective, as a noun applied to persons, and as an abstract noun,[2] *eleuth-* is used only as an adjective, only in the *Iliad,* and, with one exception, in a single fixed formula, "taking away the day of freedom" (*eleutheron ēmar*),[3] which has an exact correspondence in "to ward off the day of slavery" (*doulion ēmar*).[4] Both belong to a larger group of formulas consisting of an adjective combined with "day" (*ēmar*), which primarily designate—especially in the realm of human fate determined by war, natural forces, or divine power—a specific day or, more precisely, a moment of experience, when a turn or fulfillment of fate has occurred.[5] Their secondary, and clearly later, meaning is the condition established or terminated by such a turn of fate. Various indications suggest that "day of freedom" was constructed on the model of "day of slavery," and that both phrases belong to the latest formulas constructed with *ēmar* and thus to a relatively late stratum of the stock of epic formulas.[6] Given the outlook typical of the epic, which focuses on the part, the individual, or the moment instead of the whole, the collective, or the enduring,[7] we should not interpret *eleutheron ēmar* simply as the equivalent of a permanent state of freedom and hence as a paraphrase of the noun *eleutheria,* which did not yet exist;[8] during the archaic period, this meaning was only beginning to emerge.

From its earliest appearance in Greek literature, *eleutheros* thus forms a pair of opposites with *doulos.* In Homer *doulion ēmar* and *eleutheron ēmar* illuminate the same event from two sides.[9] Both expressions are used only when attention is focused on the fact and moment of the loss of freedom. That *eleutheros* appears exclusively in the context of war and, with one exception, only with respect to women is to be explained by the action of the *Iliad* and early Greek customs of war.[10] Because lack of freedom is determined on the one hand by subjugation to force and a foreign will—in other words, by restricted freedom of action[11]—and on the other by loss of protection, home, and country,[12] the Homeric idea of "being free" must at the very least include control over one's own person and actions and the security of living in an intact, stable community. Yet this is not expressly stated, and nowhere is freedom defined positively.

One of the factors behind the crisis reflected in the poems of the early-sixth-century Athenian lawgiver Solon is the loss of personal freedom by many farmers, resulting from economic misery and debts or personal obligations.[13] Justifying his actions, Solon describes how he freed the land by removing the debt markers (*horoi*), and how he freed many citizens from slavery abroad or servitude in Attica, inflicted upon them by debts.[14] Twice Solon contrasts the previous state of *douliē* with the act of liberation; in both instances—and only here—Solon mentions *eleutheros.* In the Law Code of Gortyn, *eleutheros* defines the status of the free (citizens), *doulos* is used for both serfs (for whom other terms are common as well) and chattel slaves, and yet other words describe bondsmen (*katakeimenos,* the freeman who pledged his person in payment for debt, and *nenikamenos,* a "free man who was condemned for debt and handed over in bondage to his creditor").[15]

The contrast between slave and free first appears as a general structuring principle around the end of the sixth century in Heraclitus's statement "War is the father of all and king of all, and some he shows as gods, others as men; some he makes slaves, others free" (*VS,* no. 22 B53, tr. Kirk).[16] This categorical distinction must have been a regular issue much earlier in archaic legislation. The Code of Gortyn offers ample illustration; I cite but two examples:

Whosoever may be likely to contend about a free man or a slave is not to seize him before trial. But if he make seizure, let (the judge) condemn him to (a fine of) ten staters for a free man, five for a slave. . . . And if one party contend that he is a free man, the other party that he is a slave, whichever persons testify that he is a free man are to prevail . . . (col. I.1–6, 15–18). If a person commits rape on the free man or free woman, he shall pay one hundred staters; . . . and if the slave on the free man or the free woman, he shall pay double . . . (col. II.2–7).[17]

The extant code was inscribed around the mid–fifth century but is generally agreed to contain older material. How much of it is older, and how much older it is, remains uncertain, and not everybody would agree that "in terms of general development, the Code may be compared with the legal system of Athens in the seventh and sixth centuries."[18] Nevertheless, it seems safe to assume that status distinctions, including that between slave and free, and conflicts about status were issues in archaic legislation at least as early as the late seventh century.

Scarce hints in extant Athenian laws offer some confirmation, though not without problems. *Eleutheros* occurs in Draco's homicide law (probably 621/620) but in a fragmentary section concerning the lawful killing of a thief in defense of one's own property. Most scholars think that the crucial gap may have contained some reference to the status of the lawful killer or, more likely, a provision that prevented any status distinction concerning the victim. Such distinctions should be expected—after all, this was a slave-owning society—and are well attested in later times. Yet there is no way of knowing whether they were really part of Draco's law (in the gap mentioned or elsewhere), and it is quite possible that in its original version this law considered only citizens; it is even possible that *eleutheros,* as preserved, meant simply "free from (punishment vel. sim.)."[19] Nor is the use of *eleutheros* in the Hekatompedon Decree on the Acropolis (inscribed in the mid-480s but again containing much older material) any clearer.[20] It is noteworthy that, with these two exceptions, *eleutheros* "is wholly absent from the inscriptions in the first volume of *IG*."[21]

Literary references to Solonian laws, however, put us on firmer ground; they leave no doubt that by the early sixth century the lawgiver recognized the need to include in his laws specific references to slaves and free: "A slave (*doulos*) . . . shall not take exercise or anoint himself in the wrestling schools. . . . A slave shall not be the lover of a free boy nor follow after him."[22] (If the term here corresponds to the original wording of the law, this is the earliest extant attestation of the noun *doulos*.)[23] Furthermore, there are good reasons to think that the law regulating the "indictment of *hubris*" (*graphē hubreōs*), well known from the classical period and covering a variety of actions dishonoring individuals, was also introduced by Solon. This law, as cited by Demosthenes (21.47), begins with the clause, "If anyone commits *hubris* against another, whether child or woman or man, whether free or slave."[24]

Typology of slave and free. Homer makes no explicit reference to such a typology, just as he has no positive definition of personal freedom. But the fact that at least the beginnings of a typology of slaves can be found in the *Odyssey* helps us understand the conditions under which such a typology developed or, indeed, could develop at all. There, a slave, who in losing his freedom loses half his value as a man (*aretē*), is characterized not only by his negative attitude toward work and responsibility but also by his unkempt appearance.[25] *Eleutheros* first appears in a typological context in a somewhat ambiguous fragment of Alcaeus in which immoderate drinking seems to be criticized as a trait unworthy of the free and even more of the noble.[26] References in Hipponax (second half of the sixth century)[27] and in parts of the corpus of Theognis (last third of the sixth century, at the earliest) confirm the existence, at the end of the archaic period, of a typology in which everything base in a person's feelings, behavior, physical traits, and habits is represented as characteristic of slaves. Traces of a corresponding typology of the freeman specifically emphasize his generosity and proud, upright bearing.[28] This spectrum of traits is refined and extended further in the literature of the fifth century.[29]

Collective or communal freedom. In conversation with his brother, Paris, Hector envisages a victory celebration (*Il.* 6.526–29), "setting up in our houses the wine-bowl of liberty [528] to the immortal gods, after we have driven out of Troy the strong-greaved Achaeans." Presumably, *krētēr eleutheros* is constructed on analogy with, and perhaps even modeled on, *eleutheron ēmar.*[30] The "wine-bowl of liberty," accordingly, means the bowl from which one drinks and offers libations to the gods in gratitude for the departure of the enemy; the act of setting it up thus symbolizes the reestablishment of secure freedom—a true "day of freedom."[31] The underlying conception is specific and close to that of *eleutheron ēmar*: the *doulion ēmar,* with all its consequences—described previously in Hector's conversation with Andromache (6.447–63)—will not descend upon the threatened individuals.[32] Whatever one thinks of the Homeric polis and its communal spirit, under the conditions prevailing at the time "freedom of the community" could be understood at best as the sum of possibilities for individual freedom (especially since what was at stake in Homeric wars was not the independence but the very survival of a polis).[33] Hence, it seems anachronistic to interpret the polis inhabitants' sense of community as an "awareness of freedom," let alone to describe this polis as a "space of freedom."[34]

Caution is all the more called for because I know of no certain testimony that explicitly emphasizes the value of the (external) freedom of the polis.[35] The closest we get is in the second half of the sixth century, when Anacreon praises a friend who died "warding off slavery from his homeland," probably either fighting with the Teians against the Persians or, after their emigration to Abdera, against the local Thracians.[36]

Freedom within the community. Solon's poems repeatedly describe Athens as threatened by a tyrant's seizure of power. In 4W (= 3GP), a programmatic poem,[37] Solon warns that the injustice and immoderation of the "leaders of the people" (that is, the rich and noble) will certainly (*pantōs*) prompt punishment by the gods and inflict slavery upon the city (7–22). It is unlikely that Solon alludes here to the much later tyranny of Peisistratus, but he could easily have deduced from the experiences of other poleis a causal relationship between the *hubris* of the nobility, the impoverishment and dissatisfaction of the demos, and civil strife (*stasis*), resulting in tyranny.[38] Solon here postulates the general validity of this causal relationship. Thus, the "bad slavery" (*kakē doulosunē*) that inescapably threatens the entire polis and every polis (*pasa polis*) in a comparable situation can be none other than that resulting from tyranny.[39] Two other fragments deal more specifically with the threat and then reality of Peisistratus's rise to power (11W = 15GP; 9W = 12GP). They emphasize the responsibility of the demos for their own fate and describe the *doulosunē* under an autocrat as the consequence, inevitable almost by law of nature, of political gullibility.

Strikingly, all these passages emphasize servitude but not the condition of "being free"; *eleutheros* is never mentioned. The reason may simply be that the poet focuses his attention on the threat of communal enslavement by a tyrant. Yet we need to ask whether a plausible explanation may also be found in underlying conceptions and ways of thinking.

Conclusions and Questions

In sum, then, while the noun *eleutheria* is not attested in the entire archaic period, the adjective *eleutheros* occurs in the *Iliad* but is primarily used in a single fixed formula referring to the moment when freedom is lost; that is, it refers not directly to a person but to a change in the condition of that person. *Eleutheros* in Homer never designates the status of individuals or a group among the free or dominant part of society in contrast to those who are unfree or dependent. Thought of the community is prompted by only one phrase containing *eleutheros*. Remarkably, the word does not appear in the *Odyssey*, although this epic dwells on daily life in elite estates, and is missing entirely in Hesiod's vocabulary. In Solon the term specifically describes those liberated from debt bondage, and in Alcaeus, probably the behavior expected of a freeman. It denotes free status in legal contexts from at least the early sixth century and once in Heraclitus. Except for some uncertainly dated occurrences in Theognis, these are the only extant references.

The corresponding terminology referring to slaves (derived from the stem *doul-* and thus in exact semantic opposition to *eleutheros*) occurs earlier throughout: in Homer *doulē* (female slave) is already applied to persons,[40] the beginnings of a typology of slaves are unmistakable, and what it means to be unfree is clearly grasped both objectively and emotionally. Hence, the absence of analogies pertaining to *eleutheros* is striking. An explicit reference to a city's enslavement when threatened by external enemies occurs in the late sixth century; and Solon speaks of the servitude imposed on a polis by a tyrant—yet nothing in the surviving literature of the archaic period suggests that the contrary, positive condition of the polis was conceptualized and designated by a term formed with the stem *eleuth-*. Moreover, in Homer the formulaic "day of freedom" is apparently constructed on the model of "day of slavery"; the epics already use several words derived from *doulos* (again in contrast to *eleutheros*), including the noun *doulosunē*, and they contain a rich terminology relating to the function, and in part also the status, of unfree or dependent persons and servants.[41] The conclusion thus seems inescapable that experiences associated with the lack or loss of freedom were conceptualized and formulated, and the corresponding terminology of servitude developed and differentiated first; the contrasting terminology concerning the status and experience of being free evolved only in reaction to those of being unfree, and then only slowly.

Even if we assume that being free was initially taken for granted as the normal condition of life, and lack of freedom was regarded as abnormal and therefore attracted attention, this fact itself deserves careful examination. For, as the extant evidence indicates, the strictly status-related division between free and unfree, expressed by *eleutheros* and *doulos*, although familiar to the epics, receives surprisingly little notice: not only are concepts associated with *eleutheros* less frequent and developed, but words derived from the stem *doul-* are relatively rare as well among the terminology employed for the unfree and dependent. Moreover, while terms for servitude (such as *doulosunē*) are attested in a political sense from the early sixth century (concerning the domestic sphere of the polis and later also its relationship to other poleis or powers), this is not true of terms for freedom. The extant terminology suggests that the archaic period did not develop a political concept of freedom at all.

Our instinctive reaction is to dismiss this out of hand as improbable. Whoever speaks of political servitude, we naturally assume, is also able to speak of political freedom and to think of the two together just as easily as he contrasts slave and free in social life. It is tempting to conclude that the extant evidence, scarce as it is, must be distorted by the chance of loss and survival. According to the methodological premise I sketched in the previous chapter, however, we must not reject what the evidence suggests before we have made an effort to find a plausible explanation for it.

Hence, in the remainder of this chapter we will try to answer the following questions. If the corresponding specialized terms were readily available, why is the free or unfree status of a person not emphasized more frequently in the epics? Why are the conceptions associated with slavery developed more and earlier than those pertaining to the free? Put differently, what conditions made it impossible or unnecessary, during and even after the period represented in the epics, to devote the same attention to freedom as to servitude? What factors prevented the condition of freedom from being highly valued, even—indeed especially—in the political arena? Why did the terminology in question develop so late? The answers we find to these questions will help us define the conditions that made it possible to place high value on freedom in the political sphere and, as a consequence, to develop a concept of political freedom.

2.2. THE LIMITED VALUE OF FREEDOM IN EARLY GREEK SOCIETY

Homeric Society

Ernst Risch and Fritz Gschnitzer propose that the rare occurrence in the epics of the specifically status-related terms *eleutheros* and *doulos* is due to the nature of poetic language, which, they think, avoids the technical vocabulary of, for example, work or legal relationships.[42] Whether or not this stylistic argument is valid, other possible explanations should be examined as well. Most of all, we should consider the possibility that the poet had no (or little) reason to mention such matters, either because his description rarely

touched on them (which is not the case here) or because the social and political conditions he described did not induce him to emphasize them, or
did so only in specific contexts.

The attempt to find an answer to this question assumes the basic historicity of "Homeric society." I have presented my views on this issue with
detailed arguments elsewhere and merely summarize them here. The epics
allow a historical evaluation because (unlike characters, actions, and events)
the economic, social, and political conditions, the background in and against
which the characters act and react, and the system of relationships and values that influences their actions are sufficiently consistent and realistic so
that a late-eighth- or early-seventh-century audience would have been able
to understand them and identify with them. As Walter Donlan puts it:

The society depicted in Homer may be, as some maintain, a fictional construct; if so,
it is an internally logical one, whose complexities, throughout 28,000 lines of epic
verse, form an intelligible and coherent pattern. To that extent Homeric society is
"real"; and it is more likely that such a social structure existed in space and time than
that it was made up, or that it is an amalgam of institutions concocted from bits and
pieces of social background extending over a period of four (or more) centuries.[43]

This society should probably be dated within living memory of the poet's
own time, that is, in the eighth or, at the very earliest, the late ninth century.[44] Even so, the poet's artistic freedom in selection, emphasis, and representation precludes us from assuming that the epics offer a complete picture
of social conditions and relationships, and the poet's traditional role of being not only an entertainer but also an educator allows for the possibility
that his views might not always correspond entirely with those prevailing
among his contemporaries, particularly the elite.[45]

The epic testimonia on free and unfree are entirely part of the social
background description. They indicate that the free—or, more precisely,
the noble elite on whom the poet focuses[46]—did not ordinarily regard their
freedom as a fact worth noting. Freedom was thus either unimportant or
taken for granted. Moreover, since in the epics awareness of freedom, or of
its absence, is primarily linked to the painful experience of its loss, members
of Homeric society seem to have thought and talked of freedom only when
they perceived a threat to their own freedom, which they had hitherto taken
for granted. Their observation of slavery as a condition and their daily co-
existence with those who were not free apparently did not suffice to make
the free constantly aware of the value of their own freedom.[47]

I offer two closely related explanations. First, generally, the status difference between free and unfree may have meant less in Homeric society than
it did later because other social distinctions and criteria were more important and contributed to minimizing that difference. Second, in particular,
the scant attention paid to freedom reflects and is based upon specific traits
of the elite. Their social organization and relationships, norms and values,
ways of thinking, and relations to the community apparently afforded no
means by which freedom could attain a high value.

More specifically, the position of the unfree within society appears to
have differed somewhat from later times. The boundary between free and
unfree, marked sharply later on, existed but tended to be blurred and was,
in certain contexts, relatively unimportant. In the elite's self-perception and
self-presentation, as reflected in the epics, the crucial dividing line in society
runs between the nobles and the various categories of free and unfree non-
nobles, who, from the perspective of the nobles, seem to coalesce into a mass
of lowly persons who count for little.[48] This undoubtedly is an idealized—
or, rather, ideologically distorted—picture; it is belied, for example, by
the description of Odysseus's relationship to his companions. In fact, there
is every reason to believe that the process of institutional solidification
and demarcation of the nobility was by no means complete, and the socio-
economic differences between the elite and the broad class of independent
farmers who owned their own (albeit more modest) *oikos* (household, estate)—and were therefore part of the communal army and assembly—were
still relatively slight.[49] As we should expect, and Hesiod demonstrates, the
free commoners for their part distinguished themselves emphatically from
those possessing no oikos of their own (day laborers, settled or itinerant
craftsmen, or foreigners), whether or not they were free.[50]

Undoubtedly, many servants were, strictly speaking, slaves.[51] But this
status normally did not need to be emphasized; it was even irrelevant. The
social terminology of early societies, closely corresponding to a complex reality, tends to be highly differentiated.[52] The rareness of status words (*doul-*,
eleuther-) and the predominance and variety of terms designating functions
and relationships and applying, it seems, to both free and unfree servants[53]
therefore suggest an important fact: a person's real position within the primary social unit, the oikos, was determined less by dependence on or subjection to a master's power—which was true in varying degrees for almost
every member of the oikos—than by function and personal relations.[54]

The conditions prevailing in Odysseus's oikos illustrate this well. Position
there is defined by closeness to the master: some trusted slaves (especially

Eumaeus) enjoy a high degree of personal responsibility and independence; reward and advancement consist not in manumission but in movement toward the center, into or close to the master's family and the group of his followers (*hetairoi*).[55] Social advancement is thus achieved within the dependence that applies to most members of the oikos, not by release from dependence.[56] This is hardly surprising: as is typical of early societies, the public sphere was relatively undeveloped, and power rested in the private oikos. The resulting lack of public protection forced the weak to attach themselves to the powerful. As the vulnerability and misery of the thetes (hired laborers) in Homer and the phenomenon of voluntary debt bondage illustrate, freedom was far from an absolute value.[57]

All this helps explain as well why the elite paid so little attention to freedom. The nobleman (*basileus*) was the head (*anax*) of an oikos; this was his primary function and was essential in determining his status in society. Of course, he was free; indeed, in a certain sense he was the only one who was really free because the other members of the oikos all depended on him and were subject to his will and power. But such freedom was elementary, taken for granted. What really mattered to the *basileus* were status and power. The constant need to prove themselves and to maintain influence in all situations formed the natural framework within which the elite thought and acted. As a consequence, the aristocratic value system was entirely focused on status, honor, and achievement.[58]

Hence, freedom was such a basic precondition of noble status that the elite did not even think of it. Loss of freedom was the ultimate dishonor and thus worse than death. Moreover, it was such a remote possibility that it seemed irrelevant, for the consequences of defeat in war were dire: death for the men, enslavement for women and children, destruction for the city—in short, annihilation and the end of noble existence. A man thus fought for his status, his family, and his life, and for the survival of his community, not for his freedom.[59] That its loss concerned "only" women prevented the idea of freedom, not from being considered occasionally, but from entering general consciousness as a primary value. This was equally true of capture by an enemy or pirates, another cause of loss of freedom;[60] it was an exception brought about by chance or fate and therefore beyond the individual's control.

Much the same can be said for the realm of political life and interstate relations.[61] External threats to the independence of a community might have prompted a communally based (individual or collective) awareness of freedom; but in Homeric society war is waged, not to subjugate cities and rule over them, but for status and booty. Raids against neighboring cities and to more distant shores are commonly undertaken for the purpose of capturing flocks and valuable objects. Only in exceptional cases—for example, those motivated by the desire for revenge—are cities besieged, conquered, and destroyed; but even then, the ultimate goal is booty, the restoration of stolen goods, and compensation for injury suffered. Hence, for individual, family, and community, not freedom but survival was the primary concern.[62]

Accordingly, a much more important concept, in the *Iliad* and generally in archaic literature, is that of "deliverance." It played a crucial role in all aspects of life, in war and peace.[63] It could be applied to anything: objects, such as treasures and ships (or the corpses of fallen heroes), animals, and human beings threatened by misfortune. Especially in war, "deliverance" in the basic sense of survival was upmost in people's minds: for the warriors in battle, the women and children fearing to become the conquerors' booty, and the city as a whole which the attacking army hopes to destroy.[64] Annihilation—of the army as well as the city—is invariably felt, and often said, to be the alternative to deliverance.[65] Athena, on whose knees the women of Troy lay costly garments, is called the "savior of the city" (*rhusiptolis*: *Il.* 6.305), and the leader's claim to honor and power rests essentially on his function as protector and rescuer of his city, his men (*laoi*), and his people.[66] Because Hector, the "protector" par excellence, uniquely meets this expectation, the people name his son Astyanax, "lord of the city." [67] Battle exhortations on both sides encourage the men to fight bravely for their own survival and the rescue of the city; the Trojans, naturally, think here also of their women and children (who are missing in the fortified naval encampment that serves the Achaeans as a temporary or "substitute" polis).[68] What Hector means concretely when he speaks of setting up a "wine-bowl of liberty" (*krētēr eleutheros*), once the Achaeans have been defeated,[69] probably corresponds closely to the encouragement he gives to his companions: "If any of you is hit and dies, then so be it. Death in defense of your homeland is no dishonor. Your wife is safe and your children's future, your house and estate are inviolate—if the Greeks sail off to their own native land" (*Il.* 15.496–99; tr. Lombardo 1997). In sum, the vast preponderance in the epics of terms referring to deliverance over those referring to freedom and servitude indicates clearly what primarily concerned those threatened by war.

Awareness of freedom might have arisen as well *within* the community if there existed, over and beyond the sum total of oikoi, a sufficiently developed communal sphere with which members of the community could identify, not merely in emergencies but permanently, and within which freedom was an essential criterion for belonging, status, and communal identification. In Homeric society, however, these conditions were still developing and far from fully and formally established.

The question of whether the elite leaders—the only persons whom the epics describe in any detail—feel much or little attachment to the community has been discussed often. While Hermann Strasburger and M. I. Finley, among others, think that the leaders' loyalty and concerns focus almost exclusively on the oikos and the community is little more than an agglomeration of largely autonomous oikoi, other scholars draw a more balanced picture.[70] That the elite's concern lies largely, even primarily, in the private sphere should not be denied; this remained true through most of Greek history. After all, the power of the individual and his status and influence in the community are largely determined by the size and wealth of his oikos (in land, flocks, valuables, and the number of followers he can muster). But power and influence do not operate in a vacuum; they are sanctioned by the community, and status and honor are awarded by the community for distinguished service to the community.[71] The individual's identity and loyalty thus focus on both the oikos *and* the polis.

This, of course, does not mean that tensions between private and communal interests are lacking. Quite the contrary, throughout the archaic period, intellectual and political concerns, clearly visible already in the epics, focused precisely on this tension and on possible ways to shift the individual's thinking and actions away from primarily private priorities toward responsibility for the community.[72] What matters for our present purposes, however, is that freedom plays a negligible role in all of this. The leader is a freeman; this is obvious, not worth mentioning. His efforts are dedicated to protecting his oikos and increasing its wealth, and to securing and increasing his status and power in the community—which requires thought about protecting the community but not normally about his own or anybody else's freedom.[73]

Furthermore, the epics describe political institutions, especially public and military assemblies, though somewhat vaguely and not without contradictions. The nature and function of these institutions have been much discussed.[74] According to the long-prevalent view, here, as in most aspects of life, the elite seem to enjoy a monopoly: they alone take part in debates, while the masses, from the elite's perspective "of no account whatever in battle or council" (*Il.* 2.202), are confined to the modest role of onlookers and listeners, shouting their approval or disapproval. Moreover, assemblies are convened only in crisis situations and only to discuss the most basic issues. Occasion and issues, furthermore, are determined entirely by members of the elite, and neither they nor the paramount leader seem to be bound by the assembly's opinion. Dissatisfaction and criticism, though not lacking, seem far from having any serious impact. In fact, whenever, over and beyond vital issues of defense and communal survival, concerns such as peace within the community, justice, or the relationship between the common good and individual demands are raised—often by outsiders who criticize the views and interests taken for granted by the majority of the elite—such opinions are suppressed or the assembly is dismissed summarily: such issues, it appears, are not in the assembly's sphere of competence (which, at any rate, was defined and fixed only much later).[75]

This traditional view of an assembly that is essentially powerless and depends entirely on elite leaders, although correct in some respects, is one-sided, overlooks important aspects, and mistakes elite ideology and self-presentation for reality. As Eric Havelock and others have pointed out, assemblies in fact play a communally essential role: they are convened whenever an important issue needs to be discussed and decided upon; they are a crucial feature of communal life; and the procedures are firmly established by tradition. The elite speakers, although all entitled in principle to address the assembly, are ranked in a hierarchy determined by status, age, and accomplishment; they often establish their credentials before expressing their opinion, and they try to convince the assembly—hence the importance attributed, among the leaders' qualities, to excellence in speaking. The leader ignores strong popular sentiment at his peril: if he fails in executing his plan, he risks censure and revolt.[76]

Even this revised assessment of the assembly's communal significance, however, does not change the fact that "freedom" played no role in the political realm. Freedom of speech was no formalized right; it was simply taken for granted by those who enjoyed it. Freeman status was not recognized as a criterion to determine "rights," such as participation in assembly or debate; and the freedom of individuals or the community was no issue of public discussion. The preconditions for a high valuation of freedom thus were completely lacking even in the polis's internal realm.[77]

To sum up this brief discussion, despite early intimations apparent in the epics, the development of a collective awareness of freedom was prevented by social and political structures and relationships, by the specific ways of thinking and forms of identification, and by the nature of political conflicts within and among early poleis. Neither the wars that tested communal solidarity nor political life within the community offered an incentive for linking political consciousness to freedom. As long as elite leadership and social domination remained unchallenged, other values and priorities prevailed.

This explains why freedom was appreciated at most on the individual and private, not the communal and political, levels. Although it was all-important to belong to and identify with various social and political entities and collectives (oikos, polis, or elite) because everything, from survival to status and power, depended on them, freedom had little to do with all this. To be sure, the Trojans could be free only as long as Troy was free; but this observation is both too elementary and anachronistic. In reality, the Trojans were not fighting for their individual or collective freedom but for survival and the preservation of their community—in later terminology, for *sōtēria* (deliverance), not for *eleutheria*. Only when they reflected on the consequences of their possible failure to achieve *sōtēria* did the loss of freedom enter their minds, and then only concerning individuals or weak groups within the community (primarily women).

We must make a careful distinction here: without doubt, to the individual in Homeric society his personal freedom was important. But apparently the awareness or appreciation of such freedom was limited to certain situations, most significantly the loss of freedom itself. Slavery was a widespread institution, firmly embedded in society; the epics often dwell on the misery associated with it—especially the traumatic experience suffered by the formerly free (and especially former members of the elite) who have lost their freedom.[78] The *Odyssey*, in particular, exploits to great effect the peculiar tension generated by the fact that the best friend and most capable assistant of a noble leader (who claims himself to have experienced enslavement) is a slave (and himself an owner of slaves) but was born a prince, that a person can thus be both free and unfree, noble and slave, king and beggar, and thanks to disguise and imaginative speech not just successively but at one and the same time.

Individual awareness of the value of personal freedom thus existed from early times. Such awareness increased over time (prompted, for example, by the spread of commercial slavery and debt bondage) but for centuries remained limited to this personal and individual aspect. Due to the structure of archaic society, this type of status difference received relatively little attention in everyday life. In the self-perception and values of the ruling elite, personal freedom was a low priority; in their practical experiences, it was rarely an important issue, but more an "epic" theme. And in political life the conditions were lacking that would have allowed freedom to become a value concept of more than occasional significance.

The World of Hesiod

One might object that all this is valid at most for the elite; especially the non-elite free farmers would have viewed the matter differently.[79] To determine to what extent this is true we turn now to Hesiod. He provides further insight into the conditions that facilitated the emergence of both the awareness and the concept of freedom. The question of whether Homer's world is historically comparable to Hesiod's is no longer in dispute. The picture of early Greek society drawn especially in *Works and Days* (*WD;* probably composed in the early seventh century) has been used by scholars as a valuable complement to that presented in the Homeric epics.[80]

Hesiod is especially important for our present purposes because he is the first not only to mention the core values of the growing polis community but to make them central to his deliberations. Moreover, he presents himself as spokesman for the commoners and as such speaks out against some traditional claims of the elite. Given the "political" nature of his poetry and his concern for what is needed to ensure the well-being of individual and community, it is striking that he uses neither *eleutheros* nor *doulos* nor their derivatives. Closer examination shows that these are not simply chance omissions owing to a particular direction of his thought that gave him no opportunity for introducing this subject.

The concept of justice, protected by Zeus, is crucial to Hesiod's thinking; with many variations, it runs as a leitmotif through the first part of the *Works and Days*.[81] In particular, the poet establishes a causal relationship between the uprightness of the individual and the well-being of the community; considering not only physical prosperity but also political aspects of communal life, he goes far beyond some parallels found in Homer.[82] For my present purpose, though, what Hesiod does *not* say is equally important. For example, in an antithetical description of the just and unjust cities, "men whose justice is straight" (*WD* 230, cf. 225) are blessed not only with health, fertility of humans and animals, and rich harvests but also with "youth-nurturing [*kourotrophos*] peace"; neither do they suffer war, famine, and other disasters, nor do they need to sail the sea to make a living (227–37). Conversely, the unjust city, ruined even by a single man's wickedness (240–41),[83] will be afflicted with hunger, epidemics, and infertility "through the counsels of Zeus . . . who punishes wrong by wiping out large armies, walls, and ships at sea" (238–47, tr. Athanassakis 1983).

External peace thus is seen as one of the factors guaranteeing the flourishing of the polis, and war as one of the evils threatening it. War in turn brings twofold destruction: of the army—and with it the death of the community's men (hence peace is *kourotrophos*)—and of the city walls, followed presumably by the capture of the city. The consequences of the city's defeat and conquest for the inhabitants—a recurrent theme in Homer—are not even hinted at. Nor is domestic peace mentioned as one of the blessings of a just city, or discord among its citizens as one of the evils suffered by an unjust city.[84] This eliminates both aspects under which freedom could be perceived as a value, as we saw it in Homer and will see it in Solon.

In the *Theogony*, Hesiod lists the monstrous offspring of Strife (*eris*), which pose manifold threats to a community (226–32):

> Then loathsome Strife bore Ponos, the bringer of pains,
> Oblivion and Famine and the tearful Sorrows,
> the Clashes and the Battles and the Manslaughters,
> the Quarrels and the Lies and Argument and Counter-Argument,
> Lawlessness [*Dusnomia*] and Ruin [*Atē*] whose ways are all alike,
> and Oath, who, more than any other, brings pains on mortals
> who of their own accord swear false oaths.

"These are all consequences of strife, but at the same time they are often its manifestations" and appear chiefly in the two most important areas of a man's self-assertion: in battle and debate.[85] Again, the effects of *eris* in war are not pursued beyond slaughter on the battlefield. But among its civil manifestations, Hesiod lists two general concepts that together encompass broadly the disturbed internal order of the community: *dusnomia* and *atē*, "civic disorder" and "self-destructive action," "ruin," "which are closely related."[86] The symptoms of this negative condition, however, are not spelled out. Again, Solon will be much more specific here, not least in thinking of the loss of freedom to a tyrant.

Another passage in the *Theogony* is even more revealing: Zeus's "second wife was radiant Themis; she bore the Horai: Good Order [Eunomia] and Justice [Dike] and blooming Peace [Eirene], who watch over the works of mortal men" (901–3). The relationship between these divine powers is as important as are the qualities they represent. In the epic world, Themis embodies the divinely sanctioned traditional order.[87] By presenting her as Zeus's wife and mother of the Horai, Hesiod emphasizes the importance of the Horai and establishes an intimate link between the guiding principles of the old order (Themis) and those of Zeus's new order.[88] The Horai are usually goddesses of the seasons, of growth and the flourishing of nature, and their care for human works accordingly focuses on the fertility of fields. By transferring this function to the political realm, Hesiod sets a new order of priorities.[89] We do not need to go into details here,[90] but that these three personified values together embody the new order established and guaranteed by Zeus can only mean that Hesiod sees them as *the* decisive factors for the well-being of a community—a view confirmed by other passages—and that concepts not included here have a lower priority.[91]

The Horai here are sisters and thus of equal importance. Conversely, in the images of the just and unjust cities, peace is the consequence of respect for *dikē* and war of its disregard. Freedom, however expressed, is mentioned in neither passage; hence, it is not one of the primary requisites of good order.[92] If, in keeping with the rationale visible in Hesiod, a sequence were to be constructed, causally or systematically connecting political values, freedom would appear only at a later stage, as an effect or manifestation of *dikē,* *eunomia,* or *eirēnē.* In a corresponding negative sequence—as we learn from Homer and Solon—concern about *doulosunē* would emerge as a consequence of bad order (*dusnomia*), injustice, and lack of peace (war or civil strife, *stasis*).

In sum, in all the passages cited above, Hesiod fails to use even the Homeric formulas *eleutheron* or *doulion ēmar.* Among the many evils he repeatedly enumerates in both works, he never once mentions servitude or enslavement as divinely imposed plagues or the consequences of human injustice, although he is perfectly aware of slavery and has ample opportunity to draw such connections.[93] Surely, this means that freedom was no primary value and its absence no major concern to him, and that, consequently, neither was worth thinking about much.

This is remarkable in a writer who sought to recognize and systematize the factors and phenomena essential to human life, to conceptualize life in all its complexity, and to show his contemporaries a way out of their difficulties. It is even stranger because we think of his time as filled with wars, raids, and violence, and because the tradition of heroic epic presented him with numerous examples of misery resulting from the loss of freedom. If he failed to respond to these stimuli, it must be either because he deliberately ignored the issues pertaining to freedom and slavery or because he saw no substantial problems in them.

Given Hesiod's intentions, the former is unlikely. True, he seems to take pains to ignore some important aspects of life, but motives are not difficult to find. Two examples will illustrate this. One concerns politics and communal institutions. The activities taking place in the Agora, including assemblies and arbitration of quarrels, are highly suspect to him, because they distract the farmer from his vital work: they are a waste of time, which those struggling on the margins of subsistence can ill afford. This much the poet needs to say, but any closer involvement with the subject would contradict the general intention of his advice.[94] The same might be true for war, largely ignored in both poems. As H. T. Wade-Gery puts it, this is as remarkable as if a modern author failed to mention love. He concludes that Hesiod, who "sets no value on military courage or leadership," may be reacting strongly to the *Iliad* and suggests the "narrowness of the peasant" as a possible explanation.[95] More plausibly, we might think of the difference in outlook between this poet and Homer: Hesiod's world is not that of the elite. The nobleman's military excellence, highlighted in Homer because of the epics' subject matter and their focus on elite values, is of no immediate relevance to the working farmer. Hesiod is interested in only one of the nobleman's activities, his function as a judge.[96] Hence, he is not concerned with aristocratic values and, if his negative feelings about seafaring are an indication (*WD* 618–91), would presumably have condemned participation in wars and raids as an incalculable risk and irresponsible distraction from the farmer's primary obligations.[97]

Thus, Hesiod's failure to pay much attention to war, let alone to glorify it, has a basis similar to that for his silence on the details of political life. Such omission represents a deliberate choice, for he clearly is familiar with war and introduces it as a matter of course, together with some of its consequences, when describing the evils of human life.[98] In fact, his independence from the epic tradition is demonstrated by his vivid depiction of the blessings of peace and by his pointed reference to Eirene as one of the primary representatives of Zeus's new order.

These reasons, however, are decidedly not valid for Hesiod's omission of the concepts of freedom and slavery. As Solon's later example shows (which will be discussed in the next section), their inclusion could have lent further emphasis and urgency to Hesiod's arguments. If, then, such omission was not deliberate, these issues must have been largely unproblematic to him. This means, on the one hand, that a freeman like Hesiod, while certainly recognizing the condition of servitude as such, and thus also its contrast to personal freedom, would not have had sufficient reason to regard it as a problem or a subject for reflection. Presumably, therefore, in Hesiod's world the institution of slavery was taken for granted: slaves were integrated into the oikos; usually their treatment differed little from that of free servants. For the freeman himself, on the other hand, the chances of losing his own freedom and thereby personally experiencing the negative sides of slavery were remote.

If this is correct, it suggests that war, at least in the extreme forms of conquest and enslavement of cities, was a less troubling and pervasive reality in the experience of Hesiod and his contemporaries than it appears to have been in a somewhat earlier world described by Homer.[99] At any rate, the poet's main concerns lie elsewhere. His instructions are rightly seen as an early reflection of economic and social crisis, forcing smallholders to fight desperately for their survival. Hesiod believes their problems can still be resolved: if they are lucky to escape setbacks and disasters and take no risks, if they work diligently and earn the gods' blessings by living justly, they can achieve prosperity and higher social standing. Debt certainly is a real danger, but its ultimate consequence, debt bondage, is no matter of concern.[100] Hence, the development that reached its climax in Athens at the time of Solon, when an alarming number of indebted farmers lost their land and freedom, can have been only in its initial stages in Hesiod's time. The poet's thinking therefore remains focused on justice, his appeals to the nobility on the sphere of arbitration and jurisdiction; the value of personal freedom and the misery caused by its loss fail to catch his attention.

Conclusions

Pursuing a different line of thought, Hans Schäfer concludes that "there were deep-seated conditions in the aristocratic way of life which prevented freedom, in whatever context, from being brought to general attention and entering the political arena as a programmatic rallying cry in its own right."[101] This sums up equally well our own considerations. In the social and political life of the early Hellenic poleis, dominated by an emerging aristocracy, as reflected in Homer and Hesiod, the dawning awareness of freedom as a value concept was severely limited. Although the significance of the loss of freedom was thoroughly understood, such loss was a rare occurrence, suffered mostly by the weak members of society (women and children). This in itself sufficed to prevent the condition of being free from gaining high and enduring esteem. It was probably less the sum of such individual experiences of lost freedom than their daily contacts in the oikos with those who were unfree that made people aware of the negative aspects typical of the slave's life. Eventually, such observations were combined in a typology of the slave, which, however, did not trigger the simultaneous development of a comparable positive typology of the free. The most important reason for this must have been that in everyday life it was less the slave who was compared to the free than the servant, whether free or slave, who was compared to the master (*despotēs*). Among the elite, the *despotēs* or lord (*anax*) of an oikos was identical with the *basileus*—of whose typology, of course, the epics contain many examples.[102]

In his very impressive and comprehensive study *Freedom in the Making of Western Culture*, Orlando Patterson comes to a diametrically opposed conclusion. He is an expert on modern slavery, a comparative sociologist, and an anthropologist. He is interested less in the terminology used by ancient societies than in their experiences as we can reconstruct them from their literary testimonies. In particular, he examines the experience of slavery from the perspectives of both slaves and masters in order to gauge their perceptions and reactions, changes in consciousness these might have caused, and the value that might have been attached to freedom—whether or not these societies used "freedom" or related words to describe this value. He thus postulates "freedom consciousness" long before the corresponding terminology existed (at all or in socially and politically effective forms); in his view, terminology offers valuable confirmation, when attaching itself to already existing values, but is not essential to the argument. This approach obviously differs from mine, which (as described in the introductory chapter) takes presence or absence of specific terminology as indicators of consciousness or lack thereof.[103]

Patterson essentially argues for two theses. One is that freedom "was generated from the experience of slavery" (xiii). "Freedom began its career as a social value in the desperate yearning of the slave to negate what, for him or her, and for nonslaves, was a peculiarly inhuman condition" (9, cf. 48 and often). The other thesis is that freedom "began its long journey in the Western consciousness as a women's value. It was women who first lived in terror of enslavement, and hence it was women who first came to value its absence, both those who were never captured but lived in dread of it and, even more, those who were captured and lived in hope of being redeemed" (xv, 51). Later, when there emerged two other forms of freedom ("civic" and "sovereignal," 3–4), this value became a men's and a communal or civic issue as well, although even then, Patterson thinks, the experience of slavery and of women remained fundamental and indispensable (chaps. 4–7).

Both theses deserve a detailed discussion. Here I have to confine myself to a few brief remarks. Despite many valid and stimulating insights, I ultimately find neither thesis convincing. The first is correct in a general and basic way: without the reality or the threat of loss of freedom, there could be no consciousness and high valuation of freedom. Nor, as pointed out above, can there be any doubt about the early Greeks' acute awareness of the misery of slavery and the value of personal freedom. The question is to what extent such consciousness transcended individual sentiments, was shared by the collectivity, and eventually compelled the community to attribute high value to freedom and even conceptualize it. Early Greek society was completely male dominated, strongly status oriented, and highly competitive.[104] In this kind of society, I suggest, it was not the experience of the slaves themselves, however sad and harrowing it may have been, nor the feelings of freewomen that were decisive; in other words, what mattered for the creation of public consciousness and values was not the perception and reaction of the weak members of society but that of the strong ones: the freemen and especially those who mattered most, the elite. As long as the freemen, whether high or low, did not in their majority adopt the view that freedom was an essential issue—which essentially means, as long as freedom did not become for *them* an important, let alone urgent or dominant, concern—freedom remained, beyond those affected directly or indirectly by its loss, a low-priority value. In this chapter, I have tried to demonstrate what factors caused this to be the case.

For the same reasons, I have doubts about Patterson's second thesis, that women played a crucial role in the "making of freedom." Unlike men, Patterson argues, women were enslaved frequently; for them, integration as wives into their master's family and thus redemption from slavery were distinct possibilities. Women thus empathized with the fate of slaves and realized the value and desirability of freedom (50–55). Even in classical Greece, by "empathizing with the slave end of the master-slave relation . . . , women became more conscious of freedom by the ever present experience of powerlessness, natal alienation, and dishonor." In other words, since women were "excluded from the public household" and had no means of wresting concessions from the elite, they inevitably empathized with the slave condition (78). In all of this, Patterson seems to me to misjudge the women's identity and underestimate the men's exposure to slavery. Whether women were as oppressed in democratic Athens as Patterson thinks is much debated. Unlike the slaves, however, many of whom were not born as such, the women's condition was not the result of a sudden, catastrophic change in their lives; rather, they were used to this condition, which had prevailed for generations, took it as a given, and developed strategies to cope with it. It is a priori more likely that they would decidedly empathize and identify with the master end of the master-slave relation. Despite the restrictions placed on them, they belonged to the master class and were *astai*, "citizen women," holding a crucially important position in the oikos and community.[105]

In early Greece, as particularly illustrated in the *Odyssey*, men were enslaved as well, though much less frequently and not usually as the result of war. Slave women who ended up as wives of their masters must have formed a small minority. Moreover, the voice we hear in the epics is rarely the woman's own or one attributed to her by the (male) narrator; in most cases, as Hector's conversation with Andromache illustrates beautifully, it is the men who talk and think about the women's enslavement.[106] Men thus shared with the women concerns about the loss of freedom and the fate of slaves. Hence, if such thoughts and experiences were conducive to evoking freedom consciousness among the free, it is not convincing that freewomen, whatever their disabilities, should have been in a substantially different position from freemen—except that they were not able to draw from such consciousness political consequences. Neither, of course, did the men: for the reasons discussed above (and on which Patterson seems to agree with me), they did not develop a high level of freedom consciousness or create corresponding values or concepts—until, as we shall see in the next chapter, dramatic changes in social relations and economic conditions confronted many of them in new ways with the loss and value of freedom.

Returning, then, to my own argument, our survey of missing preconditions makes it possible indeed to define the changes that might cause freedom to become a conscious social and eventually political value. This could happen in a number of ways. The customs of war might change so that armed conflicts resulted no longer in the destruction of cities but in their subjugation, and in the enslavement not just of women and children but of men as well. As a result, male slaves would become less exceptional, and with increasing frequency, slavery might change its character, prompting a change in awareness among the free as well. Moreover, free farmers might come to depend on the nobility not merely for the arbitration of conflicts but also economically, which might lead to exploitation and new forms of dependence. Consequently, the loss of freedom would no longer be blamed only on intangibles—war, piracy, or god-sent fate—but on individuals, members of the same community, who were known and could therefore be criticized or attacked. All this might happen not simply in isolated cases but in increasing frequency and according to recognizable patterns. Then again, the aristocratic value system might be questioned and elite power challenged; in the aristocratic self-perception, new alternatives to status based on predominance might emerge: not only nonexistence as Homer's epics seem to imply but loss of status or of dominance, even subordination to a ruler. Finally, the relationship within the community between the private and public spheres might shift; the latter might become more intense and be structured by regulated institutions, procedures, and laws; new forms of accruing power might emerge, new identities become possible or be demanded, and the principles previously determining the individual's ability to participate in government lose their validity. Under the influence of such changes, in whatever combination, it might eventually become possible for the concept of freedom to gain attractiveness as a value and political slogan. The example of Solonian Athens illustrates the possibilities and, again, limitations of such a development.

2.3. POLITICAL AWARENESS OF FREEDOM:
BEGINNINGS IN SOLONIAN ATHENS

Individual Freedom as a Political Issue: Liberation from Debt Bondage
When Solon was elected magistrate (archon) in 594, Athens was immersed in civil strife. He was given special powers to resolve conflicts and institute necessary reforms. The extant fragments of his poems offer precious insight into various aspects of the crisis he was confronted with, some of the measures he enacted, and, above all, his thinking. These poems, elegiac and iambic songs, were most likely performed at elite symposia; hence, they are not identical with his public statements but probably reflect the gist of these statements.[107] Moreover, as in the case of Hesiod's, Archilochus's, and other archaic poetry, it is possible here, too, "that the persona of the poet . . . is but a function of the traditions inherited by that poem." I have argued elsewhere, however, that the unusual specificity of some statements in the poems preserved under Solon's name and especially the compelling political logic expressed in them link the poet to the Athenian lawgiver and allow us to treat these poems as expressions of a specific person in a specific time, place, and circumstance.[108] Nevertheless, they were, of course, embedded in a poetic tradition and widespread poetic culture, and they were attractive to Panhellenic audiences because they dealt with issues that, although historically specific, were of immediate importance to many outside Athens.

Apparently, Solon was confronted with the problem of servitude and freedom on two different levels. One was the economic and social plight of a substantial number of farmers who had lost their freedom and were either held in bondage in Attica or had even been enslaved and sold abroad. So much is clear from Solon's own statements.[109] In some way or other, these problems were connected with the tenure or occupation of land, which Solon claims to have liberated by pulling out the markers (*horoi*) that were fixed in many places.[110] Exactly what categories of dependent persons were involved, what had happened to the land, what the *horoi* signified, and how and why all this had come about: these questions are still debated intensely. It suffices here to note that restrictions and loss of freedom resulting from debt and obligations (a variety of statuses usually combined in the term "debt bondage") had become an increasingly serious and frequent problem, widely visible in Attica. According to a long-standing view, in this near-revolutionary situation two principal demands were voiced: "land reform" and "liberation of the farmers."[111] If this interpretation, though recently challenged, is correct, Solon emphatically rejected egalitarian tendencies aiming at *isomoiria* (equal distribution of land). But he restored the freedom of the bonded or enslaved farmers, "shook off the burden of debt" (*seisachtheia*), instituted an amnesty law, and prohibited lending on the security of the borrower's person.[112]

Similar crisis factors had facilitated the establishment of tyranny in other poleis. Solon refused to take this step, apparently thwarting the expectations of some of his supporters. He repeatedly warned his fellow citizens against the servitude (*doulosunē*) with which a tyrant would threaten the polis, although he was ultimately unable to prevent it and perhaps lived to see the first stages of Peisistratus's seizure of power.[113]

In both contexts, Solon mentions "servitude"; but only in that of debt bondage does he explicitly speak of "liberation," of "being free." Is this due to the incomplete preservation of Solon's poetry,[114] to a peculiarity of his vocabulary, or to an uneven usage in the language of the time which perhaps attests to an essential conceptual difference? It seems clear, in any case, that Solon himself worried more than most Athenians about the loss of freedom threatened by tyranny.[115] By contrast, the problem of debt bondage was of great concern to many people. Even without Aristotle's and Plutarch's comments it would be clear from Solon's remarks (on which the former are largely based) that in the context of the agrarian crisis freedom had become a political battle cry: the problem of the personal freedom of a large number of individuals (though probably still a minority in the community) had developed into a major political issue affecting the entire community and forcing it to take a stand.[116] This was true, even though, as Solon says himself, not all the practices resulting in dependence and servitude violated the customary rules concerning the handling of debts and obligations.[117] Several factors may have contributed to bringing freedom to such political prominence.

First, the persons affected were not imported foreign slaves, whose presence continued to be taken for granted. Rather, they were Athenians, who as dependent debtors presumably found themselves in a status of suspended citizenship; theoretically, they could resume their original rights and duties, whatever these were at the time, once they met their obligations.[118] Second, this type of servitude did not result from war or piracy; it was not imposed by fate or an outside enemy but by Athenians, fellow citizens. Third, it was not the phenomenon as such that was new—debt bondage, in fact, was quite normal in archaic societies—but its occurrence on a massive scale, its pervasiveness and visibility. The victims had once been free farmers; after losing their independence, they often continued to work in Attica for their masters until, in extreme cases, they were sold abroad. The *horoi,* whether debt markers or boundary stones on formerly public lands, provided conspicuous evidence of what was happening throughout Attica.[119]

It is difficult to see why these issues erupted in a crisis precisely in this period. Long-standing economic difficulties among small and middling landholders, fueled especially by continual division of inheritances and overuse of land, may have contributed. Other factors are likely to have been involved. According to a plausible hypothesis, economic opportunities and social attitudes changed rapidly in the seventh century, prompting the elite, in their competition for prestige and power, to place increasing emphasis on the possession of goods of all kinds (especially land, horses, and valuables) and a lavish lifestyle. Rivalries among elite families intensified, impelling them to make more effective use of their own resources and perhaps also to appropriate formerly communal resources. Hence, traditional disparities in economic and social power were exploited more intensely and recklessly by old elite families and newly rich upstarts who strove to emulate them. In the process, some of them kept within the bounds of traditionally tough debt laws; others resorted to measures far exceeding traditional norms.[120] The victims, whose situation, strained in the best of circumstances, worsened drastically, at least knew exactly who was responsible for their plight.

All this helps explain why in this specific situation the problem of servitude prompted intense reactions. But it only partially explains why, for example, elite despotism was no longer tolerated, as it was in the well-known Thersites scene in the *Iliad* (2.211–77), or why people no longer accepted the grim work ethic recommended by Hesiod or simply resigned themselves to their fate but were instead led to solidarity and open revolt. For both solidarity and rebellion must have been decisive preconditions for Solon's election as an official mediator and his success in realizing his reforms. Since, in his own words, he rallied the people behind his program of liberating those bound in servitude (36W = 30GP.1–2), massive pressure from below must have played a crucial role;[121] the issue was by no means simply one of mediating quarrels between noble factions and preventing tyranny, which could easily have resulted from such quarrels.

We do not know how such solidarity was achieved; nor do we know what political processes made it possible to forge the compromises required to secure a peaceful resolution of the crisis.[122] We are not completely ignorant, however. Athenian developments should probably be seen in the context of a widespread economic and social crisis that plagued the world of Greek poleis in the late seventh century and the emergence of a broad range of new opportunities, connected with colonization, trade, and the expansion of crafts. Although the extent and significance of such changes are difficult to assess with any precision, the changes themselves are undeniable, and they may have made the lot of the debt bondsmen seem even worse: alternatives now became available to them, and their impulse to free themselves from bondage now had a concrete goal.[123] The free farmers had long been a crucial component of polis society, firmly integrated in its military and political structures. Such structures were increasingly formalized in the seventh century; regulations were introduced defining who had what rights and obligations and who did not and what qualifications were required for certain civic functions. Although such demarcations initially may have been dictated by elite interests, institutional fixation, just like the enactment of written law, was a means of overcoming crisis situations; it was based on broad communal support and an indicator of increasing political awareness.[124]

Combined, these changes severely threatened established power structures and greatly increased social mobility.[125] In stark contrast to archaic Rome, Greek elites, mired in rivalries and power struggles (as attested in Athens both before and after Solon), were not strong enough to defend their traditional position of comprehensive predominance; moreover, restraint and reform as means to reinforce aristocratic self-discipline must have been seen by many as preferable to civil strife, violence, and collective loss of power to a tyrant.[126] Compromises involving mediators and lawgivers with extraordinary powers were not infrequent in archaic Greece; the influential role of these persons attests to a remarkably developed political culture and at the same time helped advance political thinking.[127] One generation earlier,

Draco had set an example of how a crisis that threatened domestic peace could be resolved by enacting specific written legislation.[128]

Furthermore, increasing availability of imported slaves offered easier means of satisfying the demand for dependent labor, typical of all ancient societies. Although slave trade existed already in Homeric society, a tradition connected with the island of Chios indicates that it was a fairly recent innovation; this tradition perhaps preserves the memory of rapid changes in scale and significance of "chattel slavery." At any rate, the abolition of domestic debt bondage was interconnected with the rise of chattel slavery, both in Athens and in Rome. The radical concept of guaranteeing the citizen's personal freedom, realized in Athens by Solon, thus was directly related to the expansion of what would henceforth be the dominant form of slavery in the strict sense, which was characterized by almost total lack of freedom.[129]

Finally, the emergence of an energetic, visionary, and charismatic leader, standing above all parties, as Solon apparently was, must have been a catalyst in the evolving crisis and a condition for its resolution. He facilitated the expression of needs and dissatisfaction and helped mobilize those affected to a far greater extent than might otherwise have been the case. He had a program and was known for his integrity; his leadership thus made the argument that reform was imperative widely acceptable.[130] The crisis and its symptoms most likely were not confined to Athens, but similarly radical measures are not attested elsewhere; although debt bondage was apparently abolished at least in the poleis of mainland Greece, we do not know to what extent Athenian experiences can be generalized.

It was not, therefore, just the circumstances in which freedom was lost, and the specific form of that loss, that prompted the politicization of the issues of freedom and servitude. It was also the long-term social, economic, and political changes in the Greek world and especially the evolution of the polis and its institutions that effected new political awareness among broader segments of the population and enabled them to take action. Even though all this was still in its beginning stage, it encouraged a sense of community among victims, prompted solidarity among others, and made possible a successful struggle to regain lost status and abolish the customary institutions responsible for that loss. As Finley points out: "The element of social conflict hovers about the history of debt-bondage everywhere in the ancient world. There are distinctions, however . . . : in Greece and Rome the debtor-class rebelled, whereas in the Near East they did not."[131] Eventually, a strong sentiment that emphasized the fundamental difference between imported slavery (through purchase or capture) and domestic servitude must have spread widely. To push fellow citizens into bondage or, worse, to enslave them became intolerable, and the community was forced to take action.[132] Solon must have contributed significantly to the general acceptance of these views, not least by pronouncing his convictions that inaction would inevitably result in disaster, all would be affected by it, and, consequently, every citizen was responsible for the community's well-being.[133]

That Solon was in a position to realize such radical measures as the cancellation of debts and the abolition of debt bondage shows the strength and broad base of his support. At this early stage, however, such solidarity probably aimed chiefly at rectifying social and economic abuses and preventing their recurrence.[134] Even though the sphere of public concern, responsibility, and participation was greatly extended by involving the community in guaranteeing the citizens' personal status, Solon was neither a political revolutionary nor a democrat; his statements demonstrate that he was far from radically redistributing political power.[135]

Freedom and Citizenship

Solon's measures, which established the irrevocable right of every citizen to personal freedom, provided a minimum of equality among the citizens, who were thereby distinguished more sharply from all others.[136] Every positive definition of citizen status, no matter how modest, inevitably brought with it a corresponding negative definition of noncitizen status. The question then is whether, as a result, freedom came to be recognized as an essential criterion for Athenian citizenship. In the second half of the fifth century, when democracy was fully developed, this certainly was the case: not high birth or wealth but merely free status was seen as the crucial condition for the enjoyment of all rights, including full political participation—but, of course, from 451/450, only the citizens who narrowly defined themselves as a closed descent group met this requirement. As a criterion for determining citizenship and delimiting the citizen body, freedom thus was an obvious and necessary but not a sufficient condition. The situation in Solonian Athens was radically different and more complex.[137]

So far, I have used the terms "citizenship" and "citizens" loosely. Generally speaking, at some point in its development, every polis underwent a process of self-delimitation, establishing strict criteria for membership, creating a specific concept of citizenship, and consciously excluding and assigning to a lower status a potentially large group of free and permanent fellow residents. This process did not result from abstract or legal considerations, although eventually it was expressed in such terms; rather, it followed upon changes in group consciousness, increased communal integration, and the formalization of active political participation by broader segments of the nonaristocratic population. Put simply, citizenship was defined restrictively when it was perceived as a privilege or key to enjoying privileges, or when it seemed threatened by massive changes (such as an unprecedented influx of foreigners).[138] These conditions did not apply to Athens in the early sixth century. The polis was far from unified: local or regional power centers, dominated by elite families, served as bases for fierce factional rivalry; integration, though stimulated by legal measures and reforms enacted by Draco and Solon, was advanced decisively only half a century later when the tyrants suppressed factional strife and focused the community on its center in Athens, but this process was probably not completed before the end of the sixth century.[139] Strict and legal definitions of citizen and metic (resident alien) status are most plausibly dated to the first half of the fifth century; they were a consequence of the social and political reforms enacted around 508/507 under the leadership of Cleisthenes and of changes such as massive immigration connected with unprecedented economic developments especially after the Persian Wars.[140] In the sixth century, membership in the polis was defined much more vaguely, the citizen community resembled the community of free inhabitants more closely than it did in later centuries, rights and privileges were few and overshadowed by dependencies, the boundary between members and nonmembers was permeable, and immigrants could still be assimilated fairly easily.[141] With few exceptions, these conditions were still relatively close to those reflected in Homer's epics, which provide evidence for both the integration of foreigners and the presence of *metanastai*, residents who apparently were not full members of the polis; one exception is that Solon's law subjected the former, previously controlled by elite families, to a communal decision.[142] Conversely, participation in the processes of communal decision making most likely was restricted, not by law but by traditional norms, to those who mattered and had sufficient social prestige (which was determined by land ownership and economic capacity, defined in agrarian terms), that is, the elite and the free farmers who qualified for the polis's hoplite army.[143]

The debt bondsmen and enslaved Athenians who were freed by Solon's measures presumably had been in the status of *atimoi* (unprotected members of the community) and became *entimoi* again; that is, they enjoyed the "rights" and protection to which all members of the community were entitled, including the guarantee of personal freedom. To what extent they could be active politically depended not on their personal status but on their economic capacity.[144] Similarly, "official" immigrants, though *entimoi* and protected and thus presumably covered by the prohibition on lending on the security of the borrower's person, would be incapable of owning land and thus remain excluded from active political participation. In this respect, they were hardly distinguishable from the Athenian thetes.[145] All these categories of Athenians, though free members of the polis, did not possess the right of full political participation and thus were second-class citizens. But they did participate, for example, in the community's religious activities; typically, the Hekatompedon Decree, dated 485/484, still seems to distinguish between *eleutheroi* and *douloi*, while later the free Athenian citizens were always designated as *Athēnaioi*.[146]

A similar limitation holds for the potential political significance—and effect on political awareness—of social distinctions in archaic laws. Such legislation had to consider, in various contexts, the differing roles of free persons (who were divided into various categories as occasion demanded) and slaves (along with other status groups). It both set new rules, reacting to recent changes and needs, and fixed traditional norms in writing, reflecting attitudes that had developed over a long period of time.[147] If for a given offense slaves had to pay a higher penalty than free persons, and, conversely, harm done to a slave incurred only a portion of the penalty levied for a crime against a free person, this merely expressed in the sphere of law a long-standing and generally accepted social distinction. What was new was neither the distinction nor the underlying attitude but the procedure, which transferred punishment from private to communal control. This is equally true of other regulations.[148] By and large, the publication, fixation, and standardization of law did not create a new awareness but at most intensified already existing awareness. Long-accepted status differences thus might be felt more acutely, and the free might think more highly of their personal freedom.

Still, in the particular case of Athens, it is tempting to think that Solon's legislation, prompted by a crisis in which freedom had become a central political issue, must have greatly enhanced public consciousness and helped establish this value permanently in the political sphere. The former probably is true but the latter remains doubtful. The status difference between free and unfree was emphasized more sharply as the polis developed and as membership was both given a minimal definition and subjected to communal control. Yet despite its politicization in the Solonian crisis, this contrast was significant primarily in the individual citizen's private sphere.[149] In the public and political sphere, it did not replace the previously dominant distinctions between elite and commoners or between those who mattered and those who did not—distinctions that, in fact, remained essential for a long time. Rather, in a long process a new antithesis began to emerge that perhaps appeared in the political limelight for the first time after the overthrow of tyranny and was fully developed only by the mid–fifth century. This antithesis pitched citizens against noncitizens; in this constellation slaves, though of much lower status, were grouped together with freedmen and free foreigners.[150] As a result, the value of personal freedom came to be subordinated to that of citizenship; only under the exceptional conditions of Athenian democracy both were eventually combined in the concept of the "free citizen" and assumed new and unique social and political significance.[151] This development needs to be mentioned here because Solon created the conditions that made it possible. Paradoxically, however, once he established freedom as an irrevocable right of every citizen, it ceased to be a problem and an issue. His reforms thus removed a crucial cause that might have prompted the emergence of a concept of freedom in political life.

The Citizen as Slave of a Tyrant: A Political Concept of Servitude

We still need to ask whether other factors could have assigned an essential and enduring political role to the concept of freedom—for example, if it was combined in a significant way with political institutions or if it became relevant in the context of a negative experience that had a similar effect on the entire community as the crisis the polis had just overcome. In the former case, we should expect that in addition to the measures related to debt and debt bondage the Athenians linked other parts of Solon's legislation or institutional reforms explicitly to freedom. This is unlikely because no evidence survives to support it, and, from all we know, such ideas did not arise until the fifth century.[152] Negative experiences might have included threats to communal freedom through outside aggression or tyranny. As we shall see in the next chapter, however, the preservation of external independence was not an acute issue for Athens until the end of the sixth century and especially the Persian invasions.

It is therefore tyranny that comes to mind most readily when we look for the beginnings of a political concept of freedom. Solon's poems, after all, clearly attest to a connection between tyrannical rule and the servitude of the polis.[153] Moreover, whereas debt bondage resulted in dependence and servitude of individuals and became a political issue involving the community only when large numbers of citizens were affected, in the confrontation with a tyrant it was the collectivity of citizens, the polis as a whole, that was seen as enslaved (oppressed into *doulosunē*) by an individual. Solon thus uses a political concept of servitude.[154] The fact, observed earlier in this chapter, that *eleutheros* does not occur in these contexts raises the question of whether this reflects historical reality or is purely accidental, due to the chance of text survival. If the latter is the case—which, of course, remains possible— Solon must have known the corresponding political concept of freedom; that is, it would have been natural for him to describe nontyranny as freedom of the polis and its citizens. Despite lack of positive evidence this is usually taken for granted, especially since an established pair of semantic opposites is involved.[155] Yet there are reasons for doubt.

First, what seems self-evident to us, particularly in view of later conceptual developments, need not have been so for Solon and his time. True, the perception of the negative was probably needed to perceive and express the positive: without experiencing, understanding, and being able to describe with a specific term political "unfreedom"—that is, without a political concept of servitude—the idea of political freedom could not have been conceived. But the existence of the former merely made the latter possible; it did not necessitate its immediate realization. It is perfectly possible that this potential was developed only much later when different circumstances placed new emphasis on this aspect. As noted before, the form and substance of the concept of servitude generally developed earlier than those related to freedom;[156] the existence of a particular word form or meaning in the one area thus does not guarantee the existence of a corresponding one in the other.

Second, *doulos* stands in semantic opposition not only to *eleutheros* but also to "master" (*despotēs*). The etymology of the latter word and its use in the *Odyssey* indicate that the primary setting for this antithesis was the oikos.[157] What prompted its transfer to the political sphere probably was not the conquest of foreign territories and the concomitant changes in control of power and property but the emergence in the polis of forms of individual rule that were comparable in nature to that of the *despotēs* in the oikos; hence, this term was applied to the "master, ruler of the city" and, by extension, *doulos* and *doulosunē* to his subjects and their condition. The phenomenon of foreign rule was virtually nonexistent in the archaic Greek world, while that of individual rule was frequent, at least in large and active poleis.[158] This fact and obvious typological parallels—above all, the unrestricted, authoritarian, and unaccountable power the master exercised in both spheres—suggest that the concept of *despotēs* was indeed politicized in the context of tyranny.[159] Such analogies later encouraged the characterization of the Persian king as tyrant and "despot" par excellence and in theoretical discussions led to the equation of tyranny with "despotic" rule.[160] Moreover, the term was used early on to describe the rule and power of the gods, often in connection with the sphere or locale in which they were thought to be effective.[161] This transfer from the private to the religious realm exactly parallels that to the political sphere. All this is even more plausible if the original meaning of *turannos*—a word probably imported from Asia Minor—was indeed "master."[162] I suggest, therefore, that in political contexts *doulosunē*, as part of an independent pair of opposites (*doulos-despotēs*), did not automatically presume the politicization of the other pair (*doulos-eleutheros*): nontyranny was not necessarily identified with freedom. Rather, this identification was latent, waiting to be activated when a sufficiently strong impetus demanded it.

Third, in both the emerging polis and early political thought other political concepts apparently were more important than that of freedom. Homer and Hesiod pay much attention to justice.[163] The value concept describing the ideal of a well-functioning polis was "good order" (*eunomia*).[164] *Doulosunē* resulting from tyranny and debt bondage was seen as the direct consequence of *dusnomia* (disorder), and the Greeks always equated tyranny with *anomia* (lack or suspension of order).[165] As we shall see, from this perspective freedom could represent only a partial aspect of the condition of nontyranny, and the opposite of *doulosunē* was *eunomia* understood in its broadest sense. A little later, another aspect of "order" became predominant in the struggle against tyranny: political equality, or *isonomia,* a term that was to be highly prominent in the evolution of democracy as well.[166] As long as political thinking remained focused primarily on the concepts of justice and order, and then on that of equality, there was, aside from problems connected with personal status, no cause that might have prompted the politicization of the concept of freedom.

These three points lend some weight to the argument from silence, that is, the failure of all extant archaic sources, Solon foremost among them, to mention *eleutheros* explicitly in a political context. By Solon's time, apparently, *doulos* but not *eleutheros* had been transferred from the private to the public and political sphere, and *eleutheria* as the opposite noun to *doulosunē* had not yet been forged. Since plausible explanations are available for these facts, it is methodologically preferable not simply to reject the testimony of the extant evidence.[167]

Conclusions

Paradoxical though it may seem, Solon's reforms at least temporarily prevented the emergence of a political concept of freedom. This conclusion can be supported by a brief examination of Solon's political thinking, as it is formulated in a poem on *eunomia* (4W = 3GP). Presumably by empirical observation, Solon recognized that political developments follow certain logical patterns, comparable to those in nature. Just as thunder follows upon lightning, so ambitious men, if given too much power, will seize tyranny, and irresponsible behavior by individuals inevitably affects the whole community.[168] Contrary to traditional beliefs, injustice done to an individual thus concerns not only the victim but everyone, because the consequences will be felt by all. Hence, Solon feels compelled to promulgate the need for civic solidarity and shared responsibility. The practical results of this thinking are evident in his measures to improve legal protection for citizens and in those dealing with the problem of freedom and nonfreedom: the individual's loss of freedom is no longer a matter merely of private but one of communal concern, for if many citizens lose their personal freedom, a predictable chain of escalating factors can lead to civil strife (*stasis*), tyranny, and thus to servitude for all. The elimination of one kind of nonfreedom is thus indispensable for avoiding the other. Solon's far-reaching measures in this area are the logical consequence of such insights.[169]

Although from this perspective the political value of freedom is potentially high, Solon's understanding of sociopolitical causality in fact has the opposite effect: in his thinking, freedom and nonfreedom are parts of a causal chain or hierarchy of values that is topped by *eunomia* and *dusnomia*, followed by *dikē* and *hubris* or *koros* (satiety, excess). Freedom and nonfreedom are functions of the more comprehensive, primary concepts of order or disorder, which are based especially on the rule of justice or injustice but determined by a variety of other factors and expressed in a variety of phenomena.[170] Freedom and nonfreedom each are only one such factor or phenomenon among many that could gain political significance under specific circumstances. This should warn us against singling out or overemphasizing any one of them. Important as freedom may sometimes have been in politics, it was too closely tied to specific and very concrete conditions to gain permanence as a primary or even abstract value concept.

Despite these limitations, the progress in political awareness attained in Solon's time should not be underestimated. For the first time, freedom became a political issue. The consequences for an entire community of loss of freedom in various forms were experienced in a context other than war and not mainly regarding women and children; freedom (in the form of the citizen's freeman status) was recognized as a basic precondition for the polis's well-being; the citizens forged ties of solidarity that reached far beyond the immediate victims of social abuse and assumed responsibility for the individual's freedom so that the entire community could survive and prosper. For the first time, the significance of freedom was understood in its political implications, and awareness of its value became general.

The particular circumstances surrounding this series of events made it unavoidable that the specific aspect of freedom involved, once realized and protected by law, was soon taken for granted. For the time being, no other social or political problem prompted freedom to become a permanent political issue. Other values dominated in political debates. "Nomistic thinking," which traditionally focused on *nomos* (order) as a primary value and opposed *eunomia* to tyranny, made it less urgent to emphasize the aspect of freedom from tyranny—even though the latter's "despotic" character had provoked comparison with the relationship between the master of an oikos and those subjected to his power, especially his slaves, and thus caused, in the domestic sphere of the polis, the development of a political concept of servitude.[171] The question we must now ask is when and under what circumstances the political concept of freedom did finally break through.

The Emergence of the Political Concept of Freedom

3.1. POLIS INDEPENDENCE AND THE PERSIAN WARS

Our survey, at the beginning of the last chapter (2.1), of the earliest uses of *eleutheros* and *doulos* has shown that the issue of polis freedom is absent in the extant literature of the archaic period, while the possible "enslavement" of a polis is mentioned only once, and then only late. Yet, quite apart from the epics, from the middle of the seventh century lyric poetry often focuses on the subject of war or the defense of a community against an external threat (one need only think of Callinus and Tyrtaeus).[1] Moreover, praise of those who died nobly for their country is immortalized in numerous epitaphs of the sixth century.[2] The first person of whom we are told explicitly that he helped prevent the enslavement of his city is Anacreon's friend who died in battle against either the Persians or some other non-Greeks.[3] The earliest references to the external freedom of a polis, too, concern wars of Greeks against the Persians or other non-Greek powers. This is where we start our investigation of the rise of a Greek concept of freedom.

There is general agreement that the experience of the Persian Wars was crucial for the development in Greece of an awareness of the value of freedom and consequently for the conceptualization of freedom, as attested impressively by many contemporary and later sources.[4] Why exactly this was the case, however, has not been explored in detail. Most scholars take it for granted that the experience of anticipating and enduring a threat of such unusual scope, or else the subsequent overwhelming sense of relief at having been saved from it, necessarily brought about a decisive surge in the awareness of freedom among those who lived through this crisis.[5]

Fear and relief may well have been pervasive, but was focus on freedom an inevitable reaction? In what ways was freedom threatened, and how was that threat perceived? Did this particular experience differ from other war experiences other than, perhaps, in degree? More generally, how was war experienced before this time? Was a threat to freedom always part of that experience? When, and in what connection, did the Persian Wars attract the label of "wars of freedom"? Can we observe differences—at the time or over time—in the emphasis placed on this aspect or the validity of its content and meaning? Were there other, different assessments, links to specific political interests, or ideological influences?

At any rate, what seems logical and obvious from hindsight need not have been so at the time, and it is easy to lose sight of the fact that the impact of such an experience on the awareness and conceptualization of freedom could have made itself felt in various ways. It need not, or not only, have resulted from the experience itself or its immediate consequences, nor need it have been perceived at once and in the same way by everyone. To understand the processes involved here, we need to determine exactly how awareness and assessment of freedom as a political value changed over time and place these changes in a broad historical context.

The Persian Wars as Freedom Wars: Origins of a Historical Tradition

Herodotus's account offers a clear picture of the views current in his own time (440s to 420s): at Salamis and Plataea the Greeks blocked the expansionist drive of the Persians, whose goal was to conquer not only Athens, or even Greece, but all of Europe. What the Greeks of Asia Minor had failed to accomplish against the Lydians, against Cyrus, and in their revolt from Persia—that is, to avert the yoke of slavery—was gloriously achieved by the mainland Greeks. The free Greek polis had proved superior to the oriental, barbarian, despotic slave state. The merit for saving the Hellenes belonged above all to the Athenians: at Marathon, they stood firm, virtually alone; the size and quality of their fleet and the strategic skills of their clever leader, Themistocles, were decisive for the victory at Salamis; they then resisted all temptations to enter a profitable separate peace with Persia and, after the battles of Plataea and Mycale, assumed responsibility for continuing the war for freedom.[6] Thucydides and the orators inform us of the political and ideological consequences that the Athenians extracted from these events: their unique responsibility for the freedom of Hellas and their selflessness and moral superiority, they claimed, entitled them not only to political and military leadership but to rule over other Greeks.[7]

All this, fixed in a series of topoi and embedded in a long sequence of great Athenian deeds in the service of Hellas that stretched from mythical times to the present, was constantly repeated in festive and patriotic speeches: this we learn from the funeral orations. Thucydides indicates that such topoi were used as serious arguments in diplomatic negotiations to justify Athenian foreign policy.[8] Non-Athenian funeral epigrams and pointed references in Herodotus to Spartan thinking show that other poleis, too, claimed special credit for the preservation of Greek liberty. Pindar attests to similar ideas among western Greeks, and as Thucydides indicates in respectful memory, even tiny Plataea tended to think in this vein.[9]

From the mid–fifth century at the latest, therefore, the account we grasp in Herodotus and later authors was generally accepted in Athens and, apart from specifically Athenian features, at least among those poleis that had participated in the fight. The question is when the elements of this account emerged, whether those living at the time already regarded the Persian Wars as "freedom wars," and in what other ways they might have expressed their experiences.

Although the earliest extant historians wrote at least half a century later, substantial evidence is available to answer these questions. Aeschylus's *Persians* shows that already in 472 many aspects essential to Herodotus's interpretation dominated the Athenians' understanding of the (still recent) events.[10] Thucydides asserts that after the victory of 479 the Greek commander-in-chief, Pausanias, dedicated an altar and sacrificed to Zeus Eleutherios (the "God of Freedom, Liberator") in the Agora of Plataea.[11] Several epigraphical and literary documents survive from the Persian War period and the two subsequent decades; these include dedicatory prose inscriptions on monuments and votive offerings from the Persian War booty,[12] funerary, dedicatory, and honorary epigrams,[13] other epigraphical documents, fragments of poems by Simonides on events of the Persian Wars, including the recently published elegy on the victory of Plataea, and allusions to the Persian Wars in some of Pindar's odes composed shortly after 480. This evidence confirms that Herodotus's account is based on an old tradition and affords valuable insights into the process by which this tradition took shape. Its evaluation, however, is hampered by uncertainties of authenticity and date. Preferring to err on the side of caution, I eliminate from among the documents mentioning the subject of freedom or servitude all those whose authenticity and/or contemporaneity are doubtful. The following testimonia remain.[14]

Aeschylus's *Persians* (472) emphasizes Xerxes' intention to take revenge for Marathon, conquer Greece, and compete with the conquests of his predecessors by extending his rule over an entire continent. The graphic expression "yoke of servitude" occurs repeatedly. This yoke is to be imposed on Hellas, but as the dream of the Persian queen mother, Atossa, makes clear, to bear it is contrary to Greek nature.[15] The Greek battle cry at Salamis expresses succinctly what was at stake: "Forward, you sons of Hellas! Set your country free! Set free your sons, your wives, tombs of your ancestors, and temples of your gods. All is at stake: now fight!" (*Pers.* 402–5; tr. Vellacott). In response to Atossa's question about the leader (*poimanōr*, "herdsman of men") and master (*despotēs*) of the Athenian host (*stratos*), the chorus exclaims, "No one's slaves [*douloi*] are they called, not subjects [*hupēkooi*] to any man!" (242), thereby anticipating what was to become a topos: the Greeks were free, while the Persians and other Asians, subjected to the tyranny of the Persian king, willingly accepted their "slavery." The same contrast is embodied in the two women of Atossa's dream.[16]

In 470 Pindar composed a "cantata" for the dedication of the new Sicilian town of Aetna, built by Hieron for his son Deinomenes (*Pyth.* 1). Here hope for domestic freedom and peace (60–70) is accompanied by prayers for lasting external freedom, preserved recently in the battles of Himera against the Carthaginians and Cumae against the Etruscans. These two victories, pulling "Hellas out of [the danger of] heavy slavery" (71–75), are ranked with those of Salamis and Plataea (75–80). They represent the Syracusan ruler's claim not only to have saved western Greece from barbarian onslaught but to share equally with Athens and Sparta the glory of having rescued the freedom of the Greek world as a whole.[17] The *Twelfth Olympian Ode* (470 or 466) begins with an invocation to Tyche Soteira (Savior Fortune), daughter of Zeus Eleutherios, and a plea for the protection of the Sicilian town of Himera (1–2). The gods' epithets evoke an experience of rescue and liberation; they probably allude not only to the recent overthrow of the tyranny of Thrasydaeus or of Syracusan rule but also to the victory of 480 over the Carthaginians near Himera.[18]

Other testimonia can be dated at least roughly. Pindar probably wrote *Isthmian* 8 in 478, while memory of an overwhelming danger was still fresh. This poem speaks of release from great suffering, "since some god has turned aside the stone of Tantalos that loomed over our heads, an unbearable strain for Hellas. But now it is gone, and my strong anxiety is at an end. . . . Mortals can recover even from this, if they are free" ("with freedom," *sun g'eleutheriai*: 10–16; tr. Nisetich 1980, modified). Many scholars have seen here an allusion to the threat of the victorious Greeks to destroy Thebes for siding with Persia. An alternative interpretation is surely more plausible: that Pindar echoes not primarily a narrow Theban point of view but more broadly that of the Greeks, who regarded their rescue from Xerxes' attack and the danger of Persian enslavement as a merciful, essentially unexpected deliverance from an unbearable fate.[19] At any rate, this poem provides one of the earliest occurrences of the noun *eleutheria;* given the uncertainties surrounding the documents mentioned below, it may well be the earliest.

A traditional Homeric formula is echoed in one of the Persian Wars epigrams from the Athenian Agora that extols the undying fame of the brave men who "both on foot and on swift-sailing ships kept all Greece from seeing the day of slavery." After much debate, a consensus seemed to have emerged that the poems were engraved on a monument to the Athenian heroes of the Persian Wars who fought at Salamis and Plataea; the discovery of new fragments now makes it more likely that the epigrams, much more extensive than anticipated, focused on Salamis; at any rate, they can confidently be dated to the years immediately following the war.[20] Pindar's encomium on the battle of Artemisium, "where the sons of the Athenians erected the glorious foundation of freedom," probably belongs in the second half of the 470s; the outcome of the battle—from the Athenian perspective a Greek success to which their fleet contributed decisively—was seen as a precondition for the later victories and hence for the preservation of freedom.[21] An epigram that begins with the words "We strove to augment the day of freedom for Hellas and the Megarians" must originally have been engraved on a cenotaph serving as a memorial for the Megarians who died in the Persian Wars. As Felix Jacoby suggests for an analogous monument to the Corinthians, it probably dates at the earliest from the end of the 460s.[22] An anonymous scolion (drinking song) mentioning a "beautiful garland of freedom" was engraved on a used cup that turned up in the Persian rubble on the Athenian Acropolis and was thus naturally dated to about 480; Werner Peek suggests as its historical context the victory celebrations of 480–479, which would make this our earliest evidence for the use of the noun *eleutheria,* but that date is highly uncertain. The fact that the scolion is a later addition and the difficulty of establishing an exact chronology for the various finds from the Persian rubble allow for any date to at least the mid-460s.[23]

Other early testimonia, though either reconstructed or often contested, have received sufficiently strong scholarly support to be mentioned here. In a recently published fragment of an elegy on the battle of Plataea, which is likely to have been performed soon after the event, perhaps even at the official victory celebration, Simonides seems to have used Homeric language to emphasize the Greek achievement of "warding off the day of slavery from Sparta and Hellas."[24] An epitaph for men fallen in an unidentified battle

claims, "We strove to crown Greece with freedom and lie here in possession of unaging praise." Several scholars identify this as the epitaph of the
Athenians at Plataea, mentioned by Pausanias. If authentic, it presumably
was composed soon after the battle and thus might be another candidate for
earliest extant mention of *eleutheria*.[25] Another epitaph praises Adeimantus,
who commanded the Corinthians at the battle of Salamis, "thanks to whom
all Greece put on the garland of freedom [*eleutheria*]." If he indeed lived to
give his four children names reflecting his martial glory, the poem should be
dated to the late 470s, at the earliest.[26]

   To summarize, three pieces of evidence from the time between the battles
of 480–479 and about the mid-470s are useful for our present purposes and
sufficiently certain in content and chronology: the report of Pausanias's offering to Zeus the Liberator after the battle of Plataea, Pindar's reference (particularly important because of his use of the noun *eleutheria*) to the preservation of Greek freedom, and the epigram on the Athenian war memorial
which hails the averting of the "day of slavery" from Hellas. Other, less certain testimonia of the same period offer possible support. From the next
pentade we have another allusion to the Athenian claim of having bestowed
the gift of freedom on Hellas, possibly Adeimantus's epitaph, and Aeschylus's *Persians,* which demonstrates beyond doubt that by 472 the themes of
freedom, of Xerxes' intention to conquer and enslave Hellas, of the natural
antithesis of Greek freedom and oriental slavery, and of the role of Athens
as savior of Greece were all well familiar, even taken for granted. At the very
end of the decade, Pindar's *First Pythian Ode* and perhaps his *Twelfth Olympian Ode* add Sicilian echoes to confirm the picture.

   This evidence leaves little doubt that in 480–479 the Greeks did see their
confrontation with the Persians in the light of a struggle for freedom and
against servitude. But the documentary basis for this conclusion is small, especially when compared with all the other relevant sources that survive from
the years during and immediately following the war. These indicate, if nothing else, that the ideas in question were much less emphasized then than they
were even a few years later. The extant evidence includes (*a*) several dedicatory inscriptions for monuments set up from the Persian booty in Panhellenic sanctuaries; these are paralleled by dedications for Sicilian victories;
(*b*) a dedicatory epigram for the polemarch Callimachus of Aphidnae, who
died at Marathon; (*c*) an epigram from the Athenian Agora relating to Marathon (possibly originally from the funeral mound [*soros*] at Marathon), probably dating from the 480s; (*d*) the three funeral epigrams of Thermopylae
cited by Herodotus (7.228) and generally believed to date from the time of

the war; (e) a dedicatory inscription from the sanctuary at Artemisium, probably composed a few years after the war; (f) a funerary poem on the Corinthians who died at Salamis; (g) the distich on the "Serpent Column" at Delphi commemorating the Hellenic victory at Plataea, which Pausanias had engraved to enhance his personal glory and which was erased soon afterward; (h) the extant official inscription engraved in its place giving only the names of the participating poleis; some fragments of Simonidean poems that concern events of the Persian Wars, including (i) a distich ascribed to an elegy on Marathon or Salamis and (j) a piece from an ode composed perhaps in honor of those who died at Thermopylae; (k) Pindar's *Fifth Isthmian Ode*, which was composed at the latest in 478 but probably before the battle of Plataea and contains an explicit tribute to Aegina's contribution to the victory of Salamis; and finally (l), a couple of elegies in the corpus of Theognis with prayers to Apollo for deliverance from the Persian threat.[27] Other, less certain, documents might be added here as well: (m) the Spartan epitaph at Salamis, analogous to that of the Athenians mentioned above; (n) a dedication by Corinthian women to Aphrodite; (o) an epitaph for the Locrians who fell at Thermopylae; and (p) a poem on Democritus of Naxos, hero of Salamis, among others.[28]

All these testimonies were composed at or near the time of the events but none of the themes that later became so familiar appears in them. There is no mention of servitude or freedom, the deliverance of all of Greece, or victory over barbarians. What is striking is that even Athenian dedicatory inscriptions mention only the victory "over the Medes" or "over the enemy" and that the epigrams are simple: they merely repeat what we read on many public and private tombs of sixth-century soldiers, that those who died did their duty in battle for their community and proved their *aretē*.[29] Although, undoubtedly, what has survived is due to chance, overall the extant evidence seems to provide a fairly representative cross section, and the picture we derive from it is unlikely to be completely false.

The result is clear enough: even though the contemporaries may have been strongly aware of the danger of being enslaved by the Persians and greatly relieved to have preserved their liberty, initially this apparently was only one way among others in which the Persian threat was perceived and expressed. Despite the difference in scope, the outcome of this particular war was, essentially, presented no differently from any other the Greek poleis had experienced: the community had been saved from great danger, the gods were thanked for this deliverance, and those who died while fulfilling their civic duty were honored. Yet less than ten years later, all the components of the specific assessment of the Persian Wars as "freedom wars," including the corresponding terminology, were in place that were to dominate the Greek, and especially the Athenian, view of these events. Before we search for the factors that brought about this sudden reversal, some further issues need to be clarified.

Meanings of Freedom in the Persian Wars

First of all, what exactly did contemporaries (in contrast to later generations) understand by "warding off servitude" and "preserving freedom"? Aeschylus's plays offer two clues. In the Greek battle cry at Salamis in *Persians*, thoughts of the "liberation of the fatherland" (*patris*) are associated with the liberation of wives, children, shrines, and ancestral tombs: "now the struggle is for all" (405). Freedom here essentially means survival, and liberation means the restoration of everything vital for the polis in its social, religious, and political sense.

In *Seven against Thebes*, performed in 467, the chorus of Theban maidens implores the gods to protect the city from enslavement; the yoke of slavery, as it were, is already hanging over the community. The images evoked throughout the first part of the tragedy—destruction of the city, enslavement of its inhabitants, and subjugation of the country—combine epic traditions with remembrance of the fate suffered by Greek poleis in the Persian Wars. These obviously were the models available to describe the atmosphere in a city struggling for its survival and freedom.[30]

There were good reasons for linking these particular ideas to an attack by the Persians. Numerous Greek cities in Asia Minor had been devastated during their struggles against Lydian and Persian conquerors.[31] The fate of Miletus at the end of the Ionian Revolt certainly was remembered as a terrifying symbol. The Persian expedition of 490 was expressly intended to punish Athens and Eretria for supporting the Ionians: Naxos, which had resisted Persian designs in 500, and Eretria were destroyed, their population enslaved before the Persian fleet landed at Marathon. Since Xerxes' attack was motivated, at least partially, by the desire to avenge the defeat of 490, the same fate threatened all who had demonstrated solidarity with Athens and rejected the king's demand for formal recognition of Persian supremacy.[32] Hence, the Greeks had good reasons to think of freedom and servitude in very elementary and concrete terms.[33] These basic components of the concept of freedom were self-evident and therefore usually unmentioned, but they were always important to Greek thought, as is confirmed by the linkage of the concepts of freedom and deliverance, frequently attested throughout the period.[34]

But these aspects were hardly the only ones at issue in 490 and 480–479. It would have been difficult to believe at the time that the Persians merely wanted to satisfy their desire for retaliation, to force the mainland Greeks to recognize formally the sovereignty of the Persian king, and thereby to prevent them from giving any future support to the restless Ionians. In view of the enormous and systematic preparations undertaken, the actions of Mardonius in the 490s, who extended Persian control along the northern coast of the Aegean to the borders of Macedonia, and the traditional expansionist policies of the Persian Empire, the Greeks could hardly have failed to interpret the Persian expeditions as attempts to subjugate them permanently.[35] Observing the fate of the Ionians, they must have realized that Persian rule would result not only in tribute payments (which later were considered particularly humiliating and symptomatic of enslavement) but in significant restrictions, especially on constitutional autonomy and foreign policy.[36] To accept these without resistance was out of the question, at least in principle, because it contradicted the very nature and self-perception of every Greek polis. This is why no city tolerated infringements upon its territory or interference in its internal affairs by another; why the Ionian cities defended themselves desperately against the Lydians and fought against Cyrus when he refused to grant them the same favorable conditions they had enjoyed under Croesus; why many citizens of Phocaea and Teos, when resistance seemed futile, preferred emigration to subjection; why at every sign of Persian weakness some Greek poleis refused obedience to the king; and why Sparta, Athens, and Corinth considered the need to oppose Persian interference in their spheres of influence self-evident. This was a fundamental attitude, to which it made no difference whether the opponent was Greek or Persian, more or less powerful, and for which no developed concept of freedom or autonomy was necessary.[37]

Hence, the aspect of independence from external domination could well have been essential for the contemporaries' understanding of the freedom at issue—even if it was not (yet) formulated as such.[38] A variety of factors, however, induced many poleis to modify their principles. Not least, the poleis leading the defensive effort against the Persians had previously exposed themselves; they had every reason to feel threatened and thus everything to gain by uncompromising resistance. In fact, the Greek alliance seems to have comprised primarily these poleis and their allies.[39] To those who lived through the Persian Wars, the freedom they were prepared to defend therefore was elementary, a basic necessity for both the polis and the individual. Still far from being what was later made of it, it was a self-evident fact of life rather than an ideal, let alone an ideology.

Another approach to determining whether and to what extent the concept of freedom might have been available and easily usable at the time of the Persian Wars, and how its meaning and use might have changed as a result of these wars, leads to an examination of the political background. What role did freedom play in Greek political and military conflicts of the sixth century? What was the relationship between Greeks and Persians from the time of the latter's appearance in the Aegean? Were the Greeks really accustomed to regard the Persians always as oppressors and a constant threat to their freedom?

Wars and Loss of Freedom in Greece before the Persian Wars

In answering the first question, I proceed from three premises. First, it was the nature and purpose, not the frequency and intensity, of wars between poleis, and the organizational and political capacity of the poleis involved, that determined whether or not the problem of freedom would become relevant. Second, conditions after the Persian Wars differed substantially from those before. Third, for the period before the Persian Wars, the situation in the Greek mainland must be distinguished from that in the border areas of Greek settlement. I offer here a brief sketch that cannot claim completeness.[40]

Toward the end of the "Dark Ages" and in the early archaic period, clusters of poleis emerged in parts of the Greek mainland, on the coast of Asia Minor and the Aegean Islands, and in areas where Greeks founded new settlements (colonies). Territories and spheres of influence were gradually defined, but for a long time boundaries remained unclear. Population pressure made it increasingly necessary for poleis to cultivate all usable land and to seek additional resources.[41] Emigration, cultivation of marginal land, and conquest were possible means to resolve the problem. Hence, apart from traditional rivalries and raids, often conducted by elite warrior bands, there was ample incentive for feuds among the emerging poleis. These wars, brief but intense, were accordingly fought primarily between neighboring communities over control of contested tracts of land. Until well into the fifth century, this was the normal and commonly accepted form of warfare between Greek poleis, and the hoplite phalanx as the predominant fighting instrument, composed of citizen farmers, was perfectly adapted to it.[42] Whatever the situation may have been earlier, from the late seventh century, at the latest, such wars did not usually result in the destruction of cities or the enslavement of their populations. Conflicts were limited by balances and alliances among a system of poleis, by a dense network of kinship and "guest-friendship" (*xenia*) relations among elite families, and by the cautious policies of tyrants, who in most cases were intent on protecting domestic power. At that stage of their evolution, the poleis had neither the organizational structures nor the personnel needed for systematic expansion and the subjection of and permanent rule over entire poleis. Hence, conquered territories ceased to exist as separate entities; they were integrated into the victorious polis, with or without their populations. An extreme example is Sparta, where both Messenia with its helotized inhabitants, although always remembered as once independent, and the perioicic towns were integral parts of the Lacedaemonian state.[43]

Early attempts at maintaining control over other poleis, based on personal power and relationships, were undertaken by some tyrants, but these remained exceptional, loosely structured, and rarely survived the originator's death.[44] The notorious "thalassocracy" of Polycrates of Samos (died 522) as well was the product of one man's rare ambition, unscrupulousness, and success. He built up a strong navy, controlled a number of smaller islands, defeated larger ones in sea battles, and maintained close ties with other potentates (esp. Amasis of Egypt) who were similarly threatened by the expanding Persian Empire. But his power, however it was organized, was entirely personal and probably based mostly on domination of the sea, shameless piracy, and material exploitation of the defeated.[45]

Athens, which achieved complete control over all of Attica only during (and perhaps late in) the sixth century, apparently was never confronted by a threat to its independence.[46] Writing from the perspective of later periods in which communal wars had become the norm, historians and antiquarians interpreted early conflicts with neighbors, remembered in oral tradition, as full-scale intercity wars resulting from territorial disputes. However, before the very end of the sixth century—the triple war of 506—some of the fights with Megara, Thebes, and Chalkis perhaps were private or semi-private actions rather than wars involving the entire community. Scarcely anything is known about the causes of early wars with Aegina, which may equally have been prompted by neighborhood rivalries and private raids; they extended into the fifth century and by that time were certainly communal. Territorial claims in the Hellespontine region resulted from private initiatives, even if they were later supported by the polis.[47] Finally, the conflict with Sparta in the time of Cleisthenes, which resulted from domestic power struggles, touched upon the issue of Athenian autonomy only momentarily, if at all; the issue remains muddled because the earliest report in Herodotus is heavily tainted by much later experiences, and the Spartan king, Cleomenes, may have pursued his own as much as communal policies; at any rate, the conclusion that Athens was forced into a temporary alliance with the Peloponnesian League is unwarranted.[48]

Typically, Sparta's extraordinary power and influence in the late archaic period resulted from its large territory (including from the late eighth century all of Laconia and Messenia), its unique social structure and military organization, and its leadership in a hegemonic alliance system (the Peloponnesian League). Expansionist tendencies, caused by special circumstances, ended in the early sixth century with Sparta's defeat by Tegea. Subsequent wars against Tegea, Argos, and others were fought primarily over disputed territory, hegemony in the Peloponnese, and membership in the system of alliances that was gradually developing.[49] Outstanding individuals, Cleomenes above all, certainly undertook efforts to extend Sparta's sphere of power, but such attempts usually were unsuccessful, and they failed to establish firm and lasting dependencies, let alone Spartan rule over other poleis. Even within the Peloponnesian League, with very few exceptions, the autonomy of members was strictly respected, and clear limits were set to Sparta's freedom of action despite its undisputed position of leadership; at least from the late sixth century, the participation of members in decisions about league actions and the possibility of a veto against Spartan intentions were guaranteed. Thus, although membership was in some cases achieved and maintained by military force, there is no evidence that members of the league regarded themselves as "subjects" or "unfree" until the last third of the fifth century, when relations changed dramatically.[50]

The case of Thessaly, the other outstanding military power of the sixth century, at first sight appears somewhat different. Modern scholars are virtually unanimous in attributing to it a determined expansionist policy that resulted in the subjugation of and long-term rule over whole communities and regions. This thesis merits reconsideration. Significantly, Thessaly was a "tribal state," where poleis had barely begun developing and few restraints were placed on the ambitions of the heads of powerful elite families.[51] Our understanding of events, developments, and political, as well as military, institutions is greatly hampered by the inadequacy of extant sources; they are scarce and mostly date to the fourth century and much later. Hence, they interpret early history from the perspective of a time when state integration was far progressed and communal warfare and decisions about war were the norm. Their statements must therefore not be taken at face value—a principle that is too often ignored by modern scholars.[52]

Three aspects need to be distinguished in Thessaly's expansion of power. First, the population of some surrounding areas was suppressed into a status of virtual serfdom (*penestai*), somewhat comparable to that of the helots in Sparta. Second, some more distant tribes were forced into a status of permanent allegiance that obliged them to provide military assistance in kind and manpower. Such services, however, were owed exclusively to the military king (*archos,* often also called *tagos*) and thus limited to the duration of any particular war. The tribes in question seem to have retained at least their communal independence and right to conclude treaties. In the judgment of Fritz Gschnitzer, aside from the obligations agreed upon, and above all so long as no war was being fought, "they were probably free." Greater emphasis might be put on aspects of dependence, but overall, the relationship seems to have been similar, in some respects, to that between Sparta and its perioici, between Athens and Plataea, or, for that matter, to the alliance between independent but unequal partners (*foedus iniquum*) typical of Rome and its *socii.*[53]

By the late fifth century, these perioici were nevertheless regarded as "subjects" (*hupēkooi*) of the Thessalians, and their status was appraised more negatively than, for instance, that of their Lacedaemonian counterparts.[54] This may have been because, unlike the latter, they were not integrated into the Thessalian state but were separate but obligated communities; because they did not assume this obligation voluntarily and in their own interest (as did Plataea with respect to Athens) but were forced into it; and because they had no voice in deciding upon the actions they were obliged to support (as did members of the Peloponnesian League) but had to obey the *archos*'s unilateral decrees. To a time that had matured politically, become highly sensitive to the issue of freedom, and, above all, learned to categorize precisely the distinguishing marks of political servitude—conditions that did not apply in the sixth century—their status and obligations, especially to pay monetary contributions, thus perhaps seemed more closely comparable to those of the Athenian allies who had become subjects.

Third, in the course of the sixth century, the Thessalians extended their influence southward. They supported Peisistratus and, later, his sons in the last years of their rule.[55] We know of conflicts with the Phocians and Boeotians but not their exact dates, extent, and nature. While most accounts mention only Thessalian invasions, Plutarch alone speaks of an actual conquest of the Phocians.[56] A Thessalian attempt to interfere in Boeotia as well ended in a more serious setback near Ceressus. In 510 a large cavalry corps sent in support of Hippias was defeated by Sparta. The revolt of the Phocians against Thessalian rule is usually explained by the loss of power and prestige the Thessalians suffered because of these defeats. According to Plutarch, on a single day all archons and tyrants the Thessalians had established in Phocian cities were murdered, whereupon the Thessalians killed their Phocian hostages and embarked upon a merciless campaign of destruction and enslavement. Because of the heroic courage of the Phocian men and women, however, the Phocians were victorious and able to secure their freedom.[57]

Plutarch's account, with its details about the methods of Thessalian rule and oppression, has rarely been doubted. That he alone, not Pausanias or Herodotus, recounts these specific details has been attributed to his interest in the regional history of his native Boeotia and his intimate knowledge of local traditions. Both are true but neither guarantees the historical reliability of his facts or interpretation.[58] That the Thessalians were successful in extending their influence over the Phocians, at least temporarily, is probably correct, but given the organizational structures of the Thessalian *koinon* (federal state) at the time, this was presumably done through forced allegiance imposed by military victory. However the community was involved in decision making, the military campaigns in the south were probably initiated (even more than in contemporary Sparta) by individual leaders who were ambitious and eager to secure the preeminence of their families through great victories. Despite increasing centralization and state consolidation, compelling analogies to this pattern are visible in events and personalities of the Persian War period and again of the fourth century.[59] By contrast, Plutarch's description of fully established foreign rule by Thessalian officials ("archons") and local "tyrants" favored by and obligated to the Thessalians is an obvious anachronism, inspired by later phenomena.

It would be equally anachronistic to interpret the Boeotian and Phocian successes against the Thessalians as victories for freedom. Those of the Phocians were remembered more for etiological than political reasons: proverbial stratagems and the festival of Artemis Elaphebolia in Hyampolis were connected with them.[60] What the earliest source, Herodotus, says is revealing: he is well informed about those stratagems and the long-standing enmity between the Phocians and Thessalians. He knows of the "Phocian wall" at Thermopylae, which allowed the Phocians to hold off attacks by the Thessalians until the latter discovered the pass that in 480 proved detrimental to Leonidas. He even refers to the Thessalian intention to subjugate (*kata-*

strephesthai) the Phocians.[61] Yet he fails to mention that this intention was realized, the Thessalians ruled over the Phocians, or the Phocians revolted to regain their independence. If all these conflicts took place not long before the Persian Wars (as Herodotus, Plutarch, and some modern authors assume),[62] and if they were the reason for the deep hatred between these archenemies that prompted them to join opposing sides in the Persian Wars, how could Herodotus have ignored such an important contribution to his main subject, the Greek struggle for freedom? Presumably, the information he gathered led him to view the whole affair as one of many traditional feuds among neighboring cities and tribes. Compared, for instance, to the long-standing conflict between Argos and Sparta, it offered few surprises, probably even in its intensity and the number of engagements.

This interpretation allows for the possibility, mentioned before, that apart from recurring raids and invasions, the Thessalians defeated and temporarily dominated the Phocians. The view found in Plutarch, however, that they formally ruled over the Phocians must be a later elaboration, which, in fact, can be dated fairly precisely. Both Plutarch and Pausanias indicate that after 371 a parallel was drawn between the victories of Leuctra and Ceressus: Theban-Boeotian pride gave credit to both for having "liberated the Greeks."[63] In analogy to Leuctra, where Spartan domination in Greece had come to an end, Ceressus, which had at best released the Phocians from a compulsory alliance with the Thessalians, was viewed as causing the collapse of foreign rule. Accordingly, the details of the Thessalian domination over the Phocians were imagined to correspond to methods used by other imperial powers (Persia, Athens, Sparta) to maintain control over the cities they ruled. The legend of the Phocian fight for liberation was then enhanced by further details (the assassination of the tyrants and archons, the murder of the hostages, the "Phocian desperation") until it received its final form, which was common in Plutarch's time.

My examination of the two outstanding military powers in Greece in the sixth century thus confirms my thesis: military conquest with the purpose or result of subjecting previously independent communities to formal outside rule was unknown in warfare among Greek poleis before the Persian Wars. To repeat, this is not to deny the fact that there existed in sixth-century Greece marked differences of power, some significant power formations, and various methods by which one community could extend its influence over others. But where the defeated community was not absorbed into the victorious one, thereby ceasing to exist as a separate entity, influence and superiority were expressed in terms of alliance rather than outright rule. The

weaker partners thereby lost their control over foreign policy (partly or entirely) and had to supply troops to "common" wars, but they maintained a
separate and autonomous communal existence. As much as they might re-
sent such restrictions, these were apparently not perceived and expressed as
infringements on their liberty. Hence, the loss of communal freedom as a
result of war did not pose an acute political problem.

Other evidence offers further support for this conclusion. With one exception, freedom of the polis is nonexistent as a subject in lyric poetry of
the seventh and sixth centuries; this exception concerns Teos and a confrontation with non-Greeks.[64] Historians of the fifth century were aware of
a marked difference between the relations among Greek city-states before
and after the Persian Wars. In Herodotus the idea of freedom, crucial for his
conception of history, is prominent in his description of Near Eastern developments before the Persian Wars, but in his flashbacks on earlier Greek
history it appears only in connection with tyranny; in his view, therefore,
the numerous wars between Greek poleis in the sixth and early fifth centuries were not fought over *doulosunē* or *eleutheria*.[65] In his sketch of the early
history of Greece ("Archaeology"), Thucydides agrees. He uses *douleia* for
the subjection of weak states by stronger ones in the "heroic age" and of
Greek poleis by the Persians in Asia Minor and on the islands. He also takes
the existence of temporary thalassocracies for granted but expressly denies
that such power formations occurred on the mainland: "There was no warfare on land that resulted in the acquisition of an empire. What wars there
were, were simply frontier skirmishes; no expedition was sent far from the
country of its origin with the purpose of conquering others [*ep' allōn katas-
trophēi*]. There were no alliances of subject states [*hupēkooi*] under the control of the great powers, nor again did they undertake common military
actions on a basis of equality among themselves [*apo tēs isēs*]. Wars were
simply local affairs between neighbours."[66] Moreover, Thucydides emphasizes repeatedly how war changed due to Athens's policy of empire building
and the consequent subjection of formerly free poleis.[67]

Reports about actual conquests of cities and the enslavement of their
inhabitants are rare. Scholars have found evidence in the period from the
early sixth century to the Persian Wars only for the destruction of Sybaris by
Croton in 511, the enslavement of the inhabitants of Pellana by Cleisthenes
of Sicyon (ca. 600–570), and perhaps a couple more cases; moreover, the
sensation created by some of these events suggests that they were exceptional.[68] The oath taken by members of the Delphic Amphictyony to "raze
no city of the Amphictyonic states, nor shut them off from flowing water ei-

ther in war or in peace," apparently goes back to another early case, the destruction of Crisa during the First Sacred War (ca. 590, at the latest). This kind of effort to protect cities from destruction, and especially their populations from enslavement and expulsion, must have contributed significantly, during the century when the Delphic sanctuary was most influential, to a certain "humanization of warfare." [69] At any rate, what matters most for my present purposes is that none of these conquered cities was kept intact and in subjection, henceforth to be ruled by an outside power.

The causes of the phenomena discussed in this section merit more general and thorough study, which I cannot provide here. As suggested above, the Greek poleis (and, for that matter, *ethnē*, or "tribal states"), still in the process of developing, did not yet possess the institutional apparatus necessary for ruling over others or the resources to free large numbers of citizens on a long-term basis for primarily communal (military or administrative) tasks. Interstate relations, though controlled by the communities, were the domain of the elite, whose values influenced collective behavior patterns as well.[70] Sparta, which in this respect had advanced far beyond other Greek poleis by exploiting the resources of the helotized Messenians, was prevented by its narrow definition of citizenship and its precarious internal situation —its constant fear of those very helots—from continuing its aggressive expansionist policy, which was still in evidence at the beginning of the sixth century and might otherwise have led to the formation of an empire.[71]

Hence, throughout the archaic period, in the rare case of conquest of an entire community, there were only two ways in which the victors could exploit their victory: by withdrawing after looting the defeated territory and settlements or by incorporating them into their own territory.[72] Remarkably, despite frequent warfare, in the sixth and early fifth centuries neither happened to full-scale poleis in more than a handful of cases. The mainland Greeks thus witnessed only very rarely the destruction of a city or extinction of a polis and the enslavement or expulsion of its population. All this justifies my conclusion that the contemporaries of the Persian Wars were not accustomed to associating war among Greek poleis with political freedom or servitude.[73]

Limited Polis Independence before the Persian Wars

In the same period, new forms of interstate relations developed by which one polis could gain supremacy over others. In bilateral alliances the hegemonic state, as the partner with the greatest military capacity, claimed considerable authority and prerogatives. Some tyrants, exploiting personal relationships or dependence based on kinship or friendship, succeeded in extending their control over several poleis other than their own.[74] In all these cases, the poleis involved lost some of their freedom of action. Thus, even without military subjugation, the experience of restricted polis independence might have prompted a perception that freedom was lacking and desirable and, consequently, the formulation of a concept of freedom. Two case studies—Plataea's relationship to Athens and that of the Corinthian colonies to their metropolis—will help us determine whether this might actually have occurred.

In the late sixth century, Herodotus reports (6.108), the Plataeans felt so threatened by severe pressure on the part of Thebes that they turned for help to Cleomenes, king of Sparta. Cleomenes referred them to Athens, and as a result they "offered themselves to the Athenians." The latter assumed the role of protectors as requested and thwarted an attempt by Thebes to achieve a military fait accompli. A delegation of mediators from Corinth then marked out precise territorial boundaries and decreed that no one should be forced to join the Boeotian League. Unwilling to accept this verdict, the Thebans attacked the Athenians, were defeated, and suffered further loss of territory. Three issues have given cause for debate: the date (which is unimportant for our purposes), the nature of the conflict between Plataea and Thebes, and Plataea's status in relation to Athens.[75]

In explaining what kind of pressure the Thebans exerted on Plataea, the earliest extant sources, dating from the late fifth century, refer to experiences relevant in their own time: as the *hēgemōn* of the Boeotian League, Thebes insisted on Plataea's unambiguous membership, confirmed by payment of contributions, and was determined, if necessary, to enforce compliance.[76] Information on the rise and organization of the Boeotian League is sparse and contradictory. It seems to have been an unstable system of alliances based on common ethnic and religious traits and originating perhaps in the last third of the sixth century in reaction to a common threat posed by Thessaly. From the start, it did not include all Boeotian poleis, and Thebes had trouble gaining general acceptance of its leadership. By contrast, there are indications of an early tendency toward centralization and tight leadership that gave the league surprisingly "modern" structures.[77] At any rate, such attempts at consolidation probably put Plataea under pressure to join, which it evaded by attaching itself to Athens.

Yet indications are that, here as in the Peloponnesian League, the ties imposed by a system of alliances and the hegemon's claim to leadership did not significantly curtail the internal and external independence of the poleis concerned. In fact, Plataea's freedom of action was probably significantly more restricted by its relation to Athens than it would ever have been in the Boeotian League. Hence, the Plataeans' refusal to submit to Theban pressure is probably to be explained by ancient rivalries and especially territorial conflicts with their mighty neighbor, which were perhaps intensified by internal factional disputes.[78] Just as Orchomenos perhaps did with the Thessalians, the Plataeans sought outside support and eventually, "offering themselves to the Athenians" as suppliants, concluded a protective alliance with that city. This agreement imposed on Plataea the obligation to accept Athens's leadership, including decisions about war and peace, and to supply troops upon demand.[79] Although it was anything but an "equal alliance," the thesis that the Plataeans did not in fact conclude an alliance until after the Persian Wars but instead surrendered themselves and their land to the Athenians and were integrated into the Athenian state with a status comparable to Sparta's perioici is not supported by the sources.[80]

Ernst Badian has gone even further, proposing that until their liberation after the battle of Plataea, the Plataeans were regarded and saw themselves as subjects and slaves (*douloi*) of the Athenians. The arguments Badian advances to support this view require careful attention.[81] First, he suggests, the formula "to give themselves" (*didonai heautous*) is invariably used by Herodotus "of the surrender of an inferior to a superior (normally a king, twice a god), thus into a condition that would technically be described by Greeks as *douleia*" (117). However, *didonai* and *paradidonai* often appear as technical terms describing a capitulation after military defeat; as always in such cases, the victor disposes of the defeated at will; enslavement may or may not result. That in most cases of surrender in Herodotus the superior party happens to be a king or god does not imply that the sole case in which this occurs between Greek poleis—a century before the author's writing— must be assessed in the same way.[82] Second, in the context of the Thebans'· attack of 506, Herodotus describes Hysiae and Oenoe, which they occupied, as the "outermost *demoi* of Attica" (5.74.2). "Simple geography makes it clear that he must have thought of Plataea as also annexed to Attica, and his story of how the Asopus boundary came to be established confirms this interpretation, since in this no distinction is made between Hysiae and Plataea" (Badian, 117). If anything, geography and the Theban action suggest that Plataea was not Athenian territory: Plataea was much farther out than Oenoe, and the Thebans avoided it when attacking Athens; more important, that Athens, after its previous victory over Thebes, established the Asopus boundary against Thebes for both Hysiae and Plataea implies only that both communities enjoyed Athenian protection, not that they had the same status.[83] Third, according to Thucydides (2.71.2), the Plataeans reminded the invading Spartans in 429 that after the battle fought on Plataean land in 479, the Spartan leader, Pausanias, had "restored" (*apedidou*) to them their city and territory and given them a guarantee of autonomy and protection against any future aggression and subjection (*douleia*). Whatever the authenticity of the terms used by Thucydides, it is more likely that the "restoration" mentioned here refers to the previous occupation of Plataea by Persians and Thebans rather than, as Badian suggests (119–20), to an emancipation from Athenian possession. It is highly unlikely that such an act of blatant interference in the affairs of Athens, one of the most important allies, by simple fiat of the commanding general, would have been tolerated by this ally or, for that matter, some of the others. Athens accepted Spartan leadership in the interest of common survival, but once victory was won, it did not hesitate to oppose Sparta decisively.[84] Moreover, if Plataea was part of Attica at the time, would the Athenians, so adept in taking ideological advantage of their role in the Persian Wars, have failed to emphasize that all three big Persian War victories were won on their territory?

Fourth, Pausanias describes the tumulus (*soros*) the Athenians erected for their dead at Marathon, topped by stelae with their names, and a second mound "for the Boeotian Plataeans and for the slaves, for slaves fought then for the first time by the side of their masters" (1.32.3; cf. 10.20.2; tr. W. H. S. Jones). Badian assumes that Pausanias's statement is based on an inscription on one or more stelae that identified those buried in this mound as well. The fact that the Plataeans were buried with the Athenian slaves, he concludes, confirms "Herodotus' view that Plataea's status was technically one of 'slavery.'" "There should never have been any dispute about the fact that the Athenians regarded the Plataeans as in some sense *douloi.* . . . The Athenian action was deliberate and implied a public statement regarding the status of Plataea; and it is clear that the Plataeans had no objection to this" (117–18). Despite claims to the contrary, a mound excavated in the Vrana Valley near the battle site is unlikely to be this second burial. More important, Pausanias elsewhere says explicitly that the slaves had been freed before the battle (7.15.7); "slaves" should thus be read as "freedmen," and their burial together with the Plataeans is perhaps best explained by the fact that both were free noncitizens. At any rate, the issue is more complex, and other evidence shows that Badian's argument (those buried together with slaves must have been considered slaves, too) is not valid.[85]

In sum then, I do not believe the case for Plataean *douleia* under Athenian supremacy or Plataea's territorial integration into Attica can be maintained. Given this result, the argument from silence is not negligible: it is noteworthy that Herodotus and Thucydides (and in the latter the Plataeans themselves) use comparatively mild terms to characterize the conduct of Thebes toward Plataea: at a time when, as a result of Athenian imperialism, the Greeks had become highly sensitive to the issue of oppressed cities, and words like "freedom," "servitude," and "tyranny" were common fare in this context, the historians speak of compulsion, use of force, unfairness, and hegemony; they clearly did not find this case comparable to the situation in the Athenian Empire.[86] This should be taken seriously—at least as testimony to how the historians interpreted the information available to them. All in all, then, it is far more likely that Plataea's relationship to Athens was a particular kind of symmachy, known elsewhere as well, in which a threatened polis secured the urgently needed support of another polis by surrendering unconditionally (*didonai heautous*) but voluntarily and by assuming stringent obligations and yielding part of its sovereignty but doing so in a contractual relationship that bound both sides.[87]

In this special situation—where, moreover, strong and permanent outside pressure permitted only limited freedom of action anyway—restrictions accepted voluntarily and in self-defense in a chosen alliance were preferable to any that were forcibly imposed by a hated neighbor. I suggest that in Plataea's relations with Athens freedom and servitude were not issues, because voluntary subordination under a friendly power was not a condition that was regarded as a loss of freedom and thus did not by itself raise awareness of freedom.[88]

What about the Corinthian colonies? At the time of the Peloponnesian War, Corinth maintained close political ties with a network of outposts. Thucydides often refers to these as "Corinth's cities." They supported Corinth in its wars by providing troops and military bases and fought under Corinthian commanders. Potidaea, an important polis, and perhaps others received their annual officials from Corinth and adopted Corinthian coin types and standards. Clearly, therefore, the status of such basically independent communities involved restrictions on their freedom.[89]

The close bonds among these cities originated in their founding as Corinthian colonies by members of the Cypselid family. Kinship ties between tyrants were succeeded by relations between poleis that contained stronger than usual elements of dependence in the sense that the colonies were considered part of the Corinthian territory. Political dependence, however, was compensated for by the colonies' conscious sense of affiliation with their mother city and presumably by significant common interests. This was still true in the late fifth century when they had become much more independent; their close connection with Corinth may have "continued to exist more through force of habit and a sense of belonging than through force of law and power."[90] Although by then "servitude" and "tyranny" were commonly used as negative designations for interstate relations based on sharp disparities of power, Thucydides applies *douleia* to these poleis only in the polemical rhetoric of Corcyra, which competed with the mother city for influence over some of them. Nor is there any suggestion that Corinth maintained an actual empire (*archē*). Even during the Peloponnesian War, when opportunities were not lacking, these poleis did not attempt to escape from Corinthian control by attaching themselves to Athens, which succeeded only occasionally, through military pressure or conquest, in separating them from Corinth.[91]

If, then, in the late fifth century these cities were generally not considered unfree and oppressed (as were, e.g., the "allies" of Athens), we should not make a case for their oppression in the sixth century. Their status, comparable to some of the Athenian outposts, represented the closest bond conceivable at the time between colonies and their mother city.[92] Since even in its extreme form this relationship failed to create an awareness of servitude and desire for freedom, it can safely be ruled out as a factor triggering the development of a political concept of freedom. As we will see, relations in the Peloponnesian League confirm this conclusion.[93] All in all, then, in the Greek mainland before the Persian Wars, incentives for the emergence of an awareness and corresponding concept of polis freedom were indeed lacking.

The Defense of Freedom against Non-Greek Powers: Principle and Limitations

In other areas of Greek settlement things were—or were soon presented as —somewhat different. In Sicily, relations between Greeks and Carthaginians in the sixth century were only rarely marked by violent conflicts, and these did not touch upon issues of independence. The war of 480, however, which ended with the battle of Himera, soon became characterized as a defense of Greek liberty against barbarian enslavement, just as was the Greek and Etruscan conflict that resulted in the battle of Cumae in 474. A tradition that developed over a long period of time but probably originated with the Syracusan tyrants established a close chronological and ideological parallel between the victory of Himera and the Persian War victories of 480–479.[94] The reality, however, was different. Even Herodotus, ever alert to the issue of freedom, sees the conflict culminating at Himera entirely as a power struggle among groups of tyrants, tied together by alliance and kinship, one of whom enlisted the help of his *xenos,* Hamilcar of Carthage. At stake was the tyranny over Himera primarily, and the control and expansion of spheres of influence secondarily; it was a struggle among ambitious personalities, in which polis or ethnic boundaries were insignificant—Peisistratus's reliance on outside support and Aristagoras's intervention in Naxos that triggered the Ionian Revolt come to mind as analogies. It was a type of conflict in which the citizens of Syracuse refused to be involved (those of Carthage presumably were not asked), and several Greek poleis or their leaders preferred an alliance with the side supported by the Carthaginian to one with the Syracusan tyrant—just as Gelon himself supposedly had no qualms about considering an alliance with the Persians against Carthage. The threat of being subjected to Carthaginian rule obviously was far from people's minds. Not surprisingly, the monuments dedicated by Gelon and Hieron say nothing of freedom; that of Gelon presents Himera as his personal victory. The "empires" established in the 490s by Hippocrates of Gela and subsequently by Gelon and Hieron, tyrants of Syracuse, certainly established the rule of one Greek city over others, but on a personal, rather than communal, level, and the mechanism used to maintain such rule was primarily that of kinship ties among tyrants. As David Asheri puts it, the rule of Hippocrates "was not a centralized empire but rather something between a league and a true hegemony." When freedom entered the picture, as we know it did in the 460s, it thus concerned liberation from tyranny as much as liberation from foreign domination.[95]

The situation in Asia Minor was more complex. Several Greek poleis waged long and costly wars, first against the Lydian kings and, after Croesus's defeat by Cyrus, against the Persian general Harpagus. Having long been threatened by or exposed to foreign rule, some of them demonstrated their desire for independence in spectacular ways: most notably, many citizens of Phocaea and Teos escaped Persian subjugation by emigrating collectively.[96] Whatever the causes that prompted the Ionian Revolt, once it was suppressed by Persian military power, the reality of the eastern Greeks' status of dependence under foreign rule could not be ignored. This, if not the earlier experience of subjection, could have been sufficient to raise polis freedom to the level of a conscious value and to forge it into an attractive political concept. Hence, although extant evidence allows us neither to confirm nor reject it, the possibility that this concept developed in Ionia earlier than in mainland Greece cannot be ignored.[97]

Yet the potential political dynamics of this concept were weakened and obscured by other factors. In part, these, too, were intrinsic to Persian rule; in part, they were determined by the social structure and politics of the Greek poleis. I suggest, therefore, to think of a latent, rather than actual, desire for freedom, one that at best became conscious in specific situations and perhaps only as a secondary consideration, and not equally for all parts of the citizen body involved.

To explain briefly, scholars have rightly stressed the difference between the Lydian and Persian domination of the Ionians.[98] Yet, once their resistance was broken, the Ionians seem to have come to an understanding even with the Persians relatively quickly and easily. An intensive economic and cultural exchange occurred between the two areas: close bonds were forged between elite Ionian and Persian families, and political relations often far exceeded what we might expect between rulers and subjects. Having entered into a special agreement, the most powerful polis, Miletus, offered no resistance at all to the Persian takeover in Ionia.[99] Local self-government remained largely intact: the Persians exercised their rule through the local elite, generally placing authority in the hands of a particularly reliable "tyrant" family who became part of the Persian vassal system. Soon the Greeks became accustomed to involving the Persians not only in conflicts between cities but even in their domestic social and political disputes. Although in such cases the satrap became an (inevitably crucial) power factor, he simply assumed the function usually performed by allied tyrants, elite circles, or poleis; that is, he became a player in traditional elite rivalries for power.[100] Hence, their immediate political goals were more important to the Greeks involved—whether individuals, groups, or entire communities—than were the opposition between Greeks and Persians or the aspects of freedom or oppression.

Characteristically, even the events that resulted in the Ionian Revolt began with factional strife in Naxos. The Persian satrap became involved through the agency of Aristagoras, tyrant of Miletus, who was driven by personal ambition. Unlike Hamilcar in Sicily, however, the satrap acted in his official capacity, with the Great King's approval; the failure of the expedition thus spelled big trouble for Aristagoras, who sought to rescue himself by defecting from Persia. The same man who first sought to gain power and influence within the Persian Empire by helping the Persians assume control over the Cyclades and thus the Aegean then became the instigator of a major revolt. In Herodotus's presentation, the revolt originated in the politics of aristocratic individuals, as was typical in the archaic age. On one level, this is plausible and important.[101] On another level, however, the revolt gained mass support only because the instigators exploited strong opposition against tyrannical rule. In mainland Greece tyrants had long disappeared, and political systems that were more egalitarian ("isonomic") were widespread, corresponding to ongoing social change. This development was blocked in Ionia by Persian reliance on tyrannical regimes. It is quite possible, therefore, that many cities revolted not primarily because of dissatisfaction with Persian rule but because a more isonomic form of government could not be obtained unless Persian rule was overthrown with the tyrannies they supported.[102] In reaction to the general mood in Ionia, tyrants were expelled in many cities at the beginning of the revolt and, after being reinstated by the victorious Persians, deposed again in 493 by Mardonius, who apparently tried to secure the loyalty of the Greeks before he started his expansionist drive into Europe. However much the Greeks of Asia Minor may have desired freedom, this desire thus was not focused only on the external independence of a polis, it was not felt equally by all citizens, and it was counteracted and restricted by a variety of special interests.[103]

Similar tensions and contradictions are visible in the Greek mainland. The Athenian request for an alliance with Persia in the time of Cleisthenes, though unclear in many respects, probably was a rather desperate attempt to break out of political isolation and find an ally, above all against Sparta. The Athenian ambassadors even felt empowered to accept the formal submission the satrap demanded as a condition of alliance. This act was disavowed, and soon Persian support for Hippias gave rise in Athens to a decidedly anti-Persian attitude. But the incident shows clearly that less than ten years before the Ionian Revolt the Athenians showed no hesitation in drawing the "oppressors" of the Ionians, with whom they claimed ancient kinship ties, into a feud with fellow Greeks.[104]

Nor was it as certain as it may appear that the Athenians would fight the invading Persians. The extant sources, which particularly in this case are colored by later political constellations and the outcome of events, do not permit us to tell to what extent the question of resistance was debated in Athens before the expeditions of Datis and Xerxes.[105] Although it would surely be a mistake to assume that a genuinely pro-Persian or pro-tyrannical "party" existed at the time, scattered indications suggest that there was opposition and contention. Herodotus hints at the possibility of a change of mind in Athens before Marathon; the Alcmaeonids were accused of attempted treason after that battle; comments on some shards from ostracisms in the 480s characterize various "contenders" as traitors and sympathizers with the Per-

sians or the tyrants; and late but credible traditions report that leading fig-
ures who had suffered political reversals were considered potential collaborators with the enemy. Whatever the reliability of each of these pieces of information, taken together they provide important testimony that the issue
of how to react to the Persian aggression was indeed debated, that not everybody saw in the Persians a threat to survival, that the fear of treason was no
negligible factor, and that especially in the fierce political struggles of the
480s, attested precisely by the series of ostracisms, foreign policy played a
considerable role.[106] After Hippias was sighted on the Persian ships in 490,
the tolerance shown so far to persons related to or associated with the tyrant
family was no longer feasible, and it is reasonable to suppose that at least in
political polemics those who advised, for whatever reason, against a seemingly hopeless fight were denounced as friends of the Persians and tyrants.

I think it altogether likely that more than a few Athenians advocated appeasement, especially before the final decision fell in favor of resistance—
some because they considered it the only possibility to save their city, others
because they saw it as a means of gaining material and political benefits for
themselves and their supporters. The absence of such a group would have
been an anomaly. A consistent pattern can be traced from Isagoras and the
Ionian tyrants, those Athenians who conspired with Sparta after the reforms of Ephialtes, the likes of Alcibiades and Phrynichus after 415, and the
oligarchs of 411 and 404 to those favoring Macedonia in the time of Demosthenes: in the Greek world, domestic politics and foreign relations were always intertwined, especially for the elite, many of whom regarded foreign
assistance in achieving and defending power in their community a viable
option—even at the price of sacrificing the latter's full independence.[107]

What ultimately remains uncertain regarding Athens is attested well for
other states on the Greek mainland. Their decision about whether or not to
oppose the Persians was often determined by considerations that had little
to do with the ideal of preserving independence but a great deal with domestic political conflicts and partisan interests, traditional rivalries and hostilities among neighboring communities, exigencies, calculation, and oppor-
tunism. Thebes, Argos, and Aegina are but three especially telling examples.
Herodotus thinks that the Phocians refrained from joining the Persians only
because of their hatred of Thessaly. "If Thessaly had remained loyal, no doubt
the Phocians would have deserted to Persia" (8.30).[108] The revenge taken on
"traitors" after the victory undoubtedly was as often as not a pretext for settling old disputes and outstanding political debts. Where the advocates of a
pro-Persian policy can be identified, they invariably belong to a small elite

faction.[109] Not surprisingly, according to Herodotus, the Thebans advised Mardonius to seek victory less by military means than by bribing the most prominent politicians in each city.[110]

If the choice between freedom and nonfreedom could thus be decided by money or on the basis of neighborhood feuds and a host of other, primarily local factors, this choice cannot have been a matter of principle. For the communities involved, and for various groups and individuals within them, other considerations must have been at least as, or even more, important.

Such behavior should be explored further. For the most part it seems to follow certain characteristic patterns that had developed under the specific conditions prevailing in a world of small states and were necessary for maintaining balances of power and thus ultimately communal independence.[111] One of these patterns, apparently, was to regard the closest rival the worst enemy, so that the next closest was perceived as a potential ally against the former—no matter how dangerous he might be and whatever regional or ethnic differences were involved that in other contexts might have played a decisive role.[112] Another was the tendency (or need) to accept a certain degree of dependency (by no means always regarded as nonfreedom) in order to avoid a dependency felt to be even worse.[113] A third was the inability of most communities to forge internal bonds strong enough to allow the resolution of domestic conflicts within the community; one "felt closer to the like-minded in other cities than to opponents in one's own city."[114] A fourth was that, propagandistic and ideological claims notwithstanding, the contrast between Greeks and non-Greeks was hardly ever felt to be absolute except perhaps in the years immediately after the Persian Wars; hence, the inclusion of the "barbarians" in conflicts among Greeks always remained an option. In conclusion, then, where domestic and foreign policy was determined by such patterns of thought and behavior, narrow limits were inevitably set to the emergence of freedom as a dominant value concept.

The Emergence of the Term "Freedom" in the Persian Wars

To sum up, first, in the Greek mainland of the sixth century wars normally were still the result of rivalries between neighboring communities, not least over disputed borders; wars for other purposes were rare; and very rarely was a polis destroyed and its population enslaved. The military subjection of and subsequent rule over entire communities was virtually unknown. Hence, presumably, the threat of war continued to prompt the thought of *sōtēria* rather than *eleutheria;*[115] the problem of communal independence was not yet a political concern.

Second, from our perspective, relationships of dependency or partial freedom were not lacking, but the underlying conditions prevented this aspect from assuming primary importance or becoming conscious enough to create an articulated desire for freedom. In the sixth century, then, interstate relations in the Greek mainland failed to provide the stimuli necessary to develop a political concept of freedom.

Third, such stimuli were undoubtedly present in other parts of the Greek world, especially in the confrontation of Greek poleis in Asia Minor with the different social structures, political ideologies, and imperial aspirations of non-Greek states. Conceivably, therefore, an awareness of servitude and a desire for freedom might have shaped political thinking earlier there than among the mainland Greeks. Yet even there typical Greek mentalities and patterns of action—whether of individuals, groups and classes, or entire communities—as well as the great variety of competing interests seem to have kept the idea of freedom from rising to general prominence.

Even if this concept did become popular in Asia Minor, say, in connection with the Ionian Revolt, what influence might this have had on patterns of thinking in the mainland, with its very different problems? How much did it matter to Athenians or Corinthians what Ephesians or Milesians thought or propagated? Reactions in mainland Greece to the Ionian request for help in 500 do not suggest a lively interest in, let alone identification with, Ionian concerns.[116] To be sure, the Ionian defeat made a strong impression, but what sent shock waves through the Greek world was perhaps the destruction and enslavement of the great city of Miletus rather than the Ionians' renewed subjugation, which, after all, basically restored a status that had been in existence for more than half a century.[117] As a matter of principle, when dealing with early societies that have not yet developed the pertinent terminology, we should not take it for granted that a political concept can simply be transmitted from one area to another unless conditions are favorable for its reception.[118] Given the intense interaction among Greeks around the Aegean, this presumably was the case. The experiences of the Ionians, their political and intellectual reactions to those experiences, and the terminology they may have adopted in response thus are likely to have created among the mainland Greeks a favorable disposition that enabled them, once they were exposed to identical or very similar problems, to categorize and describe them in the same terms. This happened in 490 and again in the late 480s. As a result, we might expect that a political concept of freedom that was developed in Ionia between the middle of the sixth century and the big revolt, although hitherto not an issue on the mainland, would have been applied there as well as soon as they had to confront the possibility of a war against the Persians.

Since no evidence survives, we cannot go beyond speculation. To some extent, such a scenario would fit the evidence that has survived from the mainland and was discussed at the beginning of this chapter. The Persian Wars were indeed conceptualized at the time as a struggle for freedom and against servitude; a noun (*eleutheria*) was created to express this concept, and Zeus Eleutherios was the first to receive thanks after the victory of Plataea. Yet the idea of freedom, still understood in concrete and elementary ways, was by no means ubiquitous or dominant; nor did it, in commemorations of the dead and in early literary celebrations of the events, replace ideas and topoi that were traditionally voiced at such occasions. A major change in emphasis, now focusing strongly on freedom, seems to have occurred only a few years after the events, around the mid-470s.

The question then is when and in what context this change, visible particularly in Aeschylus and Pindar, took place. Several factors probably contributed. First, unlike the Ionian Revolt, the Persian Wars ended in a Greek victory. Just before and during this war, all efforts were concentrated on immediate needs, on survival. It was perhaps only after the battles of 479 and the final retreat of the Persians that people began to realize fully the gravity of the danger they had overcome, and how small, on sober reflection, their chances of success had really been. The new awareness of the unusual scope and circumstances of their experience made them think in different ways about what had been won or avoided and what had been the cause of the "Greek miracle." Hence, traditional topoi were soon found inadequate to describe this experience; as time went by, the Greeks placed increasing emphasis on their achievement and adjusted its interpretation as well as the prevailing value concepts. The former is reflected in the tendency, now attested already for the immediate postwar period, to equate the heroes of the Persian Wars with the epic heroes of the Trojan War.[119] As for the latter, freedom was propelled to prominence because the Greeks recognized a decisive cause of their victory over the Persians in the superiority of their natural disposition toward freedom (as opposed to the "slave mentality" typical of oriental barbarians) and in the free form of government characteristic of the Greek poleis (as opposed to Persian despotism).[120] Overall, the experience of this particular war inevitably enhanced consciousness of the value of communal independence. In the words of Max Pohlenz, "A really major experience was still necessary, it would appear, before the concept of freedom and enslavement could become central in the thoughts and feelings of the national community."[121]

Second, freedom soon became important as a weapon of propaganda. Immediately after the events, and even more so once the unity imposed by the common threat dissolved and political tensions reemerged, a lively competition began among the victors to determine who had made the greatest contribution. Herodotus preserves a record of some of these altercations, in which slander and misrepresentation of facts abounded.[122] To formulate such claims, succinct catchwords, such as "preservation of freedom" or "rescue from enslavement" were needed. The praise of merits achieved for a person's community, traditional on tombstones, gave way to higher claims on behalf of all of Greece. Even the western Greeks entered this contest: at Himera and Cyme, the Syracusans insisted, they had saved all of Hellas from the threat of servitude as surely as the Athenians and Spartans had done this at Salamis and Plataea; such assertion of equal achievement served also to refute malicious explanations circulating in Greece for Sicily's failure to send support against the Persians.[123]

Third, the tendency of "freedom" to develop into a political and propagandist catchword must have been enhanced significantly by the continuation of the war against Persia. In contrast to a defensive war, in which normally the objective is self-evident, an offensive war needs to be justified by arguments that are simple, convincing, and easily remembered; motivation and propaganda, supported by pithy slogans, assume great importance.

The question of whether to continue the war at all was apparently much debated.[124] The withdrawal of Sparta and her allies and the transfer of hegemony to Athens at the end of 478 terminated the joint pursuit of the war by the Hellenic alliance founded in 481, although formally it continued to exist. The naval expeditions of 478 could be justified as a means to securing what had already been won, but the reorganization of the alliance and founding of the "Delian League" in the winter of 478–477 necessitated a redefinition of its goals—not least to accord with its intended unlimited duration. Contemporary sources are lacking. Thucydides says simply that the objective was to "retaliate for the harm they had suffered by ravaging the king's territory" (1.96.1). This motive should not be doubted.[125] But it is hardly conceivable that the entire organization, including exactly specified contributions in money or ships by each member, and for an indefinite period of time, was created merely, or even primarily, with this end in view.

The Delian League presented itself unambiguously as the successor of the Hellenic symmachy of 481.[126] Thucydides indicates that in his time—even if only in polemics directed against Athens—the original purpose of the alliance could be described as the liberation of the Greeks from the Persians. Based on an examination of the traditions preserved by Herodotus, Thucydides, and later historians on the one hand, and of the historical situation and the problems confronting the victorious Greeks on the other, I have suggested elsewhere that the primary goal of the league was an offensive war to secure permanently the freedom of the mainland and to liberate the Greek cities in Asia Minor that were still under Persian rule. Moreover, references in Thucydides suggest that, in order to fight a "just war," the allies needed to avoid any appearance, let alone declaration, of open aggression—and any invasion of the king's territory essentially was an act of aggression; hence, the Greeks emphasized the aspect of retaliation and represented the war as a campaign of revenge for the destruction of temples and cities in Greece. Thucydides clearly characterizes this as a "pretext"; the actual purpose of the alliance was the preservation of the freedom of the Hellenes.[127] To be sure, ulterior motives aiming at a long-term buildup of power may soon have influenced Athenian thinking; given the still uncertain balance of power and corresponding uncertainties about the outcome of the war, no euphoria broke out among those who were to be liberated, and allied actions more often than not resembled forced "liberations." Later, the theme of liberty was used for propagandistic purposes to justify its exact opposite, the oppression of the allies, and Athenian hymns of self-praise recited it ad nauseam. Still, expectations and experiences at the time of the league's foundation were different and, as Edouard Will concludes, "it appears doubtful that the principle of liberty of the Greeks was not invoked as the motif of the new alliance."[128]

At any rate, freedom is likely to have played an important role, as a primary or secondary motive, in the beginnings of the Delian League and the continuation of the war against Persia. Therefore, this probably was the context that contributed most to the rapid popularization and subsequent propagandistic exploitation of this concept. The foundations of the typical representation of the Persian Wars that we grasp in the late 470s thus must have been laid in the years immediately following the great victories.

It is easy to think of occasions that prompted this development. Celebrations and debates took place at the official events of the Delian League, including festivals and meetings on Delos of delegates from the member states, and diplomatic negotiations within the league and with other states must have been frequent. Religious and political events in Athens offered no less fertile ground. The funeral orations (*logoi epitaphioi*), given at the annual celebration (*patrios nomos*) honoring those who had died in the past year, tended to repeat the same topoi with only minor variations. The few surviving examples, the earliest dating from the early fourth century, Isocrates' *Panegyric*, which resembles such a speech, and Diodorus's account of the Persian Wars, which is based on Ephorus and thoroughly influenced by this tradition, illustrate how Athens had placed its contributions to the Persian War victories and the rescue of Hellas's liberty in the center of its ideological self-representation and the extent to which these "commonplaces of nationalistic rhetoric" had become "a jumble of platitudinous slogans and threadbare propaganda."[129] The canon of topoi in these speeches is much older, however, as is confirmed not only by Thucydides' allusions to its use in the political rhetoric of his time but by clear indications in Herodotus and in the suppliant plays of Aeschylus and Euripides.[130] Since the *patrios nomos* was introduced relatively soon after the founding of the Delian League, perhaps as early as 475, it probably was one of the main vehicles for the development of the representation of the Persian Wars that was soon to become canonical.[131] Moreover, the topic undoubtedly held a firm place in the political discussions of the Athenian assembly.[132] The ground was thus well prepared for Aeschylus's interpretation of 472 — although *The Persians* shows just how different the thinking of that time still was from the bombastic and hackneyed emphasis of later years.

3.2. TYRANNY AND THE CITIZEN'S FREEDOM IN THE POLIS

Sources and Problems

Analysis of Solon's terminology has shown that a political concept of servitude linked with tyranny was current in Athens in the early sixth century; yet probably no corresponding concept of freedom existed at the time.[133] This raises the question of when and why it became common to contrast tyranny explicitly with the freedom of a polis and its citizens. Again, we begin by surveying the extant evidence.

In the second half of the fifth century, in Sophocles, Euripides, Herodotus, and Thucydides, this contrast is taken for granted. Aeschylus's *Libation Bearers* (458) provides the first unequivocal identification of the liberation of a city with the overthrow of tyranny.[134] This association is already presupposed in Pindar's *Twelfth Olympian Ode*, of 470 or 466, if, as is likely, the invocation of Tyche Soteira as the daughter of Zeus Eleutherios alludes to the overthrow of the tyranny of Thrasydaeus of Himera. In 466 a colossal statue of Zeus Eleutherios was erected in Syracuse to celebrate the liberation of the city from the tyranny of Thrasybulus, and the decision was made to hold "freedom games" (Eleutheria).[135]

Use of the noun *eleutheria* to characterize the free internal order of a community is first attested in Pindar's *First Pythian Ode,* of 470: for the king of Aetna, his son Deinomenes, "Hieron founded that city with liberty built by gods [*theodmatōi sun eleutheriai*] and according to the ordinances of Hyllus' rule" (61–62). This has sometimes been interpreted as an allusion to external freedom, secured by the victories of Gelon and Hieron, without which the city could not have been founded. Pindar does indeed mention this aspect of freedom a few lines later (71–80), but here he seems to refer rather to the internal condition of the new polis.[136] The association of freedom with monarchy, surprising at first sight, is best explained by the emphasis the poet places on the Doric tradition (61–66): like Sparta's kingship, that of Aetna was to be perfectly compatible with the polis's internal freedom. Hence, the poet prays to Zeus for mutual respect, harmony, and a proper distribution of honors and political authority between king and people (67–71). In keeping with his far-from-uncritical stance toward tyranny, Pindar admonishes rather than praises his benefactor, expressing the hope that Deinomenes will be a "Spartan" and good king, a protector of liberty, not a tyrant or despot.[137]

In the figure of Xerxes in Aeschylus's *Persians* (472), we encounter the fully developed prototype of a tyrant. The servitude prevailing under his rule is explicitly designated as *doulosunē.* A sharp distinction is drawn between the Asians, oppressed by their despotic king, and the Greeks, who are not forced to obey an autocrat.[138] The chorus's fear that free speech might result from the collapse of despotic power in the Persian Empire offers the earliest extant indication that the opposite of the unfree condition imposed by tyranny includes elements of freedom.[139]

Several sources thus lead us to a *terminus ante quem* at the end of the 470s. This terminus would have to be moved back by half a century if Herodotus's account of events on Samos after Polycrates' death in 522 were historically reliable. According to this report, Maeandrius, left in charge by Polycrates, erected an altar to Zeus Eleutherios to demonstrate the seriousness of his intent to renounce tyranny (3.142–43). Yet this story is suspect for several reasons, and the alleged establishment of a cult of Zeus Eleutherios is so far removed from the chronological framework marked out by other attestations of this cult that the event can hardly be authentic. If so, the assumption, generally taken for granted, that the concept of freedom as opposite to tyranny was conceived of in the sixth century has no documentary support; for other reasons, too, it is questionable.[140]

Aristocratic Equality and Opposition to Tyranny

Remarkably, the archaic poets, contemporaries of the early tyrants and often critical of them, seem to have ignored the aspect of freedom.[141] Besides Solon, Alcaeus of Lesbos serves as a useful witness. His faction of elite families was involved in an intermittent feud with other such *hetaireiai* and powerful individuals, foremost among them Pittacus, Solon's contemporary. The poet warns against seizure of power by the tyrant, predicts that the city will suffer badly from it, and complains angrily about the stupidity of the people, who themselves have installed Pittacus as tyrant.[142] Several longer fragments describe the situation and hopes of the exiled aristocrats: their oath to fight on to victory over the tyrant and to remain true to one another, their rage against the traitor who enjoys festivities and public recognition while they themselves wait for the day when "we forget this anger [and] relax from the heartbreaking strife and civil warring, which one of the Olympians has aroused among us, leading the people to ruin, but giving delightful glory to Pittacus." We learn of the poet's longing to hear the herald's summons to the assembly and council, where father and ancestors grew old, debating among "the mutually destructive citizens." [143] There is talk of sending the tyrants to Hades and "saving our people from disgrace." Here we are close to the idea of liberation, but thinking in traditional patterns, the poet speaks of rescue from disaster.[144] In his view, the overthrow of the tyrant would restore peace and the old order; it would permit him and his noble friends to return to their traditional positions of dominance in the polis, which had been wrested from them by Pittacus's rise to power. As the emphasis on *kratos* (power) in several of the poems suggests, Alcaeus's judgment of tyranny is determined by the contrast between one person's omnipotence and the impotence of everyone else. To him, tyranny means disaster for and destruction of the polis in its traditional form; like Solon, he chastises the demos for their stupidity in ignoring this danger, but unlike Solon, he is not worried about the polis's loss of liberty.

At least for Alcaeus and others like him, freedom thus was not an objective that readily came to mind when tyranny was mentioned.[145] Therefore, even if the concept of freedom had already been adopted in this context, it played at best a secondary role, because it corresponded too imprecisely to the actual needs of those who led the struggle against tyranny. This struggle was therefore waged primarily under a different slogan, to be explored presently.[146] Only much later and in a very different context did conditions demand a reassessment of priorities and a change in concepts and terminology, such as the evidence indicates for the late 470s.

I concluded earlier that in the context of tyranny *doulosunē* meant primarily subordination to a master, that is, "servitude" rather than "lack of freedom." We should assume therefore that, as long as no abstract, generally applicable concept of freedom existed, freedom would have come into play only if this particular type of subordination entailed restrictions that prompted a specific association with nonfreedom or, when lifted, with freedom. Athens is the only polis for which the extant evidence, scarce and debated though it is, permits us at least to attempt to determine who among the citizens might have thought this way, and under what circumstances they might have done so. Since even after Solon's reforms the elite controlled power and decision making, it makes sense, despite the simplification involved, to pose this question separately for elite and commoners.[147]

It is difficult to see why the latter should have striven for freedom and with what they could have associated it. They had merely exchanged one kind of ruler for another, who certainly was no worse; in fact, their social and economic situation seems to have improved in the period of Peisistratid domination. Tyranny prevented the abuses of power and factional strife that were typical of aristocracies and affected all members of the community adversely. By reducing elite power, tyranny contributed to loosening the demos's traditional dependence on the nobility. That Peisistratus's rule was remembered, however tendentiously, as the "Age of Cronus" is testimony to his popularity and thus, surely, to the advantages his regime had for large segments of the population. Even after the assassination of Hipparchus in 514, the harsher rule imposed by Hippias, which was directed primarily against the elite anyway, failed to inspire the demos to resistance and a desire for freedom. The fight against tyranny was carried almost exclusively by the nobility—or, rather, by some families or factions among them. An attempt at invasion by exiled aristocrats was aborted when the support presumably expected from the population did not materialize. Clearly, this struggle for power was of no interest to most non-elite Athenians.[148]

As was the case everywhere, it was the elite that was most severely affected by tyranny. Our understanding of the prehistory and early stages of Peisistratus's tyranny is marred by the lack of contemporary sources as well as misunderstandings and biases on the part of later ones.[149] At least two facts seem certain. First, the decades after Solon even more than the preceding period were marked by intense power struggles among aristocratic factions dominated by a few families that attempted to best each other through shifting alliances and occasionally by adopting unconventional methods. The defeated lost their political voice and often went into exile, trying to reverse their fortune through the formation of new alliances or the adoption of more radical methods.[150] Second, every leader of such an elite faction, every holder of more than average power, was a potential tyrant.[151] Hence, Peisistratus's success in establishing a tyranny in 546 represented only an extreme and absolute form of such widespread rivalries.[152] It was achieved by military force, and nothing suggests that Peisistratus would ever have permitted a really free play of power by the elite after he took control. He may have ruled with relative mildness and generosity, he may have reached an accommodation in the course of time with some of his earlier opponents and significantly broadened his base of support, but this cannot change the fact that the conditions under his rule in Athens completely contradicted traditional aristocratic customs—which were in fact revived for a short time after the fall of the tyranny—and that peace was maintained only by force and a superior will. The intentions and particular measures of his rule were either directed against or in their effects harmful to the aristocracy. Despite their temporary submission and cooperation, at least the leading families thus always tended toward opposition and revolt, even if action was possible only after Peisistratus's death.[153]

The same ideas we find in the poems of Alcaeus must therefore have been important to the Athenian elite: the real evil was the long-term domination (*kratos*) by one person or family which could not be overcome easily by the means traditionally at the disposal of rival families. Tyranny placed an individual above his peers.[154] It eliminated the free play of forces, thereby depriving other aristocrats of the possibility of exercising real power, and it made them dependent on the goodwill of the tyrant or else banished them to private life or exile.

If anyone had reason to regard tyranny as despotic and oppressive, therefore, it was undoubtedly the elite. But they did not therefore necessarily long for freedom. This concept would not have expressed what was most important for them. Freedom would simply have meant release from the power and will of an individual (i.e., the negation of a specific form of oppression), without defining the resulting condition in any precise or positive way. Put simply, the elite were not interested merely in getting their weapons back and paying no taxes, that is, in abolishing especially odious practices introduced by the tyrant. Nor did they simply wish to toil for themselves rather than for a master, as Herodotus puts it (5.78). What they were demanding was more than the elimination of the tyrant: it was their traditional share in holding power and collectively ruling the polis.[155]

By the middle of the fifth century, the Greeks recognized that power meant freedom, that complete freedom was ultimately possible only through sovereignty.[156] In the sixth century, however, political reflection was able to comprehend sovereignty only within the framework of a concept of order that broadly included the constitution or condition of the polis as a whole and focused on the quality of such order. If (among other things) the right people ruled well, in accordance with law and traditional norms, a condition of good order (*eunomia*) prevailed. When the elite or an individual ruled arbitrarily and by force, ignoring custom and law, the good order was suspended (*anomia*) or bad order resulted (*dusnomia*). The elite's objective in the face of tyranny might thus have been to restore *eunomia*.[157]

Practical experience showed, however, that tyranny not only abolished good order but did so in a particular way: by monopolizing the privilege of exercising power.[158] Who held power and how power was distributed in the community thus became crucial for the aristocrats' definition of good order. This in turn made it possible to specify the type of good order that was to be restored after the fall of tyranny: it had to include equal shares in government (at this point, of course, only for the elite) and an equal or fair distribution of power.

Even if the extant evidence does not permit proof, I therefore suggest that *isonomia,* an "order based on equality," became an ideal and catchword in the aristocracy's struggle against the tyrant's usurpation of power.[159] If so, the term may have originated elsewhere much earlier; in Athens it was probably used first by the aristocratic opponents of the Peisistratids. Its meaning was soon expanded, when "equality" became, as I believe it did, the code word for the new political order introduced by Cleisthenes after the fall of tyranny.[160] Because *isonomia* remained within the framework of "nomistic" constitutional thought and expressed succinctly, concretely, and positively what was lost by those subjected to the rule of a tyrant, it rose to prominence in this context long before the concept of freedom did.

The term *isonomia* is not directly attested in sixth-century sources, although the adjective *isonomos* occurs in the well-known scolia on the Athenian tyrannicides, which probably date, not immediately, but relatively soon after the events. They praise Harmodius and Aristogeiton for having killed the tyrant, Hipparchus, "and made Athens isonomous." Indirect testimonies—the name of Isagoras and Anaximander's famous fragment describing a system of balances among cosmic powers—lend support to the assumption that the concept expressed by *isonomia* was known in the sixth century.[161] *Isonomia* first appears in a fragment by the physician Alcmaeon of Croton, dated variously between the late sixth and the mid–fifth century.[162] It occurs several times, though not often, in Herodotus, Thucydides, and various authors of the fourth century, as well as in paraphrases by Sophocles and Euripides.

The term presents numerous problems of interpretation.[163] For my present purpose it is crucial that *isonomia* always characterizes a political system that stands in sharp contrast to tyranny or other forms of despotic rule, including narrow oligarchy, and that the notion of equality inherent in the term is not necessarily that of democracy.[164] Although denoting equality within the relevant group, it extends to only those citizens who have full rights of citizenship or are qualified to participate in government. In other words, the notion of equality is flexible here, capable of comprising larger or smaller groups, according to circumstances; thus, in the second half of the fifth century, the term could both serve as a banner for the fully developed democratic "order of equality" and describe a much more limited oligarchic system.[165] It is perfectly possible, therefore, that the term changed its range along with constitutional developments: the word was created to describe the equality customary among aristocratic leaders when it was threatened by the tyrant's claim to sole power; it was then applied to the extended equality typical of systems in which the participation of at least the hoplite-farmers was formally acknowledged (such as that introduced in Athens by Cleisthenes), and finally even to full democracy.[166]

Herodotus uses *isonomia* exclusively in contexts that concern opposition to, or suppression of, tyranny; he sees it as a positive constitutional quality, realized to a special degree in democracy and therefore emphasized most strongly by the latter's supporters. In this, and only this, context, he introduces two other terms for political equality: *isēgoria* (equality of speech) and *isokratia* (equality of power).[167] Precisely because Herodotus otherwise takes the contrast between tyranny and freedom for granted, this marked appearance of designations for equality perhaps indicates that in his time the awareness of a conceptual link between the overthrow of tyranny and the establishment of equality had not been lost. This link is also suggested by the name of Cleisthenes' opponent, Isagoras; his name understandably was not popular in Athens after 508/507, but its choice half a century earlier reveals much about the political concerns of the elite at that time.[168]

Finally, I consider it significant that the protection of freedom never appeared as an issue of concern either in Athenian laws against subversion of the constitution and the establishment of tyranny (the earliest cases of which are perhaps as early as, or even earlier than, Solon) or in the oath of the councilmen (which was instituted at the very end of the sixth century). Nor was the cult of Zeus Eleutherios, whose origins had become obscure by the fourth century, ever linked to the overthrow of tyranny in 510, not even at times when Athens's antityranny ideology was most intense. All this supports the conclusion that, from the perspective of tyranny, the idea of freedom, if it had been imported into this context at all, was at first entirely overshadowed by that of equality.[169]

The Emergence of the Term "Freedom" as a Contrast to "Tyranny"

The question now arises as to when and in what connection "freedom" finally did become the predominant word to express the opposite of "tyranny." Our previous considerations suggest that this change occurred some time after the fall of tyranny but before the performance of Aeschylus's *Persians* in 472. Since it is not documented by reliably datable contemporary evidence, both time and circumstances need to be inferred by arguments of plausibility.

The possibility that in the early fifth century freedom was linked with specific political institutions or rights, such as free speech, can safely be excluded. As Finley points out: "Changes in the matrix of rights that prevail in any society normally begin in a struggle over specific issues, not over abstract concepts or slogans. The rhetoric and the abstractions come later, and then are reified." *Isēgoria* probably was important to the Cleisthenic order, but equality of speech is not the same as freedom of speech. All early witnesses to the value of free expression interpret it as an individual right; they draw no connection with political institutions.[170] In other words, although the right of free speech, as the hallmark of the freeman (who was subject to no master), had been transferred from the private to the public sphere and there became the hallmark of the free citizen (who was subject to no tyrannical ruler), it was not yet politicized; clear signs of such politicization are found only much later.[171] This in turn means that even in its pointed contrast to tyrannical oppression the right of free speech was regarded as a mark of the free citizen first generally by virtue of the free condition of the polis and only later specifically by virtue of democracy: *political* rights were linked with freedom not because they were contrasted with tyranny but because they reflected the particular freedom that was typical of democracy.[172]

In other respects, too, it is not easy to see how and why freedom should have come to the fore as an internal value concept in Athens before the Persian invasions. Some brief comments on the intent and effect of Cleisthenes' reforms of 508/507 may help to clarify this.[173] In 506 Athens won victories against a triple alliance of Thebes, Chalkis, and Sparta, signaling a remarkable increase in power and confidence. In an important chapter (5.78), Herodotus explains these successes as due to *isēgoria*, here perhaps meant as equivalent to "democracy," which he explicitly presents as the result of Athens's liberation from tyranny. The historian's observation that newly found external strength was the result of energies unleashed by liberty and of the citizens' new commitment to the common good, which now coincided with their self-interest, seems fundamentally correct. The latter, however, occurred as the direct result, not of the overthrow of tyranny, but of the reforms introduced by Cleisthenes a few years later, after a brief but tense interlude. Fierce rivalries among elite factions culminated in a duel between groups led by Isagoras and by Cleisthenes, in which both sides resorted to extraordinary means. By appealing to the demos and, as Herodotus puts it, adding the people to his followers (*hetairoi*), Cleisthenes transformed an electoral defeat into victory. Isagoras in turn sought the support of his guest-friend, King Cleomenes of Sparta, who duly intervened with a small force, drove Cleisthenes and his followers into exile, and was about to establish Isagoras and his faction in firm control of Athens when demos and council united in a spontaneous revolt, besieged Cleomenes and Isagoras on the Acropolis, and forced them to leave the country.[174] Cleisthenes was recalled and realized the reforms that, in all likelihood, he had promised previously and that had attracted the demos in the first place to join his side against Isagoras.

It seems certain, therefore, that it was the renewed outbreak and disastrous escalation of factional strife among the aristocracy, not the overthrow of tyranny in itself, that prompted among a majority of Athenians those momentous changes in thought and action without which Cleisthenes' reforms would have been impossible.[175] This majority must have included, on the one hand, a large number of elite families whom the most recent experiences had finally convinced, as Solon had warned long ago, that the polis could not tolerate excessive aristocratic abuses without endangering its communal survival; in particular, uncontrolled power struggles were likely to result in tyranny again.[176] On the other hand, the large class of independent farmers, whom already Solon and later the exiled aristocrats, attempting to oust the tyrant, had sought to engage, now emerged as a crucial political factor.[177] They had profited most from the positive aspects of tyranny, shed previous

dependencies on elite families, and had much to lose from renewed aristocratic power struggles and misgovernment. The involvement of these citizens was thus primarily prompted by and directed against the negative aspects of aristocratic rule. But complacency with past tyranny did not mean
that they would easily accept a new one; having gained self-confidence and,
in leading Cleisthenes to victory over Isagoras, experienced the powerful
impact their engagement could have, they shared with most of the elite an
ardent desire not to see tyranny restored—least of all by an outside power:
hence their vehement reaction against Cleomenes' plan to establish Isagoras
and a narrow clique in power and their fierce determination to resist Spartan and later Persian attempts to reinstall Hippias as tyrant. What united a
vast majority of Athenians, whether farmers or elite, from 508 to the Persian
Wars and far beyond was precisely the need to eliminate the potential for
both tyranny and destructive factional strife.[178]

The involvement of the demos, however, probably had a positive purpose as well. It attests to Cleisthenes' political genius that he sensed this.
The promises he gave, in an extreme aristocratic power struggle, to win the
support of the demos apparently corresponded to a strong and widespread
but previously latent need. Cleisthenes focused this need constructively and
proposed means and structures to express it effectively. The demos in turn
seized upon these proposals and helped turn them into a new reality. If so,
this new reality must have been founded essentially on the non-elite farmers' willingness, even eagerness, to become involved and assume responsibility.[179] Hence, the reorganization and revaluation of the demes, the creation of the Council of Five Hundred, and the restructuring of the army as
the cornerstones of the reform must offer the key to its understanding.

The much discussed "tribal reform," illuminated by archaeological and
epigraphic evidence and recent detailed reconstruction, was not an end in
itself (in the sense of destroying old ties, integrating new citizens, or accom-
plishing whatever else has been proposed since antiquity) but rather a means
to fundamentally reorganize the citizen body politically, socially, and militarily. The extraordinary complexity of this reorganization, however, cannot
be explained merely by the need for an efficient army, for the installation
of a representative council, or even for greater participation by the non-
elite citizens—all this could have been achieved by much simpler means.
Such complexity rather suggests a farther-reaching objective which could be
achieved only by this specific type of arrangement.[180] Two complementary
explanations seem most plausible. Both take into account that Attica was an
exceptionally large polis that still lacked unity, encompassing as it did di-

verse regions, each with its separate interests, traditions, and dominant elite families; outlying settlements were separated from the civic, religious, and cultural center in Athens by two-day journeys and not yet fully integrated. One explanation is based on the principle of integration and solidarity: the artful and artificial system of combining demes into *trittues* (thirds) and *phulai* (tribes) was designed to make sure that in their civic function in army, council, and festivals the citizens of various regions collaborated, got to know and trust each other, and grew together as members of the same community.[181] The other explanation utilizes the principles of "civic presence" and communication. As Christian Meier suggests, Cleisthenes intended to engage and anchor institutionally the political will of the citizens, to ensure their participation, through an elaborate and dense system of representation, in communal deliberative and decision-making processes, to enhance communication between center and periphery, and to give the commoners an effective voice alongside the elite, who continued to provide leadership and thus would remain highly influential.[182]

As a result, political responsibility was to be shared among the elite and at least those citizens who owned land, qualified as hoplites, and thus had the requisite social prestige. These citizens had played a communally indispensable, though little defined and formalized, role in army and assembly virtually from the beginning of the polis; they were now formally integrated into the new political structures; their political role was clearly defined and greatly enhanced. That is, the political functions of large segments of the non-elite citizenry were assimilated to those of the elite, whose predominance, though not leadership, was reduced considerably.[183]

Despite the factor of external intervention, which certainly was not insignificant, political thought and programs of the time were dominated by demands for equality, sharing, and solidarity. As the preceding analysis has shown, such claims could be expressed perfectly well by the same terms (*isonomia, isēgoria, isokratia*) the aristocracy had used in their fight against the tyrants, despite changed circumstances and objectives. This is confirmed by the fact that *isēgoria* was still used much later to characterize the condition of those who had achieved assimilation to a socially and politically superior class through emancipation from prior subordination.[184]

Overall, it seems likely, therefore, that the political struggles of the Cleisthenic period were no more suitable than the previous fights of the elite against tyranny to give rise to a political concept of freedom. And it was that same newly acquired equality which the Athenians defended against later efforts by Cleomenes of Sparta to reinstate Isagoras, or even Hippias, as tyrants.[185] As long as such struggles were inner-Greek affairs and fought essentially by time-honored means and on a traditional scale, the common goal continued to be the assertion and consolidation of *isonomia*.

This changed dramatically when the Persians began their expansion into Europe and planned the conquest of Greece. In 490, moreover, the Athenians did not simply have to deal with a temporary intervention of a foreign power in their internal affairs. Rather, they were confronted with the very problem the Ionian cities had faced a decade earlier: in order to rid themselves of their tyrants, they had to throw off Persian rule. The double threat of subjection to Persia and restoration of tyranny was obvious to the Athenians, especially since they knew that Hippias was on the Persian ships at Marathon. Awareness of the same twofold danger seems to have had a significant impact on Athenian politics in the late 480s.[186] It seems reasonable to conclude, therefore, that the increase in the popularity of freedom as an external political value concept, attested around and after 480, was paralleled in the sphere of domestic politics. The emergence of (internal) "freedom" as a primary term to designate the contrast to "tyranny" thus most probably was prompted by the experience of the Persian Wars as well.[187]

Another factor contributed significantly to this process. Without placing much emphasis on it, the Greeks had long been aware of specific differences between themselves and non-Greek peoples; such awareness probably increased markedly in Ionia after the Persian conquest. Information was readily exchanged across the Aegean, and the mainland Greeks were not unprepared mentally for the confrontation with the foreign world represented by the Persians. Even so, the experiences especially of 480/479 gave an enormous impetus to both intellectual and popular thinking about this phenomenon, greatly enhanced the Greek-barbarian antithesis, and, above all, added a new political dimension to it.[188]

Several aspects of this multifaceted development are particularly important here. First, the Greeks perceived as the characteristic form of Persian government an absolute type of monarchy that seemed diametrically opposed to their own. In comparison to this king, they believed, however erroneously, even the highest Persian dignitaries were little more than slaves.[189] Second, because of certain basic analogies—for example, his immense personal power, his standing above the law, his lack of accountability, and his ostentation—the image of the Great King, as embodied especially by Xerxes, was equated with the negative concept of tyranny that was emerging at the time, and in turn helped shape this concept: henceforth, the Persian king was regarded and presented as the ultimate tyrant.[190] Third, in explaining their astonishing victories, the Greeks pointed most of all to the independence and strength they gained from the individual and collective freedom typical of their society. The Persians, accustomed to bearing the yoke of the despot and patiently suffering his whip, had merely fought on command and for his sake. Their bravery, imposed from above, was insufficient to withstand the determination of the Greeks, who, "neither slaves nor subjects of any man" and incapable of tolerating a yoke, had thrown themselves into the battle of their own accord, for the sake of family, community, and everything that was sacred and important to them. All these aspects are present already in Aeschylus's *Persians;* elaborated, differentiated, and reinforced by scholarly explanations, they reappear in Herodotus and in Hippocrates' treatise *Airs, Waters, Places.*[191]

As a result of all this, *doulosunē* caused by tyranny appeared in a new light. The perspective in defining its opposite was no longer that of elite or non-elite citizens who were qualified and willing to participate in government but barred by one of their peers from doing so; rather, it was that of citizens who already shared in political responsibility and perceived a sharp contrast between the social and political order typical of their communities and the total subjugation of the Persians under their tyrant king. *Eleutheria* fit this slot perfectly: from this perspective freedom naturally became the distinguishing characteristic of a community that was not subject to a tyrant. Not that this said anything specific about the constitution of such a community; on the contrary, such freedom was applicable to a broad spectrum of political systems, from Spartan *eunomia* and Athenian *isonomia* to more specifically oligarchic constitutions. Seen against the harsh backdrop of Persian imperial tyranny, the simple negation of a negative—not to be unfree (*doulos*)—now appeared highly valuable in itself; it appealed not only to one class of citizens or another, and not only under particular circumstances, but generally and to the entire citizen body.

In conclusion, then, it is most likely that the concept of freedom was imported into the context of tyranny only in the time of the Persian Wars. Even if the terminological transfer had occurred earlier, "freedom" would still have become the chief antonym to "tyranny" only at this time and under these specific circumstances. Once again the experience of these wars proved a crucial catalyst for the development of Greek political concepts and thought. Quickly, however, this new insight, won from bitter experience, hardened into a schema, was perverted by ideology and propaganda, and was misused to construct an illusionary claim, far removed from reality, that the free Greeks were superior to and hence qualified to rule over the "slave populations" of the Orient.[192]

3.3. REFLECTIONS IN THE RELIGIOUS SPHERE: THE CULT OF ZEUS ELEUTHERIOS

Early Cults of Zeus Eleutherios and Their Common Features

James Oliver devoted a broad, bold, and thought-provoking study to the reflection in the religious sphere of the ideology of freedom.[193] He assumes, rightly, that political and constitutional changes in Greek communities from the eighth century on must have been mirrored in changes in the protective function of certain divinities that had always been "political" in the sense of being closely associated with the well-being of communities and the leadership function of those in power. So long as archaic communities were ruled by *basileis*, they were under the protection of *theoi basileioi*. When "republican" governments ("civic constitutions," in one form or another) emerged, efforts were made to ensure continuation of the indispensable divine protection by changing the function, and with it the epithet, of those gods: "Zeus and Athena are still Zeus and Athena, but they no longer are the Zeus and Athena who protect kings. They become the Zeus and Athena who protect the community of free men directly in other ways, even against kings." They become *theoi eleutherioi* or, identical with them, *theoi Hellēnioi* or *sōtēres*.[194]

Hence, in Oliver's view, there already existed in or soon after the eighth century a religious concept of divine protectors of a "civic constitution" and of an internal political ("civic") freedom explicitly opposed to the claims of monarchical rule. The beginnings of the cult of *theoi eleutherioi*, accordingly, are supposed to have emerged in this early period. This view is wrong in several ways. I shall review the evidence for the rise of the cult and the concept of "freedom gods," restricting myself to the period before the mid–fifth century and beginning with two exemplary cases.

The origin of the best-known cult, in Plataea, is connected with the battle of 479, though it is not documented until much later. Thucydides, the earliest extant source, writes that after the victory of Plataea and the liberation of Greece from the Persian threat, the allied commander, Pausanias of Sparta, sacrificed to Zeus Eleutherios in the Agora of Plataea and, in the name of the allies, returned their city and land to the Plataeans with a sol-

emn guarantee of inviolability; even at the beginning of the Peloponnesian War, the Plataeans appealed to the oaths sworn at that time (2.71.2, 4).
Herodotus does not mention any of this, let alone the additional details
given in later sources. His silence is disturbing, not only because the course
of his narrative offered ample opportunity for comments on these events,
but especially because he had a consuming interest in the aspect of freedom.[195] Still, what Thucydides says is probably correct, makes sense—given
that the Plataeans were entrusted with the care of the graves and the annual commemoration of the dead—and has been generally accepted in
scholarship.[196]

It seems, however, that all this remained somewhat informal; the cult
was relatively unimportant throughout the fifth century and was limited to
this annual commemoration.[197] The cult rose to considerable prominence
only much later and in an entirely new historical context. In the second half
of the fourth century, when Philip II and Alexander planned to resume the
war against Persia, the ideology of freedom and Greek unity, traced back
to the Persian Wars of the early fifth century and emphasized already by
Isocrates and others, was systematically revived.[198] In the process, attention
naturally turned to the place that bore so symbolic a name and was already
linked to the ideology of freedom through the tradition we grasp in Thucydides. Both kings gave Plataea generous support, and a veritable "legend of
Plataea" seems to have developed, sustained by a number of supposedly authentic "documents" from the time of the Persian Wars.[199] At this time, too,
the "Freedom Games" (Eleutheria) seem to have received a major boost; in
the Hellenistic period they stood in high regard, and the victor of their most
prestigious competition, a hoplite race to the altar of Zeus Eleutherios, was
honored with the title "Best of the Hellenes." Because fifth-century archaeological or epigraphical evidence is lacking, scholars tend to think that these
games either were held on such a modest scale that they left no traces or were
soon abolished as a result of the breakup of the Greek alliance—if they were
really introduced after the battle of Plataea. Three bronze prize vessels from
ca. 480–440, inscribed "The Athenians [gave these] prizes for those [who
died] in the war" and awarded for games outside Athens, have tentatively
been assigned to the Eleutheria; if confirmed by future finds, this would
support the occurrence of competitions in the fifth century.[200] By contrast,
the elegant marble altar described by Pausanias and bearing the commemorative epigram cited in later literary texts may have been erected in the fourth
century or even later as a fitting expression of the cult's new prominence.[201]

Like all the victories over the Persians, Plataea encouraged the creation of legends. According to Plutarch (*Arist.* 11, 20), Aristides supposedly received word from Delphi that the Greeks would be victorious if they sacrificed to Zeus, among others, and fought the battle at a particular place, described in a riddle that Zeus Soter (the Savior) explained to the leader of the Plataeans in a dream on the night before the battle. After the battle, the Greeks were instructed by Pythian Apollo to make their first thank offering to Zeus Eleutherios, but only after the fire contaminated by the barbarians had been replaced by new, pure fire from the communal hearth in Delphi. Apollo and Zeus thus frame the event; the victory is largely owed to their help.

This narrative undoubtedly reflects efforts by the Delphic oracle to claim some credit for the victory and so dispel doubts about its loyalty during the preceding years. The oracle before the battle is clearly a construction *ex eventu,* but the involvement of Delphi after the battle is plausible, since the desecration of the sanctuaries by the barbarians certainly made it necessary to light a pure fire. Whether Delphi really provided the impulse to sacrifice to Zeus Eleutherios is another question.[202] Plutarch thus offers little information of more than anecdotal value. Yet we should note—and here the legendary character of his account is no disadvantage—that Zeus appears first as Soter, then as Eleutherios.

Diodorus reports that in 466–465, after the overthrow of the tyrant Thrasybulus, the Syracusans decided unanimously "to make a colossal statue of Zeus Eleutherios and each year to celebrate with sacrifices the Eleutheria festival and hold games of distinction on the day on which they had overthrown the tyrant and liberated their city" (11.72.2, tr. Oldfather, modified). Here the incentive to found the cult was the fall of tyranny and hence the restoration of internal freedom. Syracuse is often attested as one of five important centers of the cult of Zeus Eleutherios, which was later recorded on coins and revived repeatedly.[203]

Both these cases are linked to experiences that had extraordinary significance for the community or communities involved and concerned important political events. Since it was primarily the community as a whole that was affected, not the individual oikos, citizen, or human being, such a cult could be fostered only by the entire community. It was thus really a political cult. The god's new epithet was derived directly from the nature of the collective experience that had prompted the establishment of the new cult: Zeus was venerated as "Liberator" (or, rather, "God of Liberty") because he was credited with the decisive support needed to achieve liberation from enemy or tyrant.[204] Here political events had an immediate impact on cult and religion.

The close connection in the ancient world between religion and politics is well known. Martin Nilsson has shown, for example, that political claims and changes were reflected in the reinterpretation of myths, and the annexation of communities was often supported by the transfer or exchange of local cults. In such cases, a religious act usually served both religious and political purposes: to appease the gods of the annexed community and to integrate it as fully as possible into the territory of the annexing community.[205] The history of late-sixth- and fifth-century Athens abounds with well-documented cases in which religion and myth were exploited for political or ideological ends.[206] It will be important, therefore, to ask whether in some cases this applies to the cult of Zeus Eleutherios as well. First, however, we need to survey the cult's other early occurrences to reconstruct the circumstances in which both the cult and the concept of freedom gods emerged.

The names Zeus Hiketas and Zeus Eleutherios appear together on a stone marker found in Sparta. Lilian H. Jeffery rejects the usual sixth-century date in favor of the fifth. That the freedom god is here linked with the protector of suppliants—an important function already in the archaic period—perhaps points to a different sphere, in which not the community but the individual turned to Zeus for help. I have suggested therefore that Zeus Eleutherios might here be understood as the protector of freedmen, which would make this the earliest attestation of an unpolitical use of the epithet. Lukas Thommen emphasizes, however, that the cult of Zeus Hiketas (or Hikesios) could play a political role as well, as it did specifically in Sparta in an important incident after the Persian Wars, and that Sparta was known among contemporaries for its passionate emphasis on communal freedom. The question thus remains open.[207]

In 522 the tyrant of Samos, Polycrates, came to an inglorious end. According to Herodotus, Maeandrius, the man he had left in charge, was willing to renounce tyranny voluntarily. He erected an altar to Zeus Eleutherios, marked off a sacred precinct (*temenos*), convened an assembly, and declared his intention to "put power [*archē*] in the middle" (that is, to return power to the community), proclaim *isonomia,* and restore liberty (*eleutheria*) to the citizens. For himself he requested six talents from Polycrates' treasures, and for his family the priesthood of the new cult in perpetuity. The hostility of the noble Samians to his plan convinced him, however, to hold on by force to the tyranny he had inherited. "Apparently," concludes Herodotus, "the Samians did not want to be free" (3.142–43). As we shall see, this story is highly dubious in almost every respect; at this point, we should merely note the connection between abdication from tyranny and erection of an altar to Zeus Eleutherios.[208]

Pindar's *Twelfth Olympian Ode* begins with the words "Hear me, daughter of Zeus Eleutherios: watch over Himera, gird her with strength, O Tyche Soteira [Savior Fortune]. Under your guidance, swift ships pilot the seas, wars veer over the earth, assemblies pass their motions" (1–5, tr. Nisetich 1980). The reference to Tyche Soteira as the daughter of Zeus Eleutherios once again establishes a close relationship between the deity of deliverance and deity of freedom. The emphasis on these aspects was most likely prompted by a concrete recent experience. The ode is usually dated to 470, when the overthrow of the tyrant Thrasydaeus resulted not in liberation from Syracusan rule but at least in restoration of freedom in the city itself (hence the characterization of Tyche as protectress of the assembly), or to 466, when tyranny was overthrown in Syracuse and Himera regained its external independence as well. Moreover, praise of Himera's liberty probably also (and perhaps especially) reflects the victory won near that city in 480 over the Carthaginians; the reference to Tyche's assistance in war, combined with the epithets denoting rescue and liberation, is especially meaningful from that perspective.[209] This poetic invocation is not in itself proof that a cult of Tyche Soteira or Zeus Eleutherios existed in Himera; however, coins from the second quarter of the fifth century show on the reverse a female divinity making an offering at an altar and the inscription *sōtēr*. This conceivably refers to the city goddess, Himera (or even Tyche herself), clearly invoked here as a deity of deliverance or linked with an experience of deliverance.[210]

Pausanias (2.31.5) mentions an altar of Helios Eleutherios in Troizen, supposedly going back to the city's deliverance from the Persian threat.

Finally, in Athens the cult of Zeus Eleutherios is attested probably in the early second half of the fifth century by a fragmentary inscription on a stone marker and certainly in the early fourth century by a decree and literary testimonia. The cult site was on the west side of the Agora, next to the Stoa Basileios; from the late fifth century, it was adorned by the magnificent Stoa of Zeus and a statue of the god.[211] Two versions were known about the origins of this cult. One, told by the orator Hyperides, claimed that the stoa was built by *exeleutheroi* (freedmen or otherwise liberated persons); this version was refuted by the first-century grammarian Didymus, who connected the name with the liberation from the Persian threat. Whether or not, as some scholars assume, Hyperides' interpretation is simply an indirect or metaphorical allusion to the same event, it is obvious that Didymus's etiology is preferable and freedmen were linked to the stoa only long after Zeus had been given the epithet Eleutherios.[212] This most likely occurred between 479 and roughly the middle of the century, presumably, following the Plataean model, shortly after the Persian Wars.[213]

These are all the early cults of freedom gods known to us: they are surprisingly few, and with the exception of that in Sparta, they can all be placed and explained in a rather precise historical context. If we exclude for the moment the case of Samos, all these cults were established and fostered by communities (or a group of communities) that had been involved in a struggle for freedom. Moreover, with the exception of Helios in Troizen, it was always and exclusively Zeus who was venerated as Eleutherios; remarkably, Athena, who often shared political functions with Zeus, was never given this epithet. Again, these cults all came into existence after, if not in direct response to, the Persian Wars. A plausible conclusion therefore is that the cult of Zeus Eleutherios was a political cult that first emerged under the immediate impression of the Persian War experience.[214] The aspect of external freedom thus was primary; that of internal freedom (from tyranny), secondary. Finally, in several cases the god of freedom was closely related to a god of deliverance.[215]

The case of Athens takes us one step farther. There is not a shred of evidence that the Athenian Zeus Eleutherios was ever linked with the overthrow of tyranny in 510. In this city a strong antityranny ideology developed in the fifth century that kept the events of the late sixth alive in people's minds. The tyrannicides of 514 became the heroes of democracy and were honored, among much else, by statues in the Agora. The question of who deserved most credit for the expulsion of the tyrants was still an issue of controversy and rivalry many decades later. If anywhere, the argument from silence is valid here: had a special cult arisen in this connection, we would know about it.[216] Hence, I consider it certain that the cult of Zeus Eleutherios was motivated in Athens not by the overthrow of the tyrant but, at the earliest, by the subsequent deliverance from the Persian threat.[217] Since all this concerns not just any city but Athens, which soon became the center of the Greek "ideology of freedom," this fact adds weight to my earlier suggestion that at the end of the sixth century the potential for activating "liberty" as a primary slogan against tyranny was still slight and far from self-evident.[218]

Zeus Soter and Zeus Eleutherios:
Cult Change and Conceptual Development

The fact that the Athenian cult of Zeus Eleutherios was closely linked with another cult of Zeus provides useful evidence for the former's "ancestry" and hence its origins. In Aristophanes' *Wealth* (1174–75) a priest of Zeus Soter appears onstage. The scholiast comments, "In the city they honor Zeus Soter, and there too is a shrine of Zeus Soter. Some say that he is the same as Zeus Eleutherios." The lexicographer Hesychius says the same thing, but the other way round. Harpocration provides more detail: "That he is called Eleutherios too, though the inscription says Soter, is made clear by Menander." Assembly decrees that were published in inscriptions placed near the Stoa of Zeus confirm that both the stoa and statue were referred to as Zeus, Zeus Soter, or Zeus Eleutherios. Hence, the two cults were undoubtedly identical. Moreover, since, according to Menander as cited by Harpocration, the inscription on the statue base read "Soter," this must have been the god's primary epithet. Apparently it was also the older: excavations at the site of the later stoa have unearthed a small sixth-century shrine with an altar in front of it. Homer Thompson and R. E. Wycherley assume reasonably that this was already a shrine of Zeus; if so, it must have been dedicated to Soter.[219]

In all likelihood, then, a cult of Zeus Soter, which had existed at the Agora since it became the polis's political center, received the additional epithet Eleutherios after the Persian Wars, and this double appellation was retained by both the stoa and the statue. The Athenian Zeus Eleutherios was thus a specification of an older cult of Zeus Soter, arising in response to a particular political experience. A Soter cult is also attested in Plataea. It has been suggested that there, too, this cult was identical with that of Eleutherios—which is perhaps supported by the appearance of both gods in the legends cited in Plutarch's *vita* of Aristides and discussed above.[220] In Plataea too, therefore—and there certainly earlier than anywhere else—under the profound impression of the Persian victories, Zeus, who was traditionally venerated as Soter, was given the new name of Eleutherios.

Why it was Soter who became Eleutherios is immediately apparent: he had long been the rescuer and protector in times of danger and need. Though in the realm of private life he shared this function with numerous other gods —often *theoi sōtēres* were even invoked collectively—he was clearly dominant in the communal and political realm; as "protectress of the city" Athena alone held an equally prominent position. And it was only as Soter that Zeus had a function in war as bringer of victory and savior from all kinds of distress and destruction.[221] As long as defeat in war meant either material loss or annihilation for individual and community, the concept of deliverance was sufficient to cover the entire range of experiences: the difference between this and other life-threatening situations like shipwreck and starvation was merely one of degree, and Zeus Soter could be called upon to give divine assistance in all of them.[222] This remained unchanged until the extraordinary danger posed by the Persian invasion—a danger that specifically threatened the freedom of the polis both externally and internally—brought this particular aspect among many covered by *sōtēria* to full awareness and gave it the independence reflected in the coining of a new name for Zeus Soter. Because Eleutherios specified a more comprehensive function of Zeus, in some places his cultic identity with Soter was retained for a long time; he could be invoked even in contexts where the issue was less freedom than more generally success in war, and conversely Soter could continue to assume the function of Eleutherios along with his own.[223]

We can take the argument further. Since the cult of Zeus Eleutherios was political insofar as its establishment was a political and communal act that responded directly to a political experience, and since the specific nature of this experience was reflected in the epithet given to the god, there could be no such cult without an experience of liberation or, more precisely, without the ability to perceive a specific event in exactly these terms. Thus, this communal cult necessarily presupposes the existence, or at least the simultaneous development, of a political concept of freedom. We have already examined the question of why no political concept of freedom developed, or was needed, during the archaic period. The extant poetry illustrates eloquently the central importance of the concept of deliverance (*sōtēria*) in all aspects of life and especially in war. I explained the wide predominance of this concept primarily by the nature of wars and the absence among archaic Greek poleis of the phenomenon of foreign rule over entire communities.[224] It was not until the sixth century, when the Greeks were confronted with the very differently structured states of Lydia and Persia, that they (and for a long time only those in Asia Minor) experienced territorial expansion of a new kind and the possibility of being subjected to foreign rule entailing the loss of communal freedom. Even so, initially they still seem to have dealt with these new consequences of war from the perspective of *sōtēria* and entrusted their fate to Zeus Soter. *Sōtēria* thus was flexible and comprehensive:

it still included what later came specifically to be viewed as freedom. It was only when pressure increased drastically during the Persian campaigns to conquer Greece, and when the Greeks achieved their dramatic successes in repelling them, that a new awareness broke through and freedom was fully recognized as a separate and crucial value. At that point, this particular aspect of deliverance was emancipated, as it were, from among the many meanings of *sōtēria* and became an independent concept.[225] A new noun was forged to express it (*eleutheria*), and a new name was given to the god responsible for it. And just as the new god remained closely related to the old god, even sharing his cult, the political concepts of *eleutheria* and *sōtēria* continued to be closely connected and the idea of survival remained an essential component of Greek freedom.[226]

Hence, the cult's primary concern was indeed with external freedom— that is, the community's rescue from the danger of subjugation by an external enemy. The cult's connection with freedom from tyranny was secondary but followed closely, paralleling the conceptual development examined in section 3.2 above. The extant evidence suggests that a cult with this orientation was established first in Syracuse in 466–465.

The Samian Cult of 522: A Historicizing Fiction

Yet there still is Herodotus's report about Maeandrius and his attempt to establish a cult for Zeus Eleutherios after Polycrates' death in 522.[227] This story has generally been taken seriously. Skepticism, however, has been expressed concerning a rather long section of "Samian *logoi*" that includes this particular story.[228] The basic fact underlying it, that a certain Maeandrius distinguished himself by attempting to replace tyranny with a more aristocratic and in that sense "isonomic" government after Polycrates' death, is conceivably based on accurate tradition.[229] The details certainly are not. The entire episode receives stark relief if it is read against Athenian experiences, highlighting both parallels and contrasts. More specifically, in its mode of thought and terminology, Maeandrius's speech, like all of Herodotus's speeches, reflects thoughts and sentiments of the historian and his time, not of the late sixth century; its intellectual affinity to the "constitutional debate" (3.80–82) is unmistakable.[230]

The same must be said about Maeandrius's supposed founding of a shrine of Zeus Eleutherios. This cult is unusual in every respect. It would have been in existence almost half a century before the earliest of the other political cults of this type. It was founded, not by a community in gratitude to the god for its liberation, but by the tyrant himself as a gesture of goodwill before his intended abdication. In fact, it looks as if Maeandrius had wanted to make his intention more credible by scrupulously following the protocol usual in such cases—except that the protocol was in fact different, was established only decades later, and was known to Herodotus but most likely not to Maeandrius. Moreover, Maeandrius's plan to step down was never carried out; he held on to power, his tyranny turned out to be more brutal than that of his predecessor, and soon it was replaced by a Persian vassal tyranny: "until 480 Samos was mostly a pawn in the hands of Persia."[231] Neither for Maeandrius and his successors nor for the community of Samos was there any reason to continue fostering a cult of Zeus Eleutherios. Had it been founded, it would have survived the ceremony only by a few hours. Finally, given these arguments against historicity, the total absence of a corresponding cult connected with the actual overthrow, a good ten years later, of the Athenian tyranny makes the Samian account even less believable. In short, this is not an authentic tradition but a historicizing fiction, a depiction of events as they might have been imagined in Herodotus's time, after the Persian Wars and after the founding of the cult of Zeus Eleutherios in Syracuse.[232]

Herodotus, admittedly, seems to have seen the shrine himself in a suburb of Samos (3.142.2). Since he lived on Samos for a while and his information about conditions there—to the extent that it can be verified—seems reliable, there is no reason to doubt the existence of such a shrine in his time. But this does not mean that he offers, or was presented with, the correct explanation of its origin. His informants may well have given him a false account, either to serve their own ends (such as the family interests of the descendants of Maeandrius who held the cult's priesthood) or because they themselves lacked precise knowledge; alternatively, Herodotus himself, unable to obtain precise information, may have established a connection that corresponded to empirical knowledge available in his time, seemed reasonable to him, and served his interpretive purposes. In any case, I consider it virtually certain that the cult of the Samian Zeus Eleutherios originated no earlier than the autumn of 479, when Samos was liberated from both Persian and tyrannical rule, and that the story of its much earlier origin could have been invented only after that time.[233]

Conclusions: Zeus Eleutherios and Power Politics

Oliver's thesis, cited at the beginning of section 3.3, that a religious concept of divinities functioning as protectors of "civic" freedom—and hence cults of *theoi eleutherioi*—may have come into existence as early as the eighth century, when kingship in many communities was replaced by "civic constitutions," has proved untenable. Oliver's further assumption that other, earlier cults served a similar function can be shown to be even more improbable.

Oliver interprets the "Great Rhetra" at Sparta as the "initiation of a civic regime for the whole community," which, according to the extant tradition, was linked with the founding of a cult of Zeus Syllanios and Athena Syllania. So far, this epithet has not been explained convincingly; proposals to emend it abound. Oliver, like others before him, suggests Hellanios/a, which is paleographically plausible and concurs with a Hellenion attested in the vicinity of the Spartan Agora, but has not been received enthusiastically in recent scholarship.[234] At any rate, according to Oliver, such *theoi Hellēnioi* are identical in function to *theoi eleutherioi,* and *Hellēnios* is thus synonymous with *eleutherios.* He deduces this from the "parallels" in Samos and Syracuse (which, as indicated above, are only superficial and have no value anyway for this early period); from the repeated invocation of *theoi Hellēnioi* in Herodotus in contexts where elsewhere in the text we find the concept of *eleutheria* (though not of *theoi eleutherioi*); from the contrast drawn between these *theoi Hellēnioi* and *theoi basileioi;* and from the function of the later cults of Zeus Eleutherios (which, again, tell us nothing about the archaic period).[235]

In Herodotus *theoi basileioi* represent the "royal gods" who protect the Persian monarchy; from the Greek perspective, these are Persian or "barbarian" gods with no relevance to the Greeks.[236] They are contrasted not with gods of a "civic constitution" but with *Greek* gods: Zeus Hellenios and *theoi Hellēnioi* are the native gods of the Greeks, to whom, for example, a Greek can turn when abroad and in trouble and who are invoked when Greeks swear to maintain solidarity against the Persian "national enemy."[237] For the same reason, the political function of *theoi Hellēnioi* lay primarily in the area of Panhellenic ideology. Only secondarily, because the Persian Wars were seen as freedom wars par excellence, did the "gods of the Greeks" also become "freedom gods," protecting Greek *eleutheria* against the barbarian threat.

All this is visible clearly in the earliest known cult, that of Zeus Hellanios, located below the highest point of Aegina. Zeus here was originally the weather god; the epithet perhaps points to a connection with the small tribe of Hellenes in the Spercheios Valley in Thessaly, as is certainly the case with the name and family of the Aeginetan hero Aeacus. In the earliest literary references, dating from the first half of the fifth century, the epithet is interpreted, quite naturally, in the sense of "Panhellenios"—as in fact the god was later called explicitly. Because of his name and location, he came to be regarded as the true protector of "the Hellenes" allied against the Persians and later, in idealizing retrospective, as symbol of Panhellenic solidarity and the fight for freedom.[238]

According to Oliver, in Athens the cults of *theoi sōtēres,* especially of Zeus Soter and Athena Soteira, were consciously contrasted with the old royal cults on the Acropolis by their location in the Agora; their function exactly paralleled that of the Spartan *theoi Hellēnioi.* All we know, however, is that in the classical period Zeus Eleutherios was identical with Zeus Soter in the Agora. We do not know when and in what circumstances the cult of Soter arose; in this particular location it apparently goes back only to about the time of Peisistratus. Moreover, only Zeus, not Athena, was given the new epithet of Eleutherios. Literary references and inscriptions, though not always entirely clear, suggest that the cult of Soter in the Agora belonged exclusively to Zeus and that, when both Zeus and Athena are mentioned together, reference is to the well-known shrine they shared as *sōtēres* in the Piraeus.[239] The assumption of a cultic parallel to Sparta therefore has no foundation.

In sum, contrary to Oliver's thesis, the extant evidence shows that the political conceptualization of liberty was achieved only around the time of the Persian Wars or even later, and this concept prompted an echo in the religious sphere only at that time. The concept of *theoi sōtēres,* however, is considerably older. The same is probably true for the concept of *theoi Hellēnioi,* which, at first, merely reflected the awareness of a Hellenic cultic and religious community and assumed occasional overtones of Greek freedom only after the Persian Wars, when it was politicized and assimilated to the similarly politicized concept of freedom. Before then, the comprehensive epithet *sōtēr* seems to have included the essence of what was later, under exceptional circumstances, expressed by *eleutherios.*

Yet Oliver's point of departure is correct: Greek religion did reflect important social and political changes that occurred in Greek communities, and it was indeed in new epithets of Zeus and Athena that such changes were chiefly, though not exclusively, expressed.[240] The cult of Zeus Eleutherios confirms this link between religion and politics, which we can understand even better by looking briefly at the cult's subsequent vicissitudes.

Two questions arise immediately. First, if in the archaic period Zeus and Athena were equally venerated and not infrequently even shared a cult as protectors and saviors of cities, and if the idea of a god of freedom evolved from that of a god of deliverance, why were there no cults of Athena Eleutheria? Second, why was the cult of Zeus Eleutherios not more important and widespread during the fifth century? There is in fact an enormous discrepancy between what we know about the cult on the one hand and the role of the political concept underlying it on the other. The Plataean cult is mentioned only once in all the literature surviving from the fifth century: in a speech in Thucydides written around the very end of this century. Had the grammarian Didymus not corrected a remark by Hyperides, we would not have a single ancient comment on why the Athenian Zeus Eleutherios was given that name. His statue was inscribed with "Soter," and his priest remained the priest of Soter; evidence for a priest of Eleutherios is found only centuries later.[241] Unless the extant sources deceive us badly, the historians and orators, who tirelessly invoked the memory of the Persian Wars and especially the proud Athenian tradition of freedom, did not deem this "god of liberty" worthy of mention. Why was he paid so little attention?

A glance at the sacral aspects of Athenian "imperial ideology" suffices to show that in the fifth century the religious repercussions of political developments did not lose their significance. Rather, it probably was the political situation arising after 479 that prevented the cult of Zeus Eleutherios from achieving the importance it potentially had because of its connection with the collective, emotion-laden Greek experience of victory over the Persians. This potential might have been realized if the fight against Persia had continued beyond 478 as a Panhellenic undertaking with the participation of Sparta and her allies. For such a comprehensive alliance, Plataea would have offered itself as an obvious center. Sparta and the Peloponnesians withdrew, however, leaving the field to the Athenians and a new alliance of poleis in and around the Aegean. As a result, Plataea was marginalized, and soon after his triumph of 479 the Plataean god of liberty was upstaged by other deities. Place and god regained their central importance only in the fourth century, when agitation for a new Persian War brought the old one and with it the Plataean Panhellenic freedom ideology back into the limelight.[242]

The founders of the Delian League tried to represent it as a direct and kindred successor of the Hellenic League of 481. But in its composition, organization, and goals, as well as in its religious aspects, this league was different. Delos was probably chosen as its meeting place and treasury because it was a widely known cult center and the site of a festival attended since ancient times by Ionians and island Greeks; it thus offered a counterweight to Delphi, with which Sparta had long maintained a close relationship. As a result, Apollo became the league's divine protector. We do not know in detail how this function was institutionally expressed, especially since no evidence has survived of a reorganization of the cult festival, which presumably had lost some of its reputation and function after the Persian conquest and the disaster of the Ionian Revolt.[243]

Although Delos and Apollo continued to play a crucial role in Athenian imperial conceptions, divine protection was transferred to Athena when the center of the alliance was moved to Athens in 454.[244] In connection with the increasingly complex organization of the empire, this function was apparently emphasized in several new ways. The treasury of the Delian League and that of Athena were linked closely, though somewhat obscurely. The accumulated tribute was stored in the form of golden statuettes of Athena Nike. Not only did Athena receive as first fruits a fixed quota (one-sixtieth) of the tribute paid by the allies, but some of the accrued funds were used to rebuild and magnificently enhance the goddess's sanctuary on the Acropolis, which had lain in ruins since the Persian Wars.[245] Athena's ancient olive-wood statue as Polias in the Erechtheion, her monumental statue as Promachos, and her chryselephantine statue in the Parthenon all emphasized her central role as goddess of both Athens and the empire, while the Parthenon and its splendid frieze could also be interpreted as both a civic and an imperial celebration. Probably soon after 454 the allied and subject cities were granted the "privilege" of contributing a cow and panoply to the Panathenaea and marching in the procession. The elegant temple of Nike on the bastion of the Acropolis, constructed in the late 420s to celebrate the victory of Pylos, added even more to Athena's luster. Epigraphic evidence attests to the presence of the cult of "Athena, the protectress of Athens," in some cities; whether it was indeed promoted throughout the empire remains debated.[246]

The conclusion is obvious: the foundation of the Delian League and its later transformation into an Athenian empire gave such central importance first to Delian Apollo and then to Athena that, although the Athenians explicitly continued the crusade for liberty from Persia, on the Panhellenic level Zeus Eleutherios was reduced to a marginal role. In Athens, his cult was introduced and combined with that of Soter, probably soon after the Persian Wars, but the reconstruction of the temples ruined by the Persians, including the shrine of Zeus Soter-Eleutherios in the Agora, was delayed for decades, perhaps on the basis of an agreement reached among the Greeks during the war against Xerxes.[247] By the time construction began, Zeus found himself in the shadow of the triumphant Athena, whose sanctuary received priority. Although for ideological purposes he was occasionally pulled into the limelight (see below), his place generally remained in the background.

This also suggests an answer to the second question: why, despite their shared function as *sōtēres,* did only Zeus and not Athena become a god of freedom? As the city goddess of Athens, Athena rose to promote Athenian claims to hegemony and power. Zeus, on the other hand, was credited with the victory and liberty won at Plataea. This victory symbolized the ultimate success of the Hellenic League founded in 481 and led by Sparta. The members of this league understood and presented themselves as the true Hellenes and their alliance as a Panhellenic organization. Hence, it stood under the protection of the Panhellenic god par excellence, Zeus, the king of the gods, who as Zeus Hellanios sat enthroned on Aegina and was particularly suited to be the symbol of Panhellenic solidarity. Logically, therefore, he became "Eleutherios." It was precisely the connection of this epithet with the great Panhellenic experience of the Persian victories that in general precluded other gods from assuming this function.

It made sense to introduce him in his new capacity to Athens as well; for this city, which regarded the victories of Marathon and even Salamis as virtually its own, had much to thank him for. Yet as the result of unforeseeable events, he stood no chance against his powerful daughter. He was given proper recognition some fifty years later by the erection of a stoa in his name, but only after the buildings on the Acropolis were completed and when strong political pressures drew renewed attention to the values and accomplishments he represented. The extant evidence suggests that around the outbreak of the Peloponnesian War, the specifically Athenian ideology of freedom was greatly revalorized; the resulting "doctrine" of absolute Athenian sovereignty and liberty is reflected impressively in Euripides' *Heraclidae* and in the first speech Thucydides gives to Pericles, both performed at that very time. The erection of an especially magnificent stoa for Zeus Eleutherios at precisely that time thus made a strong political statement that was underscored by the use of Nike statues as acroteria: just as Athens, refusing to yield to the demands of the Persian king, had become the champion of Greek freedom, so Athens now judged surrender to Spartan pressure as incompatible with its proud tradition of freedom and the self-respect of its free citizens.[248]

All in all, then, the cult of Zeus Eleutherios confirms the close connection between religion, cult, and politics. The genesis of the cult directly reflects basic changes in the realm of political awareness and concepts, without the influence of political calculation, as is typical of the archaic period. Its later fate testifies to the impact new propagandistic and ideological demands had on religious phenomena. Henceforth, the cult served specific political aims; it became the instrument and—through temporary neglect—the victim of power politics. Other, specifically Athenian examples are perhaps more useful to demonstrate the variety of ways in which cults and myths could be used to serve ideological purposes in justifying power and domination. Conversely, the cult of Zeus Eleutherios teaches us that political aspects were not always mirrored with equal intensity in the religious sphere. Indeed, because of the specific political conditions that developed in the fifth century, the ideology of freedom in this respect received surprisingly little attention. After the decline of Greek freedom, however, it was powerfully resurrected by Philip and Alexander.[249]

Note added in proofs: Josh Ober and John Ma kindly brought to my attention a new inscription, recently discovered in Thebes and as yet unpublished, but presented to the public in newspaper articles and discussed at conferences (see *Ta Nea* of Aug. 8, 2002, with a photograph on which the crucial words are legible). It perhaps comes from a late sixth-century victory monument, celebrating an invasion of Attica and the "liberation of Chalkis," one might imagine (although this is not attested elsewhere) by expelling the Athenian cleruchy that was established there after the Athenian victory over Chalkis in 506 (Hdt. 5.77 with reference to the Athenian victory monument on the Acropolis and the epigram recorded there). Details and context cannot, of course, be assessed before the inscription is fully published. What matters here is that "setting Chalkis free" is expressed not by a formula containing *eleuth-* but by *Chalkida lusamenoi,* "having loosened (the bonds of) Chalkis." (On "to loosen" [*luein*] as an early word for "to liberate," see Raaflaub 2000d: 258–59.) If this is really a late-sixth-century inscription it thus adds another piece of evidence supporting the thesis argued for in this chapter.

— 4 —

The Concept of Freedom after the Persian Wars
Its Meaning and Differentiation in Interstate Relations

4.1. CONTEMPORARY EXPECTATIONS AND THE
RISE OF THE ATHENIAN EMPIRE

Empire, Subjection, and Freedom: Problems and Questions
In the winter of 478/477, the Hellenic League, formed in 481 to ward off the
Persians and augmented in 479 after the victory of Mycale, broke apart,
without being formally terminated. Differences in assessing the need to continue the war, widespread dissatisfaction with the leadership of Sparta and
its appointed commander, Pausanias, and the clever diplomacy of the Athenian leader, Aristides, finally prompted a majority of the league's members
to entrust hegemony to Athens. Sparta and the members of the Peloponnesian League withdrew from the war. A new alliance was established under
Athens's leadership: it is commonly called the "Delian League." [1]

The alliance was initially one of free and equal poleis bound by oath for
an indefinite time to maintain mutual defense, to conduct wars jointly, and
to contribute to the actions of the alliance according to individual ability. Its
immediate purpose was to maintain preparedness against another Persian
attack, to liberate the Greeks still under Persian rule, and to seek revenge for
the devastations caused by Xerxes' army in 480 – 479.[2] The allies determined
policy in council by joint consultation and equal vote and entrusted military
leadership and the management of finances to the hegemonic power, Athens. Given the circumstances of the alliance's origins, its generally accepted
purpose, and the traditions prevailing in the world of Greek poleis on such
matters, the extent and use of the authority thus falling to Athens were
largely self-evident. The advantages and disadvantages that contemporaries
associated by experience and observation with membership in such an alliance gave no cause to expect what the Athenians later would make of it.

Hence, it seemed unproblematic to leave the prerogatives and authority of the *hēgemōn* unspecified, to formulate objectives and oaths in traditional and general terms, and to set no specific limit to the duration of the alliance.[3]

Whatever Athenian leaders thought initially about their city's hegemonial role—which they had tried to realize, at least partially, already two years before—they must have perceived quickly that it offered them great new opportunities.[4] Exploiting the very vagueness of the terms agreed upon, the need for protection felt acutely by many allies, their city's supremacy within the league, and its ever increasing military superiority, they soon turned the situation to Athens's advantage. In the course of a single generation, with but few exceptions, the allies became subjects and the symmachy was transformed into an Athenian empire. This process was essentially completed by the time of the Thirty Years' Peace with Sparta in 446 but reached its crucial stage much earlier, by the late 460s or early 450s.[5]

In this context, Athens's imperial rule and the changed status of its former allies became political issues that were significant far beyond Athens's immediate sphere of control. The Spartans were repeatedly forced to deal with the effects, and in the period before the Peloponnesian War Athens's oppression of its allies and the threat its policies posed to the freedom of many more Greek poleis became central issues of contention within and between the two "power blocs." Exploited by a fierce and skillful war propaganda, these issues retained their relevancy until the collapse of Athens in 404.

In all these developments, the concept of freedom played a variety of significant roles. Moreover, Athens's rise to power and the dramatic change in its relations with its allies decisively transformed the nature, use, and value of this concept. To begin with, Athens's *archē* (rule, empire) represents the first extensive and long-term rule of one Greek polis over other Greek poleis.[6] Various measures adopted to systematize such rule distinguish this experiment from anything that may seem comparable before and during this period. Here, for the first time, the contrast between freedom and servitude became important in Greek interstate relations. This raises a number of questions: when and why did this occur, how did contemporaries become aware of it, what aspects of freedom came to the fore in this process, and how did those particular experiences influence the concept's further development?

Second, new words, such as "autonomy" (*autonomia*) and "self-sufficiency" (*autarkeia*) introduced distinctions and nuances to the concept of freedom itself. What prompted the coining of these new terms, and how did their emergence affect the terms that already existed?

Third, on various levels, freedom quickly became a versatile propaganda tool and eventually a formula that could be used nearly ad libitum. Yet the concept never lost its tangible value and great appeal. We thus have a rare opportunity to observe in some detail how a value concept was ideologized and to examine in specific contexts the relationship between freedom as a value concept and as a propaganda slogan.

Fourth, the problems caused by Athenian domination stimulated political thinking and analysis. As a result, the place and role of freedom in the system of political values, and the factors that determined them, were explored and understood better. For example, the interdependence of freedom and power or of external and domestic freedom came to be recognized, scrutinized critically, and exploited politically, affording us important insights into the nature, potential, and limitations of this concept.

Some of these issues will be discussed in subsequent chapters. Here I will begin by asking how contemporaries' perception and judgment of the Athenian Empire affected their understanding of the nature and value of polis freedom. The extant evidence enables us to understand the distinctive elements that were perceived as determining the nonfreedom or servitude of a polis. This will in turn allow us to define more precisely the idea of polis freedom and the internal and external conditions for its realization or preservation.

The history of events and developments is not the subject of this study, but some preliminary remarks may be helpful. The purpose for which the Delian League was founded was realized swiftly and effectively. Remaining Persian garrisons were driven out of the coastal cities of the Aegean and Hellespont, the league's sphere of influence was extended to the borders of Pamphylia, and Persian fleets were kept far from Aegean waters. Around 450, warfare with the Persians ceased: the league had fulfilled its original goal of liberating and protecting the Greeks from the Persians.[7] This was clearly seen as a turning point; like the earlier disaster in Egypt (454), it prompted a crisis in the alliance. The process of transforming the symmachy into an archē had begun much earlier; the crisis of the late 450s may have prompted the Athenians to accelerate this process and make it more systematic; it came at least to a preliminary conclusion in the early 440s.[8]

Little is known about the beginning and the causes of this process.[9] What is clear is that Athens soon used force, not only against those who refused to join, but against poleis intent on leaving the league. Thucydides brands the subjugation of Naxos (early or mid-460s) as the first "enslavement" of a formerly autonomous polis, and Russell Meiggs describes that of Thasos (465 or

463) as "the first unambiguous sign of tyranny." [10] Whatever their frequency, these were unrelated, variously motivated actions, undertaken mainly in fulfillment of Athens's hegemonic function and presumably with the consent of a majority of the allies. Such experiences must have led Athenian politicians to recognize and then to test the possibilities available to their city; gradually, such efforts must have become more systematic, eventually driven by a conscious policy. This stage was clearly reached by the time of the crisis that developed in the Delian League in the aftermath of the Egyptian catastrophe. The measures the Athenians undertook in the following years to consolidate their power not only made the changes in the relationship between *hēgemōn* and *summachoi* (allies) obvious, but advanced those changes even further. Now not only defectors but all the poleis were affected: this was not merely a quantitative change but a qualitative one as well.

Athens's domination thus arose gradually and haphazardly. The allies, formerly equal, were not all subjugated uniformly and in a single act. Rather, the process was scattered, varied, and to some extent hidden, affecting in dramatically obvious ways only individual rebellious poleis. For a long time the great diversity of statuses among the poleis within the Athenian sphere of power probably made it difficult to perceive global changes. Hence, the allies' awareness and assessment of their own condition and of ongoing general changes must have differed considerably and hindered the development of a terminology that described such changes adequately. The emergence of such terminology can certainly not be linked to a single event or specific date.

Moreover, it is uncertain how easily the terminology of freedom or servitude was transferable at that time. One might think that, once power relations outside and within the polis came to be viewed at all from the perspective of *douleia* and *eleutheria,* these terms could be readily applied in any given circumstance. [11] Yet they had emerged only recently, in response not to an ordinary and familiar kind of political oppression but to an extraordinary and monumental threat and in connection with foreign, "barbarian," domination; they were thus imbued with "national" elements and intense emotions. In contrast, subjection by a Greek polis was a previously unknown phenomenon in relations among Greeks themselves and in this case resulted from a lengthy and complex process. [12]

It is thus worth asking when and why the subjection of Athens's allies was perceived (by themselves or others) clearly enough so that the corresponding terminology of servitude could be applied to them. Since servitude presupposes domination, we must also ask when and in what circumstances the dominance of Athens became so marked that it was recognized, and finally also designated, as rule (*archē*) or even oppression (*turannis*) rather than hegemony.

To appreciate the significance of these changes fully we need to remind ourselves that they represented something entirely new in the experience of those affected by them. Because what happened here was not only unexpected but unprecedented, fundamentally un-Greek, and therefore literally inconceivable, awareness and terminology needed time to adjust to it. This can be clarified by a brief analysis of the horizon of experience against which the founding members of the Delian League were able to measure their expectations in 478/477. Naturally, they would have thought first of relations within the Peloponnesian League, a hegemonic alliance led by Sparta that was considerably older and therefore served as an obvious model for later alliances, including that concluded in 481 against the Persians. They might also have remembered the situation of the Greeks of Asia Minor, who had lived under Persian rule and thus carried with them a very different bag of experiences.

Relationships in the Peloponnesian League

The system of alliances known to moderns as the "Peloponnesian League" (the ancients called it simply "the Lacedaemonians and their allies") developed from the middle of the sixth century out of a number of bilateral symmachy treaties in which the respective partners accepted the military and political leadership of Sparta and were obliged to support it militarily in return for protection against external threats and, possibly, internal stasis.[13] It is uncertain whether the league ever adopted some form of "federal constitution" or remained informal and loose, its effectiveness largely dependent on common interests and the leader's ability to prevail. Of course, it made a considerable difference for those involved whether particular obligations or restrictions were based on mutual, perhaps even legally contracted, agreement or imposed by the superior will of the hegemonic power. It is not known, for instance, whether the habit observed in the fifth century of initiating league action—apart from certain specified cases—only after consultation with the allies and with their consent was a set rule and, if so, whether it was based on custom or a formal decision.[14] For my present purpose, however, it is sufficient to consider the actual procedures, whatever the legal or contractual background. The following aspects seem particularly noteworthy.

First, alliances resulted either from military defeat (thus Tegea) or from voluntary attachment (e.g., Corinth); these differences apparently did not affect the status of an allied polis in the symmachy. The treaties were not limited in time; withdrawal was regarded as rebellion and fought whenever possible, but there is no evidence that renewed subjugation resulted in discrimination against the offending member.[15] Until the late fifth century, no extant testimony accuses Sparta, as Athens was accused, of "enslaving" its allies. Rather, status differences among members were pragmatic in nature and the result of obvious factors such as size, power, and location: because of their immediate proximity and the enormous discrepancy in power, small Arcadian poleis were necessarily more exposed to Spartan influence and therefore more "dependent" than such distant and powerful allies as Corinth and Thebes.[16]

Second, as in all Greek symmachies, the *hēgemōn* held a position of clear supremacy. According to the formula used in oaths and treaties from an unknown time, the allies were obliged unilaterally and unconditionally to support Sparta by supplying troops in case of war, and they were bound by majority decisions of the assembly of league representatives.[17] In this respect they yielded an essential part of their freedom of action and thus of their sovereignty. But there were mitigating circumstances. Usually, Sparta sought the consent of its allies before making important decisions. It was therefore difficult for the *hēgemōn* to abuse the unrestricted allegiance owed it by treaty.[18] Moreover, depending on their political and military importance, league members had considerable opportunity to influence decisions; Corinth, in particular, often played a leading role in shaping and opposing Spartan policy.[19] Yet the great powers were not all that counted. Thucydides explains that the lack of a unified, authoritative will (in contrast to the Athenian sphere of power) under the system of *isopsēphia*, "equality of vote," forced the leadership to take the opinions of individual allies into account. Given their relatively small number, the divergence of interests among them, and their unwillingness to be subordinate, this was significant. Nor was the members' right to participate in decisions merely theoretical; its violation during the Peace of Nicias triggered vehement reactions.[20]

Moreover, wars among allies or between allies and outsiders were prohibited only during campaigns undertaken by the league. In some cases the allies' freedom of action proved substantial and had far-reaching consequences.[21] The loss of sovereignty caused by membership in the alliance therefore was indeed limited in time and scope; the Spartans certainly did not have permanent authority over their allies and could fully exploit opportunities theoretically available to them only in situations of compelling urgency and as long as their leadership remained unchallenged.

Third, except for the states near the Isthmus, the Peloponnesians were predominantly land-based and agrarian states that were economically undeveloped and had little money at their disposal.[22] The states contributed to common war efforts by supplying contingents of citizen hoplites. When the league was not at war, as was normally the case, they could use their armies in any way they chose. Sparta's strength, too, was based entirely on its hoplite army; its manpower supply was never abundant and, if anything, shrinking. Therefore, the allies were useful to the league and its leader only as partners with military capacity. It was inconceivable for them to make monetary payments instead of furnishing hoplites or to make regular financial contributions, let alone pay tribute.[23] That the leader thus was dealing with weaker but never defenseless partners determined their relationship.

Fourth, through most of the fifth century Sparta continued to respect its allies' right to internal self-determination. At the time when the treaties were concluded, this right was taken for granted and thus not mentioned explicitly.[24] Even much later, it was unthinkable that Sparta might station garrisons or place colonies on allied territory or dispatch functionaries with authority over internal affairs, or that the Spartan assembly might pass laws intended to bind other league members.[25]

True, in the late fifth century Sparta was accused of encroaching upon the constitutional sovereignty of its allies, but it is uncertain whether and to what extent this applies to earlier periods. Already by the end of the sixth century, Sparta had supposedly gained the reputation of having suppressed tyrannies in its sphere of influence and of being opposed in principle to tyranny. This seems incompatible with its intention to reinstate Hippias in Athens and probably reflects much later ideology; even if not, it was a positive reputation.[26] Later, Sparta came to be regarded as a firm supporter of oligarchy.[27] We do not know when it began actively to pursue such a policy (or when such a policy became necessary). No action apparently was taken against the "democracies" that developed, for example, in Elis and Mantinea,[28] and it appears likely that the predominance of "oligarchic" governments observed by Thucydides in the Spartan sphere of influence was noticed and became an object of suspicion only when, as a result of increasing polarization between democracy and oligarchy in the second half of the fifth century, it was contrasted to the Athenian tendency to promote democracy in its empire.[29] Some incidents indeed occurred during the Peloponnesian

War that seemed to corroborate this assessment;[30] Sparta probably adopted a pronounced pro-oligarchic policy only at that time.

Fifth, my comments do not intend to minimize the leader's political influence on the allies. Membership in this permanent symmachy clearly restricted individual sovereignty, especially in external affairs. Normally this was accepted, either because the advantages outweighed the disadvantages (as for Corinth in its long-standing conflict with Argos) or because only thus could a relatively high degree of freedom be maintained (as in the case of Tegea after its military defeat). Attempts to withdraw from the league occurred, but for good reasons, dissatisfaction rarely went so far. The special circumstances existing in each polis, the nature of the league, and the safeguards built into its normal procedures long prevented differences from outweighing common interests. Moreover, the alliance remained primarily defensive well into the Peloponnesian War; its main purpose was not to expand the power of the *hēgemōn* but to maintain the status quo. Given its specific interests and limitations, caused especially by fear of the helots and concern for domestic security, Sparta continued to find more advantage in maintaining access to the military capacity of independent partners than in suppressing its allies.[31]

Accordingly, the aspects of dominance and dependence in the relationship between *hēgemōn* and allies were not pronounced enough before the Peloponnesian War to warrant accusing Sparta of "subjugation," even in polemical debate. Thucydides' treatment of this issue in his discussion of the prehistory of the war (432) is illuminating. Athenian envoys in Sparta, confronted with this very accusation, counter by remarking that the Spartans have themselves everywhere imposed an order that serves their own purposes (i.e., oligarchies). But they concede that, by withdrawing from the Persian War, Sparta has avoided the dilemma between establishing a forceful *archē* or risking its own safety—a dilemma that Athens has been compelled to resolve by assuming power and rule over its allies. Thus, they admit indirectly that the condition of the Spartan allies differs fundamentally from that of the Athenian subjects—despite the "establishment of oligarchies." Moreover, when Pericles rejects Sparta's demand of autonomy for the cities of the Delian League, he disputes neither that the Athenian allies have generally lost their autonomy nor that Sparta's have basically retained theirs; he merely criticizes an arrangement that too strongly serves the advantage of the *hēgemōn*.[32]

Later, indeed—especially after widespread allied disgruntlement with Sparta's handling of the Peace of Nicias—Athenian diplomats polemicized against Sparta's *archē,* and even Herodotus, commenting on Sparta's leading position in mid-sixth-century Greece, claims that it had already "subjugated" the greater part of the Peloponnese.[33] Athenian propagandists thus had a ready answer to the accusation that their city ruled over subject poleis. But in extant fifth-century sources Sparta is never called a *polis turannos,* and the explicit terminology of servitude is never applied to its allies. Even more important, only if relationships in the Peloponnesian League differed substantially from those in the Delian League could the Corinthians in 432 agitate as they did against Athens's enslavement of its allies and the Spartans claim so convincingly to be the "liberators of Hellas."[34]

In 478/477 this Spartan symmachy, whose basic features probably were copied by the Hellenic League of 481, provided the only model to illustrate how members of a league might be affected if they accepted, by treaty of alliance, to yield certain rights of sovereignty to a hegemonial power and league assembly.[35] Thucydides (6.92.5) lets Alcibiades, seeking refuge at Sparta in 415, characterize the allies' relationship to Sparta as the voluntary acceptance of *hēgemonia* that is based not on force but goodwill: a flattering and idealizing description but not devoid of truth, especially for the beginning of the war—and one that fits the beginnings of the Delian League as well. True, many poleis desperately needed Athenian help and would probably have accepted even significant restrictions on their sovereignty. But on the whole there was no reason to fear such consequences. Moreover, as the example of Plataea shows, the obligation to render military assistance, even if it was unrestricted and linked with a great power difference between the partners, was not regarded as a loss of freedom, as long as it was based on mutual interests and needs.[36] It is understandable, therefore, that no one thought it necessary to limit the duration of the alliance, to formulate protections against abuse of power by the *hēgemōn,* or even to define and guarantee the status of the allies. The traditional formulas seemed sufficient, based as they were on mutual trust. Why else would league members have volunteered to surrender their means of self-defense?[37]

The *Douleia* of Greek Poleis under Persian Rule

To later observers it may have occurred that turning over the defense of freedom against the Persians to Athens was, so to speak, like driving off the devil with Beelzebub. Unfortunately, we know even less about the details of Persia's exercise of rule than about the Peloponnesian League. Apart from general considerations, specific clues are offered almost exclusively by the motives that can be deduced for the Ionian Revolt.[38]

Persian rule was based on military conquest and subjugation, both directly and indirectly, by virtue of Cyrus's defeat of Croesus, the previous ruler over the Greeks in Asia Minor. Hence, with the partial exception of Miletus, which had concluded a special treaty, the Greeks were unambiguously Persian subjects.[39] They were obliged unconditionally to obey the orders of the Great King and his satraps, to supply troops for their wars, and to pay tribute. This system was formalized by Darius; from his reign on, at the latest, the concept of foreign rule must have been associated chiefly with these three obligations, which therefore must have been perceived early on as components of servitude.[40]

Moreover, Persian rule in the Greek cities was exercised indirectly through "tyrants" who were members of the local aristocracy and had either risen to power earlier or were installed by the satrap. Therefore, tyranny here was linked with foreign rule and exempted from the dynamics of competition that usually prevailed in Greek poleis. Persian rule thus curtailed constitutional autonomy, perpetuated artificially a condition that increasingly ran counter to general developments elsewhere in the Greek world, and provided one of the most salient reasons for the widespread dissatisfaction underlying the Ionian Revolt.[41] At the same time, however, these tyrannies served as shields against outside interference: as long as they functioned reliably, more extensive and direct intrusion in internal affairs remained unnecessary. Hence, overall, the judicial and administrative autonomy of the poleis was respected; even when Darius introduced a standardized imperial coin, not all local coinage was required to conform. There is no evidence of centralized legislation affecting the internal affairs of the poleis, and interference in their religious life would have been contrary to the principle of religious tolerance observed generally by the Persians.[42]

Finally, the poleis retained their military potential and with it their defensive capability, although in some places fortifications were dismantled.[43] They were even able, to a certain extent, to maintain an independent foreign policy; in fact, the consequences of one such action, in which the satrap of Sardis became embroiled, triggered the revolt.[44] Moreover, the Persians exhibited some flexibility in their exercise of rule: after suppressing the Ionian Revolt and destroying the ringleaders and the principal city involved (Miletus), they enacted reforms that took into account the most important causes of dissatisfaction, changed conditions, and local needs.[45]

Persian rule thus was not all negative. In view of the attendant advantages—or perhaps the risks involved with resistance or the lack of real alternatives—especially the upper classes were prepared then as later to come to terms with their Persian overlords. Still, the state of subjection to the despotic will of a distant, alien king, his satraps, and his puppet tyrants, as well as everything connected with that condition of servitude, must have been widely felt to be unbearable.[46] This surely intensified when Darius resumed expansion toward the west and Persian domination became more conspicuous and oppressive. Yet extraneous factors were crucial in encouraging many poleis to overcome initial reluctance and join the revolt: recent Persian failures were perhaps interpreted too quickly as signs of weakness, and the involvement of Athenian and Eretrian contingents propelled the revolt in a direction that was perhaps not fully anticipated.[47]

At any rate, the revolt failed. More than a decade later, the Hellenic League, upon Athens's insistence, liberated the island and Ionian Greeks from Persian "slavery" and admitted them to their alliance. The Delian League continued this policy. All signs indicated that this marked the end of the days of servitude; not even the worst pessimist would have expected them to return—let alone so soon. How did the *douleia* of these same cities under Athens compare with that under the Persians? Despite significant differences (such as the absence of tyrants and of an ethnic contrast between rulers and ruled) Athenian domination had much more in common with Persian rule than with Spartan supremacy. Moreover, for several reasons (Athens's interference with its subjects' domestic affairs, the constant presence of a variety of Athenian officials, and Athens's tendency to insist on centralized control and conformity to its own standards), Athenian rule eventually must have been far more visible in the individual poleis, and servitude accordingly more immediately palpable, than under the Persians.[48]

4.2. FREEDOM AND SERVITUDE OF A POLIS: TERMINOLOGY AND DEFINITIONS

The Terminology of Servitude

What exactly was the purpose of using *douleia* and related terms to describe the status of a polis under Athenian rule? What was the significance and function of this word among the terms for dependence existing at the time? I begin by examining how the word was used in the last third of the fifth century, when documentation is richest, and will then try to determine the time and conditions when such usage emerged.

At first sight, Thucydides seems to use *douleia* without special emphasis; though stark and at times rhetorically colored, its meaning is hardly distinguishable from that of other terms for the same status, such as *hupēkoos* or *hupocheirios*.[49] Thucydides thereby puts the subordination of poleis under Athens on a par with that of the subjects of the Great King, of the helots under Sparta, citizens under a tyrant, and the demos under an oligarchic regime. Generally, the word *douleia* is versatile. It can be used for every aspect of life and encompasses various degrees of servitude. In the political sphere it is situated between "freedom" and "autonomy" on the one side and "enslavement" in the strict sense (*andrapodismos*) on the other.[50] *Douleia* of a polis thus basically means that its independence is restricted but the personal liberty of its citizens remains intact. Within these limits, there exists a broad spectrum of forms of political dependence, which have in common only that a polis in *douleia* in some way has to obey (listen to) a master (hence, *hupēkoos* from *hupakouein*) and is subject to outside rule (hence, *douleuein* is frequently identical with *archesthai*). Such seemingly nonspecific usage has misled scholars into interpreting *douleia* as a primarily rhetorical or metaphorical expression that is legally imprecise and therefore not to be taken at face value.[51] We should avoid, however, approaching our mostly nonlegal sources (such as drama and historiography) with inadequate expectations: if they were not interested in legal precision, they could still have been precise, specific, and consistent from a political and pragmatic perspective.[52] The following discussion intends to pursue this possibility.

First, *doulos* is distinguished in two respects from other terms applied to slaves.[53] It is contrasted to *eleutheros;* thus, we might expect the subordination of a polis to be characterized as *douleia,* when the author intends to stress its lack of or desire for freedom. And it is firmly antithetical to *despotēs;* thus, *douleia* emphasizes the "despotic character" of the domination of one state over another. These two aspects often suffice to explain the choice of *douleia* rather than another term.[54]

Second, in Thucydides *douleia* and related words almost always appear in speeches, and especially in those delivered by opponents and victims of Athens.[55] These terms are thus not neutral in value but decidedly negative and appropriate for use in polemics and propaganda.

Third, apart from speeches, Thucydides uses these terms in their marked sense only in three passages; each time their appearance is readily understandable. In one, he simply picks up the thread of earlier speeches (6.88.1). In another, however (the suppression of the revolt of Naxos), he offers a comment: "This was the first of the allied cities which was deprived of its freedom ["enslaved," *edoulōthē*] contrary to Greek custom" (1.98.4).[56] The pointed formulation here stresses the fact that this is the first, and therefore especially appalling, case of enslavement of an ally; it emphasizes the violation of customary behavior among Greek states that hitherto had been taken for granted; and it implies a contrast to the initial autonomy of the allies, mentioned just before (1.97.1). A similar contrast is brought out when Thucydides describes the mood among the retreating Athenians after their defeat by Syracuse: "They had come to enslave others, and now they were going away frightened of being enslaved themselves" (7.75.7). Otherwise, when reporting events, Thucydides uses only neutral terms, even in contexts that highlight the general hatred of Athenian rule.[57] Nor does he repeat the term *douleia* when describing the suppression of other revolts.[58]

Fourth, with few exceptions, Thucydides lets the Athenians themselves avoid words related to *douleia,* while they speak without inhibition of their *archē* and their "subjects" (*hupēkooi, hupocheirioi*), terms obviously regarded as more neutral in value.[59] The exceptions are readily explained by their context or by deliberate authorial choice. For example, Alcibiades, trying to convince the Persian satrap that the Athenians would be preferable to the Spartans as partners in power, argues that the former were "prepared to collaborate in conquering and enslaving [*xunkatadouloun*] the sea for themselves, and for the king all the Hellenes inhabiting his country, while the Spartans, on the contrary, came with the intention of liberating them [*eleutherōsontas*]."[60]

Finally, the same distinctions can be grasped from the variations appearing in a given context. Thus, in the Melian Dialogue (5.84–111), whenever the debate focuses on those subjected to Athenian rule or the impending fate of the Melians, the latter speak of "slaves" and "enslavement" and the Athenians of "subjects" and "those who are governed," of "rule" and "survival" (*sōtēria*).

Clearly, then, *douleia* is not simply a casual, value neutral, readily interchangeable, or even technical term designating the status of a subject city. Rather, the word has strong emotional, moral, and propagandistic overtones. It emphasizes the negative aspects of being oppressed by foreign rule, depending on another's commands, and lacking freedom of decision and action. Hermann Strasburger points out rightly that it evokes the intentions of the Persians in the Persian Wars and thus puts the Athenians on a level with the barbarians.[61] Those who use the word are not interested in the legally precise definition of a particular degree of dependence. Rather, they desire to characterize a given relationship of dependency as especially hated, feared, and reprehensible, or to emphasize pointedly the development or existence of this negative type of dependency even in cases that are commonly viewed differently. Hence, in Corcyra opponents of a proposed alliance with Athens provoke the specter of *douleia,* although the proposal envisions neither the allegiance nor the tribute typical of Athenian subjects in the empire, and Pericles regards even the smallest concession to Spartan ultimatums as a clear sign of *doulōsis.*[62]

Other sources confirm that the word usage we find in Thucydides was widespread and reflects a politically differentiated terminology common in the last third of the century. The "Old Oligarch" in this context uses the extreme formulation only once, when observing that, as a consequence of Athenian regulations concerning legal procedures, the allies have become virtual slaves of the Athenian people.[63] Euripides denounces the "enslavement" of small and weak poleis by the big powers.[64] Due to the loss of crucial plays, the picture is less clear in comedy. In *Knights,* old man Demos is hailed as *monarchos* and *basileus* of Hellas whose splendid rule all people fear like that of a tyrant (1111–14, 1329–30, 1333). According to a common (though not unchallenged) interpretation, in 426, shortly after the suppression of the Mytilenian revolt, Aristophanes in *Babylonians* graphically embodied the lot of the allies in a chorus of mill slaves who, despite their barbaric costumes and masks, supposedly were recognizable as citizens of Samos.[65] In *Poleis,* Eupolis personified the cities of the empire as women who brought tribute to their master, the Athenian Demos, thereby eliciting all the stereotypical associations connected with the power relationship between (male) masters and (female) subordinates, whether free or slave. In doing so, he not only conflated "in one stroke several sociopolitical categories—the political ally, the female, the slave"—but apparently took advantage of the opportunity to criticize some Athenian methods of exploiting its slavelike allies without challenging its right to rule over them.[66]

It is likely, therefore, that within Athens this negative terminology and the associations connected with it were employed, much as they were by Thucydides, deliberately (though rather exceptionally) for specific purposes, not least to draw attention to or criticize Athenian methods of exercising rule over the allies.[67] Such intentional, differentiated word use probably was common long before the last third of the century, when Athens drastically tightened its control over the allied cities.[68] Two *testimonia e contrario* suggest a *terminus ante quem* of 446.

At a meeting of the Peloponnesian League in 432, representatives of Aegina complained "that they were not, as specified in the treaty, autonomous." During the negotiations preceding the war, accordingly, Sparta demanded that Aegina's autonomy be restored. The treaty in question is probably the Thirty Years' Peace of 446 rather than the treaty sealing Aegina's capitulation to Athens in 457. Thus, Aegina's condition after its surrender must have been experienced and described as servitude and at least partially improved by the autonomy clause agreed upon in the Thirty Years' Peace.[69] Not constrained by the language of diplomacy and treaties, Pindar expresses Aegina's aspirations more pointedly: he appeals to "Mother Aegina," Zeus, and the island's native heroes to guide this polis "on her voyage of freedom" (*eleutheroi stoloi, Pyth.* 8.98–99). This ode is dated to 446: in view of Athens's recent setbacks in Boeotia, Euboea, and Megara, hopes of regaining freedom must have been rising. The word used here is *eleutheria;* its opposite clearly *douleia.* The general theme of the ode and the contrast evoked between the bright world of justice and peace and the deadly shadow of violence and the breach of peace unmistakably condemn Athens's oppression of its allies.[70]

Both testimonia concern Aegina, a polis incorporated by force into the naval alliance at a relatively late date; they do not by themselves constitute proof that by then the allies' condition had become one of *douleia* and was generally perceived as such. But again this can be ascertained indirectly: in an ultimatum issued before the war, Sparta demanded autonomy for all the Greeks in Athens's sphere of influence. Accordingly, Sparta believed that the affected poleis lacked autonomy and—as the later promise of *eleutheria* to those very cities indicates—suffered *douleia* under Athens.[71] In the Thirty Years' Peace, Sparta had tacitly acknowledged Athenian rule over its empire. Since to our knowledge the status of the allies did not change significantly in the intervening time, the situation of 432 may be presumed to have existed already in 446.[72]

That the terminology of servitude must have been fully developed by midcentury, at the latest, can be established further by considering the characterization of Athens's rule and the words applied to it in the extant sources.[73]

The Terminology of Domination

It is hardly necessary any longer to demonstrate how unhesitatingly the terms "dominance" and "empire" (*archē*) are used in Thucydides' work, by the author himself and by the Athenians, who were both interested, though for different reasons, in using value-neutral terminology.[74] What is significant, again, is that many contemporary works contain precise parallels that help us assess the use of terminology and the representation of dominance among the Athenian public.

The Old Oligarch takes the Athenian *archē* for granted. He comments on the suppression and exploitation of Athens's allies and the mechanisms developed by the Athenian demos to control them at home and in Athens.[75] References in contemporary comedies illustrate that average Athenians accepted their rule over the Greeks as a political reality which filled them with pride and a sense of importance and with which they identified strongly.[76] In *Wasps,* performed in 422, the passionate judge Philocleon is convinced, thanks to the crucial role played by the courts in Athenian political life and in controlling the allies, that he is "lord of all," and that his power is comparable with that of any monarch. The natural basis of parody and mockery is Athens's power, her rule "over a thousand tribute paying cities, from Pontos to Sardinia."[77] In *Knights* (424), the demagogue-slaves contending for the favor of Master Demos know that what really counts are their own impressive merits gained by extending his rule. At the end of the play, when Demos, rejuvenated, reappears onstage, the chorus cheers his rule over the Greeks.[78] It would be in keeping with this tendency if Aristophanes, in a rather unclear remark in the *parabasis* of *Acharnians,* boasted not merely of having, in a previous play (*Babylonians*), shown the Athenians the true face of democracy in the allied cities—as the passage is usually understood— but of having demonstrated to them "the way that the *dēmoi* in the cities are ruled by the *dēmos* [of Athens]."[79]

There used to be a clear *terminus ante quem* for the development of such Athenian awareness of their rule in the empire and the terminology connected with it. The earliest decrees collectively designating the allies as "cities over which the Athenians have power [*kratos*]" or "which the Athenians rule [*kratousin*]" were long dated to the early 440s, which seemed all the more striking because the Old Oligarch and Aristophanes indicate that even in their time the usual, and official, designation was still "allies," or at most "tribute-paying allies." Recent epigraphical discoveries now make a considerably later date for these decrees more likely.[80] On the other hand, Sophocles' use of *summachoi* in *Ajax,* an early play probably performed in the 440s if not 450s, marks an "ally" as inferior, liable to receiving orders, and lacking full control over his own affairs.[81]

In the intense debates that must have taken place in and outside Athens over its methods of imperial rule, its domination was occasionally even equated with a tyranny.[82] This unflattering characterization was probably introduced by opponents or victims of Athens's policies. In Thucydides, it is first brought up by the Corinthians, who urge war at a meeting of the Peloponnesian League. It is then adopted cautiously by Pericles and more forcefully by Cleon.[83] The theme seems to have appealed particularly to the comic poets. They compared Athens's rule over its allies not only with that of a master over his slaves—thus Eupolis in *Poleis* and Aristophanes in *Babylonians* and *Wasps*, mentioned earlier—but also with that of an autocrat and tyrant. In *Knights*, the chorus cries out, "Demos, glorious is your rule [*archē*], when all men fear you like a tyrant" (*andra turannon*, 1111–14), and later, "Hail, king [*basileus*] of the Hellenes!" (1333).[84] The fascination of tragedy with the figure of the tyrant may in part have been prompted by the same experience. According to an attractive suggestion by Bernard Knox, in *Oedipus Rex* Sophocles employed the already familiar characterization of Athens as a *polis turannos* effectively to place his tragic hero within a complex associative frame of reference. Around the same time, Herodotus based his interpretation of an important Athenian event of the late sixth century— Cleomenes' unsuccessful attempt to reinstate the tyrant Hippias in Athens —on the same contemporary associations evoked by the term *turannos*.[85]

All in all, there can be little doubt that, in the form and at the time described by Thucydides, it was a firmly established part of the political and rhetorical arsenal to compare Athens's imperial rule with a tyranny. But it is just as clear that "tyranny" in this sense was not a technical term that could be introduced at will to describe any form of predominance or rule.[86] Rather, it was used almost exclusively either to evoke negative associations in polemics and propaganda against Athens or by the Athenians themselves to emphasize dramatically, by drawing on those same associations, certain problematic traits of their rule and so to underscore criticism and warning or to justify the need for drastic political measures. "Tyranny" thus served among the terms of domination a similar function as *douleia* did among those for subservience.[87]

According to Plutarch, Thucydides, son of Melesias, already used this comparison in the 440s, during a period of bitter debate over the purpose and limits of Athens's exercise of power in the Delian League. Although Plutarch's description of this debate abounds in anachronisms, this particular detail is not implausible. If so, the extant traces of evidence again lead us back to the years just after the middle of the century, to the time, that is, when the organizational and "ideological" evolution of the Athenian *archē* had come to an end.[88]

The Emergence of the Terminology of Servitude: Time and Reasons

The differentiated terminology of domination and servitude that was commonly applied to the relationship between Athens and its allies in the last third of the fifth century can be traced back to the early 440s. It is unlikely, however, that it came into usage only at that time. Since contemporary sources are lacking, it is more difficult to determine at what point in the preceding decades and under what circumstances this could have occurred.[89] We thus need to examine the purpose and effect of various political and military changes by which the naval alliance was transformed into an Athenian *archē* and, in doing so, take into account also the reactions and sentiments of those affected.

The terms of the alliance and the lack of precise definitions in the initial treaties were described at the beginning of this chapter. I should add here that the autonomous or free status of the allies was in all probability not defined by treaty either. It was taken for granted, and that it might ever be challenged was beyond the horizon of experience and expectations of those concerned.[90] By the start of the Peloponnesian War, all the allies except for Chios and Lesbos had lost their autonomy and become subjects of Athens. Except for Samos, which lost its autonomy in 439, and Aegina, which regained it in 446, this apparently was the situation already before 446.

The unsuccessful revolts of several allies certainly contributed significantly to this fundamental change. Thucydides emphasizes the importance of these events.[91] He was aware that this was only one of several factors in a complex process of transformation but does not cite specific measures intended to bring about or further the Athenian *archē*, which he explains mostly by Athens's unscrupulous exploitation of an increasing military imbalance and by widespread complacency among the allies. Yet the tendency, apparently common in the second half of the fifth century, to simplify the situation by presenting military subjugation as the general cause of the allies' *douleia* has its problems.[92] Epigraphic evidence confirms that more allies rebelled than Thucydides mentions, either individually or in groups. Still, only a fraction of the roughly 150–200 members of the Delian League could have been affected directly by the consequences of military subjugation following a revolt.[93] Even if *douleia* was mentioned in such cases, we should not assume that it was therefore applied to all other allies as well. Military superiority and strict leadership did not in themselves create *douleia*.[94] At most, they were preconditions for behavior or measures that could be perceived by those affected as direct violations of freedom and autonomy or else cumulatively made them aware that their status had deteriorated decisively. It is necessary, therefore, to analyze not only the conditions imposed after the suppression of rebellions but also Athens's behavior toward its other allies and measures imposed on them that might have made perceptible the changes in status that were eventually expressed by the terminology of servitude.

First, then, the conditions of surrender. Thucydides gives no details about Naxos. Both Thasos (463) and Aegina (457) were forced to conclude a treaty of capitulation (*homologia*), tear down their walls, and turn over their fleet. Thasos lost its mainland possessions and mines and had to pay enormous reparations. Aegina had to close its mint.[95] These are the earliest known cases; the next, illuminated by inscriptions, occurred in the late 450s and early 440s.

All three poleis were subjugated by war, as Thucydides mentions expressly, and *homologiai* were treaties of capitulation.[96] In accordance with the conventions of war, the victor—the alliance's *hēgemōn*, Athens—had the right to deal freely with the defeated, theoretically even to impose direct outside rule, which would have made *douleia* obvious. Although Athens never went so far, the fact remains that by military defeat these poleis were forced to accept the dictates of the victor.[97]

The conditions laid down in treaties of surrender were reinforced by mutual oaths with formulations indicating the precise degree of obligation and dependency of the capitulating city. Some of these oaths, the earliest dating to the late 450s, have survived in inscriptions or can be reconstructed from them.[98] No evidence exists for earlier years. Although the oaths were adjusted to reflect local conditions or broad changes within the alliance, the surviving formulas show much consistency. It is thus not impossible that similar formulations were used in earlier cases.

The most important parts of these oaths are the pledges of allegiance and obedience.[99] The first is merely a stronger and more detailed renewal of the promise given on entry into the alliance.[100] The obligation to obey ("I will obey the orders of the Athenians," or "I will obey the Athenian people"), however, is by its very nature irreconcilable with the principles of equality and autonomy on which the alliance was originally based.[101] Initially, there could have been at most an obligation, comparable to one operating in the Peloponnesian League in the fifth century, to recognize majority decisions of the league's assembly as binding on all.[102] This sweeping pledge of general obedience to Athens marks a fundamental change in the relationship between leader and ally—a change in status from equality to subordination. Wolfgang Schuller rightly emphasizes that this unqualified obligation and the corresponding power given to the victor must have prompted a direct association with the condition of a slave.[103] Here we grasp clearly the origin of the *douleia* of individual allies.

Restrictions on freedom are contained as well in other conditions dictated by the victor: "defortification" and surrender of the fleet stripped away the conquered city's ability to defend itself and thus to determine its own fate. Since usually only the walls on the seaward side were affected, the purpose of these measures—to give Athens permanent access from the sea—was all too obvious.[104] To illustrate the impact of such measures, we might think of Athens's own experiences: its resolute defiance of Spartan efforts to prevent it from fortifying the city after the Persian Wars, and Sparta's demand, in 404, that precisely those defenses (fleet and important parts of the fortifications) be eliminated which had made the city immune to Sparta's invasions of Attica. The Athenians saw this as a dire symbol of servitude.[105]

Instead of supplying independent naval contingents to the allied war effort, defeated rebels had to pay the annual "contribution" (*phoros*).[106] Initially the allies were free to choose whether to contribute money or ships; that both categories originally were equal follows from the initial equality of all allies. We do not know how many began by maintaining their own fleets. Over time, most allies opted for the apparently less costly and arduous method of paying the *phoros,* which, as is often attested, was compatible with autonomy.[107] Hence, the failure to supply ships was at first not perceived as dishonorable and the *phoros* not as an infringement on liberty, despite its potential association with the tribute formerly owed to the Persians. Even later, contributions to a common war effort were not interpreted negatively, so long as they were voluntary, based on a joint decision, and therefore open to discussion and influence.[108]

This situation changed—at first only for the poleis affected—when freely made decisions were replaced by the dictates of the conqueror. The *phoros* became a tribute. Indirectly and over time, this negative assessment was adopted by the other allies as well. As the change from ships to money proved irreversible and the *hēgemōn* unwilling to lower or abolish obligatory payments according to circumstances, the element of force became obvious. The more Athens tightened the reins, the more the poleis became aware that their tribute was financing its rule over them. The *phoros* thus came to be seen as an instrument of oppression and was generally discredited.[109] Consequently, in the Second Athenian League, tribute payments were rejected as incompatible with freedom and autonomy and were replaced by a different system of financial contributions.[110]

A clear picture emerges. The measures imposed by Athens on rebellious allies in treaties of surrender contained such unmistakable restrictions of freedom that the resultant status could not but be perceived and then described as *douleia*.[111] The inclusion in the oath of allegiance of an unqualified pledge of obedience that established an active obligation only made this explicit.

Additional measures undertaken later by Athens to increase the dependence of individual poleis highlighted this new reality. Garrisons stationed in allied territories, whose commanders were given military, as well as political and legal, authority, and officials dispatched from Athens with equally broad legal and political powers drastically boosted the potential for outside influence and control.[112] The establishment of settlements of Athenian citizens (cleruchies) on confiscated allied land, serving both as punishment and to prevent renewed rebellion, had the same political and psychological effect. Moreover, it violated one of the basic principles of all Greek poleis: that only citizens were entitled to own land.[113] Obviously, direct intervention in the constitutional sovereignty of a polis—likewise documented for the first time in cases of suppressed rebellions—was perceived as especially damaging to the freedom of a polis, even if such intervention might have been welcomed by considerable numbers of citizens.[114]

It is not unlikely, therefore, that the terminology of servitude emerged already in connection with the first instances of status change resulting from an unsuccessful revolt. The question then is when and why it was extended to the majority of poleis that never revolted.

The change in status especially of an increasing number of important poleis could of course have influenced that of the others.[115] The imbalance in military and political power between Athens and its many small allies, which had existed from the start despite initial equality, could certainly have led in time to actual subservience. Athens's increasingly arrogant behavior and its willingness to use the alliance's resources in part for "private" imperial purposes could have been important factors.[116] Even if the institutions and procedural methods of the alliance remained in place, all this may have sufficed eventually to equate a creeping erosion in status with outright *douleia*. It is also possible that for such a deep change in perception a much greater interference in existing relationships was necessary: one that could be recognized by everyone as unmistakable evidence of a new reality.

Two stages should be distinguished in this process. In joining the alliance, the members had renounced some of their freedom of action in foreign and military affairs and thus accepted a reduction of their sovereignty. Most of them had done this willingly, in exchange for protection, knowing and expecting that the superior authority and sovereignty created by the sum total of such concessions would be shaped and controlled by a council (synod) in which every league member was represented and had a vote. With this proviso, a limited surrender of sovereignty was compatible with the freedom of the individual poleis.[117]

But then Athens restricted the active role of the synod and usurped part of its authority, gradually claiming for itself the right to determine league policy. Binding majority decisions of the joint leadership council were thus replaced by the dictates of the hegemonic power. As a result, those elements of sovereignty that the members by implication had surrendered only conditionally were lost permanently. Voluntary restriction of polis sovereignty had turned into one imposed by outside force: significant elements of nonfreedom emerged. This process entered its decisive phase when the treasury of the league was moved to Athens in 454. From then on, the synod led at best a shadow existence with no political power.[118] By then, at the latest, Athens had assumed full political and diplomatic representation of the allies in external affairs and sole responsibility for making decisions.[119] With these changes, and with Athens's subsequent decision to use league money for a building program on the Acropolis, any semblance of the conditions upon which the league had been founded disappeared.[120]

As Thucydides shows, even such complete loss of freedom of action in foreign affairs could be reconciled with a somewhat flexible concept of autonomy. In a later phase of the formation of its empire, however, from about the middle of the century, Athens also began to interfere more systematically in the domestic sphere of the league members. This was done through regulations enacted by the Athenian assembly without participation or consultation of the allies; with few exceptions they were binding on all (hence they are sometimes called *leges generales*).[121] Some pertained to individuals or groups of persons (such as decrees protecting Athenian citizens and "honorary consuls," *proxenoi*, in allied cities); others to specific situations (e.g., the Megarian Decree).[122] Yet others more generally concerned Athens's relationship to the allies as well as to important areas of their public life, including the standardization of the assessment and collection of tribute; the imposition of Athenian standards in measurements, weights, and currency; regulation of court procedures (including one determining that in cases of serious crimes the allies had to submit to jurisdiction in Athens); contributions to the Panathenaea (and later to other important Athenian festivals), which the allies were all obliged to make because of their fictitious status as Athenian colonists; and religious laws establishing, among others, the cult of "Athena, mistress of Athens," in cities of the *archē*. As Schuller has shown, there was hardly an area of domestic politics in which formally autonomous local institutions were not diminished in importance by an Athenian "superstructure."[123] Although most of these decrees cannot be dated and some of them are now thought to belong in the 420s rather than 440s, they were not introduced ex nihilo. The practices involved are likely to have emerged much earlier—but again, we do not know when.[124]

I should think that the realization even of parts or beginnings of such policies was more than sufficient to make the allies aware of their changed status.[125] By assigning later dates to some of the public decrees concerned with the empire, "many of which suggest an iron-fisted rule—or at least a desire for such," our understanding of the development of Athenian rule over the allies has been both clarified and somewhat confused. The full impact of the new discoveries that influence the dating criteria needs to be sorted out.[126] But it would be a mistake to conclude that the tightening of Athenian control now needs to be moved wholesale to the 420s. As Schuller points out, even without the documents affected by the dating controversy enough evidence remains for a major shift in Athenian attitudes and policies around the middle of the century. The transfer of the league treasury to Athens meant that the Athenian demos assumed financial control;[127] the Athenian assembly arrogated the synod's power; and Athena took over from Apollo the role of the empire's protector deity. Accordingly, she received a quota of the annual tribute. The amounts were recorded in a large inscription on the Acropolis in annual entries numbered by years. Like the tribute's display during the opening ceremony of the Great Dionysia, this was an unmistakable expression of Athenian rule. The fictive "colonial status" of the allies was also established by then. It entailed their obligation to send contributions to the mother city's annual festivals. This was only the first step in a series of measures that organized the empire more systematically. Hence, Thucydides remarks at the end of the Pentecontaetia: In these years (that is, long before the 420s), "the Athenians had established their rule more strongly" (*tēn te archēn enkratesteran katestēsanto*, 1.118.2).[128]

It is not surprising, therefore, that the measures connected with the abandonment of Delos as center of the league seem to have aroused strong opposition primarily in the Ionian cities and on the islands.[129] I consider it likely that in the emotional and polemical debates of those years, at the latest, the terminology of servitude was applied to all allies—at least by themselves and by third parties. Some confirmation may be found in Thucydides, who lets the Mytilenians establish a connection between the end of hostilities against the Persians and increased efforts on the part of the Athenians to subjugate the allies.[130]

Hence, whenever the *leges generales* were enacted, they did not create fundamentally new conditions but aggravated an already existing situation or trend. They had a palpable impact on life and autonomy of the individual poleis and made them aware even more of their subservient status. Although, with few exceptions, extant contemporary literature, including even Thucydides, pays little attention to such matters,[131] we may conclude that henceforth primarily Athens's infringements on polis autonomy through laws and functionaries were associated with *douleia*. Aristophanes, who parodies this situation especially in *Birds,* and the Old Oligarch offer us an informative, even if exaggerated, description of the reality created by Athenian policies at least in the sphere of jurisdiction and an explicit confirmation of the resulting *douleia* of the allies.[132]

The Emergence of the Phrase *Polis Turannos*

A brief examination of the reasons that may have prompted contemporaries to describe Athenian rule over the allies as a tyranny will be helpful to corroborate the results gained previously.[133] In Greece, "tyranny" originally was a term used only within a state or community to designate the extraordinary power, in whatever form, of an individual over his fellow citizens. It may seem to have been easy to transfer this term to the sphere of foreign relations, but given the novelty of the situation and the still relatively undeveloped political terminology, the transfer cannot have been self-evident or have ensued automatically. Before the word could be applied to Athens, there had to be a strong motive and one or more triggering associations.[134]

The sources mention two relevant criteria. One—usually considered sufficient in modern scholarship—involves the element of force, uncontrolled power, rule without checks, accountability, or legal foundations, and *hubris,* which are sometimes said to generate hatred and fear among the subjects.[135] No doubt such concerns played a significant role. Here I will focus on the other criterion, mostly ignored but perhaps no less effective in evoking the idea of arbitrary tyrannical power: the nature of the ruler and the origin of his rule. Usually, tyranny was established when an individual, whose achievements had perhaps given him a special place within the polis's ruling elite, usurped autocratic power by disregarding law and tradition and arrogating the substance and opportunities of aristocratic rule to himself, his family, and his friends. By so doing he reduced the rest of the elite, who were initially entitled to share equally in the exercise of power, to a position of inequality, impotence, and subservience. Hatred of and resistance to such a tyrant were naturally concentrated among the excluded nobles, whose main goal was to regain their share of power and their position of equality.[136] With few exceptions, tyranny was rule achieved from inside the polis, from among a group of peers; it was usually not forcibly imposed from outside.

This model can be transferred to the realm of intercity relations only if essential conditions are comparable. In fact, a hegemonial symmachy is an association of politically equal entities, among which the *hēgemōn* is *primus inter pares*. Power is built up and monopolized from within this association; that is, the *primus inter pares* rises to sole power by exploiting opportunities and disregarding accepted "rules of play," and by so doing reduces former peers to a status of subservience.[137] That this particular way of establishing power facilitated the application of the notion of tyranny to Athens's rule seems to be confirmed by arguments that are highly prominent in Thucydides but were probably much older.

According to the historian, Athens lost its popularity as leader because it no longer treated its allies as equals (1.99.2). He lets the Athenian envoys in Sparta ascribe the lack of popularity of their city's rule primarily to its subjects' resentments about receiving commands from a power with which they had once dealt on a level of equality (1.76.3–77.4): subjects find rule imposed by force—through war, for example—easier to bear than dictatorial rule by a *hēgemōn;* the former establishes clear legal and power relationships that accord with traditional norms and expectations, whereas the latter results from illegal usurpation by a state that is still remembered as a former equal. "Men's indignation, it seems, is more excited by legal wrong than by violent wrong; the first looks like being cheated by an equal, the second like being compelled by a superior" (1.77.4). The Mytilenians (3.9.1–11.8) distinguish between an early period in which the Athenians were leading "on the basis of equality" (*apo tōn isōn*) and a later phase when they pursued the subjection (*doulōsis*) of their allies (3.10.4). They conclude that only mutual fear, based on equal resources, can safeguard an alliance (3.11.3). Pericles goes even further: to submit, without arbitration, to a demand raised by one's equals amounts to enslavement (*doulōsis,* 1.140.5–141.1).[138]

The strong emphasis Thucydides places on these aspects suggests that, and helps explain why, Athens's manner of establishing its rule by gradual encroachment was resented bitterly by the allies.[139] It is likely, therefore, that the comparison of Athens's rule with tyranny arose not only because of its use of force in suppressing individual revolts but also because of its harsh and self-serving leadership practices and its increasing tendency to disregard the allies' equality and autonomy as it was presumed initially in treaties and institutional practices. Reasons to draw this comparison probably existed long before the incisive changes in the alliance in the late 450s and early 440s—the time of the earliest surviving traces of the use of "tyranny" in this context. At any rate, once the comparison had taken hold, every time Athens was denounced as *polis turannos,* the allies could not but be reminded forcefully of their *douleia.*

Conclusions: Elements of Polis Freedom

To summarize, evidence for the terminology of both domination and servitude suggests the early 440s as the common *terminus ante quem* for their appearance in the context of Greek interstate relations. My analysis of political developments and perceptions corroborates this and suggests that fundamental changes in the relations between leader and allies in the Delian League may have made the latter aware of the emergence of imperial domination and thus prompted the creation of a corresponding terminology even much earlier. Revolts of some important poleis were forcibly suppressed. These allies were reduced—by stipulations in the treaties of surrender, by oaths of obedience, and by subsequently tightened mechanisms of control—to a status that could hardly be regarded as anything but *douleia.* While the relationship between Athens and the other allies remained formally unchanged, the hegemonic power's rapidly increasing military and political superiority, its oppressive leadership, and its self-serving policies soon came to be seen as despotic. The status of most allies deteriorated gradually. The initial spirit of equality and autonomy was increasingly ignored. Hence, Athens was regarded as the tyrant city, and its former allies its *douloi,* which prompted widespread resentment and dissatisfaction.[140]

This process was accelerated by changes in the organization of the alliance in the late 450s. With few exceptions, all allies were now equally treated as subjects; realization of their changed position, and the terminology pertaining to it, must have become common at that time, if not earlier. Although legally the differences among various status categories of allies continued to exist, they were blurred even further by the *leges generales,* enacted at various times, which became binding on all and must have dispelled any lingering doubts about the allies' *douleia.*[141] Eventually, the Athenian sphere of power comprised only three categories of poleis: the great mass of "tribute-paying subjects" (those who were "enslaved"); a few "autonomous allies," distinguished by certain privileges but no less burdened with a series of restrictions on their freedom; and "free allies," who were not members of the Delian League but had concluded special treaties with Athens.[142]

All this says nothing about the extent of rejection or acceptance of Athenian rule by individual allies or about the motives that prompted such reactions.[143] I have merely established that at a particular time, for identifiable reasons, Athens's rule over its allies was recognized and categorized as such and that in specific situations and for specific, similarly identifiable reasons, the negative terminology of tyranny and servitude was applied to it. Perceptions and terminology in turn must have prompted thoughts about the allies' freedom, now lost but still desirable. Hence, the entire process analyzed above must have had a profound effect on freedom as a concept and value. How then, as a consequence, was the idea of polis freedom redefined and reconceptualized?

As noted above, when the Delian League was founded, the status of its members was left undefined, as it was in all early symmachy agreements. Athenian exploitation of what was not expressly regulated by treaty[144] destroyed the foundations previously taken for granted in interstate agreements; henceforth, long-standing customs and unwritten rules could no longer be relied upon. It became necessary to guard against the possibility, which was now foreseeable, that what was left undefined would be exploited.[145] Eventually, the leader's powers and rights were made explicit,[146] and the allies' status was defined with increasing precision. Such specifications highlight those aspects of a polis's independence that were considered most significant and about which, as a result of Athens's methods of exercising its power, contemporaries had become especially sensitive. The central issues were equality and autonomy.

First, the specific circumstances of Athens's amassing of power strengthened the general perception, reflected in political speeches and soon in the wording of treaties, that in interstate relations respect for equality was crucial. An older formula mutually granting full equality of rights, which apparently originated in interstate agreements regulating mutual legal assistance (sumbola) and was tied to conflict resolution through negotiation or arbitration, now assumed the broader meaning of mutual recognition of the full political equality of both partners to a treaty.[147] To guarantee such equality, partners sometimes agreed to "share hegemony equally" by alternating leadership or making it dependent on the theater of war.[148]

Second, in treaties of the second half of the fifth century, the status, or capacity for self-determination, of individual poleis or of all those affected or involved was recorded with increasing regularity. The term used is always *autonomia*. This term is attested in literary sources for the treaty of the Thirty Years' Peace in 446 (concerning Aegina), for the negotiations of 432, and for several treaties drawn up during the Peloponnesian War that sometimes include precise details. Inscriptions preserve guarantees of autonomy in an Athenian decree of around 427–426 for the citizens of Mytilene, then in one for Selymbria (probably 409–408), and in one for Samos (405, a renewal of an earlier decree of 412–411).[149] In these cases, autonomy primarily means free choice of constitution. In treaties concluded by Athens after 404, the guarantee of autonomy is a firmly established component.

The treaty of the Peace of Nicias is particularly informative. It contains a guarantee of autonomy for several poleis in the Chalcidice that had broken away from Athens and were being returned by Sparta in exchange for others. They were to pay Athens the *phoros* set by Aristides (in 477, thereby avoiding later increases) and remain independent unless they chose to ally themselves with Athens.[150] This is our most important evidence for the compatibility of autonomy and payment of *phoros*. The treaty also includes a guarantee of autonomy for the sanctuary and citizens of Delphi and specifies control of jurisdiction and taxation as elements of their self-determination. The intention obviously was to safeguard the sanctuary's full internal self-government, to keep it free from foreign influence, and to insulate it from conflicts between the two power blocs.[151]

The peace concluded between Argos and Sparta in 418/417 guaranteed the autonomy of the other cities of the Peloponnese.[152] In a slightly later treaty of alliance between the same partners, the status of any other polis that might join the agreement was defined as autonomous and "independent" in the sense of a "polis in its own right" (*autopolis*); its territorial integrity would be fully recognized, and disputes would be settled on a fair and equal basis.[153] Such clauses, which stressed the independence of a polis as an individual legal entity, were no doubt intended to protect small communities and prevent the kind of power buildup that Mantinea, for example, had recently achieved through its expansionist policy.[154] Significantly, the word *autopolitēs*, used only once by Xenophon in order to stress civic self-determination as the defining characteristic of polis autonomy, appears in a comparable context of foreign policy: resistance in 382 to the expansionist plans of Olynthus.[155]

How effective such guarantees of autonomy were is unimportant here. What matters is that they were formulated at all, and that they became a firmly established component of treaties. The autonomy formula was expanded in the early fourth century: the stipulation that participating poleis should be "free and autonomous" was repeated in all proclamations of "general peace" (*koinē eirēnē*) and adopted in Athenian treaties in the late 380s and 370s.[156] Finally, the detailed specifications mentioned variously in documents from the late fifth century—such as exemption from tribute, the right to levy taxes, control over constitution and jurisdiction, civic self-determination, and territorial integrity—were brought together in the Decree of Aristotle, which passed in 377 in the Athenian assembly and formulated the invitation to join a new naval alliance against Sparta.[157] This document is our most valuable source for the expanded definition of polis freedom. It states that the alliance's primary purpose is to ensure the freedom, autonomy, peace, and territorial integrity of its members (lines 9–12). Their status is described as follows: they shall remain "free and autonomous, living under whatever constitution they want, neither receiving a garrison nor having a governor imposed upon them nor paying tribute" (20–23).[158] Prohibition of public and private ownership of property by Athenians in the territory of allies is recorded in particular detail (25–46). Essentially, the same stipulations appear in the treaty of alliance concluded shortly afterward between Athens and Chalcis.[159]

Both documents place remarkably strong and detailed emphasis on territorial integrity, which we may therefore assume to have been regarded as the most important condition and foundation of the sovereignty of a polis. In contrast, the remaining components—constitutional sovereignty and renunciation of tribute, garrisons, and foreign functionaries—were probably, despite the paratactical formulation, subordinate to the main stipulation, that is, to the guarantee of freedom and autonomy. In these individual aspects we should recognize those Athenian means of controlling their fifth-century empire that were perceived as the most palpable infractions of the allies' freedom and autonomy. The Decree of Aristotle and the treaty with Chalcis thus provide further corroboration that it was primarily Athens's exercise of imperial rule that made the Greeks more acutely aware of the foundations and substance of polis freedom and caused them to introduce specific clauses into their treaties in order to prevent the recurrence of such developments.[160] These were unable to stop aggression and subjugation, but henceforth such actions represented an overt breach of legal agreements and were thus far more serious than the violations of custom and expectation committed by Athens in the fifth century.[161]

4.3. EMERGENCE AND MEANING OF THE CONCEPT OF *AUTONOMIA*

Evidence and Questions

In the treaties that guaranteed and specified the independence of poleis, the technical term is invariably *autonomia;* in the fourth century, we find the expanded formula "*autonomia* and *eleutheria*" but never *eleutheria* alone. Since, overall, *eleutheria* continued to be used far more often, *autonomia* was probably preferred in certain contexts in which it presumably met specific needs. If we assume, as remains to be shown, that *eleutheria* is the older term, even in the political sphere, and that *autonomia* belongs within the conceptual field of *eleutheria,* a number of questions arise. When, why, and in what context did the term *autonomia* originate? What was its meaning and political function? What was its relationship to, and how did its emergence affect, the usage of *eleutheria?*

Most studies of *autonomia* have taken a systematic approach based on international law rather than a political-historical one.[162] This has caused major difficulties. Much effort has been expended, unsuccessfully, in searching for a legally unambiguous definition of the term,[163] while the possibility was neglected that what fails to be legally unambiguous may nevertheless be adequately clear politically. Those using a systematic approach also tend to treat evidence from different times as one body of source material, thereby neglecting historical development and change. This danger was admirably avoided in a study published by Hans Schäfer in 1932, which, although in some respects outdated, shows unusual understanding and retains its value. Elias Bickerman's article of 1958, thoroughly systematic, and Martin Ostwald's book of 1982, clarifying the context within which *autonomia* arose, remain the points of departure for any further examination, despite a flurry of activity in recent years. The analysis presented here agrees with some of Ostwald's conclusions but differs substantially from his and Bickerman's studies in approach, method, individual interpretations, and above all in its assessment of the relationship between *eleutheria* and *autonomia.*[164]

In the fifth century, *autonomos* and *autonomia* appear almost exclusively in political contexts. They are occasionally applied to an individual (as in the earliest extant reference) but so rarely that we can safely assume that the words were primarily political in nature and probably in origin.[165] Although *autonomia* differs in this respect from such related terms as *eleutheria* and *autarkeia,* it accords with composite terms derived from the same root, such as *eunomia* and *isonomia.*[166]

Moreover, the evidence for the word is relatively late. It appears, only as an adjective, once in Sophocles' *Antigone* (perhaps 442), twice in Herodotus, thrice (in identical contexts) in the Hippocratic treatise *Airs, Waters, Places,* then frequently in Thucydides and Xenophon's *Hellenica;* epigraphically, it is attested from 427–426 on.[167] It does not occur as a noun and verb before Thucydides. In keeping with the principles followed in the present study, I take this record seriously. That it cannot be attributed to the late emergence of prose literature or the loss of its earliest representatives is clear: *autonomos,* as *Antigone* demonstrates, fits the verse. It is surprising, therefore, that the word in its political meaning is completely absent from extant drama—particularly of the last third of the century, when, as prose literature and inscriptions show, it was common in political language. Apparently, what was expressed by *autonomia* was not significant among the political problems dealt with in even the most political tragedies, such as Euripides' suppliant or Trojan plays, or in Aristophanes' political comedy.

Herodotus and Thucydides apply the word to events of 479–477, more than thirty years before its earliest direct attestation. Since we lack independently corroborating evidence, these references must be regarded as anachronistic, reflecting the historians' use of terminology common in their own time.[168] On the other hand, the guarantee of autonomy for Aegina in the Thirty Years' Peace of 446, inferred from Thucydides, is so close to the date of *Antigone* and so well anchored historically by the negotiations of 432 that its authenticity seems certain. These negotiations in turn are close enough to the earliest direct evidence for the political use of *autonomos* in the works of Herodotus and Hippocrates, and to the earliest inscription mentioning the word, to rule out any doubt about authenticity. Solid evidence thus suggests, at least for the emergence of the adjective *autonomos,* a *terminus ante quem* in 446.[169]

To establish the word's precise meaning is more difficult. Despite similarities, simple equation with modern "autonomy" only adds to the confusion.[170] Clearly, for several decades *autonomia* played an essential role in Spartan (and to a modest degree also in Athenian) foreign policy.[171] The concept thus had a programmatic function and was capable of describing a political idea. It also had significant propaganda value. It appeared in treaties, and hence in legal documents, and served as a means of dividing the cities in the Athenian sphere of influence roughly but comprehensibly into two categories. In all these contexts, we should suppose, at least adequately clear ideas could be associated with the term; there must have been one or perhaps several principal areas of meaning that were in people's minds when a polis was promised, guaranteed, or denied *autonomia*.[172]

When trying to be more precise, however, we run into trouble. To be sure, in the period between the Peace of Nicias and the founding of the Second Athenian League, we discern a number of elements that could be subsumed under the category of *autonomia;* I discussed these at the end of the last section. But we should be wary of constructing on their basis a generally applicable definition of the term. As Bickerman rightly insists, "the content of a legal fact is not the arithmetic sum of its components."[173] Moreover, such specifications may represent a later stage of development and thus indicate reactions to the concept and changes in its meaning. Finally, no consistent scheme is discernable: in different situations, our sources mention different aspects of the concept, and they never define it comprehensively and precisely.[174] The reason probably lies not only in the primarily nonlegal nature of our evidence but in the concept itself, although, to repeat, this does not mean that contemporaries perceived it as imprecise in usage or meaning.

In view of these difficulties, I set aside for the moment the problem of defining the content and historical development of *autonomos* and focus first on its actual use, especially in Thucydides, trying to distinguish it from *eleutheria* and to understand its political function.

The Function of *Autonomia* and Its Relationship to *Eleutheria*

The negotiations before the outbreak of the Peloponnesian War offer a starting point. From Aegina's complaint at the first assembly in Sparta to Pericles' rejection of Sparta's final ultimatum, the issue is always *autonomia*. It seems clear that Sparta at this stage was striving, not to gain complete independence for Athens's subjects, but to restore their original status within the symmachy.[175] Beyond these negotiations, however, and after their failure, the goal of the war was formulated clearly and consistently as "liberation of the Hellenes." This went far beyond the demand of autonomy and could only signal a complete end to any form of dependence on Athens.[176] In his speech to the citizens of Acanthus in 424, the Spartan general Brasidas makes the same distinction. He refers repeatedly to Sparta's promise to "free Hellas" and underscores his expectation that the subjects of the Athenians will prove willing allies in the struggle for their freedom. Since in all these passages he uses *eleutheria,* his promise to the poleis he hopes to win over is particularly striking: they will become autonomous allies (*xummachoi autonomoi*). In order to explain this distinction in terminology, Bickerman suggests that the citizens of Acanthus were to be *eleutheroi* in view of their deliverance from Athenian domination but *autonomoi* with respect to their alliance with Sparta, which of course was a condition of the former.[177]

From these and a number of analogous references, Bickerman establishes a distinction between *eleutheria* and *autonomia* that is grounded in international law. *Eleutheria* denotes an unqualified, comprehensive freedom that is not curtailed by restrictions on sovereignty resulting from membership in an alliance; *autonomia*, in contrast, denotes the independence possible within an alliance or other relationships of dependency, that is, a restricted or derived independence.[178] Since such restrictions have an effect chiefly in the spheres of foreign policy and war, *autonomia* must apply primarily to the internal realm of the polis.

This definition is based on two observations: no matter how closely the two terms sometimes seem to come to each other, they are never entirely synonymous and interchangeable, and *eleutheria* is the superior, more comprehensive concept.[179] This is undoubtedly correct. Nevertheless, Bickerman's definition is problematic insofar as it bestows on *autonomia* a degree of precision to be expected in public or international law. Even from a political or pragmatic perspective, it seems to me one-sided and incomplete, and in any case merely secondary. Since Bickerman's distinction focuses on the extent and origin of a polis's independence, it differentiates between categories such as absolute and restricted, self-reliant and conditional or derived, or the absence and presence of external ties. Such distinctions are certainly pertinent in many cases and help explain them, but in others they create insurmountable problems. I suggest therefore that they are merely the result of another, more fundamental difference between the two concepts, one that is not at all comprehensible in legal terms.

Bickerman's distinction is applicable especially to the treaties of peace or alliance discussed at the end of the previous section, insofar as these offer guarantees of autonomy to poleis belonging to a symmachy. It holds as well for Aegina in 446 and the cities of the Chalcidice in the Peace of Nicias, whose freedom to choose whether or not to enter an alliance was expressly mentioned, even though there was never any doubt that they belonged within the Athenian sphere of power.[180] Other examples could be cited to support the plausibility of Bickerman's definition. But why did the treaty of the Peace of Nicias guarantee Delphi only *autonomia* and not *eleutheria*, although context and qualifying clauses indicate that the sanctuary was to be protected from any form of dependency?[181] Was it just because such independence required the guarantee of the signers of the treaty? Why did the

Syracusan Hermocrates contrast the Ionians, since time immemorial slaves of some master, to the Sicilians, "free Dorians from the autonomous Peloponnese" (6.77.1)? Must we really suppose that he wanted here to invoke the Peloponnesians' membership in the Spartan symmachy that de facto reduced their liberty to mere autonomy?[182] And why did Thucydides write (1.113.3–4) that after the battle of Coronea the Athenians withdrew and all Boeotian cities regained their *autonomia* (rather than their *eleutheria*)? Is it plausible that, although he did not mention the subsequent reestablishment of the Boeotian League, he simply anticipated this (generally known) fact?[183]

Bickerman does not ignore that Thucydides was interested in power relationships rather than legal ones. Accordingly, he suggests, in such cases the definition of *autonomia* must be modified to refer to "cities and tribes that, although in a given moment independent, still remained in the sphere of influence of another power. Again, the notion of *autonomia* reflects the background of dependency."[184] One may wonder whether this is still sufficiently precise; at any rate, it does not apply to some of Bickerman's cases. For example, Thucydides comments on Athenian attempts in the winter of 415–414 to win the Sicels over to their side: "those more in the low lands, and subjects [*hupēkooi*] of Syracuse, mostly held aloof; but the peoples of the interior who had never been otherwise than *autonomoi*, with few exceptions, at once joined the Athenians." The autonomous Sicels were thus precisely those not included in the Syracusan sphere of influence.[185] Passages like these and the fact that both Herodotus and Thucydides use sometimes *eleutheros* and sometimes *autonomos* in the same context and concerning the same subjects, have prompted some scholars to conclude that in certain cases *autonomia*, after all, was indeed synonymous with *eleutheria*.[186]

There is another difficulty. Thucydides seems to draw a rough distinction between three categories of Athenian allies. For instance, Euphemus, an Athenian envoy addressing a meeting of Sicilian communities, explains that his city arranges its leadership over the allies in Hellas to gain optimal advantage: "The Chians and Methymnaians are *autonomoi* and furnish ships; most of the rest have harder terms and pay tribute in money; while others, although islanders and easy for us to take, are free allies altogether [*panu eleutherōs xummachountas*], because they occupy convenient positions round the Peloponnese" (6.85.2).[187] Two questions suggest themselves. First, if inclusion in a symmachy meant a decline in status from *eleutheros* to *autonomos*, how could some allies have been "altogether free," and what was their relationship to the "autonomous" allies? Second, what was the difference between subjects who were held by the *hēgemōn* in a relationship of force and the autonomous allies, and in what way were the latter autonomous?

Regarding the first question, undoubtedly, the free allies were partners who did not belong to the Delian League but had concluded individual treaties of alliance with Athens.[188] Even they, however, were subject through this alliance to Athenian hegemony and thus restricted in their foreign policy and military freedom of action. Hence, Thucydides himself emphasizes elsewhere that these "free allies" were not totally free but were independent only to the extent covered by the concept of *autonomia*.[189] The question must therefore be rephrased: why can the same poleis be described sometimes as free and sometimes as autonomous?

As to the second question, apart from the special case of Aegina (446–431), "autonomous allies" were those that enjoyed a long-standing, especially close relationship with the *hēgemōn* and were singled out as "pillars of Athenian rule": Samos (until 439), Lesbos (until Mytilene revolted in 428/427; afterward only Methymna), and Chios. It is evident that the autonomous status of these poleis constituted a well-known fact to which one could appeal and that this status could be lost or regained, that it preserved remnants of the equality and autonomy that originally characterized all allies, and that only these poleis continued to provide ships.[190] Furthermore, the last two factors are causally linked: the privilege of supplying ships was not extended to allies who by agreement or decree newly acquired or regained autonomous status. Despite its symbolic and emotional significance, therefore, this privilege was not a constitutive element of *autonomia,* just as, conversely, the payment of *phoros* was not constitutive of the subjects' lack of autonomy.[191] Nor, apparently, was the inviolability of domestic authority the principal criterion for autonomous status: at least some of the *leges generales* seem to have been applied to autonomous allies as well.[192] The extant sources clearly do not permit us to determine specifically in what ways the autonomous allies, compared with the mass of "subjects," were still privileged after the middle of the century, and thus how *autonomia* was legally defined.[193] The question is only whether this is a decisive issue.

We can, however, be certain of something that has escaped Bickerman and Ostwald in their attempts to distinguish *autonomia* from *eleutheria.* As far as the "autonomous allies" are concerned, *autonomia* is not so much a negative condition, to be contrasted with complete freedom, as a positive one, if compared with the unfree status of "subjects." If the term *autonomia* had always implied primarily "that the city is not in complete charge of its politics,"[194] it could not have played such an important role in politics and propaganda. On the contrary, our evidence is consistent in suggesting that the term was perceived as strongly positive and propagandistically effective and that this made it possible to make *autonomia* the subject of a specific political agenda. Otherwise, a guarantee of *autonomia* would not have made it more attractive for a polis to join an alliance. Nor, one should expect, would the "autonomy policy" practiced by Sparta in the late fifth and early fourth centuries, however self-serving and hypocritical, have been so dangerous for the dominant poleis targeted by it, unless it promised a significant and desired improvement in the status of those hitherto subjugated.[195] This positive valuation finds expression in Thucydides as well. In Hermocrates' proud proclamation that Sicily was populated not by Ionian *douloi* but by free Dorians who had emigrated from the autonomous Peloponnese, the juxtaposition of free and autonomous has the cumulative effect of creating a superlatively positive notion.[196] To be sure, as Bickerman suggests, *autonomia* frequently corresponded de facto to a status of limited freedom. But viewed from a different angle, the same condition could be judged very positively. Thus, what chiefly mattered was the speaker's or commentator's point of view or his political attitude. This had little to do with international law but much with political pragmatism and psychology.

This approach permits a new understanding of a passage that at first sight seems to suggest synonymy of *autonomia* and *eleutheria*. Herodotus reports that in 479, when trying to induce the Athenians to defect from the Hellenic League, Mardonius offered them a treaty of alliance, quoting his king's orders: "Return their land to them, but also let them . . . choose any extra territory they want—and let them be *autonomoi*" (8.140α.2). It was presumably the reference to a treaty that led Bickerman to believe that in this case, too, the choice of the word *autonomos* instead of *eleutheros* was determined by the restriction on freedom imposed by an alliance—a freedom, moreover, granted by the Persian king.[197] But Herodotus himself rejects this interpretation; for Mardonius underscores the king's offer by saying: "Be free [*eleutheroi*] and make an alliance with us [*homaichmiē*], without treachery and deceit" (8.140α.4). How could Mardonius say *eleutheros* when the king wrote *autonomos?*

The solemn and rare word *homaichmiē* (spear brotherhood) places particular emphasis on the equality of the allied partners. Thus, in Herodotus's interpretation, the Persians offered an alliance "on fair and equal terms."[198] Of course, even Mardonius could not deny that certain commitments would be involved and above all that equality and autonomy would depend on the continued goodwill of the king. If he nonetheless promised the Athenians *eleutheria,* he must have meant that in keeping with the Greek war objective they would remain free, in the sense of being protected from the dreaded subjugation (*douleia*) under the Persians. *Eleutheros* here means "not ruled over," neither by the king, his satrap, nor a tyrant installed by him. Herodotus's Xerxes must have the same condition in mind, but he expresses it positively: what he wants to emphasize with "let them be *autonomoi*" is that "they shall be their own masters and govern themselves."

Therefore, I suggest, the choice of *autonomia* instead of *eleutheria* indicates a change of perspective and a different accentuation. Whoever says *eleutheria* is looking outward, referring to the absence of, or defense against, subjection to foreign domination; emphasis is placed on the fact that the community involved is not ruled by someone else. Whoever says *autonomia* is looking inward, stressing the self-determination of that community. Since both concepts are concerned with the contrast between self-government and being ruled by another, they are often very close. But *autonomia* stresses self-determination, and *eleutheria* the absence of foreign rule; *eleutheria* is passive, *autonomia* active; *eleutheria* is a double negative concept ("not unfree"), *autonomia* a positive one; *eleutheria* implies "freedom from something," *autonomia* "independence for something." Despite their affinity, therefore, the two terms are clearly and consciously distinguished—as is evident in Thucydides' usage.

The speech of the Mytilenians provides a good illustration. Their envoys to Sparta in 427 describe how their situation became precarious when Athens began to pursue, instead of war against the Persians, the *doulōsis* of the allies: "Unable to unite and defend themselves, on account of the large number of voting members, all the allies were enslaved [*edoulōthēsan*], except ourselves and the Chians, who continued to participate in campaigns, being *autonomoi* and at least nominally *eleutheroi*" (3.10.5). The Mytilenians would have been neither prudent nor correct in describing themselves as "free allies" like Corcyra and others outside the Delian League. What they could say is: sure, we are autonomous and, at least on the face of it, not yet enslaved like the others. Their polis's status is defined negatively by *eleutheroi,* positively by *autonomoi.* The same distinction resolves the apparent contradiction in the simultaneously free and autonomous status of those outside allies: they are free because they are not subject to direct rule by Athens as are the members of the Delian League; they are called autonomous when Thucydides stresses their unrestricted capacity for internal self-determination, in contrast to their external freedom of action, which was restricted by the alliance with Athens. Both terms are correct; which one was chosen depended on the aspect to be emphasized.

Bickerman's definition thus generalizes a more specific, and therefore secondary, usage resulting from such differing perspectives. Precisely because emphasis is placed on the domestic sphere and self-determination, *autonomia* is compatible with certain forms of external dependence, even payment of tribute; in this specific sense, a polis is autonomous if it maintains domestic self-determination even though it has partially or completely lost its external freedom of action.[199] On the other hand, a political entity can be described as autonomous when, in a specific context, the intention is to establish a contrast to a neighboring power. In such cases, *autonomos* does not mean, as Bickerman interprets it, that a city or a tribe is still within the sphere of influence of another power and accordingly enjoys only limited independence; on the contrary, it means that in spite of its powerful neighbor, a city or tribe is not limited by foreign influence and is in full control of itself.[200] Although *eleutheros* might be used here as well, the particular aspect being emphasized determines the choice of *autonomos*.

The distinction proposed here makes it possible to explain every case in which Bickerman's definition presents problems or breaks down.[201] In the example, previously mentioned, of the Boeotian cities that have regained independence from Athens, the purpose is not to emphasize the overthrow of Athenian foreign rule; hence, *eleutheros* is not used here. But neither does *autonomos* refer to the superior sovereignty of the Boeotian League or the superior power of Thebes. Rather, it highlights the restoration of complete self-determination made possible by the return of exiled oligarchs and the elimination of democracies imposed by and aligned with Athens.[202] Conversely, as we shall see, *eleutheros* is preferred in tragedy, especially in the suppliant plays, because they stress the aspect of averting foreign domination.[203]

Autonomia, accordingly, designated only roughly a particular side of a polis's independence. It did not have a fixed meaning, and the range it covered and the elements it comprised were not clearly determined from the outset.[204] Although it could serve to indicate certain limitations (especially those caused by foreign influence or power), the word was primarily associated with a number of general and comprehensive positive ideas—most important that the citizens themselves should be able to determine their *nomoi*: the constitution, way of life, and policies of their community. Since this touched upon an area fundamental for the citizens' identification with their polis, the term was politically potent and effective, despite its lack of precision. It was a purely political term, and for political purposes it was eminently useful exactly because it was broad and both concrete and vague.[205] Hence, it played an important role in interstate relations, although it was insufficient as a concept of international law. Moreover, discrepancies might have existed between a looser and a stricter standard of *autonomia* current in the Athenian and Spartan spheres of influence, respectively. This made frictions almost inevitable when the term entered the language of treaties.[206]

For all these reasons, *autonomia* needed to be augmented from case to case by explicit definitions (for example, concerning sovereignty over juris-diction, constitution, or taxation). Through such clauses the term became legally precise and useful; without them, the door remained open for arbi-trary interpretation and political abuse.[207] Significantly, it was again Athens that brought this development to its logical conclusion. After the experi-ences of the fifth century, the inclusion of a simple autonomy clause in the treaty would have been far from satisfactory for those invited in 377 to join the second naval alliance. Nor would it have been enough to make such a clause more precise by emphasizing one or two important aspects. Hence, an expanded clause that had emerged recently was chosen for this purpose; it guaranteed both *autonomia* and *eleutheria,* meaning that the allies would both enjoy full internal self-determination and be subject to no form what-soever of outside domination, let alone imperial rule.[208] Moreover, every detail of this guarantee was spelled out, and whatever had been experienced in the past as a violation of autonomy was explicitly excluded. Nonetheless, the role *autonomia* played in the fourth century demonstrates that it served as little more than a label in the game of power politics.[209]

I draw three conclusions. First, such specifying elements are potential but not necessary components of *autonomia.* Failure to recognize this ex-plains the diversity and lack of success of modern attempts at definition. Victor Ehrenberg's suggestion that, considering the time of origin, the word could "hardly ever have meant anything . . . but *tois hautōn nomois chrēsthai,* possession and use of one's own laws," should be accepted, provided the meaning of *nomoi* is kept broad enough: "laws" is too narrow. Ostwald's minimal definition is entirely adequate: a state "which is free to determine the norms by which it wants to live." [210]

Second, for the reasons explained above, the relationship between *auto-nomia* and *eleutheria* vacillates and allows for various possibilities. Applied to a completely free community, the terms can be equal in value in that they illuminate opposite aspects of the same reality: *eleutheria* the absence of foreign domination; *autonomia,* self-determination. *Autonomia* can be subordinate to *eleutheria* in that it describes the (limited, internal) capacity for self-determination of a polis that is externally dependent on a superior power or an alliance, while *eleutheria* denotes its complete freedom. In this sense, every free city is also autonomous, but not every autonomous city is free. Even on this lower level of "partial freedom," the two terms can again be seen as equivalent. A city that is not completely free though autonomous can be called free in the sense of "not subjected, ruled, or enslaved," emphasizing the double negative meaning of *eleutheros.* Because they ensue from the very nature of the two concepts, all these possibilities coexist in our sources. Such variety of possible interpretations and nuances in meaning must drive modern specialists in international law to despair. For the Greeks, who were used to it, circumstances and context determined clearly enough how the two concepts should be interpreted, individually and in relation to each other.

Third, we can now assess as well the influence of the new term *autonomia* on the meaning of *eleutheria.* In certain types of situation, such as "freedom wars," in which the aspect of eliminating, or preventing, foreign rule clearly predominated, probably only one perspective was possible, and only *eleutheria* could be used. Presumably, with the emergence of the term *autonomia,* the polis's external independence became even more the proper domain of *eleutheria.* As we shall see, the two terms eventually fused into a single formula for complete internal and external freedom. Moreover, the acknowledgment of the possibility of "partial freedom" (concentrating on the capacity for internal self-determination and neglecting external dependency) required as a corollary the conceptualization of "unrestricted, complete freedom." *Eleutheria,* which, although valued highly, initially defined its content negatively (free from, rather than for, something), was thereby given an additional, strongly positive meaning.

The Coining of *Autonomia:* A Reaction to Athens's Imperial Rule

The changes in terminology analyzed above were triggered when new needs emerged and it became necessary to differentiate the concept of polis freedom. The question then is what this need was, and when and under what conditions the term *autonomia* was coined. Since *eleutheria* is the more comprehensive and superior political concept, we should logically expect *autonomia* to be a later creation. The *terminus ante quem* in the middle of

the century suggested by the extant evidence indeed points to a period substantially after the Persian Wars. The condition for the word's emergence is
that the particular aspect it accentuates had become an urgent problem that
impressed itself on public consciousness, was clearly recognized, and could
be formulated as such. In other words, we have to look for a condition of
marked and undesired dependency that caused noticeable dissatisfaction; a
completely free community did not need to develop a concept of *autonomia*. However such external dependency was perceived, a crucial additional
factor must have been that those affected insisted on preserving or restoring
what was regarded as self-determination par excellence: being master in one's
own house.[211] In short, *autonomia* could be recognized as a problem and
formulated as a concept only when attention focused on self-determination
and self-government rather than liberation from foreign rule or influence.

If the chronological parameters indicated above are correct, possible
contexts for the emergence of *autonomia* exclude a priori two sixth-century
phenomena: tyranny and Persian rule over the Greeks of Asia Minor.[212]
Thus, we need only consider the possible impact of the two Greek "power
blocs" around the mid–fifth century. That the term was coined in the sphere
of the Peloponnesian League seems unlikely.[213] To be sure, many of the parties involved in interstate treaties recorded by Thucydides, beginning with
the Peace of Nicias, were Peloponnesians, and Sparta did advocate *autonomia* for the Athenian allies, but this is hardly sufficient reason to conclude
that autonomy clauses originated in the Peloponnese or that Sparta invented
the concept. In fact, until well into the last third of the fifth century there
seems to have been insufficient incentive within the Spartan symmachy for
the creation of such a term, because the dependency of the allies on the
hegemonic power was limited and relatively weak, and unwelcome intervention in their internal authority remained rare.[214] The autonomy clauses
in Peloponnesian treaties therefore represented reactions to recent changes
and new needs, and Sparta's policy of propagating autonomy, in the Peloponnesian War and beyond, merely adopted demands and a catchword that
had originated elsewhere.

The word *autonomia* thus most likely emerged by the middle of the fifth
century, at the latest, within the framework of the Delian League or Athenian Empire.[215] By that time, Athens not only had arrogated the sole right
of disposal over the resources of the alliance and decision-making authority over allied policy but had begun in various ways to interfere in the self-
governance of the allies. Several examples had already demonstrated that ef-

forts to break away from Athens and regain full *eleutheria* were hopeless. In view of the discrepancies in power and Athens's increasingly dictatorial attitudes, equality (*isonomia*) among the allies had become illusory as well.[216] The more perceptible all this became, the more important it seemed that each ally should at least retain self-determination in its own sphere. As a result of such experiences and considerations, I suggest, *autonomia* was created as a new value concept and catchword, intended to express a specific need and partial aspect of the larger concept of polis independence. We saw earlier that it was probably the same experience that prompted Athenian rule to be characterized as tyranny. Hence, conceivably the antithesis, strongly emphasized by Herodotus and Hippocrates, between *autonomia* and despotic rule within a community, people, or state played a role in this conceptual development.[217]

All this represents a close analogy to the emergence, a generation earlier, of the political concept of freedom itself. In the specific emergency of the confrontation with the Persians, the pressure of changed circumstances and new needs had caused the Greeks to recognize the crucial importance of a polis's freedom from foreign oppression. This aspect, long subsumed under the more comprehensive notion of "deliverance and survival" (*sōtēria*), thus gained independent value. It was emancipated, so to speak, and became a new and separate concept, expressed by the new noun *eleutheria*.[218] The same word was subsequently used to contrast the polis's internal freedom to its servitude under a tyrant. For some time this sufficed; greater precision was unnecessary. "Self-determination," which had previously been unproblematic and covered by *eleutheria*, became significant as a specific problem and need only as a result of the conditions that evolved in the Athenian Empire. It soon acquired enough importance to crystallize into an independent concept and merit a new term, *autonomia*.

Yet most allies were eventually reduced to the level of "subjects." The only exceptions were the three "guardians of the *archē*," for whom *autonomos* specifically designated their privileged position within the Athenian power system—although limits were imposed on their self-determination as well, and their special standing was recognizable as such only in comparison to that of the other members of the league.[219] We do not know when the term "autonomous allies" was adopted. Possibly only the three islands were capable of fully applying it to themselves—and only until their respective revolts. But this designation and the debate waged in the second half of the century about the allies' *autonomia*, desired by them and eventually demanded for them by their advocate Sparta, prompted historians and other observers to retroject the term *autonomos* to describe the status of all allies at the time when the Delian League was founded.[220]

4.4. POLIS FREEDOM: A CONCEPT OF RELATIVE VALUE

By the second half of the 450s, if not 460s, contemporaries had become fully aware of Athens's subjugation of and rule over its allies, and this was reflected in an increasingly differentiated terminology. Such widespread deprivation of freedom was unprecedented in relations among Greeks; hence, we should expect it to have appeared shocking both to those who were affected and to outsiders.[221] We need to ask, therefore, how those who were "enslaved" reacted, what role the desire for freedom, so splendidly demonstrated by many Greek poleis during the Persian Wars, played in this process, and what effect these developments had on freedom as a value concept.

To begin with, there certainly was no lack of resistance against subjugation by Athens. As early as the 470s, Carystus tried in vain to evade incorporation in the naval alliance, as did Phaselis in the 460s, Aegina in the 450s, and later Melos. We can also be sure that strong reservations or opposition had to be overcome in many other poleis.[222] Numerous revolts are attested; presumably, there were more, not mentioned in the selective reports of the historians nor documented by extant inscriptions.[223] Nevertheless, the discrepancy between the very large number of subject cities and the small number of revolts is striking. So is the fact that these revolts—at least before the Ionian War after Athens's Sicilian debacle—were undertaken singly or in very small groups.

Greek responses to the Persian conquest offer illuminating parallels. Having failed in their attempt to forge a common defense after the fall of the Lydian kingdom, most of the Ionian poleis fought the invading Persian army individually, with great determination but unsuccessfully. The emigration of the citizens of Phocaea and Teos was later praised as a shining example of the Greek spirit of independence. Yet the most powerful city in Ionia, Miletus, entered into a separate advantageous agreement with Cyrus and took no part in the fighting at all.[224] After Darius's failed Scythian campaign, a number of apparently uncoordinated uprisings erupted in the area of the Hellespont; these were suppressed by the Persians with little difficulty.[225] Following his defeat at Salamis, Xerxes had scarcely marched past in his retreat to

Asia when Potidaea and the poleis on the Pallene peninsula in the Chalcidice rebelled against the Persians; with much luck, they were able to hold out, even though Mardonius's expeditionary force still occupied Thessaly and strong Persian forces in Thrace were in a position to take immediate action against them.[226]

These and other examples show that Greek attitudes and actions in fighting for independence were characterized by isolation and lack of coordination, impulsive reaction to specific opportunities and necessities (apparently without much consideration of long-term chances for success), and both remarkable determination to incur sacrifices in the struggle against foreign domination and an inclination to avoid resistance altogether in exchange for a privileged position. Yet during the Ionian Revolt, many (though by no means all) of the poleis cooperated with one another; they voluntarily submitted to a supreme command, strove for a common goal, and by doing so achieved success in some stages of the war. Although they ultimately failed precisely because the Persians were able to break their unity, the Hellenic League against Xerxes provided a compelling lesson about what could be accomplished by collaboration, cohesion, and perseverance. Hence, two examples were at hand to demonstrate how a successful "war for freedom" could—and should not—be waged.

The lack of coordinated action on a substantial scale against Athens and the relative rareness of individual revolts therefore need to be explained. Thucydides is virtually our only source of information on these issues, and he focuses, with few exceptions, on the circumstances prevailing just before and during the Peloponnesian War. Overall, he seems to have been firmly convinced of one basic fact: among Athens's subjects the desire for freedom was widespread, and for this reason Sparta's war propaganda, advocating the liberation of the Hellenes, succeeded.[227] He thus confirms on the part of those affected a marked contradiction between a strong desire to act and a limited willingness or ability to do so. Presumably, this contradiction was equally pronounced in earlier decades.

It can be resolved in two ways. Either Thucydides' assessment is incorrect, that is, biased or exaggerated—in which case the inactivity of the Athenian subjects is the lesser problem, and what needs explaining is rather their presumed willingness to subordinate themselves and perhaps the "popularity" of Athenian rule. Or else Thucydides is right; then reasons must be found for widespread unwillingness to break with Athens despite hatred of its rule and a corresponding desire for freedom. In this form, the alternative is certainly put too crudely, but it captures the essence of a scholarly controversy over the popularity of Athenian rule that was initiated by G. E. M. de Ste. Croix in 1954 and pursued since by a number of scholars.[228]

I do not need to recapitulate this controversy here in detail. It has shown, in any case, that de Ste. Croix's attack on Thucydides' reliability is too strong and too general to be tenable: despite some exaggerations, the essentials of Thucydides' account must be accepted. At the same time, the debate has given us a more subtle understanding of the prevailing attitudes and needs in the poleis of the Athenian *archē*. This understanding (to which de Ste. Croix himself has contributed significantly) helps us answer the question of the value, potential, and limits of polis freedom.

First of all, we need to consider two facts of power politics. One is military superiority: Athens had already become the uncontested master in the Aegean when dissatisfaction grew among the allies.[229] The vast majority of poleis kept no substantial military fleets of their own and were thus deprived from the outset not only of the possibility of sustained resistance but of the means of communication and cooperation that were essential for success.[230] Moreover, Athens's military and political control over the cities, exceptionally intensive and varied for the time, made preparations for revolt difficult to hide. The second factor was Athens's skillful exploitation of a strategy the Persians had used successfully with Miletus and tried unsuccessfully with Athens itself: to grant privileged status to an especially powerful polis and thus to split the opposition.[231] In this case, three large islands, later called the "guardians of the *archē*," were among the leading founders of the Delian League and seem to have held a special status from the start. They collaborated closely with Athens and even later enjoyed greater autonomy and more equality than the rest.[232] Concerted action by these three naval powers, especially during a time of widespread unrest, could have proved dangerous to Athens. Yet their primary concern apparently was to maintain their privileged position, and this prevented them from intervening on the side of their subjugated allies. They even agreed on occasion to aid in their suppression,[233] so that they were as isolated as the others when they felt compelled to revolt themselves.

While these factors explain the isolation and relative rareness of revolts, a second group of factors further dampened any willingness to break free. For example, the Delian League comprised many small communities that were able to protect their political independence against the pressure of powerful neighbors only by maintaining close ties with Athens: the *douleia* under Athens, a distant master, at least saved them from closer peril.[234] A similar situation had earlier prompted Plataea to seek safety from Theban encroachment by placing itself under Athens's "protective rule," and for a while pressure by Corinth caused Megara to do the same. Poleis in border areas, which had to withstand strong pressure from Persian satraps, were in the same position.[235] Given Athens's control of the seas, in some cities concerns about trade and communication may have carried greater weight than loss of independence.[236] Such cases, however, were balanced by others: in the course of time apparently a substantial number of poleis were induced by their proximity to Persia to revolt or tacitly withdraw from the league.[237] Here the issue was not freedom but an exchange of Athenian for Persian subjugation, either because Athens's protection in the long run was not able to avert Persian pressure or because the disadvantages of Athenian domination were perceived, at least by the most powerful group in each polis, as greater than its advantages.

This brings up aspects of domestic policy. The extant evidence suggests that Athens began already in the late 450s or 440s to establish or support democracies in allied poleis as a means of buttressing its rule and preventing uprisings.[238] This policy (which was applied more generally only later) was encouraged by several factors. Democracies remained relatively rare and even more rarely came into existence without Athenian influence; constitutions that were described, from the perspective of democracy, as oligarchies were therefore the norm.[239] Hence, resistance to Athenian rule was usually initiated by oligarchic circles or regimes, which naturally sought the support of states that empathized with both their political orientation and their intention to defect from Athens: Persia and Sparta. In these same poleis, there usually existed substantial "democratically inclined" groups that were unable to succeed on their own and could secure a share of power, or even exclusive power, only with the support of Athens.[240] These groups were often so intent on controlling power domestically that the loss of external freedom imposed on them by Athens seemed a lesser evil.

The stabilization of Athens's rule through its "policy of democratization" thus rested on the fact that tensions between the dominant power and subjected cities coincided with a growing political polarization within these cities between "democratic" and "oligarchic" factions and were thereby either enhanced or neutralized.[241] Ever since this polarization had entered political consciousness, problems of political participation and distribution of power in the polis tended to be assessed from the perspective of freedom or nonfreedom.[242] To gain or preserve their domestic power and freedom of action must have seemed more important to many—whether "democrats" or "oligarchs"—even at the price of sacrificing their polis's collective independence, than attaining such independence at the risk of losing their own domestic freedom.[243]

For various reasons—not least because Greek poleis were normally rather small and opportunities for "exporting" conflicts by focusing on outside wars and expansion were lacking—domestic political struggles were often fought with extraordinary vehemence. As a result, to secure their power, both "democrats" and "oligarchs" felt compelled to eliminate their opponents not only politically but also physically by exiling or destroying them. As Thucydides' "case study" of stasis in Corcyra demonstrates most impressively, this led to deep divisions, civil wars, masses of refugees, and perpetually unstable conditions that forced the victorious parties to rely even more on the protection of a superior power.[244] "Democratic" factions that reached power in cities of the empire with Athenian help (whether through political change or social conflict) thus depended on Athens's protection in far more than a political sense. External dependence became the precondition not only for their internal rule and freedom but for their social survival.

That democrats therefore generally preferred to remain in the Athenian sphere of power does not mean that Athens's rule was altogether popular with them.[245] On the contrary, as T. J. Quinn suggests, these democrats in fact often may have hated Athens and endured "political subordination only for the sake of party." This "is shown by their readiness to desert her in circumstances where they believe they can do so without injury to themselves or democracy."[246] The same is true of "oligarchs": they did not hesitate to exchange their polis's dependence on Athens for dependence on the Persians (or, later, Sparta) if this helped them preserve their internal dominance in the face of claims made by the "demos." Even without such pressure resulting from stasis, they might, in view of specific advantages or constraints, prefer subordination to Persia rather than Athens.[247] Yet even these groups strove to regain their polis's freedom as soon as an opportunity presented itself—and as long as they could do so without jeopardizing their internal dominance.[248]

It is clear, then, that the question of how strongly the poleis in the Athenian Empire felt their lack of freedom and how highly they actually valued the possibility of regaining their independence cannot be answered solely by observing their actions. Their unwillingness to resist or revolt certainly indicates neither that they lacked the desire for freedom and willingly subordinated themselves to Athenian rule nor that the latter was welcomed by the majority in each case.[249] Combining these observations on the behavior of the cities with Thucydides' description of situations and motives and his explicit comments, I conclude that polis independence remained a central value concept that was realized if at all possible and was common to all citizens. In most cases, however, its realization was prevented by several countervailing factors: powerful external pressure exerted by the two Greek superpowers and the Persians but also neighboring cities, internal political conflicts and factional strife, and divergent interests. In particular, the issue of sharing or controlling political power domestically was often so predominant that it seems justified to speak of a relativization of the value of polis freedom.

Yet even this conclusion needs to be modified. While focusing on the changes that occurred in the decades after the Persian Wars, we should not overlook essential elements of continuity. Certainly, the possibilities of outside pressure had become more diverse and intensive, internal differences more absolute, and the two were more frequently combined and for that reason fraught with more severe consequences. In general, all this created much more complex conditions. But the basic patterns corresponded to those already present, for instance, in Ionia before the great revolt and in the Greek mainland before the invasions of Darius and Xerxes.[250] Ever since subjugation by an external power had brought with it the awareness of the community's nonfreedom and thus of the value of freedom, such freedom had never meant the same or been of equal value to all citizens or communities. Not everyone, thus, found it equally worth striving for, and once it was no longer the normal condition of a Greek polis, taken for granted by everyone, it could, when lost, seldom be regained. The chances to succeed in doing so were best when rejection of non-Greek foreign rule was linked with rejection of internal rule by a tyrant or a narrow oligarchy; this gave the polis's struggle for freedom a broad base and great effectiveness. Under the more complex conditions of the post–Persian War period, such circumstances often prompted acceptance of Athenian domination as the lesser of two evils. The quiescence of the subjugated cities and their sometimes enduring "loyalty" were caused chiefly by a combination of fear of the Persians and of domination by an elite faction, or else by the combined effect of internal stasis and fear of the power and vengeance of Athens.[251]

Thus, the question of "freedom for whom?" had not become a burning issue only recently, even if the basis for answering it had changed and the spectrum of possibilities had broadened. Polis freedom was always a relative value due to the specific conditions prevailing in the Greek world, and such relativity was intensified as political conditions became more complex.

"Freedom" in Ideology and Propaganda

5.1. ATHENS: FREEDOM JUSTIFIES DOMINATION

The Athenian *archē* was the first Greek empire, extensive and relatively long-lasting, centralized and organized to a remarkable degree. Contemporaries were here confronted in a new way with the phenomenon of power: its manifestations, dynamics, and consequences, its possibilities and limitations, and the euphoria and rejection it prompted.[1] For the first time, the necessity emerged in Greece of explaining and justifying domination, of developing an ideology and propaganda of power and rule over others, and of thinking critically, systematically, even theoretically, about such issues. Political thought matured quickly under rapidly changing conditions and was ready to formulate and refine such ideas, to adapt them as new challenges evolved, and generally to examine human and interstate relations with ever deeper understanding. Although Athens was not the only political, cultural, or intellectual center in the Greek world, in this respect, too, it occupied a leading position.[2] Certainly, in the political exploitation of freedom it took the initiative, breaking new ground and setting an example for centuries to come: ever since the Athenians discovered the versatility of this concept and how easily it could be used and abused for political purposes, freedom has remained a central concept of political ideology and propaganda.

Presumably, the Athenians were confronted with the need to explain and justify their rule only when its negative manifestations had become issues of intense debate. Before the time of the Peloponnesian War, no evidence survives about how they reacted to this challenge. From the foundation of the Delian League, however, and increasingly from the 460s and 450s, negotiations and confrontations focusing on Athenian methods and policies must have occurred frequently within the alliance and in relations with outsiders.[3]

For Athenian politicians abroad, issues concerning their city's relationship to its allies are likely to have become a common subject of debate. They
knew what to expect, anticipated problems and criticism, and had their answers ready. As a result, a fixed range of arguments developed rather quickly.
This assumption is at least in part corroborated by explicit comments in
Thucydides.[4]

In Athens itself, things may have been different. It is an open question
whether the Athenians found it necessary at all to justify their domination
in their own political debates. Thucydides and Aristophanes—despite the
latter's occasional harsh criticism of individuals and specific abuses—largely
convey the impression that such domination was taken for granted (or at
least assumed to be obviously justified and represented as such) and that at
most some excesses were criticized. The Athenian people had also long become accustomed to accepting pragmatic and utilitarian arguments.[5] This
impression, however, is somewhat deceptive. The extant sources do not adequately reflect the nature and content of discussions held among Athenians about these issues. These sources were written mostly at a time when
Athens was exposed to strong outside pressure and hostile propaganda and
when the possibility of a breakup of the *archē* was perceived as a vital threat
to Athens's survival. Hence, there was little incentive for dispassionate discussion. Moreover, political speeches that would offer the most revealing insight into such debates are almost completely lacking for this period. Orations that survive from later decades show what this loss means, particularly
for the investigation of propaganda, the justification of policies, and the
use of the past in political debate.[6] Philosophical and theoretical concepts,
as well as his own interpretive intentions, influenced Thucydides' representation of the aspects that interest us here.[7] Finally, Athenian policies toward
the allies developed dynamics of their own which even "conservative" politicians found difficult to escape.[8]

It may well be true that most Athenians on all social levels rarely questioned their city's rule over the allies as such, but it would be wrong to assume that they did not often (and particularly when major challenges arose)
discuss, generally and in detail, the forms, goals, and consequences of their
exercise of such rule.[9] The Mytilenian Debate, as formulated by Thucydides,
offers a good, if rather extreme, example, while Euphemus's speech in Camarina illustrates the need to justify imperial rule abroad, just as the Melian
Dialogue documents the tendency to ignore this need when there was no
strong compulsion or incentive.[10] The rhetoric of fourth-century panegyric
speeches suggests that the Athenian demos felt a deep and constant need for

legitimization. Thus, the standard arguments recurring in funeral orations include the demonstration that Athenian rule over the allies was justified. No matter how much it was taken for granted, people constantly needed to be reassured that it was deserved, necessary, and good.[11]

Such patriotic speeches tended to be soaked in chauvinism and hyperbole. They cannot be taken altogether seriously, but if they were successful, they must have reflected to a considerable extent the attitudes and expectations of their audiences. Herodotus and Thucydides indicate that core arguments recurring in the funeral orations also played a crucial part in foreign policy discussions.[12] Evidence for the full range of such arguments survives only from the early fourth century, but its almost canonical persistency apparently extends far back in time.[13] Clues offered by historians and tragedians, the regular recurrence of similar occasions for such speeches, the frequency in the assembly of intense debates on issues relevant here, and other reasons leave no doubt that the Athenians indulged in an idealizing representation of their imperial rule long before its collapse. A significant number of the arguments known from later periods probably originated well before the Peloponnesian War. They were possibly formulated already in connection with (or soon after) the formation of the Athenian Empire and quickly became fixed as set pieces in political, as well as panegyric, speeches.

In justifying their rule, the Athenians claimed, first, to be entitled to hegemony and rule because of their city's unique merits. They supported this claim on two levels: empirically, by emphasizing that their efforts had been decisive in saving Greek freedom in the Persian Wars, and theoretically, by referring to the doctrine of the natural right of the stronger to dominate the weaker.[14] Second, they combined both these reasons in pointing out that the Ionians, long accustomed to being "slaves," had proved unworthy of freedom. In addition, by treacherously supporting the Great King against their fellow Hellenes, they had forfeited any right not to be treated as subjects. Third, postulating as the purpose or effect of their rule the enhancement of the welfare of those ruled, the Athenians stressed a number of partly indisputable, partly questionable positive aspects, above all the guarantee of both external and internal freedom of the poleis in their *archē*. Fourth, because of the hatred of their subjects and Sparta's hostility, the Athenians insisted that they had to hold on to their rule in order to preserve their own safety and freedom. And fifth, they presented their thalassocracy as the foundation of the sovereignty and self-sufficiency of their own polis and thus as the prerequisite of a higher, even absolute form of freedom, impressively formulated in the concept of the "freest of all cities" (*eleutherōtatē polis*). The strong emphasis placed on various aspects of freedom in all these arguments leaves no doubt that this concept was highly prominent in political thought, propaganda, and political debates of the time, on the part of both critics and supporters of Athens's rule.[15]

The Preservation of Greek Freedom and Athens's Claim to Rule

Leadership among Greek poleis was based not solely on a city's military superiority but also on its ability to serve a political function that was greatly important to many others. At least from the late sixth century on, Sparta was widely recognized (and sanctioned by divine authority at Delphi) as the "head" or "patron" (*prostatēs*) of the Greeks.[16] Its claim to holding this *prostasia* rested largely on its reputation, however authentic, of having always stood at the forefront of the struggle against tyranny,[17] but the obligation inherent in it reached farther: to protect any Greek·community threatened by injustice. This is why the Ionians appealed to Sparta when they were threatened by Cyrus after the defeat of Croesus, why Aristagoras of Miletus turned first to Sparta for assistance in the planned revolt of the Ionians against Persia,[18] and why hegemony in the Hellenic League against the Persians in 481 naturally fell to Sparta. It was only Sparta's lack of commitment to the continuation of this war after 478 that cleared the way for a new hegemonic power, and at first only in this particular struggle; the function of *prostatēs* of all Greeks, though weakened, remained Sparta's.

Apparently, at least a few decades later, Athens challenged Sparta and presented itself as *prostatēs*. In fighting certain battles (for example, at Tanagra and Oinophyta), it claimed to have served the interests of Greek freedom, which was threatened by other Greeks.[19] The maxim formulated by Thucydides' Pericles, that Athens's selfless willingness to help others was rooted in the self-confidence of the free, seems to have served as justification for foreign policy decisions.[20] Even during and right after the Persian Wars, Athens supposedly demanded not only military leadership because of its strong fleet but also political leadership rivaling Sparta's *prostasia*.[21] In order to support this claim, the Athenians needed to demonstrate that they had long fulfilled the protective function expected of a *prostatēs*. They had assisted the Ionians in their revolt (a risk Sparta had refused to take) and as a result been threatened gravely by Darius's intended revenge. They had defeated the Persians at Marathon (without Sparta's help). They had shown exceptional willingness to accept extreme sacrifice for a common cause, involving even the destruction of their city (a fate the Peloponnesians were spared). They had made a decisive threefold contribution to the victory at Salamis (unmatched by Sparta) that included the largest fleet, the most experienced crews, and in Themistocles a brilliant strategist. Finally, the performance of the Athenian hoplites at Plataea rivaled that of the Spartans. All this proved the Athenians' ability and willingness to assume the function (now abandoned by Sparta) of protecting the Hellenes against the Persians.[22] Athenian opposition to Spartan plans that would have hurt the Ionians (including their resettlement in mainland Greece) and their determined advance to the Hellespont in the autumn of 479 (after the Peloponnesians went home) provided final confirmation.[23] These merits were soon honored by the transfer of hegemony.

In religious authority, Delian Apollo, though crucial for an alliance involving the Ionians, did not match his counterpart at Delphi. Thus, in the case of Athens the religious sanction that, in addition to political and military stature, had supported Sparta's *prostasia* needed to be offset by proven achievement: the legitimacy of its claim to leadership rested exclusively on its merits in the struggle for Greek freedom. This connection was essentially developed already by the time the Delian League was founded.[24] It remained central among Athenian arguments of political justification and was emphasized ever more strongly the more the same merits were subsequently used to justify not only hegemony but domination. Tangible political necessities thus drove the Athenians to elaborate the catalogue of their glorious deeds, to transform the representation of the Persian Wars, and especially to enlarge, at the expense of other participants, their own contribution to the rescue of Greek freedom.[25]

The link between the claim to leadership and past achievements naturally is most evident in speeches. Lysias and Isocrates took it up frequently and, pursuing their own political agenda, developed it with special emphasis.[26] Thucydides allows us to trace it back to the late Periclean period. The speech he gives to the Athenian envoys in Sparta in 432 (1.73–78) provides particularly valuable information. It confirms that Athens's historical merits in preserving Greek freedom (73–74), familiar from the funeral orations, were indeed enlisted to support its claim to hegemony (75.1–3). Since hegemony was assumed to develop into imperial rule almost by natural law, these merits served also to justify domination (75.3–76.4).[27]

The description of such achievements in the Athenian speech is interwoven with thoughts that recur in Herodotus. His positive assessment of the Athenian contribution to Greek freedom was probably intended to correct a widespread tendency among his contemporaries, prompted by the negative impact of Athenian imperialism, not only to reject the political claims based on this contribution but to diminish the importance of this contribution itself.[28] Such attitudes had long been common, and the Athenians were apparently accustomed to arguing in the manner Thucydides presents here in concentrated form. The ambassadors will avoid repeating the "old stories," that is, the mythical elements in the catalogue of Athenian achievements, "but we must refer to the Persian War, to events well known to you all, although you may be tired of constantly hearing the story" (73.2).[29]

The Athenian speech in Sparta, clearly not a celebratory oration, confirms that arguments typically recurring in funeral orations were also used quite naturally in political speeches.[30] Their purpose could vary considerably, from defense (as in the *Panegyric* of Isocrates) to justify Athenian leadership and refute accusations, to offense (as here in Thucydides) to deter potential opponents by a sober description of that rule and its rationale. This aggressive line of reasoning, like the doctrine of the natural right of the stronger to rule over the weaker that it incorporates, reflects the political climate prevailing before and during the war and was perhaps adopted only then. The defensive use of such arguments, however, was common much earlier. According to Wilhelm Kierdorf, the mythical elements of the catalogue of achievements, based on very old traditions, gained their topical relevance precisely because of the experience of the Persian Wars and the continuation of this war after 479. This also explains their popularity in drama and visual representations, as can be shown easily for the battle against the Amazons.[31] In the suppliant stories dramatized, for example, in Aeschylus's and Euripides' *Suppliant Women* and in the latter's *Children of Heracles,* the primary element of comparison was not the Athenian fight for the rights and freedom of Hellenic communities threatened by other Hellenic powers but rather, on a more general level, Athenian willingness and proven ability to accept the responsibility of protecting those in need. Athens's acceptance of hegemony in 477 in response to pleas by allies who felt variously mistreated and threatened therefore offered a powerful incentive to propagate the topical relevance of all these mythical examples.[32] The emphasis placed on Athens's merits in the Persian Wars was part of the same argument (and must therefore have emerged at the same time), enhancing the "old" (mythical) by recent (historical) achievement. "Freedom" thus must indeed have become a dominant catchword already in the events and discussions surrounding the change in hegemony and the foundation of the Delian League.[33]

In this connection, very old conceptions (better known from Rome) of reciprocity and obligations arising from services and assistance gained new significance. Athens's sacrifice for and commitment to the freedom of all Greeks gave it more than merely a moral claim to receive services and allegiance in return. Recognition of its hegemony in the new alliance was an appropriate consequence.[34] The extension of the same kind of justification to imperial rule, however, exceeded the framework of traditional ethics and deprived the Athenian claim of its previously credible basis, thus revealing its largely propagandistic purpose.

Two later events document both the continued significance and the limits of such mutual obligations. According to Thucydides, in 427 the Plataeans, forced to capitulate and standing trial before their Spartan conquerors, emphasized that it was gratitude for "the courage and goodwill" they had displayed "in those perilous times" that had prompted Pausanias in 479 to bestow upon them a guarantee of autonomy and protection. This promise, given in the name of all Greeks, was now violated by Sparta and Thebes. Archidamus, the Spartan king, promised to respect that guarantee, provided that the Plataeans abided by the condition underlying it, that is, if they committed themselves, as they had done then, to side with the liberators rather than the oppressors of Greece or at least to remain neutral. With this proviso, it seems, the force of such old obligations would have sufficed to cause the Spartans to spare the city, even though their political interests at the time inclined them toward satisfying the wishes of Plataea's inveterate enemy, Thebes.[35]

At the end of the Peloponnesian War, the Athenians expected, and several Spartan allies demanded, extreme forms of punishment for the losers: enslavement of the population and destruction of the city. Yet, as Xenophon puts it, "the Spartans said they would not enslave a Greek city which had done such great things for Greece at the time of her supreme danger." Thus, even at the end of a war so marked by hatred and cruelty, it was still possible to acknowledge the obligations owed the Athenians because of their great merits—although the Spartans hardly acted without ulterior motives.[36]

Rule over Those Unworthy of Freedom

Another line of argument emphasized by Thucydides is certainly late. Their subjects, the Athenians seem to have maintained, did not deserve a better fate because in their previous actions and attitudes they had proved unworthy of freedom. In a meeting at Camarina in the winter of 415/414, the Syracusan Hermocrates tries to discredit the Athenian proclamation of freedom for Sicily by pointing to the enslavement of the Ionians. In response, the Athenian envoy, Euphemus, justifies the subjugation of the Ionians and island Greeks. Echoing Hermocrates' harsh description of the eastern Greeks as "always slaves," he says, they

joined the Persians in attacking their mother country—namely, Athens—and, un- like us, when we abandoned our city, did not have the courage to revolt, which would have meant losing their property. Instead of this they chose to be slaves them- selves and wanted to make us slaves too. We therefore deserve the empire which we have, partly because we supplied to the cause of Hellas the largest fleet and a cour- age that never looked back, while these subjects of ours harmed us by being just as ready to act in the service of Persia.[37]

In other words, those who accept *douleia* and help their masters subju- gate other free peoples have no claim to be treated by these as anything but *douloi*. Freedom must be earned; those not capable of such commitment are not worthy of freedom. The cruel tone of this statement must surely be attributed to political rhetoric and the pressure to counter Hermocrates' clever polemics.[38] But the pointed arguments of the two speakers make sense only if they could count on a widespread inclination among other Greeks to look down upon the Ionians. Close parallels are found in certain aspects of Herodotus's description of the failure of the Ionian Revolt.[39]

In Athens such an inclination perhaps became pronounced when the empire was firmly established and feelings of superiority prompted attitudes of "might makes right." Moreover, a common Dorian awareness of freedom developed in response to the growing antagonism between Peloponnesians and Athenians. It was based essentially on the perceived contrast with the Ionian "slave mentality" which so readily accommodated subjugation by Athens. Thucydides' Hermocrates expresses it pointedly: what the Atheni- ans have to deal with in Sicily "is not Ionians, Hellespontians, and islanders who may change masters, but are always slaves either to the Persians or to someone else, but free Dorians from the independent Peloponnese living in Sicily."[40] The polemical emphasis placed here on the inferiority of the Greeks of Asia Minor must have served the purposes of Athenian propa- ganda equally well.

Rule in the Best Interest of the Subjects

The merits of the Athenians in the Persian Wars, Isocrates writes, were gen- erally recognized to support their claim to hegemony. "But from this point on some take us to task, urging that after we succeeded to the sovereignty of the sea we brought many evils upon the Hellenes" (4.100). Although Isocra-

tes, for reasons of his own, restricts the circle of critics to Laconophile oligarchs,[41] such accusations must have been more widespread and a challenge
to Athenian politicians. This can be inferred from Lysias's and Isocrates' explicit attempts at refutation and from transparent efforts in Plato's *Mene-
xenus* and Aelius Aristides' *Panathenaicus* to avoid this stumbling block and
to focus instead on Athens's military and political successes.[42]

Despite their tendency to idealize, Lysias and Isocrates offer the most serious and differentiated apology of Athenian rule that survives. Because both
authors were deeply engaged in contemporary political issues, they include
arguments that were available as such only after Athens's collapse and the establishment of Sparta's empire. But much of the debate they reflect is older,
echoed as well in remarks of speakers in Thucydides.[43]

The following arguments are obviously late. First, the harshness and unpopularity of Sparta's rule and of the Committees of Ten (decarchies) it imposed on many subject poleis prompted the conclusion that, in comparison,
Athenian rule had been less oppressive, therefore better, and, indeed, basically rather good.[44] Second, in the last years of the war, Sparta's agreements
with the Persians that recognized the Great King's power over the Greeks in
Asia Minor in return for Persian financial assistance caused widespread out-
rage and intensified anti-Persian feelings in Athens. Sparta saw itself accused
not only of delivering Greeks into slavery under barbarians but of betraying its own propaganda of liberation.[45] In comparison, Athenian rule again
appeared more positive. At least it had never subjected Greeks (who were by
nature free) to barbarian brutality.[46] Third, other positive sides of Athens's
rule were, again by contrast, illuminated by describing the conditions prevailing in the Aegean after its defeat. The seas were now controlled by pirates
and the cities by hordes of mercenaries; stasis raged everywhere; wars, raids,
and the conquest of cities were common. From an Athenian perspective,
even the principles formulated in the King's Peace (the guarantee of freedom and autonomy) could not possibly seem more attractive than the reality achieved by their own empire.[47]

Despite exaggeration and occasional deception, the intended contrast to
earlier conditions contained some truth.[48] Above all, the political and military presence of the Persians in the Aegean, the terms imposed by the King's
Peace, and the abandonment of the Greeks of Asia Minor threw bright light
on the indisputable Athenian merit of having deprived the Persians not only
of their conquests in Europe but of some of their Asian territory, and of having for decades barred the Persian fleet from the Aegean.[49]

This line of argument did not make it necessary to deny or defend Athenian rule as such in any detail. Yet efforts were not lacking to refute criticism and to emphasize its blessings. When the Second Athenian League was announced in 378, prospective allies were explicitly promised, along with freedom and autonomy, that earlier methods of maintaining control over them would be avoided.[50] Isocrates repeatedly addresses the criticisms prompting this promise. In his attempts to justify excessively harsh treatment of subjects, tribute payments, interference in constitutional autonomy and local jurisdiction, confiscation of territory for cleruchies, and other grievances, he mixes factual accuracy with arrogant denial, omission, excuses, and deception. This reveals not only the embarrassment of a later observer but the difficulties with which Athenian politicians and diplomats had long been confronted.[51] Correspondences are found in the attitudes of the Athenian demos (as described by Aristophanes and the "Old Oligarch") and radical politicians (as reflected in Thucydides).[52]

It was thus indispensable to find ways to represent Athens's imperial rule positively, especially by proving that even in this phase of its history—as in the old (mythical) times and during the Persian Wars—it had unselfishly bestowed great blessings upon all Greeks. More specifically, it was crucial to show that Athens had exercised its rule for the good of its subjects and thus was qualified, and had the right, to exercise it. This served as well to refute the two most serious accusations leveled against the Athenians: despotism (tyranny) and disregard for the allies' constitutional autonomy. The relevant chapters in Lysias's *Funeral Oration* (probably of 392), which may have served as a model for the analogous section in Isocrates' *Panegyric* (around 380), offers the earliest compilation we have of the arguments developed for this purpose.[53]

Surprisingly, those aspects (increasing and widespread private and public prosperity) that would have shown most readily how much even Athens's subjects had profited from its thalassocracy receive little attention.[54] Instead, political aspects predominate, and among these especially the promotion of democracies in the allied cities.[55] Democracy is characterized here as the political system that serves the interests of all citizens and has enabled Athens's power and prosperity. Athens, the argument goes, had chosen for itself the best possible and freest constitution; by passing it on to its allies, it had selflessly allowed them to share in its own privileges.[56] It had not, therefore, deprived them of freedom but rather given it to them. The accusation of having violated constitutional autonomy was thus unfounded. Rather, the democratization of the allied cities was to be understood as a service that gained in value the more generally it was applied; hence, the argument con-

cludes, Athens had not, as critics maintained, bestowed this benefit se-
lectively but upon all. Clearly, here the need for justification drove the
argument far beyond what was necessary and historically accurate. In its
generalized form this is unquestionably late; in its basic, more modest version it could well be much older.

Freedom within the allied communities, according to Isocrates, was further secured by the general principles of Athenian leadership. We "governed
all the cities under the same laws, deliberating about them in the spirit of
allies, not of masters [*despotai*], guarding the interests of the whole confederacy but leaving each member free to direct its own affairs" (4.104–5). This
corresponds (again for reasons of contemporary politics) to the definition
of a good *hēgemōn* and at the same time refutes the long-standing accusation
that Athens was a *polis turannos.* As Edmund Buchner comments, "If the
Athenians were not *despotai,* the allies were not *douloi* as was always said; on
the contrary, they were *eleutheroi,* and the *eleutherōsis* so loudly proclaimed
by Sparta would have been altogether unnecessary."[57] All we know about
the Athenians' own representation of their rule in the fifth century suggests
that this too must be a late line of argument that confirms the vehemence
and long aftereffect of criticism provoked by Athens's suppression of its allies' internal and external freedom.[58]

The encomium on the positive achievements of the Athenian *archē* culminates in the statement that, thanks to Athenian power and efforts, allied
poleis had for seventy years experienced neither tyrannical rule nor enslavement by barbarians; Persian triremes had not dared to invade the Aegean;
and both internal and external peace had reigned everywhere. Although
again exaggerated, much of this is true.[59] In particular, that "freedom from
the barbarians" prevailed throughout their sphere of influence must have
ranked at the top of the Athenians' list of proud accomplishments ever since
their victories against the Persians in the 470s and early 460s. "Freedom
from tyrants" had a strong tradition especially among islanders and eastern
Greeks, where it had long been associated with the idea of freedom from the
Persians.[60] In these two respects, therefore, emphasis could be placed on continuity from the beginning to the end of the alliance; during this entire period, although relations with the allies changed, Athens had indeed met its
original obligations.

To summarize, the greater part of the defensive arguments discussed here
can have gained significance only after the Peloponnesian War and in connection with a specific political purpose: to demonstrate, despite the allies'
negative experiences with the fifth-century *archē,* that Athens was worthy of

renewed hegemony. This is especially true of comparisons made with the appalling conditions after Athens's defeat, but probably no less of the often embarrassing attempts to refute criticism of particular methods by which Athens had exercised its power. Such explanations, which Thucydides invariably relegates to the realm of pure propaganda, may well have been offered while the *archē* still existed.[61] Yet, as Thucydides and Isocrates show, the fact that the *archē* was based on superiority in power and on force was usually not disputed. At most it was glossed over with arguments used at all times in such situations: circumstances had left no other choice, no one in the same situation could have acted differently, and credit was deserved for moderation.[62]

In contrast, most elements of the encomium on the blessings of the *archē* probably went back far into the fifth century. The Athenians most likely began to claim responsibility for freedom from tyrants and barbarian rule already in the early years of the Delian League, although the latter acquired added significance in the last decade of the Peloponnesian War.[63] The slogans of "general peace" and "security and freedom of the seas" certainly were current at least from the time when hostilities with the Persians ended in the midcentury and when Pericles announced his plan of a Panhellenic congress (if it is authentic) in the early 440s.[64] As the contrast between oligarchs and democrats intensified, Athens also increasingly claimed credit for supporting democracies and thus preventing stasis and securing the allies' domestic freedom.[65]

Overall, then, precisely the elements of justification that emphasized freedom date to the time of the *archē*, and often quite early. Athenian propaganda insisted that the empire benefited its subjects because it guaranteed their internal and external freedom. From the late 430s, this was Athens's primary response to the challenge presented by Sparta's proclamation of liberty for the Hellenes. Earlier, it helped refute the accusation (which by 432 gained new relevance as well) that Athens exercised its rule as a tyranny.[66] Although even Athenian politicians occasionally adopted this negative perspective to shake up their audience, and the demos basked in the glory of its "magnificent rule," to be branded a tyrant was still insulting and incompatible with Athens's self-image as benefactor and savior of the Greeks.[67]

The Empire as Guarantor of Athens's Own Freedom

Contemporary observers did not fail to recognize that the empire had developed its own dynamic, which Athens could not ignore without endangering itself, and which therefore restricted its freedom of action. According to Thucydides, in 432 the Athenian envoys in Sparta explained that after Athens assumed the hegemony in the war against the Persians,

the actual course of events first compelled us to increase our power to its present extent: fear of Persia was our chief motive, though afterwards we thought, too, of our own honor and our own interest. Finally there came a time when we were surrounded by enemies, when we had already crushed some revolts, when you had lost the friendly feelings that you used to have for us and had turned against us and begun to arouse our suspicion: at this point it was clearly no longer safe for us to risk letting our empire go. (1.75.3–4)

Had the Spartans retained hegemony after the Persian Wars, they would soon have been confronted by the same alternative: to assert their rule forcefully or to endanger themselves (1.76.1).

Fear, honor, advantage: twice the Athenians insist on these three factors.[68] Fear of whom? Above all, and initially, certainly the Persians. For no matter how much their propaganda extolled their ancestors' selfless efforts on behalf of the freedom of all Greeks, the Athenians were always aware that they had fought just as much for their own liberty.[69] In 432, however, this factor was hardly very significant anymore. Fear of the hatred and vengeance of the subjects had superseded it. The speech of the Athenian envoys in Sparta, Pericles' last oration, and Cleon's warning in the Mytilenian Debate illustrate how much the Athenians were thinking in terms of their own security and freedom. The experience of the last years of the war and Athens's collapse may have caused Thucydides to emphasize these aspects more than was warranted by earlier horizons of expectation, but hatred and desire for retaliation on the part of some of Athens's subjects were real enough to keep a sense of at least potential danger alive.[70] Moreover, as tensions with Sparta became critical, many—though by no means all—Athenians seem to have become convinced that they were facing a decisive struggle, unavoidable almost by law of nature, between the two leading powers in Greece, in which the freedom of the two antagonists was at stake: the loser would necessarily be enslaved by the victor.[71] Thucydides brings this out sharply in the first and last speeches of Pericles and elaborates on it in that of Euphemus in Camarina. The Athenians, Euphemus says, were long dominated by the Peloponnesians; after the Persian Wars, their navy enabled them to break free. The Spartans had no more right to give us orders than we had to give orders to them, except that at the time they were stronger. Our view is that . . . [by maintaining our empire] we are least likely to fall under the domination of the Peloponnesians, since we have the power to defend ourselves. . . . No one can be blamed for looking after his own safety in his own way. . . . It is because of fear that we hold our empire in Hellas, and it is also because of fear that we have come [to Sicily] to settle matters for our own security, together with our friends; not to enslave anybody, but rather to prevent anybody from being enslaved. (6.82–83)[72]

The idea that rule over others is a prerequisite for freedom is fully developed here: "We say that in Hellas we rule in order not to be ruled" (6.87.2). We will see later how the Athenians developed this concept even further.[73] Thucydides suggests that they used this as an argument by the beginning of the war, which is confirmed roughly by Herodotus's incidental reference to the harm that, in the wake of the Persians, the leading Hellenic powers (*koruphaioi*) themselves brought upon their country in their struggle for domination (*archē*, 6.98.2).

Conclusions: Freedom as a Propaganda Slogan

Freedom apparently was central from the very beginning among the motives, arguments, and propaganda of the Delian League. The alliance was founded, among other reasons, to secure recently preserved and newly won freedom and to liberate those not yet free. Athens's claim to leadership was based exclusively on its proven ability to fight for such freedom and its continuing commitment to this fight. As long as this claim aimed only at supporting hegemony in a symmachy of free and equal partners, it met with no objection. The merits and ability of the leader were uncontestable; its ambition to lead, the interests of those who were led, and their obligation to Athens were in complete agreement. The meaning of freedom, then, still largely coincided with reality even if it was already used for propagandistic purposes.

But when the alliance was transformed into an empire, Athens greatly increased the claims it derived from the same merits and changed them qualitatively. Although its efforts to safeguard freedom from the barbarians continued successfully, it now began itself to violate the allies' freedom and thus abandoned the basis and self-evident condition of their voluntary recognition of its leadership. Not even the greatest services for freedom in past and present would have sufficed to justify the destruction of the liberty of those just liberated. What had previously been credible because of the commensurability of merits and claims now needed to be postulated and proclaimed with ever more extravagant rhetoric. The more freedom became an object of political debate and polemics, the more the Athenians insisted on their past and continuing achievements on behalf of freedom. Accordingly, the word developed rapidly into a tool of propaganda, a catchword that appealed to something that was covered ever less by contemporary and (because of the exaggeration involved) even past reality, and in which the proportion of pretense and falsehood became ever greater. Eventually, freedom became a means of defending its opposite: for the first time in world history, it served to justify oppression and imperial rule.

It was not, to be sure, the only justification, especially not after Athenian politicians learned from some Sophists to use the doctrine of the law of nature in their arguments. But it seems striking that, according to Thucydides, at the very time when they were advancing these new theories of power politics as the foundation of their city's policies, they were also expanding, refining, and differentiating its freedom propaganda. Occasionally, Athenian diplomats or writers dismissed criticism of their city' rule by pointing out that its subjects had by their actions proved unworthy of freedom long before Athens assumed power over them. Sometimes they attempted to refute individual points of criticism or emphasized that Athens's rule was better —better than its reputation and enemy propaganda made it out to be, better than that of any other polis in a comparable position would be, better than Athens might itself exercise it considering its immense power, and better, finally (and much later), than it was in fact exercised by Sparta and Persia after Athens's collapse. But such attempts were not very effective. It was more useful to insist upon those positive aspects of freedom that Athens had bestowed upon its subjects precisely through its leadership and power: prevention of enslavement by the Persians or by oligarchic factions or tyrants.

Naturally, what the Athenians gave so generously to their subjects they were justified in claiming for themselves: security and freedom. In order to protect themselves from revenge on the part of the oppressed and from Sparta's competing claim to predominance, they regarded it as indispensable to hold on to their *archē*. Imperial rule was thus recognized as an essential precondition for the preservation of Athens's own freedom. Furthermore, as we shall see in the next chapter, in affording the ruling city a higher form of freedom and making it completely independent and sovereign, imperial power was, if not vital, at least highly desirable. Here it was not fear but pride, or, in Thucydides' formula, honor and advantage, that determined the relation between power and freedom.[74]

By the time of the Peloponnesian War, then, the concept of freedom was freely usable in every way one wished; it had developed into the centerpiece of political programs and the subject of intense propaganda. Claim and reality, what was said and what was thought, might differ greatly and even contradict each other completely. Freedom thus became the multipurpose propaganda slogan it has remained to this day. Yet, compared to what we are used to, ancient Greek propaganda remained relatively modest and simple.[75] For a long time it also retained a remarkably large measure of truth. To use freedom as a justification for imperial rule in so many ways and on several levels at once was possible only because the concept itself had become differentiated and subdivided and because the needs and interests of those addressed differed markedly and encompassed contradictory, even mutually exclusive, tendencies. Everywhere a multitude of factors, both external and internal, determined the judgment of Athenian rule and often made it acceptable or preferable to the alternatives available, despite obvious disadvantages.[76] For varying reasons, therefore, Athenian freedom propaganda remained attuned to the varying interests of substantial numbers of citizens in the communities of the empire. Hence, it was relatively successful as a political weapon, even against the Spartan propaganda of liberation, though for obvious reasons the latter was popular and effective.[77] It is probably only toward the end of the Peloponnesian War that Athenian propaganda dramatically lost its effectiveness—only to be corroborated to a greater degree than could ever have been expected by the conditions emerging after 404.

5.2. THE ATHENIAN CONCEPT OF ABSOLUTE FREEDOM

While they consolidated and intensified their imperial rule, the Athenians developed their own version of the concept of polis freedom, raising it to a uniquely high, virtually absolute, standard. Encompassing three complementary ideas—absolute sovereignty, absolute self-sufficiency, and absolute liberty—this became Athens's most potent response to Sparta's propaganda of liberation.[78]

Absolute Sovereignty

The beginnings of the concept of absolute sovereignty date to the time of the Persian Wars.[79] However the Athenians may have justified their demand for shared hegemony during that conflict,[80] after it ended their actions were determined by the objective of preventing potential dependency on Sparta. The destruction of their city had made them vulnerable to outside interference. They rebuilt the walls in great haste, ignoring objections by Sparta and its allies. Thucydides attributes considerable importance to this episode, formulating the arguments on both sides with great care. That he did so from the perspective of his own time goes without saying, and it is perfectly possible that he accepted elements (for example, concerning Themistocles' deception) that resulted from early legendary elaboration. But the hasty construction of the walls is confirmed archaeologically; therefore, it is unnecessary to doubt Sparta's protests and the Athenians' determination to carry out the reconstruction at all cost.[81]

Already by the end of the sixth century, Athens had surprised its neighbors and the *prostatēs* of Greece, Sparta, by vigorously defending its independence. Even earlier, it had expanded its sphere of influence into the area of the Hellespont.[82] More recently, it had achieved the splendid victory at Marathon almost single-handedly, become the strongest naval power in Greece, advanced claims to share the hegemony, and demonstrated an independent political will. It had thus become a threat to the traditional distribution of power in Greece. If Sparta succeeded in preventing the Athenians from rebuilding the fortifications destroyed by the Persians, they could, despite their fleet, be kept under control—a goal, Herodotus believed, the Spartans had tried to achieve once before by restoring Hippias as tyrant.[83] Without a means of defending themselves against Sparta's unrivaled land army, the Athenians would always remain subject to outside pressure and largely lose their freedom of action in foreign affairs. They understood what was at stake and acted quickly and resolutely.

What began at that time was realized more fully in the following decades, through Athens's naval policy, the construction of the Long Walls, which turned the city and its harbor into one impregnable fortress, and other measures. As a logical consequence, the Athenians consciously developed the underlying political principle into a doctrine that was of prime importance in determining the city's policies. In 432 this doctrine played a crucial role in shaping Athens's response to Sparta's challenge. This is attested clearly by Thucydides and reflected in interesting ways in the suppliant dramas of Euripides.

The subject matter of the *Heraclidae,* performed probably in 430, was part of Athens's catalogue of glorious deeds, regularly recounted in funeral orations: the children of Heracles, persecuted by their uncle Eurystheus, had sought refuge on Athenian soil; accepting responsibility for protecting them, the Athenians had defeated an invading Peloponnesian army. One of the most burning political issues of the time—how a polis should deal with an ultimatum posed by another—is dramatized here through the problem the Athenians must resolve in the myth: whether or not to grant asylum to victims of persecution and thus to defend humanitarian ideals and a Panhellenic *nomos*—an issue, significantly, that did not immediately concern their own interests or advantages.[84] Despite the great danger involved in accepting the refugees and thus risking the armed intervention of a mighty power that pursues a brutally self-interested policy, the Athenians find it impossible to decline the request. As a free polis, Athens must not allow its decision on such a fundamental issue to be determined by outside pressure; otherwise, its sovereignty will be diminished, its freedom destroyed. The Athenian leader thus dismisses the ultimatum posed by the herald from Argos:

> Go hang yourself! Your Argos holds no terror for me.
> Your hope was to bring shame on me by dragging off
> these suppliants; that was not for you. This city of mine
> owes no subservience to Argos; she is free.[85]

A few years later, in the *Suppliants,* Euripides returned to the theme of a polis unconditionally asserting its sovereignty in the face of an ultimatum threatening war, and there, too, its rejection is based on a clear affirmation of freedom.[86]

In Thucydides, Pericles' response to Sparta's demands before the outbreak of the Peloponnesian War offers a close parallel. Rescinding the Megarian Decree, he says, might seem a trivial matter, if this really helped avoid war. But this is not the point. It is impossible in principle for equal powers that have committed themselves to settling their differences by arbitration to yield to any order or ultimatum.[87]

> If you give in, you will immediately be confronted with some greater demand, since they will think that you only gave way on this point through fear. But if you take a firm stand you will make it clear to them that they have to treat you properly as equals. . . . When one's equals, before resorting to arbitration, make claims on their neighbors and put those claims in the form of commands, it would be slavish to give in to them, however big or small such claims may be. (1.140.5–141.1)

Yielding out of fear thus means abandoning one's sovereignty and submitting to a foreign will, and that is nothing less than *doulōsis.*[88]

The notion of freedom presented here presupposes an unqualified willingness to resist outside pressure and an absolute insistence on equality and sovereignty in all its territorial, political, and ethical-moral aspects. Accordingly, in debates described by Thucydides emphasis is frequently placed on the fact that interstate arbitration and agreements can succeed only if conditions are similar on both sides, if both partners match each other in power, and if they are willing to deal with each other on equal terms. Treaties of this period thus began specifically to stress equal treatment and equal rights among partners.[89] Moreover, precisely because it equated concessions with loss of independence, this concept of sovereignty was potentially aggressive; it could be realized only on the basis of power that guaranteed equality or superiority in every conceivable conflict.[90] Such power could be gained by keeping military preparedness at the highest level, eliminating competition wherever possible, subjugating weaker poleis, and exploiting the resources of others, thus achieving the greatest possible degree of material independence.[91] It is no accident, therefore, that precisely in this context we encounter new ways of linking, on the one hand, freedom with an enhanced and politicized concept of self-sufficiency and, on the other, freedom with domination.

Absolute Self-Sufficiency (*Autarkeia*)

In the Funeral Oration (2.36.1–3), Pericles juxtaposes the merits of the Athenians' ancestors, to whom the city owes its liberty, with those of their fathers, who built up the *archē,* and those of the present generation: "We ourselves . . . have enlarged most parts of this empire, and we have prepared our polis to be most self-sufficient [*autarkestatēn*] in all respects both for war and for peace" (3). The sequence of freedom, rule over others, and complete autarky thus corresponds to the sequence of generations:[92] the status of *polis autarkestatē,* achieved by Athens in Pericles' time, presupposes both the polis's freedom and its domination over others. This statement as such is not surprising. Thucydides and his contemporaries observed frequently that its power enabled Athens to exploit the resources both of those it ruled and of outsiders and thus to satisfy all its needs.[93] But the political use of the concept of self-sufficiency is of great interest; it requires us to survey, at least briefly, the development and meaning of the term *autarkeia.*[94]

The word is rare even in the fifth century.[95] The adjective and its use in describing individuals seem older than the noun and political usage. Early on, the word was linked by some thinkers with the ideals of moderation and frugality as well as independence from external needs and pressures, then by the Socratics with the notion of self-control (*enkrateia*), and, eventually, by Aristotle with the doctrine of happiness (*eudaimonia*) as an essential component of "inner freedom."[96] The personal and ethical components of the concept always outweighed the political ones. The latter appear only in Thucydides and fourth-century political philosophy; they are absent in tragedy, comedy, and Xenophon, and rare even in the orators. Herodotus knows them but alludes to them only indirectly. Since, in addition, the adjective continued to be used much more frequently than the noun, it seems hardly doubtful that *autarkeia* never gained widespread importance in the language of politics and propaganda.[97]

In Thucydides' Funeral Oration, Pericles refers a second time to this specifically Athenian character trait, now concerning the individual citizen, who finds in his city the best conditions for the free development of a personality distinguished by versatile and independent virtue, hence of individual self-sufficiency.[98] The political meaning is confirmed by the context and the addition of "with us": not by himself but only by relying on the support and exploiting the resources and opportunities afforded by his polis can an individual develop his full potential, become *autarkēs*.[99] Moreover, in a different but again political context, the historian mentions the "self-sufficient location" of the island of Corcyra that allows its inhabitants largely to avoid the mutually binding contractual relationships usual among poleis and to tyrannize those visitors who are forced to stop there in their passage to the West.[100]

In Thucydides, therefore, the concept of *autarkeia* is not only clearly politicized but, in its application to Athens, considerably enhanced: thanks to Athenian rule, the city as a collective, and each citizen individually, are completely self-sufficient. The question is how this claim should be understood and explained, especially since all other authors agree that self-sufficiency is unattainable by an individual; it can be achieved only by gods, the wise, and those who have absolutely no needs.[101] It is precisely the frailty of the human condition that provides a crucial incentive for the formation of communities, and it is the primary aim of the polis as the best possible form of community to secure the essential needs of its citizens and to realize collective self-sufficiency. Upon closer inspection, however, not even the polis can attain this goal; in order to satisfy its needs, it is frequently forced to reach beyond its boundaries. Hence, for Aristotle, too, self-sufficiency is a goal, an ideal condition, to which the polis comes as close as is at all possible.[102]

Thucydides agrees inasmuch as he believes that the polis should be self-sufficient and enable citizens to live self-sufficient lives; moreover, he takes it for granted that *autarkeia* is unthinkable without freedom.[103] Yet his concept goes further both by presenting as virtually realized what is otherwise understood to be merely an ideal and by extending the concept in an unusual way.[104] While elsewhere it is directed inward, as it were, and indicates that an entity—whether a person or a political collective—is capable of satisfying its needs by and within itself and thus needs nothing from outside itself, Pericles' formulation of the concept is also directed outward, cutting through the polis's normal limitations. Athens certainly depends on the outside world, even beyond the boundaries of its *archē*, but it is nonetheless self-sufficient because it is capable of ensuring by its own power and means that all its needs will be permanently satisfied. The same can be said for the concept of the individual Athenian's personal autarky.

The idea and ideal of individual self-sufficiency (applied to family and *oikos*), in the sense of economic independence, was certainly very old.[105] Yet for centuries it was apparently unnecessary to coin a special term for it. When such a term finally appeared, it signified not only economic but every form of individual independence that focused on the self and was therefore unconcerned with the outside world. Even in the political realm concern with self-sufficiency was much older than the term. Problems of food supply had long been a central issue in politics and legislation of many poleis; Athens was only a somewhat extreme example.[106] Yet, although they constantly had to deal with this problem, neither the politicians in Thucydides nor their colleagues in the fourth century spoke of *autarkeia* in this connection. We can only surmise why this should have been so. In contrast to the concept of autonomy, for example, that of autarky was probably too abstract, too absolute, and too broad to be usable in practical politics. Moreover, given the general primacy of political over economic concerns in Greek politics, it was perhaps too deeply rooted in the economic realm to provide a convenient political catchword.[107]

These considerations make it possible to define the function and purpose of the political concept of *autarkeia*. It clearly was not used chiefly in practical politics, and the frequent observation by modern scholars that it attracted constant attention is correct for the issues involved but not the concept itself.[108] Rather, the latter probably gained significance primarily in political theory. At any rate, this particular concept could only have arisen in a polis whose citizens had become accustomed to take power and rule over others for granted in all their political deliberations, and who had learned to analyze such rule with its possibilities and limitations, practically and theoretically, and to include it in their calculations and long-range planning. As a primarily theoretical concept, *autarkeia* may have influenced the political thinking of Pericles. This secured its place in Thucydides' formulation of the Funeral Oration—not as the description of a concrete goal but as the triumphant characterization of an extraordinary, almost superhuman, and virtually absolute capacity for self-determination which only one city had been able to achieve and which in the superlative form, *autarkestatē polis*, encompassed Athens's greatness, rule, and complete independence.[109]

That such monopolization of self-sufficiency by the dominant polis necessarily corresponded to noticeable restrictions on the part of the subject cities goes without saying. We need think only of the concentration of Aegean commerce in the Piraeus and Athens's control of trade and communication in the Aegean, highlighted notoriously by the Megarian Decree.[110] One might wonder why such restrictions did not elicit stronger responses. The answer perhaps is that the cities within the Athenian sphere of influence also profited in many ways from this situation and that here, too, economic aspects were subsumed under the political and expressed in terms of general dissatisfaction over the increasing lack of political freedom.

Absolute Freedom

The third element of the specifically Athenian concept of freedom is the explicit causal linkage of freedom and rule over others. We do not know when this idea arose. One of the formative experiences underlying it probably was the intellectual confrontation with the phenomenon of the Persian king's unrestricted power. In *Prometheus Bound* only the king of the gods, Zeus, showing here the traits of both a "supertyrant" and the Great King, is recognized as really free: "All tasks are burdensome—except to rule the gods. No one is free but Zeus" (49–50).[111]

That the Athenians had been accustomed to connecting the freedom of their city with its power or greatness is attested in the years after Athens's collapse, when it was weak and dependent on Sparta, and the contrast to earlier times was felt bitterly.[112] Yet we can safely project the basic tenor of this late evidence back to Pericles' time; it fits well into the framework of ideas on power politics that were developed then. Moreover, speakers in Thucydides, especially Pericles, Nicias, and Alcibiades, frequently establish the same connection.[113] Its essence is summarized by Diodotus in the Mytilenian Debate: the highest stakes a polis can play for are freedom and the power to rule over others (3.45.6).

We find discussions of this idea also in Euripides and several times in Herodotus, who apparently recognized its importance, not least for the political thinking of his time.[114] Two episodes in the *Histories* are particularly relevant here. One concerns two Spartans, Sperthies and Bulis, who offer themselves up to the Persians in order to expiate a sacrilege committed by their polis in killing Persian heralds. When asked by the general Hydarnes why they refuse to become friends of the Great King and important dignitaries in his service—indeed, rulers over Greek territories—they have a ready response. A Persian knows how to be a slave but nothing about freedom. "If you ever did come to experience it, you would advise me to fight for it not with spears only, but with axes too" (7.135.2–3). These are Spartans, but the Athenians exhibit the same attitude when they reject a special treaty offered by Mardonius.[115]

Xenophon attributes a comparable argument to the Spartan king Agesilaus, who in the early fourth century tried to win over the satrap Pharnabazus by guaranteeing him freedom and wealth. Although freedom, he explains, is the greatest of all possessions, Pharnabazus will certainly be expected, not to choose freedom in poverty, but to fight for power of his own instead of that of the Great King. "You should bring into subjection to yourself those who are now, like you, slaves of another. And so, if you become free and rich at the same time, what else could you desire to make you completely happy?" (*Hell.* 4.1.35–36).

When faced with the alternative of freedom without power (in poverty) or rule over others without freedom, the Greeks of the Persian Wars had proudly chosen freedom; this, at any rate, is Herodotus's interpretation, obviously based on the perspective of his own time. Presented with the same alternative, Xenophon's Agesilaus would have made the same choice. But, in contrast to Sperthies and Bulis, Agesilaus understands the Persian satrap's contrary decision, and he knows of a third possibility which Herodotus's Greeks realistically could not yet have taken into account: freedom with power. In his opinion, this comes closest to the perfect happiness achievable in the realm of politics.[116]

The other episode—Herodotus's final chapter (9.122)—should at least be mentioned in passing. It reports the advice Cyrus supposedly gave the Persians who desired to leave the barren mountains of their native land and settle in the fertile plains they had conquered. Cyrus replied with "the warning that, if they did so, they must prepare themselves to rule no longer, but to be ruled by others. 'Soft countries,' he said, 'breed soft men. It is not the property of any one soil to produce fine fruits and good soldiers too.'" This episode is part of an interpretive pattern pervading the *Histories*. It contrasts the struggle for freedom and quest for power of a people living in a poor land, accustomed to hardships, and therefore tough and capable of highest achievements with the decline of the same people when they have been spoiled by the riches of empire, grown soft, and thus become vulnerable to the bravery of other poor and simple peoples. To illustrate this pattern that he judges inevitable by law of nature, Herodotus uses the example of the Persians, starting with their liberation from the yoke of the Medes and Cyrus's conquest of Asia and ending with their failure in Greece. The defeat of the enervated Persians by the simple and brave Greeks represents the latter's struggle for freedom, the first stage of their rise. The second stage, the establishment of imperial rule, lies beyond the chronological limit chosen by Herodotus. Yet he alludes to it and there is no doubt that, when writing about the Persians, he was reflecting on the brilliance and greatness as well as the limits and possible end of the Athenian *archē*.[117] Such interpretation of history was the product of a time that had become accustomed to thinking of freedom and imperial rule as connected in a close and complex relationship.

In Athens, where under democracy the demos's freedom and participation in power were interdependent, the significance of this connection was recognized in domestic politics as well.[118] Thucydides went yet a crucial step further by combining the domestic rule of the Athenian citizens (in democracy) with their external rule (in the empire) to create a comprehensive "hyperconcept" of power and rule, and connecting this with freedom under the same double perspective. Thus, he comments on the oligarchic coup of 411, "It was no easy matter about one hundred years after the expulsion of the tyrants to deprive the Athenian people of its liberty—a people not only unused to subjection itself, but, for more than half of this time, accustomed to exercise power over others."[119] As Jacqueline de Romilly remarks, "the act of ruling" appears here "as the perfect expression of both internal and external freedom, and, in fact, as a superior freedom. . . . This . . . brings out the full force of the superlative '*eleutherōtatē*,' which he uses . . . when speaking of Athens, the city whose people enjoyed, in addition to their democratic liberty, the complementary pleasure of ruling over those around them."[120] Thus, Nicias, in his final appeal, speaks of the *eleutherōtatē patris* (7.69.2), and Alcibiades in Sparta justifies his earlier prodemocratic position with the remark that his family's "principles were that we should all join together in preserving the form of government . . . under which the city was most great and most free" (*megistē polis kai eleutherōtatē*, 6.89.6).

If, as Kenneth Dover suggests, we were here to translate the superlative *eleutherōtatē* negatively as "least subject to domination or pressure by other states," the effect would be lost and the impression conveyed completely wrong.[121] Athens's freedom was based internally on the rule of the demos and the city's specific free way of living[122] and externally on its rule over the empire, which offered it almost unlimited possibilities. This was the positive reason why Athens could be proclaimed the "greatest and freest of all cities"; this was the proud creed of the city that had reached the peak of its power. Even if this had become a topos repeated all too frequently, it was not for that reason any less meaningful.

Conclusions: Freedom through Power

The three elements of the specifically Athenian concept of freedom discussed above complement one another, forming a coherent whole that culminates in the formula of *eleutherōtatē polis*. This in itself indicates that we are indeed dealing here with a set of important political ideas that reflect the self-understanding of the Athenians in the late Periclean era. Only in the exceptional situation in which Athens found itself at that time could such an extraordinary concept not only have been conceived of but have been described as largely realized.

This raises the question of exactly when and how this concept originated and whether it was a purely theoretical construct or in fact played a role in politics and propaganda and shaped the attitudes and actions of Athenian politicians. Its coherence and the very fact that most of its attestations and its most poignant formulations are found in Thucydides might cause us to think that it should be attributed largely to the historian himself and thus to the realm of theory and historical interpretation. On closer view, however, the following thesis seems more plausible. The three elements of the concept of absolute freedom did not necessarily represent a fixed political doctrine but rather a nexus of political arguments that assumed great importance in Athens in the late 430s. The underlying ideas arose in different contexts and at different times. As confrontations with the Peloponnesians intensified and criticism of Athens's interventionist foreign policy and its oppression of the allies turned increasingly polemical, these ideas were combined by some of the leading thinkers and politicians and tied in with theories of power politics developed in sophistic circles. They served primarily to strengthen the pride and self-confidence of the Athenian citizens. Their purpose in an increasingly vicious propaganda war was above all to create an explicit and highly positive Athenian ideology of freedom as a means to counter

Sparta's popular slogans of "liberty for the Hellenes" and "down with the *polis turannos.*"

It would be worth pursuing this in detail.[123] Here I point out only a few important aspects. Parallels to and echoes of most of the ideas and principles so impressively formulated by Thucydides are found in the works of many contemporary authors. Their presence in Euripides' *Heraclidae* (430) and *Suppliants* (late 420s), Sophocles' *Oedipus Rex* (429–425), Aristophanes' *Knights* (424) and *Wasps* (422), Herodotus's *Histories,* and the Old Oligarch's pamphlet confirms that they were widely familiar in the years just before the war and during its first phase. Hence, beyond question, they were prominent in Athens during the time and political situation defined by Pericles' speeches in Thucydides.[124] The historian himself may have harmonized, refined, and sharpened these ideas, perhaps even drawn farther-reaching conclusions from them and used them for his own historical interpretation, but he did not invent them.

Moreover, a remarkable building, the Stoa of Zeus Eleutherios, offers additional confirmation.[125] In design and execution it was grand, dwarfing the venerable Royal Stoa next to it; its importance was thus underscored by its appearance. Archaeological examination of the remains confirms that construction began around 430. This is significant in our present context. The cult of Zeus Eleutherios had, after all, been introduced in the Agora and combined with the older cult of Zeus Soter almost fifty years earlier. In the Agora itself little had changed since the early 450s, after the buildings destroyed by the Persians had been restored or rebuilt and the Tholos and other structures had been erected in the Cimonian era.[126] The Periclean building program focused on the Acropolis and on serving the needs of the Athenian imperial ideology. Hence, it promoted Athena as the protectress of the *archē.*[127] The area where Zeus Soter/Eleutherios was worshiped had been obscured by the workshops and stalls of artisans. Only the altar was still in use. Now suddenly, about 430, Zeus Eleutherios was remembered— not long after Sparta launched its program of "liberation of the Hellenes" and Pericles warned against the *doulōsis* that would ensue from accepting Sparta's "orders," and around the time when Euripides' *Heraclidae* was performed.[128] Construction began on an ambitious stoa in Zeus's honor. His statue was placed in front and a figure of Nike on each wing. Now suddenly the ideals embodied by this Zeus (*sōtēria* and *eleutheria*) became important. This is hardly a coincidence. I suggest that this building was intended both as the monumental representation of the Athenian ideology of freedom and as an emphatic response to the challenge posed by Spartan polemics and propaganda. What the Parthenon was for the imperial city, the Stoa of Zeus Eleutherios was for the "freest of all cities": the monumental reflection of an idea central to Athens's self-image—the same idea that we find interpreted historically and rhetorically by Thucydides, mythically and dramatically by Euripides.

The time when the Athenian ideology of absolute freedom rose to prominence, its significance, and its purpose can thus be determined with reasonable probability. Two consequences still require attention. This ideology, carried as it was to such extremes, throws new light on the *douleia* of the allies. The more the ruling polis insisted on its own absolute freedom and linked it to its imperial rule, the more it emphasized, even if only by implication, the lack of freedom of those it ruled. The only freedom that really counted for Athens was its own. By realizing it in such absolute ways, it turned freedom into tyranny. Vigilance, commitment, and sacrifice were necessary to maintain it; but what other city could pride itself upon such greatness? [129]

Remember that the reason why Athens has the greatest name in all the world is because she has never given in to adversity, but has spent more life and labour in warfare than any other state, thus winning the greatest power that has ever existed in history. . . . It will be remembered that of all Hellenic powers we held the widest sway over the Hellenes, that we stood firm in the greatest wars . . . , that we lived in a city which had been perfectly equipped in every direction and which was the greatest in Hellas. (*polin euporōtatēn kai megistēn,* Pericles in Thuc. 2.64.3)

The subject cities should be happy—so said the Athenian propaganda—not to have to suffer Persians and tyrants as masters. Yet, what was such freedom worth when compared with that of the "freest of all cities"? Dazzled by the "glory of Athens" and the beauty of its artistic achievements in Pericles' "Golden Age," we tend to forget that glory and beauty were paid for, as always in history, by the blood, labor, and oppression of the exploited. [130]

As has rightly been observed, in Greece the tendency to amass power and rule over others was not restricted to Athens. Sparta, Thebes, Argos, Mantinea, Syracuse, and a number of other poleis at various times developed more or less pronounced imperialist tendencies. Persuaded by such phenomena, some scholars represent the link between love of freedom and striving for power over others as a characteristic deeply rooted in Greek nature. They conclude that, as the logical consequence of various specifically Greek factors, an "imperialist impulse" was firmly embedded in the Greek idea of freedom.[131] This view seems to me questionable for a number of reasons.

Argos and Thebes had long been involved in attempts to unite a well-demarcated region under a single will, that is, in a process that elsewhere, even in Laconia and Attica, had been completed in a much earlier period and was generally accepted.[132] Syracuse was by far the largest and most powerful polis in Sicily; it had served an important hegemonial function in warding off the Carthaginians and was heir to expansionist ambitions of its tyrants as well. Overall, among the western Greeks it played a role that is indeed comparable to that of Athens in mainland Greece. The other examples postdate the formation of the Athenian Empire and thus were partly influenced by it. Mantinea satisfied its expansionist desires at the time of the Peace of Nicias, and the Spartan Empire and Theban predominance date to even later decades.[133] In earlier chapters, I established that the phenomenon of rule over others in any precise sense was unknown in the Greek world before the confrontation with the Persians, and that in the archaic period the desire for power and predominance was not yet linked with the concept of freedom.

It is unlikely, therefore, that the Greek idea of freedom comprised from the beginning an essential imperialist component that could not fail to express itself whenever there was an opportunity. Imperial ambitions may have broken through frequently and forcefully, but they need not have been linked expressly with freedom in each case. Moreover, we should not make the mistake of underestimating the seminal impact of the Athenian model that was realized under unique conditions, opened up immense opportunities previously unknown to the Greeks, and apparently provided an irresistible incentive for imitation. This question should be pursued further and in greater depth, as should that of the extent to which Athenian imperialism may have been inspired in turn by the Persian example.[134] On present understanding, it seems preferable to regard the deliberate and explicit linkage of freedom and rule over others—like the political concept of freedom itself—not as natural and inherent in Greek character but as the result of a specific historical constellation.

5.3. SPARTA'S FREEDOM PROPAGANDA

The tension between claims and reality, value concept and propaganda slogan, that characterizes the use of the term "freedom" in the last third of the fifth century can be observed particularly well in Sparta's propaganda of liberation. It was less complex than Athens's own propaganda and essentially concentrated on a single aspect and purpose. Thanks especially to Thucydides, its background, application, credibility, and success can be traced rather precisely. Although the historian avoids giving too much room to Athenian propaganda, which he presumably disdained as too obvious and misleading, he pays enough attention to that of the opposing side to enable us to form an adequate picture. Yet, sensitive as he is to all propaganda, he marks it sufficiently as such to prevent any misunderstanding on the part of his readers. To demonstrate this (and only this) is the purpose of the following brief sketch.[135]

The Legitimacy and Intensity of Sparta's Propaganda of Liberation

The intensity and importance, and perhaps also the effectiveness, of Sparta's freedom propaganda can be inferred from the frequency with which Thucydides mentions it. The Corinthians raise the call for the "liberation of the Hellenes" (that is, of the Greeks oppressed by Athenian tyranny) at both congresses of the Peloponnesian League in Sparta. The full significance of Sparta's adoption of this motto is visible for the first time when the historian describes the mood prevailing in large parts of Greece immediately before the war: "People's feelings were generally very much on the side of the Spartans, especially as they proclaimed that their aim was the liberation of Hellas. States and individuals alike were enthusiastic to support them in every possible way. . . . So bitter was the general feeling against Athens, whether from those who wished to escape from her rule or from those who feared that they would come under it." [136] This professed purpose of Sparta's war resurfaces in the *History* repeatedly at crucial events, such as the siege and destruction of Plataea, Mytilene's plea for Spartan assistance, Brasidas's speeches in the Chalcidice, the Melian Dialogue, and the deliberations of the Sicilians.[137] In the course of the war, the Spartan program of liberation and the resulting ideological contrast to Athens became fixed quantities, which, as Thucydides lets Alcibiades demonstrate unscrupulously in his negotiations with the Persian satrap Tissaphernes, could be utilized in political calculations.

Alcibiades said also . . . that the Athenians were the better people with whom to share power: they were not so ambitious to acquire an empire on land, and both their policy and their actions in the war fitted in best with the King's interests, since an alliance with the Athenians would be on the basis of conquering the sea for Athens and conquering for the King those Hellenes who lived in the King's territory, whereas the

Spartans . . . had come as liberators and it was hardly likely that, after liberating Hellenes from their fellow Hellenes, they would not also free them from subjugation to foreigners. (8.46.3) [138]

Undoubtedly, therefore, in Thucydides' view the Peloponnesian War was waged no less as a war for liberty than the Persian Wars had been in Herodotus's presentation.

How did Sparta legitimize its claim to be the liberator of Hellas? As Thucydides lets the Corinthians argue, Sparta had failed to prevent the buildup and expansion of Athenian power. It was thus held responsible for the loss of freedom on the part of Athens's subjects, and it might bear responsibility for that of its own allies as well: "When one is deprived of one's liberty, one is right in blaming not so much the man who puts the fetters on as the one who had the power to prevent him, but did not use it—especially when such a one rejoices in the glorious reputation of having been the liberator of Hellas" (1.69.1). How should we understand Sparta's claim, as presented here? Since this speech dates considerably before the official proclamation of the war's purpose, the Corinthians cannot yet be referring to the actual war slogan of liberation. Rather, this must be an appeal to the ideological foundation on which any action on the part of Sparta beyond its own sphere of influence would have to be based, that is, Sparta's traditional function as leader (*prostatēs*) of Hellas. In this function Sparta was thought to have liberated the Greeks from tyrannies, led them to victory over the Persians, and thus helped liberate the Greeks as much as Athens did, whose propaganda claimed this merit arrogantly and exclusively for itself. This *prostasia* had been overshadowed by Athenian actions and claims after the Persian Wars, but it was not forgotten. Hence, Thasos and other poleis appealed to Sparta when they revolted from Athens, and for this very reason Sparta in 432 "issued an invitation" not only to its own allies but "to anyone else who claimed to have suffered from Athenian aggression" (Thuc. 1.67.2–3). [139] Sparta's *prostasia*, like that assumed by Athens, was morally and politically legitimized by the commitment to protect victims of injustice.

In 432, those who claimed to suffer from, or to be threatened by, injustice were above all Sparta's own allies, particularly Megara and Corinth. They concluded from recent Athenian actions—the notorious Megarian Decree and events in Corcyra and Potidaea—that the Athenian expansionist policy posed a direct threat to poleis remaining outside its *archē*. [140] In the Thirty Years' Peace, Sparta and Athens had agreed to mutual recognition of their respective spheres of influence. Hence, as the arguments of the Peloponnesians indicate clearly, only Athenian violations of treaties or intrusions into the opposing sphere of influence could serve to justify war.[141] Athenian methods to maintain control in its own sphere were an altogether different matter. Legally, the Athenian allies were none of Sparta's business—which therefore did not react to appeals by Samos and Mytilene.[142] The only way to legitimize intervention on behalf of the allies' autonomy—and later their complete freedom—was to invoke the higher norms of "Hellenic *nomoi*"[143] and to hark back to Sparta's traditional *prostasia*. This step, which Corinth had been preparing ever since the Corcyrean crisis, was taken only shortly before the outbreak of the war. At that point Sparta presented Athens with an ultimatum demanding autonomy for all its subjects and, when Athens refused and negotiations broke down, issued its proclamation of a war of liberation.

It is important to separate these two aspects clearly. Sparta could use recent events as justification for going to war only to protect the interests and security of its allies. Despite Athens's protests, which were to some extent justified, and Sparta's own doubts, there were grounds for concluding that Athens had violated, if not the letter, at least the spirit of the Thirty Years' Peace.[144] On the other hand, Sparta could legitimize its much more extensive campaign to liberate the Hellenes only by appealing to its traditional *prostasia*, not to any Athenian treaty violation. Athens had once waged war to liberate the Hellenes and now enslaved them. This represented an injustice that Sparta, as *prostatēs* of Hellas, was called upon to redress.[145] Not even the Athenians denied that their rule, though justified, might well be unjust; they merely contested Sparta's authority in this matter.[146] It is thus no accident that Athens's opponents, when launching a propaganda campaign against the tyrant city, drew renewed attention to Sparta's supposedly long-standing reputation of being opposed in principle to tyranny—a reputation that lay at the roots of its *prostasia*. Nor is it by chance that Herodotus, working on his *Histories* in those very years, draws attention to the same constellation of ideas and, in his introduction, programmatically pronounces the "enslavement" of free Greek cities an injustice.[147]

According to Thucydides, the Corinthians formulated the common goal of the Peloponnesian allies as follows: "As for that tyrant city which has been established in Hellas, let us make up our minds that it is there to dominate all alike and is planning to subdue what has not been subdued already. Let us then go forward against it and destroy it, let us be able to live our own lives in the future without fear, and let us liberate the Hellenes who are now enslaved!" (1.124.3). Everything said before this shows that the latter component (liberty for the Hellenes) was of secondary importance. This conclusion is supported by the fact that King Archidamus and the ephor Sthenelaidas, speaking before the vote of the Spartan citizens, do not even mention this goal.[148] Further confirmation is found in the negotiations that the Spartans continued, even after passing the resolution for war, in order to obtain the best possible pretext if, as could be expected, the Athenians refused to accept any ultimatum. The Spartan ambassadors brought up religious issues first, then the grievances of their Peloponnesian allies, and only after these the issue of the autonomy of Athens's subjects. Had Athens pulled back its troops from Potidaea or simply promised Aegina a more courteous treatment or even, as Thucydides lets the envoys say explicitly, done nothing more than to revoke the Megarian Decree, war would have been avoided and the "liberation of the Hellenes" would have become a nonissue—even if it was placed in the center of Sparta's final ultimatum.[149]

Thucydides thus took pains to expose Sparta's proclamation of Hellenic liberty, even before the war began, as a pretext, a strategic ploy, and a weapon of propaganda. Even if Sparta initially intended to realize this promise, especially since it elicited widespread enthusiasm, the war was waged primarily to protect the members and supporters of the Peloponnesian League. The "liberation of the Hellenes" was nothing more than a means to that end.[150]

The Realization of the Program: Liberation under Dark Clouds

Sparta, then, emphasized its *prostasia* over Hellas merely in the interest of its *prostasia* in the Peloponnese. It was thus rightly reproached for having stood back so long and watched the Athenian buildup of power, for even formally recognizing it in the Thirty Years' Peace, and for not responding earlier to appeals by oppressed Athenian allies.[151] It was not long before darker clouds gathered.[152] In 427, the Spartan admiral Alcidas was criticized harshly for massacring captives who had not fought against him and were allies of Athens only by compulsion: "This was hardly the right way to free Hellas" (3.32.1–2). In the same year the Plataeans surrendered. After a trial clearly characterized by Thucydides as a sham, the survivors were executed by the Spartans as accomplices in the subjugation of Hellas. They were sacrificed, the historian asserts, for political reasons because Sparta was eager at the time to get the Thebans actively involved in the war.[153] A year later, Sparta founded the colony of Heraclea Trachinia north of Thermopylae. Resistance by the local population was substantial from the beginning and gave the new polis no peace; both its disproportionately large size and the use Sparta made of it suggest ulterior political motives.[154]

Three years later Brasidas embarked upon his great expedition to liberate the Chalcidice. In the speeches Thucydides gives him, he emphasizes his one and only objective, to collaborate with the poleis of the region and put their collective energy into realizing the promise made at the beginning of the war. Spartan help had indeed long been requested by some of these poleis, but Thucydides' account of Spartan motives for answering that request at this particular time decidedly places the emphasis elsewhere.[155] Brasidas himself was soon impelled openly to threaten "compulsory liberation," since for propagandistic and strategic reasons Sparta could not afford to have its offer rejected.[156]

Some cities opened their gates out of fear or else submitted to force.[157] They were all "liberated," but to what end? Brasidas had expressly promised nonintervention in internal affairs. Yet Sparta soon installed military governors, at least in Amphipolis and Torone—predecessors of the later harmosts.[158] Mende got off lightly when it was reconquered by Athens. Torone and Scione were destroyed, and the population was enslaved. Brasidas was unable to prevent it. When agreement was reached in the Peace of Nicias to return conquered areas to their original spheres of influence, those cities were promptly handed over, protected only in part by feeble agreements. The same treaty contained a clause that amounted to an explicit abandonment of the program of liberation and acknowledgment of the Athenian *archē:* "With regard to Scione, Torone, Sermylie, and any other cities in Athenian hands, the Athenians may act as they please." Some of Sparta's allies voiced strong opposition to this—but, Thucydides remarks, this, too, was a pretext intended to conceal very different motives.[159]

Oligarchic governments had traditionally prevailed within Sparta's sphere of influence. Hence, it was probably only at a relatively late date that such prevalence was attributed to Sparta's disregard for the autonomy of its allies and to a deliberate policy of harmonizing constitutions in its alliance system. Essentially, such charges were a consequence of the widespread polarization between "democrats" and "oligarchs" that was linked with the conflict between the superpowers, and a reaction to criticism of Athens's policy of imposing democracy in some poleis of its empire.[160] During the war, however, Sparta's relationship to its allies changed. In 418/417, upon the conclusion of a treaty of peace and alliance with Argos, Sparta intervened and established narrow Laconophile oligarchies in Sicyon, Argos itself (against strong democratic opposition), and later in some Achaean cities. What had hitherto been somewhat natural because of an extensive correspondence of interests now and henceforth needed to be corrected or maintained by force.[161]

Such change of policy became necessary in part because Sparta's attitude in concluding the Peace of Nicias alarmed some of its allies. Some rejected the treaty altogether, feeling especially threatened by a clause in the supplemental treaty of alliance that made any changes in treaties with Athens dependent only on Sparta's agreement. These allies went so far as to voice openly the suspicion that Sparta was plotting with Athens to "enslave" the Peloponnesians.[162] Subsequently, too, it was hard to overlook the fact that Sparta tended to direct the policy of its alliance more and more highhandedly, obtaining the agreement of the allies only after the fact, if at all.[163] Moreover, Sparta intervened repeatedly and ruthlessly in domestic affairs of allied poleis.

In the name of autonomy and sovereignty for all Peloponnesians, Sparta freed some communities from their dependence on, or their territorial integration in, allied poleis and bound them instead directly to itself by an alliance treaty.[164] This "policy of autonomy" was obviously intended to weaken those allies that were considered dangerous and unreliable, and hence primarily served Sparta's own interests. While all of this may have seemed necessary under the pressure of a war that had hitherto achieved little and in view of the increase in secessionist tendencies within the alliance, it contributed little to upholding Sparta's reputation as a champion of freedom and autonomy.

During the war, primarily two fears seem to have provoked skepticism of the program of liberation on the part of many of the "beneficiaries." Liberation meant breaking with Athens and entering into an alliance with Sparta —not total freedom, certainly, and a great risk besides. Moreover, Sparta's reputation led those it liberated to expect aggressive intervention in their constitutional autonomy. Such fears were often well founded.[165] The contradiction between program and reality, already visible early on, became amply apparent during the last phase of the war, when new challenges forced Sparta to use unconventional measures in its pursuit of victory. These involved not least an alliance with Persia, which had been considered much earlier but was realized only in 412, and then at great cost. In return for Persian military and financial assistance, Sparta acknowledged Persia's sovereignty over all territories and cities ever held by the Great King and his forebears. This initial formulation, too broad and partly misleading, prompted strong protests even among the Spartan commanders; it was replaced by a revised clause restricting the king's rights to the king's land "as far as it lies in Asia." [166]

The case of the Milesians illustrates well what this meant concretely. They had defected earlier from Athens. Now their anger over Persian-Spartan leadership erupted in violence against the Persian garrison. The Spartan admiral, Lichas, had to insist nevertheless "that the Milesians and all others in the King's territory should acknowledge their dependence [*douleuein*] on Tissaphernes [the Persian satrap] and court his favor, until the war was satisfactorily concluded." [167] There is no need to pursue this further in detail. It suffices to note, as did Lichas, that for the sake of victory over Athens, its primary goal in the war, Sparta was willing to hand over to the Persians a considerable number of the poleis that had been freed, or still waited to be freed, from Athenian rule. While this helped Sparta prevail in the end, it also greatly diminished its prestige and did not prevent its involvement, a few years later, in a war against the Persians, who insisted on executing the rights they had gained. Despite Sparta's efforts, this war failed to change the facts established by the treaty of 412. The result was cemented in the King's Peace of 386. [168]

In the last phase of the war, Sparta developed a new system to secure areas won by conquest or defection. It concluded alliances with the poleis involved and stationed in them largely independent garrisons under the command of harmosts. This system became the foundation of Sparta's imperial rule after the war. Until 404, it was possible to justify all the measures imposed on former Athenian subjects as restrictions on freedom that were unavoidable for military reasons but limited to the duration of the war. [169] The permanent abolition of the program of liberation became apparent only when the restrictions were not revoked after Athens's capitulation. Those who had been liberated failed to regain their full independence (at least to the extent possible in a hegemonic symmachy) and were instead permanently bound to Sparta under conditions that hardly seemed to differ from those in the Athenian *archē*. [170]

Sparta may have had pressing reasons in those circumstances for deciding to establish an *archē* of its own. [171] Yet all instruments of control, except for the decarchies imposed by Lysander, had long been in place. Hence, having proved willing to betray the Greeks of Asia Minor even to the Persians, Sparta was suspected of having acted with sinister motives from the beginning. It was easy to think that it had never seriously intended to fulfill its promise of liberating the cities in the Athenian Empire but had used this promise simply as an effective propaganda weapon to weaken Athens by encouraging the defection of its allies. Isocrates, in particular, later untiringly denounced the mendacity of Sparta's freedom propaganda.[172] For all these reasons, in the historical tradition the connection between Sparta's struggle against Athens and its own formation of an empire was sometimes reduced to one of direct causality.[173]

The Effectiveness of Sparta's Freedom Propaganda

To posterity, judging from hindsight, the principle determining Sparta's actions from the very start seemed all too obvious. To the contemporaries, who were affected and deceived by it, it became apparent only gradually. Thucydides, ever suspicious of ideology and propaganda, recognized it and brought it out sharply in his nuanced account. In his view, among Sparta's motives the freedom of the Hellenes was always a secondary goal, subordinate to its own interests and power and to the security of its system of alliances.[174] Certainly, the Spartans did not launch their "war for freedom" in order to gain an empire of their own. Alcibiades, the Athenian renegade in 415, probably describes accurately what most of them had in mind. Having overthrown Athens's power, which had become too much of a threat to all other Greeks, he says, "you yourselves will live in safety and be the leaders of the whole of Hellas, which will follow you voluntarily, not because of force, but from goodwill" (6.92.5).[175]

Nevertheless, as Thucydides makes clear, Sparta's freedom propaganda was a successful weapon with significant impact on the war. It was propaganda, but as such it was good and effective for a number of reasons. First, it responded to a strong and widespread need. However "popular" Athens's rule and however diverse and contradictory the interests of the communities in its empire, enough evidence survives to show that there was a strong mood in favor of regaining independence—as long as this could be achieved under acceptable conditions.[176] Second, the call for liberty was launched offensively and in response to a situation that gave it a large degree of credibility. Unlike Athens, Sparta did not have to direct its efforts and propaganda toward maintaining and justifying a status quo that was rejected by many of those affected. Nor did it have to operate with two different concepts of freedom, one for itself and one for the others. Third, Sparta profited from the fact that initially perceptions about the leader's function and the role of allied autonomy differed radically in the two camps. Whereas in Athens imperial rule and the subject status of the allies had long been acknowledged facts, Sparta had so far shown restraint as a *hēgemōn,* and its prestige had largely remained intact from the time of its archaic *prostasia* and its leadership against tyrants and Persians. Compared to Athens, therefore, Sparta seemed predestined to lead the fight for the restoration of liberty in Hellas. Finally, although in Sparta itself few illusions may have existed about the real value of the program of liberation, some Spartan commanders represented it during the war with great personal commitment, thereby preserving Sparta's credibility and prestige until the final phase of the war.[177]

— 6 —

Meaning and Function of Freedom within the Polis

6.1. FREEDOM AND DEMOCRACY

Freedom versus Tyranny

Freedom was discovered as a value within the community during the Persian Wars, when it was threatened by tyranny imposed by a foreign power. The antithesis between freedom and tyranny established at that time retained its significance throughout the fifth century. Especially in Athens it had a lasting effect on the self-understanding of the isonomic and later democratic polis.[1] In contemporary thought it apparently prevailed even over the more recent and clearly more immediately significant antithesis between democracy and oligarchy. The latter, according to Thucydides, dominated domestic politics in many communities, especially during the Peloponnesian War, though it was less evident in Athens before 411.[2] Shortly before this war, for example, the Athenians renewed and expanded ceremonies honoring the descendants of the Tyrannicides.[3] In 415, shortly before the departure of the Sicilian expedition, hysterical fear of tyranny pervaded the city in reaction to the sacrilege of the mutilated herms. This prompted Thucydides to reflect on the question (which apparently was still, or again, intensely debated at the time) of the precise circumstances under which Athens had been liberated from tyranny almost a century earlier.[4]

The figure of the tyrant and fear of tyranny, manifesting themselves as well in the polemics of daily politics and in laws enacted against tyranny and subversion, thus remained highly relevant.[5] This fact requires explanation —for tyranny scarcely existed in the Greek world of the second half of the fifth century. Even the Persian king, long seen as a "supertyrant," hardly attracted much attention anymore. Moreover, given the changing political realities, one would expect the image of "the enemy at home" to have been defined increasingly by the contrast to oligarchy. Helmut Berve suggests that democratic Athens needed the counterimage of tyranny for its self-affirmation and that the Athenians, looking at real or presumed tyrannies of the past, became aware of their own freedom with great pride. This seems true enough, but other factors probably played a role as well.[6]

A sharp and emotionally loaded contrast might have been needed to foster not only pride in but a deeper understanding of the achievements and deficiencies of the isonomic or democratic form of government. The contrast to oligarchy was less pronounced, sometimes blurred, and thus probably less suitable for this purpose. After all, oligarchy—like democracy—came in many forms, and moderate oligarchies, based on considerable citizen participation, were close to moderate democracies.[7] It is not surprising that in a political system that was defined by an exceptionally strong claim to equality, citizens would harbor fear especially of individuals who might exceed the limits implied by such equality, become too powerful, and therefore be suspected of aspiring to sole power. This tendency was exploited by politicians in their rivalries for power and was enhanced by a pronounced—and only seemingly paradoxical—need for democracy to rely on a strong, charismatic, and effective leader.[8] Criticism and suspicion of Pericles, and even more of Alcibiades, expressed in the comic theater no less than in the political arena, provide evidence. Cleon's relentless campaign in the 420s, which fomented fear of tyranny, and reactions to democratic egalitarianism (elaborated by some Sophists in Plato's *Gorgias* and *Republic* 1) that idealized the self-centered, all-powerful individual offer further confirmation.[9] Finally, as Edmond Lévy emphasizes, fear of tyranny seems to have increased markedly in the course of the war. This is easily understandable, given the war's psychological impact, the opportunities for influence, power, and enrichment it offered to elite leaders, and the long absence from Athens that service with the fleet entailed for many of the citizens most committed to democracy. Such fear apparently was further enhanced by the ever more ruthlessly demonstrated ambition and thirst for power of some younger members of the elite who took sophistic theories of natural law rather seriously. At the same time, sources associate some of the traits most feared in tyranny with the ideals of Laconophile oligarchs deeply hostile to democracy and freedom. All this made tyranny a practical and sweeping but nonspecific symbol of the negation of all democratic values and achievements.[10]

In sum, then, throughout the century the contrast to tyranny retained a strong influence on the concept of internal communal freedom. Like Aeschylus, Sophocles and Euripides dealt effectively with the problem of tyrannical rule precisely because they viewed it from the perspective of freedom. Herodotus, who pays close attention throughout to liberty won in the struggle against tyranny, emphasizes two additional factors that undoubtedly originated in contemporary debates on democracy and freedom.[11] He recognizes that internal and external freedom are of equal value and that the polis can achieve complete freedom only by combining them.[12] Yet he and the contemporary author of the Hippocratic treatise *Airs, Waters, Places* try —for the first time in the extant evidence—to trace the effect of liberation from tyrannical rule in the realm of social and political psychology. Herodotus contrasts Athens's weakness under tyranny with its surprising military successes after the overthrow of tyranny. His explanation is that the Athenians, "so long as they were held down, deliberately shirked their duty, as slaves working for their master, but when freedom was won, then every man among them most eagerly worked on his own behalf" (5.78).[13] Since, according to the view prevailing in Herodotus's time, Cleisthenes had founded democracy, Athens's success described here is taken as evidence for the value of this constitution: Athens "thus proved, if proof were needed, how excellent a thing democracy is, not in one respect only but in all" (5.78).[14]

Although this passage connects democracy and citizens' liberty, the context still defines freedom by its contrast to tyranny. In fact, all comparable references say only that one is free if not ruled by a tyrant. At the time, this was certainly a positive assessment (especially in historical or ethnographic comparison), but the concept remained unspecific and largely determined negatively. Its value was established by contrast and comparison: to be free was not to be unfree (for example, in the way the Persians were).[15] Freedom was, above all, not connected with a specific constitution. Any nontyrannical system—even a "constitutional monarchy"—could claim to realize it.[16] In this sense, freedom was popular already by the late 470s.

The Identification of Freedom with Democracy: Evidence

In his *First Pythian Ode* (dated to 470), Pindar approvingly linked the constitution of the newly founded Sicilian polis Aetna with "liberty built by gods."[17] His outlook was still determined by the antithesis to tyranny, but it would seem to have been relatively easy to reverse the perspective from negative (the polis is free because it is not ruled by a tyrant) to positive (it is free because it is governed by a specific constitution). At least so it appears to us. Moreover, by about the same time, the political system in which "the people" were the determining factor had come to be recognized as a specific type of constitution and was distinguished from others by the criterion of who controlled power.[18] Yet even under the exceptional conditions of constitutional development in Athens, the conscious identification of democracy with freedom seems to have occurred much later. It is attested explicitly only after about 430. This is puzzling and we should ask whether the extant evidence is reliable in this respect.

Obviously, the possibility of making this identification did not depend on the existence of the noun *dēmokratia*—although strong evidence suggests that this word was coined in the 460s.[19] Earlier concepts of equality of political rights or speech (*isonomia, isēgoria*) that continued to be applied to the same constitution would have served equally well. Nor is it impossible that these terms, or approximations such as *dēmos, dēmos archōn/kratōn* (the ruling people), or *stratos* (army), which perhaps functioned as forerunners of *dēmokratia,* were understood even earlier as signifying the guarantee of the polis's internal freedom.[20] Yet two important documents survive from before 430 that consciously and revealingly discuss essential characteristics of democracy without emphasizing freedom. Moreover, there are good reasons to think that the conditions that made this identification possible emerged only after the middle of the century.

In *Suppliants,* most likely performed in 463, Aeschylus contrasts two forms of political decision making: an autocratic monarchy, which the suppliant women, refugees from Egypt, take for granted, and the sovereign assembly of polis citizens to whom the mythical king of Argos defers as if he were a democratic leader.[21] The poet uses terminology that comes remarkably close to the word *dēmokratia.*[22] He repeatedly emphasizes essential principles of democracy (especially the process of decision making in open assembly, the relationship between leader and citizen body, and the responsibility of *all* citizens for the welfare of the community), which he opposes sharply to the Eastern system dominated by an authoritarian tyrant-king. It can hardly be doubted, therefore, that Aeschylus considered these issues extremely important—and it is all the more striking that he did not mention freedom at all as a positive trait of democracy. Forty years later Euripides did not miss such opportunities.[23]

The same is true of the Constitutional Debate in Herodotus (3.80–82). Scholarly discussion over the problem of its sources and date continues. Whether or not in content and formulation this section is slightly older than most of the *Histories*,[24] two observations are worth noting. One is that the constitution later (and elsewhere in Herodotus) called *dēmokratia* is described by its advocate as having "the most beautiful name of all" (*isonomia*) and as featuring some essential institutions ensuring rule by the people, but such rule is not linked with freedom. Yet freedom appears in the debate: its realization, by liberation from outside rule, is presented as evidence for, of all things, the superiority of monarchy.[25] A possible explanation is that by the time this piece was composed, the connection of liberty with the democratic constitution was, if familiar, at least not yet as obvious and natural as it was later on. The other observation is that this very connection is marked in other parts of the *Histories*. For example, in 5.78 freedom, realized by the overthrow of tyranny and guaranteed by *isēgoria* (used here virtually as an equivalent to *dēmokratia*), fosters external success and increase of the polis's power.[26] In 3.142–43 the story of Maeandrius, Polycrates' successor in Samos, combines all the essential elements: the founding of a sanctuary of Zeus Eleutherios (as a symbol of the liberation brought about by Maeandrius's renunciation of tyranny) and, "after placing political power [*archē*] in the middle," the proclamation in the assembly of *isonomia* and *eleutheria*.[27] The equation of liberty and democracy (represented by *isonomia* and decision making in the assembly by all citizens) is conceptually achieved here; what is missing is the final step of giving it an explicit and abstract formulation.[28]

Conclusions drawn from silence are never certain. In this case, however, the assumption that democracy was regularly identified with freedom by the time the bulk of Herodotus's work was composed or revised (in the 420s) is firmly grounded. For it is precisely in the last third of the fifth century that this equation occurs explicitly and in a variety of sources. While references in Thucydides cannot be dated precisely,[29] the constitutional debate in Euripides' *Suppliant Women* was written in the late 420s, and the treatise of the "Old Oligarch" on the constitution and political principles of Athens was written between 431 and 424, at the latest.[30] The latter formulates the essential aspects sharply: "The people do not want a good order [*eunomia*] under which they themselves are slaves; they want to be free and rule. Bad order [*kakonomia*] is of little concern to them. What you consider bad order (the opposite of *eunomia*) is the very source of the people's strength and freedom." If one were to try instead to introduce *eunomia* and exclude the common people from deliberation, decision making, and holding office, the result would be excellent but "the people would swiftly fall into slavery" (Ps. Xen. *AP* 1.8–9). Moreover, as will be discussed below, both this author and Euripides define for the first time individual components of the demos's freedom in democracy.[31]

The Equation of Democracy and Freedom: Causes and Time

Why, then, was freedom recognized and claimed at all as a special characteristic of democracy, and why, on current evidence, did this not occur until several decades after the emergence of both democracy and the concept of political freedom within the polis? It will be helpful to remember the principle that what to later generations seemed self-evident (and seems so to us) did not need to appear in the same way to contemporaries. If the polis's internal freedom was defined by the contrast to tyranny and, accordingly, every nontyrannical constitution could be described as free, freedom was not necessarily understood as a specific (nor the most important) characteristic of the constitution prevailing instead of tyranny. Rather, freedom constituted the precondition, the outer frame, as it were, within which other aspects or values such as law and justice, order, or equality predominated. If, to extend the metaphor, not only this frame but also its content were to be identified expressly with freedom, a further impulse was needed, a tangible experience or contrast that forced upon the citizens the awareness of the fundamental importance of their particular form of constitution for establishing or preserving their freedom.

This is true not only of a constitution as a whole but also of individual institutions. Whereas later generations might automatically link these to freedom, their ancestors were preoccupied with other aspects (such as those just mentioned). Since all that mattered was encapsulated in these values and formulated succinctly by the concept of *isonomia,* it was not necessary to bring freedom into the picture. In fact, nothing speaks against the assumption that even the democratization achieved by the reforms of the late 460s and 450s was pursued mainly under the banner of further improving political equality and the empowerment of *all* citizens.[32]

It is not easy to pinpoint the experiences or thoughts that eventually prompted recognition of the particularly free quality of democracy. Observation of conditions prevailing elsewhere may have offered important insights. In poleis that were governed more or less exclusively by elites, the ordinary citizens did not enjoy the same rights and might feel oppressed in various ways. Moreover, *stasis* between *oligoi* and *dēmos* was frequent and had a severely negative impact on the communities involved.[33] The contrast to Sparta was even more pronounced. The Athenians must have recognized that, compared with the strictly disciplined regime imposed on the Spartan citizens, their own system was more liberal and attuned to the nature of freemen. Not that the Spartans were not proud of their freedom, but their understanding of such freedom was much closer to elite ideals that eventually crystallized in an aristocratic concept of freedom.[34] Once the Athenians realized that the general condition of freedom typical of their city was in important ways tied to democracy, they might easily have linked democracy itself with freedom. This is roughly the line of argument Thucydides lets Pericles pursue in the Funeral Oration (2.37).[35] It could have played a role much earlier.

It is uncertain, however, whether such comparisons were likely to focus on the aspect of freedom before the Athenians had become aware themselves of the fact that their social and political system was in essential ways characterized by freedom and, more important, that this system and their freedom depended on each other. For, as previously noted, democracy and oligarchy did not always and necessarily stand in sharp antithesis, and given Sparta's tradition of pride in its own freedom, there was no a priori reason to judge the Spartan order as fundamentally unfree, despite its strictness and nondemocratic nature.[36] Moreover, the specifically Athenian freedom ideology, which responded to outside challenges and represented Athens as the freest of all cities, was probably not developed and propagated systematically until shortly before the Peloponnesian War.[37] Especially in Athens's case, internal and external affairs, democratic government and the policies of the democratic city, and the claims and criticism of each were intertwined. Internal factors thus may well have been primary and crucial for the identification of democracy with freedom. These factors will be analyzed here. External factors may have enhanced and broadened this identification once it was made.

From around 470, at the latest, it had been common to distinguish various constitutions by the criterion of who ruled and thus to regard control of or participation in power a decisive determinant of a constitution.[38] When emphasis was placed on the number and the type of persons controlling power, and thus on the nature of rule as such, attention was inevitably drawn also to those who were subjected to such rule. This aspect had long been recognized in the Greeks' confrontation with tyranny and Persian monarchy, prompting in such contexts the use of loaded words like *douleia* and *douloi*. In connection with the concept of "rule by the people," such terminology could have contributed to activating the association with freedom. We thus need to discuss how and when this could have happened.

Although *dēmokratia* is often used in surviving fifth-century sources either critically or apologetically, it is unlikely that this was the predominant use and that, as has been suggested, the term was introduced by opponents of this constitution.[39] But once the word was created, negative interpretation was possible, and where that occurs it provides valuable information about the political mood of the time, for it presupposes one of two assessments. Either, based on a traditional meaning ("non-elite people" as opposed to "all the people"), *dēmos* was distorted to designate only the "lower classes," "rabble" (thus ignoring the large class of hoplite-farmers), and *dēmokratia* accordingly was taken as "rule of the masses." Or the *kratos* component was pointedly interpreted as control of power and exercise of rule,[40] thus indicating that the demos, as sovereign, had completely taken over the management of politics, thereby depriving the elite of one of their most important traditional functions. Either or both alternatives may have applied, but neither could have been regarded as realized or realizable before the evolution of democracy had reached a specific (and ascertainable) stage.

When contemporaries in the first third of the fifth century identified rule by "the people" as a new form of government, they understood this to mean above all that neither a single individual nor the aristocracy but the people were sovereign. In other words, responsibility for the welfare of the city and for making final decisions on all important political issues belonged to the citizen body. I suspect that initially this was qualified, by custom and general consent, in the sense of "all citizens who mattered," that is, who were sufficiently well-off economically and therefore possessed enough social prestige to serve in the hoplite army.[41] At any rate, the understanding was clear and could be expressed adequately by the simple word *dēmos* or equivalents. It was based on the fact that through the assembly and the reorganized Council of Five Hundred the citizens at large at this stage played a much more important political role than before. But leadership by the traditional aristocratic institutions at first remained unchallenged; the *dēmos* still followed rather than led.[42]

By the mid-460s this was no longer the case. For almost two decades the Athenians had waged nearly incessant war, fighting the Persians and extending the reach of their empire. Their fleet, almost nonexistent before the Persian Wars, had come to dominate the waters of the Aegean and far beyond. The lower-class citizens (thetes), whose property was insufficient to qualify them for service in the hoplite army and who therefore, in my view, had not "mattered" enough to be taken seriously in politics, had recently emerged as the mainstay of Athens's security, power, and prosperity. Their views and voices could no longer be ignored.[43] In the *Suppliants* of 463 Aeschylus dramatized precisely this situation. Knowing that a decision forced upon his polis by a group of refugees will have far-reaching and potentially disastrous consequences affecting all citizens, the mythical king refuses to decide by himself and insists that *all* citizens, the *entire* city (*pasa polis*), must be involved.[44]

Only a year later, led by Ephialtes, the Athenians enacted reforms that transferred crucial powers (most important, control over the officials) from the Areopagus Council to the Council of Five Hundred, the *ekklēsia,* and the law courts and that eliminated institutional guarantees of elite predominance, thereby paving the way for the demos to become the ruler of the city in the full sense of the word. Additional reforms were passed in subsequent years that enabled the lower-class citizens actually to assume the role assigned them in the new system.[45] Even so, it probably took some more time until they had become accustomed to this new role and played it more assertively. The "democratic" king in Aeschylus's *Suppliants* could not yet have said what Euripides' Theseus said in another suppliant play forty years later and Pericles might have said in the 440s and 430s, countering criticism of his own overwhelming influence: "I have established the demos as monarch!"[46] Leadership by members of Athens's elite continued for several decades, and democracy claimed in theory and self-presentation to be comprehensive and integrative.[47]

As long as democracy was understood as rule (in the sense of sovereignty, participation in, and control of government) by *all* citizens, no part of the citizen body needed to feel dominated, suppressed, or excluded, and there was no urgency to equate democracy with freedom.[48] In other words, although at any given time some ruled and others were ruled, there was no concern about oppression of those not in power because such rule was exercised through the entire citizen body (in the assembly) or its representatives (in council, offices, and law courts) and by applying the principles of constant rotation and wide distribution of authority. Hence, in essence there were only rulers, even if they did not all rule simultaneously.[49] In this comprehensive concept of democracy, *isonomia* was realized in the broadest possible sense. As long as this integrative claim of democracy was convincing (even to the great majority of the elite) and therefore generally accepted, *doulosunē* and *eleutheria* served merely to distinguish democracy from tyranny.

This changed when a narrower, more exclusive concept of democracy became prevalent or was perceived as such by a sufficiently large number of citizens. It is uncertain how and when this occurred and what in particular caused this change. Apart from a few highlights, the extant sources—most of all Thucydides—are largely silent about the internal history of Athens between about 460 and 430.[50] Yet we know of at least three periods of major domestic conflict, and it is important to determine how deeply and permanently these may have affected the perception of democracy. Moreover, we can identify major changes that must have been decisive in bringing about the identification of democracy with freedom. I begin by sketching the most important of these in a deliberately broad and general outline that will be followed by a more detailed analysis.[51]

For whatever reasons, the integrative claim of democracy lost—or never fully gained—credibility. Democracy began to be regarded as a partisan system pursuing policies that served the interests of the lower classes rather than those of the entire polis, let alone the elite. Significant parts of the elite felt rebuffed and excluded, first occasionally, in particularly contested decisions, then more frequently or even permanently. Their frustration, expressed in increasingly hostile and intensive forms, prompted democratic leaders to denounce such sentiments as expressions of the partisan interests of a small power-hungry aristocracy (or even of only a particular faction). These leaders might even accuse their opponents of intending to deprive large parts of the citizenry of their political equality, thus aiming at oligarchy or even tyranny. Whether such accusations and the fears they raised were realistic and based on tangible evidence or were simply played up polemically and opportunistically in political debates is less important than the possibility that such arguments could be used in principle, and potentially to great effect.

With the emergence of a polarization between oligarchy and democracy—and especially their more radical versions—the two constitutions came to be perceived by different parts of the citizen body not simply as different but as mutually exclusive forms of partisan rule. At that point, *doulosunē* and *eleutheria* became relevant terms of reference: the few (*oligoi*) felt dominated by the demos (especially the masses of thetes who manned the ships); the demos, in turn, feared *doulosunē* under the few. The conceptual equation of freedom with democracy thus probably arose among those who championed democracy and feared—or claimed to fear—that the rule of the demos was threatened by an oligarchic seizure of power. This idea, importantly, was linked with another that combined freedom with power and rule over others:[52] uncompromising determination to maintain control of power was recognized as the one vital prerequisite for the freedom of the demos. Once it arose, this view was probably strengthened by the observation of factional strife in other poleis, now interpreted in this light, and by the "ideological" contrast, now keenly felt, to the distinctly less free system of Sparta.

This explanation of why democracy came to be identified with freedom assumes a strong and articulated opposition between supporters and opponents of democracy. It contradicts an opinion, widespread in scholarship, that before the coup of 411 (and the preceding crisis following the Sicilian disaster of 413) there existed in Athens no serious and active opposition to democracy, no overt contrast between democrats and oligarchs, and accordingly no debate over the fundamentals of this contrast.[53] To be sure, scholars used to assume too easily that a marked ideological contrast had developed early on. But to reject such a contrast completely seems to me wrong, for various reasons. The problem needs urgent reexamination; here I can offer only a few explanatory remarks, focusing on four aspects: terminology, the attestation of ideological contrasts, instances of factional strife, and attitudes toward democracy among the elite.[54]

First, terminology points to a much earlier period of contention. *Oligarchia* was probably coined by opponents of this form of government. It presupposes rule over the many or the masses and is thus unlikely to be older than *dēmokratia*. Although both *oligarchia* and *dēmokratia* occur first in Herodotus, strong clues suggest that at least the latter emerged in the 460s. As we shall see, most likely it was soon used negatively and polemically as well. For both terms advocates could substitute more positive ones— *aristokratia* and *isonomia*.[55]

Second, the ideological contrast between the two political systems is fully developed in the pamphlet of the Old Oligarch and in Herodotus's Constitutional Debate. Both documents present them as fundamentally irreconcilable and presuppose the possibility of replacing one by the other. In his pragmatic analysis, the Old Oligarch concludes that hopes for an oligarchic coup are unrealistic, but he is keenly aware of the measures that would need to be taken to accomplish it.[56] Although his piece is usually dated in the 420s, a date in the late 440s has been proposed as well; the same is true for Herodotus's debate. At any rate, neither gives the impression that the ideas it presents were new at that time.[57]

Both approaches thus yield a firm *terminus ante quem* long before 411— not, of course, for the existence of a politically active and organized opposition to democracy but for the radical rejection of democracy in certain circles and for an ongoing debate reflecting the wide acceptance of the belief—discussed and justified theoretically as well—that democracy and oligarchy were incompatible in principle. Plutarch's comment on the political rivalry between Pericles and Thucydides, son of Melesias, that it "sharply widened" a previously existing rift among the citizens "and caused the one side to be named the party of the many [dēmos], the other of the few [oligoi]" (Per. 11.3), is factually exaggerated, influenced by the perspective of his fourth-century sources, but probably not too far off chronologically.[58]

Third, Athens witnessed a series of fierce political struggles that each time seem to have opposed factions representing more conservative elite circles and their followers to more consciously or radically democratic groups, which, of course, were also led by aristocrats.[59] The first of these conflicts is connected with the reforms of Ephialtes in 462. They were preceded by accusations against individual members of the Areopagus Council and passed at precisely the time when Cimon, long predominant in Athenian politics, was abroad with several thousand Athenian hoplites, assisting Sparta against a helot revolt. Whether or not this was decisive for the reform's acceptance in the assembly, it is clear that in this case constitutional change was closely connected with a change of direction in foreign policy, from alliance to open competition and confrontation with Sparta. When Cimon returned, he tried to invalidate the changes that had been enacted, but he failed and was soon ostracized. Ephialtes was assassinated. Athens was filled with fear of open stasis and even a coup d'état assisted by Spartan intervention. In Eumenides, only a few years later, Aeschylus urged his fellow citizens to rely on tolerance and mutual respect to restore civic unity. This illustrates how dire the situation must have seemed to him. Although details and chronology are much debated, there is no doubt that the reforms of 462 were heavily contested.[60] The losers perceived them as the result of a partisan victory of one part of the citizen body over the other. This was ominous: a strong minority of citizens, presumably including many members of the elite, initially did not see the new democracy as an integrative system; in their view, the reform merely served as a tool in a factional power struggle.[61]

I suggest that this was precisely the type of situation in which divergent interpretations of dēmos, long inherent in the word, suddenly became highly prominent. Supporters of the reform argued that the entire demos, all citizens, the whole polis, needed to be involved in decisions, especially on war and peace, that were bound to affect their lives profoundly. Opponents, by contrast, represented these changes as nothing but a sellout to the lower classes.[62]

Still, facing great challenges in Greece and abroad, the Athenians seem to have pulled together and restored domestic unity. When Cimon returned

from exile in 452, he was elected *stratēgos* again, was instrumental in nego-
tiating a truce with Sparta, and undertook a major naval campaign against
Cyprus, where he died. We have no direct information about what sort of resistance Pericles had to overcome in effectively ending the war with Persia
(whether informally or by a formal agreement) and, conceding recent losses
in central Greece, in concluding the Thirty Years' Peace with Sparta in 446.[63]
The extant evidence focuses on only one major domestic conflict, that with
Thucydides, son of Melesias, about use of league funds for the building program on the Acropolis. Again, it seems, debate about domestic issues was
intertwined with Athens's foreign policy, in this case its relation to the allies.
In the end, Thucydides was ostracized, probably in 443, and Pericles' long
tenure as the undisputed "first man" in Athenian politics began.[64]

For some ten years, Athens was successful, most Athenians prospered,
and disaffection probably remained low. In the later 430s, however, tensions between Athens and members of the Peloponnesian League, especially
Corinth, increased. By 432, pressured by its allies, Sparta confronted Athens
with a series of ultimatums. The process by which the Athenians eventually
reached the decision to reject Spartan demands and accept war must have
been intense and messy. Enough hints survive, scattered in many sources
and, unfortunately, not always of unquestionable reliability, to indicate that
Thucydides offers an unrealistically smooth narrative and presents Pericles
far too positively. Pericles' hawkish policies were bitterly contested, and contemporaries continued to hold him responsible for the war and its consequences—so much so that they fined and deposed him after only two years.[65]

During the war, tensions and polarizations increased, especially when
democratic leaders squandered opportunities for peace gained by military
successes (in the later years of the Archidamian War) and led Athens into the
disaster of the Sicilian expedition. Such tensions are illustrated by Cleon's
reactivation of antityranny rhetoric and ideology, the surprisingly strong reaction of the Athenians to the religious scandals of 415, and the prelude to
the oligarchic coup of 411.[66]

Fourth, in view of this series of political struggles that all combined both
external and internal issues of contention and were probably influenced by
differences in political principles and ideology, it is not surprising that the
organizational structures for an oligarchic coup were fully in place in 411
and perhaps long before.[67] By then a hard core of committed opponents of
democracy had apparently been joined by a rapidly growing number of elite
citizens who, whether from conviction, a sense of obligation, or opportun-
ism, had previously held leading positions in democracy but were now frus-

trated by massive political mistakes, military setbacks, and heavy taxation.[68] The three broad categories evident at that time had probably been represented among the elite from the 460s (although in varying strength, composition, and importance): at the two extremes, a relatively small group of determined supporters and opponents of democracy;[69] in the center, a large majority who, so long as democracy was legitimized by success, saw in its policies an opportunity for exercising power, gaining prestige, and enriching themselves. As soon as that legitimacy collapsed (and personal profit could no longer be gained through democracy) or when a promising alternative presented itself (for example, in the appearance of a compelling "conservative" leader), varying parts of this group turned their backs on democracy.[70] Thucydides lets Alcibiades, now turned enemy of democracy, explain in Sparta in 415 why his family continued to be involved in democratic leadership, despite the system's patent absurdity. Democracy was firmly established and welcomed those pursuing integrative policies ("being leaders of the whole"); most of all, "our principles were that we should all join together in preserving the constitution which had been handed down to us and under which the polis was greatest and freest" (6.89.3–6). This probably reflected a widespread attitude.

To be sure, the complexity of Athenian politics should not be underestimated. Profound changes occurred during the half century and especially the two decades before 411, and these also affected the conditions under which political power could be gained and exercised and opposition could express itself.[71] It would be a mistake, therefore, to concentrate only on the contrast between democracy and oligarchy and to assign the same weight to it throughout this period. But some essential traits persisted because they were deeply rooted in the thoughts and traditions of the elite, and they became still more firmly marked in the face of the democratic challenge. Not everyone who held high office and emerged as a leader under democracy was a democrat.[72] Because everyone, especially among the elite, profited in one way or another from democracy,[73] a large majority participated, at least temporarily, but this did not mean that they unconditionally accepted a system that was profoundly opposed to essential elements of aristocratic self-understanding and, moreover, presented every leading politician with a number of serious disadvantages.

Some of these are mentioned in contemporary criticism of democracy; despite polemical exaggeration, they should be taken seriously. I cannot discuss them here in detail,[74] but there can be little doubt that some of those who held positions of responsibility under democracy had good reasons to be uneasy and dissatisfied, even if such feelings could rarely be articulated publicly. Nor can there be any doubt that a permanent dichotomy existed between supporters and opponents of democracy. Although such opposition was usually insignificant in practice, it had the potential of being effective and dangerous. All this is important for understanding the conditions that fostered an ideological conflict between democracy and oligarchy, which in turn resulted in divergent interpretations of political terminology and in the linkage of freedom with democracy.

If this linkage, as I suggest, presupposes a sharp antithesis between oligarchy and democracy, it might be possible to determine more precisely the period in which this happened. The question is when contemporaries (especially critics of democracy) must have realized that the democrats' claim to represent the community as a whole did not correspond to reality and that democracy was in truth the partisan rule by one part of the citizen body over the other. Three conditions were probably necessary to bring this about.

First, institutions had to be created which guaranteed full civic equality by enabling the lower-class citizens to exercise their political rights. Decisive progress in this direction was made between 462 and 450 by the reforms proposed by Ephialtes and Pericles. The former significantly strengthened the power of the institutions representing the entire citizen body. The latter removed the biggest obstacles to giving all citizen classes adequate representation in the democratic institutions by introducing pay for jurors and perhaps other functions and opening the archonship to the *zeugitai* (which later virtually amounted to abolishing a minimal census for that office).[75] The citizenship law of 451/450 probably marks the time by which the democratic institutions were fully developed. A few years later, the effects of these reforms may have been evident enough in day-to-day politics to allow critics to conclude that Athens had turned from isonomy to "ochlocracy" (rule by the masses).

Second, this conclusion presupposes that the institutions of democracy were in charge of government not only in theory and marginally but fully and in daily practice. Here an observation offered by Eberhard Ruschenbusch is useful. In the world of Greek poleis, domestic politics afforded few opportunities for political development. As a consequence, the activity and decision-making authority of the popular assembly could be expanded only in the area of foreign policy.[76] Yet few poleis were able to conduct an active and independent foreign policy. Hence, in most cases citizens made relatively few, and very seldom important or controversial, decisions. In Athens, between the 470s and 450s, as the empire took shape and its rule over the allies became more incisive and comprehensive, as revolts needed to be suppressed and wars were fought against both Persians and Greeks, the policies determined by the *ekklēsia* entailed a rapidly increasing number of decisions of varying scope and complexity. Correspondingly, the business of the democratic council and the importance and activities of the law courts increased rapidly as well. All this is reflected in a suddenly growing number of inscriptions recording bills and treaties and probably, in the context of the reforms of 462–450, in modifications to the structure and working of council and law courts that were intended to meet the new needs.[77] The cumulative impact of all these changes left no doubt that Athens was now (and only now) truly ruled and governed by the people. As the assembly became more active and assumed greater responsibility, citizens gained self-confidence. On the other hand, the growing number of important decisions with long-term consequences also caused more tensions and conflicts. We know that the change of foreign policy in 462 and the war against the Peloponnesians thirty years later provoked strong opposition. The same is probably true for the beginning of the "First Peloponnesian War" in the early 450s, and I find it difficult to believe that the "enslavement" of the allies provoked in Athens no resistance at all. It was possible to approve of Athens's rule in the naval alliance without condoning all the methods by which it was established and exercised.[78]

If so, the third condition was met as well. There had to be sufficient reason for opponents to conclude that this democracy fostered policies—at least on certain important issues—that corresponded more to the interests of the demos than to those of the community as a whole, let alone the elite. As a result, the latter could gain the impression that "insofar as they wanted to realize policies according with their norms, beliefs, and connections, they regularly and necessarily met with defeat."[79] Whether or not this impression was correct, it could easily prompt the perception that this democracy was consciously partisan—to the extent of willingly running the risk of alienating many members of the traditionally leading class who so far had still been politically involved.

I suggest that all these factors began to have an effect around the same time, in the 440s. True, as we saw above, the political reorientation of 462 resulted in the first violent clash of fundamentally irreconcilable positions. But at that time crucial stages of the institutional development of democracy still lay ahead. Athens's policies toward its allies were still in flux and largely uncontested. The war against the Persians continued, and the enormous expenditure of energy required by an expansionist policy pursued on several fronts apparently made it possible to close ranks. Moreover, Athens was still militarily engaged on both land and sea. The hoplites thus bore major responsibilities in their city's wars, and in 457, in Boeotia, they achieved one of Athens's most momentous victories.

Such renewed solidarity increased after Cimon's return from exile but came to an end after his death. Around the middle of the century it became clear that the war on several fronts was overtaxing Athens's strength. Pericles once again systematically reoriented Athenian policies. Peace with Persia and Sparta and some measures tightening the organization of the empire, on the one hand, and the citizenship legislation of 451/450, the purging of the citizen list in 446, and the beginning of a large-scale building program on the Acropolis, on the other, are the markers of that reorientation. With these measures, Pericles laid the foundation for a lasting position of personal power based not least on his popularity among the masses. Moreover, the military setbacks of the early 440s and Athens's loss of almost its entire sphere of influence on the mainland reduced—though far from eliminated—the role of the hoplites in supporting Athenian power politics. The polis thus came to depend even more on the fleet and the performance of the thetes.[80]

The implementation of at least parts of this program provoked strong and bitter opposition against Pericles. According to Plutarch, the primary issue of contention was the use of league funds for the building program. Something more fundamental must have played a part. Some scholars recognize in the citizenship law a strong antiaristocratic component.[81] Sophocles' *Ajax* and *Antigone,* performed in the 450s and 440s, reflect profound tensions caused by ongoing sociopolitical developments.[82] In any case, an unusually violent and long-lasting confrontation took place in the mid-440s between Pericles and Thucydides, son of Melesias, and their supporters and seriously threatened Pericles' position. Thucydides' ostracism in 443 sealed the defeat and dissolution of his faction and at the same time marked the end of organized resistance to Pericles' program and the beginning of his fifteen-year "principate" in Athens.[83]

After 443 at the latest, probably after the essential features of the new Periclean program and his political methods had emerged, those opposing Pericles may well have become convinced that he was forging a policy that one-sidedly favored the interests of the demos. Whether or not Pericles promoted this interpretation in order to further his goals, in the opinion of his opponents *dēmos* no longer designated the entire citizen body. The integrative claim of democracy had lost its credibility beyond the circle of those promoting it and benefiting directly from it. If this had not happened twenty years earlier, now it was inevitable that the term *dēmokratia,* in the opponents' view, should be restricted in meaning to "partisan rule by the masses." As a consequence, the perception must have emerged now that democracy and rule by the few, best, or most powerful were mutually exclusive forms of partisan rule, each representing only the interests of parts of the citizen body. Those who did not belong among the ruling part had no choice but to be ruled, dominated, "enslaved." Overall then, the conditions for identifying democracy as rule of the demos with freedom for the demos existed from about the middle of the 440s. As we saw earlier, extant evidence confirms that the identification was current by the late 430s and early 420s.

Under the political conditions prevailing at the time, debates about specific issues or persons could seldom be wholly separated from the more general question of the community's order or constitution. Democratic ideology, emphasized heavily in Pericles' Funeral Oration, demanded of the democratic citizen to put the interests of the polis above his own, to be a "lover [*erastēs*] of his city." As especially Thucydides and Euripides illustrate, democracy bred and required a specific type of citizen who thought and behaved in specific ways and pursued specific policies, all of which were different from those in an oligarchic polis. Even democratic warfare differed from that in other poleis. Particularly in the case of Pericles (and even more so in that of Cleon), the personality of the leader, the political programs and policies accepted by the polis, and the political system were inextricably intertwined.[84] Once it was recognized that democracy depended upon the demos's active involvement and control of power, and that certain political programs and styles of leadership were better suited to this goal than others, it was easy to arouse fears that opponents were aiming at abolishing especially "democratic" policies and thus endangering the rule of the demos itself. Although at the time no realistic politician dared to present a radical alternative to democracy, such fears could be raised, as Cleon did, without citing concrete evidence. It might be done with even greater effect if an opponent (such as Thucydides, son of Melesias) strongly emphasized aristocratic traditions and advocated a more moderate course in Athens's relations with its allies.

In the political conflicts of the 440s, Pericles was accused of aiming at tyranny.[85] Given the new state of awareness of those years, even this familiar accusation took on new significance. Exceedingly ambitious or influential individuals or small groups were no longer seen as a general threat to the free polis but more specifically to the now fully established comprehensive rule by the Athenian demos. From here, too, it was only a small step to conceptualizing this democracy as the constitution that guaranteed the freedom of the demos, and therefore to identifying it with freedom itself.

There are thus a number of reasons for believing that the process of equating democracy with freedom was a result, directly or indirectly, of the political debates and conflicts of the 440s. This at any rate seems the earliest possible context in which this equation could have been made. Explicit confirmation in the sources is lacking, however, and the late 430s remain equally possible, when a similarly vehement debate about a crucial decision tied to political principles took place, one concerning the war with Sparta.[86] Around that time—or a little earlier—a terminological change occurred in a closely related area that confirms the conclusions just reached.

Confirmation: From Equality of Speech to Freedom of Speech

For the citizen's "right of speech" the Athenians used no fewer than three terms, which emerged one after another and, despite considerable overlaps in meaning, continued to exist side by side.[87] Such terminological plurality is noteworthy, especially since it concerns a concept that was crucial to the self-understanding and self-representation of democracy.

The origins of this particular terminology must be sought in a very early time and an entirely different setting. With the emergence of an antithetical typology of slave and free it became apparent that the ability to express one's opinion—"to speak freely" (*eleutherōs legein*) or "to use one's mouth freely" (*eleutherostomein*)—was one of the most important properties of the free person. Correspondingly, the inability to do so was recognized as an especially clear mark of the slave's lack of freedom. The earliest references occur in Aeschylus's plays, but both the idea and the expression probably are significantly older.[88]

The freeman's right of free speech was then transferred to the realm of politics. This is first attested in the context of the contrast to tyranny, which deprived the freeman of even this elementary right—a sure sign of his *doulosunē*. In *Persians* (591–94), Aeschylus accordingly used the restoration of free speech as an indication that with the overthrow of tyranny freedom was restored. Freemen, that is, could once again fully enjoy their personal freedom in their community; no reference to a particular form of government was implied here. In this general sense, *eleutherōs legein* retained its significance as a battle cry against tyrannical behavior.[89]

At the time Aeschylus wrote, however, an association between free speech and a specific form of government had long been established, but it emphasized a different aspect. From the sixth century, particularly perhaps since the reforms of Cleisthenes, *isēgoria* (equality of speech), like *isonomia,* played a central role in Athenian political terminology. What mattered here was apparently not so much that a citizen, without being oppressed by a tyrant, could express his opinion freely—that is, express it at all—but that his opinion had the same weight as that of all other citizens who enjoyed full citizen rights.

Equality of speech thus became the most important hallmark of the isonomic constitution.[90] This explains why in Athens freedom of speech, contrasted to tyranny, long remained secondary to equality of speech, even after the emergence of a political concept of freedom. For the same reason, it was unnecessary to coin a noun for free speech: *eleutherōs legein* remained adequate. *Isēgoria* in fact was the word that best described the unique freedom enjoyed by citizens in an isonomic and later a democratic system. Euripides explicitly characterizes the herald's call in the *ekklēsia,* "Who wants to speak?" as the optimal realization of democratic freedom and equality: *isēgoria* is *eleutheria* (*Supp.* 438–41). In a similarly crucial passage, Herodotus substitutes *isēgoria* for *dēmokratia,* recognizing in it the real value of the democracy he thinks Cleisthenes created. In his view, *isēgoria* thus was the primary institutional consequence of the latter's reform and the condition that enabled the Athenians, now changed from *douloi* under the Peisistratid tyrants to *eleutheroi,* to develop an entirely new capacity for achievement.[91]

This reminds us of the Old Oligarch's depiction of the blurring of class and status boundaries in democratic Athens. He explains this remarkable phenomenon with the conditions created by Athens's naval empire. Since the citizens are involved in communal service to an extraordinary degree, the community has to rely to an unusual extent on the labor and activity of slaves and metics, who, accordingly, are allowed a large amount of personal initiative and freedom of action. To characterize such emancipation of dependent and noncitizen classes, the author repeatedly and pointedly uses *isēgoria.* Here, of course, the word has no political function. Its use in this passage, however, illustrates its great social importance. Even in the case of the lower-class citizens, on whose service in the fleet the welfare of the entire community depended, the capacity to speak up was symbolic of status and full political participation.[92]

Isēgoria was thus the quality best describing the condition—achieved by emancipation from prior subordination—of assimilation with a socially or politically higher class in society: for slaves with the free, for metics with the citizens, and for the lower-class citizens, who hitherto lacked full rights, with those citizens who had enjoyed them before. This explains why it was possible for *isēgoria* to represent *isonomia* as a whole (as in Hdt. 5.78) and why it assumed such enormous value in the self-understanding of democracy. For the same reason, the right of speech as a basic characteristic of the freeman could virtually be equated with the citizen's rights in a democracy.[93]

Although *isēgoria* continued to claim a central position among democratic value concepts, a new term emerged around the last third of the fifth century: *parrhēsia* (*pan-rhēsia*), the "right to say all." Covering a similar range of meanings and serving a similar political function, this term did not, however, replace or supersede *isēgoria* but was juxtaposed to it.[94] In many cases, the word meant nothing more than the ability to "speak out openly, freely," and accordingly also to "speak the whole truth."[95] In this sense, it agrees exactly with *eleutherostomein* and *eleutherōs legein,* which had long been common but could not easily be turned into nouns. This fact, like the new initial component of the word, indicates that now the emphasis was placed on freedom and the free person's unrestricted right to express his opinion.[96] This needs to be kept in mind whenever *parrhēsia* appears in competition with *isēgoria* in the political sphere.

Three passages in Euripides' plays are especially important here. Polynices, in exile, says that the worst part of being a refugee is to be robbed of *parrhēsia,* like a slave. In a similar situation Ion, having found his father, expresses the hope that his mother is also an Athenian citizen, so that he will not, as a "half-citizen," be denied *parrhēsia* in the community, like a slave. Finally, Phaedra fears that, as a result of her defilement of the family's honor, her sons, like slaves, will lose the *parrhēsia* taken for granted by free persons and citizens.[97] Although the causes are different, the consequences for those affected are the same and of equal importance. For the same reason, as we learn from Theognis, impoverished noblemen in the late archaic period saw themselves deprived of their ability to speak in communal meetings, while in fourth-century court orations Athenian citizens, whose rights were suspended because of conviction or debt, primarily complain about the loss of their *parrhēsia.*[98]

Parrhēsia thus describes the chief characteristic of the fully entitled citizen; free speech is almost synonymous with citizenship.[99] To be deprived of this right makes the citizen slavelike; its possession thus realizes the elementary quality of a free person. Only democracy, which guarantees this right in political life, can help the freeman achieve full self-realization. Not surprisingly, therefore, *parrhēsia*—like *isēgoria* for the Old Oligarch—became the favorite target of democracy's critics. They considered it fundamentally flawed, inevitably degenerating into licentiousness and "unrestrained speech" (*akolasia*) and causing the democratic city to decline into chaos.[100]

Parrhēsia therefore was a value term that enjoyed great prominence in both democratic ideology and antidemocratic polemics. Hence, it is all the more striking, as pointed out before, that this term did not replace *isēgoria* but was used together with it. The likely explanation is that despite its versatility and high value, *isēgoria* was unable to express certain aspects that assumed importance in the period when *parrhēsia* emerged. A marked change in political conditions and awareness must therefore have occurred that made it necessary, in certain political situations, to assess the citizen's right of speech primarily from the perspective of "freedom" rather than, as before, of "equality." That a noun was now needed, and a completely new term was coined to express this specific aspect, suggests, in any case, that it had greatly risen in significance. Conversely, that it was possible for so long to do without such a noun clearly indicates that the concept of equality retained its priority until the final stage in the evolution of democracy.[101]

The period in which *parrhēsia* was coined can be determined with reasonable certainty: Euripides' *Hippolytus* gives us a *terminus ante quem* in 428, which suggests the time just before and at the beginning of the Peloponnesian War. The three authors who provide the most important evidence for *isēgoria*—Herodotus, the Old Oligarch, and Sophocles—all fail to mention *parrhēsia;* the former two wrote in precisely this period and even a few years later. It is unlikely, therefore, that this word was prominent much earlier. Hence, the conclusion seems justified that freedom of speech gained significant importance in comparison to equality of speech precisely in the late 430s and early 420s.

It was at this time, in connection with the outbreak of the war, that political polarization reached a new height and the goals and methods of Pericles' politics were once again intensely contested.[102] In the years since the debates of the 440s, both opponents and advocates of democracy had apparently become fully aware of the fundamental importance that *isēgoria* had for the realization of democratic policies and for democracy's defense against any kind of opposition. The shift of emphasis in the valuation of the democratic right to speech must have occurred in the context of such recently intensified polarization. As was well known—and is saliently illustrated by the remarks of the Old Oligarch—the opponents of democracy (and sympathizers of oligarchy) considered the exclusion of the lower-class citizens (*kakoi*) from full citizen rights, and especially the revocation of their unrestricted right to speech, the first step toward eliminating the partisan rule of the demos and ending what they considered an utterly bad political system. Aware of this threat, the democrats realized that the issue was no longer primarily one of equality of speech (understood in purely formal terms) but of freedom of speech (which defined both the form and the content of that right). In other words, it was crucial to maintain in political life not only the principle that all citizens were allowed to speak but the farther-reaching principle that they could say whatever they wanted. The reason was precisely that opponents of democracy objected to the fact not only that whoever wished to speak publicly could do so but that he could say whatever he thought right and important, thereby serving the interests of demos and democracy rather than those of the "better ones." [103] Hence, this "right to say everything" was manifestly of particular importance. More than anything else, it constituted democratic freedom. Freedom of speech, long overshadowed by *isēgoria,* thus gained new prominence and became a new catchword. *Parrhēsia* supplied a term for it that clearly and simply expressed everything that mattered, and it soon became the key word for the freedom of the citizen in democracy.

6.2. FREEDOM IN DEMOCRACY AND IN OLIGARCHY

Questions

In Thucydides, Brasidas's address to the citizens of Acanthus in 424 includes a remark that succinctly characterizes the close connection, common at the time, between constitution and external dependency. He has not come, Brasidas says, to interfere in internal conflicts and hand over power in the city to a particular group; he does not intend to disregard the polis's constitution "and enslave the many to the few or the few to all" (4.86.4–5). The fear was obviously widespread that Sparta would attempt to consolidate its influence in newly won cities by establishing oligarchies.[104] In this particular passage Brasidas, strikingly, avoids the usual contrast between the "enslavement" of the majority (*to pleon*) by the few (*hoi oligoi*) and that of the few by the majority; rather, he substitutes for the latter the enslavement of the smaller number (*to elasson*) by all (*hoi pantes*), that is, by the entire citizen body. This paradoxical expression is easily explained by the ambiguity inherent in *dēmos,* discussed previously, and by the tendency, especially frequent in democracy, to equate the majority with the totality.[105] At the same time, it illuminates the dilemma that caused the dissatisfaction of the "few." In a polis governed by an oligarchy, the demos (in the sense of lower classes or even "all but the elite") was excluded from political participation and thus subordinate to (polemically, "enslaved by") the ruling elite. But in a democracy, the few who by virtue of descent, wealth, education, and ability regarded themselves especially, or even solely, qualified to govern were captives of a system in which they participated but, because of the disparity in numbers and perhaps also the difference in interests, were rarely able to prevail. They were "slaves" of a communal will that included theirs without being theirs.

If we turn Brasidas's remark around, we should expect that freedom was viewed by the many as the opposite of "enslavement" under the few, and was also viewed by the few as not being subordinate to the will of the totality. Logically, therefore, it should be possible to trace the existence not only of a democratic, antioligarchic concept of freedom but of an oligarchic, antidemocratic one as well. One of the objectives of this chapter is to examine this assumption and explain the ensuing results. The other will be to divide the democratic concept of freedom, only roughly distinguished from oligarchy in the previous chapter, into its most important components, to define their content, and to determine their origin and significance. Overall, this will clarify the function and importance of the late-fifth-century concept of freedom in the self-understanding and self-representation of democracy and its opponents, in both theory and practice.

I proceed from the basic fact, emphasized several times already, that *eleutheros* initially denoted "not unfree," "not ruled." Accordingly, the equation of democracy and *eleutheria* meant above all that the demos was subject neither to the rule of a minority (oligarchy) nor to that of a single individual (tyranny). This condition could be achieved and protected only if the demos had power and actively participated in government. Since, moreover, democracy as the rule of the entire citizen body was distinguished from other constitutions with restricted participation, the democratic concept of freedom must have emphasized the demos's involvement in government. The question then is how this specifically democratic linkage of freedom with control of power was defined and conceptualized. Was it connected with specific civic rights and institutions? In short, what ideas were associated with it, and how did these affect the judgment of democracy and its self-understanding?

In this chapter, "aristocracy" and "oligarchy" will be used synonymously to designate the social and constitutional system that competed with the fully developed democracy. Whether *oligarchia* was ever used in an entirely positive sense is unclear. In their self-representation, in any case, oligarchs relied upon traditional aristocratic values and concepts. Actual rule by an aristocracy was, of course, a matter of the distant past. Families belonging to an old nobility and a more recent group of wealthy families formed a new elite that claimed to be "better" and thus entitled to exclusive leadership and control of power, in part within democracy, in part and at times in opposition to it. The term *aristokratia* is not attested before Thucydides and perhaps was not coined until late in the century, but even where it is not used the positive catchphrase for "oligarchy" is "rule of the best." [106] For our purposes, therefore, further distinction is unnecessary.

Definitions of Democratic Freedom

According to the Old Oligarch, the demos does not want to be subjugated in a well-ordered state (in *eunomia*) but wants to be free and rule; for it is precisely from a bad order (*kakonomia*) that the people derive their strength and freedom. In a good order (*eunomia*) only the "good ones" make political decisions and rule over the commoners, who, being incompetent, must be excluded from all political deliberation and decision making; *eunomia* thus inevitably "enslaves" the people (*AP* 1.8–9). Although the author, true to his political viewpoint, regards democracy as partisan rule by the masses, he is the first to state explicitly that the demos's freedom depends on their participation in power. The demos's rule is manifested by the participation of all citizens in offices, council, and assembly, with the right of free speech. Even from this opponent's perspective, greatest importance is assigned to *isēgoria*: he sees the absurdity of the democratic idea embodied in the fact that unqualified and uneducated people ("madmen," *mainomenoi*) are able to take the floor at any time about anything.[107]

In Euripides' *Suppliants*, Theseus expressly has "the entire polis," all citizens (349), approve his decision to intervene in Thebes, militarily if necessary, on behalf of the suppliants (the mothers of the "Seven against Thebes") because, he says (352–53), "I have placed the people in the position of a monarch [*es monarchian*]; I have given this polis liberty and made it a community of equal vote [*eleutherōsas tēnd' isopsēphon polin*]." [108] In his debate with a Theban herald about the positive and negative aspects of democracy, Theseus mentions other distinguishing characteristics of democratic freedom. Athens is ruled not by a tyrant but by the people in annual rotation, and the poor are entitled to equal participation with the rich (403–8).[109] While in a monarchy the laws are virtually in the possession of one man, therefore withheld from the communal realm, and are incapable of effecting equality, in democracy they are written down and are communal property, thus establishing full equality of justice for weak and strong (429–37). Most important, every citizen can take the floor in the assembly: the essence of freedom (*t'eleutheron*) is embodied in the herald's opening call, "'Who has some good advice for the community and wants to bring it in the middle?' Whoever wishes to do this gains praise; who does not remains silent. What greater equality than this could there be for the polis?" (*ti toutōn est' isaiteron polei?* 438–41).[110]

Thus, as the main elements of democratic freedom, Euripides singles out democracy itself as the rule of the entire citizen body and the full equality of all citizens before the law and in politics. Rule by the people is characterized by the sovereignty of the demos in the assembly and their representation in the annually rotating organs of government.[111] Equality is achieved precisely by such regular rotation, by the guarantee of equal opportunities for all, by laws that are written and therefore equally binding on all, by the right of speaking freely in the *ekklēsia,* and by the equal value of every vote in decision making. Even if the specific terms are not explicitly mentioned here, they are so clearly paraphrased that the essentials can be summarized in the following formula: democracy is freedom in that it guarantees *dēmo-kratia* and *iso-kratia,* in the sense of both *isonomia* (understood as equality before the law and equality of political participation) and *isēgoria.*[112] Here, too, the citizen's unrestricted right to speak is emphasized as the crowning feature of democratic equality and freedom.

What Euripides lets Theseus present here is an ideal depiction of democracy and a collage of its most important positive characteristics, balanced, in the comparison with tyranny, by negative arguments from a critical perspective. Although formally a debate about three constitutions, it focuses mainly on the weaknesses and strengths of democracy.[113] That the poet found it important to insert it here confirms that such discussions were "in the air" and politically significant at the time.

Pericles' Funeral Oration in Thucydides belongs in this same context. In the form in which it is presented it must have been influenced by the experiences of Athens's defeat in 404, and it fulfills an important function in the structure of Thucydides' narrative and interpretation of history. Yet it undoubtedly contains a considerable substratum of authentic Periclean ideas. Here, too, the positive aspects potentially inherent in democracy are combined in an ideal, though somewhat defensive and, some scholars think, not overly enthusiastic, summary; how close this comes to reality does not concern the author yet.[114]

In the passage most important for our purpose (2.37), Pericles analyzes, as announced in 2.36.4, the characteristics of the political organization and communal life (*politeia, tropoi*) that have made Athens great.[115] Because not a few but the majority decide, the system is justly called a democracy. But (he implies) the negative implications of the word *dēmokratia* do not apply here because (he explains) every citizen enjoys equality of law in private disputes, while his public esteem depends on his accomplishments, not on his (positive or negative) social standing or financial circumstances. All that matters are his personal qualities and his ability to serve his community well (37.1).[116] Freedom marks the political life of the community; it is also critical for trust and generosity in the citizens' daily lives (37.2). This comment on freedom both summarizes the preceding remarks about the particular nature of Athenian democracy and emphasizes the principle on which harmony in social life is based: "Our communal life is founded on freedom" (*eleutherōs politeuomen*). Freedom, then, is the hallmark of democracy as a whole and of its constituent elements, majority decision and *isonomia* (again comprising two aspects: equality before the law and equality of opportunity and participation in political life).[117] Moreover, as Thucydides adds, such freedom is compatible with respecting (literally, fearing) both written and unwritten law and those who at any given time hold office (37.3).

This concept of democratic freedom is broader than that of Euripides and is oriented differently. In Euripides, freedom is linked with various elements of democracy that are concrete and rooted in institutions. Here, political and social life is characterized as free in a much more comprehensive, almost anthropological sense:[118] democracy is freedom because it is the form of government appropriate for a freeman and because the democratic citizen *is* a freeman and behaves accordingly in both his private and his political capacity. It is significant, therefore, that emphasis is placed here not on the contrast to tyranny, as in Euripides, but on conceptions linked with the typology of the freeman[119] and on the contrast to Sparta's rigid political and social order.

Within this comprehensive concept, several components can be distinguished which recur in significant places in Thucydides' work.[120] Decision by majority precludes domination of the majority by an oligarchic group just as, conversely, partisan rule by the masses is made impossible by high regard for the personal qualities of each citizen.[121] In private as in public life, democracy guarantees the highest possible degree of individual freedom and offers the citizens the opportunity of developing the qualities inherent in them as freemen.[122] This in turn shapes political life and the conduct of the city in foreign affairs.[123] Democratic freedom, however, is far from anarchy; it recognizes the limits imposed by written and unwritten *nomoi* and by the authority of those holding office. We are reminded of the remarks of Herodotus's Demaratus on the subordination of Spartan freedom to the rule of *nomos,* and we generally sense the contrast to Sparta which, at once proudly and apologetically, pervades much of the Funeral Oration.[124]

Elements of Democratic Freedom

This much is certain: by the last third of the fifth century, the Athenians had long passed the stage when political freedom was understood simply as the opposite of nonfreedom. A number of positive criteria had been recognized, though on various levels and with varying degrees of generality. To begin with, they can be divided into the two broad categories later used by Aristotle to define democratic freedom:

The foundation of the democratic constitution is liberty. People constantly make this statement implying that only in this constitution is there any share in liberty at all; every democracy, they say, has liberty for its aim. "Ruling and being ruled in turn" is one element in liberty. Then there is the democratic idea of justice as numerical equality, not equality based on merit. . . . That is one aspect of liberty, one which all democrats regard as part of the definition of their constitution. Another is the "live as you like" principle. For this too is the mark of a free man, just as its opposite, living not as you like, is the mark of one enslaved. This is the second defining feature of democracy and from it has come the principle of "not being ruled," not by anyone at all if possible, or at least only in alternation. This is an element of liberty that is based on equality.[125]

The first criterion, to rule and be ruled in turn, occurs in Euripides' *Suppliant Women,* where it forms, like other institutions, a central element of *isonomia.*[126] All these institutions, combined in the broadest possible understanding of political isonomy, are marks of political freedom. The latter's most important foundation is therefore isonomy itself, the ability of all citizens to share in power and participate in government. In surviving discussions of democratic freedom, various institutional characteristics of democracy are emphasized in varying combinations, but the view is always directed beyond such isolated aspects to the underlying totality, the principle of *iso-*

nomia itself.[127] In other words, apart from free speech (which will be discussed below), they count less individually than in their function as essential components of a political system that is capable only in its entirety of establishing and guaranteeing freedom. The dominant point of view is always: the demos rules—that is, all citizens participate in government—and hence the community is free.

Aristotle's second criterion, "to live as one likes," is underscored repeatedly already by Thucydides. I emphasized above that this criterion interprets democracy as the constitution appropriate for the freeman. To be deprived of such freedom is thus tantamount to living a slave existence. Only in a democracy can a freeman expect to lead a life commensurate with his personal freedom. Several important aspects are connected with this idea.

For example, from this point of view, the understanding, self-evident in the fourth century, that in democracy a person's free status is the sole criterion for full citizenship seems so obvious that its familiarity can be safely assumed, even though it is not explicitly documented in the fifth century.[128] Furthermore, the hallmark of the democratic polis is not only that a free person can live more freely there than elsewhere but that the entire life of society is imbued with such freedom, which, as a result, extends even to noncitizens. According to the Old Oligarch's pamphlet, the blurring of social boundaries in Athens, which were caused by the social impact of Athenian naval policies (and thus indirectly of democracy), was criticized already in the 430s and 420s.[129] Such criticism of what opponents considered a perverted interpretation of freedom in democracy was expanded and intensified particularly by Plato, whose characterizations of the anarchic "democratic person" and "democratic city" are remarkable for their biting sarcasm.[130] In substance, though, Plato agrees with more sober comments of Aristotle: since freedom is identified with the ability of everyone to do as and what he likes, "in such a democracy each lives as he likes and for his fancy of the moment, as Euripides says. This is bad. It ought not to be regarded as a denial of liberty to have to live according to the constitution but rather as self-preservation."[131]

Finally, the strong emphasis placed on the two criteria mentioned above (*isonomia* as a superior, indivisible principle, and a way of life appropriate to a freeman) helps explain the rudimentary development of actual "freedom rights" or "civil liberties" in the democratic polis.[132] I am not thinking of those rights that were connected directly with participation in government and associated primarily with democracy or citizenship and only indirectly, through these intermediaries, with freedom. Nor am I concerned here with legal protections of the citizens, such as the right of any person (*ho boulomenos*) to take legal action on behalf of an injured party (the *"Popularklage"*) or on his own behalf (for example, through *ephesis* or perhaps *eisangelia*) or rules that prohibited torture or execution of a citizen without due process of law or interference with the property of a citizen.[133] Although some of these come close to modern interpretations of "rights" or "civil liberties," they were not categorized as such by the Athenians. Rather, I mean those rights that were explicitly perceived as guarantors of the citizen's freedom within the social and political parameters of his community.[134] Equality before the law undoubtedly qualifies as such a right.[135] Otherwise, it seems to me justified in only two cases to describe specific rights expressly as "liberties."

One is the principle of the integrity of an Athenian citizen's person and home. Demosthenes describes the right to offer as security, not one's person, but only one's property as an essential privilege of the freeman as opposed to the slave—especially in democracy, where laws and customs support the principle of mutual consideration, "as it befits free men."[136] The rights in question are thus those of freemen in general (hence, Demosthenes includes the metics), but they are so only because of democracy and the protection it affords; they therefore apply chiefly to citizens and radiate, as it were, from them to other, noncitizen categories of freemen.[137]

The extremely high value placed on the principle of freedom of speech (as discussed earlier) is even more instructive. In the late fifth and fourth centuries, this concept represented the most tangible embodiment of the citizen's freedom in democracy. Among others, Demosthenes describes *isēgoria* as civic liberty par excellence, offering basic protection to poor and weak citizens against reprisals by their rich and powerful fellow citizens.[138] Even in political contexts this concept always contains a clearly perceptible social component, while in the nonpolitical realm all three terms used for it (*eleutherōs legein, isēgoria,* and *parrhēsia*) describe the ability typical of the freeman, in contrast to the slave, always to express his opinion freely. That the concept's political and social elements were so closely intertwined is remarkable. It can be explained by the need for identity and self-assertion perceived by the citizen masses supporting democracy, by the emphasis placed on the indivisibility of the free life in a democratic polis, and by the fact that *politeia* can describe the entire order and way of life of a community rather than merely its political constitution.[139]

Another factor that undoubtedly contributed importantly to the rudimentary development of civil liberties in Greece is the absence of a strong state authority and a powerful, independent magistracy. This factor can be defined more sharply by a comparison with the Roman concept of freedom; we will return to this later.[140]

Freedom and Law in Democracy

Heavy emphasis placed on the ideal of social and political freedom inevitably caused conflict with another concept immensely important to the Greek polis, that of *nomos*. The ensuing problems were discussed intensely and exploited polemically by political writers and philosophers of the fourth century. According to judgments that, although exaggerated, were widespread among such authors, democracy tended to confuse freedom with lack of restraint, lawlessness, anarchy (*akolasia, paranomia, anarchia*), and in general the rejection of all authority and leadership, whether by individuals, institutions, or laws.[141] Precisely because of its much debated relationship to democracy and freedom, the concept of *nomos*, encompassing broadly a variety of notions from way of life, custom, and tradition to unwritten and written law, had acquired crucial importance already in the fifth century.[142] As problems and dangers inherent in "radical democracy," with its apparently excessive drive for freedom, were perceived and their causes understood, and as the effects of self-centered individualism and ambition on the community were recognized, it became clear that *nomos* had a unique and indispensable protective capacity. Respect for *nomos* made it possible to defend the community's freedom from its own excesses, attacks by authoritarian opponents, and the threat posed to communal values and norms by relativist theories. The conclusion conveyed with great urgency by political leaders and theoreticians alike was that obedience to constitution and law, and to those whom, on the basis of the constitution, the community placed in positions of power, was not to be confused with a form of subordination unworthy of freemen. On the contrary, such obedience was indispensable to creating in the community the very prerequisites for true freedom, prosperity, and happiness and for the fullest development of individual capabilities.[143]

Herodotus offers an early discussion of these issues in a conversation between Xerxes and the former Spartan king Demaratus (7.101–5). Seeking an explanation for the Greeks' determination to resist the vastly superior Persians, the historian lets the interlocutors focus on the differences in social order and government between Persians and Greeks.[144] Intelligence (*sophiē*) and the strength of law (*nomos ischuros*), Demaratus explains, have brought out the virtue (*aretē*) that has helped the Greeks in general and the Spartans in particular overcome the poverty of their land and the rule of despots (102). Whereas the bravery of the masses of Persian subjects rests on brutal force and fear of their godlike king (103.4), the strength of the Spartans, who are unbeatable especially as a collective, springs from another source: "They are free, yes, but not entirely free; for they have a master, and that master is Law," which they fear much more than Xerxes' subjects fear him. And this *nomos* always demands the same: to stand firm in the line of battle and to conquer or die (104).

The Greeks are thus free because they are not subject to any king or imposed law but have created for themselves in their independent communities a common way of life and set of laws to which they must accommodate but which provide them with the best possible opportunity to develop their individual and collective *aretē*.[145] Here, as in another discussion, between two Spartan envoys and a Persian satrap (discussed earlier), freedom, the primary characteristic of the Greek polis, is contrasted to the *doulosunē* of the Persians, including even high officials, under their Great King.[146] In both cases Herodotus lets Spartans stand up to Persians and correct their misperceptions about freedom. Yet because Sparta's community is dominated by a strict *nomos*, its pride in freedom is balanced by a counterweight, as it were: the Spartan variant of Greek freedom is far from total and prevented effectively from transcending sound limits.[147] In addition, as Herodotus makes clear and Thucydides confirms, despite its commitment to freedom Sparta tended to focus on its own immediate interests.[148] The Athenian conception of freedom, by contrast, was less narrowly concentrated on Athenian advantage; it is not an end in itself but is more idealistic, generous, and committed to a higher communal and Panhellenic objective. This, at any rate, was the view propagated in the Periclean era, variously reflected in Herodotus, Thucydides, and Euripides' suppliant plays.[149]

Such differences mirror the divergent views of the two poleis about the most desirable form of community. Significantly, we find no Athenian statement that so succinctly underscores the precedence of *nomos* over freedom as does that of the Spartan Demaratus. But this posed a major problem to democracy's self-representation. A rigid *nomos*, such as that accepted by Sparta, was incompatible with the Athenian commitment to a free way of life. Yet rejecting the power of *nomos* or openly subordinating it to freedom would have been counterproductive and dangerous; above all, it would have confirmed the distorted image of democracy propagated in opponents' polemics.[150] The affirmation of freedom in the democratic way of life thus needed to be balanced by an equally clear affirmation of the validity of *nomos* and *nomoi.* This tendency, sometimes visibly prompted by the need to defend democracy against oligarchic criticism, is reflected in various arguments that focus precisely on the problem at hand.[151]

Euripides (*Supp.* 429ff.) and Thucydides (2.37.1) illustrate that equality of justice for all citizens was considered an essential condition for democratic freedom.[152] Thucydides lets Pericles (2.37.3) and the Syracusan Athenagoras (6.38.5) emphasize the necessity of complying with written and unwritten laws and respecting the power of those holding office. Despite some "accidents," the Athenians were fully aware of the problems lurking here and tried to keep them under control with carefully thought-out regulations.[153] Conversely, at the end of the fifth century, negative experiences with oligarchy proved useful politically, psychologically, and propagandistically. After all, the oligarchs, once in power, were able to maintain their rule only by disregarding customs and laws—to an extent that by far overshadowed everything experienced in and feared from democracy.[154] Finally, the Athenians were frequently accused of having violated a higher, Panhellenic *nomos* by enslaving their allies. They countered that they had always, in the distant and recent past, lived up to this principle by unconditionally supporting the freedom of the Hellenes.[155]

All of this, to be sure, took place within the realm of Athenian democratic propaganda and self-justification. But this only confirms that even the champions of democracy were well aware of how vulnerable democracy really was. Precisely because it was committed to the fullest possible realization of freedom in all aspects of communal life, it could easily degenerate into lawlessness and anarchy and just as easily be misunderstood or misrepresented in this way by its opponents.

Democratic Freedom versus Oligarchic Claims to Exclusive Power: The Theory

Dismissal of democratic freedom as anarchy was only one of a broad range of criticisms leveled at democracy by its opponents. It is not my purpose here to present a detailed analysis of such criticisms.[156] My question is only whether opponents, who invariably strove to limit both the number of citizens participating in government and the scope of their participation, were able to propose any positive alternative to the democratic interpretation of freedom they so despised.

The Old Oligarch's treatise serves as a point of departure, for it presents the terminology and argumentation of the "oligarchic opposition" in unusually concise and pure form, while still remaining relatively objective.[157]

The author sees the preservation of the freedom and material interests of the demos as the sole purpose and justification of democracy. Conversely, he takes it for granted that oligarchy serves only the interests of the elite and necessarily results in the "enslavement" of the lower citizen classes.[158] In his view, democracy represents rule by the poor, low, base, uneducated, incapable, and unfit, while oligarchy or aristocracy gives power to the good, noble, educated, capable, and rich. Democracy, the epitome of "bad order" (*kakonomia*), thus stands in a natural and insurmountable contrast to aristocratic or oligarchic "good order" (*eunomia*).[159] Even democracy's opponents recognize that participation in government is an indispensable condition for maintaining the demos's freedom, but they claim for themselves, on the strength of their pervasive qualitative superiority, an exclusive right to rule because they alone are capable of governing "well" and for the best of the polis. In their thinking, political power is an end in itself, a means to aristocratic self-fulfillment, not to realizing or preserving freedom. They see life in a democratic polis, not primarily as servitude, but as entirely incompatible with aristocratic self-understanding. Therefore, participation in democratic politics needs to be thoroughly justified.[160] In sum, in this author's view self-interest is predominant on both sides; democrats focus on institutions, oligarchs on the citizens' social status and personal qualities.

In the constitutional debates in Herodotus and Euripides the arguments are similarly presented on two different levels. The advocates of democracy rely on institutions that guarantee equal participation in government by (and thus the liberty of) all citizens and protect them from abuses and despotism.[161] The opponents of democracy insist, instead, on the lack of personal qualities that is decisive in rendering the lower classes unfit for participation in government. The masses, we hear in Herodotus,

are a feckless lot—nowhere will you find more ignorance or irresponsibility or violence. . . . A king does at least act consciously and deliberately; but the mob does not. Indeed how should it, when it has never been taught what is right and proper, and has no knowledge of its own about such things? The masses handle affairs without thought; all they can do is to rush blindly into politics like a river in flood. . . . In a democracy, malpractices are bound to occur. (3.81.1–2, 82.4, tr. de Sélincourt and Marincola)[162]

The constitutional debates remain focused on the contrast between monarchy and democracy; they do not consider the aristocratic or oligarchic alternative at all—or only marginally and superficially.[163]

By contrast, the speech of the Syracusan Athenagoras in Thucydides includes an explicit argument in defense of democracy and a critique of oligarchic aspirations. Athenagoras is described as a democratic demagogue in the manner of Cleon.[164] He alleges that his opponents intend to use extraordinary powers decreed for them during a crisis (which he denounces as faked in the first place) to establish an oligarchy or even a tyranny (6.38.1–3). He then enumerates the main points of the oligarchs' propaganda and their criticism of democracy. Instead of age restrictions imposed on office holding by democratic law, oligarchs prefer more flexible regulations that give free rein to the political competence and energy of the best and wealthiest; instead of democratic "numerical equality" realized by equal participation of all citizens in political decision making (*isonomia*), oligarchs insist on "proportional equality" that is graduated, in the aristocratic tradition, according to social status (38.4–39.1).[165] Athenagoras contrasts these claims with the reality as seen from the democrats' perspective: oligarchy is the selfish rule of a few who, based on their wealth, boast sole political competence and demand exclusive control of power. They let the people share only in dangers while reserving all advantages for themselves (39.1–2). Only democracy protects the interests of everyone, the well-being of the entire community, and the freedom of all. As is typical of democracy, *dēmos* is emphatically interpreted here in its integrative meaning, designating the totality of citizens (39.1).

Despite differing political points of view, the extant sources agree in all essential respects. Oligarchs aim primarily at monopolizing power for their group, emphasizing the principle that only the best and most capable should govern. Democrats want to ensure isonomy and freedom for all citizens by preventing just such monopolization of power by small groups. Oligarchs usually focus on citizens' personal qualifications, democrats on institutions. Athenagoras's speech, however, also contains a democratic counterargument that is exceptional in focusing on citizens' personal qualities and thus meeting oligarchic claims head on: the many may not be financial wizards or the smartest political advisors, but collectively they "are best at listening to the different arguments and judging between them" (6.39.1). This argument, perhaps also suggested in Herodotus's Constitutional Debate, was later elaborated upon by Aristotle and supported by a theory of "cumulative qualification." Individually, this theory says, the commoners may be inferior to the "better ones," but cumulatively, by adding up their talents and qualities, they are far superior even to the best.[166] This assumes in principle —as do Thucydides' Pericles and Plato's Protagoras, but in stark contrast to global criticism by democracy's opponents—that every citizen is politically competent and able to make reasonable and informed decisions.[167]

On the political level, freedom thus played no role at all in the theory and self-representation of fifth-century oligarchs: they did not challenge the monopolization of freedom by democracy but tried to invalidate it through vehement and polemical criticism of its content.[168] This will be confirmed by a brief analysis of the political and ideological arguments advanced in connection with the oligarchic coups of 411 and 404 in Athens.

Corroboration in Practice: The Experiences of 411 and 404

After the Sicilian disaster, Athens found itself in great military and financial difficulties. In 411, after an extended period of preparation, democracy was overthrown by an oligarchy, the "Four Hundred." Their violent regime was soon replaced by a more moderate one, of "Five Thousand," that in turn yielded to democracy again only a few months later. Because of partly contradictory statements in the sources, both the sequence of events and the successive constitutions are much debated. Moreover, Thucydides' eighth book, our primary source, is incomplete and contains no speeches. Hence, political goals and ideological aspects are not summarized succinctly in one or two passages, as they are in Athenagoras's speech, though they can be inferred and combined from numerous scattered remarks.[169]

Alcibiades lets the "most influential" (dunatōtatoi) and "best" (beltistoi) Athenians know that he will return to Athens only under an oligarchy, not under the "wicked system" that is democracy (Thuc. 8.47.2). Powerful (dunatōtatoi) elite Athenians, convinced that they are suffering most from the war, begin to hope that they can gain control over politics (48.1; cf. 63.4).[170] In their view, oligarchy is a reasonable government of order and moderation (sōphrosunē, 53.3, 64.4–5). It guarantees power to those who contribute most with their bodies (sōmasin) and money (chrēmasin); it is therefore rule by those who are wealthy and bear arms (65.3; as opposed to rule by the poor, who man the ships). In reality their only concern is to dominate the city and to monopolize power, which they then seek to maintain by every means, even by murdering, arresting, and exiling their opponents.[171] Thucydides' narrative and comments leave no doubt that competitive ambition and lust for power were rampant even within the oligarchic group.[172]

Apart from occasional references to the displeasure of the masses and their helplessness in the face of external crisis and oligarchic terror, we learn little in this context about the democratic counterposition.[173] Yet Thucydides repeatedly mentions the demos's loss of freedom—an experience unknown to the Athenians for almost a century and one so unexpected that even the enemy hardly dared to accept it for real.[174] Furthermore, certain details in the historian's description of the oligarchic exercise of power reflect essential features of the typology of tyranny.[175] This endowed the democratic concept of freedom with additional legitimacy and relevance.

The alliance with the Persian satrap Tissaphernes, promised by Alcibiades and of great significance for the continuation of the war, was tied to the establishment of an oligarchy in Athens.[176] This allowed the oligarchs to argue convincingly that the rule of the few "had not been established to do any harm to the city or the citizens, but in order to preserve the state as a whole";[177] hence, this was not self-interested rule by a small clique. Initially, the oligarchs hoped to gain the upper hand in the war as well, but they soon tried to enter into peace negotiations with Sparta.[178] Although these were no more successful than those with the Persians, they added a marked foreign policy component to the conflict between democrats and oligarchs. While the former insisted firmly on continuing the war, the latter, as their situation became more precarious, first advocated peace and then were willing even to betray their city to the enemy, as long as this would help them save their power or at least their lives.[179]

Even though on this issue moderate oligarchs eventually refused to follow the relatively small group of extremists, the attitude of the latter heavily influenced contemporary judgments and helped discredit the entire oligarchic movement.[180] Thus, the events of 411/410 enhanced the credibility of democracy's claim to be the guarantor of the polis's internal and external freedom and to be fully committed to maintaining its greatness and power. Oligarchs, on the other hand, did not hesitate to sacrifice their city's empire and independence in order to preserve their domestic rule and save their own skins.

The experiences of 404/403 were to prove this judgment all too correct. It was the rule of the Thirty that gave finality to the Athenians' equation of the idea of oligarchy with that of tyranny[181]—understandably, given this regime's brutality and despotism, which the sources condemn unanimously. It is not unlikely, however, that this experience affected Thucydides' depiction of the regime of the Four Hundred in 411/410. At any rate, the loss of most contemporary sources bars us from access to evidence that might permit a more neutral and generally valid assessment of oligarchy, including the role freedom might have played in this context. Isocrates, typically, offers no more than criticism of the tyranny of the Thirty and elsewhere of Lysander's decarchs—that is, of extreme oligarchies.

The program proclaimed by the oligarchs can be deduced from Xenophon's account and the speeches written by Lysias in the years just after the events. Power was to be exercised by the noble and best (*kaloi k'agathoi, beltistoi*), who, because of their personal qualities, would be able to govern for the good of the city.[182] At the same time, they would eliminate the negative effects of participation by the *kakoi* in government and guide those citizens who were as yet unqualified to rule toward competence and justice.[183] The criteria determining competence to rule were debated even among the oligarchs: for the moderates it was "those who have the means to be of service, whether with horses or shields" (those serving in cavalry and infantry; that is, the top three census classes), while the radical oligarchs apparently were concerned only with keeping the number as small as possible.[184]

The proclamation that oligarchy was "rule by the best" could not long hide the fact that this "fairest name" was merely a cloak for "most monstrous acts" (Lys. 12.78). From the beginning, the goal of the Thirty was to gain absolute power over the city and to have a free hand in government. Their internal discussions centered neither on policy issues nor on the welfare of the citizens but on how to safeguard their power and distribute it among themselves.[185] Hence, their regime was marked by despotic measures and terror, and they ruthlessly silenced opposition even within their own ranks. Like their decision to disarm the citizens, this was enough to recall the practices of tyrants. According to Xenophon, representatives of the radical wing even admitted openly that despite their large number they were a tyranny and intended to act accordingly.[186] Finally, these oligarchs, too, were willing, and this time realized their intention, to betray the city's independence in order to preserve their own power. A Spartan garrison was installed on the Acropolis only after the Thirty requested it,[187] and in their fight against the democrats in exile the Spartans were their strongest supporters.

Hence, in this case, too—indeed, here especially—the democratic catchword of freedom served several purposes: it was directed against the *douleia* of the city under a tyranny, of the demos under the few, and finally of Athens under the foreign domination of Sparta.[188] A crucial factor in the self-understanding of the Athenian democrats after 403 was that their heroic struggle had restored both the internal and the external freedom of their city. Awareness that Athens's power and greatness were intimately connected with its democratic government, which in turn drew its strength from navy and empire, was probably widespread already before the Peloponnesian War.[189] It was so clearly confirmed by the experiences of 411 and especially 404/403 that in the thinking of Athenian democrats the interdependence of internal and external freedom became a virtual dogma, and freedom, power, and greatness of their city were joined inseparably with democracy. In contrast, it was taken for granted that for the sake of their own advantage and power, oligarchs would accept the weakness and insignificance of their city and even deliver it up to foreign rule.[190] Examples of this, too, were known from earlier times, though they had never had such drastic consequences. The same constellation would again play an important role a few decades later in the confrontation between the Greek poleis and Philip of Macedon.[191]

Freedom as the Monopoly of Democracy

Contemporary statements concerning the democratic concept of freedom are thus consistent. They unanimously present it in stark contrast to exclusive claims to power and tyrannical tendencies typical of oligarchy, and they reflect the importance of external aspects even in this context. This concept thus proved remarkably comprehensive: it covered the whole range of concerns of the polis, both internally and externally. It is not surprising, therefore, that the notion of absolute freedom, similarly based on the internal and external rule of the demos, was also conceived in democratic Athens.[192]

The extant evidence leaves no doubt that within the community freedom was the monopoly of democracy. Brasidas's statement, mentioned earlier, is thus unique; no trace can be found of an oligarchic concept competing with that of the democrats.[193] This makes sense, for such a concept would have been coupled with a restrictive definition of citizenship, which in turn, like the aristocratic notion of proportional equality, would have emphasized the political superiority of a limited group. Inevitably, highlighting the exclusion and thus the "servitude" of all the rest, this would have deprived such a concept of all its propaganda value and provoked suspicion and resolute opposition. Boasting of its power, the imperial democratic city could afford to glorify itself as *eleutherōtatē polis,* deriving its supreme power and freedom precisely from its rule over the allies. No one else could do this. By voicing similar claims, oligarchic circles, normally not in power in Athens, would have advertised their intention to rule not just over outsiders but especially over citizens, and thus been accused of tyrannical ambition. Unlike demands for adequate political consideration of economic, social, or intellectual differences, the nonfreedom of citizens could be justified neither morally nor politically by qualitative (that is, positive) arguments. By contrast, however much the oligarchs contested it, the democratic concept of freedom presupposed the participation in government of all citizens and was therefore comprehensive and integrative, both in theory and in practice.[194]

Two other considerations must have helped prevent the development of an oligarchic concept of freedom. Since nonparticipation was interpreted as being ruled, dominated, and, in the polemical terminology of the time, "enslaved," only institutionalized political participation could guarantee freedom. For the democrats, therefore, sharing in power was essentially a means to an end: their goal was life in freedom and happiness. For the oligarchs, it was an end in itself, a self-evident claim with intrinsic value, based on a manifold sense of superiority. The oligarch had to rule, not to be free, but to realize a social and political function that he considered his by natural right and long tradition.[195]

We know, moreover, that the concept of equality was divided, claimed, and interpreted differently by democrats and oligarchs.[196] The reason was that equality had originally been and always remained an aristocratic notion. It could thus become an important oligarchic principle. The idea was then adopted and reinterpreted by constitutions that extended political participation to nonaristocratic parts of the citizen body. The result, as democracy gradually developed, was an increasingly broadened democratic concept of equality. Similarly, democrats and oligarchs interpreted the concept of *dēmos* in starkly contrasting ways.[197] An analogous development was not possible with freedom because it had never been an aristocratic value concept. The concept of political freedom within the community first arose in the isonomic polis of the early fifth century. So long as it was directed only against tyranny, it was unobjectionable to the elite. However, when it became the palladium of democracy in its defense against oligarchic claims to exclusive power, it quickly became the target of attacks by opponents. Not only, therefore, was it impossible for the oligarchs to turn to an alternative notion of political freedom, but the denunciation of the democratic understanding of freedom became one of their main ideological weapons: what democracy passed off as freedom was really anarchy, lawlessness, and chaos, to which they opposed the higher value of aristocratic *eunomia*.

Evidence for this ideological battle is found from the early fourth century on. It was expressed most pointedly in the demand to restore an "ancestral constitution" (*patrios politeia*), in which freedom was not confused with lack of restraint and lawlessness, and *nomos* controlled political life.[198] Similar views, however, are undoubtedly much older. Already in Pindar and Herodotus the demos's rule is characterized negatively by identifying the demos with impetuous, undisciplined crowds.[199] Most likely, therefore, when the concept of freedom was monopolized and ideologized by democracy, it immediately became the object of oligarchic polemics.

An Aristocratic-Oligarchic Counterconcept: The Fully Free Citizen

Still, oligarchic circles were apparently not content merely to polemicize against the democratic concept of freedom. There is some evidence to show that they tried to undermine it through a radically different interpretation of one of its primary assumptions and thereby to exploit the concept's political and propagandistic value for their own purposes. Typically, they focused on an aspect that had always been their main concern: the personal qualities needed to participate in government. The following remarks are based mostly on fourth-century statements. The rise of the views presented in them cannot be traced precisely. Hints in the extant evidence suggest, however, that, like the democratic ideology of freedom, they probably go back, at least in their essentials, to the second half of the fifth century. It is reasonable, therefore, to assume that the debates to be analyzed here, focusing on the concept of the "free citizen," also go back to the period of marked polarization between democracy and oligarchy.[200]

The characterization of aristocracy as rule by the noble and educated, oligarchy as rule by the rich, and democracy as rule by the free indicates that democracy emphasized personal freedom as the sole condition for the full exercise of citizen rights.[201] This was simply a succinct formula implying the rejection of further qualifications and the recognition of every citizen as a full citizen. The oligarchs countered with the claim that the constitution they preferred made possible the participation in government not of everyone who was legally free but of all who were truly and in every respect free. Only those who were economically independent qualified as such: they did not need to work for a living and (apart from operating their farms or estates) were able to devote themselves to the "liberal arts," to a higher "liberal education," and to service for the community. The concept of the "free citizen" was thus defined restrictively: most citizens recognized by the democrats as free were not really free; by aristocratic criteria they were dependent or unfree and therefore no more qualified to exercise full civic rights than metics, foreigners, or slaves.

The redefinition of the concept of the free citizen was therefore central to the oligarchic argument. The result, a split into two totally divergent interpretations of this concept, is closely analogous to the previously mentioned divergent definitions of the concepts of civic equality and *dēmos*. The oligarchic interpretation was based on a high valuation of social status and prestige and, like most aristocratic ideas, derived its (secondary) political effect from the general and primary social superiority claimed by the aristocratic and wealthy upper class. The democratic interpretation, in contrast, arose from the collective claim to freedom of the entire citizen body; it was rooted primarily in the political realm but, because it upgraded the citizen's social status, had an impact on the social realm as well. Reduced to a simple formula, this conceptual contrast mirrors that between the recent, primarily political identity of the democratic citizen and the traditional, primarily social identity of the aristocrat.

The oligarchs did not invent this idea but rather utilized for their own purposes a long-established, specialized meaning of *eleutheros*. In the sixth century at the latest—probably much earlier—a detailed typology of the slave and, by contrast, of the freeman had emerged that included traits of physical appearance, character, and behavior. The word *eleutherios*, coined specifically for this context, could be used flexibly within this typology in the sense of "what is owed to, appropriate for, or typical of a freeman" but also assumed the specialized meaning of "generous," "liberal."[202]

This specialization seems to be very old.[203] It has an exact correspondence in Latin (*liberalis*), is represented in German (*freigebig*), and in both ancient languages is closely linked with the conception of good and noble descent (*eugenēs, gennaios, ingenuus, generosus*). This conception in turn can be connected with the original contrast (inferred etymologically for *eleutheros* and its opposite) between those within and those outside the descent or tribal group (including among the outsiders war captives and slaves).[204] It is thus possible that the archaic elite, although showing little interest in the political potential of freedom, nevertheless appropriated some elements essential for status and social prestige. At any rate, numerous statements in late-fifth- and fourth-century authors name as characteristics of the freeman the ability to avoid manual and dependent labor, to participate in political life, and to enjoy a higher education and a refined lifestyle. Just as these abilities are available not to every freeman but only to the wealthy elite, *eleutheros* and *eleutherios* not infrequently assume in specific contexts the explicit meaning of "aristocratic," "noble," "respectable."[205] Some fourth-century writers distinguish the "free" not only from slaves but also from *banausoi* (those involved in base and vulgar professions): artisans, craftsmen, shopkeepers, day laborers, and similar persons who earn their living through an "unfree occupation." Thus, by that time "being free" included a marked aristocratic component far exceeding legal status. In the view of writers critical of democracy, only those citizens who were fully free in this elevated sense ought to enjoy full political rights.[206]

Some scholars have accordingly felt justified in postulating an early aristocratic concept of freedom, for which they advanced bits of circumstantial evidence. As we saw in earlier chapters, this view is likely to be wrong, especially in such a generalized form.[207] At most it holds for the special concept of *eleutherios,* which split off very early from *eleutheros.* The fact that in the fifth century one particular interpretation of the concept of the freeman overlapped with that of the highborn is not to be explained by the assumption that aristocrats saw themselves always as freemen par excellence and that "being free" always also meant "being noble, rich, and powerful." The answer rather lies in the opposite direction.

The typological traits of the free person were based in their entirety (not only in the special components suggested by *eleutherios*) on those of the elite, not the non-elite freemen. The reason is that ancient lines of social demarcation, never completely erased, naturally suggested such an orientation. Greek elite society, predominant for centuries, was accustomed to regarding all non-elite persons, including the overwhelming majority of freemen, as "mean," "base," and "bad" (*kakoi, ponēroi*)[208] and to placing the most important social dividing line between aristocrats and nonaristocrats. From this perspective, aesthetic, psychological, and moral distinctions of a typological kind could be drawn, not between slaves and non-elite free, but only between slaves and non-elite free on one side and the elite on the other. A positive value concept could become conscious and effective as such only if it was aligned with the ways of living and thinking, and the values and characteristics, of the elite. Thus, what was typical of the freeman had to be as close as possible to what was typical of the nobleman.

The more the value of individual freedom entered consciousness, was formulated explicitly, and became important in social and political life, the more it was probably elevated (at least in particular contexts) by integrating aristocratic elements. Although "what is typical of a freeman" and "what is typical of a nobleman" were not identical, the latter was useful to enhance the former, and the two tended to converge.[209] This tendency was probably accelerated and received political importance when an increasingly clear distinction emerged between various status categories among the free polis population (citizens, metics, freedmen, foreigners). Citizen status thereby was not only separated clearly from that of other categories of freemen but also elevated and imbued with the characteristics of higher quality. A new and increasingly effective dividing line emerged between citizens and noncitizens. It deprived the traditional separation between elite and non-elite of its unique significance and gradually replaced it, at least in contexts that were most important for public life.[210] This process began in the early sixth century, gained momentum toward the end of that century and after the Persian Wars, and essentially came to an end about the middle of the fifth century, marked by Pericles' citizenship law of 451/450. The consequence must have been that the citizens as an exclusive group, now sharply separated from others, clearly privileged, and distinctly elitist in their thinking, saw themselves as the real freemen and applied the typological characteristics of the free—perhaps in heightened form—primarily to themselves. From this specific perspective, then, it was natural to advance the criterion of personal freedom as the only qualification for full citizenship in democracy, and as virtually synonymous with citizenship, just as, strikingly, the sole references to specific democratic "civil liberties" concern rights belonging to a freeman in general (in contrast to the slave's lack of rights and protections).[211]

It is thus likely that the tendency, visible early on, to assimilate elements of the concept and typology of the freeman to the image of the nobleman was enhanced by the changes in awareness connected initially with the delimitation of the citizen body and the emergence of the concept of the citizen and then with the perfecting of democracy and the social and economic effects of the empire.[212] This tendency, to identify with the ideas, norms, and behavior of the elite, to "adapt upward," goes far beyond this particular context; it seems to be a pattern in all Greek (and probably all ancient) social and political thought and behavior. I cannot pursue this here but need only to point out, as has long been recognized, that in the course of democratization aristocratic forms of thinking and behavior were to a remarkable extent taken over by broader citizen classes.[213] One might tentatively speak of a tendency in the demos toward "aristocratization." This factor must have contributed significantly, for instance, to the increasing sense of exclusiveness among citizens, highlighted by the citizenship law, to their jealous protection of their economic and political privileges, and to their contempt for "dependent labor," that is, their reluctance to work for another person and thus to depend on someone else for their living.[214]

I see a connection with this factor as well in the absence of any effort to develop a differentiated system of representative government. The tendency instead was to turn the citizen into a professional participant in public life, a full-time citizen (polités), and to enable him to meet his ever-expanding civic duties by introducing daily pay for certain offices and functions.[215] The underlying idea—although never consciously or openly formulated and only very incompletely realized—probably was that in a democracy even the poor citizen should have the opportunity of doing what the nobleman had always done as a matter of course: to use his time as he wanted and to dedicate himself to service for the community. Hence, when democracy boasted that the only qualification it demanded for full citizenship was freedom, this concerned not only the citizen's personal status as a freeman but implicitly as well a whole range of ideas that reached far beyond legal status and moved the freeman, as a full citizen, close to the aristocrat.

It is precisely this claim that the oligarchic opposition resisted with great determination. They seized upon the long-established typology of the freeman, took it seriously with all its implications, and, enhancing it even further, postulated its validity only for those who, because of descent, wealth, education, and innate ability, were truly able to live and act in accordance with its claims. The image of the freeman, modeled after the image of the nobleman, was now for the first time appropriated by the elite with a conscious view to exploiting its potential in political life. The oligarchs, therefore, did not reactivate an archaic aristocratic concept of political freedom —a concept that had never existed in the first place. Rather, they took over and developed further an understanding of the value and significance of personal freedom for the citizen as (in Aristotle's words) a "political being" (*zōon politikon*), an understanding that had arisen without, even in opposition to, the elite and had long since been politicized by democracy.

6.3. CONCLUSIONS

The contrast to autocratic, tyrannical rule that had emerged as vital in the experience of the Persian Wars remained essential for the concept of internal political freedom throughout the fifth century. In fact, during the Peloponnesian War it became even more pronounced. For a long time freedom was not associated with a specific form of government. Its association with democracy can be traced in extant sources only to the beginning of the last third of the century and is probably not much older. In substance, this association presupposes a marked opposition between oligarchy and democracy; external factors—in particular, the acutely felt contrast to the radically different social and political system of Sparta—may have intensified it. The conflict in the 440s between Pericles and Thucydides, son of Melesias, offers the earliest possible context for this development, but lacking support in the sources, proof is impossible; thus, the similarly intense conflicts of the late 430s remain equally possible.

This time frame for the identification of freedom with democracy is corroborated by an analogous change in the terminology of the citizen's right to speak: a new term for "freedom of speech" (*parrhēsia*) was coined for similar reasons at the end of the 430s at the latest and was used alongside a long-familiar and greatly popular term for "equality of speech" (*isēgoria*). Both these developments in the "conceptual field" of internal freedom reflect fundamental changes in the self-perception and self-representation of democracy and its citizens. They occurred at the time when the contrast between democracy and oligarchy became ideologically marked and polarization increased, not only on specific policies but also, as the Old Oligarch's pamphlet illustrates, on constitutional principles. At the same time, as this text as well as the constitutional debates inserted in Herodotus's *Histories* and Euripides' *Suppliant Women* document, discussions were rampant about the best constitution and especially the advantages and disadvantages of democracy.[216]

Precisely because of its association with full civic equality, this aspect of freedom remained the monopoly of democracy. It comprised various components that can be deduced from late-fifth-century discussions and were later brought together in Aristotle's succinctly formulated principal categories of "alternatively ruling and being ruled" and "living as one likes." They correspond to a more political-institutional and a more social orientation of freedom and became highly important for the self-understanding of democracy. Both aspects were attacked by opponents in intense polemics that globally condemned the democratic concept of freedom as a chaotic miscreation. For both ideological and practical reasons, however, the aristocratic-oligarchic opposition to democracy failed to develop its own concept of freedom that might have competed directly and equally with the democratic concept. Instead, they insisted on the elite's traditional claim to superiority and power, restricting the qualification to govern to their own class and, at most, the "middle classes" fit for military service according to the traditional criteria of hoplite warfare.

The global exclusion of the lower classes, deemed unfit in every respect, from participation in government was not only justified in theory but in 411 and 404, in times of great crisis and defeat, also realized in practice. On both occasions, extreme oligarchic tendencies soon prevailed: a terrorist regime was installed, and the sacrifice of the polis's independence was considered not too high a price for preserving oligarchic rule. As a result, oligarchy was discredited as a viable alternative to democracy, and the democratic concept of freedom was strengthened in its manifold aspects, which emphatically included the assertion of the polis's power and independence. Only in a particular area, concerning the notion of the fully free citizen (which was elaborated upon by fourth-century political philosophy), was an attempt made to turn the appeal of freedom against democracy and to the benefit of aristocratic ideas of society and government.

$$\sim 7 \sim$$

Summary and Final Considerations

7.1. SUMMARY

My methodological principle has been that the use of the concept of freedom needs to be studied in each period separately, strictly on the basis of the sources available for that period. This naturally requires that the preserved record be taken seriously, despite enormous loss of evidence. This requirement is in turn based on the working hypothesis that it is indeed possible to understand and explain a concept's use and development, as it is retrievable from contemporary sources, by placing it in its political and social context.

The question posed by this hypothesis can certainly be answered positively. Even though it remains possible that the preserved record may have misled us on occasion, the sources offer a clear picture. A political concept of freedom was not developed before the early fifth century—neither in the sphere of foreign relations nor in that of domestic politics. The idea of a citizen's freedom within his community, initially seen in contrast solely to his oppression by tyranny, was given a positive content and associated with a particular constitution even much later. We can clearly discern the conditions that made the development of such conceptions possible, desirable, and finally necessary, and we understand why without these conditions—especially in a time that lacked a ready-made terminology—an awareness of the value of political freedom, and corresponding terms and concepts, did not and could not arise earlier.

These results also allow us to conclude, with all due caution, that on the whole the surviving sources inform us reliably on these matters. Our methodological premise has thus proved correct. The reason probably is not only that, after all, a representative selection of the most important texts from each period did survive but still more that, because of the highly political character of Greek society, even texts without explicitly political content evince a strong political engagement. We were able to observe in many cases that politically relevant terms indeed tend to show up in archaic and early classical poetry at about the time in which, for reasons that make historical sense, they assumed great importance. This in turn justifies our frequent reliance on the argument from silence, that is, the deliberate use in our historical reconstruction of that which did not (yet) exist. I readily admit that this inevitably entails an element of uncertainty: conclusions reached in this way can never claim to be more than the most plausible that are achievable under given circumstances, and new discoveries may force us to revise these conclusions. This is true for all investigations that are forced to work with highly incomplete data. Only with this premise is it possible at all to undertake a study of Greek concepts that have their roots in, and thus must be traced from, the early archaic period. What is crucial here is to work with a clear and explicit methodology; otherwise, all we can achieve remains guesswork.

That a political concept of freedom emerged in the early fifth century corresponds to the *terminus ante quem* suggested by the extant sources. The concept apparently did not yet exist in the archaic period. Awareness of the positive value of any kind of freedom (and thus the ability to coin a term for it) presupposes a strong and general consciousness of the negative value of the corresponding kind of nonfreedom (and with it, as a rule, the corresponding negative terminology). Moreover, the ability to translate such general consciousness into *political* thought, terminology, and action depends on the significance of such consciousness on the communal level and/or among those classes that matter most in the community.[1] In early Greece both the dominant elite and the large (and communally important) class of independent farmers took their personal freedom for granted. They considered its loss a remote possibility, hardly ever to be experienced in real life, and beyond ordinary human control. As long as this was the general attitude, freedom could not become an object of reflection and a nucleus around which further development of the concept could crystallize.[2]

Archaic evidence shows that awareness and terminology were more advanced in the sphere of nonfreedom than in that of freedom and that there was apparently no sufficiently strong impetus to thematize the value of personal and even less of political freedom. Several reasons account for this: the specific structure of society (in which large *oikoi* under powerful elite leaders formed the centers of power and protection), the value system of the nobility (which focused on competitive virtues, status, and honor based on excellence in fighting), and the slow development of a clearly defined political sphere (in which new systems of reference and norms of behavior could take root). Moreover, although *douloi* were occasionally contrasted as unfree persons with *eleutheroi* (especially when emphasis was placed on their loss of freedom), like other categories of dependent persons they were seen far more often as servants in opposition to their master (*despotēs*).

In this specific context, it was the terminology of servitude that first assumed political meaning. Subjection (*doulosunē*) to a tyrant, later equated directly with "slavery" and thus with nonfreedom, was initially understood primarily as subordination, servitude: the citizen was *doulos* in the sense of having to serve or obey the tyrant as his master (*despotēs*).[3] The alternative opposition *doulos-eleutheros*, which had long been used in private life, apparently was not politicized at the same time, perhaps because two concepts that already existed in contemporary political thinking were capable of expressing adequately the essential aspects of the contrast to tyranny. One was that of good order (*eunomia*), which was suspended by *dusnomia* or *anomia* ("bad order" and "lack of order" brought about by tyranny) and needed to be restored for the sake of the community's well-being. The other was that of political equality (*isonomia*), in the sense that all citizens who met the qualifying criteria valid at the time had an equal right to participate in the exercise of power (which was temporarily monopolized by the tyrant). Thus, as long as political thinking focused on order (*nomos*) and equality— and as long as the fight against tyranny was carried on almost exclusively by the aristocracy, who were interested first in power, then in equality— tyranny could not spur a concept of political freedom, even though it was blamed for the *doulosunē* of the polis and its citizens. And when tyranny was overthrown and broader citizen classes achieved political equality, it was for the longest time the defense and further development of such expanded *isonomia* that held highest priority.

In the sphere of relations between communities, too, conditions were lacking that could have prompted a high valuation of freedom, and here, too, another concept was initially more important. Wars were usually fought not for conquest but for spoils or over disputed boundaries. Conditions and institutions were lacking that would have made it possible to rule over other communities or to create a territorial empire. As the result of territorial expansion, when it occurred, both on a large scale (as in Sparta's conquest of Messenia) and in smaller ways (when polis territories were "rounded off"), the territory of the defeated was integrated into that of the victorious community; the former ceased to exist as a separate entity and became, in whatever form, part of the latter. Individually, some of the defeated may have suffered the loss of personal freedom, although enslavement of conquered populations seems to have been rare in the century or so before the Persian Wars. On the polis level, it was normally the problem of protecting possessions and territory, rarely that of communal survival, and hardly ever that of the preservation of independence that challenged the citizens. Thus, at least in mainland Greece, freedom was not an issue. The concept of being saved and surviving (*sōtēria*)—of central importance already in Homer for both individual and community—proved adequate to needs and political conditions until the end of the archaic period.

This conclusion is perfectly compatible with the existence of various forms of political dependency that may later have been perceived as partial freedom or, indeed, nonfreedom. Even in the private sphere, voluntary subordination under the protection of a powerful figure was compared with the relationship of follower or retainer to leader or lord, not to the status of a slave; a client was never considered a slave. Accordingly, a voluntary alliance concluded between a weak polis that was threatened by an overpowering neighbor and a strong polis that demanded from its partner unconditional political and military allegiance in return for protection of its communal independence (such as that between Plataea and Athens in the late sixth century) did not, by contemporary standards, in and of itself constitute a relationship of rule or domination and hence did not affect freedom. This is also true of the sometimes close dependence of colonies on their mother city (as in Corinth's case) or the extensive Spartan alliance system in the Peloponnese. The origin and purpose of such relationships and the form in which they were established played as important a role in the assessment of any given case as did preexisting traditions, mutual interests, and opportunities to influence decisions that affected both partners. Such exceptionally close ties between independent poleis were not described as *douleia* even in the late fifth century, when the concept of political freedom had long become common fare. Hence, it is highly unlikely that at the time of their emergence such relationships had sufficient power to shape awareness in the direction necessary to produce a concept of freedom.

The archaic period, then, did not create a political concept of freedom because it did not need one, that is, because those political aspects on which this concept focused never reached a sufficient level of importance. But a decisive condition for its genesis did appear in this period in the evolution and social and institutional consolidation of the polis, which remained the politically and culturally predominant form of community in Greece until the end of the classical period.[4] The Near Eastern empires of the third to first millennia B.C.E., the Achaemenid Persian Empire, and probably to some extent also the Greek palace states of the Bronze Age were characterized by authoritarian governments and steeply graded, hierarchical social structures. Subordination and obedience were consequently regarded as the highest virtues, and this prevented a high valuation of freedom.[5] By contrast, the polis communities that evolved roughly from the tenth to seventh centuries in a process that is still somewhat obscure were shaped, on the one hand, by the collective predominance of family groups that increasingly developed the characteristics of an aristocracy and, on the other, by large numbers of non-elite citizens, independent farmers, who played an indispensable role in the polis army and assembly. From the start, therefore, the values of the polis were not those of subordination and obedience. Rather, the elite focused on individual achievement, status, leadership, and influence, based on collective participation (equality) in power, while for the community as a whole and the non-elite class of farmers and soldiers, it was most important to realize a traditional good order (*eunomia*) that guaranteed justice and protection from abuses of power.

Freedom (as a claim and individual right) became a political issue for the first time when debt bondage, long familiar in Greece and common among early societies around the Mediterranean, spread rapidly and was used with increasing ruthlessness as a resource in elite power struggles. Threatened by bondage and enslavement, large numbers of both dependent and still independent farmers banded together and confronted the elite with their demands. In Athens, this crisis was resolved by Solon's reforms. The abolition of debt bondage established individual freedom as the citizens' inalienable right. The issue, as a result, lost its immediate political relevance. Freedom disappeared from the political agenda without having found expression as a lasting political concept.

The crisis of Solon's time was part of a widespread process of change, marked by social conflicts and the emergence of powerful individuals in the roles of tyrants and lawgivers. This process resulted, in the course of the sixth century, in the formal political integration of at least those citizen classes that had enough economic capacity to qualify for the increasingly formalized hoplite army, in the development of "isonomic" constitutions and differentiated political institutions,[6] and in the creation of organizational structures required for ruling over others. All these changes also prompted sharper distinctions within the polis between citizens and non-citizens, an increased consciousness of the community's place and role in international relations, and new forms of political thought and behavior.[7]

It is in these fully developed poleis, with a broadened and solidified base and a more self-conscious and self-confident citizen body, that tyranny was finally perceived as incompatible with a community of free citizens: here lies the origin of the antityranny ideology known in the classical period. However implacably individual tyrants may have been opposed by their fellow aristocrats, accommodation to tyranny was made easier for the aristocracy by common class traditions and claims to exclusive power and by the growing need to ward off demands raised by non-elite classes. The latter had long profited from the suspension of elite rivalries and abuses brought about by tyranny. Eventually, however, having attained isonomy and facing the unpredictable attitudes of aristocratic families, they began to judge tyranny from a different perspective: freedom from tyranny became the crucial precondition for maintaining political equality.

It was probably only this new form of integrated polis that was able—though not always willing—to muster the uncompromising determination to face such seemingly insurmountable odds as the Athenians and later the allied Greeks did in fighting the Persian invaders at Marathon and Salamis. To be sure, aristocrats contributed decisively to this struggle, but they did so within the framework of their changed poleis. Elsewhere, aristocracies, ruling their communities in more or less narrow oligarchic regimes, were still thinking and behaving according to long-standing traditions of their class. They felt connected primarily to their peers in other poleis or even abroad and failed to develop an exclusive commitment to the needs of their own polis.[8] Lacking sufficient integration into the polis, being flexible and interested primarily in maintaining their own power, they were often able to accommodate themselves early on with their community's potential enemies. Although aristocrats did not necessarily consider this desirable, their primary goal of maintaining their domestic rule was compatible with conceding, to various degrees, the independence of their community. This was as evident to foreign powers that counted Greek poleis among their subjects as it was to the Greeks themselves, and it confirms that political freedom was not a prime value for the elite. During the Peloponnesian War, when political ambition and rivalries soared, this phenomenon came to haunt even the Athenians.[9]

Such flexibility in foreign relations was not an option for non-elite citizens who had only recently achieved political equality. If they did not want to sacrifice what they had gained, they had to risk everything and fight. Safeguarding the independence of the polis became for them the condition for maintaining their equality in the polis. Thus, whether in domestic politics or foreign relations, political consciousness of the value of freedom could arise only when on the basis of far-reaching changes isonomic constitutions emerged, when in many poleis broader citizen classes came to share power, and when a new political awareness developed. In short, only the isonomic polis had the ability to form a political concept of freedom.[10]

The potential inherent in this development was realized when a profound and unique experience hugely enhanced the associations latent in the concept of freedom, concentrated them, as it were, and filled them with enough urgency to make the creation of a new concept necessary. This was the experience of the Persian Wars. True, the Greeks of Asia Minor had long been familiar with domination by a foreign power, the concomitant loss of freedom, and various infringements on the autonomy of their communities. Although we lack positive evidence, we cannot rule out the possibility that to these Greeks the notion of polis freedom had already become a value and ideal and thus also an important political concept—not least during their great, though ultimately unsuccessful, revolt against the Persians in the 490s. Athens and Eretria had supported this revolt and perhaps brought such ideas back home. All other mainland Greeks lacked such experiences; they probably felt no incentive to revise their traditional canon of values and to find a prominent place among them for freedom.

In 490 and in 480/479, however, these very Greeks, facing Persian invasions that aimed at revenge and subjection, were confronted with a threat of hitherto inconceivable proportions. In this situation, a vast leap in the consciousness of freedom occurred. According to the extant evidence, it was only and exactly in those years that the noun *eleutheria* was coined—a sure sign that the values embodied in this word had gained greatly in importance and that an urgent need was now felt for a convenient way to express them. Emphasis now shifted from traditional conceptions to a coherent group of new concepts that were dominated by polis freedom and a collective distinction from the barbarians, who were perceived as inferior and slavish. By the end of the 470s, the basic traits of the representation of the Persian Wars as Greek "freedom wars" were fully developed.

At the same time, the Athenians (and potentially other Greeks) faced the danger that foreign rule would cause the imposition of tyranny—a linkage experienced previously by the Ionian poleis. Now for the first time they had compelling reasons to associate subjection to tyranny not only with servitude under a master but also specifically with nonfreedom, and the prevention or overthrow of tyranny with freedom. As a result, the idea of the polis's internal freedom emerged as an independent counterconcept to tyranny and was juxtaposed to the concept of equality that had previously been predominant in this sphere.

This reconstruction of conceptual developments is confirmed by a striking religious analogy. Investigation of the origins and function of the cult of Zeus Eleutherios has revealed a direct connection in time, and partly also in locale, to the victory over the Persians. The god's primary function as protector of the polis's external independence was soon extended to cover the polis's internal freedom as well. Yet the Athenians never associated the cult of this god with the overthrow of tyranny in their own city in the late sixth century, although this event and the subsequent veneration of the Tyrannicides soon became the core of an elaborate civic ideology focusing on democracy and liberty. This suggests that it was indeed only the potential repercussions of a Persian victory on their constitution that prompted them to realize the value of freedom in opposition to tyranny.

Religious evidence also confirms the priority, visible in archaic poetry, of the concept of *sōtēria* (survival, deliverance) over that of freedom. The cult of Zeus Eleutherios most likely arose from a widespread and much older cult of Zeus Soter—a change that reflects the recent emancipation of one specific aspect among many included in the broad concept of *sōtēria*. It would seem, then, that throughout the archaic period the concept of *sōtēria* comprised a range of contents that potentially overlapped with freedom. It became indispensable to formulate the latter aspect as a specific and independent concept (*eleutheria*) when drastically changed conditions placed great emphasis on it and endowed it with sufficient value. An analogous process of conceptual emancipation occurred later when—again due to a drastic shift in emphasis caused by wholly new conditions—the aspect of political self-determination was separated out from the range of meanings included in *eleutheria,* and a new word (*autonomia*) was coined to express it.

The origin of the political concept of freedom is thus firmly anchored in the historical context of the Persian Wars. It is worth repeating that this concept, so basic and central from then on, was discovered as a political value when a specific form of community, evolving under exceptional conditions (the Greek polis supported by equal citizens), dared to resist subjugation by a vast territorial and authoritarian empire.[11] Empires, of course, had existed before, and all of them were created by subjecting peoples and cities. But neither those who submitted to their rule nor those who resisted successfully had previously viewed the outcome of such confrontations primarily from the perspective of freedom and servitude. The reason essentially is that neither the social and power structures nor the value systems of these com-

munities and states had ever accorded this particular aspect great importance, let alone priority.[12]

But in Greece the necessary conditions existed, and the way was paved
by the earlier emergence of the idea of political servitude. In conceptual development, the experience of the Persian Wars thus had the effect of activating a latent potential. The highly dramatic forms of this experience not
only gave the newly discovered concept great and lasting prominence but
directed its further evolution into specific channels. By spectacularly rising
to the challenge, the isonomic polis proved successful and was strengthened
decisively. Freedom and equality became its proudly perceived and propagated hallmarks. Initially, however, freedom primarily indicated, negatively,
that the polis was "not being ruled" by an outside power, nor the citizens by
a tyrant. Equality, in contrast, was the positive designation of the condition
attained by the citizens under their constitution. For a long time, therefore,
the political development toward democracy took place under the banner
of equality, while *eleutheria* served primarily as a catchword highlighting the
defense of this "constitution of equality" against actual or imagined threats
by potential tyrants.

Moreover, the non-Greek ("barbarian") world was for the first time seen
collectively in contrast to the Greek world as a whole, and this contrast was
equated with a pointed opposition between the world of the free and that of
slaves ruled over by a despotic king. Although the Greeks thus recognized
freedom as the true general characteristic of their social and political order,
it did not take them long to distinguish within this free Greek universe various degrees of freedom. The most important models were, on the one side,
the freedom of the Spartans, perceived as self-centered and restricted by
the compulsion of a rigorously applied *nomos,* and, on the other, the more
open, more liberal freedom of the Athenians, which, although also committed to observing the *nomoi,* was presented as based far more on the ethos
of voluntary subordination to and responsibility for the good of the community (their own as well as the larger community of Hellas). The experience of the Persian Wars thus supplied the impulse for the development of
a variety of ideas and perceptions connected with freedom. Their beginnings
are visible in the first decade after 480, and the works of Herodotus, Euripides, and Thucydides reveal the entire spectrum in various stages of elaboration and critical analysis.

In yet another respect the Persian Wars initiated a process that profoundly influenced the development of the freedom concept. The Athenians
used their hegemony in the Delian League and the continuation after 478 of

the war for freedom against the Persians to establish and consolidate their rule over the allies. For the first time, one Greek polis exerted power on a large scale over many other Greek poleis, and for the first time, this process, involving both the formation of power and empire and the loss of freedom, was observed, discussed, and criticized by the vast public of the entire Greek world. Freedom and its opposite thus became increasingly important factors in interstate debates and negotiations. As a result, the Greeks applied the political terminology of servitude, domination, and freedom to relations not only between Greeks and barbarians but among Greeks themselves. Distinctions between a value-neutral and a negative-polemical terminology (*archē* and *hupēkooi* versus *turannis* and *douloi*) were now sharpened and intensified. Moreover, as soon as Athenian rule was recognized as such and the situation of the allies was understood as *doulosunē*, Athenian mechanisms of exercising power began to be perceived specifically as elements of nonfreedom, and the concept of political servitude was defined more precisely. Thus, it became possible, not simply to understand *eleutheria* in the general sense of "not being ruled" or "unfree," but rather to conceptualize it positively and precisely by distinguishing individual elements of freedom. As a result, the texts of treaties began expressly to record such elements of freedom in order to protect the partners by closing "loopholes" and reducing undefined areas that might encourage abuses. Athenian imperial rule thus contributed significantly to prompting reflection on interstate relations and to their definition, classification, and regulation.[13]

The allies' loss of sovereignty, caused by the transformation of the Delian League into an Athenian empire, was first perceived in the sphere of interstate relations. But soon Athens began to interfere in the allies' internal affairs as well. As this tendency intensified, the allies' ability to maintain communal self-determination became one of their primary concerns. Consequently, this aspect of polis freedom attracted much more attention than before. It was separated out from *eleutheria* and given expression in a new term, *autonomia*. The importance the concept of self-determination gained in the second half of the fifth century is reflected as well in the appearance of other terms formed with the *auto*-component. They either give a particular slant to the general idea (for example, by emphasizing citizenship or power, as in *autopolitēs* and *autokratōr*) or focus on individual aspects of it (such as jurisdiction or taxation, as in *autodikos* and *autotelēs*). The concept of communal self-sufficiency (*autarkeia*) also describes a specific aspect of a community's independence; it soon became an important part of Athens's ideology of power and freedom.

The first signs of a propagandistic use of the newly discovered concept of freedom appear immediately after the Persian Wars. In fact, *eleutheria* quickly emerged as a central component of political propaganda and as a formula that could be used almost arbitrarily—occasionally even to denote its opposite. In particular, the Athenians based their right to hegemony and imperial rule on their unique merits in maintaining Greek freedom during the Persian Wars and on their claim to having protected the freedom of their allies ever since (externally against the Persians and internally from tyrants and oligarchs). Conversely, the more opposition and hatred they met within their sphere of influence, and the more challenged they felt from outside it, the more concerned they became to preserve their own freedom. As its politicians repeatedly emphasize in Thucydides, Athens found itself in the position of a tyrant who was able to maintain his freedom only by oppressing his subjects.

As tensions increased in the late 430s and war broke out between the Athenian and Spartan "power blocs," freedom became the object of an intense war of propaganda. Critical observers, however, could scarcely doubt that the catchword of "freedom for the Hellenes" (that is, for the Athenian subjects), propagated by Sparta and her allies, served the Peloponnesians as a useful pretext but as a war objective ranked far behind the requirements of their own security. Nevertheless, despite shortcomings in its implementation, such propaganda proved successful throughout the Peloponnesian War. Freedom was especially suitable for propaganda purposes because it corresponded to distinct needs and strong desires. Despite negative experiences and severe disillusionment, it retained the power to awaken new hopes and create new illusions. Nothing has changed in this respect to the present day. During the Peloponnesian War, this scenario was acted out on a grand scale for the first time in world history.

Orlando Patterson defines as "sovereignal freedom" "the power to act as one pleases, regardless of the wishes of others. . . . The sovereignally free person has the power to restrict the freedom of others or to empower others with the capacity to do as they please with others beneath them." On the individual level, he thinks, this concept is as old as that of "personal freedom." On the collective level, he agrees, it arose after the Persian Wars.[14] In my view, however, in Greece before the Persian Wars this component was not consciously perceived and expressed as a form of freedom. Rather, it was part of the concept of "master and lord." That a *despotēs* was naturally free was so obvious that it did not need to be said. All that mattered was his status and the power he had over others. The explicit connection of freedom with this concept was secondary, following upon the politicization of freedom.

Eleutheros, in fact, represented only one corner of a conceptual triangle at whose other corners stood *doulos* and *despotēs*. In this triangle, "freeman" and "master" were initially opposed independently to the dependent person (*doulos*) who in one case was unfree (a slave), in the other a servant (one who had to obey commands). *Eleutheros* was not yet explicitly contrasted to *despotēs*; the triangle remained open. When the master-servant antithesis was applied to political situations, it was at first, in the context of opposition to tyranny, *doulosunē* alone that became a political concept. Freedom became politicized when the slave-free antithesis gained political relevance in the Persian Wars. It now became clear that being politically free meant not only (or not primarily) being "not unfree," that is, not being a slave, but not being ruled in any way, that is, having no master at all. Now each of the three concepts stood in opposition to each of the other two; the triangle was closed.

Yet another relationship was soon added. The two antitheses to *doulos* were linked positively and eventually equated with each other: only the master who ruled over others was truly free. This was recognized originally in thinking of tyranny (or the tyrant-like absolute power of the Persian king or of Zeus, king of the gods), but it was the Athenians at the height of their imperial rule who first forged a specifically political conception of "sovereignal freedom." Literary and monumental evidence places this conception in the late Periclean period. It came close to serving the Athenians as a political doctrine. In its pursuit, they insisted resolutely on the absolute territorial, political, and moral sovereignty of their polis, demanded unrestricted recognition of the principle of equality in relations between major powers, and acted upon the understanding that power was an indispensable foundation of equality and therefore also of freedom. Since sufficient power could be won only by ruling over others, imperial rule became the prerequisite for freedom, and freedom in turn served again—but on a different level—as justification of imperial rule. This idea manifested itself most notably in the combination of "freedom and greatness" or "freedom and power" in Athenian self-representation and in the characterization of Athens—based on such greatness and power—as the "freest of all cities." The concept of self-sufficiency (*autarkeia*) gained political relevance in the same context: thanks to its *archē*, Athens had the means to satisfy all its needs and, to a degree previously unknown, to make itself independent of the outside world, self-sufficient, and powerful—in short, completely free.

Overall, I suggest, these concepts represented the Athenian ideological response to the massive challenge their power policies faced on the part of the Peloponnesians. Such claims were designed to boost the self-confidence of the Athenians themselves and to present to the outside world the defiant pride of the imperial city that was denounced by others as being a tyrant (*polis turannos*). In monumental form, the ideology of the "freest city" (*eleutherōtatē polis*) found its expression in the magnificent Stoa of Zeus Eleutherios in the Agora, begun about 430. Zeus Soter/Eleutherios, who had long been neglected in favor of Athena on the Acropolis, the protectress of Athenian imperial rule, was now, in the face of great new danger, revalued, elevated, and placed in the center of Athenian civic life.

All in all, then, Athens's rule over its empire is as important as the Persian Wars to understanding the development of the Greek concept of freedom. To this we must add a third crucial set of changes and experiences, which would not have existed without the other two but developed its own dynamic and brought to the fore some central components of freedom. This was Athenian democracy.

The democratic concept of freedom—or, more precisely, the identification of democracy with the freedom of the demos—resulted, like all other components of the concept of freedom, from a change in consciousness brought about by far-reaching political changes and shifts in political values. In its application to the polis's internal sphere, freedom was long defined only by contrast to tyranny; that is, it was not explicitly linked to a particular constitution. The development of democracy was initially dominated and stimulated by *isonomia,* the ideal of equal political rights for all full citizens. From about the 470s, the citizens' control over political institutions began to be viewed as the crucial element in all constitutions. Hence, the number and quality of those participating in government became the most important criteria to distinguish various constitutions and to create a new constitutional terminology that was brought to the fore by a series of important changes.

Such changes included the full realization of democracy in 462–450, with an increasingly active and self-confident participation of the middle and lower classes in political life, a new role played by the assembly in policy making, and the formulation of more specifically democratic policies. As a result, aristocratic or oligarchic beliefs and attitudes appeared increasingly incompatible with democratic ones. Awareness of such changes and differences prompted the coining of the word *dēmo-kratia* (probably in the 460s), which focused on control of power (*kratos*) by the demos and came to imply as a contrast the nonparticipation in power, and therefore subservience, of the demos under the rule of the few (*oligarchia*). *Dēmokratia* and *oligarchia* thus became mutually exclusive opposites. The shift of emphasis to the alternative of ruling or being ruled prompted an association with freedom and nonfreedom—especially in the polemical atmosphere of polarized political debates as they are attested in various periods of the fifth century. From then on, in the democrats' self-understanding, the citizens' freedom depended on the condition not only that they were not ruled by an individual or a small faction but that they themselves shared in and controlled power and government.

Accordingly, one essential element of the democratic concept of freedom was its foundation in institutions; protection of democratic freedom was assured above all by the strict implementation of rotation of offices (the principle of "ruling and being ruled in turn") and by virtually unrestricted freedom of speech in political meetings. Both of these principles could be expressed by the traditional value concepts of *isonomia* and *isēgoria,* which were now explicitly identified with freedom and given a new, comprehensive interpretation. Institutionally guaranteed political equality thus became a crucial condition for the freedom of the democratic citizens.

Another, equally important component was of a different nature. The Athenians became increasingly aware of the sharp contrast between their own political system and that of Sparta. They realized that democracy guaranteed them the greatest possible freedom in their private, social, and communal lives: it imposed the fewest restrictions and afforded them the most freedom of action and the best opportunity for self-fulfillment. It soon became a fixed topos that democracy allowed the citizen "to live as he likes."[15] More was behind this principle than unrestricted freedom, although opponents misinterpreted and attacked it as license and lawlessness, while supporters defended it as compatible, even necessarily linked, with respect for the *nomoi.* What mattered rather was that democracy wholly accepted the free citizen in his capacity as a free person and thereby enabled him fully to realize his personal potential in both private and public life. Here presumably lay one of the basic preconditions for the Athenian citizens' ability to develop a specifically political identity and to commit themselves to public service in extraordinary intensity—without being forced to do so by rigid social pressure.

As a corollary, it was recognized that those fundamental individual rights to which the freeman could lay claim were protected better in a democracy than in other political systems: equality before the law, protection of person and property, and most of all the elementary right of freely expressing one's opinion. It is instructive, therefore, that in the sequence of terms used for the right of speech a substantial change occurred around 430, at the latest (that is, not long after democracy appropriated freedom itself). The coining of *parrhēsia*, henceforth used alongside *isēgoria*, confirms both the shift in value from equality to freedom and the deep connection between the democratic concept of freedom and the values and characteristics essential for the freeman's liberty.

The identification of freedom with participation in government, so important to the democrats' self-understanding, was nothing other than the domestic equivalent of the specifically Athenian conception of "freedom through power" developed in the sphere of foreign relations. Yet the relationship between the internal and external spheres went considerably further. Internal freedom, realized by the rule of the demos in the polis, proved an indispensable prerequisite for the polis's external freedom based on imperial rule—which, in turn, guaranteed the continuity and stability of democratic freedom. Internal and external freedom were thus closely interconnected. Politicians and writers from the last third of the fifth century accepted this as a matter of course. Elaborating upon such ideas, Thucydides (or his source, perhaps even Pericles himself) combined the demos's internal rule (in democracy) and external domination (in the empire) into a comprehensive concept of power and rule which he connected with the idea of freedom, understood under the same double perspective: here lies the substance of Athens's characterization as the "freest city" (*eleutherōtatē polis*).

The relation between internal and external freedom also presented itself, though in a different way, as a problem to smaller poleis living in the shadow of the great ones. For them a broad concept of freedom along the Athenian model was illusory. They were too weak and torn apart by conflicts between factions that called themselves "oligarchic" and "democratic." Externally, they thus had to content themselves with sacrificing parts of their sovereignty in exchange for gaining a share in the collective freedom, as it were, that the hegemonic power guaranteed against third parties. (This was also the main argument the Athenians used to justify their rule.) Internally, democrats and oligarchs alike tried to secure power and freedom for their own group and to preserve the highest possible degree of domestic autonomy by attaching themselves closely to one or the other "protective power." Because resources and conditions in these small poleis were limited and there were few opportunities to develop new policies or deflect energies and tensions away from the community, domestic conflicts were often carried on with extreme intensity and violence, and the question of domination in the polis became one of simple survival. Such conflicts at the same time afforded the hegemonic or imperial powers opportunities for intervention, which they often used to establish constitutions that were in tune with their own and thus likely to secure their rule. The conclusion reached by Alfred Heuss, that only relatively large and strong poleis could afford completely independent (and, consequently, relatively tolerant) domestic policies is certainly correct.[16]

7.2. CHARACTERISTICS OF THE GREEK CONCEPT OF FREEDOM

In a different kind of summary, I will finally attempt to isolate five characteristics of the Greek concept of freedom that I consider central. These are its focus on collectivity and community, its foundation in the non-aristocratic middle and lower classes, its politicization and ideologization, its broad claims and comprehensive scope, and its tendency to interweave political and social concerns. Some observations on the contrasting content and characteristics of the Roman concept of freedom and the context in which it emerged may help define certain of these distinguishing features more sharply. The following brief sketch is intended solely for the purpose of comparison and does not aim at completeness. It is based necessarily on the richly documented late republican period. I have discussed elsewhere what aspects are applicable to earlier centuries—and why just these.[17]

Neither in Rome's early period nor in the age of imperial expansion did external freedom (the community's or state's independence) ever become a determining factor. Especially during the early republic, when the freedom concept first took shape, Rome often struggled for survival; later it fought for predominance and expansion of its territory, but hardly to preserve its freedom.[18] *Libertas* therefore assumed significance and a political function exclusively in the sphere of internal politics.

The late Roman republic knew a decidedly aristocratic concept of freedom that focused on the traditional aristocratic order as a whole. It included in particular the *auctoritas* (influence, authority) of the senate, representing the collective claim to leadership of the whole senatorial class, and the *dignitas* (rank, status, based on merits of individual and family) of individual senators. These components of *libertas* served primarily to protect the senate's supremacy, which was challenged from two sides: by the demands of populist politicians (*populares*), who, in rejecting traditional aristocratic prerogatives, emphasized the freedom of the people (*libertas populi*), and by the ambitions of powerful individuals, who threatened the very foundation of aristocratic equality and rule. This component of the freedom concept essentially emerged during the crisis of the republic in the late second and first centuries B.C.E. and was therefore late and secondary.

What constituted the liberty of the Roman people was not their ability to govern and participate actively in public deliberation[19] but their sovereignty to make decisions in the assembly (to the extent that such authority was not limited by the powers and traditional prerogatives of senate and magistrates). More importantly and concretely, the *libertas populi* consisted of a number of exactly defined rights and legal protections. These concerned, on the one hand, some controls intended to prevent excessive individual accumulation of power (and therefore also to preserve aristocratic equality): the principles of annuity and collegiality (the latter including the right of veto) and detailed regulations of the senatorial career (*cursus honorum*). On the other hand, *libertas* entailed equality before the law (*aequa libertas, aequum ius*), even if it remained limited by the general acceptance of social inequalities. *Libertas* did not therefore justify demands for equal opportunity in office holding or challenges to judicial patronage. A third sector covered by *libertas* was protection against abuses by magistrates, offered especially by the extraordinary powers of the tribunes of the plebs. The tribuneship was thus regarded as the ultimate "protector of freedom," and the rights of giving assistance (*auxilium*) and of appealing for help (*provocatio*), both closely linked with the tribuneship, were hailed as "the two bulwarks to guard freedom" (*duae arces libertatis tuendae,* Liv. 3.45.8). The codification of law in the *Twelve Tables,* also celebrated as *libertas,* served in the same sense to protect the citizens from abuses of power by their social superiors. The last components of *libertas* mentioned here were the oldest. Probably originating in the first half of the fifth century, they resulted from the very causes that prompted the emergence of the Roman concept of freedom.[20]

Even this brief survey reveals the essential characteristics of this concept. It was sharply differentiated according to social stratification. Altogether different aspects were important for the senators and especially the members of the highest elite (the *nobiles*) than for their non-noble fellow citizens. Aristocratic freedom consisted in collective predominance and equality of political rights and participation. For the people, in contrast, freedom meant primarily individual protection from aristocratic, especially magisterial, arbitrariness and oppression. Hence, the Roman concept focused closely on institutions and rights and was connected with individual laws. In fact, it is possible to delineate the content of *libertas* by referring to relevant laws, and it is only logical that freedom could be identified with the validity of, and respect for, law and justice (*lex et ius*). This striking need for legal support corresponded to the primarily negative orientation of *libertas,* which in turn was the result of concrete experiences: in Rome freedom was almost without exception—for aristocrats and commoners alike—protection against (excessive) power, force, ambition, and arbitrariness.

The causes of the negative, defensive orientation of *libertas* are to be found in the circumstances of its rise and the social and political structures of early republican Rome. Shaped by Etruscan influences, conflicts with a powerful kingship, and an almost permanent threat to communal survival on the part of hostile neighbors, Rome's patrician aristocracy developed an exceptional degree of solidarity, discipline, and communal ethos. Leadership ability, demonstrated by service to the community, was valued highly and complemented by an exclusive claim to leadership. The collective social and political authority of the aristocratic heads of family, united in the senate, was strong enough to tolerate an independent magistracy, which, though institutionally controlled, still had the exceptional power required to ward off danger from without and to deal with internal crises and social conflicts.

In response, the non-elite plebeians initially focused their efforts mainly on protecting individual citizens against abuses by the patricians and patrician magistrates, whose overwhelming power affected every area of life. It is in this context that the concept of freedom gained political importance in Rome, and not, as in Greece, in that of the community's defense against foreign rule and tyranny.[21] Freedom thus was connected early on with the special protective authority of the tribuneship, which was created for this very purpose. Freedom was then extended to cover other rights of protection that the plebeians won in the course of long-lasting social conflicts, and eventually to other areas of political life. For historical reasons, it makes sense, therefore, that the freedom concept remained focused, even much later, on the needs of individual citizens, that its function was markedly negative and defensive, and that it was linked primarily with individual rights that eventually were fixed by law.

In Greece, by contrast, once the system of poleis had emerged, communities were involved in raids and rivalries with their neighbors but hardly ever in wars that threatened their survival. For problems caused by over-

population and social conflict, a safety valve was available in an almost unlimited opportunity to emigrate and create new settlements along the coasts
of the Mediterranean and Black Sea. Because external and constant internal
pressures were lacking, there was no incentive for solidarity and discipline
among the aristocracy, nor any need for strong and cohesive leadership.
Early on, therefore, the elite's superiority and leadership were challenged.[22]
When serious social conflicts broke out in the late seventh and sixth centuries, the aristocracy suffered a deep crisis and lost not only what was left
of its unity and discipline but also, bit by bit, its political predominance.
Hence, political reforms (such as those of Solon, who was rather conservative in his outlook, or of Cleisthenes, who came from the highest aristocracy) inevitably diminished the exclusiveness and strength of aristocratic
rule. Political offices, which did not have much power to begin with, were
rarely able to gain independent authority. When the functions of the popular assembly were enhanced and institutionalized, in several poleis (including Athens) the traditional aristocratic council lost the important function
of preparing and deliberating the assembly's agenda to a new council that
was open to nonaristocrats as well.

In Rome, the patrician aristocracy was long able to withstand plebeian
demands that debt laws be mitigated and debt bondage abolished. These and
other pressing problems were resolved only in the second half of the fourth
century, when this could be achieved at the expense of third parties in the
aftermath of external victories and conquests, that is, without loss to the Roman elite.[23] The issue of protecting the citizens' personal freedom thus remained for decades at the center of political debates and conflicts, and it is
in all likelihood this very fact that raised freedom consciousness in Rome to
a level that was sufficient to create a corresponding political catchword and
concept. In Athens, by contrast, these same problems, once they caused serious conflict, were resolved once and for all by Solon's reforms, thus stifling
the further evolution of freedom consciousness in the political realm. As
a result, in Greece freedom gained political importance in connection not
with the issue of the individual citizen's personal liberty but much later with
that of the community's collective freedom from outside oppression. Like
the concept of servitude, that of freedom was thus politicized first with regard to the collectivity, not the individual. In the fifth century, this aspect, focusing on the preservation of communal independence, constantly retained
high prominence because of the nature and frequency of military conflicts
between Greeks and non-Greeks and among the Greeks themselves.

Within the community, freedom gained importance in opposition to tyranny; it thus again pertained to the entire community and focused on the collectivity of the citizens. In Athens in the fifth century, the elite's predominance continued to be weakened. As democracy was fully developed, the council and officials were increasingly reduced to the function of assisting the assembly, which reigned with full, sovereign power. It was therefore not the contrast to a powerful aristocracy or magistracy that gave more precise definition to freedom. Rather, as a result of tensions between aristocratic or oligarchic claims to exclusive power and democratic will to freedom, equal participation in government by all citizens came to be seen as the main constituent of the demos's freedom. Moreover, it was soon recognized that such freedom had to cover all aspects of the citizen's life in his polis. Once again, therefore, freedom became politically significant with respect to the whole community, not to the rights and needs of individuals.

This primary concern for the collectivity of citizens and the community as a whole is an important characteristic of the Greek freedom concept. It comprised and guaranteed the interests, rights, and freedom (or freedoms) of the individual citizens; therefore, normally these did not need to be stressed separately. This explains the strikingly low emphasis placed on "civil liberties" in Greece, especially when compared to Rome and the later Western tradition shaped by Roman thought. In contrast, the aristocratic-oligarchic concept of the "fully free citizen," developed in reaction to democracy's collective claim to freedom, was oriented solely toward the individual: it emphasized the nobleman's higher, "real" freedom, based on descent, wealth, ability, and education, as an indispensable prerequisite for responsible participation in government.

This brings up the next point. Neither in Greece nor in Rome was the concept of freedom invented and made politically useful by the elite. In Rome, on the contrary, its political dynamism and attractiveness as a catchword in social conflict was apparently generated by the non-elite citizen's need of protection against the elite, who, despite all their power and social superiority, depended on the citizens for the defense of the community. In Greece, the protection of the external independence of the polis became an issue only when in some of the leading communities equal political participation had already become a crucial concern for broad non-elite classes that were both militarily indispensable and interested in stabilizing the polis. It is only on this basis that a large segment of the citizenry could view the possibility of losing such participation through usurpation of power by a tyrant or exclusive government by a group of elite families as a problem of political servitude versus freedom, and that this viewpoint could become critical enough to prompt political action and involvement. In Rome, however, the non-elite classes' involvement in the "struggle of the orders" was initially motivated entirely by social issues. The demand for political equality was raised only in a later phase, and then only by members of a plebeian elite that had emerged by a process of social and economic differentiation and by immigration after the "closure of the patriciate." [24] Whether this part of the plebeian struggle was also supported by the call for liberty is entirely uncertain and rather unlikely.[25]

In the Greek aristocratic value system, individual political power and predominance were placed above the freedom of the polis: if necessary, domestic rule was compatible with lack of communal independence. Exceptions notwithstanding, this was a constant element in political behavior, traceable from relations in the Ionian cities under Persian rule in the sixth century to the difficulties Demosthenes faced in arousing Greek resistance to Philip II. By contrast, for the non-elite classes who upheld the isonomic polis and identified with it, collective independence from foreign domination was indispensable for maintaining internal freedom and equality. Only because they recognized this and valued independence sufficiently could freedom become the object of a great struggle, a watchword, and a concept during the Persian Wars. True, aristocrats played an important role in this particular struggle, but overall the Greek concept of freedom was still primarily the achievement of the non-elite citizens. After the creation of the Athenian Empire and the development of full democracy, freedom became the domain of the citizens at large (including now the lower classes), who ruled in, and through, their city and whose civic identity rested on their political liberty. Freedom remained the monopoly of democracy. In contrast to their Roman peers, the Greek aristocratic-oligarchic upper classes never developed an alternative political concept of freedom. They merely reinterpreted the concept of the free citizen, claiming that status on an elevated level exclusively for themselves.

In his analysis of the transformation of "politicosocial concepts" in the fifth century, Christian Meier defines "politicization" as the most important and pervasive principle. Indicative of this tendency was the "politicization of the entire society" characterizing Athenian democracy and the development of a true "political identity" among Athenian citizens. Meier understands "politicization" as a "change toward the comprehension of a social world that was constituted by the citizens acting in their capacity as citizens and, to this extent, became political." Politicization "denotes the central tendency of a collective change that made politics the very stuff of civic life—in which the community found its collective identity in voting and decision making, in performing public functions, and in supervising and enforcing public order."[26]

This process of separating out an independent and primary sphere of politics began in the Solonian period, gained momentum at the time of Cleisthenes, and substantially came to an end under Pericles. The political concept that stood at the center of this process from beginning to end, however, was that of equality, contributing to, and being part of, the politicization of community and individual citizens. Freedom was drawn into this process and became politicized only at the very end. True, it had enjoyed brief political prominence in Solon's time, and from the time of the Persian Wars, it was regularly applied in political contexts (and in this sense was political). But the thinking underlying its use long remained traditional and "nomistic," directed toward restoring a preexisting order that was disturbed by abuses or undue monopolization of power.[27]

To be sure, protection of the community against despotism and tyranny was increasingly ensured by the political engagement of larger segments of the citizenry. Indeed, this engagement gave rise to "an entirely new kind of freedom . . .—the freedom to participate in politics, and in particular to vote." Hence, institutions quickly grew in importance. All these changes were increasingly recognized, reflected upon, and subjected to conscious planning and action. But apparently the terminological instruments needed for their formulation and realization initially relied on other concepts: power, participation, and, above all, equality. Freedom remained primarily a delimiting and defensive (and, in this sense, negative) concept that offered a frame of reference, was highly valued, but was not explicitly made positive and concrete or defined. For this reason it could not be a normative influence on, or anticipate, constitutional development or be linked with specific rights. Both functions were decidedly true of equality. Ever since the claim that control of political power was the hereditary right of the aristocracy had lost its self-evident validity, and institutions had been adjusted to allow the propertied non-elite classes qualified to serve in the army to share in such power, the possibility of extending *isonomia* and *isēgoria* further, eventually to include all citizens, had existed at least in theory. This potential was realized when, as a result of the Persian Wars and Athens's naval policy, the criterion of qualification for military service unexpectedly proved flexible as well.

Thus, the concept of freedom did not so much, as Meier suggests, undergo "a distinct shift in the direction of politicization" in the course of the fifth century;[28] rather, it was taken over relatively late and somewhat suddenly by an already fully politicized citizenry. It now became part of a new system of political thinking and acting and was made to serve an altogether new political function. Henceforth, it played a central role in the autonomous "political sphere" characteristic of Athens, bearing markedly on political status and relations, on possibilities for action and ways of behaving, on rights and institutions, and on self-understanding and expectations. It thus indeed was politicized in a wholly new and comprehensive way.

But this is hardly the whole explanation. On the one hand, despite the concept's primarily political orientation, a strong social component remained notable. (Or perhaps, rather, the concept of freedom was politically effective precisely because it combined political and social components.) On the other hand, the politicization of the citizenry was a condition, but not the direct cause, of the politicization of the concept. The latter found its concrete expression in the equation of freedom with democracy. Apparently, this equation was not realized as long as the claim of democracy to represent the interests of all citizens and the welfare of the whole community was broadly and sufficiently convincing. As long as this was the case, freedom remained a firm but static framing concept that was directed against tyranny but not linked to a specific nontyrannical constitution nor affected by changes carried out under its protective cover by and between such constitutions.

This situation ended when the integrative claim of democracy lost its general credibility and two rivaling and, in their narrow interpretations, incompatible alternatives developed within the free and isonomic community: democracy and oligarchy. In insisting more vigorously on their claims to superiority and exclusiveness, the oligarchs reacted to the politicization of the citizenry—particularly the active and self-assured engagement of the lower classes, with all its (from their perspective) undesirable manifestations. Precisely this oligarchic reaction and its potential consequences, which the democrats anticipated and feared, prompted them to appropriate and monopolize freedom for their own political purposes. Freedom was now—and only now—combined with equality, designating no longer simply the freedom of the community from tyranny but above all that of the demos from oppression by oligarchs. It became a motto and claim of the politicized citizenry and in the process was itself politicized.

A sharply perceived and expressed contrast to oligarchy was thus decisive in this process. This left its mark on the concept of freedom. In its connection with democracy, it was not only politicized but also ideologized. In this respect as well it is important that it gained prominence only when democracy had matured institutionally and sociologically and had developed its own political programs, and when its impact had become unmistakable. Like all Greek polis constitutions, democracy was more than merely a political system. It affected not only the modalities of making decisions, the number of those participating in decisions and the range and intensity of their participation, and the style and methods of political leadership but all aspects of life in the polis. It created new norms and realities everywhere: in the communal and private lives of and relationships among the citizens; in relations between elite and non-elite, rich and poor, citizens and noncitizens, slaves and freemen; in the function of laws and administration of justice; in the cultural, religious, economic, and military spheres; and even—indeed, above all—in foreign policy. All these changes—including those within the polis and those directed outward—were closely and visibly interconnected, and all were linked causally, whether directly or indirectly, to democracy.

Democracy was thus a comprehensive social phenomenon, a way of life. Its supporters represented this claim energetically and with conviction and, as a result, often gave offense. In Athens itself, for a number of reasons, open, direct, and organized opposition to democracy was impossible. The ideological conflict with those who favored oligarchy was forced underground, so to speak, or at least confined to private clubs and theoretical discussion.[29] The presence of such principled opposition was certainly known, but it was seldom tangible and concretely identifiable. It was therefore disquieting, appearing more dangerous than it actually was—all the more so because populist politicians like Cleon enhanced such fears by constantly warning of an ever-present danger of tyranny. Furthermore, democracy was attacked from outside Athens because of its oppression of the allies and its specific brand of aggressive and interventionist foreign policy. In both respects, it fared badly in comparison to Sparta's disciplined, cautious, and predictable leadership. Finally, those Athenian elite leaders who were actively involved in democratic politics were accused of betraying traditional aristocratic values by their peers who were opposed to democracy, while the "new men" (wealthy upstarts), despite their efforts to align themselves with the nobility, were never accepted as equals.[30] And the thetes, on whom after all both democracy and Athens's power largely depended, were in small ways and large, despite much praise and flattery, often made to feel the contempt of the upper classes and were perpetually in need of self-affirmation and legitimation by success.[31]

On the whole, therefore, several factors contributed to keeping the democrats (whether high or low) somewhat insecure. This manifested itself, on the one hand, in a marked tendency toward defensiveness and self-justification (visible even in Pericles' Funeral Oration) and, on the other, in a need for recognition and a tendency toward restlessness and hyper-activism (*polupragmosunē*).[32] Both these tendencies prompted strong emphasis on achievements in which one could feel pride and on values that were able to counter the negative reputation nourished by enemies of Athens and of democracy: Athens's merits, power, and imperial rule, and the ideals of justice, equality, and freedom. These concepts thus became strongly imbued with ideology or, as especially in the case of *eleutheria*, were appropriated by democracy precisely for their ideological usefulness.

Democracy, as said before, was (and was understood as) a way of life that influenced all activities and relations in and of the polis. Accordingly, the democratic concept of freedom was broadly conceived and effective, eventually covering the entire sphere on which democracy had an impact. Thucydides' formula, attributed to Pericles, that "freedom is typical of life in our community" (*eleutherōs politeuomen*, 2.37.2) expresses this succinctly. Hence, for example, in Athens freedom also affected the status and function of noncitizens, even slaves, and found its fulfillment both in the ideals of equality and solidarity of all citizens and in the principles of individual self-sufficiency (*autarkeia*) and freedom of action enjoyed by all free inhabitants of the polis. In relation to the outside world, it justified, on the one hand, generosity in assisting the oppressed (thus meeting the demands of a higher *nomos* shared by all Greeks) and, on the other, will to power in exerting despotic rule over other Greeks (thus violating another Panhellenic *nomos*).

The same applies on a larger scale as well. The concept of freedom claimed by the Greek polis came to cover the entire sphere influenced by the polis. The Greeks perceived a close connection between the spheres within the polis and among poleis. The latter appeared to them like an enlarged version of the former—a macrocosm operating by the same principles as the domestic microcosm. The world of poleis was seen as a group of political entities analogous to the citizens in the polis. As a result, for example, the terminology required to understand, define, and categorize positions, relationships, and patterns of behavior in interstate relations was usually created by transferring concepts previously developed within the polis, and the interaction among poleis and their behavior in relation to third parties was analogized to the behavior of individuals or groups within the polis and their relations to outsiders. Significantly, the political concept of equality, developed in domestic politics and fundamental to the isonomic polis, likewise gained central importance in interstate relations as a result of Athens's rise to power and predominance in the Delian League.[33]

The connections suggested here would need to be analyzed in greater detail, but it is worth noting that in the decisive phases of the emergence and elaboration of the concept of freedom—in the contexts of the Persian Wars, Athens's rule in the empire, and democracy—both aspects, the internal and the external, were involved and equally important. The question thus arises whether such interweaving of internal and external aspects was not in fact a determining factor in the emergence, dynamism, and success of the Greek concept of freedom. In this sense, freedom was all-encompassing and indivisible. Without freedom within the community, the freedom of the community could neither have become a value concept nor have been preserved as a reality; without the possibility of achieving or maintaining the freedom of the polis, there could in the long run have been no freedom in the polis. Such interlocking of both spheres then reached greater complexity and a higher, almost absolute value in the self-understanding of democracy, when it was linked with the interdependence of freedom and rule over others.

In this same context, we should note yet another aspect. Reflections on the content of democratic freedom focused on two distinctly different levels, one institutional, the other societal. The importance of institutions for the establishment and preservation of democratic freedom was recognized early on. It is striking, however, that freedom was rarely associated directly with individual institutions; instead, the association was made primarily with democracy or isonomy as a whole. Apparently, in political thinking individual institutions were subsumed under democracy and their function was analyzed within its framework. Only in a second stage was the "rule of the people," which was guaranteed by the sum total of such institutions, identified with the freedom of the demos. In other words, in the Athenians' consciousness full citizenship was so inseparably linked with the principle of participation in government that the connection with freedom was primarily made by way of *dēmo-kratia* as a whole. Freedom thus became a function of democracy. What chiefly mattered was whether a measure, law, or institution was democratic or "friendly to the people" (*dēmotikos*); this in itself determined whether it was free or supportive of freedom. "Democracy" and "democratic" (*dēmotikos*) thus converged in meaning with *eleutheria* and *eleutheros* and, as the terms designating the precondition of freedom, often attracted the primary association with this value or ideal. What the Athenians perceived as free easily corresponded to, and was expressed by, *dēmotikos*.[34]

The only exception was the citizen's right of speech. Ever since democracy and freedom had been equated, this right—a cornerstone of democracy—had been linked directly with freedom. The logical consequence, in a political constellation conducive to it, was the coining of *parrhēsia*, which expressed that association more directly than *isēgoria* (the term used previously for the same right). Such emphasis on a single civic right resulted not only from the central importance of this right for the functioning of the democratic constitution but just as much from the fact that it was an elementary right of the freeman that was validated and rigorously enforced in political life. *Isēgoria*, or *parrhēsia*, thus embodied the intimate connection, as it were, between the institutional and social components of freedom.

This social component, underestimated by previous scholarship, may well offer a key to understanding what, for the average Athenian, was the core of the value of freedom guaranteed by democracy. It constituted an important condition that enabled him to develop a political identity and over time made it so attractive that it became his primary identity. For those who could not compete in ancestry, education, or wealth with the (old and new) upper classes, which, after all, continued to set the tone, it was crucial to be taken seriously in every respect for, as it were, the only presentable quality they possessed: being freemen, with all the traits that set them apart from the unfree. Democracy gave every citizen the right "to live as he liked" (and thus made it clear that upper-class norms were no longer mandatory to be valued as a full citizen)[35] and to express his opinion at any time and on any subject (and thus disconnected the citizen's ability to speak up in politics from the economic and social requirements previously taken for granted). Democracy guaranteed him the integrity of his house and person,[36] put him on a par with all other citizens in all essential areas of life (especially before the law and in politics), and made him independent of the power of the mighty. For all these reasons, democracy met an extraordinarily important sociopsychological need: it was the only political system that enabled the freeman to develop and realize his potential to the fullest. This claim applied on an elementary level[37] and was at the same time extremely comprehensive: democratic freedom offered to all citizens (and, in varying degrees, to all inhabitants of the polis) a unique degree of liberty in living and shaping their lives. The democratic polis was in truth a community of the free. Democracy not only presupposed but also realized the personal freedom of the freeman to an extent that had never been known before and was not to be achieved again for over two millennia.

Abbreviations

For abbreviations of classical sources see *The Oxford Classical Dictionary*.

A&A	*Antike und Abendland.*
AAHG	*Anzeiger für die Altertumswissenschaft.*
ABG	*Archiv für Begriffsgeschichte.*
AC	*L'antiquité classique.*
AHB	*Ancient History Bulletin.*
AJAH	*American Journal of Ancient History.*
AJP	*American Journal of Philology.*
AP	*Constitution of the Athenians* (*Athenaiōn Politeia*).
ASNP	*Annali della Scuola Normale Superiore di Pisa.*
ATL	Meritt, Wade-Gery, and McGregor 1939–53.
AW	*The Ancient World.*
BCH	*Bulletin de correspondance hellénique.*
BICS	*Bulletin of the Institute of Classical Studies, University of London.*
BMC	British Museum. *Catalogue of the Greek Coins.*
BSA	*Annual of the British School at Athens.*
C	Campbell 1982–93.
CA	*Classical Antiquity.*
CAH	*Cambridge Ancient History.*
CEG	Hansen 1983.
CJ	*Classical Journal.*
C&M	*Classica et Mediaevalia.*
CP	*Classical Philology.*
CQ	*Classical Quarterly.*
CR	*Classical Review.*
CSCA	*California Studies in Classical Antiquity.*
CT	Hornblower 1991–96.
CW	*Classical World.*
D	Diehl 1925, 1949.
DNP	*Der neue Pauly: Enzyklopädie der Antike.* 15 vols. to date. Stuttgart, 1996–.
Edm.	Edmonds 1957–61.
Entdeckung	Raaflaub 1985.

FGE	Page 1981.
FGrH	Jacoby 1923–98.
GG	Brunner et al. 1972–97.
GP	Gentili and Prato 1988.
G&R	*Greece and Rome.*
GRBS	*Greek, Roman, and Byzantine Studies.*
HCT	Gomme 1945–56; Gomme, Andrewes, and Dover 1970–81.
HdAW	Handbuch der Altertumswissenschaft.
HSCP	*Harvard Studies in Classical Philology.*
HWPh	*Historisches Wörterbuch der Philosophie.* 11 vols. to date. Basel, 1971–.
HZ	*Historische Zeitschrift.*
ICS	*Illinois Classical Studies.*
IG	*Inscriptiones Graecae.* Berlin.
IM	*Istambuler Mitteilungen* (*Mitteilungen des Deutschen Archäologischen Instituts, Istambuler Abteilung*).
Inscr. Cret.	Guarducci 1935–50.
JDAI	*Jahrbuch des Deutschen Archäologischen Instituts.*
JHI	*Journal of the History of Ideas.*
JHS	*Journal of Hellenic Studies.*
JMH	*Journal of Modern History.*
JÖAI	*Jahreshefte des Österreichischen Archäologischen Instituts.*
KlP	*Der kleine Pauly: Lexikon der Antike.* 5 vols. Stuttgart, 1964–75.
LCL	Loeb Classical Library.
LCM	*Liverpool Classical Monthly.*
LIMC	*Lexicon Iconographicum Mythologiae Classicae.* Zurich, 1981–.
LP	Lobel and Page 1955.
LSJ	Liddell, Scott, and Jones 1940.
"Materialien"	Raaflaub 1981.
MGR	*Miscellanea Graeca et Romana.*
MH	*Museum Helveticum.*
ML	Meiggs and Lewis 1969.
N	Nauck 1889.
OCD	*Oxford Classical Dictionary.* 3d ed. Oxford, 1996.
P	Page 1962.
PCG	*Poetae Comici Graeci.* Ed. Rudolf Kassel and Colin Austin. 8 vols. to date. Göttingen, 1983–.
PCPhS	*Proceedings of the Cambridge Philological Society.*
PdP	*La parola del passato.*
Pearson	Pearson 1917.
P.Oxy.	*The Oxyrhynchus Papyri.* Ed. with tr. and notes by Bernard P. Grenfell and Arthur S. Hunt. 67 vols. to date. London, 1898–.
P&P	*Past and Present.*
PRIA	*Proceedings of the Royal Irish Academy.*
QS	*Quaderni di storia.*
QUCC	*Quaderni Urbinati di cultura classica.*
RAC	*Reallexicon für Antike und Christentum.*
RD	*Revue historique de droit français et étranger.*
RE	*Realencyclopädie der classischen Altertumswissenschaft.* 49 vols. Stuttgart, 1893–1978.

REA	*Revue des études anciennes.*
REG	*Revue des études grecques.*
RFIC	*Rivista di filologia e di istruzione classica.*
RH	*Revue historique.*
RhM	*Rheinisches Museum.*
RIDA	*Revue internationale du droit de l'antiquité.*
RM	*Römische Mitteilungen (Mitteilungen des Deutschen Archäologischen Instituts, Römische Abteilung).*
RPh	*Revue de philologie.*
RSA	*Rivista storica dell'antichità.*
RSI	*Rivista storica italiana.*
SCI	*Scripta Classica Israelica.*
SEG	*Supplementum Epigraphicum Graecum.*
SHAW	Sitzungsberichte der Heidelberger Akademie der Wissenschaften, phil.-hist. Kl.
SI	*Studi italiani di filologia classica.*
SMEA	*Studi micenei ed egeo-anatolici.*
Sn-M	Snell and Maehler 1970, 1971–75.
SO	*Symbolae Osloenses.*
SV	Bengtson 1975.
Syll.	Dittenberger 1915–24.
TAPA	*Transactions of the American Philological Association.*
Tod	Tod 1946–48.
TrGF	*Tragicorum Graecorum Fragmenta.* Ed. Bruno Suell et al. 4 vols. to date. Göttingen, 1977–.
VS	*Vorsokratiker:* Diels and Kranz 1961.
W	West 1992.
WS	*Wiener Studien.*
ZA	*Ziva Antica.*
ZPE	*Zeitschrift für Papyrologie und Epigraphik.*
ZRG	*Zeitschrift für Rechtsgeschichte, Romanistische Abteilung.*

Notes

1. Introduction

1. Finley 1982: 119–20; see also the entire chapter 7, "Between Slavery and Freedom" (first published in 1963/64).

2. See, e.g., Constant 1874 (first published in 1819).

3. See, e.g., Croce 1930; Bleicken 1972: 7–10; Finley 1982: 77–80; Hansen 1989, 1996; de Romilly 1989, 1990; Murray 1995; Momigliano 1996. See also, e.g., Jenkyns 1980; Mossé 1989; Roberts 1994. On the history of the concept of freedom from antiquity to the modern age: e.g., Brunner et al. 1972–97: 2.425–542; Patterson 1991 (vol. 2 still to appear); Davis 1995.

4. Ehrenberg 1967: 19; cf. Pohlenz 1955: 3 (= 1966: IX). Examples include, apart from Ehrenberg, Lana 1955; Lauffer 1960; Gomme 1962: 139–55; van Straaten 1972; Schwabl 1974; see also Larsen 1962; Welles 1965. See further n. 15.

5. All dates are B.C.E. unless indicated otherwise.

6. To my knowledge, Loenen 1930 had little impact on subsequent scholarship.

7. Pohlenz 1955: 5 (= 1966: IX).

8. Thus also Schäfer 1963: 316 n. 3; cf. the reviews by Georg Luck, *Gnomon* 27 (1955): 487–91; Erich Bayer, *HZ* 182 (1956): 88–91; Sartori 1968; Lanza 1977: 239–43.

9. See esp. the review by Dieter Nörr, *ZRG* 85 (1968): 435–38. Guazzoni Foà 1974–76 is also oriented primarily toward the history of philosophy and *Geistesgeschichte* but in large part is devoted to searching for the roots of modern ideas of freedom in the works of ancient authors. Muller 1962 is even more a work of cultural history: "My main concern is the living tradition of freedom: what has entered the broad stream leading to the consciousness of modern man, and lately to the almost universal acceptance in theory of the once-revolutionary principle of 'human rights' or the rights of man. . . . While I have of course tried to understand the mentality of ancient peoples, . . . I have dwelt rather on their contributions to *us*, and their shortcomings by *our* standards" (xvi).

10. E.g., Ferrabino 1929 (with Gaetano de Sanctis's review in *RFIC* 8 [1930]: 230–45); Diller 1962a; Gomme 1962: 139–55; Larsen 1962; von Fritz 1965; Welles 1965; Pointner 1969: 8–24; Gelzer 1973; Dover 1976; Finley 1976b; Momigliano 1979; de Romilly 1983.

11. Meier 1975; Heuss 1965; Schäfer 1957. See also Festugière 1947: pt. 1, with chapters on political freedom, a philosophical critique of the concept of freedom, and the freedom of the wise man.

12. To mention only a few: Finley's analyses of terminology "between slavery and freedom"

(collected in Finley 1982); Meier's work on the evolution of predemocratic and democratic terminology and political thinking (collected in Meier 1970, 1990); Strasburger's thoughts on individual vs. community and on the historians' reactions to Athenian ideology (1954, 1955, 1958); Ostwald's investigation of *nomos*, equality, and democracy (1969) and of *autonomia* (1982); and studies by many scholars on the terminology of equality (see chap. 3.2, nn. 159–67, below).

13. See esp. Kloesel 1935; Wirszubski 1950; Bleicken 1962, 1972; Kunkel 1969; and now Brunt 1988. For a comparison between Greek and Roman concepts: Raaflaub 1984b.

14. Gschnitzer 1981: 9.

15. See H. Schlier in *Theologisches Wörterbuch*, vol. 2 (1935), 484–500; E. Fuchs in *Religion in Geschichte und Gegenwart*, vol. 2.3 (1957), 1101–4; D. Nestle in *RAC* 8 (1972): 269–306; W. Warnach in *HWPh* 2 (1972): 1064–83. Cults: Waser, *RE* 5.2 (1905): 2346–47 (Eleutheria); Karl Kock, *RE* 13.1 (1926): 101–3 (Libertas). Nothing on the concept of freedom in *RE*, *KlP*, *Lexikon der Alten Welt*, *Lexikon der Antike*, and the 2d ed. of *Oxford Classical Dictionary*; see criticism by J. Bleicken et al. in *Gnomon* 39 (1967): 746–47. Articles on freedom (often with an introductory section on antiquity) can be found, e.g., in *Staatslexikon: Recht, Wirtschaft, Gesellschaft*, 6th ed., vol. 3 (1959), 528ff.; *Sowjetsystem und demokratische Gesellschaft*, vol. 2 (1968), 660ff.; see also Brunner et al. 1972–97: 2.425–542.

16. De Romilly 1989, 1990; Hansen 1989, 1996; Murray 1995; Ostwald 1995; Momigliano 1996 (lectures given in Cambridge in 1940); Wallace 1996; Nakategawa 1998; *OCD*, 609–11; *DNP* 4 (1998): 650–52 (both by myself); Squilloni Vignoli forthcoming. The explanation in Patterson 1991 of the emergence of the freedom concept differs markedly from mine; see chap. 2.2 at n. 103 below.

17. Finley 1982: 114–15: "The pre-Greek world—the world of the Sumerians, Babylonians, Egyptians, and Assyrians; and I cannot refrain from adding the Mycenaeans—was, in a very profound sense, a world without free men, in the sense in which the west has come to understand that concept. It was equally a world in which chattel slavery played no role of any consequence. That, too, was a Greek discovery." On Mesopotamia: below at n. 78. In Egypt, the word seems to have played at most a role as the opposite of personal repression: Aristide Théodoridès, *Lexikon der Ägyptologie*, vol. 2 (1977), 297–304; Assmann 1990: index, s.v. *Freiheit*. The Hebrew of the Old Testament has no word for political freedom; hence the Septuagint uses *eleutheria* and related words only in connection with private law concerning slaves. See Ostwald 1995: 43 and, in more detail, Nestle 1972: 288 (who emphasizes that the theme of freedom is nonexistent in rabbinical literature as well; it first appears, under Hellenistic influence, in Maccabees). F. Stanley, *The Anchor Bible Dictionary*, vol. 2 (1992), 855–59: "The OT knows of freedom almost exclusively only as a social state. . . . Thus the Hebrew terms for 'free' and 'freedom,' . . . which are not witnessed very frequently, often occur in discussions of slavery and manumission. . . . Though the redemption of Israel from slavery in Egypt is cited in support for the manumission of Hebrew slaves in the 7th year . . . , the OT does not develop a theology of freedom on the basis of the Exodus. Rather, Israel was ransomed in order to be God's servants . . . , and the language used to describe this event is primarily that of 'redemption,' not of 'freedom.'" On the dissenting view of Snell 2001 see n. 78 below. Freedom is missing in the index of Briant 1996 (on the Persian Empire). On China: generally, Reinau 1981: 25–28; more specifically, Finley 1982: 119; Lloyd 1996: esp. chap. 6.

18. Meier 1975: 429 (tr. here and elsewhere mine).

19. Heuss 1965: 67.

20. Meier 1970: 15; cf. Koselleck 1972a: 127. Middle position: Koselleck 1972a: 120; 1972b: xxiii.

21. Richter 1996: 10–11. See Koselleck 1972a, 1972b, 1987, 1989; for further discussion, see,

e.g., Koselleck 1979; Richter 1986, 1987, 1990, 1995; Busse 1987; Lehmann and Richter 1996; Dipper 2000. I thank Christian Durand for suggestions about recent bibliography.

22. Koselleck 1972b: xiv–xix (see also for the following paragraph); cf. the summary in Richter 1996: 11–12.

23. Meier 1977 (expanded and revised in subsequent versions).

24. See H. G. Ritter, in *HWPh* 1 (1971): 797–98.

25. See, e.g., Schultz 1973; Berding 1976; J. Sheehan's review of *GG* in *JMH* 50 (1978): 312ff.

26. Koselleck 1972b: xxii–xxiii.

27. See J. Sheehan's review of *GG* in *JMH* 50 (1978): 318.

28. "Materialien," pts. 2, 4 (analysis), 3 (sketch).

29. Koselleck 1972b: xxi ff., 1972a: 125.

30. On the terminology of slavery and other categories of dependent persons: Gschnitzer 1964, 1976b; Klees 1975; Kästner 1981; and bibliography cited in nn. 49–50 below and in chap. 2.1, n. 41.

31. See esp. Larsen 1962; Heuss 1965; Martin 1978, 1979a; Meier 1982. On the concept of master and ruler: Klees 1975; Cobet 1981. See further below, chap. 5.2.

32. See Dieter Nörr's review of Nestle 1967 in *ZRG* 85 (1968): 428; see also, more generally, Spahn 1977: 42–43, 45–46.

33. Bleicken 1972: 7–10. This observation obviously does not intend to blur the differences between ancient and modern concepts of freedom; see bibliography cited in n. 3.

34. Thus also Meier 1970: 14–15; Frei 1981: 206. Differences: e.g., Sabine 1963: 3; see also (on one particular aspect) Schäfer 1932: 175ff., esp. 176. Meier 1980: 51 (= 1990: 29): "The Greeks had no Greeks to emulate."

35. Bleicken 1972: 10. On concepts and ideas in social history: Austin and Vidal-Naquet 1977: 20–26.

36. Heuss 1973: 4–8.

37. On the comparability of early social conditions: e.g., Heuss 1973: 8–17; Raaflaub 1986: 29–36, 1990: 512–13; see also Davies 1997; Ando 1999. On the anachronism of Rome's enduring city-state myth: Cornell 1991. On etymology: n. 74 below. For a comparison of the two concepts of freedom: beginning of chap. 7.2 below and Raaflaub 1984b.

38. Chambers 1973; Nouhaud 1982. The "false" documents showing up in the fourth century reveal themselves as such mainly by their anachronistic terminology: Habicht 1961; Seager 1969; de Romilly 1972; Robertson 1976. Aristotle's sources and his treatment of early Athenian history: Hignett 1952: chap. 1; Day and Chambers 1962: chap. 1; Ruschenbusch 1979: chap. 1; Rhodes 1981: 5–30, 1993; Chambers 1993; Gehrke 1994; Maddoli 1994. Aristotle and freedom: Mulgan 1970, 1984; Barnes 1992.

39. On Herodotus's intellectual context: Lateiner 1986; Thomas 2000. On his topicality: Strasburger 1955; Fornara 1971b; Meier 1973, 1987b; Raaflaub 1987, 2002a, 2002b; Stadter 1992; Moles 1996. The date and mode of publication of the *Histories* is much debated (Bakker 2002); I accept Fornara's arguments (1971a, 1981) that Herodotus was still working in the late 420s: Raaflaub 2002a: 36–37.

40. See Raaflaub 2000d. On Herodotus and *eleutheria:* von Fritz 1965: 5ff., esp. 22ff. In the chapter on Herodotus in his history of Greek historiography (1967), von Fritz pays particular attention to the theme of freedom, which, he argues, became a leitmotif only in the final phase of revision and therefore is not represented equally throughout the work.

41. So, too, Fornara 1970a: 177–78.

42. See, e.g., Meier 1980: 154–58 (= 1990: 87–89); Raaflaub 1988b, 2000c; Hammer 2002.

43. The concept of *autonomia* offers a good example: chap. 4.3 below.

44. See also, in a different context, Strasburger 1954: "It lies in the nature of questions as I pose them here that the right answers cannot be found by firmly asserting or denying intellectual facts but only by aiming at a historically decisive graduation. One first has to describe the Greeks without bias as one sees them" (227, my tr.).

45. See also, in a different context, Meier 1970: 26–27.

46. Murdoch 1968: 165, quoted by Starr 1977: 18.

47. Athens as an exception rather than a prototype: e.g., Schäfer 1963: 99ff., 269ff.; Finley 1976b: 15, 20–21; Starr 1977: 12, 101. See also Meier's criticism of Ehrenberg's representation (in 1965b) of Athens as an ideal type of polis: Gnomon 41 (1969): 367ff., esp. 370–71.

48. Similarly, the works of the three Athenians Aeschylus, Sophocles, and Euripides are commonly described as "Greek tragedies."

49. See esp. Finley 1982: 77 and chaps. 7–9 (on which the following paragraph is mostly based). See also Lotze 1959, 1962; Mossé 1979; Beringer 1982; and particularly de Ste. Croix 1981: esp. 133ff.

50. On individual categories: Busolt and Swoboda 1926: 939ff., 948ff.; Harrison 1968: esp. 181ff.; Austin and Vidal-Naquet 1977: 111ff. On metics: Clerc [1893] 1979: esp. 327ff.; Hildebrecht Hommel, RE 15.2 (1932): 1413ff.; Whitehead 1977, 1984, 1986b; Fraser 1995. Davies (1977–78: 106–7) suggests further differentiation.

51. Perioikoi: see bibliography in OCD, 1141; DNP 9 (2000): 582–83; Lotze 1993–94; and recently Hall 2000. See also Roy 1997 on the perioikoi of Elis. Neodamodeis: Lotze 1959: 42ff.; Mossé 1981: 355–56; Furuyama 1988; and bibliography in DNP 8 (2000): 823. Hupomeiones (Xen. Hell. 3.3.6): Busolt and Swoboda 1926: 659; Shimron 1979. Mothakes: bibliography in DNP 8 (2000): 421. On the latter and additional categories: Cartledge 1987: index, s.v. "Sparta, citizenship."

52. Eleutheroi: Willetts 1955: 33ff., 1967: 10ff. In the Law Code of Gortyn, too, eleutheros is mostly used in opposition to "unfree" or "slave." Col. 2.2ff., however, offers the only example known to me where it reflects the original meaning of the word as deduced by etymology (see n. 74 below): "member of the descent or tribal group," "insider," hence "citizen," in contrast to "nonmember," "outsider." Apetairoi: Willetts 1955: 37ff. (with the rev. by Jochen Bleicken, Gnomon 29 [1957]: 270), 1967: 12–13; see also Willetts 1954 with Larsen 1936.

53. On the Roman half-citizens: Cornell 1995: 349–52. Eleutherai: Gschnitzer 1958: 82–83; Buck 1979: 99, 113. Davies (1977–78: 107) sees another analogy to cives sine suffragio in the status of metics who were offered isoteleia. That the status of the Plataeans should be seen as an Athenian analogy to that of the Lacedaemonian perioikoi (e.g., Kahrstedt 1934: 353; Kirsten 1950: 2285) is unlikely. Their partial and temporary enfranchisement during the Peloponnesian War must be separated from the alliance they concluded with Athens at the end of the sixth century: Gawantka 1975: 174ff.; Kapparis 1995; and chap. 3.1 at nn. 75ff. below. The case of the Salaminioi is again different: Lambert 1997; Taylor 1997.

54. Gschnitzer (1964: 7–8, 1976b: 2ff.) sees having control over their persons and work as constitutive; see also de Ste. Croix 1981: 117; Finley 1982: 40–41; Aristot. Rhet. 1367a33: eleutheron . . . to mē pros allon zēn.

55. See the Hekatompedon inscription and Jordan's commentary, cited in chap. 2.3 at n. 146.

56. See further chap. 7.2 below.

57. See Reinau 1981: 45ff.; chap. 7.2 below.

58. See, e.g., the arguments on debt bondage in Finley 1982: 118–19, 162ff.

59. For all these reasons I disagree with Patterson 1991 (see chap. 2.2 at n. 103).

60. See esp. Finley 1982: 146–49 with ref. to Diod. 1.79.3; Aristot. AP 9.1.

61. For an example of a diachronic analysis: Raaflaub 1980; for a comparative study: Raaflaub 1984b; and below, beginning of chap. 7.2.

62. See below at n. 78. Dandamaev's large work on slavery (1984) and other seminal works, written for nonspecialists (such as Kuhrt 1995; Sasson 1995), now offer some help.

63. Preparation: esp. Ryder 1965. Continuing history: e.g., Jones 1939; Pohlenz 1955: 113ff. (= 1966: 106ff.); Welles 1965: 38ff.; Heidemann 1966; Bernhardt 1971: 10ff.; Orth 1977; de Ste. Croix 1981: 300ff.; Seager 1981; Gehrke 1990: index, s.v. *Freiheitserklärungen.*

64. See, e.g., Mossé 1962: esp. 216ff., 333ff.; Lévy 1976; Hamilton 1979: pt. 1; Gschnitzer 1981: 144ff.; Strauss 1986; Cartledge 1987; Lewis 1994: 24ff.; Tritle 1997; Munn 2000: pt. 3.

65. Exceptions concern especially uses of freedom in philosophy, but see below.

66. For a survey of fourth-century sources on *eleutheria:* "Materialien," pt. 4.

67. Gschnitzer 1976b: 3–4, 1981: 10ff., esp. 16–17, 24–25. See also Cassola 1964a: 276ff. Beringer (1982: 18, 22–23) is more cautious.

68. Thus, in particular Mele 1976: 115ff., esp. 122ff.; more generally, Maddoli 1970: 42ff. The views of van Effenterre on the structure of Minoan society, based on his finds in Mallia (van Effenterre and van Effenterre 1969) are summarized in van Effenterre 1985. His identification of an agora and prytaneion is patently influenced by his wish, in the interest of continuity (see below at nn. 82ff.), to recognize archaic society in its Minoan predecessor—an interpretation which Edouard Will in his review (*RH* 238 [1967]: 391 n. 1) rightly judges to be "quite adventurous."

69. E.g., the carpenter described as *Athēnaiēs dmōs* in Hes. *Erga* 430 (for parallels: West 1966: 188 at *Theog.* 100) or the biblical "servant of God" or "servant of the Lord." See Heubeck 1966: 106; Mele 1968; Walser 1984: 23 n. 51a; contra: Gérard-Rousseau 1968: 76. See also Lindgren 1973: 2.38–39. Gschnitzer (1981: 16–17) interprets these persons as temple slaves (*hierodouloi/-ai*). Privileged position: Garlan 1988: 27–28.

70. Garlan 1988: 26; I thank Cynthia Shelmerdine for showing me an unpublished chapter on Mycenaean society. See Lejeune 1959; Lencman 1966: esp. 151ff., 180ff. (with the comments of Gisela Wickert-Micknat, *Gnomon* 39 [1967]: 587ff.; Debord 1973: 225ff.); Wundsam 1968: 169ff. Summaries of the controversy in Lindgren 1973: 2.35ff.; Hiller and Panagl 1976: 108ff., 287–88. Morpurgo-Davies (1979: 93 n. 20) emphasizes the uncertainty about the status of Mycenaean "slaves," which contrasts sharply with the formal identity of *doero* and *doulos.* See further Olivier 1987 (on the sale of slaves); Garlan 1988: 25–29 (on qualitative differences between Mycenaean and later Greek forms of slavery); Hiller 1988 (on dependent personnel); Deger-Jalkotzy 1972; Chadwick 1988 (on the [slave?]-women of Pylos). I thank Thomas Palaima for bibliographical advice.

71. Uchitel 1988: 29.

72. For discussion of some of the relevant documents: esp. Ventris and Chadwick 1973: 298–99; also Lejeune 1958; Palmer 1963: 306ff.; Duhoux 1976: 161ff., esp. 165ff.; Hiller and Panagl 1976: 199ff.; Mele 1976: 118ff.; Garlan 1988: 29.

73. Contra: Mele 1976: 122ff., esp. 152–53, but see the discussion of Mele's theses by J. F. Goetschel and P. Debord (145ff., 151–52). For discussion of Cassola 1964a: Duhoux 1976: 168–69; and, on methodology: Hiller and Panagl 1976: 332–33.

74. See n. 66. Contra: Gschnitzer 1981: 24–25. The etymologies of the words involved might help, but they too are contested. *Doelos-doulos* is usually considered to have been borrowed from the Near East or Anatolia (Benveniste 1969: 1.355–61; Frisk 1954–72: 1.412), but Tovar (1971) and Gschnitzer (1976b: 7–8) suggest an Indo-European origin. *Ereutero-eleutheros,* like Latin *liber,* is usually connected with the Indo-European root **leudh-* (*leudhe-ros,* cf. German *liut-, Leute,* "people"), designating initially "growth," hence the community of growth and

descent, those who belong to the group, the people, the insiders, as opposed to the outsiders (Frisk 1954–72: 1.491; Pokorny 1959: 684–85; Walde and Hofmann 1965: 791; Benveniste 1969: 1.321–33; Gschnitzer 1976b: 3 n. 6). Insofar as the latter eventually include the dependent and unfree, those who belong are also seen as free. Szemerényi (1977: 108–16), however, accepts this derivation only for *liber;* the Greek word "originally applied to things only in the sense of 'free of impost.' It was borrowed from Anatolian **arawatar(a)* 'free(dom) of impost.'" Its meaning was extended "from (thing) 'free of impost' to (a person) 'free of obligations (characteristic of a slave)'" only in post-Mycenaean times. The discussion goes on; for its current state, see Squilloni Vignoli forthcoming: chap. 1.

75. Garlan 1988: 29.

76. E.g., Maddoli 1970: 17ff.

77. Starr 1961b: 42ff.; Vidal-Naquet 1963: 712–13; Finley 1982: chaps. 12–13. Deger-Jalkotzy (1988) and Uchitel (1988) suggest the Hittite Empire or Ugarit as the closest parallels. See also Lévy 1987. Generally on Mycenaean states and society: Chadwick 1976; Treuil et al. 1989; Dickinson 1994; Laffineur and Niemeier 1995; Bennet 1997.

78. Slaves: Dandamaev 1984; Kuhrt 1995: index, s.v. "slaves." Neither "free(dom)" nor "liberty" is listed in the indexes of these works; cf. Ostwald 1995: 43, and n. 17 above. Snell (2001) now attempts to demonstrate the importance of freedom in Mesopotamian and Israelite culture. His evidence, however, focuses entirely on the flight of slaves and the reaction of those in power to such flight. As far as I can see, none of this leads much beyond an appreciation (by deed more than word) of personal liberty and beyond the class of persons lacking it. Of course, the root of any freedom concept ultimately lies in this appreciation, but its historical impact is minimal if, to stay within the metaphor, no shoots, plants, and trees grow from this root. See chap. 2.2 at n. 103. Still, Snell's suggestions deserve a careful discussion, in which the evaluation of the linguistic evidence he adduces should play an important role.

79. See chap. 3.2 at nn. 188–90.

80. Jacobsen 1946: 202; see also Reinau 1981: 23ff. On ancient Israel: n. 17 above.

81. Above all, analogies should be sought in the economic system, which was directed centrally from the palace. See n. 77. For discussion of the nature of monarchy: Wundsam 1968: 16ff.; Hiller and Panagl 1976: 280–81; Thomas 1976; Milani 1981; Rehak 1995.

82. The discussion between Anna Morpurgo-Davies (1979) and Fritz Gschnitzer (1979), based chiefly on terminology, is instructive.

83. E.g., Starr 1961b: 46ff.; Snodgrass 1980: 15ff.; Finley 1982: chaps. 12, 13 (esp. 218ff.).

84. For this and other reasons, the views presented by Mele (1976) seem to me highly problematic.

85. *Dmōs* is probably linked with *dōma* (house) and thus, like *oiketēs* (*oikos,* "house"), is a functional term (see chap. 2.2, n. 53 below).

2. Awareness of Freedom in Archaic Greek Society

1. Compiled from "Materialien," secs. 4–5.

2. *Douleion eidos: Od.* 24.252–53; *doulē: Il.* 3.409; *Od.* 4.12; *doulosunē: Od.* 22.423. On *doulion ēmar,* see n. 4.

3. *Il.* 6.455; 16.831; 20.193. Exception: 6.528.

4. *Il.* 6.462–63. Cf. *Od.* 14.340; 17.320–23. Among others, Risch (1972: 192) emphasizes that in these formulaic phrases *eleutheros* is opposed not to *doulos* but to *doulios:* "le sens n'est pas 'libre,' mais '(jour, etc.) de la libération.'"

5. Examples in "Materialien," nn. 60–61. See Santiago 1962; Accame 1962: 313–14; Kirk 1985: 338, 1990: 221 ("most of evil import"). For the concept of time and the personal experience expressed by *ēmar,* see Accame 1962: 299ff., esp. 311ff.; Fränkel 1962: 4–6; Mele 1968: 93ff., 99ff.

6. "Materialien," n. 62; see Santiago 1962, citing linguistic arguments; and Mele 1968: 100–101, 171ff.

7. Mele 1968: 93ff., 99ff.

8. So used by Hesych. s.v. *eleutheron ēmar*. See "Materialien," n. 64; Santiago 1962: 148–50; Bömer 1957–63: 4.66 n. 4.

9. Gschnitzer 1964: 6–10, 1976b: 8–13, esp. 9.

10. On the custom of killing the men and enslaving only the women and children, see Ducrey 1968b: 113–15; Wickert-Micknat 1983: 33–45.

11. As also Gschnitzer 1976b: 9; cf. Patterson 1991: 52. See *Il.* 16.831, 835–36; *Od.* 14.271–72; 17.440–41; also 24.210: *dmōes anankaioi*.

12. See esp. *Il.* 6.455–58; Tritsch 1958: 416 n. 22; Mele 1968: 134; Beringer 1982: 24–28. Nestle (1967: 14–15; followed by van Straaten 1972: 108–9) too narrowly and absolutely interprets *eleutheron ēmar* as the day "on which one could live one's life at home" (11, my tr.); although this certainly was an essential factor, it was not the only or primary one for those affected (8–9): "Materialien," sec. 2 with n. 41.

13. Sol. 4W = 3GP.23–25; 36W = 30GP.5–15 (see n. 14). See Aristot. *AP* 2.2–3; 5.1; Plut. *Sol.* 13.3–5. For bibliography on the "Solonian crisis" and debt bondage, see n. 107.

14. Fr. 36W = 30GP.5: (*Gē*) *prosthen douleuousa, nun eleuthera;* 15: *eleutherous ethēka*. Aristot. *AP* 6.1: *ton dēmon ēleutherōse*. See chap. 2.3 below.

15. Willetts 1967: 13–17, 1965: 95–102. On the code: n. 18.

16. Kirk 1954: 245–49; Guthrie 1962: 446–48; Fränkel 1973: 375–76; Kahn 1979: 207–10.

17. Tr. Willetts 1967: 39–40; the code contains many more regulations with status distinctions (see n. 148 below). For discussion: Willetts 1967: 53ff., 1955, 1965.

18. Willetts 1967: 8, referring to Bonner and Smith 1930: 71 n. 13; cf. Guarducci 1935–50: 4.126 and, e.g., Gagarin 1982: esp. 138–46 (145: "from at least the early sixth century"); Davies 1996; Hölkeskamp 1999: 117–28.

19. Preserved in a version republished in 409/408: ML, no. 86 = *IG* I³ 104.36–37. Discussion and later sources: Morrow 1937; Maidment 1941: 151–52; MacDowell 1963: 20–22, 94–96, 126–27; Stroud 1968: 57; Grace 1973; Gagarin 1978: 119, 1979: 306; Mactoux 1988: 333–34; Tulin 1996: 18 n. 43.

20. The word is isolated and reconstructions vary greatly, as a comparison of *IG* I² 3.31–32, 35 with *IG* I³ 4.9, 13–14 shows. Date: *IG* I³ 4; Jordan 1979: 36–38.

21. Jordan 1979: 39.

22. Aeschin. 1.138–39 (tr. Adams, LCL) = F74 Ruschenbusch 1966; cf. also F20, cited by Dem. 23.53, without mentioning Solon. For discussion of these and other possibly Solonian laws mentioning slaves: Mactoux 1988.

23. Mactoux (1988: 339) thinks the original term was *oikeus*.

24. See Fisher 1992 for general discussion. Solonian origin: Fisher 1992: 68–82; Murray 1990.

25. *Od.* 17.320–23; 24.249–55. See also 4.244–50; Bömer 1957–63: 4.63–68 (commenting on the replacement of *aretē* by *nous* in Plat. *Laws* 6.777a); Lencman 1966: 298–300 (with additional references); Mele 1968: 170.

26. Alc. 72LP/C. See Page 1955: 171–75; Gomme 1957: 255–57; Bowra 1961: 147–49; Rösler 1980: 170–81. More in "Materialien," sec. 4.2.b with bibliography. Cassola (1964a: 270) here takes *eleutheros* as synonymous with *esthlos*, and *eleutheroi* with the aristocracy; so, too, Nestle 1967: 16. To characterize *eleutheros* as a word for "nobility" on the basis of this problematic fragment is not warranted: "Materialien," n. 227; and chap. 6.2 at nn. 200ff. below.

27. Hipponax fr. 26W(= 36 Degani 1983).5–6: barley as food for slaves (*doulion chorton*).

28. On the Theognis corpus, including its date: Lesky 1966b: 168–72; van Groningen 1966:

4. See generally Bowra 1938: 137–70; Adkins 1985: chap. 7; Figueira and Nagy 1985. None of the passages essential here belong to the poems addressed to Kyrnos; hence, they are probably not part of the old core of the collection (Ford 1985). Typology of slaves: Theogn. esp. 530–31; of the free: 535–38, 903–20, esp. 915–16 ("Materialien," 350 nn. 90, 92).

29. "Materialien," secs. 6.3, 8.3. On the political use of such typology: Ober 1989: 270–77.

30. Chantraine 1958: 2.14.

31. So, too, LSJ, 532, s.v. *eleutheros;* Schwyzer 1939–53: 2.178; Wickert-Micknat 1983: 51. See also schol. *Il.* 6.528: *ton ep'eleutheriai histōmenon.* Cf., e.g., Eumelus 1P (n. 35 below) and Xenarchus fr. 5 (2.596 Edm.): *eleutheron oinon* ("Materialien," n. 98). Comparable phrases in Bowra 1963: 152. Beringer's view (1961: 289–90; cf. Beringer 1985: 46–53; Garlan 1988: 45) that *eleutheros* means primarily the person who belongs to the community while *doul-* designates the person who does not belong (the "un-person") seems to me as problematic as Nestle's attempt (1967: 10–11)—based partly on Beringer—to postulate a "native krater"; see also Mele 1968: 173 with n. 166. This may have been the original meaning of the word (chap. 1.7, n. 74, above), but in Homer other aspects have moved into the foreground. On the cultural significance of the krater: Luke 1994.

32. On the concreteness of such conceptions, see Strasburger 1954: 230–31.

33. War: below at nn. 62ff. Sense of community: at n. 71 below. The community in Homer: Starr 1957, 1986; Thomas 1966; van Wees 1992: chap. 2; Raaflaub 1993 (with bibliography), 1997a: 629–30, 1997c; Olson 1995: chap. 9; Cook forthcoming.

34. As do Pohlenz 1955: 8–9 (= 1966: 4–5); Bömer 1957–63: 1.485 (freedom of the homeland); Beringer 1961: 288–91, 1985; Nestle 1967: 11 n. 33, 14; Mele 1968: 79; Wickert-Micknat 1983: 50–51; Garlan 1988: 31. See also below at n. 69.

35. On the problems posed by Eumelus 1P (mentioning "sandals of freedom," *eleuthera sambala*), see "Materialien," 192 with nn. 103–9.

36. Anacreon 419C (*amunōn patridos doulēiēn*). See Wilamowitz 1913: 105–6; Bowra 1961: 269–70; Fränkel 1973: 302 (= 1962: 345). Historical context: Graham 1992: 48–52.

37. Vlastos 1946; Solmsen 1949: 111–17; Jaeger 1960: 315–37 (= 1966: 77–99); Fränkel 1973: 220–22 (= 1962: 253–55); Stahl 1992 with more recent bibliography.

38. A close parallel is in Theogn. 39–52; see Nagy 1983 and generally Lintott 1981: chap. 2. Date of Solon's archonship: Raaflaub 1996c: 1052–53 with bibliography.

39. So, too, among others, Ferrara 1964: 72–73; Spahn 1977: 125, 128; Stahl 1992: 392–93. For a different view (the many under the few): e.g., Linforth 1913: 141, 201–2; Solmsen 1949: 112 n. 23; Masaracchia 1958: 264.

40. On the lack of a masculine equivalent: Gschnitzer 1976b: 8–10; Beringer 1982: 25–28 (with an improbable explanation).

41. See Beringer 1961, 1964, 1982, 1985; Gschnitzer 1964, 1976b; Lencman 1966; Mele 1968: 135ff.; Debord 1973; Ramming 1973.

42. Risch 1972: 193ff., 198 (summarized by Panagl and Hiller 1976: 14); Gschnitzer 1976b: 9, 12–13; Kirk 1990: 221 ("a technical term and restricted in usage"). Contra: "Materialien," 374 n. 501; Beringer 1982: 23 with n. 33. Richter's explanation (1968: 21), postulating a "humane Tendenz," seems implausible. Lawrence Tritle reminds me that the *Song of Roland* abounds in terminology that reflects social and institutional developments.

43. Donlan 1981–82: 172. See in detail Raaflaub 1998a; more briefly Raaflaub 1997a: 625–28; cf. esp. Strasburger 1953; Schadewaldt 1965: 87–129; Adkins 1971; Hampl 1975–79: 2.51–99; Finley 1977; Qviller 1981; Carlier 1984: pt. 2; Morris 1986; Ulf 1990; Auffahrt 1991: chap. 5; Patzek 1992; van Wees 1992; Murray 1993: chap. 3; Seaford 1994; Olson 1995: esp. chap. 9; Cook forthcoming. Contra, among others: Long 1970; Snodgrass 1974; Sherratt 1990; Thomas 1993; Cartledge 1996b: 687–88; Osborne 1996: 147–57 (who attributes at least the value system to Homer's

world). Date of the composition of the extant epics: Lesky 1967: 687–93; Heubeck 1974: 213–28; Kirk 1985: 1–10; Latacz 1996: 56–65 (second half of eighth century) vs. West 1966: 46–47, 1995; Burkert 1976; Taplin 1992: 33–35; van Wees 1992: 54–58; Crielaard 1995 (first half of seventh century). On the problem of the epics' fixation in writing, see the differing views of Powell 1991; Cook 1995; Nagy 1996. Dihle (1970: 165–73), Andreae and Flashar (1977: 260), and Finley (1977: 31–33), among others, think that the two epics were composed by the same poet but, if not, that they are still close enough in date to be considered together.

44. Finley (1977: chap. 2, esp. 48; followed by Austin and Vidal-Naquet 1977: 37–40; Donlan 1980: 2–3, 1981–82: 172–73, 1985: 298–305; and others) argues for the tenth to ninth centuries. Morris (1986), Ulf (1990: chap. 6), van Wees (1992: 261–65), and others favor the poet's own time; see also Welwei 1981. My own view (near but not entirely contemporary with the poet's time): Raaflaub 1991b: 211–15, 1997a: 628, 1998a: 181.

45. Selection: Calhoun 1962: 431; Raaflaub 1993: 46. Educator: Herington 1985: 67–71; Gentili 1988: 155–61; Raaflaub 1991b: 249–50 with more bibliography. See also Seaford 1994: chap. 1.

46. Latacz 1996: 32–35. Homeric "heroes" and "nobles" (*basileis*) should not simply be equated with a "nobility" or "aristocracy"; nor are they "kings" in any specific sense of the word. See Starr 1961a: 132–33, 1977: chap. 6, 1992: chap. 1; Spahn 1977: 38–47. Donlan (1980: chap. 1) speaks of "protonobility," observing that "in anthropological terms, the 'ranked' society of the tribal chiefdom had just begun to move in the direction of the 'class' or 'stratified' society of the archaic aristocratic state" (18). Lacking a better alternative, like Donlan (25), I use "nobility" and "nobles" as collective terms for the elite glorified in the epics. On early Greek elites, see Gschnitzer 1981: 38–47, 55–56, 60–67; Stein-Hölkeskamp 1989: chap. 2; Raaflaub 1991b: 230–38, 1997a: 634–36; Murray 1993: chap. 3.

47. Contra: Pohlenz 1955: 7 (= 1966: 3). Further discussion: below at nn. 102ff.

48. Finley (1977: 53–54; cf. Hasebroek 1931: 14–15, 20–21; Strasburger 1953: 98) takes for social reality what is essentially elite perception, representation, or ideology.

49. Thus, esp. Starr 1977: 121–28 (but see Millett 1984); Donlan 1980: chap. 1; Murray 1993: 68. Idealization: van Wees 1992: index s.v. The elite's refined lifestyle (e.g., Latacz 1984; Hölscher 1989: 21) does not contradict this assessment: Raaflaub 1991b: 237–38, 1997a: 635–37. Military and political importance of non-elite farmers: Latacz 1977; Gschnitzer 1981: 35–38; van Wees 1994, 1997: 692–93; Raaflaub 1997a: 642–46, 1997c, 1997d. Relations between elite and non-elite: Raaflaub 1997a: 634–36; see also Donlan 1999: 345–57; Haubold 2000.

50. See, e.g., Spahn 1980: 539; and next section below. For a different view: e.g., Gschnitzer 1976b: 12–13 with n. 36; Welwei 1981: 14.

51. This is true, above all, for the *dmōes, dmōiai,* but valid quite generally. See Beringer 1961, 1964 (where, however, "the argument unfortunately is constantly pushed to an absurd extreme" [Vidal-Naquet 1965: 123 n. 31, my tr.]); Lencman 1966; Gérard-Rousseau 1969; Ramming 1973; Gschnitzer 1976b: 60–68; Garlan 1988: 29–37. Beringer (1982, 1985) presents a different view.

52. As is evident especially in their kinship terminology (Miller 1953).

53. See, e.g., Westermann 1935: 895–98; Richter 1968: 17–23, esp. 19; Debord 1973: 236–37; Finley 1977: 53–55; Garlan 1988: 30–31; and, with modifications, Mele 1968: 130ff.; Beringer 1982. If the derivation of *dmōs* from *dōma* (house)—suggested, e.g., by Buck and Petersen 1945: 26; Fraenkel 1953: 23; Benveniste 1969: 1.297, 305, 358; and supported by Strasburger 1976: 24; Beringer 1982: 18—is correct, the original meaning of this term would also be functional; cf. the analogy of *mnoïtēs* (linguistically = *dmoïtēs,* LSJ) and *oikeus* in Cretan society: Willetts 1967: 13–17.

54. "Legal status" seems inappropriate, since in this early period legal forms were undeveloped and relationships based on power and influence predominated: see esp. Debord 1973:

234–35. Oikos: Lacey 1968: chap. 2; Finley 1977: 57–63; Donlan 1989a, 1989b: 7–13; Ulf 1990: chap. 5; van Wees 1992: 41–44; Hanson 1995: chap. 2; on a later period: Cox 1998.

55. Manumission, not documented before the end of the sixth century, probably was possible but rare and informal: Willetts 1954: 216; Rädle 1969: pt. 1; Garlan 1988: 73. Eumaeus's closeness to the master's family: Od. 15.361–79. The advancement Odysseus promises the two herdsmen Eumaeus (certainly a slave) and Philoetius (probably a slave) for their help in the fight against the suitors consists of a wife, property, and a house "close to his"; they will be "companions and brothers" to Telemachus (hetairoi kai kasignētoi): Od. 21.213–16; cf. 14.61–66. Plut. Quaest. Gr. 14 (Mor. 294d) speaks of manumission and enfranchisement; although echoed by many moderns, this certainly is anachronistic. See, e.g., Ehrhardt 1951: 88–89; Beringer 1964: 18–20; Lencman 1966: 300–301; Mele 1968: 160–61; Strasburger 1976: 35; Welwei 1981: 15; Wickert-Micknat 1983: 203–4 (all differing in details of their interpretation). Debord (1973: 234) emphasizes the importance of bearing arms for assimilation with the free; on bearing arms: van Wees 1998.

56. See generally Vidal-Naquet 1965: 123–24; Austin and Vidal-Naquet 1977: 44–45; Debord 1973: 234–38.

57. Thetes: see esp. Od. 11.488–91 (considered the lowest category in society, even below the slaves) with Finley 1977: 57–58, 71; but see Austin and Vidal-Naquet 1977: 44–45; Welwei 1981: 16; Garlan 1988: 35. See also Od. 18.356–75; Il. 21.441–52; Mele 1968: 120ff.; Richter 1968: 17–19; de Ste. Croix 1981: 179ff., esp. 185–86; Gschnitzer 1981: 33–34. Debt bondage: below at n. 111. The Roman clientele system offers another impressive illustration: e.g., Cornell 1995: 289–91.

58. See esp. Il. 6.207–11; 11.783–84; 12.310–21; Jaeger 1954–61: 1.chaps. 1–2; Adkins 1960: chap. 3, 1972: chap. 2; Finley 1977: 113–14; Donlan 1980: chap. 1; van Wees 1992: chap. 3. Dependence of all others: Frost 1994: 46.

59. E.g., Il. 6.476–81; 15.494–99. On the consequences of defeat: below at nn. 62ff.; Ducrey 1968b: 113–15; Wickert-Micknat 1983: 32–45 and passim. Annihilation: cf. Patterson's characterization of slavery as "social death": 1982, 1991: 10.

60. Pirates: e.g., Od. 14.294–97; 15.415–84; cf. Wickert-Micknat 1983: chap. 2.

61. Spahn 1977: 29–37; Gschnitzer 1981: 41–47, 1983, 1991; Donlan 1989b; van Wees 1992: chap. 2; Raaflaub 1993: 54–57, 1997a: 642–46, 1997c.

62. The significance of Il. 6.528–29 (setting up the "wine-bowl of liberty") should therefore not be overestimated (see above at n. 34; Meier 1975: 426 with n. 3). What really mattered is expressed quite differently by Paris (Il. 3.70–75) and Hector (15.496–99, quoted below). Raids and booty: see esp. Il. 18.509–40; 11.670–761 (with Bölte 1934); Bruck 1926: 41–58; Hampl 1975–79: 3.3–5; Starr 1977: 47–48 (cf. Starr 1961a: 136–37); Karavites 1982a: 13–16; Wickert-Micknat 1983: pt. 1; Nowag 1983; Jackson 1993. On forms of war and war in interstate relations: Raaflaub 1997c, 1997d.

63. See the Homer lexica, s.v. saoō and soos (sōtēria first occurs in plays of the fifth century, sōtēr in Pindar and Simonides), as well as s.v. eruō/rhuomai (related to Latin servare), listing well over fifty occurrences in the Iliad alone. Among lyric poets, Alc. 129LP; Tyrt. 11.13W; Carm. pop. 858.17P; Hipponax 81.3D; Theogn. 68, 235, 675, 868, are especially informative. See further Fatouros 1966: s.vv.

64. Warriors: see, variously, Il. 1.117, 344; 5.23; 7.307–9; 8.243–44; 9.248; 11.363; 15.290, 563; 16.252; 20.93, 194–95, 311; 21.608–11; 22.232. Women: Il. 6.94–95 (= 275–76); 15.496–99; 17.221–28; 24.728–32. City: Il. 6.95, 276, 306; 15.496–97; 17.144–45. Destruction of the city: e.g., Il. 6.326–31, 447–49; 8.241; 13.772–73.

65. E.g., Il. 1.117; 8.246; 9.78, 230; 15.496–99, 502–3; 17.221–28.

66. *Il.* 9.396; 16.542; Stegmann von Pritzwald 1930: 26; Haubold 2000: 10 and passim. Athena: cf. *Hymn. Hom.* 11.1, 4; 28.3; Mastrocinque 1981: 5 with bibliography in n. 12; cf. later *sōsipolis* (Aristoph. *Ach.* 163) and the deity Sosipolis, appearing in various places (Roscher 1924–37: 4.1221–28; *LIMC* 7.1.799); on the corresponding coins from Gela: e.g., Gielow 1940–41: 112; *LIMC* 7.1.799–800.

67. For this meaning of *echō* and Hector's name, see 6.402–3 (Astyanax, "since Hector alone saved Ilion": *erhueto*; cf. 22.506–7); 5.473; 24.730; see also 24.499, 728–30; cf. Nagy 1979: 145–46.

68. Esp. *Il.* 15.496–99 (below) with 502–3, 659; 17.144–45, 220–28. See Latacz 1977; and, on the Achaean "polis," Raaflaub 1993: 47–48.

69. Above at n. 30.

70. E.g., on Strasburger's (1954) side: Adkins 1960, 1972; Finley 1977: chap. 4; Austin and Vidal-Naquet 1977: 40–44; Spahn 1977: chap. 1; Donlan 1980: chap. 1; Reinau 1981: 9–14; Murray 1993: chap. 3. Contra: Hoffmann 1956; Greenhalgh 1972; Gschnitzer 1981: chap. 2; van Wees 1992; Raaflaub 1993: 51–59.

71. Power of the oikos: e.g., *Il.* 1.281; see Donlan 1981–82, 1989b: 7–13; Gschnitzer 1981: 40–41; van Wees 1992: 41–53. Recognition by community: *Il.* 12.310–28 with Redfield 1975: 99–103.

72. See Adkins 1960, 1972; Herman 1987; and, on early political reflection, Donlan 1973; Rose 1975; Gschnitzer 1976a; Welwei 1981: 13 and passim; Raaflaub 1988a: 197–261, 1988b, 1998a, 2000c; Nicolai 1993; Spahn 1993.

73. A rare exception is Hector's worrying about Andromache's fate if Troy falls (*Il.* 16.440–65).

74. See, e.g., Busolt and Swoboda 1926: 333–41; Martin 1951: 17–62; Finley 1977: 78–82, 108–16; Spahn 1977: 29–37; Andreev 1979; and following nn.

75. The assemblies in *Il.* bks. 1–2 and *Od.* bk. 2 offer good examples. *Od.* 2.25–34: war and other "public matters" (*dēmion*: 32, 44) as the assembly's business. New themes and criticism: *Il.* 2.225–42 (rejected: 246–77; cf. Gschnitzer 1976a); *Od.* 2.40ff., esp. 63ff., 166ff., 229ff. (dismissal of the assembly: 252–57; cf. Rose 1975: 136–37). See Raaflaub 1988b: 9–16, 1989a: 11–18.

76. Speech: *Il.* 1.258; 9.53–54, 442–43; Kennedy 1963: 35–39; Raaflaub 1980: 24–26; Martin 1989. Assembly: Havelock 1978; Gschnitzer 1983, 1991; Carlier 1984: esp. 182–87; Bannert 1987; Raaflaub 1993: 54–57, 1997c: 8–20; Flaig 1994, 1997; Hölkeskamp 1997.

77. Hence, again, attempts to characterize the polis as a "space of freedom" or to establish that "freedom of the state" was a relevant concept (above at n. 31) seem to me misguided.

78. Thus, rightly, Welskopf 1964: 332–33.

79. On the existence and significance of this class: e.g., Hasebroek 1931: 33–39; Richter 1968: 16. More above, n. 49. I use "farmer" (rather than "peasant") in a generic sense; for discussion, see Millett 1984; Hanson 1995.

80. Especially since Hesiod describes contemporary sociopolitical conditions in *WD*, the work is useful for understanding Greek society of the archaic period; see Donlan 1980: 26–34; Raaflaub 1993: 59–64. On Hesiod's intellectual importance and his relationship to the Homeric epics: Solmsen 1949: pt. 1; Jaeger 1954–61: 1.55–76; Munding 1959; Kirk 1960; Lesky 1966b: 91–106; West's introductions to 1966, 1978; Barron and Easterling 1985. On Hesiod's date: also Janko 1982: 94–98, 228–32. Assessments of his autobiographical remarks vary: see Gagarin 1974; Erler 1987; Lamberton 1988: chap. 1; Nagy 1990: 36–82, who emphasizes the poet's Panhellenic significance. On his sociohistorical usefulness: e.g., Burn 1936; Nussbaum 1960; Detienne 1963; Spahn 1980: 533–44; Millett 1984; Stein-Hölkeskamp 1989: 57–63; Hanson 1995: chap. 3; Tandy and Neale 1996. Osborne (1996: 143–47) reminds us that Hesiod, too, is selective, his picture influenced by his particular agenda.

81. *WD* 1–297; cf. *Theog.* 81–93. On justice in Hesiod: esp. Wolf 1950: 120–51; Gagarin 1973, 1986: 46–50, 1992; Havelock 1978: chap. 11; Erler 1987; Erbse 1993; Nagy 1993; and the bibliography cited in n. 87.

82. Esp. *Il* 16.384–92; *Od.* 19.109–14.

83. Likewise in the Prometheus-Pandora myth, humankind collectively suffers for the wrongdoing of one individual, its divine *promachos*, Prometheus (*WD* 47–50, 54–59, 90–106).

84. See, in contrast, e.g., *Il.* 9.63–64: "Out of all brotherhood [*aphrētōr*], outlawed [*athemistos*], homeless shall be that man who longs for all the horror of fighting among his own people [*polemos epidēmios*]." See Andrewes 1961; Kirk 1985: 154 (mention of phratries as "intrusion" from the poet's own time).

85. Marg 1970: 138–41 (quot. 138, my tr.); Solmsen 1949: 29–32; Fränkel 1960: 320–23; West 1966: 230–32.

86. Fränkel 1960: 322–23; Marg 1970: 140–41; on *atē*, Stallmach 1968.

87. Hirzel 1907: chap. 1; Ehrenberg 1921: 3–18; Wolf 1950: chaps. 1, 4, 5; Latte 1968: 140–45, 233–51.

88. Solmsen 1949: 34–36, 66–75; Ostwald 1969: 63–64. For a comparable case, Snell 1975: 45.

89. Bowra 1958: 238; West 1966: ad loc.; Marg 1970: 286.

90. On *eunomia*, see n. 164 below. The combination is probably Hesiod's own, just as the personifications of Eirene and Eunomia are found here for the first time. See Pind. *Ol.* 13.6–8 (cf. Will 1955: 620–24); fr. 57Sn-M (cf. Ostwald 1969: 64).

91. See, e.g., Fränkel 1960: 323. On the nature and function of Hesiod's personifications: esp. Solmsen 1949: chap. 1; Fränkel 1960: 316–34, 1973: 96–108; Snell 1975: 45–55; see also Ehrenberg 1921: 127 on *Il.* 9.145; more generally, Feldman 1971.

92. It is suggestive that no noun existed yet for "freedom" and the term could thus not be personified. This, however, does not affect the possibility of referring to the issue of freedom in one of the traditional contexts, for which, for example, the formula of *eleutheron/doulion ēmar* (still popular in poetry of the early fifth century: chap. 3.1 at nn. 20, 22 below) would have sufficed.

93. *WD* 459, 502, 573, 597, 608, 766 (*dmōes*); 430, 470 (*dmōios*); 405–6 (a "bought woman," *gunaika ktētēn*; cf. Sinclair 1932: ad loc.). On slavery in Hesiod: Nussbaum 1960: 215–20.

94. Hesiod's purpose in the Hecate hymn (*Theog.* 430–34; see West 1966: 128 for text, 285–86 for comm.) is different; see Boedeker 1983: 83–84. Lawsuits: *WD* 27–34; cf. Detienne 1963: 21; Spahn 1980: 543–44.

95. Wade-Gery 1949: 91–92.

96. An exception is *Theog.* 431–41 (again in the Hecate hymn): Boedeker 1983: 84–85.

97. Osborne 1996: 146–47: the world of *WD* has to be without war, "for the sudden gains and losses which the violence of war brings would upset the plausibility of a direct connection between labour and prosperity."

98. Wade-Gery's assessment (at n. 95 above) is extreme; so is Detienne's (1963: 19). On *Theog.* 228, see the parallels listed by West 1966: ad loc. On *WD* 160–73 (the "race of heroes"), see Wade-Gery 1949: 92 n. 9.

99. Otherwise we would expect these aspects to have been reflected more strongly in *WD*, not least in the description of the Iron Age (Wade-Gery 1949: 92). See also Nussbaum 1960: 217–18; Detienne 1963: 19; Ruschenbusch 1978: 76. Alternatively, the motif of war, not between neighboring cities but about the conquest and destruction of cities, might have been a more traditional epic theme; but see Raaflaub 1991b: 222–25, 1997d: 51–53.

100. Debt: *WD* 344–60, 394–404. Chances for improvement: *WD* 298–316, 335–41, 361–65, 381–82; cf. especially the admonition to be content with one son: 376–80. See Will 1957: 9–

10, 12–24; Detienne 1963: 21–27; Spahn 1977: 52–58; Donlan 1980: 26–40; Millett 1984; Link 1991: 30–31. Ernest Will's reconstruction (1965) has been contested: Will 1967: 422 n. 5.

101. Schäfer 1963: 313 (my tr.).

102. As noted by Drexler 1976: 21. See further, chap. 2.3 at n. 157 below. Typology of the master: e.g., *Od.* 24.249–55. See also Rose 1975: 135, 139–40; Donlan 1980: 4–8.

103. Patterson 1991. For his approach and methodology, see his introduction. I focus here on his chap. 3 and parts of chap. 4, which deal with the emergence of the consciousness of freedom in early Greece. See also chap. 7.1 at n. 14 below and, for a more detailed critique, Raaflaub forthcoming. Patterson's expertise on modern slavery: 1982.

104. See only Adkins 1960, 1972; van Wees 1992.

105. Patterson 1986. I have collected bibliography on women's condition in classical Athens (with a brief summary of relevant debates) in Raaflaub 1998c: 32–36.

106. *Il.* 6.407–65. On women in Homeric society, see the summary and bibliography in Raaflaub 1997a: 639–41. Male voice: for an early discussion of this and related issues, see Arthur 1973; more recently, Doherty 1995.

107. For discussion and bibliography: Raaflaub 1996c: 1038–42, 1997b: 104–8. On Solon's date: Raaflaub 1996c: 1052–53 with bibliography.

108. Nagy 1990: 67–71 (quot. 71); cf. Anhalt 1993. Raaflaub 1996c: 1041–42, 1997b: 107–8.

109. Fr. 36W = 30GP.8–15: "To Athens, to their home of divine origin, I brought back many who had been sold, some unjustly, some justly, and some who had fled out of dire necessity, who no longer spoke the Athenian tongue after wandering in many places. Others, who were subjected there to shameful slavery, fearing the whims of their masters, I set free" (tr. Rhodes 1984: 52); cf. fr. 4W = 3GP.23–25.

110. Fr. 36W = 30GP.5–7. On *horoi*, n. 119 below.

111. See Aristot. *AP* 2.1–2, 5.1–2; Plut. *Sol.* 13.3–6. Earlier scholarship on the various statuses involved and the causes of the crisis is cited in Manfredini and Piccirilli 1977: 169–78; Rhodes 1981: 94–97; Chambers 1990: 143–47. See also Gschnitzer 1981: 75–84; Andrewes 1982: 375–91; Gallant 1982; Oliva 1988; Rihll 1991; Welwei 1992: 150–61; Murray 1993: chap. 11; Osborne 1996: 221–25; Harris 1997; Foxhall 1997. On the thesis of Cassola (1964a: 276, 1964b: 45–46, 1973: 77–78) that the issue was public land occupied by the elite, and "liberated" here means "returned to the people," see Will 1967: 424–25; Lévy 1973: 89–90. The thesis has been revived by Link (1991: 13–34) and merits careful attention. Debt bondage: de Ste. Croix 1981: index s.v.; Finley 1982: 150–66.

112. *Isomoiria:* fr. 34W = 29bGP.8–9; cf. Vlastos 1946: 75–82, 1953: 352–54. Rosivach (1992) offers a different interpretation. See generally the references in n. 13 above. "Freeing the earth" (fr. 36W = 30GP.3–7) seems used here as a metaphor—conjuring up the entire symbolic, religious, and emotional content of the idea—for "freeing the farmers." See, e.g., Pohlenz 1955: 11 (= 1966: 7); Masaracchia 1958: 143, 342, 350ff., esp. 352–53; Edouard Will 1965: 66–67 with n. 1; Nestle 1967: 25 (with parallels in n. 56). Harris (1997) proposes a different interpretation of *seisachtheia.*

113. 9, 11W = 12, 15GP (cf. above at nn. 38–39), if these poems are autobiographical. Solon: 32–34W = 29–29bGP; cf. Aristot. *AP* 11.2–12.2; Plut. *Sol.* 14.4–15.1.

114. Among others, Woodhouse (1938: 12–13) and Ferrara (1964: 33 n. 26) think that whatever was politically essential has survived.

115. See Solon's unsuccessful warnings (n. 113) and his chastising of the demos for their political stupidity. See also 4W = 3GP.18. Generally, in contrast to the majority of the elite, the demos, though not necessarily supporting the establishment of tyranny, frequently tolerated it and did nothing to oppose it (chap. 3.2 at n. 148 below).

116. Minority: Aristotle and Plutarch (n. 13 above), who imply that "the majority were the

slaves of the few" (*AP* 5.1), undoubtedly simplify and exaggerate the polarization, based on Solon himself, who mentions only those groups, at the extremes of the social ladder, that were antagonists in the crisis: Ehrenberg 1968: 56; Spahn 1977: 118–19; Rhodes 1981: 95. In 4W = 3GP.24 and 36W = 30GP.8, Solon himself mentions "many"; see von Fritz 1943.

117. 36W = 30GP.9–10: *prathentas, allon ekdikōs, allon dikaiōs* (tr. in n. 109 above). See Ferrara 1964: 100 n. 28; Ehrenberg 1968: 55, 58. Archaic laws of debt in general: Finley 1982: 150–66. A possible connection with the legislation of Draco: Ruschenbusch 1960: 149 with n. 104, 1966: 7–8; Hopper 1966: 140–42.

118. See Finley 1982: 120, 150–66. Analogies in the Code of Gortyn: Willetts 1967: 14. Citizenship: below at nn. 136ff.

119. Hence, Solon's boast to have pulled the *horoi* out and liberated the earth: 36W = 30GP.5–7. On the meaning of *horoi* in this time and context: e.g., Fine 1951: 177–91; Rhodes 1981: 94–95, 175; Link 1991: 15–22; Harris 1997: 104–6.

120. See n. 109; generally, esp. Starr 1977: 46–54, esp. 52–53; Gschnitzer 1981: 60–67; Gernet 1981: 279–88, esp. 286–87. Elite rivalries: Lintott 1981: chap. 2. Similar problems, plaguing contemporary Megara, are reflected in the Theognis corpus: see Figueira and Nagy 1985: chaps. 1, 5.

121. See esp. 5W = 7GP.1–2; 34W = 29bGP; 36W = 30GP.20–27; 37W = 31GP. That the aspect of liberation was important for debtors of all categories, even those not *stricto sensu* enslaved, is stressed by Solon himself (36D = 30GP.5–15); cf. von Fritz 1976: 113, 116, 128–29, 131.

122. In *Entdeckung*, 58–59, I speculated about the factors possibly involved and the nature of ongoing changes. I think now that the extant evidence does not allow us to grasp these changes in any detail. Nor are these aspects essential for my argument. Recent summaries of the state of our knowledge are available in Starr 1977, 1982; Stein-Hölkeskamp 1989: 57–85; Welwei 1992: pt. 3; Murray 1993: chap. 11; Osborne 1996: 215–25.

123. See von Fritz 1976: 128–29; Peremans 1972; Weeber 1973; Gschnitzer 1981: 78–79. Increase in trade and crafts in this period: Austin and Vidal-Naquet 1977: 54–56; Starr 1977: chaps. 3–4, 1982: esp. 425–31. Snodgrass (1980: chap. 4) is more cautious. Crisis: above at nn. 107, 119.

124. Role of the free farmers: Raaflaub 1997d. Evidence on the development of institutions is scarce; it consists mostly of Homer and scattered references in other poetry and inscriptions. No modern systematic study exists; see, e.g., Welwei 1983; Carlier 1984, 1991; Ruzé 1984, 1997; Stahl 1987: 149–75; Stein-Hölkeskamp 1989: 94–103; Raaflaub 1997c. Eder (1998: esp. 121–34) stresses the role of the elite. Law: n. 127 below.

125. Attested well in the Theognis corpus: Figueira and Nagy 1985.

126. Eder 1986, 1998. For a comparison between Greece and Rome: Raaflaub 1984b: 553–63, 1986: 29–34. Elite rivalries in Athens: on the attempted coup of Cylon, see Rhodes 1981: 79–84; Welwei 1992: 133–37 (both with sources and bibliography); on the period after Solon, see Aristot. *AP* 13–15.1, with Rhodes 1981: ad loc.; Andrewes 1982: 392–98; Stahl 1987: 56–105; Welwei 1992: 219–27.

127. Lawgivers: Bonner and Smith 1930: chap. 3; Gagarin 1986: chap. 3, esp. 58ff.; for a reassessment, see Hölkeskamp 1992a, 1992b, 1999; Gehrke 1993; a brief summary with more bibliography in Raaflaub 1993: 69. Political culture and political thought: Meier 1990: 29–52.

128. Ruschenbusch 1960; Stroud 1968; Gagarin 1981a; Humphreys 1991; Welwei 1992: 138–46.

129. Chios: Theopompus, *FGrH* 155 F122; cf. Hdt. 6.137.3; on Hipponax fr. 27W, see Starr 1961b: 365 n. 9; Debord 1973: 239–40. Dependent labor: Finley 1982: 127–28 ("Structurally and ideologically, dependent labour was integral, indispensable."); de Ste. Croix 1981: 112–14, 133.

Interconnection: Heuss 1965: 75–78; Will 1967: 435–36; Finley 1980: chap. 2, esp. 82–92 (a crucial discussion); de Ste. Croix 1981: 141–42; Mactoux 1988; Manville 1990: 132–34. Comparison with Rome: n. 132 below.

130. Solon's standing between the factions: frs. 5W = 7GP; 36W = 30GP.15–27; 37W = 31GP.

131. Finley 1982: 118–19, 162 (quot.). See Austin and Vidal-Naquet 1977: 70–72.

132. Typically, failing debtors were sold abroad both in Rome (*trans Tiberim: Twelve Tables* 3.5; Gell. *N.A.* 20.1.47; Ampolo 1987: 76–80) and in Athens (Sol. 36W = 30GP.8–12). See de Ste. Croix 1981: 162; Finley 1982: 139.

133. Fr. 4W = 3GP, one of the prime documents of Solon's political thinking; see below at n. 168.

134. Comparison with the Roman "struggle of the orders" is illustrative but difficult. For example, it is indicative of the power and solidarity of the patrician aristocracy that they were able to resist for a long time plebeian pressure caused by debt problems, that the law of debt was fixed in the *Twelve Tables* in very harsh terms, that vigorous efforts to resolve the problems were undertaken only after the beginning of large-scale territorial expansion in the fourth century, and that debt bondage was abolished only when this could be achieved without losses to the elite. For discussion: Finley 1980: chap. 2, 1982: 156–62; Raaflaub 1984b: 552ff., esp. 561–65, 1986: 210–27; Eder 1986; Cornell 1995: index, s.v. "debt."

135. See esp. frs. 5–6W = 7–8GP; for discussion: Raaflaub 1996c: 1058–72, 1998b: 38–39; contra: Wallace 1998.

136. Finley (1982: chap. 7) emphasizes that this represents an exceptional development among ancient societies.

137. For discussion of citizenship in Solonian Athens: e.g., Welwei 1967: 427; Davies 1977–78: 105ff., esp. 114–17; Spahn 1977: 64–69; Whitehead 1977: 140–43; Reinau 1981; Sealey 1983; Manville 1990: chaps. 5–6; Walter 1993b: 176–209. 451/450: next note.

138. Frost 1994: 45: citizenship "is one of those notions that becomes relevant only when it conveys a benefit that some people receive and others do not." For general and theoretical discussions: e.g., Manville 1990: chap. 1, 1994; Whitehead 1991; Scafuro 1994; Connor 1994; Ostwald 1996. A good example is Pericles' citizenship law of 451/450: Patterson 1981; a summary of recent views in Raaflaub 1998c: 35–36.

139. Enactment of written law as means of integration: Ruschenbusch 1960: 149–52, 1983; Eder 1986; Gagarin 1986: 78–80; Gehrke 1993. Unifying effect of tyranny: Stahl 1987: pt. 3; Ober 1989: 60–68; Manville 1990: chap. 7; Eder 1992; Bleicken 1994: 28–34. End of sixth century: Frost 1994; Anderson 2000, 2003: chap. 4.

140. Economic and social changes: French 1964; Frost 1976; Davies 1992; Raaflaub 1998c: 22–30. Metic status: Hommel 1932: esp. 1424–39; Whitehead 1977: 140–54; Sealey 1983: 116–23; Manville 1990: 135 n. 35. See also next note.

141. Frost (1994: 47–51) and Manville (1990: chap. 6) suggest a higher degree of integration. Immigrants: under Solon, see Plut. *Sol.* 24.4; on the *diapsēphismos* (scrutiny of citizen lists) and enfranchisements under Cleisthenes, of doubtful authenticity, see n. 150 below.

142. Sealey 1983: 111–15, with examples. *Metanastai: Il.* 9.648; 16.59. Gschnitzer (1981: 29) points out that in both passages this status is characterized as *atimētos*, "lacking prestige"; I suggest that this concerned persons who, like the thetes (above at n. 57), were not protected by a powerful elite oikos; those who were protected became full members of the community later (Hainsworth [1993: 144] overlooks this difference). I see here similarities with the Roman system of *clientela* that should be explored further. The fate of the unprotected refugee or emigrant is illustrated in Tyrt. 10W = 6GP.3–10.

143. Whether or not this army was employed frequently: Frost 1984.

144. Since we do not know whether they were able to regain control over land previously lost, speculation on this issue seems futile.

145. Rhodes 1981: 140–41. I have argued that this did not change much even under Cleisthenes: Raaflaub 1996b: 145–47, 1998b: 39–44, 91–93; contra: Ober 1993, 1998b.

146. See n. 20 above; Jordan 1979: 39. By contrast, in the late seventh century, as attested by Draco's law (*IG* I³ 104; ML, no. 86, line 28), *Athēnaios* probably still was the designation "for all members of the community who might be affected by the pollution resulting from a homicide" (Frost 1994: 48). Free noncitizens in cult: see, e.g., the Panathenaic procession (Maurizio 1998).

147. The Roman *Twelve Tables* offer a good example: see Wieacker 1967: esp. 301–2, 315, 332. Archaic Greek legislation: Bonner and Smith 1930: chap. 3; Ruschenbusch 1960, 1983; Gschnitzer 1981: 73–75; Eder 1986; Gagarin 1986: chaps. 3–4; Camassa 1988, 1996; and esp. Hölkeskamp 1992a, 1992b, 1999; Gehrke 1993. Examples in Solonian laws: above at nn. 22ff.; in the Code of Gortyn (at n. 17 above): e.g., cols. 1.42; 3.22; 5.53–54 (status of free witnesses); 1.4–5, 9; 2.2–28 (differentiated fines, see next n.); 1.15–18, 25, 29 (contested personal status); 6.55–7.10 (next n.).

148. E.g., concerning the status of children of mixed marriages; see *Od.* 14.202; Solon F20 in Ruschenbusch 1966, with Harrison 1968: 13–14, 164; Code of Gortyn, cols. 6.55–7.10, with Willetts 1955: 34–35, 1967: 15. Communal control: Ruschenbusch 1960: esp. 145–46, 153–54; more generally, 1968. Differentiated penalties in the Code of Gortyn: see the informative charts in Willetts 1955: 33–34, 1967: 10; in Draco's law: Ruschenbusch 1960: 136–37; in Solon's laws: Ruschenbusch 1960: 137 n. 31, 1966: 13, 80.

149. But see Ehrenberg 1967: 136–37.

150. See Heuss 1965: 75–78; Davies 1977–78. On possible disenfranchisements and (re)enfranchisements after the fall of tyranny: Aristot. *AP* 13.5, 21.4, with *Pol.* 3.1275b34–39 and the comms. by Rhodes 1981; Chambers 1990; see also Welwei 1967; Bicknell 1969; Fornara 1970b; Peremans 1972; Sealey 1983: 117–18; Manville 1990: 174–89. On the entire process: Whitehead 1977: 143–54; Reinau 1981: 36–51.

151. Raaflaub 1983; and see below, chap. 6.2 at n. 119 and the end of chap. 7.2.

152. Again, the comparison with Rome is illustrative: Raaflaub 1984b.

153. Frs. 4W = 3GP.17–18; 9W = 12GP.3–4; 11W = 15GP.1–4; see above at n. 37.

154. Esp. in frs. 4W = 3GP.17–18 (where *pasa polis* means "every city" as well as "the entire city": Solmsen 1949: 112 n. 23); 9W = 12GP.3–4. Moreover, Solon addresses "the Athenians" and talks of "our city": 4W = 3GP.1, 30–31; cf. 11W = 15GP.

155. See n. 167; absence of *eleutheros*: above, after n. 39.

156. Above at nn. 40–41.

157. Opposition: Zeller 1910: 454–57; Risch 1972: 193–94; Klees 1975: 18–26. Etymology: Walde and Pokorny 1927: 787; Frisk 1954–72: s.v; Benveniste 1969: 1.304–5. The word *despotēs* is not found in the *Iliad* and appears in the *Odyssey* only in the feminine (Wackernagel 1916: 209 n. 1; for references see the lexica on Homer). The word always implies the antithesis master-servant/slave, even when the wife and mistress (*alochos despoina*) performs a task that is usually left to a maidservant (*Od.* 3.403, 7.347).

158. See chap. 3.1–2 below. Foreign conquest: Stegmann von Pritzwald 1930: 84, followed by Rengstorf 1935: 43. In Tyrt. 6.2, 7.1W = 5GP.2, 4 (Stegmann von Pritzwald's primary reference) *despotēs* applies to the relationship between the helots and their Spartiate masters.

159. Solon: n. 115 above, for criticism of the demos as being submissive to tyrants (see also n. 113). Ionians: Theogn. 847–50 (849: *dēmon philodespoton*); and, e.g., Hdt. 4.142 (*andrapoda philodespota*). In connection with the liberation of debt bondsmen (36W = 30GP.13–15), Solon applies the antithesis *despotēs-doulos* to the private sphere as well. See also Hybr. 909.5–

10P; Aesch. *Pers.* 241–42; *Eum.* 526–28, 696–97; *Prom.* 926–27; and frequent usage in the historians.

160. Details in Klees 1975: 18–26.

161. See Sappho 95.8LP (Hermes); *Hom. Hymn. Dem.* 365 (*desposseis pantōn*); Anacreon 348.3P (*despoin' Artemi thērōn*); Bacch. *Epin.* 11.117Sn-M (Artemis as *chrusea despoina laōn*), 13.95; Pind. fr. 122.17Sn-M (Aphrodite as *Kyprou despoina*), *Nem.* 1.13 (*Olympou despotas Zeus; cf.* fr. 36Sn-M). Cf. the analogy of aristocrats or monarchs: Archil. 3.5W (*despotai Euboiēs*); Pind. *Pyth.* 4.11 (Medea as *despoina Kolchōn*), 53; cf. fr. 122.13–14; *Pyth.* 4.53.

162. Berve 1967: 1.3 with 2.517; Fadinger 1993: 265.

163. Hesiod: at nn. 79ff. above. Homer: Havelock 1978: chaps. 7–10; Gagarin 1986: chap. 2; and further bibliography in Raaflaub 1993: 51 with 91 n. 34.

164. Andrewes 1938; Ehrenberg 1946: 70–93 (= 1965a: 139–58); Erasmus 1960; Ostwald 1969: 62–95 (with further bibliography in p. 62 n. 1); Meier 1970: 15–25.

165. Fr. 4W = 3GP.17–18, 31; Schäfer 1932: 147; Sinclair 1967: 21–22, 31; Ostwald 1969: 85–95; Meier 1972: 822.

166. See below, after n. 169, for the hierarchy of values, and chaps. 3.2 at n. 159 and 6.1–2 (passim) for *isonomia*.

167. Contra: Pohlenz 1955: 11 (= 1966: 7); Snell 1965: 94–95; Meier 1975: 426; Spahn 1977: 31–32; among many others, who assume that the concept of political freedom emerged as the result of experiences with debt bondage and tyranny. In this context one came to understand "the connection between the freedoms of the individuals and the freedom of the whole, the polis" (Spahn 1977: 32).

168. See esp. frs. 4W = 3GP.1–29; 9W = 12GP. Ostwald 1969: 67–69; Meier 1970: 19–25; and recent summaries in Raaflaub 1996c: 1058–62, 1997b: 109–11.

169. Vlastos 1946: 73–74; Flach 1973; Starr 1977: 184–87. On this poem: generally, Jaeger 1926; Vlastos 1946; Stahl 1992; Meier 1993a: 69–84; Raaflaub 1996c: 1058–71, 1997b: 109–11, 2001b: 89–99. Solidarity: Reinau 1981: 20–29; Manville 1990: chap. 8. Legal protection: Vlastos 1946; Ruschenbusch 1968.

170. Meier 1970: 19, 26, 28. Even in his encomium of *eunomia* (4W = 3GP.32–39), Solon emphasizes its ability, not to grant or protect freedom, but to restore order and balance. For a comparable hierarchy of values in Hesiod: at n. 92 above. *Hubris, koros:* Pearson 1962: chap. 3, esp. 70–73; Fisher 1992: 68–82.

171. "Nomistic thinking": Meier 1970: 15–25; cf. Meier 1990: chap. 7, esp. 173–76.

3. The Emergence of the Political Concept of Freedom

1. In the "Second Messenian War," the Messenians rather than the Spartans would have used a freedom slogan; hence, much mistaken trust has been placed in Eumelus 1P (chap. 2.1, n. 35, above).

2. E.g., Lattimore 1942; Friedländer and Hoffleit 1948; Peek 1955, 1960: nos. 23–52; Gentili 1968: 69–81.

3. Chap. 2.1 at n. 36.

4. "Materialien," secs. 7.2, 9.2, 15.3; and below at n. 6.

5. Among many, Pohlenz 1955: 15 (= 1966: 11–12); Gelzer 1973: 34.

6. "Materialien," secs. 9.2.a–c, 9.7. Herodotus and freedom: von Fritz 1965, 1967: chap. 5 passim. Persian goals: Walser 1987.

7. Chap. 5.1 below.

8. Esp. Thuc. 1.73; for further discussion, see chap. 5.1 below. See also the debates on the fate of Plataea: Thuc. 2.71.2–3, 72.1; 3.53–59, 62; *HCT* 2.346, 354–55; Diller 1962a: 194–95. Funeral orations: n. 129 below.

9. Pind. *Pyth.* 1.71–80. Plataea: n. 8 above. Sparta: esp. Hdt. 7.101–4, 135.2–3; von Fritz 1965; Havelock 1972: 45–52. Epigrams: discussed below.

10. Pohlenz (1937: 116 n. 3) provides a list of correspondences; see now also Saïd 2002: 137–45.

11. Thuc. 2.71.2, 4; see discussion at n. 195 below.

12. See the list in Gauer 1968: 134; a selection in ML, nos. 19, 25, 27–29.

13. In time most of these entered the corpus of Simonides (collected in Diehl 1925: 85ff.; Page 1981: 186ff.; Campbell 1982–93: 3.519ff.), whose authorship is disputed in most cases: for discussion see Boas 1905; Wilamowitz 1913: 192–209; Bowra 1938: chap. 6; Kegel 1962: 77–83; Podlecki 1968, 1973; West 1970: esp. 278–79, with n. 27; Page 1981: ad loc.; Molyneux 1992: 6–23 (history of scholarship on the question), chaps. 7–8.

14. Questionable authenticity: "Materialien," sec. 7.2; Habicht 1961; Robertson 1976. I thus ignore even such potentially important documents as the "Themistocles Decree" (for discussion: ML, no. 23; "Materialien," sec. 7.2.b; Robertson 1982; Kennelly 1990), the "Oath of Plataea" (Siewert 1972; "Materialien," sec. 7.2.c), and several epigrams ("Materialien," sec. 7.2.d).

15. Aesch. *Pers.* 50: *zugon doulion;* cf. 72, 745 (referring to the Hellespont). Atossa's dream: 181–97. Xerxes' intentions: e.g., 65–80, 177–78, 233–34, 473–77, 753–58.

16. Aesch. *Pers.* 181–97; cf. 23–24; for the Persian perspective, see n. 189 below. On *Pers.* 241–42, see "Materialien," sec. 7.3.a.

17. Pin. *Pyth.* 1.75: *bareia doulia.* See Burton 1962: 103–4; Bowra 1964: 115; Kierdorf 1966: 39–43. Gentili (1995: 18–19) emphasizes also the parallel established between Hieron and Zeus; he thinks that *eleutheria* (*Pyth.* 1.61–62) refers to external freedom as well (1995: 349–50); see below at n. 136.

18. Below, at n. 209.

19. For discussion: e.g., Kierdorf 1966: 32–35; Thummer 1968: 2.127, 130 (with bibliography). In "Materialien," sec. 7.1.a, I was overly cautious; see schol. Pind. 8.17a–b; Ruck 1969; and, very firmly, Köhnken 1975: 25 n. 2, 26 n. 7: "Pindar's concern is with the grief and loss the Persian Wars had brought upon Greece as a whole" (32). Date: Bowra 1964: 407; Privitera 1982: 118. Threat to Thebes: Hdt. 9.86–88.

20. Sim. XXa *FGE/C* (line 4: *doulion ēmar;* tr. Campbell); *CEG* 2; *IG* I³ 503 (with the new fragments). For discussion: ML, no. 26; West 1970; Welwei 1970; "Materialien," sec. 7.2.d I; Barron 1990 (including the new fragments).

21. Fr. 77Sn-M (*phaennan krēpid' eleutherias*). See Kierdorf 1966: 37–39; "Materialien," sec. 7.2.e II.

22. Sim.(?) 96D = XVI *FGE/C; IG* VII 53; Tod 2.20 (*eleutheron ēmar aexein*). Corinthians: 95bD = XII *FGE/C* (lines 3–6 most likely are a later addition: Page 1981: 204–5). Further bibliography in "Materialien," sec. 7.2.d VI. Date: Jacoby 1944b: 40 n. 11, 42 n. 21; 1945: 172 n. 57, 175 n. 77; Welwei 1970: 299–300.

23. Peek 1933 (*ele]utherias kalon . . . stephanon*). Date: Peek 1933: 120, accepted, e.g., by Siewert 1972: 53–54. Details in "Materialien," sec. 7.2.a with n. 152.

24. Sim. 11W.25–26, tentatively restored by West, on the basis of Sim.(?) XVI.1, XXa.4 *FGE/C,* as *Spartēi te kai Helladi doulion ēmar eschon amunomenoi.* On the date: Boedeker 1995: 220–25. For discussion: Boedeker and Sider 2001.

25. 118D = VIII *FGE/C.* Paus. 9.2.4. In "Materialien," sec. 7.2.d IV, I considered it unauthentic, but see Page 1981: 197–99, accepted by Campbell 1982–93: ad loc.

26. Sim. 94D = X *FGE/C* (tr. Campbell); see n. 122 below. In "Materialien," sec. 7.2.d III, I sided with the skeptics; Page (1981: 200–202) makes a strong case for authenticity.

27. (*a*) Discussed by Gauer 1968, with the texts listed on p. 134; cf. the thank offerings of Gelon for Himera at Delphi and of Hieron for Cumae (ML, nos. 28–29; cf. Harrell 2002). [Sim.] 106aD = XXXIV *FGE*/C, if authentic, represents a secondary dedication for an enlarged monument: Gentili 1958: 69–84 (who declares the second couplet, which emphasizes the contribution of four sons of Deinomenes to Greek *eleutheria*, "certamente spurio" [83]); Page 1981: 247–50 (a "literary exercise"); Krumeich 1991: 56–60. (*b*) ML, no. 18; Tod 2.13. (*c*) Sim. 88aD = XXI *FGE*/C; ML, no. 26. (*d*) Sim. 83, 91, 92aD = VI, XXIIa–b *FGE*/C. (*e*) Sim. 109D = XXIV *FGE*/C. (*f*) Sim. 90bD = XI *FGE*/C; Tod 2.16; see Boegehold 1965. (*g*) Sim. 105D = XVII *FGE*/C; ML, no. 27; Tod 2.19. (*h*) ML, no. 27; Tod 2.19; *ATL* 3.95–100. (*i*) Sim. 62D = eleg. 9C; cf. Podlecki 1968: 269–72. (*j*) Sim. 5D = 531P/C. (*k*) Pind. *Isthm.* 5.46–52; cf. Kierdorf 1966: 35–37. (*l*) Theogn. 773–82; cf. 757–64, dated to 490 by Highbarger 1937: 99–110 (accepted, among others, by Kierdorf 1966: 14); to 480/479 by van Groningen 1966: 1.299–302; Figueira and Nagy 1985: 33, 122; contra: Burn 1962: 170 (before 500). Simonides' authorship is doubtful in several cases. For further references to modern bibliography, see "Materialien," nn. 571–82.

28. (*m*) 121D = IX *FGE*/C. (*n*) 104D = XIV *FGE*/C. (*o*) 93D = XXIII *FGE*/C. (*p*) 65D = XIX *FGE*/C. On all these, see Page's comments, *FGE* ad loc.

29. Dedications: e.g., ML, nos. 19, 25. The simplicity of such inscriptions was retained in the fifth century: e.g., ML, nos. 28, 29, 36, 57, 74. Epigrams: see the summary of topoi in Gentili 1968: 69–81.

30. Aesch. *Septem* 69–77, 109–80, 253–54, 321–33, 451, 713. On echoes of the Persian War experience in this play: "Materialien," n. 146 with bibliography. At the time, a comparable vital threat from fellow Greeks hardly existed: below at nn. 40ff. (Groeneboom 1928: 98 is mistaken here); in stark contrast, Euripides' Trojan War dramas reflect the contemporary reality of the Peloponnesian War.

31. See, e.g., Theogn. 603–4, 1103–4; Highbarger 1937: 91–92, with a summary of numerous references in Herodotus (90 n. 9).

32. Miletus: Hdt. 6.18–22. The effect of Phrynichus's play *Capture of Miletus* on the Athenians: Hdt. 6.21.2. This play is dated variously to before (493) and after the Persian Wars: Badian 1971: 15 n. 44; Frost 1980: 76–77; Roisman 1988; Rosenbloom 1993. Revenge in 490: esp. Hdt. 5.105; 6.43.4–44.1, 94.2, 101.3. Naxos: 5.30–34. On the motif of revenge in Herodotus: de Romilly 1971b; more generally, Bellen 1974; Gehrke 1987. Xerxes' revenge: e.g., Hdt. 7.8β; his demand for submission: 7.32.

33. So, too, Nenci 1956: 36ff. See also Hdt. 8.3.1 ("the survival of Hellas" or "the destruction of Greece"), among many similar formulations. Aesch. *Pers.* 347–49 and the latter's emphasis (e.g., 65–66, 188) on the Persian army as "destroyer of cities" are indicative as well.

34. Chap. 3.3 below. See also Dem. 14.32; Xen. *Hell.* 2.4.17.

35. The Persians' minimal goals: Walser 1959: 233–34. More generally on all these issues: Burn 1962; Hignett 1963; relevant chaps. in *CAH* 4²; Lazenby 1993. Walser 1984; Balcer 1995; and Briant 1996: chaps. 4, 13, include the Persian perspective.

36. Chap. 4.1 below. Tribute: e.g., Hdt. 1.6.2, 27.1; 7.51.1, 108.1.

37. Whether true or not, the story of Athens's and Sparta's treatment of the Persian envoys who demanded earth and water is symptomatic: Hdt. 7.133.1; Kraft 1964: 144–53; Sealey 1976. The significance of "giving earth and water": Kuhrt 1988. A typical example of this way of thinking (considered and presented as such by Thucydides) was the reaction of Melos to Athens's threats during the Peloponnesian War: Thuc. 5.84–116; see, generally, Martin 1940: 76–87. Lydians: Hdt. 1.14–22, 26–27.1. Cyrus: 1.141, 162–69. Phocaea and Teos: 1.163–68. Rebellion: Hdt. 5.1, 26 (after Darius's failed Scythian expedition); 8.126–29 (after Xerxes' retreat from Europe); chap. 4.4 at nn. 225–26 below.

38. See Kierdorf 1966: 41, refuting Nenci 1956: 36ff.

39. See *ATL* 3.95–105, which, however, is too schematic: Brunt 1953: 144–48. Modification of principles: below at nn. 98ff., 108ff., and see chap. 4.4.

40. See, generally, e.g., Martin 1940; Hammond 1967a: 135–39, 194–203; de Romilly 1968; Karavites 1982a; Raaflaub 1990, 1994. See also Starr 1961a: 136–37; 1961b: 124, 346–47; 1977: 50; Snodgrass 1980: 85–86, 144, and index under "warfare." For recent research on issues touched upon in the next paragraph: Burstein et al. 1997: 7–13.

41. Poleis: Snodgrass 1980: chap. 1, 1993; Welwei 1983: pts. 1–2; Raaflaub 1991b: 239–47, 1993. I am skeptical of the thesis that the polis essentially continued from the Bronze Age (van Effenterre 1985; less extreme: Morris 1991; for a differentiated discussion: Thomas and Conant 1999). Territories: Starr 1961b: 346–47, 375–76; 1986: 39; de Polignac 1995. Buck (1979: chap. 6) offers an example of how polis territories were "filled out" and small settlements absorbed in the process. On population increases, in my view a decisive precondition for both the formation of the polis and colonization (esp. on the scale both phenomena assumed): Snodgrass 1980: 19–25; and summaries of recent debates in Raaflaub 1991b: 215–17 with bibliography; Osborne 1996: chap. 4; Scheidel forthcoming.

42. Thuc. 1.103.4, 122.2; 4.92.4; 5.41, 79.4; 6.88.1; cf. Brunt 1966: 84; de Romilly 1968: 211; de Ste. Croix 1972: 218–20. Examples are the "Lelantine War" between Chalkis and Eretria (see n. 66), the Spartan conquest of Messenia, early wars between Corinth and Megara, repeated fights between Athens and Megara over Salamis or between Sparta and Argos over the Thyreatis. Phalanx: Connor 1988; Hanson 1989, 1991, 1995: chaps. 6–8; Raaflaub 1997d, 1999: 132–41. Different views on the development of the phalanx: van Wees 2000; Krentz 2002.

43. Cartledge 1979: chaps. 8–10. Helots: Ducat 1990; and n. 71 below. *Perioikoi:* Shipley 1997. Personal relations: Ruschenbusch 1978: chap. 4; Herman 1987. Integration: Raaflaub 1990, 1991a. Destruction: Ducrey 1968a, 1968b; more generally, Karavites 1982a. Alliances: Tausend 1992; Baltrusch 1994. Earlier period: Wickert-Micknat 1983: esp. 61–62; Raaflaub 1991b: 222–25 with bibliography.

44. Below, n. 74 and at nn. 89ff.

45. Shipley (1987: 94–95) and Tausend (1992: 86–89) rightly challenge the concept of a "Samian Empire" implied by Herodotus and Thucydides; cf. Mitchell 1975; Wallinga 1993: 84–101; de Souza 1998: 282–83.

46. Attica: Richardson 1974: 7–11; Boardman 1975; Figueira 1985: 278–79; Starr 1986: 48 with bibliography in nn. 47–49 on p. 112; Frost 1990; Anderson 2000, 2003: chap. 5; contra: Welwei 1992: 65–66. The question is less whether there were independent poleis in Attica than whether the "polis government" centered in Athens had full control over outlying areas.

47. Eleutherai: Nilsson 1951: 26–27; Gschnitzer 1958: 86–88. Oropos: Gschnitzer 1958: 82–85. Salamis: Taylor 1997: chap. 1. Aegina: Frost 1980: 82–84; Connor 1988: 9; Tausend 1992: 106–10, 235–37; Figueira 1993: esp. chaps. 2–5 with bibliography. Generally, Frost 1984; Figueira 1985: 278–86, 1991: chap. 5.

48. Larsen 1933–34: 1.263, 1940: 180 n. 3; de Ste. Croix 1972: 333. Herodotus: e.g., Strasburger 1955. Cleomenes: Will 1955: 648–56; Carlier 1977; Cartledge 1979: 146–48; Cawkwell 1993.

49. See generally Kiechle 1963a: 242–52; Forrest 1968: 73–77; de Ste. Croix 1972: 96–97; Tomlinson 1972: chap. 8; Cartledge 1979: chap. 9. On Hdt. 1.67–68, describing the turning point: Boedeker 1993.

50. See n. 65 below and detailed discussion in chap. 4.1 at nn. 13ff. Late fifth century: chap. 5.3. Cleomenes: n. 48 above.

51. Tribal state: Sordi 1953a, 1958: 313–43; Gschnitzer 1954, 1955; Larsen 1968: 12–26.

52. Not least by Helly (1995), who argues for much more centralization at a much earlier date. Scarceness of sources: F. Gschnitzer, review of Sordi 1958, *Gnomon* 32 (1960): 167–69. The chronology of the events discussed here is much debated but not significant for my purposes.

53. For discussion: esp. Wade-Gery 1924; Larsen 1937: 831–32, 1960, 1968: 12–26; Sordi 1958: chap. 3; Gschnitzer 1958: 2–6, 173–78 (quot. 176, my tr.); Forrest 1982: 294–99; Helly 1995. Obligations: e.g., Xen. *Hell.* 6.1. Communal independence: esp. Hdt. 7.132.1; Diod. 11.3.2. *Penestai:* Ducat 1994. *Archos:* Helly 1995: chap. 1; *tagos:* Larsen 1968: 14; see, briefly, Hans Beck, *DNP* 11 (2001): 1223; Helly, *OCD,* 1471.

54. Thuc. 2.101.2; 4.78.6; 8.3.1; Xen. *Hell.* 6.1.9.

55. That Hippias was at the time "little better than a vassal of Thessaly" (Larsen 1960: 236, 1968: 113) is greatly exaggerated.

56. Hdt. 7.176.4; 8.27–28; Paus. 10.1.3ff.; 13.4ff.; Polyaen. 6.18.2; 8.65. Subjection: Plut. *Mor.* 244b, 866f. The chronology is much debated. Most scholars favor the early sixth century. A much later date has been proposed by Sordi (1953a, 1958: chap. 3) but opposed by Larsen (1960).

57. Plut. *Mor.* 244b–d (the legend of "Phocian desperation"). Explanation: based on Plut. *Cam.* 19.3, Beloch 1926: 205–6; Schober 1941: 482–83; Sordi 1953a, 1958: chap. 3; Larsen 1960: 234ff., 1968: 110–14. Ceressus: Paus. 9.14.2; Plut. *Mor.* 866f; Larsen 1960: 236–37; Buck 1972, 1979: 107–12; Ducat 1973: 67.

58. Plutarch: Sordi 1953a: 246–47; Larsen 1968: 19 n. 3, 114. That Plutarch wrote a biography of the victorious general, Daiphantos (*Mor.* 244b), does not make the details more credible. The life, work, and reliability of Aristophanes of Boeotia, on whom Plutarch relies occasionally, cannot be determined precisely; see Hignett 1963: 22; Buck 1979: 129–30; and esp. *FGrH,* vol. 3B, comm. on no. 379. Larsen, Sordi (previous notes), and McInerney (1999) accept all the details. For a far-ranging mythopoetic interpretation: Ellinger 1993.

59. E.g., Westlake 1936; Berve 1967: 1.183–85; Helly 1995.

60. Festival: Plut. *Mor.* 244e, 1099e. Stratagems: Pol. 16.32.1–2; Paus. 10.1.7; Plut. *Mor.* 244d.

61. Hdt. 7.176.4, 215; 8.27–33.

62. Hdt. 8.27.2; Plut. *Mor.* 866e–f; cf., e.g., Larsen 1960: 236–37.

63. Plut. *Cam.* 19.4; Paus. 9.14.2–3. On the oracle obviously invented after Leuctra: Parke and Wormell 1956: 2.103, no. 254. Hdt. 8.27.5 mentions a statue group dedicated by the Phocians in Delphi; a fourth-century inscription on a statue base refers to victories over the Thessalians as well: *Syll.,* no. 202b; cf. Sordi 1953a: 244.

64. Anacreon 419C (chap. 2.1, n. 36, above). See Pohlenz 1955: 13 (= 1966: 9). See also n. 73 below.

65. "Materialien," sec. 9.1.a (Persians), 9.4.c (tyranny). Herodotus and freedom: n. 6 above. His understanding of the nature of the early conflicts between Greek poleis is remarkable, especially from the perspective of the time around the outbreak of the Peloponnesian War. By contrast, Herodotus provides a harsh assessment of Sparta's "rule" in the Peloponnesian League in the mid–sixth century, presumably influenced by contemporary polemics: by that time, "most of the Peloponnese was subjected to them" (1.68.6: *katestrammenē*); see Cartledge 1979: 138–40. Drexler (1972: 131–32) is wrong here.

66. Thuc. 1.15.2 (tr. Warner, heavily modified), with *HCT* 1.126. As often, Thucydides' formulation is ambiguous: "they had not stood together [united, combined, *xuneistēkesan*] as subjects [*hupēkooi*] toward [or against] the greatest poleis [*pros tas megistas poleis*]." On the "Lelantine War" (1.15.3), vastly misinterpreted already in antiquity, see bibliography in Raaflaub 1991b: 224 n. 62; Tausend 1992: 137–45; Parker 1997. *Douleia:* Thuc. 1.8.3, 16. Thalassocracies: 1.15.1; cf. *HCT* 1, at 1.13.6, 15.1; on Polycrates, see n. 45 above.

67. Esp. Thuc. 1.122.2; 4.92.4. To understand Thucydides' interpretation, one needs to take

into account his theories of power: e.g., Kiechle 1963b; de Romilly 1963; Woodhead 1970; Allison 1989; Ober 2001; more bibliography in Raaflaub 1994: 106 n. 6.

68. The wonder generated by such conquests compensates somewhat for the gaps in the extant evidence. See Ducrey 1968b: 110–12; Karavites 1982a: 33–35. Greek reactions to wars of annihilation: Ellinger 1993. Sybaris: esp. Hdt. 6.21; Ducrey 1968b: 57–59. Pellana: *P.Oxy.* 10 (1914): no. 1241, col. 2; expressly recorded by Aristotle(?) as the first case of this kind. Customs changed drastically in the second half of the fifth century as a consequence of Athenian policies: Ducrey 1968b; Karavites 1982a. In this respect, as in empire building, Sicilian tyrants, perhaps imitating Persian customs, were ahead of the mainland: Asheri 1988a: 769 on the depopulation, enslavement, and destruction of cities by Gelon in the late 480s.

69. Thus esp. Larsen 1944; Kiechle 1958: 134–35; see also Hampl 1938: 4–6; Walbank 1951: 53–54; Schäfer 1963: 276; Karavites 1982a: 19–26. Amphictyonic oath: Aeschin. 2.115 (tr. Adams). On parallels in the "Oath of Plataea": Siewert 1972: 75–80. Kiechle offers the interpretation of *mēdemian polin . . . anastaton poiein* accepted here; Kuch (1974: 27–32) emphasizes the expulsion of the population. First Sacred War: bibliography in Bengtson 1969: 87 n. 5; Robertson 1978 (questioning the war's historicity); Lehmann 1980 (defending it); Tausend 1992: 43–47, 161–66; Davies 1994; McInerney 1999.

70. See esp. Karavites 1982a: 19–26; generally, Raaflaub 1990, 1991a: 570–78. Interstate relations: Herman 1987; Raaflaub 1997c.

71. Cartledge 1980, 1987: chap. 2; Finley 1982: chap. 2; and bibliography in Raaflaub 1993: 97 n. 99. Understanding of archaic Spartan society and institutions is currently undergoing serious revisions; see Hodkinson 1983, 1993, 1997, 2000; Nafissi 1991; Kennell 1995; Thommen 1996. Specifically on the helot problem: Ducat 1990; Figueira 1999; Luraghi 2002a, 2002b. On fear of helots: chap. 4.1, n. 31.

72. The latter must have occurred often on a small scale when poleis "rounded off" their territory by "absorbing" smaller settlements or when, on a larger scale, entire regions—such as Attica (n. 46 above), the Argolid (Piérart 1997), or Laconia (n. 49 above)—were "unified" by the dominant polis. A good analogy is the annexation of Veii by Rome: Cornell 1995: 309–13, with sources.

73. Hence also the absence of such topoi in sixth-century funerary inscriptions (n. 2 above). The fact that war rarely threatened a community's survival is directly related to the "ritualization" of hoplite warfare (Connor 1988; Raaflaub 1997d: 56) and helps explain the remarkable emphasis placed, among elite values and ideals, on nonmilitary achievements (Donlan 1980: chaps. 2–3, esp. 78–80; Stein-Hölkeskamp 1989: index, s.v. *Spiele, Sport*); a comparison with Rome is revealing here (Raaflaub 1984b: 553–57). See also the note on p. 117.

74. Examples include Lygdamis, installed by Peisistratus in Naxos (Berve 1967: 1.78, 2.564); Peisistratus's son, Hegesistratus, in Sigeion (Berve 1967: 1.62, 2.553–54); and the control over several Sicilian poleis by Hieron's family (Berve 1967: 1.147–52). Parallels are found in the Persian vassal system, where individuals (including exiled Greek nobles) were assigned cities as personal fiefdoms (Briant 1996: 359–61). The interpretation of vaguely similar cases in *Il.* 9.140–56 and *Od.* 4.174–77 is much debated: bibliography in Raaflaub 1993: 91 n. 35.

75. In the range of dates discussed most often (519–506), 509 is perhaps most likely. See Will 1955: 640–41; Amit 1970, 1973: 71–72; Buck 1979: chap. 7; Shrimpton 1984; Tausend 1992: 181–85. On the Corinthian mediation: Piccirilli 1973: 42–46. Hennig (1992) considers most of Herodotus's details an elaboration after the fall and destruction of Plataea in 427.

76. Hdt. 6.108.2–5; Thuc. 3.55.1, 61.2, 63.2, 4.

77. Busolt and Swoboda 1926: 1409–12, with Schäfer's qualification, 1932: 90; Schober 1934: 1457–58; Cloché 1952: 30–33; Larsen 1968: 26–31; Buck 1972, 1979: chap. 7. Ducat (1973: esp. 71–72) emphasizes modern structures. The form of the Boeotian League that existed at the end of

the fifth century and probably evolved only gradually after 447 (Bruce 1967: 157–64) is inapplicable to the late sixth century.

78. Hdt. 6.108.6 suggests the former. On the latter: esp. Amit 1970: 419–26, 1973: 64ff., esp. 70 (with some exaggeration).

79. Hdt. 6.108.1, 4, 6 (cf. 2). Thuc. 2.73.3; 3.55.1, 3, 63.2, 68.5 refer unequivocally to a symmachy. Orchomenos: Buck 1979: 110–11; cf. Lauffer and Hennig 1974: 334–36. See Schäfer 1932: 226; Amit 1970: 416–19, 1973: 73; esp. Will 1954: 421 with n. 1. See also the remarks given to the Thebans in Thuc. 3.61–64. Note that the Plataeans had first "given themselves" to the Spartans (Hdt. 6.108.2).

80. For this thesis: Schäfer 1932: 225–26; Kirsten 1950: 2285–86; Shrimpton 1984: 301–2; contra: Highby 1936: 59–61; Will 1954: 419–21; Amit 1973: 73–74; Hammond 1992; Hennig 1992: 20–21; Baltrusch 1994: 12–14 (strongly emphasizing the aspect of a mutually binding treaty).

81. Badian 1993: chap. 3, esp. 117–21 with nn. Contra: e.g., Hammond 1992: 144–45; Hennig 1992: 18 n. 10.

82. See Hammond 1992: 144; also Will 1954: 421 on the term *paradidonai*, used by Thucydides to express the unconditional surrender (e.g., of Mytilene) and hence the inequality in a relationship.

83. Location of Hysiae and Oenoe: Hammond 1973: 444–46 and fig. 18 on p. 421.

84. Hdt. 8.3, 106.2–3; cf. Petzold 1993–94: 1.421–27, 429. Badian's (1993: 120–21) and Shrimpton's (1984: 302) explanations for Athens's acquiescence are equally unconvincing (so, too, Hennig 1992: 20). Persian occupation: Hammond 1992: 145 (who also discusses the meaning of *apedidou*, but see Hennig 1992: 20 n. 11).

85. Esp. Paus. 1.29.7 on the tomb of the Athenians (including slaves) who fell against Aegina before the Persian Wars. More evidence and discussion in Welwei 1974: 22ff., esp. 27–28, refuting Bömer (1957–63: 4.140, 150–51), who anticipates Badian. Free noncitizens: I suggested this in *Entdeckung*, 19 n. 71 (criticized by Badian 1993: 220 n. 21). Freedmen: esp. Labarbe 1957: 169–70; Welwei 1974: 22ff.; Hunt 1998: 26–28 (with earlier bibliography). Hammond (1992: 147–50) accepts Marinatos's identification of the Vrana Valley mound with Pausanias's; contra: Welwei 1974: 25–27, 1979.

86. Hdt. 6.108.2 (*exandrapodisthentes*) alludes to the danger of enslavement for Plataea's citizens after the city's conquest by Thebes, not to political domination.

87. See Ducat 1973: 67; Tausend 1992: 180–81. Thuc. 1.25.1–2 mentions a comparable petition by Epidamnus to Corinth; cf. Schäfer 1932: 225; and esp. Will 1954: 420–21. Tausend (1992: 185–86) sees an analogy in Eretria's relation to Athens and thinks that Athens at that time was trying to follow Sparta's model in the Peloponnese in building a hegemonic alliance system. Baltrusch (1994: 12–14) suggests that Plataea tried to establish a relationship comparable to that between a colony and mother city (13 n. 59: Badian's interpretation "far too extensive"). Partial loss of sovereignty: chap. 4.2 at n. 117 below.

88. This was the situation of many Athenian allies in the early years of the Delian League: chap. 4.4 below.

89. Gschnitzer 1958: 129–30. These poleis were not represented in foreign affairs by Corinth as were those in the Delian League by Athens. See generally (with sources and bibliography), Will 1954; Gschnitzer 1958: chap. 23. Officials: Thuc. 1.56.2 (perhaps to be generalized: Will 1954: 416). Coinage: Gschnitzer 1958: 135.

90. Gschnitzer 1958: 132ff. (quot. 135, my tr.); Will 1954: 419. Foundation: Will 1954: 414; Gschnitzer 1958: 128–29; Werner 1971: 68ff., esp. 71; Salmon 1984: 209–17.

91. Gschnitzer 1958: 124–25; a possible exception in Thuc. 3.102.2; see also Will 1954: 417. Corcyra: Thuc. 1.34.1; contra: 1.38.2–3. Comparison with a "colonial empire": Gschnitzer 1958: 128 n. 8; contra: Will 1954: 418 n. 1. See also generally Finley 1976a.

92. Athens: Will 1954: 422–49; Gschnitzer 1958: chap. 20. See esp. Hdt. 6.136.2. Austin and Vidal-Naquet (1977: 126) mention as another example Sinope and its colonies in the Black Sea region.

93. See chap. 4.1 at nn. 13ff. below.

94. Liberty: Pind., *Pyth.* 1.71–80 (above at n. 17), echoing phrases of the Athenian Persian Wars epigram (above at n. 20); Barron 1990: 141; Ephorus, *FGrH* 70 F186; Diod. 11.20.1. See also [Sim.] 106aD = XXXIV *FGE*/C, perhaps a later dedication for a collective monument of the Syracusan tyrants (see n. 27). Parallel: already mentioned by Pindar; that the victory monument set up by the Syracusan tyrant imitated the Serpent Column monument dedicated by the Hellenic alliance after Plataea, as suggested by Amandry (1987: 81–92), is contested by Krumeich (1991). Hieron had Aeschylus's *Persians* reperformed in Syracuse: Aesch. T1.68–69, 56a Radt (*TrGF* 3). On the development of the tradition: Gauthier 1966; Meister 1970; Merante 1972–73; Ameling 1993: 18–33.

95. See below at n. 203. Personal politics: Ameling 1993: 33–41. Syracuse: Plut. *Mor.* 175a. Peisistratus: Hdt. 1.61. Aristagoras: below at n. 101. Monuments: n. 27 above. Gelon: Hdt. 7.153ff., esp. 163–65. For discussion: Berve 1967: 1.137–54; Will 1972: 227–52; Asheri 1988a. From the Carthaginian perspective: Hans 1983: chap. 2; Huss 1985: chaps. 10–11; Ameling 1993: chap. 1.

96. Hdt. 1.56–94, 141–76. Phocaea, Teos: 1.164, 168–69.1. Subjection of Ionia: Walser 1984: chap. 3; Balcer 1995: chap. 3; Briant 1996: 45–48.

97. Evidence: Tozzi 1978: chaps. 1–3; Murray 1988: 466–73. Herodotus, the main source, wrote from the perspective of the post–Persian Wars period (chap. 1.3 at n. 39 above); there is no independent evidence to confirm contemporary use of his terminology. On his report of the Ionian Revolt: Tozzi 1978: chap. 1; Murray 1988: 466–67, 470–72; Walter 1993a. Causes of the revolt: chap. 4.1, nn. 38ff.

98. E.g., Will 1972: 53–54.

99. Hdt. 1.141.4, 143.1; Gorman 2001: 125–28. On the same principle, Xerxes and Mardonius later tried to undermine mainland Greek resistance by granting Athens a privileged status: Hdt. 8.140–44. Relations: Walser 1959: 225; Wolski 1973: 3–4.

100. Tozzi 1978: 122–23, 129–30, with good comments. See generally Heuss 1946: 45–53; Herman 1987. "Vassal tyranny": see Schäfer 1963: 109–12; Berve 1967: 1.chaps. 3–4; Tozzi 1978: 118–24; Walser 1984: chap. 4; Graf 1985; Austin 1990; Luraghi 1998; Georges 2000: 10–23; in the Persian context: Briant 1996: chap. 8 and index, s.v. *tyrans grecs.*

101. Naxian expedition: Hdt. 5.30–34; Tozzi 1978: 128–33. Defection: Hdt. 5.35–36. See esp. Heuss 1981: 20–21; Walter 1993a; Georges 2000.

102. Esp. Hdt. 4.137.2; 5.37–38. See Walser 1959: 226–27; Schäfer 1963: 111; Tozzi 1978: 118ff., esp. 123–24; Murray 1988: 474–76; Georges 2000: 19–23 (the latter two with good observations). Sixth-century isonomic systems: O'Neil 1995: chap. 1; Robinson 1997. I would not call these "democracies": Raaflaub 1995: 30–34.

103. Hdt. 5.43.3 and previous note. See also Tozzi 1978: chap. 6, esp. 156, 172–76. Desire for freedom: e.g., Walser 1959: 223–28, 1987 (very low); Meiggs 1972: 24–30; Will 1972: 54–57 (relatively high).

104. Hdt. 5.73. Kinship: already in Sol. 4aW = 4GP. See Will 1972: 76ff., esp. 79; Nenci 1994: 267–68 with bibliography. On the Persian interpretation of the submission of Athens: Walser 1987: 162; Kuhrt 1988: 91–93, in whose opinion "the entire story . . . smacks of a later rewriting of history by the Athenians well after Xerxes' defeat." For a similar reinterpretation (of Miltiades' presence in Darius's Scythian expedition): Hdt. 4.137; Graf 1985: 98.

105. Ever since Salamis and Plataea, and probably since the founding of the Hellenic League in 481, the allies considered resistance the only morally defensible position. Whoever differed in word or action from those who wanted "what was best for Hellas" (Hdt. 7.145.1–2,

172.1; 9.19.1; cf. 7.157.2) was seen as a traitor and liable to the most serious punishment (next note). Hence, especially in Athens, no politically ambitious family could afford to admit that any of its members had ever supported an "appeasement"; to correct historical facts became imperative (Gillis 1979: 51–52; Lavelle 1993). Moreover, in every assembly meeting curses were uttered against those who established contacts with Persians or tyrants (Isocr. 4.157; Aristoph. *Thesm.* 337–39).

106. Against the existence of a pro-Persian "party": Badian 1971: 1, 10–11; Kinzl 1977a: 210–14. Karavites (1977) attempts a comprehensive reconstruction; contra: Williams 1980; see also Ruschenbusch 1979: 53–54. Bibliography: Karavites 1977: 130 n. 6; Gillis 1979: chaps. 5–6. Marathon: Hdt. 6.109.5. Alcmaeonids: Hdt. 6.115, 121–24; Gillis 1969, 1979: chap. 5. Ostracisms: Aristot. *AP* 22.4–6, supplemented by the evidence of the ostraca. Ostraca: for general discussion, see ML, no. 21; Thomsen 1972: chap. 2; Rhodes 1981: 267–71; Lehmann 1981; Dreher 2000. For a detailed analysis of all sources, including the ostraca: Siewert 2002. Relations to tyrant family: Lavelle 1988. Traitors, Medes, etc.: Schreiner 1970; Thomsen 1972: 97–98; Vanderpool 1973: 231–36; Williams 1978; Siewert 2002: 63–136. Dissent: Hdt. 9.5; Wolski 1973. Collaborators: Raubitschek 1957 (240–41 on Aristides); Plut. *Arist.* 13, with Harvey 1984 (Agasias and Aeschines); Gillis 1979. However the war against Aegina figured in Athenian preparations, even there the relation to Persia was an important consideration: Hdt. 6.49–50, with Frost 1968: 117–18, 1980: 83–84; Williams 1980: 109 n. 21; Hdt. 7.144, with Raaflaub 1998b: 96 (with bibliography).

107. Isagoras: Hdt. 5.70–72; Aristot. *AP* 20.2–3. Tyrants: e.g., the example of Syloson of Samos (Hdt. 3.139–49), and generally Hdt. 4.137.2; cf. Austin 1990. After Ephialtes: Thuc. 1.107.4–5; Raaflaub 1998b: 49, with more sources and bibliography. Alcibiades, Phrynichus, and the oligarchs: chap. 6.2 at n. 179 below; Raaflaub 1992: 24–31, 2001b: 109–10. This pattern has been observed by others (listed in Harvey 1984: 69). See generally Herman 1987: esp. chap. 5.

108. Hignett 1963: 96–104; Drexler 1972: 152–57; Gillis 1979: chaps. 6–7. On Thebes: also Gottlieb 1963: 77–78. Thessaly: Westlake 1936. Argos: Gillis 1979: 61–62 with n. 7. Aegina: Will 1955: 659–63; Figueira 1993: 95–96.

109. E.g., Eretria (Hdt. 6.100–101) or Thebes (Hdt. 9.86–88; Thuc. 3.62.3); cf. Drexler 1972: 148ff. passim. Revenge: cases are summarized in Wolski 1973; cf. Huxley 1967.

110. Hdt. 9.2.3, 41.2–3; Pol. 6.56; Gillis 1979: 74. On Pindar's caution, corresponding to the pro-Persian position of many of his patrons: e.g., Bowra 1964: 110–17; Ehrenberg 1968: 177–81. See generally the observations of Heuss 1981: 18–22.

111. A systematic investigation is an urgent desideratum. See, e.g., Schäfer 1932; Ruschenbusch 1978; Karavites 1982a; Walser 1987: 164–65; Raaflaub 1990. Martin (1940) offers rich material but an undifferentiated and superficial analysis.

112. This pattern was decisively disturbed by the emergence of the Athenian Empire: Thuc. 4.92.4; but see chap. 4.4 below.

113. A prime example is Plataea, discussed above. See Ruschenbusch 1978: chap. 1 on the very limited size and power potential of most poleis, which in cases of conflict made unrestricted independence illusory. On consequences for the foreign policy of such poleis: Ruschenbusch 1978: chap. 4.

114. Meier 1972: 825 (my tr.). See de Ste. Croix 1954; Heuss 1965: 83–86, 1973: 17–24; generally, Lintott 1981: chap. 2. The contrast to early Rome is instructive: Raaflaub 1996a: 290–92.

115. References in chap. 2.2, n. 63. In addition, e.g., Archil. 51D (*Mon. Archil.* A col. IV.4) = 95W; Alc. 428LP/C; *Carm. adesp.* 1027cP.

116. Tozzi 1978: 65; Lateiner 1982: 137–44. Even the Athenians' positive reaction was probably dictated by self-interest more than altruism: Kuhrt 1988: 91–93.

117. Hdt. 6.18–21; on the Athenian reaction: Roisman 1988; Rosenbloom 1993. We do not

know whether the sentiment expressed by Aeschylus—that Asia was Persian territory and the Hellespont separated two distinct spheres—was widespread and had developed long before the debates about the purpose of the Delian League: Aesch. *Pers.* 101–13, 739–86; Raaflaub 1988a: 285–86; Meier 1993b: 70–78; cf. Rosenbloom 1996.

118. The same question concerns the possible influence of the Greek concept of freedom on the early development of an analogous Roman concept: Raaflaub 1984b: 538–40. See, generally, Raaflaub and Müller-Luckner 1993: xxi–xxii; Raaflaub 2000a; and esp. Humphreys 1993.

119. See the beginning of Simonides' poem on Plataea (11W, with Boedeker 2001); a little later the "Eion epigrams" ("Simonides" 40[a] *FGE;* Aeschin. 3.185; cf. Plut. *Cim.* 7.6; Jacoby 1945: 185–211).

120. See at nn. 189ff. below; "Materialien," sec. 9.7.c.

121. Pohlenz 1966: 9 (= 1955: 13); cf. Gelzer 1973: 27, 32.

122. Early competitions: Hdt. 8.93.1; 9.71, 105. Distortion: e.g., the Athenian and Corinthian versions of the conduct of the Corinthian admiral Adeimantus: Hdt. 8.94 with Adeimantus's funeral epigram cited at n. 26; Plut. *De mal. Her.* 39.870b–71b; cf. Burn 1962: 444–45; Bowen 1992: 140–42. The pattern was repeated and intensified during later wars among the former allies, as Hdt. 7.139 attests; see also chap. 5.1 below.

123. Pind. *Pyth.* 1.71–80. Conflicting versions: Hdt. 7.157–65 (cf. von Fritz 1965: 11–14, 23; 1967: 262–72). See above at n. 94 on the construction of exact parallels between western and eastern events.

124. Hdt. 9.106 on the Greek war council after the last victory; 9.114 on Sparta's lack of enthusiasm; for background and analysis of the latter: Lotze 1970; Cartledge 1979: chap. 11; Steinbrecher 1985: chap. 3; Powell 1988: chap. 4.

125. At all times, booty and acquisition were important and natural aspects of warfare. See, in the present context, e.g., the combination of ideological-political and material considerations in Aristagoras's appeal for help (Hdt. 5.49, 97.1) or in Themistocles' actions after Salamis (Hdt. 8.111–12); e.g., Jackson 1969; Kallet-Marx 1993: chap. 2; more generally, Pritchett 1971–91: 1.chap. 3, 5.chap. 2; Ducrey 1977; Finley 1986: chap. 5 ("War and Empire"); Garlan 1989.

126. Hence the financial officers' title, *Hellenotamiai,* and the designation of the league as "the Hellenes." See *ATL* 3.97 with n. 12; Larsen 1940: 202; *HCT* 2.262; Giovannini and Gottlieb 1980: 21–28; Brunt 1993: 64–74.

127. Pretext: Thuc. 1.96.1. Liberty: 3.10.3; 6.76.3–4; Raaflaub 1979a. On the purpose of the Delian League: Steinbrecher 1985: 72–86; Powell 1988: 4–11; Rhodes 1992: 34–40; Brunt 1993: 65–67; Petzold 1993–94: pt. 2. On "just war" in fifth-century thought: Drexler 1976: 28ff. On vengeance as motive for war: n. 32 above.

128. Will 1972: 132 (my tr.). Counterarguments: esp. Sealey 1966 (contra: Jackson 1969; Meiggs 1972: esp. 463–64; de Ste. Croix 1972: 298–307); Rawlings 1977 (contra: French 1979; Raaflaub 1979a). See esp. Petzold 1993–94: pt. 2, with bibliography; and chap. 4.1 below.

129. On the funeral orations: Strasburger 1958; Kierdorf 1966: chap. 3; Loraux 1986. Quotation: Zuntz 1955: 18; cf. Strasburger 1958: 21.

130. On Thucydides (esp. 1.72–73): Kierdorf 1966: 100–110. On Hdt. 9.27: Kierdorf 1966: 97–100. See also Meyer 1892–99: 2.219–22. On the significance of the suppliant plays in this context: Kierdorf 1966: 92–94; Zuntz 1955: 16–20. See further, chap. 5.1 below.

131. 475: Kierdorf 1966: 83ff., esp. 95. 479: Hammond 1969: 142. 465/464: Jacoby 1944b (contra: *HCT* 2.94–101; Bradeen 1969: 154–55). For discussion: see also Stupperich 1977: 200–238; Clairmont 1983: 1.1–15; Loraux 1986: 56–72 (esp. on the *epitaphios logos*).

132. See also Badian 1971: 15 n. 44, where Phrynichus's *Capture of Miletus* is dated in the first years of the Delian League rather than, as is usually done, in 493; see, however, Rosenbloom 1993.

133. Chap. 2.3 above.

134. Orestes' revenge is not only a son's duty but also tyrannicide (Dodds 1960: 19–20) and thus also a politically meritorious act that ignites "the shining light of freedom": *Cho.* 808–11; cf. 859–65, 1044–47; Garvie 1986: at lines 130–31: "light symbolizes salvation." Tyranny in the *Oresteia:* Berve 1967: 1.193–94; cf. Griffith 1995. In the *Prometheus:* Berve 1967: 1.193–94; Thomson 1929, 1932: 6–12; Podlecki 1966: chap. 6 (all with references); see also chap. 5.2, n. 111, below. Note esp. *Prom.* 926–27. Testimonia for other authors: "Materialien," sec. 9.4.

135. Pind. *Ol.* 12.1–2 (see below at n. 209). Syracuse: Diod. 11.72.2 (below at n. 203).

136. External freedom: e.g., Nestle 1967: 33–34; Gentili 1995: 349–50 with recent bibliography. Internal freedom: see following notes. Pind. *Pyth.* 1.71–80: above at n. 17.

137. Wilamowitz 1922: 296ff., esp. 300–301; Kirsten 1941; Will 1956: 59–60; Burton 1962: 103–4. For Pindar's conception of Hieron's rule as traditional kingship closely associated with Zeus, see *Ol.* 1.12; 6.93–96; Harrell 2002 (with further references and bibliography). Pindar and tyranny: *Pyth.* 2.86–89; 11.52–53; Kirsten 1941: 60; Bowra 1964: 155–56; Berve 1967: 1.191–92.

138. See above at nn. 15–16 and below at nn. 189–90.

139. Aesch. *Pers.* 591–94: "No longer will men guard their tongues; for the people have been liberated to speak freely [*lelutai . . . laos eleuthera bazein*], now that the yoke of power has been broken."

140. For the traditional view: e.g., Ehrenberg 1940: 296; Schäfer 1963: 316; Meier 1970: 21; and bibliography cited in chap. 2.3, n. 167 above. Detailed discussion below at nn. 227ff.

141. Guazzoni Foà 1974–76: 1.102ff., esp. 104.

142. In the same sequence: the scholiast's summary of Alc. 74LP/C; 31D = 141LP/C; 87D = 348LP/C; see also 48D = 75LP/C.11–13; 119, 120, 122, 130D = 6LP/C, esp. lines 27–28. Cf. Aristot. *Pol.* 3.1285a35–b1 on Pittacus as "elected tyrant." Date: Page 1955: 150–52; Lesky 1966b: 131; Rösler 1980: 33; Burnett 1983: 107–20. On Alcaeus and factional strife: Schachermeyr 1950; Page 1955: 149–243; Berve 1967: 1.91–95, 2.572–75; Rösler 1980: 26–36; Burnett 1983: 156–81; Podlecki 1984: 62–82.

143. 24aD = 129LP/C, lines 13–24; 43D = 70LP/C, esp. lines 8–13 (tr. Campbell); 24cD = 130LP, lines 18–24 = 130bC, lines 3–9.

144. Alc. 24aD = 129LP/C, line 20; cf. Theogn. 39–52.

145. See also Xenophanes 3.2W/GP: "as long as they were without hateful tyranny."

146. Since a great variety of phenomena were subsumed under the umbrella term of "tyranny" (Kinzl 1979), the thought of *doulosunē* would have been prompted only by specific aspects or forms of single rule, whereas the exclusive predominance of one member of the elite, no matter what the specific circumstances, inevitably provoked fierce resistance from his peers deprived of shared power.

147. Forrest 1966: 163–64, 170; Pleket 1972: 71; Ober 1989: 60–65; Bleicken 1994: 17–28; and chap. 2.3 at n. 135 above. Subordination to a master: chap. 2.3 at n. 157.

148. Tyranny as the consequence of aristocratic abuses and stasis: Sol. 4W = 3GP.5–22; Theogn. 39–52; Lintott 1981: esp. chap. 2. Suppression of stasis: Kinzl 1979: 33–36. Impact of tyranny on demos: e.g., Spahn 1977: 157–61; de Ste. Croix 1981: 278–83; Stahl 1987: esp. pt. 3; Eder 1988, 1992; Bleicken 1994: 28–34. Age of Cronus: Aristot. *AP* 16.7, with Rhodes 1981: 217–18. Invasion: Hdt. 5.62; Aristot. *AP* 19.3.

149. Biases: Berve 1967: 1.190–206, 343–52; Lavelle 1993. Herodotus: Stahl 1987: pt. 1. Aristot. *AP:* Rhodes 1981 on *AP* 14–19.

150. This is the least that can be established on the basis of Hdt. 1.59–64; Aristot. *AP* 13–15. For discussion: e.g., Rhodes 1981; Asheri 1988b (both ad loc.); Sealey 1960; Andrewes 1982: 394–98; Stahl 1987: 56–105; Stein-Hölkeskamp 1989: 139–45; Welwei 1992: 221–29; Lavelle 2000.

151. Sol. 33W = 29aGP; Archil. 19W, 23W.17–21; Bacch. 20B Sn-M, C, lines 10–12; cf. Connor 1977; Ruschenbusch 1978: 71–72.

152. On the interpretation of Peisistratus's alleged first two attempts at tyranny, see bibliography in n. 150, esp. Welwei 1992: 227. The date of his successful attempt is debated: Rhodes 1981: 191–99.

153. For recent discussion: Andrewes 1982: 402–16; Stahl 1987; Lewis 1988; Stein-Hölkeskamp 1989: 145–53; Welwei 1992: 229–65. Kinzl (1979) and McGlew (1993) emphasize the tyrant's need to collaborate with the elite.

154. Expressed well by Hdt. 3.142.3 (n. 158 below).

155. Well formulated by Arist. *Pol.* 5.1311a18–20.

156. First attested in Aesch. *Prom.* 49–50. See chap. 5.2 at n. 111 below.

157. Thus, e.g., Ehrenberg 1965a: 263; Bleicken 1979: 163–64; Frei 1981: 218. *Eunomia:* chap. 2.3, n. 164, above.

158. Heuss 1946: 45–50, 1965: 72, 74; Schäfer 1963: 310, 315–16; Meier 1970: 29–30. See Hdt. 3.142.3: the tyrant as ruler over his peers (*homoioi*). See also Edouard Will, review of Ostwald 1969, *RPh* 45 (1971): 108–9; Pleket 1972: 65–66.

159. In general, see Meier 1970: 39–40, 1980: 283–84 (= 1990: 161–62). On *isonomia* as modification or specification of *eunomia:* Aalders 1968: 9–12; Meier 1980: 117 n. 68 (= 1990: 66 n. 71); Frei 1981: 216–17 (with a valuable analysis of word formation, 212ff.). The elite's tendency, initially taken for granted, to perceive *isonomia* as a privilege limited to their own class, must have been reinforced by increasing challenges "from below": e.g., Theogn. 53–60, 183–92, 315–22, 667–82; Donlan 1980: chap. 3. On "equal" and "fair": Cartledge 1996a.

160. My understanding of *isonomia* differs from that advocated especially by Vlastos, Ostwald, and Ehrenberg (in his later publications) and from that of Fornara 1970a: 171–80; it comes closer to that of Will and Pleket (see bibliography in n. 163); Meier 1968: 9–11, 1980: 116–17 (= 1990: 66). Ostwald (1969: 61) and Frei (1981: 212ff.) have shown that the old controversy, whether *isonomia* is derived from *nomos* or *nemein,* is unproductive. Despite all the scholarship existing on this and related terms (listed here only incompletely), a comprehensive modern examination of the development of the concept of equality remains an urgent desideratum; some thoughts in Cartledge 1996a; Raaflaub 1996b; Roberts 1996.

161. *Scol. anon.* 10, 13D = *Carmina convivalia* 893, 896P/C, lines 3–4: *ton turannon ktanetēn isonomous t'Athēnas epoiēsatēn;* Fornara 1983: no. 39A. Interpretation and date: Vlastos 1953: 339–44; Ehrenberg 1965a: 253–63, 279–86; Ostwald 1969: 121–36; Fornara 1970a; Pleket 1972: 68–77; Fornara and Samons 1991: 42–50, 166–67 (who consider the use of *isonomos* here an adaptation to later fifth-century terminology). A paraphrase of *isonomia* (which does not fit the meter) probably appears in Theogn. 678 (*dasmos isos:* Cerri 1969), of uncertain date (van Groningen 1966: 198–99, 267–69). Isagoras: below at n. 168. Anaximander, *VS,* no. 12 B1, as reflection of *isonomia:* Vlastos 1947: esp. 168–73, 1953: 361–63. Ehrenberg (1965a: 263 n. 2) has doubts. On attempts to restore *isonomos, eleutheros,* or related terms in fragmentary epigrams connected with monuments of the Athenian tyrannicides: Raaflaub 2000d: 261–65.

162. *VS,* no. 24 B4. See Vlastos 1953: 344–47; Ehrenberg 1965a: 284. Ostwald (1969: 97–106) is opposed by Will, *RPh* 45 (1971): 105–8; Pleket 1972: 64–65. See now Triebel-Schubert 1984.

163. Ehrenberg (1940), Vlastos (1953), Ostwald (1969: 96–136), and Borecký (1971) list and analyze the evidence. Further discussion: Larsen 1948; Vlastos 1964; Ehrenberg 1965a: 279–86; Ostwald 1969: 137–60; Fornara 1970a; Meier 1970: 15ff., esp. 36–44; 1987a: 119; 1988: 52 n. 16; Will, *RPh* 45 (1971): 102–13; Pleket 1972; Frei 1981; Heuss 1981: 22–27; Triebel-Schubert 1984; Lengauer 1987; Rosivach 1988: 46–52.

164. Thus with strong emphasis Will, *RPh* 45 (1971): 105ff., 111; followed by Pleket 1972: 64–

68. See also Meier 1970: 40–41; Frei 1981: 211. Ostwald 1969: 97: "*isonomia* is not a name for a form of government but for the principle of political equality."

165. The latter in Thuc. 3.62.3–4 (*oligarchia isonomos*). See esp. Will 1955: 618; *RPh* 45 (1971): 108–9, 111; Pleket 1972: 64–65.

166. Such extension was facilitated by the fact that a certain level of equality had been characteristic of the polis from its very beginnings: it included the independent farmers who fought in the communal army and sat in the communal assembly; see Morris 1996; Raaflaub 1996b: 150–53, 1997c, 1997d; more generally, Detienne 1965. The possibility that *isonomia* initially was an aristocratic concept was accepted by Ehrenberg (1940: 294–95; cf. 1965a: 154–55, 279–86) but rejected later, in view of Vlastos's (1953) objections: Ehrenberg 1965a: 261–63. Meier (1968: 10 with n. 27), Fornara (1970a: 176), Will (*RPh* 45 [1971]: 110–11), Borecký (1971: 24), Pleket (1972), and Gschnitzer (1981: 91), among others, favor this possibility; see also Raaflaub 1980: 26–28. Frei (1981: 218–19) and Heuss (1981: 22–27) have doubts, but their arguments do not exclude it.

167. *Isonomia:* esp. Hdt. 3.80.6 (*ounoma pantōn kalliston*); Thuc. 3.82.8; also Hdt. 5.78 on *isēgoria* (*chrēma spoudaion*). See Vlastos 1964: 4–5; Fornara 1970a: 171–80; Sealey 1974: 273–75. *Isēgoria:* Hdt. 5.78; Shimron 1979: 132 n. 2. *Isokratia:* Ostwald 1973.

168. On tyranny and elimination of equality, see also chap. 4.2 at nn. 135ff. below. Isagoras and *isēgoria:* Raaflaub 1980: 23–28. Beloch (1893: 616–17; not mentioned in the 2d ed.) emphasizes the significance of the appearance of names ending with -*agoras;* see also Ehrenberg 1940: 294; Momigliano 1971: 518. Hirzel (1907: 266 n. 5) underscores the political function of names with *Iso-*.

169. Laws: Ostwald 1955, 1986: 8; Gagarin 1981b; Rhodes 1981: 156, 220–22. Oath: Rhodes 1972: 193ff., esp. 195; cf. Meier 1968: 20–22. Cult of Zeus Eleutherios: chap. 3.3 below.

170. Aesch. *Pers.* 591–94 (n. 139); *Supp.* 946ff. (948–49: *saphōs d'akoueis ex eleutherostomou glōssēs*); see also fr. 225.31 Mette (*eleutheron legeis*); *Prom.* 180 (*agan d'eleutherostomeis*) with 309–29. Quotation: Finley 1982: 80; cf. Frei 1981: 206. *Isēgoria* and Cleisthenes: Raaflaub 1980: 28–34.

171. Eur. *Supp.* 438–41 (late 420s); cf. Soph. fr. 192 Pearson. See chap. 6.1 at nn. 90ff. below.

172. See further, chap. 6.2 at nn. 132ff. below.

173. Hdt. 5.66, 69–70, 72–73; 6.131.1; Aristot. *AP* 20–22.2; cf. the comments by Rhodes 1981; Chambers 1990; Nenci 1994: ad loc. The bibliography is immense; some of it is listed in my "Forschungsbericht" (Raaflaub 1995). See esp. Kienast 1965; Ostwald 1969: 137–73, 1988; Will 1972: 63–76; Martin 1974: 7–22; Kinzl 1977a: 200–210; Meier 1980: 91–143 (= 1990: 53–81); Siewert 1982; Ober 1993, 1998b; Raaflaub 1995, 1998b; Loraux 1996; Lévêque and Vidal-Naquet 1996; Anderson 2003. Develin and Kilmer (1997) present a minimalist view.

174. Hdt. 5.66.2 (*ton dēmon proshetairizetai*), 69.2. Herodotus's assessment of the Athenian successes in 506 (5.74ff., esp. 78) undoubtedly reflects views on democracy current in his own time (Heuss 1962: 190; Raaflaub 1994: 144–45). On the triple alliance: Tausend 1992: 118–23. Robert (1964) suggests that the account of the triple war itself is modeled on a similar crisis in 446–445. On fifth-century representation of Cleisthenes as founder of democracy: Hdt. 6.131.1; Aristot. *AP* esp. 22.1, 29.3; Ruschenbusch 1958: 418–21; Rhodes 1981: 240–42, 260–61. For contrasting assessments of the demos's revolt: Ober 1998b; Raaflaub 1998b.

175. This is not to deny the crucial role the tyranny played, in several ways, in preparing the ground for these changes: bibliography in n. 148.

176. See esp. Bradeen 1955: 29; Kienast 1965: 280; Martin 1974: 21; Kinzl 1977a: 201–2; Siewert 1982: 157–59. Eder (1986) emphasizes the elite's need for self-discipline in order to avoid tyranny.

177. Spahn 1977: 162–73; Meier 1980: 113–23 (= 1990: 64–70).

178. Such unity (emphasized but perhaps overstated by Frost 1968: 121–23; Kinzl 1977a: 210–14) is suggested by the silence of our sources on any resistance to Cleisthenes' reforms or on post-Cleisthenic troubles. The difference from the reactions prompted by Ephialtes' reforms in 462 is remarkable: the latter were clearly perceived as driven by partisan interests (Raaflaub 1998b: 49–50 with bibliography and sources; see also chap. 6.1 at n. 60 below).

179. See esp. Ober 1989: 69–71, 1993. The suggestion that the demos joined Cleisthenes merely in their capacity as clients of elite families (thus Kinzl 1977a: 201–2) seems untenable: the weakening of traditional ties of dependence was an indispensable precondition for several aspects of the reforms. See Meier 1980: 113–23 (= 1990: 64–70).

180. Tribal reform: esp. Traill 1975, 1986; and bibliography in Raaflaub 1995: 16 n. 41. Demes as foundations of the entire system: Spahn 1977: 163–65; Osborne 1985: 64–92; Whitehead 1986a: 3–38; see also Jones 1999; Anderson 2003: chap. 5. Military aspects: Bicknell 1972: 19–21; van Effenterre 1976; Siewert 1982: pts. 3–4; see also Frost 1984. Council: esp. Larsen 1955b: 13–21; Will 1972: 71–72; Zambelli 1975; McCargar 1976. Rhodes (1972: 178–210) is more cautious.

181. Raaflaub 1995: 25–27 with bibliography.

182. Meier 1980: 124–38 (= 1990: 70–78). Support for these suggestions is found, for example, in the organizational structures of the new council, which made participation of substantial numbers of non-elite citizens necessary (Raaflaub 1980: 32–33; cf. Will 1972: 71–72), and in the focus on the Agora as the new political center (Thompson and Wycherley 1972: 19–21; Camp 1986: chap. 3; von Steuben 1989; Shear 1994; Anderson 2003: chap. 3; questions in Raaflaub 1998b: 93–95). Meier (1988: 91 n. 16) suggests that "we should consider more seriously the possibility that the demand for *isonomia* initially comprised the idea of a balance between demos and aristocracy" (my tr.); cf. Meier 1987a: 119.

183. As a logical consequence, more elite prerogatives were eliminated in the 480s, when archons were appointed by lot, thus making membership in the Areopagus Council accessible to the non-elite: Aristot. *AP* 22.5, with the comments by Rhodes 1981: 272–74; Chambers 1990: 241–43; cf. Badian 1971; Martin 1974: 26–28; Kinzl 1977a: 216–22. Previous role of farmer-hoplites: Raaflaub 1997d, 1999: 132–41. For arguments supporting my thesis that the thetes continued to play a secondary political role: Raaflaub 1998b: 40–43, 92–93.

184. Raaflaub 1980: 17.

185. Hdt. 5.74–75, 90–93. The account of these episodes is at least partly colored by experiences and perspectives of Herodotus's own time: Strasburger 1955: 12–14, 22; summarized in Raaflaub 1987: 223–24.

186. 490: e.g., Hdt. 6.109.3, 121.1; 6.22.1 (Samos). 480s: nn. 105–6 above. Hence, the first three victims of ostracism were accused of being friends of both the tyrants and the Persians: Aristot. *AP* 22.4–6, with the ostraca of Callias (see Siewert 2002: 56, Kallias Kratiou Alopekethen); Karavites 1977.

187. Again, the possibility cannot be excluded that the same process had begun earlier (during the Ionian Revolt) in the poleis of Asia Minor.

188. This topic has recently received much attention. Early awareness: Schwabl 1962; Weiler 1968; Dihle 1994: chap. 1. See generally Reverdin 1962; Hall 1993; Cartledge 1993: chap. 3; Dihle 1994; Georges 1995; Ulf 1996. Specifically on Herodotus: Reverdin and Grange 1988; Hartog 1988. Tragedy: Bacon 1961; Hall 1989. Reflection in art: Bovon 1963; Miller 1997. Greeks in Persia: Walser 1984: chap. 5; Briant 1996: 359–64. The degree of knowledge of the non-Greek world was probably very uneven; among lower classes it was sparse, one-sided, and cliché-ridden, especially since the "average" Greek encountered the barbarian primarily as a slave (Baldry 1962: 174).

189. I need to emphasize that these were not facts but subjective perceptions, distorted by prejudices and misunderstandings: the stuff ideologies are made of. See generally Sancisi-Weerdenburg 1987a, 1987b; Sancisi-Weerdenburg and Kuhrt 1987. A good illustration is Darius's letter to an imperial officer in the west, Gadatas, in which the Persian term *bandakā* ("vassal," "subject": Kent 1953: 199; Briant 1996: 335–37) is translated as *doulos* (ML, no. 12: *basileus basileōn Dareios . . . Gadatai doulōi tade legei*); see also, e.g., Xen. *An.* 2.5.38; *Cyr.* 4.61. See further the references to the empire of the Persian god-kings in Aesch. *Pers.* 150–58; Hdt. 1.114.5; 7.8β.3, 11.4, 39.1, 96.2 (on generals in Xerxes' army: *douloi* like all the others; cf. *Pers.* 23–24: *tagoi Persōn, basilēs basileōs hupochoi megalou*), 135.2–3 (chap. 5.2 at n. 115 below); 8.102.2–3; also 2.172.5; 3.140.5. See (also on the following comments) Walser 1975: esp. 536–37; Klees 1975: 200–219; Drexler 1976: 23ff., 66–67.

190. Xerxes as tyrant in *Persians:* Richardson 1952; Berve 1967: 1.193, 2.625–26; Hall 1989: esp. 69–76, 154–59. Tyranny in the *Oresteia* and *Prometheus:* n. 134 above. See generally Alföldi 1934: 9–25, 1955: 25–32; Walser 1975: 531–32, 540.

191. *Persians:* at nn. 15–16 above. Herodotus: esp. 7.135.2–3 (chap. 5.2 at n. 115 below), 101–4, esp. 104.4 (chap. 6.2 at n. 144 below). Hippoc. *Aer.* 16, 23; Heinimann 1945: 170–80. See generally Backhaus 1976; Thomas 2000.

192. References in "Materialien," sec. 9.7.g; see esp. Diller 1962b; Dihle 1994: 46–53.

193. Oliver 1960. See reviews by F. Bourriot, *REA* 63 (1961): 179–82; Edouard Will, *RPh* 36 (1962): 84–91. Bömer (1957–63: 1.484–89) offers important observations on the cult.

194. Oliver 1960: chap. 1, esp. 10–11 (quot. 11). See chap. 2.2, n. 46 above for *basileis* (not "kings" in any strict sense of the word).

195. See esp. 9.81, 85, where Herodotus mentions the dedications and funerals after the victory.

196. Everything else that is mentioned only in later accounts is controversial, however. See below at n. 199 and chap. 4.3 at n. 168. Annual commemoration: Thuc. 3.58.4; Isocr. 14.61.

197. For an explanation, see below at n. 242.

198. See esp. Etienne and Piérart 1975; West 1977.

199. Royal support: e.g., Paus. 4.27.10; 9.1.8; Arr. *Anab.* 1.9.10; Plut. *Alex.* 34.2; Kirsten 1950: 2311–12. Documents: on the "Oath of Plataea": see the list of supporters and opponents of its authenticity in Siewert 1972: 3–4; among the former, Siewert himself and Meiggs 1972: 504–7; among the latter, esp. Robert 1938: 307–16; Alois Dreizehnter, rev. of Siewert, *Gnomon* 47 (1975): 379–83. On the "Covenant of Plataea": Plut. *Arist.* 21.1; Siewert 1972: 89–93; Meiggs 1972: 507–8; Sansone 1989: 197. On both: Baltrusch 1994: 44–48. Robertson (1976: esp. 18, 20–21) dates the origin of these "documents" to 378–368.

200. Established in 479: Plut. *Arist.* 21.1–2; Diod. 11.29.1–2. See further Paus. 9.2.5–6; Strabo 9.2.31. Earliest literary (Poseidipp. fr. 31 *PCG:* after 290) and epigraphic (an honorary decree of the mid–third century: Etienne and Piérart 1975: 51–58) evidence provides a *terminus ante quem* in the early third century. See, e.g., *ATL* 3.101; Meiggs 1972: 507–8; Etienne and Piérart 1975: 63–75; Schachter 1994: 125–43. *Aristos Hellēnōn:* Robert 1929. See also Kirsten 1950: 2327–28. Prize vessels: Amandry 1971: 620–25; cf. Boedeker 2001: 151–52, with recent bibliography.

201. Altar: Paus. 9.2.5; cf. Strabo 9.2.31. Epigram: Sim.(?) 107aD = XV *FGE/C* (Plut. *Arist.* 19.7; *De mal. Her.* 42.873b; cf. *Anth. Pal.* 6.50). On text and date: Wilamowitz 1913: 197–99; Jacoby 1945: 185 n. 107; Molyneux 1992: 197. As Wade-Gery (1933: 71–82, esp. 76–77) points out, *pote* in line 1 suggests a later date as well.

202. See esp. Calabi Limentani 1964: liii–lvi and on 20.4 (a later construction, intended to connect cult and games with Delphi). Fictitious oracle: Hignett 1963: 419–20 (439–47 on

Delphi's role in the war); contra: Parke and Wormell 1956: 174–76. Pure fire: Delcourt 1955: 150; Parker 1983: 23.

203. Together with Athens, Plataea, Tarentum, and Caria (on the latter, however, see Jessen, *RE* 5 [1905]: 2350; Fehrle, in Roscher 1924–37: 6.621; Farnell 1896: 62; on Tarentum, see Wuilleumier 1968: 474): Hesych. s.v. *Eleutherios Zeus;* schol. [Plat.], *Eryx.* 392a; schol. Paus. 1.3.2. Coins and revivals: Head 1911: 179–82; Fehrle, in Roscher 1924–37: 6.622; Kraay and Hirmer 1966: pl. 47, no. 133; Schwabl 1978: 1197.

204. The numerous epithets of Zeus constructed on *-ios* point to a primarily local or functional relationship (Schwyzer 1939–53: 1.466, 2.176; lists of Zeus's epithets: Roscher 1924–37: 6.592–671; Schwabl 1972, 1978: 1441–75). Strictly speaking, Zeus is thus not the "liberator" but the god associated with freedom. In comparison, for example, with Zeus Soter, this could be significant, but given the lack of an agent noun for the stem *eleuth-*, not too much should be made of it.

205. Nilsson 1951; cf. Nilsson 1967: 708–21. Livy 5.22.3–7, on the transfer of Juno to Rome after the fall of Veii, offers an instructive analogy. For various aspects of "religion and politics," see, e.g., Sordi 1981 and a growing bibliography on Athenian democracy, empire, and religion: esp. Smarczyk 1990; Shapiro 1994; Versnel 1995; Parker 1996: chaps. 8–10; Jameson 1998; survey with bibliography in Raaflaub 1998c: 36–40.

206. One need only think of the avowed purpose of the Delian League (revenge for the destruction of temples: at n. 127 above); the use of the "Cylonian curse" by Sparta as a weapon against Athenian leaders from the Alcmeonid family (Hdt. 5.70.2, 72.2; Thuc. 1.126–27); Cimon's returning the "bones of Theseus" to Athens (Plut. *Cim.* 8.5–6; Garland 1992: chap. 4; Mills 1997: 34–42); the reinterpretation of the myth of Theseus in the late sixth and early fifth centuries and its use in imperial ideology; the use made of the cult of Athena for the same purpose (on both, e.g., Castriota 1992 and bibliography cited in previous note; see also at n. 244 below); the development of the myth of autochthony (Rosivach 1987a; Shapiro 1998) or of the suppliant myths (chap. 5.1 at nn. 31–32 below).

207. *IG* V 1.700, illustrated in Cook 1914–40: 2.2.1096 n. 1. Jeffery 1961: 184: "not earlier than the 5th cent.," with which Alan Boegehold agrees (oral communication). Zeus Hikesios: Cook 1914–40: 2.2.1096–98; Roscher 1924–37: 6.631–32; Schwabl 1972: 316–17, 1978: 1027–28. Freedmen: Bömer (1957–63: 1.484, 487–89, and passim) rejects the possibility of an early or even original connection with freedmen. See also Thommen 1996: 137–41, with reference to *Entdeckung,* 130; Paus. 3.17.9 (dedication of bronze statues to Zeus Hikesios after the murder of Pausanias).

208. See at n. 227 below. On Herodotus's comment: Ostwald 1969: 166; La Bua 1978: 31ff.; Reinau 1981: 37 n. 25.

209. 470: e.g., Holm 1870: 242; Ziegler 1913: 1620; Wilamowitz 1922: 305. 466: Barrett 1973: esp. 28–35. Battle of Himera: suggested by *Pyth.* 1.71–80 (at n. 17 above); thus also Pohlenz 1955: 15 (= 1966: 12); Bömer 1957–63: 1.486; Bowra 1964: 123. Barrett (1973: 35) disagrees.

210. Kraay and Hirmer 1966: 287, no. 66, with pl. 20 (Himera); cf. Ziegler 1913: 1620; Gielow 1940–41: 122. These scholars think of an allusion to Asclepius or Heracles, but the inscription *SŌTĒR* seems unproblematic: the masculine form in combination with Tyche is found also in Aesch. *Ag.* 664; Soph. *OT* 81 (cited by Gielow 1940–41: 113). Later coins from Syracuse write *SŌTEIRA* next to a feminine head (Artemis Soteira in Kraay and Hirmer 1966: pl. 46, no. 130; and Kore Soteira on a coin in the former Virzi collection [personal communication from P. R. Franke]). The identification of a temple of Zeus Eleutherios by Dunbabin (1948: 429) is pure speculation; on the possibility of a cult: also Barrett 1973: 34–35; Lintott 1981: 187.

211. Testimonia in Wycherley 1957: 25–30. Stone marker: *IG* I³ 1056; Wycherley 1957: no. 39: *Dios E[leutherio].* Cf. Meritt 1952: 374, no. 25: other reconstructions are possible but none

seems more probable. Date: Meritt 1952. *IG* II² 43 = Tod 2.123 ("charter" of the Second Athenian League), lines 65–66. An honorary decree of 393 was to be set up near the statue of a god (*agalma*), probably this one, but no epithet is preserved (Lewis and Stroud 1979: 191–93). Xen. *Oec.* 7.1; *P.Oxy.* 39 (1972): 47–48, no. 2889, lines 5–7 (beginning of Aeschin. Socr. *Miltiades*); [Plat.] *Theag.* 121a; [Plat.] *Eryx.* 392a: all referring to the Stoa of Zeus Eleutherios. In a fragment of unknown origin and date but generally attributed to Sophocles, Liberty is called the blessed child of Zeus (*Eleutheria Dios olbion tekos; TrGF* 4, no. 927b). Stoa of Zeus: Thompson 1937: 5–55; Travlos 1971: 527–33; Thompson and Wycherley 1972: 96–103; Camp 1986: 105–7.

212. Hyperides, Didymus: Harpocr. s.v. *Eleutherios Zeus* (Wycherley 1957: no. 27); *Etym. Magn., Suda,* s.v. *Eleutherios* (Wycherley 1957: nos. 26, 35). See Farnell 1896: 62; Bömer 1957–63: 1.489; Oliver 1960: 16 n. 15. Metaphor: Wycherley 1957: 26, on no. 27; Rosivach 1978: 40–41 (referring in n. 33 to the perhaps significant use of *exeleutheros* instead of *apeleutheros*); Schwabl 1978: 1066. A simple error on the part of Hyperides cannot be ruled out, since by his time freedmen probably sacrificed to the freedom god, just as in Argos they drank "freedom water" (*eleutherion hudōr*) from the spring of Cynadra: Antiph. com. fr. 26.4–5 *PCG;* Hesych. s.v.; Wilamowitz 1884a; Bömer 1957–63: 1.488.

213. So, too, Rosivach 1987b: 264–67; 279–85 on cult practices. Robertson (1976: 17) suggests that the epithet Eleutherios was not introduced in Athens until the 370s, when the epithet first appears unambiguously in the charter of the Second Athenian League (n. 211 above). If not the stone marker (n. 211 above), at least the historical-ideological context of the construction of the Stoa of Zeus (chap. 5.2 at n. 125 below) strongly supports a much earlier date.

214. Pohlenz 1955: 15 (= 1966: 11); Bömer 1957–63: 1.484–85. On *Eleutheriōn* or *Eleutherios* as the name of a month in Halicarnassus, perhaps connected with an Eleutheria festival: *Entdeckung,* 133 n. 288; the evidence is certainly later than the fifth century.

215. The cults of *theoi sōtēres* deserve a thorough investigation. Numismatic evidence is especially helpful; see, e.g., a Zeus Soter on the only extant coin (early fifth century) of Galaria in Sicily (*BMC* 2, *Sicily* [1876]: p. 64). An unnamed lightning-wielding god on a coin from Zancle (dated ca. 460, i.e., shortly after the fall of tyranny) has been identified as Poseidon (Mertens 1947: esp. 33, with a survey of earlier interpretations) or Zeus [Eleutherios] (Gielow 1940–41; followed by Kraay and Hirmer 1966: 286, with pl. 17, no. 53). A similar Zeus on a late-fifth-century strigil reproduces a late archaic statue of Zeus Soter in Olympia (Marwitz 1979).

216. Antityranny ideology in democracy: Berve 1967: 1.190–206; Rosivach 1988; McGlew 1993: chap. 6; Raaflaub 2003; see also the beginning of chap. 6.1 below. Tyrannicides: Taylor 1991 with earlier bibliography. Controversy: Hdt. 5.62–63; 6.123; Thuc. 6.53.3–60.1 with *HCT* 4.317–29; Munn 2000: 114–18. Rivalries: Thomas 1989: esp. chap. 5.

217. Boersma (1970: 31–32, 88–89) suggests, by reinterpreting the archaeological evidence, that a shrine of Zeus Eleutherios existed at the Agora as early as the time of Cleisthenes and finds it in a small building directly north of the Bouleuterion that is usually identified as Metroon, that is, a shrine of the mother goddess (Meter) of Asia Minor (Thompson 1937: 135–40; Thompson and Wycherley 1972: 30–31; Travlos 1971: 352–56; Camp 1986: 91–94). I have stated my arguments against this highly implausible theory in *Entdeckung,* 134 n. 292, and see no reason to repeat them here. To my knowledge, no evidence has come to light that would force me to change my opinion. On building activity in the Agora in and soon after the time of Cleisthenes, see recent bibliography listed in n. 182 above. On Bouleuterion and Metroon: Miller 1995; Shear 1995.

218. Above at n. 185. Ideology: chap. 5.1–2 below.

219. Epithet: Höfer, in Roscher 1924–37: 4.1265; Fehrle, in Roscher 1924–37: 6.619. Schol. Aristoph. *Wealth* 1175; Hesych., Harpocr., s.v. *Eleutherios Zeus* (cf. schol. [Plat.] *Eryx.* 392a): Wycherley 1957: nos. 24, 28, 27 (whence the tr.). Inscriptions: testimonia in Wycherley 1957:

e.g., nos. 40–43; Isocr. 9.57 with Paus. 1.3.1. See also Schwabl 1978: 1066–67. Shrine: Thompson 1937: 8–14, 73–74; Thompson and Wycherley 1972: 96. Date: at n. 239 below. Parker (1996: 239 n. 76) accepts the identification of the two cults. See Rosivach 1978 for other functions of Zeus this cult site may have served, especially that of Zeus Agoraios; Robertson (1992: 52), however, locates the latter in the Old Agora.

220. At n. 202 above. Soter: *IG* VII 1668; Fehrle, in Roscher 1924–37: 6.620; Jessen, *RE* 5 (1905): 2349.

221. See generally Farnell 1896: 59–61; Höfer, in Roscher 1924–37: 4.1236–72; Dornseiff 1927; Nilsson 1967: 414–16. Private sphere: e.g., Aesch. *Supp.* 981–82; Soph. *El.* 281; Aristoph. *Frogs* 738, 1433; and a strigil with a stamp reproducing a statue of Zeus Soter (Marwitz 1979). Athena: Roscher 1924–37: 1.684–85; Höfer, in Roscher 1924–37: 4.1241–42; Nilsson 1967: 433–38; and chap. 2.2 at n. 66 above. War: Höfer, in Roscher 1924–37: 4.1262–63; Fehrle, in Roscher 1924–37: 6.691–92; Burkert 1985: 128, with ref. to *IG* XIV 268; Parker 1996: 239. E.g., Zeus Soter as recipient of a vow before the battle of Arginusae (Diod. 13.102.1) or as a watchword in battle (Xen. *An.* 1.8.16); the Soteria founded in Delphi in the third century after the repulsion of the Celts (*IG* II² 680, lines 5ff.; Roussel 1924; Nachtergael 1977).

222. See chap. 2.2 at nn. 63ff. above. Hence, the importance to sailors of the joint cult of Zeus Soter and Athena Soteira in the Piraeus (Höfer, in Roscher 1924–37: 4.1242, 1269). On the festival of the Diisoteria: Deubner 1932: 174–76; Parke 1977: 167–68; Parker 1996: 239–40.

223. As when in Athens the shields of exceptionally brave warriors who had died in battle were dedicated to Zeus Eleutherios (Paus. 1.26.2; 10.21.5–6), or a crater was dedicated to him after a victory (*Et. Magn. s.v. Eleutherios Zeus*). See also Aristot. *De mundo* 7 (= Stob. *Ecl.* 1.2.36). See also Rosivach 1987b: 267–71.

224. Chap. 2.2 at n. 63 above and the present chap. at nn. 40ff. above.

225. An analogous process can be observed in the rise of the concept of autonomy: chap. 4.3 below.

226. Even a cursory reading of Herodotus makes this strikingly clear. See also Aesch. *Pers.* 347–49, for a variant to 402–4.

227. See above at n. 208.

228. Acceptance: e.g., Berve 1967: 1.114; von Fritz 1967: 1.325–26; Ostwald 1969: 107–9, 165–66; Pleket 1972: 65; Roisman 1985: esp. 257, 263–67; Shipley 1987: 103–5; Rosivach 1987b: 264 n. 5; Garland 1992: 7. Doubts: Pohlenz 1955: 189–90 (= 1966: 182 n. 8); Bömer 1957–63: 1.484. Skepticism: Jacoby 1913: 221–22, 446–47; Barron 1964b; How and Wells 1928: 1.298 (concerning Hdt. 3.142); Immerwahr 1956–57: esp. 319–22 (concerning 3.139–49); Asheri 1990: 348: "Around the historical core, whose authenticity there is no reason to doubt, Herodotus has created an essentially anecdotal account, with unexpected changes of scene, dialogues, political discourses, and a series of ironically paradoxical plots" (my tr.). See also Murray 1988: 470–71 and the detailed discussions by La Bua 1975, 1978.

229. See esp. Mitchell 1975: 80, 86.

230. Esp. Hdt. 3.80.2, 6 (Immerwahr 1956–57: 319); cf. Asheri 1990: 350. On Herodotus's personal sentiments: Tölle-Kastenbein 1976: 21. On his speeches: Solmsen 1944; Waters 1966, 1985: 9–10, 64–69; Lateiner 1989: 17–26. This does not exclude the possibility that some elements of this speech could have been expressed at the time (esp. the characterization of tyranny as power usurped by an individual at the expense of his peers, the pointed contrast between tyranny and *isonomia*, and the concept of "putting power in the middle" [see Detienne 1965]), but such correspondences would be accidental: oral tradition normally does not preserve such details. Athenian experiences: Ostwald 1969: 166; Raaflaub 1987: 225–26.

231. Shipley 1987: 103.

232. On Athens, see at n. 216 above. For believers in Herodotus's credibility, my conclusion is hard to swallow: see, e.g., R. Sealey's review of *Entdeckung* in *Gnomon* 60 (1988): 164–65; E. Stein-Hölkeskamp, *Gymnasium* 98 (1991): 93; W. Donlan, *CP* 85 (1990): 58 ("This is perhaps the most controversial treatment of the evidence in R.'s book"); cf. Bleicken 1994: 544. In view of such doubts, I have rethought the whole issue (Raaflaub 2000d: 253–55), but considering what I believe to have learned about the methods and purposes of ancient historiography in general and of Herodotus in particular, I see no reason to change my view. Herodotus's purpose is, to put it simply, more didactic than positivistic; he is more interested in exploring the meaning of the past for the present than in reconstructing the past per se (see, e.g., Fornara 1971b; Nicolai 1986; Raaflaub 1987, 2002a, 2002b: esp. 164–86, with bibliography in n. 55; Gould 1989). Herodotus's story makes sense and is meaningful in his interpretive context, but for the reasons given in this section, we are not obliged to accept it as historical.

233. Hdt. 9.90–92, 106. Herodotus's knowledge: Jacoby 1913: 220–24, 428ff., esp. 430. Reliability of archaeologically verifiable information: Tölle-Kastenbein 1976: 108. Maeandrius's descendants: e.g., Jacoby 1913: 223; La Bua 1978: 31ff.; see also Mitchell 1975: 86; Shipley 1987: 104–5. Athenaeus (13.561F; *FGrH* 449 F1) cites *Kolophoniaka* of Erxias (date unknown) with a reference to Eleutheria held on Samos in honor of Eros. Nothing else is known about this.

234. Plut. *Lyc.* 6.2; Oliver 1960: 12ff., esp. 14. Hellenion: Paus. 3.12.6; Bölte, *RE* 8 (1913): 173–74. Hellenios/a: Wilamowitz 1884b: 94 n. 8; Chrimes 1949: 484–85 (doubted in A. M. Woodward's review, *Historia* 1 [1950]: 633); Edouard Will, *RPh* 36 (1962): 85; LSJ, s.v. *Hellēnios;* other emendations are listed by Oliva (1971: 77–78) and Manfredini and Piccirilli (1980: 234), who keep Syllanios/a; Nafissi (1991: 74) prefers Skyllanios. If Hellenios/a were to be accepted, two references may help explain this epithet and the Hellenion: Paus. 3.12.6 connects the latter with the Persian Wars; Xen. *Lak. pol.* 13.11 mentions Hellanodikai in the Spartan army, who apparently arbitrated conflicts among allies in the field. Schäfer (1963: 289 n. 4) connects this office with the formation of the Peloponnesian League in the sixth century, but Thommen (1996: 67) points out that such a title requires more of a Panhellenic function and fits better into the context of the Hellenic League of 481.

235. Oliver 1960: 14–17.

236. Hdt. 3.65.6 (cf. Asheri 1990: 286); Greek perspective: 5.106.6 (cf. Nenci 1994: 315).

237. Solidarity: Hdt. 5.49.2; 8.144.2; 9.7α.2; cf. Bengtson 1974: 168. Especially instructive is the appeal to *theoi Hellēnioi* in Hdt. 5.92.5, 93.1–2, in a context clearly influenced by the conditions of the late Periclean period (n. 185 above). The *theoi Hellēnioi* here are essentially identical with *theoi Hellēnikoi* (Hdt. 4.108.2) or *theoi Hellēnōn* (Ael. *V.h.* 2.9); thus also LSJ, s.v. *Hellēnios.* See also Eur. *Hipp.* 1121; Heliod. *Aeth.* 5.4; Ael. *V.h.* 12.1. This also explains the Hellenion, a sanctuary shared by several Greek poleis in Egyptian Naucratis (Hdt. 2.178.2): Lloyd 1988: 224; Bowden 1996: 18–24, with references to two other Hellenia in Hellenistic Egypt and a list of fragmentary dedications on pottery to *theoi tōn Hellēnōn vel. sim.* (23 nn. 26–28); Möller 2000: 105–8, 192–96.

238. As illustrated by the role of the Aeacidae during the battle of Salamis: Hdt. 8.64.2, hence 9.7α.2. Zeus Hellanios as weather god: Theophr. *P. sem.* 1.24; Fehrle, in Roscher 1924–37: 6.623; cf. Roscher 1924–37: 1.111. On the cult's altar: esp. Welter 1938: 91–92. On the connection of Hellanios with Thessaly: Jessen, *RE* 8 (1912): 176; Cook 1914–40: 2.2.894 n. 3. On Aeacus's origin and connection with Aegina: West 1985: 162–64; E. Kearns, *DNP* 1 (1996): 308. Earliest references: Pind. *Nem.* 5.10 (ca. 483), see Farnell 1930–32: 1.187, 2.275; *Paean* 6 (fr. 52f Sn-M).125–26 (478–460), see Radt 1958: 88–93, 132–33, 174–75. "Panhellenios": schol. Aristoph. *Knights* 1253; Paus. 1.44.9; 2.29.7, 30.3–4. On the cult legend (Aeacus freed Hellas from a severe drought by praying to his father, Zeus; in gratitude, a shrine common to all Hel-

lenes was erected to Zeus): Isocr. 9.14–15; Diod. 4.61.6; Apollod. *Bibl.* 3.12.6.9–10 (3.159); schol. Pind. *Nem.* 5.17b; 8.19a. On the Aiakeion in Athens: Hdt. 5.89; Wycherley 1957: 48–49; Stroud 1994.

239. Oliver 1960: 46ff., esp. 50. Soter in Agora: Thompson 1937: 8, 10–12; Martin 1951: 266; followed by Boersma 1970: 17. Piraeus: Wachsmuth 1890: 141ff. with references; Höfer, in Roscher 1924–37: 4.1242, 1269; Garland 1987: 137–38 with 239–40. For further discussion: *Entdeckung*, 143 n. 319; Rosivach 1987b; Parker 1996: 238–41 with ample documentation.

240. Nilsson 1950: 12ff.; see Nilsson 1967: 417–18 on the frequency of cults of Zeus Polieus or Poliouchos and Athena Polias.

241. *IG* II² 1352 (second century C.E.).

242. Above at nn. 198–99.

243. Festival: Laidlaw 1933: 45–50; *HCT* 1, at Thuc. 1.96.2; Meiggs 1972: 43; Balcer 1974: 32. Decline: Thuc. 3.104; Highby 1936: 11–13. Highby (1936: 13) concludes that the Delian League was "purely political in character." One would expect a reference to religious aspects in Thuc. 1.96.2 or 3.104 but Thucydides does not comment on the significance of Athenian festivals in the context of the empire; see *HCT* 1.388, and generally Jordan 1986; Hornblower 1992. The lack of inscriptions seems more troubling, but the quantity of inscriptions other than dedications is very small in Athens as well before the reforms of Ephialtes in 462 and increases rapidly only thereafter (Meiggs 1972: 18–19; Schuller 1984: 89), that is, at a time when Athens replaced Delos as the league's center. On the continuing importance of Delos, the Delian Apollo, and the Delia: Laidlaw 1933: 59–75; Hornblower 1992: esp. 182–83, 186–97; Shapiro 1996a.

244. See generally Meiggs 1972: chaps. 15–16; Balcer 1974: 32–34; Schuller 1974: 112–18, 169–70, 175; Smarczyk 1990; Parker 1996: chap. 8. Transfer to Athens: Pritchett 1969.

245. Nike statuettes: Oliver 1960: 138–40. On the various treasuries: Samons 2000. Tribute quota lists: *ATL*. Tribute and building program: recent discussion and bibliography in Samons 1993; Giovannini 1997; Kallet 1998: 48–52.

246. On the possible promotion of the cult of Athena throughout the empire: chap. 4.2 at n. 123 below. Athena on Acropolis: Herington 1955; Hooker 1963; Meiggs 1972: 94–95, 416–17; Fehr 1979–81. Nike temple: Meiggs 1972: 135–36, 496–503; Mark 1993; Gill 2001. Parthenon frieze: recently, Smarczyk 1990: 298–317; Osborne 1994; Shapiro 1996b. Panathenaea: Smarczyk 1990: 549–91; Maurizio 1998 (without mentioning the allies).

247. Burn (1962: 515), Meiggs (1972: 504–7), and Balcer (1974: 33–34), among others, accept the authenticity of this clause in the "Oath of Plataea"; contra: Siewert 1972: 102–6; Robertson 1980: 118–19.

248. Thus also Rosivach 1978; for details, see chap. 5.2 at n. 125 below.

249. Above at nn. 198–99. Democracy itself offers another example of an important political concept and reality that is reflected to a surprisingly small extent in religion: Versnel 1995; Jameson 1998; see also Boedeker and Raaflaub 1998: 326–27.

4. The Concept of Freedom after the Persian Wars

1. See generally *SV*, no. 130; Larsen 1940; *ATL* 3.183–243; Brunt 1953; Calabi 1953: 37–49; Meyer 1963; Meiggs 1972: chap. 3; Schuller 1974: 141–48; Pistorius 1985: 9–19; Steinbrecher 1985: esp. pt. 2; Fornara and Samons 1991: chap. 3; Rhodes 1992: 34–40; Petzold 1993–94; Baltrusch 1994: 52–64. Giovannini and Gottlieb (1980) argue, wrongly, I think, that no new alliance was founded in 478/477 despite the change in hegemony.

2. See chap. 3.1, n. 127, above.

3. Unlike most scholars, Meyer (1963: esp. 426–32, 439–40) disagrees. See further n. 90 below.

4. Earlier attempts: Hdt. 7.160–61; 8.2–3. The view, widespread a few decades later, that the predominance in Greece which Athens reached by the midcentury was envisaged by its leaders already during and right after the Persian Wars (e.g., Hdt. 6.109.3, 6, or the anecdote reported by Plut. *Them.* 20.1–2; *Arist.* 22.3–4; Diod. 11.42) is clearly anachronistic: Amit 1973: 31 n. 75; Frost 1980: 178–79; Nenci 1998: 281–82. Modern scholars who have adopted this perspective and argue, in various ways, that the Delian League thus was from the beginning an Athenian *"Herrschaftsinstrument"* include Meyer 1963; Rawlings 1977; Robertson 1980; and Steinbrecher 1985: pt. 2; contra: Will 1972: 130; French 1979; Raaflaub 1990: 542–45; Petzold 1993–94 (with detailed discussion and bibliography).

5. Historical developments: *ATL* 3.245–325; Meiggs 1943, 1963, 1972: chaps. 5–10; Schuller 1974: pt. 2; Rhodes 1985: 22–29, 1992: 40–61; Powell 1988: chap. 2; Fornara and Samons 1991: chap. 3.

6. Ancient historians commonly use terms like "empire" and "imperialism," though non-specifically, in this context; despite the modern connotations of these terms, I follow this custom here, alternating with the Greek term *archē;* see Schuller 1974: 1 n. 1, 97; Raaflaub 1996a: 274–75 with bibliography.

7. Whether the war with the Persians ended informally or by formal agreement is not important for my present purposes. On the much-debated "Peace of Callias": *SV,* no. 152 (sources and earlier bibliography); Meister 1982; Lewis 1992: 121–27; Badian 1993: chap. 1; Samons 1998.

8. Egypt: Meiggs 1972: 93–95, 101–8, 118; Rhodes 1992: 50–53; Robinson 1999. Crisis and systematization: Nesselhauf 1933: chap. 1; Schäfer 1963: 41–79; Meiggs 1963, 1972: chap. 7; Will 1972: 171–79; Schuller 1974: 172–77; Rhodes 1992: 54–61. Balcer (1978: x–xi, 12ff., and passim) dates the transformation of the confederacy into an empire exactly to the spring of 449; against this kind of approach, see Finley 1978: 103–5 (= 1982: 41–43). The view that the early 440s were a crucial period for the systematic consolidation of the empire is based in part on the "Peace of Callias" (see previous note); on Pericles' "Congress Decree" (Plut. *Per.* 17), the historicity of which is debated (pro: Meiggs 1972: 151–52, 512–15; Stadter 1989: 201–4 with bibliography; contra: Robertson 1976: esp. 10ff., 18; Meister 1982: 102–3; Podlecki 1998: 70); and on some imperial laws which were traditionally dated to this time but probably belong to a considerably later period; see n. 80 below. Fornara and Samons (1991: chap. 3) argue for completion of the transformation to empire in the mid- to late 460s.

9. For this paragraph, see the bibliography cited in n. 5 above.

10. Naxos: Thuc. 1.98.4 (*edoulōthē*). Thasos: Thuc. 1.100–101; Meiggs 1972: 86. Dates: *CT* 1.151, 154; Badian 1993: 101.

11. See, e.g., the use of *douleia* and similar words in Aesch. *Seven against Thebes* (69ff., esp. 74–75, 109ff., 253–54, 321ff., 451, 713); *Ag.* 360. Moreover, both *eleutheria* and *douleia* were used metaphorically to designate various forms of dependency and liberty: e.g., Pindar, *Pyth.* 12.15; more in "Materialien," secs. 6.1.b, 6.2.

12. Earlier relations among Greeks: chap. 3.1 at nn. 40ff. above.

13. See, generally, Busolt and Swoboda 1926: 1320–37; Larsen 1932, 1933–34; Schäfer 1932: index, s.v. "Sparta," "Symmachie," with the comments by Highby 1936: 66–74; Wickert 1961; Kagan 1969: 9–30; de Ste. Croix 1972: 94–124, 333–42; Cartledge 1979: chap. 9; Tausend 1992: esp. 167–80.

14. For a "constitution": e.g., Larsen 1932: 140–45, 1933–34: 1.257–58; Hampl 1938: 117–23; contra: Kagan 1969: 13ff. with a summary of the scholarly controversy. See also Baltrusch 1994: 19–23.

15. Unrestricted duration: Larsen 1933–34: 1.265–70; Kagan 1969: 18; Gschnitzer 1978: 16–17, 39. Revolt: Thuc. 1.18.3, 71.5; 5.30.1; Larsen 1933–34: 1.268–69; Kagan 1969: 15ff.; de Ste. Croix

1972: 94–95. An important case is Tegea, which, together with other Arcadian poleis, around 470 concluded an alliance with Argos and seceded; see Sim.(?) 122D = LIII *FGE/C* (*Anth. Pal.* 7.512)—if indeed this epigram belongs in this context (discussed in Page 1981: 278–79; "Materialien," sec. 7.1.b with nn. 142–43); Andrewes 1952; Forrest 1960: 229–32; Wickert 1961: 54–56; Cartledge 1979: 214–15; Lewis 1992: 102–8. Equal treatment: doubted by Jeffery (1988: 350).

16. Kagan 1969: 18–19, 21.

17. Thuc. 5.30.1–4. Supremacy: Bickerman 1950: 116–24. Formula: ". . . shall follow the Spartans whithersoever they may lead both by land and by sea, having the same friend and enemy as the Spartans" (tr. Cartledge 1976: 88); Larsen 1933–34: 1.270–76, 2.1–10; Kagan 1969: 11; de Ste. Croix 1972: 108–10, 298–307; Gschnitzer 1978: 26–36; Pistorius 1985: 119–25; Baltrusch 1994: 19ff. A Spartan treaty containing this formula (Peek 1974; *SEG* 26.461; ML, no. 67 bis [p. 312]) is dated by Peek, followed by Gschnitzer (1978), to the early fifth century, by Cartledge (1976) and ML to the 420s, by Kelly (1978) and Baltrusch (1994: 21–23) to the early fourth century; the last seems most convincing.

18. Larsen 1932: 141–42; de Ste. Croix 1972: 108–9.

19. Will 1955: 638–63; Kagan 1969: 21–26; Salmon 1984: 240–52.

20. Thuc. 5.27ff. *Isopsēphia* is specifically attested for the initial stage of the Delian League by Thuc. 3.11.4 (cf. 10.5); for Sparta, see 1.125.1, 141.6; 5.29.2–3, 30.1; cf. Hampl 1938: 119–23.

21. Kahrstedt 1922: 87–104; de Ste. Croix 1972: 120–22; Gschnitzer 1978: 36–39; examples also in Busolt and Swoboda 1926: 1331 n. 1. For restrictions, see Xen. *Hell.* 5.4.37; cf. Larsen 1933–34: 1.261. Contra: Ruschenbusch 1978: 79 with n. 10 on p. 94. Conflicts with far-reaching consequences: Thuc. 1.24ff., 103.4.

22. Emphasized by Thuc. 1.120.1–2; see Kallet-Marx 1993: index, s.v. Sparta.

23. See Thuc. 1.19, 121.3, 5; Kahrstedt 1922: 336–42; Busolt and Swoboda 1926: 1337. In the fourth century, under different circumstances, this too changed: Xen. *Hell.* 5.2.21. Sparta's problems: Hodkinson 1993, 2000.

24. E.g., Kahrstedt 1922: 104–18; Busolt and Swoboda 1926: 1330; Triepel 1938: 374. Contra: de Ste. Croix 1972: 98–99, but see text below and n. 34.

25. The *xenagoi* attested in the Peloponnesian War had military functions ("liaison officers" or "military advisors"; see Busolt and Swoboda 1926: 1335 with n. 1); even if they indicated a changed relationship between Sparta and the allies, the late date of their appearance is decisive.

26. Thuc. 1.18.1; Hdt. 5.92a.1; Isocr. 4.125; Aristot. *Pol.* 1312b7–8; Plut. *De mal. Her.* 859c–d; accepted, e.g., by Schäfer 1932: 147–51; Hammond 1982: 354–56. Doubts and criticism: Busolt 1878: 212–17, 304–6; Ehrenberg 1929: 1384; Cartledge 1979: 139–40, 148 (see also Cartledge 1987: index, s.v. "support for oligarchs"); Bernhardt 1987 (a propagandistic invention or massive exaggeration originating in the second half of the fifth century); *CT* 1.51.

27. Thuc. 1.19, 76.1, 144.4; Xen. *Hell.* 6.3.14; Aristot. *Pol.* 1296a32ff., 1307b19ff.; Kagan 1969: 12–13.

28. "Democracies": O'Neil 1995: 32–33, 38–39, 45–47; Robinson 1997: 108–11, 113–14, both with discussion, sources, and bibliography but using "democracy" loosely (see chap. 3.1 n. 102 above). At any rate, democracy did not necessitate defection from the league: in the 470s Elis did not participate in the alliance of Arcadian poleis with Argos, and Mantinea alone was not involved in the second battle (at Dipaea); see Wickert 1961: 54–56, 67–68; Amit 1973: 132–34, based on Hdt. 9.35.2; Paus. 8.8.6.

29. Contra de Ste. Croix 1972: 98–99.

30. Thuc. 5.81.2, 82.1, with *HCT* 4 ad loc. See further chap. 5.3 at nn. 160ff. below; Triepel

1938: 374. The examples cited by de Ste. Croix (1954: 20 n. 5) all date to the late fifth and fourth centuries; similarly *CT* 1.55.

31. See in general Lotze 1970; Andrewes 1978b. The clause in a treaty with Tegea, mostly dated to the mid–sixth century, to expel the Messenians and to "make none a citizen" (*mē exeinai chrēstous poiein*), that is, not to enfranchise fugitive helots, seems significant: *SV*, no. 112; Jacoby 1944a; Baltrusch 1994: 20 n. 89. On the significance of fear of the helots: de Ste. Croix 1972: 89ff., esp. 96–101; Talbert 1989 (with bibliography); Ducat 1990; Cartledge 1991.

32. Envoys: Thuc. 1.76.1–2; Pericles: Thuc. 1.144.2 with 145, 139.3, 140.3; cf. esp. 1.19. See Wickert 1961: 83; and n. 34 below.

33. Thuc. 5.91.1; 6.68.2–3 (both heavily propagandistic); Hdt. 1.68.6 (highly unusual; see chap. 3.1, n. 65, above). Peace of Nicias: chap. 5.3 at nn. 160ff. below.

34. See Thuc. 1.68–71, 120–24; 2.8.4; cf. 6.92.5. Contra: de Ste. Croix (1972: 96–124), whose tendency to use Sparta's severe "subjugation" of its allies to minimize that perpetrated by Athens is unmistakable. Above all, de Ste. Croix does not take sufficiently into account that the situation in the Peloponnesian League changed markedly during and after the war. Sparta's leadership became increasingly autocratic toward the end of the fifth century. Evidence reflecting this change should not be retrojected into much earlier periods. See chap. 5.3 below.

35. Hellenic League: e.g., Brunt 1953; Baltrusch 1994: 30ff.

36. Chap. 3.1 at n. 88 above.

37. Schuller 1974: 147 n. 50, 153–54. Robertson (1980: 65 and passim) overlooks these aspects.

38. See also chap. 3.1 at nn. 98ff. above. On what follows, see esp. Walser 1959: 223–28, 1984: chap. 6; Tozzi 1978; Murray 1988; Nenci 1994; Briant 1996: 158–68; Corsaro 1997: 27–36; and the bibliography, including many articles, listed by Tozzi and Nenci; see also Walter 1993a; Georges 2000; Kienast 2002.

39. Hdt. 1.162–65, 168–69; Strabo 6.1.1; see also Theogn. 603–4, 1103–4, with Highbarger 1937. Conditions after a treaty of alliance were different: Hdt. 1.76.2, 141. Miletus's special status: Hdt. 1.141.4, 143.1, with Asheri 1988b: 348; Gorman 2001: 124–28.

40. Obedience to orders: e.g., Busolt 1893–1904: 2.506; Heuss 1937: 13ff., esp. 15. Military duty (a significant aggravation compared with Lydian rule): Hdt. 1.171.1; 3.1.1; 4.83, 89, 97–98, 137ff.; 6.48; 7.93ff., and passim. Cf. Hdt. 2.1.2: the Ionians and Aeolians, as *douloi* whom Cambyses inherited from his father, are ordered to supply troops for the Egyptian campaign. Tribute: emphasized as esp. typical of *douleia* by Hdt. 1.6.2, 27.1; 7.51.1, 108.1; see also 3.67.3, 89–90; cf. Busolt 1893–1904: 2.515, 517–18; Dandamayev 1972: 43–44. Formalization: Briant 1996: 402–6. See generally Briant 1996: 510ff.

41. See chap. 3.1 at n. 102 above, with bibliography cited there.

42. See Busolt 1893–1904: 2.517; Hammond 1967a: 176, 178. Imperial coin: Christ 1967: 42; Briant 1996: 417–22, with bibliography; Dandamayev 1972: 45–48.

43. Hdt. 1.162.2, 164.1.

44. Hdt. 5.30–35. After the revolt, feuds among Greek poleis were prohibited: 6.42.1.

45. Hdt. 6.42–43; Diod. 10.25 (including a fair assessment of tribute and the replacement of tyrannies by "isonomic" governments); Briant 1996: 510–14; Georges 2000: 33–35.

46. Tozzi 1978: 114ff. passim; Gillis 1979: 10ff. (with bibliography).

47. Esp. Georges 2000, but see Kienast 2002. Herodotus (5.1, 26) reports spontaneous uprisings in the Hellespont region after Darius's failure against the Scythians: How and Wells 1928: 2.10; Tozzi 1978: 126ff.

48. It seems necessary to emphasize this even if the question of "freedom (or enslavement) for whom, and of what sort" (de Ste. Croix 1972: 36 n. 70), might cause modifications. See also

chap. 4.4 below. In Thuc. 1.77.2–5 the Athenians emphatically deny the comparison of their rule with that of the Persians implied in 1.69.5 (cf. 6.77.1; de Romilly 1963: 259–60).

49. See *ATL* 3.155–57.

50. *Doulos* vs. *andrapodon:* Volkmann 1961: 12–13; Gschnitzer 1964: 6–16; Ducrey 1968b: 23–25.

51. See Schuller 1974: 105 with bibliography in n. 157; in addition, de Ste. Croix 1954: 2, 1972: 36; Amit 1973: 39.

52. For similar difficulties posed by the concept of *autonomia:* chap. 4.3 below.

53. Gschnitzer 1964: 6–12; Klees 1975: 14–26.

54. As, e.g., in Thuc. 1.69.1, 124.3; 3.10.3, 5; 3.63.3; 4.86.1; 5.9.9; 6.76.4, 77.1, 80.5; 8.48.5. See *ATL* 3.156.

55. The speeches of the Corinthians are typical (Thuc. 1.68.3, 69.1, 121.5, 122.2, 124.3), as are those of Brasidas (4.86.1, 87.3), Hermocrates (6.76.2–4, 77.1, 80.5), and the Mytilenians (3.10.3ff., 13.6).

56. "Contrary to custom": *CT* 1.151 (whose tr. I follow); cf. Ténékidès 1954: 20–21 (with extensive bibliography); de Ste. Croix 1972: 38 n. 69; Balcer 1974: 32 n. 65; Ostwald 1982: 39. Contra (contrary to law, constitution, agreement): e.g., *ATL* 3.156; Larsen 1940: 191 n. 3; Brunt 1953: 152; Giovannini and Gottlieb 1980: 30 n. 92. Earlier in the same chapter, Thucydides uses *andrapodizein* for the fate of Eion and Scyros, where the inhabitants were sold into slavery and, in the latter case, replaced by Athenian settlers (Ducrey 1968b: 131; *CT* 1.150).

57. As esp. in Thuc. 2.8.2; 5.14.2; 7.56.2; 8.2.1.

58. Thasos (Thuc. 1.101.3), Aegina (108.4), Euboea (114.3), Byzantium and Samos (117.3). The usual terms are *katastrephesthai* (1.94.2, 114.3), *hupēkooi* (e.g., 2.23.3 [cf. 4.99]; 3.102.2; 4.108.3; 5.84.1; 7.28.4; 8.2.2, 64.1, 5; esp. instructive: 6.69.3; 8.68.1), *hupocheirioi* (1.88), *xummachoi hupēkooi* (2.99.2; 7.20.2), or *hupēkooi* contrasted with *xummachoi* (6.43.1; 7.57.3–4).

59. E.g., the Athenians in Sparta (esp. Thuc. 1.77.2, 5) or Pericles (2.41.3); see also 5.91.1; 6.21.2, 22.1; 7.63.3; to subjugate (*katastrephesthai*): 1.75.4; 6.82.3.

60. Similarly, Phrynichus (Thuc. 8.48.5), Pericles (2.63.3; cf. *HCT* 1.176), Nicias (6.20.2), and Euphemus, who echoes Hermocrates' polemics (6.76ff., esp. 76.2–4, 77.1–2, 80.5) in order to refute its implications (6.82.3–4, 83.4, 84.2) but would not have chosen this extreme word on his own (see, e.g., 6.82.3, 84.2).

61. Strasburger 1958: 29 n. 1.

62. Thuc. 1.141.1. Corcyra: 1.44.1; 3.70.1ff. (esp. 70.3, 71.1).

63. Ps. Xen. *AP* 1.16ff., esp. 18; otherwise, *summachoi* is used throughout, even in 2.1 in connection with the tribute; cf. Aristoph. *Ach.* 505–6; Schuller 1974: 149 with n. 153. For the date of the pamphlet (most likely between 431 and 424): Frisch 1942: 47–62; Treu 1967: 1947–59. Bowersock (1966: 33–38) argues for an earlier date (443–441, accepted, e.g., by Fornara and Samons 1991: 65 with n. 86); contra: e.g., Connor 1971: 207–9; de Ste. Croix 1972: 307ff. For a later date (420–415): Gomme 1962: 38–69; Ramirez Vidal 1997; see also Hornblower 2000.

64. E.g., Eur. *Supp.* 491–93 (*douloumetha*); *Belleroph.* fr. 286.10–12N.

65. Fr. 71 *PCG* (with sources); 64 Edm.; cf. Plut. *Per.* 26.3–4 with Stadter 1989: 249–51. On the political tendency and historical context of *Babylonians:* e.g., Weber 1908: 84ff.; Norwood 1930; Forrest 1975; Welsh 1983. Contra (among others): Meder 1938: 59 n. 166; Tuplin 1985: 357 n. 34. On *dēmos turannos* in *Knights:* below at n. 78.

66. For discussion: Schmid and Stählin 1946: 118; Norwood 1932: 193–97; Storey 1994: 109–12; Rosen 1997 (quot. 164).

67. Athens's rule as such apparently was hardly ever criticized; e.g., Meiggs 1972: 392; Forrest 1975: 22–23; Finley 1978: 106; Andrewes 1978a: 4–5, 1978b: 101–2.

68. Nesselhauf 1933: 69ff., esp. 84–94; Meiggs 1972: chaps. 17–18.

69. 432: Thuc. 1.67.2 (quot.), 139.1; cf. 140.3. Treaty: *SV*, no. 156; see also Nesselhauf 1934: 289–92; *ATL* 3.303; Meiggs 1972: 183–84; de Ste. Croix 1972: 293–94: Ostwald 1982: 23; *CT* 1.109; Figueira 1993: chap. 10. Contra (treaty of 457): *HCT* at 1.67.2. Substance: see esp. *ATL* (referring to analogies in the Peace of Nicias: Thuc. 5.18.5), Meiggs, Figueira (as cited). Badian (1993: 137–42) postulates a general autonomy clause in the treaty of 446, which, moreover, merely "revived and refurbished" a "sworn obligation dating back to 479" (115–16 with n. 17); I have strong doubts. See further nn. 168 and 206 below and, for discussion of the concept of *autonomia*, chap. 4.3 below.

70. Date: Pfeijffer 1999: 425. Interpretation: Finley 1955: 167–68; Wade-Gery 1958: 251–52; Burton 1962: 174; Bowra 1964: 156–57; Pfeijffer 1995, 1999: 439–40, 451, 455–56, 600–601.

71. Thuc. 1.139.3; 2.8.4.

72. 446: e.g., Wade-Gery 1958: 249; *HCT* 1.348; *ATL* 3.303–4; Meiggs 1972: 184; Badian 1993: 137. The significance of measures enacted in 443 is interpreted variously, e.g., by Schäfer (1963: 60–81), Meiggs (1972: 244–47), and Schuller (1974: 1–70).

73. Thucydides' use of *douleia* in 2.71.2 (concerning Pausanias's guarantee to Plataea in 479) is, of course, no proof of the actual use of this word at the time (see n. 168 below on *autonomia* in the same context). Nor does Herodotus, despite Badian's claims (1993: 117–18), imply or confirm that Athenians and Plataeans saw the latter as *douloi* of the former from the time they "gave themselves" to the Athenians to gain protection against the Thebans (6.108): see chap. 3.1 at nn. 75ff. above.

74. See also Hdt. 6.98. *Archē* as value-neutral term: Drexler 1976: 14–16 (with references).

75. Ps. Xen. *AP* 1.14–18; 2.2–3. On 1.15, cf. discussions in Plato (e.g., *Rep.* 587e) and Aristotle (e.g., *Pol.* 1318b6ff.) of the treatment of subjects; on 1.18 (humiliation of allies in law courts), see parallels in Aristophanes, cited below. See generally Cataldi 1984; Levi 1997.

76. Lévy 1976: 122–27 with references.

77. Aristoph. *Wasps* 700, 707. Courts: 517–18, 546ff., esp. 575, 577, 619. Contra (demagogues have all the power; judges and the entire demos are nothing but miserable "slaves"): 515–20, 602–4, 653ff. Comic exaggeration is obvious; see the comments by MacDowell 1971; Sommerstein 1983.

78. Merits: e.g., Aristoph. *Knights* 797. Corresponding oracles: 965–66, 1086–89. Praise: esp. 1111–14, 1329–30, 1333–34. See also Eupolis fr. 246 *PCG* (232 Edm.) on Chios as model ally "who takes orders wonderfully [*peitharchei kalōs*], just like an obedient horse" (tr. Rosen). Since, as in *Birds* 879–80, the tenor is positive (Dunbar 1995: ad loc.), the imagery is all the more revealing (cf. Aesch. *Pers.* 181ff.; Rosen 1997: 154–58); see also Thuc. 3.3.4; Bickerman 1958: 329–30.

79. Aristoph. *Ach.* 641ff. (642: *tous dēmous en tais polesin deixas hōs dēmokratountai*). The wordplay is ambiguous, probably intentionally; the interpretation remains uncertain. For the common view: Forrest 1963: 1 n. 3, 1975: 21–22, 27–28; *HCT* at Thuc. 4.88.2; Schuller 1974: 83 with n. 24. Contra: Popp 1968: 431–32 n. 34; Lewis 1992: 384 ("The easiest way of taking" this line "is that some scepticism might be possible about the nature of what were claimed to be democracies"). Sommerstein (1980: 189): "what democracy means for the people of the allied states: this vague expression may refer to the democratic regimes in the allied states themselves or to the way they were ruled by democratic Athens."

80. *SEG* 10.23, lines 8–9 (Hill 1951: B33; *IG* I³ 19: a proxeny decree traditionally dated before 445); *SEG* 10.19, lines 14–15 (= 12.9; Hill 1951: B34; *IG* I³ 27: according to Meritt [1952: 346–47] a proxeny decree for Delphi, ca. 450): *en [tōn poleōn hosōn A]thenaio[i kratōsin]*. Later documents in Schuller 1974: 121 n. 232: most, as here, with *kratousin*. On *proxenia* and the proxeny decrees: Gschnitzer 1973; Walbank 1978; Marek 1984. Mattingly's suggestion to date these decrees in the 420s (e.g., 1968: 479–81 = 1996: 250–52) was long opposed on epigraphical grounds

(e.g., Meiggs 1972: 425–27). This is part of a broader controversy on the date of Attic inscriptions; see Meritt and Wade-Gery 1962–63; Meiggs 1966; Schuller 1974: 211–17; Fornara and Samons 1991: 182–87. Mattingly's long-heretic efforts to redate many imperial documents to a later period (see his articles now collected in Mattingly 1996) have received recent support by the discoveries of Chambers et al. (1990); see Chambers 1992; his foreword and Mattingly's introduction in Mattingly 1996; and, on the proxeny decrees, Mattingly 1992: 136–38. Schuller (2002, with recent bibliography in nn. 6–8) offers a preliminary assessment of the impact of such discussions on our understanding of the development of the empire (see below at n. 124). *Summachoi:* n. 63 above; Schuller 1974: 149 with n. 53.

81. Soph. *Ajax* 112–17, 1097–99; cf. Knox 1961: 8 (= 1979: 132).

82. Details in Raaflaub 1979b; see also de Romilly 1963: 125–30; Hunter 1973/74; Drexler 1976: 36–40; Lévy 1976: 117–19; Connor 1977; Schuller 1978; Tuplin 1985; Barcelò 1990; Raaflaub 2003: 77–81.

83. Thuc. 1.122.3, 124.3; 2.63.2; 3.37.2; also 6.85.1.

84. See also Aristoph. *Knights* 1329–30 (*monarchos*); *Wasps* 587, referring to the judges' lack of accountability, a trait typical of tyranny (Hdt. 3.80.3). The view that there was no clear distinction between *monarchos, basileus,* and *turannos,* at least before Thucydides (Berve 1967: 1.194–95, 199; cf. Bleicken 1979: 149 with n. 3; Giorgini 1993: 81–82; Parker 1998: 149–54), is not uncontested (Connor 1977: 101–2; Ferrill 1978). See further chap. 6.1 at nn. 1ff.

85. Hdt. 5.90ff., esp. 93; see Strasburger 1955; Stahl 1983: 210–217; Raaflaub 1987: 223–24. Sophocles: Knox 1954 (= 1979: 87–95), 1957: chap. 2; accepted, e.g., by Segal 1993: 11; doubted by Tuplin 1985; Seaford 2003. On tragedy, tyranny, and *polis turannos:* Seaford 2003; cautious suggestions in Raaflaub 1988a: 294–95, 298–99; more systematically, Rosenbloom 1996.

86. I disagree with de Ste. Croix's statement (1954: 2) that "terms such as *turannos polis* do not necessarily imply . . . that Athens was an oppressive or unpopular ruler." Those who used the word "tyranny" intended to emphasize precisely this fact. See also Drexler 1976: 40; Raaflaub 2003: 77–81 (correcting Raaflaub 1984a: 73–78 and arguing against Connor 1977); see further chap. 5.2 at n. 129 below. Well established: e.g., Diller 1962a: 198–204; Popp 1968: 428–29; Meiggs 1972: 288; Schuller 1974: 121.

87. Typically, Thucydides uses *polis turannos* only in speeches. The difference between *polis archousa* and *polis turannos* is brought out well in Isocr. 8.91; cf. 8.115.

88. Plut. *Per.* 12.2; see Klein 1979: 502–7; Raaflaub 1979b: 242–43. For discussion of *Per.* 12–14 on the debate about Pericles' building program: Andrewes 1978a; Ameling 1985; Ostwald 1986: 185–88; and the comments by Stadter 1989. If *Prometheus Bound* was written by Aeschylus and performed in 457 (which is contested), lines 49–50 might offer an even earlier *terminus ante* (see chap. 5.2 at n. 111 below; Raaflaub 1988a: 294–95).

89. In characterizing the subjugation of rebellious Naxos at the end of the 470s as "enslavement," Thucydides (1.98.4) echoes sentiments and uses words typical of his own time. Whether these corresponded to those used at the time itself we cannot know without independent contemporaneous or near-contemporaneous evidence. This is true as well for the definition of the allies' original status as autonomous (97.1); see Raaflaub 2000d: 251–52; and below at n. 168.

90. See above at n. 3. On the absence of detailed regulations: e.g., Nesselhauf 1934: 291–92; Larsen 1940: 190–91; Meiggs 1972: 46; Schuller 1974: 147 n. 50. By contrast, *ATL* 3.228 n. 12, Hammond (1967b: 52, 55–56), and Giovannini and Gottlieb (1980: 28–30), among others, assume a contractual guarantee of autonomy because they consider it hard to believe that the allies in 477 would have been blind enough to surrender their freedom willingly to Athens for all time (see also Badian 1993: 137–42). This argument is valid only if (like Robertson 1980) one

disregards the contemporary horizon of experience, which, rightly, Ostwald does not (1982: 24–25 with n. 60).

91. Esp. Thuc. 1.98.4 (with *HCT* ad loc.; *CT* 1.152); 1.75.3–4 (cf. Aristot. *AP* 24.2). 1.99 explains generally why these individual uprisings failed.

92. For the tendency to generalize: Thuc. 3.10; 6.73.6. Thucydides' judgment: e.g., in 1.99.2–3; 3.10.4, 11.1–2. On omissions in the Pentecontaetia: *HCT* 1.365–89; Schreiner 1976, 1977; see also *CT* 1.133–34 with bibliography.

93. Lists of revolts: Schuller 1974: 112; Balcer 1974: 26–29; see also Bradeen 1960: 267–68; Legon 1968: 201–2. Literary sources remember only one case not mentioned by Thucydides: Miletus (Ps. Xen. *AP* 3.11; Aristoph. *Knights* 261). Aristophanes otherwise cites only the well-known big examples (Naxos, Chalcis, Euboea, Samos, and Byzantium: *Knights* 25–39; *Wasps* 236–37, 282–83, 354–55; *Clouds* 211–12), which seem to have become canonical early on. Number of league members: *ATL* 3.28; Meiggs 1972: 524–61.

94. As the case of Sparta demonstrates (above at n. 32), and see Thucydides' definition of "hegemony" (1.120.1). Baltrusch (1994: 63–64) observes that, technically speaking, the alliance was not "transformed" into an empire but the latter began to emerge during the 460s alongside the continuing alliance. What matters here is that, even without legal foundation, within a short time the treatment and status of most allies were assimilated to that of former rebels.

95. Naxos: Schuller 1974: 104–5; Ostwald 1982: 37–39. Thasos: Thuc. 1.101.3. Aegina: 108.4. Mint: Seltman 1955: 111. Aegina was probably not previously a member of the Delian League (Meiggs 1972: 51–52, 455; de Ste. Croix 1972: 334–35; Figueira 1993: esp. 108–9; contra: Mac-Dowell 1960; Balcer 1964: 68–75, 373–85), but since it was treated in the same way as Thasos, it can be considered here.

96. Bickerman 1950: 107; Balcer 1978: 58–65; Karavites 1982a: 29; Baltrusch 1994: 203.

97. This applies also to the forced incorporation of reluctant poleis into the alliance: Carystus before the Naxian revolt (Thuc. 1.98.3 mentions only the *homologia*), Phaselis during the Eurymedon campaign (Plut. *Cim.* 12.3–4: indemnity but no other punishment), and doubtless many more. See Karavites 1982a: 36, 38–39.

98. Bickerman 1950: esp. 107–16; Schuller 1974: 101–6. Extant oaths are collected in Balcer 1964: 247–51; Meiggs 1972: 579–82.

99. Erythrae (453–452?): *IG* I³ 15d, lines 40–42; *ATL* 2.D10; Hill 1951: B26, lines 70–73 (that this fragment is part of the Erythrae Decree [*IG* I³ 14] is not uncontested; see Meiggs 1972: 421–22; ML, no. 40, pp. 92–93). Chalcis (446–445): *IG* I³ 40; *ATL* 2.D17; ML, no. 52, lines 21–32. Samos (439–438): *IG* I³ 48c; *ATL* 2.D18; ML, no. 56, lines 15–21. For detailed discussion of these and other decrees: Koch 1991.

100. The partners swore to remain loyal to Athens and its allies and not to revolt, or they swore to have the same enemies and friends, perhaps both. See Hdt. 9.106.4; Aristot. *AP* 23.5; Bickerman 1950: 105–7; de Ste. Croix 1972: 298–307; Meiggs 1972: 45. According to Schwahn (1932: 1109), the second formula is found already in ancient oriental treaties. Against de Ste. Croix, Giovannini and Gottlieb (1980: 18), Robertson (1980: 71), Steinbrecher (1985: 55–62), among others, it needs to be emphasized that this formula is neutral and therefore not limited to alliances between unequal partners: Bickerman 1950; Herrmann 1968: 21; Baltrusch 1994: 52–59, 64–66. It does not, therefore, characterize the Delian League from the beginning as an alliance based on unequal treaties.

101. See n. 99 above: Erythrae, lines 72–73; Chalcis, lines 31–32; Eretria (*IG* I³ 39; *ATL* 2.D16), lines 2–3; Samos, lines 20–21 (for which the text suggested by *SV,* no. 159, seems preferable to that of *ATL* and ML).

102. See Larsen 1932: 140, 1933: 259; and above at n. 17.

103. Schuller 1974: 105–6; cf. Bickerman 1950: 109–10; Baltrusch 1994: 59–64.

104. Balcer 1964: 237–40; Schuller 1974: 11–13. This measure was later applied prophylactically (e.g., Thuc. 4.51), even as a matter of principle (Thuc. 3.33.2; Telecleid. fr. 45 *PCG* = 42 Edm.; Plut. *Per.* 16.2), presumably following Persian examples, for which see Bengtson 1953–54; Pritchett 1971–91: 1.63–64; Cawkwell 1973: 54 with n. 3.

105. Plut. *Lys.* 14; Xen. *Hell.* 2.2.20, 23. Symbolic significance: Andoc. 3.13–14 (cf. 11–12, 37–38); Lyc. *Leocr.* 61. The walls were rebuilt only after Sparta's fall from undisputed power in the Corinthian War and Conon's victory at Cnidos in 395/394 (Tod 2.107; Seager 1994: 101, 104). Another example (Sparta and Mantinea): Xen. *Hell.* 5.2.1–7; 6.5.3–5. Athens in 479: chap. 5.2 at n. 81 below.

106. Thasos: Thuc. 1.101.3. Aegina: 108.4. Samos: 117.3. Mytilene: 3.50.1. Schuller 1974: 144–45.

107. E.g., in the cases of Aegina (*ATL* 3.303; Balcer 1964: 78) and poleis in the Chalcidice (Thuc. 5.18.5). See in addition Xen *Hell.* 3.4.25. Switch: Thuc. 1.99.3 (with Schuller 1974: 153–54); Plut. *Cim.* 11.1–3 (with Kiechle 1967: 278–79). Finley (1978: 109–14 = 1982: 46–51) emphasizes financial considerations. Compatibility: Pistorius 1985: 174–76.

108. Hence, the Peloponnesians were willing to assume added financial burdens in the war against Athens (e.g., Thuc. 1.19, 121.5). Importantly, in 478/477 an assessment based on uniform criteria replaced the arbitrary collection of war contributions (mentioned, e.g., by Hdt. 8.111–12). Contra: e.g., Ehrenberg 1965b: 140 (= 1969: 114); Robertson 1980: 65ff.

109. E.g., Thuc. 1.121.5; Plut. *Cim.* 11.2–3; in addition, Thuc. 1.99.1; Aristoph. *Peace* 619–22; see Meiggs 1972: 265; Will 1972: 181. This began long before the famous debate in the 440s on the use of *phoros* for construction on the Acropolis (n. 88 above).

110. Tod 2.123; Bentson 1975: 257, lines 21–23. *Syntaxis:* Cargill 1981: 124–27; Dreher 1995: 41–89.

111. Thus also Balcer 1978: 63.

112. See esp. *ATL* 3.143. Even the garrison placed in Megara (an "independent ally," Thuc. 6.85.2) was charged with preventing defection: Schuller 1974: 35. Means of control: *ATL* 3.chap. 8. Garrisons: Nease 1949; Schuller 1974: 32–36. Officials: Schuller 1974: 39–48; Balcer 1976; Leppin 1992. On the number of officials: Aristot. *AP* 24.3, with comments by Rhodes 1981; Chambers 1990.

113. Cleruchies: detailed discussion in Schuller 1974: 13–32; Schmitz 1988: 79–115; Brunt 1993: chap. 5 (with comments on the reaction of the affected communities to the confiscation and private acquisition of land by Athenians); Salomon 1997; see also Gauthier 1973; Erxleben 1975; Finley 1978: 115ff. (= 1982: 51–53).

114. See esp. the pertinent regulations in the Erythrae Decree (ML, no. 40, lines 8ff.). On this complex of problems: esp. *ATL* 3.chap. 9; HCT 1.380–84; Balcer 1964: 89–98, 213–21; Schuller 1974: 82–100.

115. Schuller 1974: 109, 111–12.

116. Arrogance: Thuc. 1.99.1–2; 3.10.4; also Plut. *Arist.* 25.1; Aristot. *AP* 24.2. Private use: e.g., the employment of allied contingents in the "First Peloponnesian War" (ML, no. 36 with Paus. 5.10.4; Thuc. 1.107.5 on participation in the battle of Tanagra; Meiggs 1972: 96–97); see also, on the duty to perform military service for Athens (not the allies), *ATL* 2.D11; *IG* I³ 21, lines 8–15 (cf. Oliver 1935); further, *ATL* 3.256; Balcer 1964: 110.

117. See Thuc. 1.97.1 and relations in the Peloponnesian League (discussed above at n. 17); Bickerman 1950: 110; Lévy 1976: 70; Balcer 1978: 5–10; Baltrusch 1994: 52–59. On the league's synod: Meiggs 1972: 46–49; Schuller 1974: 140–41; Culham 1978.

118. Treasury: Nesselhauf 1933: 1–2; Schuller 1974: 169–77. For a significantly earlier date: Pritchett 1969; Robertson 1980: 112–19. Note Plut. *Arist.* 25.1–3: the imposition of Athenian

rule and especially the transfer of the treasury were regarded as injustice and a treaty violation. Changes in the synod: *ATL* 3.138–41; Meiggs 1972: 173 with n. 1; Schuller 1974: 70 with n. 397, 148, 171; Ruschenbusch 1979: 90–91.

119. Not documented until later (Schuller 1974: 108–9) but hardly to be doubted (Schuller 1974: 126–27); see the comment of the Mytilenians, Thuc. 3.10.4.

120. To what extent league money was really used for this purpose is debated; see chap. 3.3, n. 245.

121. A brief survey in Schuller 1974: 106–8. *Leges generales* should be distinguished from regulations, likewise adopted in the Athenian assembly, concerning individual conquered cities. On compatibility with autonomy: below at n. 219.

122. Protection: Meiggs 1972: 171–72; Schuller 1974: 49–50, 107–8; and n. 80 above. Megarian Decree: Nesselhauf 1933: 64–69; Kagan 1969: 251–72; de Ste. Croix 1972: chap. 7; Wick 1977; *CT* 1.110–12.

123. Schuller 1974: 165–66. The extension of colonial status to the allies seems to me of particular ideological importance here: Schuller 1974: 112–17. As an illustration, one might think of Corinth's relation to its colonies (chap. 3.1 at n. 89 above).

124. See n. 80 above and, for a brief systematic reassessment, Schuller 2002; for the financial decrees, Samons 2000. Tribute (the Decree of Cleinias): *IG* I³ 34; *ATL* 2.D7; ML, no. 46; see Meiggs 1972: 165–67; Fornara and Samons 1991: 180–81; Koch 1991: 249–85; Samons 2000: 189ff. (420s). Coinage or standards decree: *IG* I³ 1453; *ATL* 2.D14; ML, no. 45; see Meiggs 1972: 167–71; Schuller 1974: 211–17; Koch 1991: 369–403; Figueira 1998: pt. 4; Samons 2000: 330–32; Kallet 2001: 205–25 (420s or even later). Courts: Balcer 1964: chap. 7, 1978: 119ff.; Schuller 1974: 48–54; see also Gillis 1971: 39; and the thorough investigation of Koch (1991). Panathenaea and other festivals: Meiggs 1972: 292–95; Schuller 1974: 112–17; Smarczyk 1990: 154–298, 525–611; Parker 1996: 142–44. Religion: attested indirectly; see Barron 1964a; Meiggs 1972: 295–98; Smarczyk 1990: 58–154; Parker 1996: 144–49; see also Simms 1975: 275–78.

125. On the Parthenon as an "imperial" sanctuary: Smarczyk 1990: 31–57, 298–317; Osborne 1994; Shapiro 1996a; Parker 1996: 141–42.

126. Especially since not all imperial decrees contain the infamous three-barred sigma. Quotation: L. Kallet in a review of Mattingly 1996 in *Phoenix* 51 (1997): 419. Discoveries: n. 80 above.

127. In the Eretria and Chalcis Decrees (*IG* I³ 39–40), admittedly both recording treaties with defeated rebels, the allies promise to pay the tribute to the Athenian demos, not the league.

128. Schuller (2002) concludes that it will not be necessary to rewrite the history of the Athenian Empire. Welwei (1999: 129–30), though having doubts about a "crisis" in the empire around the midcentury (next n.), agrees that the Athenians made visible efforts to organize their rule more strictly and to optimize their control over the subject cities. For differentiated treatments of various aspects (esp. finances and judicial procedures): Figueira 1998 and Koch 1991, respectively.

129. Nesselhauf 1933: 11–13; Meiggs 1972: chap. 7; Schuller 1974: 174–75; Rhodes 1992: 54–61.

130. Thuc. 3.10.4; Fornara and Samons (1991: 82–88) point out that hostilities de facto ended after the battle at the Eurymedon.

131. One exception is Thuc. 1.77.1: see de Ste. Croix 1961, summarized in Schuller 1974: 53, and the comments in *CT* ad loc.

132. Ps. Xen. *AP* 1.18; Aristoph. *Birds* 1021–34 (with Meiggs 1972: 583–87; Dunbar 1995: 562ff.); see also, e.g., *Birds* 1422–69; *Peace* 169–72, 639–47 (with Roussel 1933; Meiggs 1949); and, more generally, *Wasps* 546–630. See Meder 1938: 59–62, 83–87, and passim; Popp 1968.

133. See above at nn. 82–88.

134. See, in more detail, Raaflaub 1979b: 243–52. The structural similarities observed by Diller (1962a: 199–200) and Schuller (1978: 10ff., esp. 13) are significant (not least for Thucydides' interpretation) but hardly obvious enough to trigger the comparison decades before Thucydides. Original use of the word: Berve 1954, 1967: 1.3–13.

135. In Thucydides, this motif is esp. marked in speeches (of the Athenians in Sparta, Pericles' last, and Cleon's about the Mytilenians): de Romilly 1963: 125–26; Berve 1967: 1.205, 2.629. *Hubris:* Plut. *Per.* 12.2; *Arist.* 25.1–2; Aristot. *Pol.* 1284a40–41; *AP* 24.2. Among others, Martin (1940: 287), Will (1972: 173), *HCT* (at Thuc. 3.37.2), and Meiggs (1972: 379) view *hubris* as the main criterion.

136. See Berve 1954, 1967: 1.3–13. Here, too, all that matters is the perspective of the affected fellow nobles; the hostility of the Mytilenian elite against Pittacus is characteristic: Berve 1967: 1.92–93; and chap. 3.2 at nn. 141ff. above. See also, e.g., Hdt. 3.142.3; Thuc. 8.89.3.

137. Vividly formulated in Thuc. 1.122.2–3; see Thuc. 120.1 (with comments in *HCT*) for a definition of the *hēgemōn's* status and responsibility.

138. On Thuc. 1.99.2: Raaflaub 1979b: 249 n. 50. See also 1.91.7; 5.11.4.

139. For factors that mitigated such sentiments: chap. 4.4 below.

140. Thuc. 1.99.1–3; Aristot. *AP* 24.1–2; Plut. *Arist.* 25.1–3; *Cim.* 11.

141. On whether even "autonomous" allies were affected by this: below at n. 219. See also chap. 5.2 at n. 87 on the meaning of giving and receiving "orders."

142. E.g., Thuc. 6.85.2; 7.57.3–4.

143. See chap. 4.4 below.

144. See, e.g., Pericles' argument in the final negotiations before the Peloponnesian War: Thuc. 1.144.2, with Nesselhauf 1934: 286ff., esp. 289–97.

145. The wordy affirmation of the trustworthiness of the partners to a treaty, as in an alliance of 433–432 between Athens and Rhegion (ML, no. 63; *SV,* no. 162, lines 10–15), points in the same direction.

146. See below at n. 148. A good example is the League of Corinth of 338–337 (Schmitt 1969: no. 403, esp. pp. 12–13). This process parallels, but is not identical with, the development of *spondai* (treaties between states at war) in the fifth century, described, e.g., in Schäfer 1932: 57–63; Baltrusch 1994: pt. 2.

147. E.g., Ténékidès 1954: 18; Thuc. 5.79.1; cf. 27.2; Hdt. 9.7a.1. See *HCT* at Thuc. 5.79.4. On *sumbola:* Gauthier 1972; Koch 1991: 45–60. Arbitration: Piccirilli 1973. On the formula *kata ta patria* in such contexts: Ostwald 1982: 3–7.

148. Thuc. 5.47.7 (with *IG* I³ 86; Tod 1.72; *SV,* no. 193, lines 24–26); Xen. *Hell.* 7.1.13–14, 5.3 (and *SV,* no. 290; Tod 2.144, lines 35–36); Aeschin. *Ctes.* 143.

149. Literary evidence: chap. 4.3 below. On the treaties: Koch 1991; on the autonomy clauses: Pistorius 1985: chap. 6. Mytilene: *IG* I³ 66.11–12; Tod 1.63; *ATL* 2.D22, lines 12–13; Meiggs 1972: 317; Ostwald 1982: 66 n. 229. Selymbria: *IG* I³ 118; *SV,* no. 207; ML, no. 87, lines 10–12 (the addition of *autonomous,* otherwise unanimously accepted, is doubted by Bickerman 1958: 334 n. 62). Samos in 412: Thuc. 8.21; *IG* I³ 96; Lewis 1954: 29–31 (the extant fragmentary text does not contain the autonomy clause mentioned by Thucydides and confirmed by the later decree). Samos in 405: *IG* II² 1; ML, no. 94, lines 12–13; Osborne 1981–83: D4–5, lines 15–16; see also Bickerman 1958: 334–35; Ostwald 1982: 45, 1993; Koch 1993; Whitehead 1993. Another example is the bestowal of autonomy by Gortyn on Rhittenia: *Inscr. Cret.* 4.80 (p. 183), line 1; Willetts 1955: 110–14.

150. Thuc. 5.18.5 (*pherousas ton phoron . . . autonomous einai . . . xummachous d'einai mēdeterōn . . .*) and, for the circumstances, 4.81. For details: *HCT* 3.668ff. Peace of Nicias: *SV,* no. 188; Kagan 1974: 342–49; Lewis 1992: 431–32; Baltrusch 1994: 169–85.

151. Thuc. 5.18.2: *autonomous einai kai autoteleis kai autodikous kai hautōn kai tēs gēs tēs*

heautōn; see *HCT* ad loc.; Ostwald 1982: 7; on *autoteleis,* also Whitehead 1993: 328–29. These clauses need to be seen against the background of the fight for control of Delphi during the "First Peloponnesian War" (Thuc. 1.112.5; Plut. *Per.* 21.2; Tod 1.39; Meiggs 1972: 175). See also *Inscr. Cret.* 4.80, line 1: *aut]onom[o]i k'autodikoi.*

152. Thuc. 5.77.5; see also 5.27.2.

153. Thuc. 5.79.1 (*autonomoi kai autopolies*); see Xen. *Hell.* 5.1.34; Ostwald 1982: 5–6.

154. For Sparta's action against Mantinea during the Peace of Nicias: chap. 5.3, n. 164. Against Elis after 404: Ryder 1965: 12ff.; Cartledge 1987: 248–53. Cf. Thuc. 5.18.6 on communities in Olynthus's sphere of influence: *oikein tas poleis tas heautōn* (*HCT* ad loc.: "They are now to be guaranteed their separate existence against encroachment by Olynthos"). For background: Thuc. 1.58.2.

155. Xen. *Hell.* 5.2.14; *autopolitai* is a plausible emendation: the contrast is *sumpoliteuein* (5.2.12).

156. A decree for Eteocarpathus of 394–390 (*Syll.* 1.129; Tod 2.110, lines 11–12) still mentions only autonomy. The expanded formula is attested in 384 (treaty with Chios, *Syll.* 1.142; Tod 2.118; *SV,* no. 248, lines 20–21: *ep' eleutheriai kai autonomiai*), in 378 (alliance with Byzantium, Tod 2:121; *SV,* no. 256, lines 6–7), and in 377 (alliance with Chalcis, n. 159 below). It has been assumed for the Peace of Antalcidas (esp. von Scala 1898: no. 122, pp. 114–15), but this treaty probably contained only the simple guarantee of autonomy (*SV,* no. 242); see Nolte 1923: 10; Hampl 1938: 8ff., 85ff.; Ryder 1965: 25ff. On the origin of the expanded formula, see also below at n. 208. On *koinē eirēnē:* esp. Hampl 1938; Ryder 1965; Jehne 1994 (all index, s.v.); Baltrusch 1997.

157. *Syll.* 1.147; Tod 2.123; *SV,* no. 257. Tr.: Harding 1985: no. 35.

158. *eleutherōi onti kai autonomōi, politeuomenōi politeian hēn an bolētai mēte phroran eisdechomenōi mēte archonta hupodechomenōi mēte phoron pheronti.* Cf. Diod. 15.29.8. See Erxleben 1975; Cargill 1981: chaps. 2, 8; Dreher 1995: chap. 2.

159. *Syll.* 1.148; Tod 2.124; *SV,* no. 259, lines 18ff. (21–26: *echen tēn heautōn Chalkideas eleutheros ontas kai autonomos kai au[   ]s mēte phroran hupodechomenos par' Athēnaiōn mēte phoron pherontas mēte archonta paradechomenos para ta dogmata tōn summachōn*). In the gap of apparently more than nine letters, one would expect a word for constitutional sovereignty, otherwise missing here (*autopolitas?*); proposals mentioned in the app. crit. of *SV* (p. 214) include *aphorologētos, autospondos, autodikountas, autokratoras.* See also the honorary decree of 387 for Clazomenae: *Syll.* 1.136; Tod 2.114, lines 22–25.

160. Parke (1930: 57) suggests, rather, a reaction to Sparta's exercise of power after 404, in which, however, territorial integrity was no issue. At the occasion of the foundation of a new alliance headed by Athens, abuses suffered in the earlier one were probably uppermost in people's minds; so, too, Ostwald 1982: 49.

161. Nesselhauf 1934: 292–93.

162. Besides the works cited in n. 164, see Busolt 1875: 645ff.; Nolte 1923: 8–14; Martin 1940: 84–87; de Ste. Croix 1954: 16–21; Ténékidès 1954; Ryder 1965: chap. 1; Bernhardt 1971: 4–10; Pohlmann 1971.

163. On this problem: Schuller 1974: 110–11 with n. 184; also Bickerman 1958: 324 n. 36.

164. Schäfer 1932: 166–75; Bickerman 1958; Ostwald 1982 (essentially written in 1977–78: ix). My own analysis was completed before 1979; it is thus independent of Ostwald's and that of Karavites 1982b. As far as I can see, it has not been superseded, nor much noticed in recent discussions: Figueira 1990; Bosworth 1992; Hansen 1995; see also Lévy 1983.

165. Contra: Schäfer 1932: 166; but see Ostwald 1982: 10–11. Application to individuals: n. 201 below.

166. Ostwald 1982: 1, 9–10 with n. 5. On *autarkeia:* chap. 5.2 at n. 92 below.

167. Inscriptions: n. 149 above. Soph. *Ant.* 821 (see n. 201 below); Hdt. 1.96.1; 8.140α.2 (420s); Hippoc. *Aer.* 16.4, 7; 23.8 (dated variously to the second half of the fifth century [Jouanna 1999: 375], shortly before 430 [Heinimann 1945: 206ff.], 430–415 [Pohlenz 1937: 45], or the fourth century [F. Kudlien, *KlP* 2.1171]). Cratinus fr. 419 *PCG* contains only the word itself.

168. Thus Ostwald 1982: 18–22, refuting Bickerman 1958: 339–43; cf. Raaflaub 2000d: 251–52. Badian (1993: 115 n. 16) and Hansen (1995: 27 n. 31, 38) remain uncertain. The passages are Hdt. 8.140α.2 (Athens); Thuc. 2.71.2, 4, 72.1 (Pausanias's guarantee of *autonomia* for Plataea); 1.97.1 (initial status of members of the Delian League). Hdt. 1.96.1 (early history of the Medes), of course, is unquestionably anachronistic. In the case of Plataea, the formulation chosen by Thuc. 2.71.2 makes clear what is at issue, even without mentioning *autonomia* (see also Plut. *Arist.* 21.1); the authenticity of the guarantee of protection for Plataea itself can hardly be doubted: Amit 1973: 63ff., esp. 83–84; Brunt 1993: 69–71. The autonomy clause in the "Peace of Callias" would provide a *terminus ante quem* in the midcentury, close enough to other firm attestations; given the continuing debate about authenticity (see n. 7 above), I have not taken it into consideration here.

169. So, too, Ostwald 1982: 23. On 446, 432, and Thucydides: at n. 69 above; n. 175 below; and esp. Nesselhauf 1934: 292. Schäfer (1932: 167) and Bernhardt (1971: 6–7) disagree.

170. Hansen 1995: 22–23.

171. Schäfer 1932: 169–70; Ryder 1965: chap. 1; Cartledge 1987; Jehne 1994 (both index, s.v.); Figueira 1990.

172. See also Schuller 1974: 110.

173. Bickerman 1958: 324 (my tr.); see below at n. 210.

174. Earliest attempts at definition appear in the scholiasts (on Thuc. 2.29.2) and lexicographers (Bekker 1814: 1.466: *autonoumenē polis: hē tois heautēs nomois chrōmenē kai ouch hupakouousa heterois*); cf. Cic. *Att.* 6.1.15, 2.4.

175. Thuc. 1.67.2, 139.1, 3, 140.3, 144.2. See, e.g., Nesselhauf 1934: 291; Herter 1953; Bickerman 1958: 324, 343. Wick (1977: esp. 85–90) offers a different interpretation of the Spartan demand for autonomy. Badian (1993: 157) overlooks here that Thucydides is speaking of *autonomia* rather than *eleutheria*.

176. See, e.g., Bernhardt 1971: 7–8. Liberation: chap. 5.3 at nn. 136ff.

177. Freedom: mentioned directly or indirectly ten times in Thuc. 4.85–87; *xummachoi autonomoi*: 4.86.1, 87.4–5, 88.1. The same distinction is used of the Plataeans by Archidamus (2.72.1). Bickerman 1958: 331. Bernhardt (1971: 8) assumes here (in anticipation of 4.86.4) a promise of nonintervention in constitutional sovereignty.

178. Bickerman 1958: 326–27, 330: Le "terme pour l'entière indépendance de la cité est *eleutheria*. . . . Toujours le terme *autonomia* indique que la cité n'est pas la maîtresse absolue de sa politique." 343: La "souveraineté originaire, possédant le caractère absolu, que les auteurs appellaient *eleutheria*, . . . la . . . souveraineté dérivée et généralement soumise aux conditions, fut officiellement appelée *autonomia*." Ostwald (1982: 1, 13–14 and passim) agrees.

179. Bickerman 1958: 324.

180. Treaties: above at n. 149. Aegina: above at n. 69; Chalcidice: Thuc. 5.18.5. This also explains arguments in the Mytilenian Debate (Thuc. 3.39.2, 46.5, with Lévy 1983: 261–64) and of the Mytilenians (Thuc. 3.10–13 passim; emphasis on autonomy: 10.5, 11.1, 3, cf. 39.2; fear of losing status: esp. 3.10.5–6, 11.1–2, 12.1–3, 13.1). See Bickerman 1958: 327 n. 39.

181. Thuc. 5.18.2; cf. *HCT* ad loc.

182. Thus Bickerman 1958: 325 n. 38; cf. here Bickerman's interpretation of Thuc. 5.58.3 (328 n. 44).

183. Thus Bickerman 1958: 328 with n. 45. By contrast, *HCT* (at Thuc. 1.113.4) takes this as

evidence that *autonomos* could also mean "complete independence." Diod. 12.6.2 also refers to the Boeotians' recovery of autonomy.

184. Bickerman 1958: 328 (here as elsewhere, my tr.). For the following examples: Bickerman 1958: 328 with n. 44; cf. Ostwald 1982: 13.

185. Thuc. 6.88.4. While Thucydides elsewhere thinks of Syracusan influence as spanning the entire island (6.6.2, 11.2), here this influence is explicitly restricted. Similarly, in describing conditions in Thrace, the historian distinguishes between the original Odrysian kingdom of Teres, the father of Sitalces, additional parts of Thrace subjugated by Teres, and the remaining territory of the "autonomous" Thracians: 2.96.2–4, 98.3–4, 101.3.

186. E.g., Hdt. 8.140α.2, 4; Thuc. 6.85.2; 7.57.7; Ehrenberg 1965b: 114 (= 1969: 93); Will 1972: 178; see also *HCT* at 1.113.4.

187. See also Thuc. 6.43, 69.2; 7.57.

188. Above all, Cephallenia and Zacynthos (Thuc. 2.7.3, 30.2; 7.31.2), Corcyra (6.85.2; 7.57.7; with *HCT* 4 ad loc. and p. 434), and Argos (6.43; cf. 69.3). For others, see the list in 7.57.9–10 with *HCT* ad loc.

189. Thuc. 7.57.7–8. Corcyra: above at n. 62 (the alliance as *douleia*). The same holds for Leontini and other Sicilian allies (6.84.2–3).

190. Aristot. *AP* 24.2 (*phulakes archēs*); see at n. 219 below; de Ste. Croix 1954: 19.

191. So, too, de Ste. Croix, 1954: 16–21; Balcer 1964: 324; Schuller 1974: 111. Although, for example, Aegina (after 446) and Samos (after 412) were *autonomoi* again, they did not provide ships. The irreversibility of the change from ships to *phoros* is decisive. On *phoros*: at nn. 106ff. above.

192. This is demonstrable for the proxeny decrees (n. 80 above) and the decree regulating the protection of Athenians in allied territory (Aristoph. *Peace* 169; with Roussel 1933; Meiggs 1949). Outside interference by exempting a citizen from local jurisdiction is attested for Chios by *SEG* 10.76; see Schuller 1974: 108. The decrees regulating colonial status, which included mandatory participation in the Panathenaea and the cult of "Athena, the mistress of Athens" (if this is the correct interpretation of the evidence), also applied to the *autonomoi* (see bibliography cited in n. 124). It is unclear whether they were exempted from the coinage decree; see, e.g., Robinson 1949; Balcer 1964: chap. 8, 1978: 14 n. 32; Meiggs 1972: 167–71—but this issue may be affected if the decree is dated to a later period (n. 124). Athens blatantly interfered in the constitutional autonomy of Samos before the actual revolt (Thuc. 1.115.3). Schuller (1974: 55–56) thinks it possible that autonomous allies did not have to accept Athenian functionaries. Balcer (1978: x, 14 n. 32, and passim) favors extensive exemption.

193. Thus esp. de Ste. Croix 1954: 18–19; Schuller 1974: 11. The apparent contradictions in Thuc. 7.57.3–5 can be plausibly explained; see (against de Ste. Croix 1954: 17–18) Dover in *HCT* 4.432ff., esp. 434; further, de Romilly 1963: 87 n. 6; Schuller 1974: 54 n. 304.

194. Bickerman 1958: 330. On the inadequacy of this definition: also Schuller 1974: 110–11. Ostwald's assessment: 1982: 14, 15–16, and passim.

195. For discussion, with sources and bibliography: Cawkwell 1976; Cartledge 1987: chaps. 13–14; Bosworth 1992: 127–36. This seems especially true for Elis and Thebes, less for Mantinea. The principle was invoked already in the treaties with Argos (418–417): Thuc. 5.77.5, 79.1; see the bibliography cited in n. 154.

196. Thuc. 6.77.1; cf. esp. 6.84.2–3 and the speeches connected with the revolt of Mytilene: n. 180 above, and 3.39.2, 46.5–6.

197. Bickerman 1958: 332 with n. 55. Ostwald's interpretation (1982: 15–16) overlooks essential points.

198. Applied to the Hellenic League of 481 by Hdt. 7.145.2; Thuc. 1.18.3; 3.58.4. See also Pol-

lux 1.153; 4.30 (who clearly relies on the historians); *Suda*, s.v. *homaichmia* (quotation of unknown origin); App. *Celt.* 15. On Mardonius's offer: also Hdt. 9.7α.1 ("on fair and equal terms," *summachous . . . ep' isēi te kai homoiēi*).

199. See also Hansen 1995.

200. See the examples mentioned above at n. 185.

201. E.g., Hdt. 1.95.2–96.1, concerning the way land was originally settled in individual autonomous villages (1.96.2); cf. Thuc. 2.16.1 (*autonomōi oikēsei*) with 15.1–2, 63.3; or Hippoc. *Aer.* 16.3–7, 23.5ff. (esp. 23.7–8), where the direct connection with *hoi nomoi* in the sense of "political order," "constitution" (denied by Bickerman 1958: 340–41), is perfectly plain (see 16.3–4, 6–7, 23.6–7; Ostwald 1982: 11–12); Hdt. 5.78, though using different terminology, is closely related. Bickerman (1958: 339ff.) helps himself in these cases by assuming an "original meaning" derived from *nemō* or *nemomai* (rather than *nomos*): "*autonomos* serait originalement celui qui a sa propre, particulière portion" (341; cf. 342: "leur propre lot; leur propre destinée"). Although accepted, e.g., by Will (1972: 178), this is rightly rejected by Ostwald (1982: 1 with n. 5, 10); the late origin of *autonomia* and its relationship to *isonomia* seem crucial as well. On Soph. *Ant.* 821–22 (*autonomos zōsa*): esp. Schadewaldt 1929: 93ff., referring to a complementary passage in 872ff. (875: *autognōtos orga*) and paraphrases it by "you were ruined by . . . your stubborn sense of self [*Eigen-sinn*], your self-will, your self-determination, your striving on your own to make assessments and decisions and to act accordingly" (94, my tr.). Hence, the interpretation of *autonomos* in 821 as the will to act according to one's own determination, following one's own law, seems irrefutable, and that of Bickerman (1958: 343: "A. . . . possède sa propre, unique portion de descendre chez Hadès encore vivante") incorrect; see also Kloesel 1935: 5; Lanza 1977: 83; Ostwald 1982: 10–11.

202. Thuc. 1.113.4 (above at n. 183); conversely, in 3.62.5 the Thebans speak of the liberation of Boeotia by their victory at Coronea (*eleutherōsamen*). The inward view also determines the choice of *autonomia* in 8.91.3.

203. Chap. 5.2 at n. 85.

204. See also Schäfer 1932: 167.

205. As suggested to me by Ernst Badian.

206. Aegina might offer an illuminating example. The autonomy guarantee of 446 probably meant nothing more than an adjustment to a "moderate" mode of rule (like that exercised over Samos, Lesbos, and Chios, albeit with tribute payments instead of naval contributions; neither, after all, had anything to do with autonomy; see also Amit 1973: 39). The discrepancy with the Peloponnesian standard of autonomy, always present, became an issue only when Sparta began to compile a list of Athenian "offenses" that might, if need be, justify a war. At that time Aegina complained that it was "not autonomous" (Thuc. 1.67.2). Hence, Athens did not need to have introduced any additional restrictions to be accused of having broken the treaty by violating that clause. For different views: Lewis 1954: 21ff.; Ostwald 1982: 42.

207. As was demonstrated by Sparta's policy of enforcing *autonomia* in the early fourth century: above at n. 154.

208. See Nolte 1923: 20. The view that autonomy is incompatible with being ruled by another is expressed succinctly in the political publicity of the fourth century: e.g., Isocr. 8.16–17, 68–69, and frequently in Isocr., *On Peace* and *Plataicus* (Buchner 1958: 128).

209. Schäfer 1932: 171ff., esp. 174–75.

210. Ehrenberg 1965a: 154 n. 1 (my tr.), following Kahrstedt 1922: 86. Ostwald (1982: 10), however, still tries to integrate individual elements firmly into the concept of *autonomia* (9ff., 26ff., 40). For modern definitions: Schuller 1974: 110 n. 184.

211. See also Ostwald 1982: 14, 28–29.

212. Bickerman (1958: 339ff.) thinks the latter probable because (*a*) he does not believe, given the specific forms of interstate relations in the polis world, that the Greeks were capable of inventing such a technical term of international law (339); (*b*) he considers Athens's infringements on the autonomy of its subjects far less serious than those of the Persians (340); and (*c*) he regards the word usage common among authors of the late fifth and fourth centuries to be a faithful reflection of what originated in Asia Minor before the Persian Wars (340–41). All three points are highly questionable; hence, the thesis itself is untenable. Moreover, Herodotus never uses the word in this context (Ostwald 1982: 1).

213. This was proposed, e.g., by Nolte 1923: 8–9; Stier 1928: 12; and opposed by Schäfer 1932: 167; Ehrenberg 1965a: 154 n. 1. See also *HCT* at 5.27.2.

214. See above at nn. 13ff.; for changes, see chap. 5.3 at n. 161.

215. So, too, Schäfer 1932: 167–68; Ehrenberg 1965b: 114 (= 1969: 93–94); Bernhardt 1971: 5–6; and esp. Ostwald 1982: 1, 30ff., esp. 36ff., 40, 46ff.

216. On *isonomia* in interstate relations: Schäfer 1932: 160–66.

217. Hdt. 1.95.2–96.1; Hippoc. *Aer.* 16.3ff., 23.5ff. *Polis turannos:* at nn. 74ff., 133ff., above.

218. Chap. 3.3 at nn. 224ff.

219. Schuller 1974: 54–55.

220. Thuc. 1.97.1; cf. above at n. 168. De Ste. Croix (1954: 17ff., 1972: 307) rejects the possibility that an official status category of "autonomous allies" ever existed. Remarkably, the majority of later bestowals of *autonomia* (above at n. 149) concerned those allies that had held this status once before (Selymbria, like Aegina, was an exception, probably due to special circumstances); such bestowals apparently remained rare, and the word was avoided even when clear elements of autonomy were stipulated in a treaty (as in the Chalcis Decree of 446: *HCT* 1.342 with n. 2).

221. Finley's important interpretation of *douleia* in this context (1982: 81) overlooks this dimension.

222. For documentation: e.g., Sealey 1966: 242–48; Balcer 1974: 24–25.

223. Above at n. 93.

224. References in n. 39 above.

225. Hdt. 5.1.1, 2.1.

226. Hdt. 8.126–29. Suspected of desertion, Olynthus, too, was besieged and punished (127).

227. See, in particular, Thuc. 2.8.4–5, 11.2; 4.121.1; 8.64.3, 5. More below, chap. 5.3 at n. 176.

228. De Ste. Croix 1954. See de Ste. Croix 1972: 5ff., 34ff.; Jones 1957: 67ff.; Bradeen 1960; Pleket 1963; Quinn 1964; de Romilly 1966; Popp 1968; Mørch 1970; Balcer 1974; Fornara 1977. See also Heuss 1965: esp. 81ff.; Woodhead 1970: 6–7; Schuller 1974: 82ff., esp. 94ff.; Davies 1993: chap. 5 and 137–39.

229. Thuc. 1.99; Plut. *Cim.* 11; Schuller 1974: 11–12, 153–54.

230. Compared with the Ionian Revolt, which was directed against an empire based on superiority on land, the situation was thus reversed and more hopeless from the start.

231. Miletus: Hdt. 1.141.4, 143.1; Athens: 8.140 (see above at n. 197).

232. Aristot. *AP* 24.2; Plut. *Arist.* 23.4; autonomy and equality: Thuc. 3.9ff.

233. Schuller 1974: 54; Balcer 1974: 30–31.

234. De Ste. Croix 1972: 42–43.

235. E.g., the Hellespontian poleis of Parion and Sigeion (451–450): Balcer 1974: 31; see also generally de Ste. Croix 1972: 37ff., esp. 40. Plataea: chap. 3.1 at nn. 75ff. Megara: Thuc. 1.103.4.

236. Thus, e.g., Nesselhauf 1933: 58–67 (partly opposed by Schäfer 1963: 75ff.); Bradeen 1960: 262–63; Schuller 1974: 76ff., 81–82.

237. Balcer 1974: 29–31.

238. For details: Schuller 1974: 88ff. The Erythrae Decree offers the earliest evidence; on its date: n. 99 above. On the dangers of generalizations: Schuller 1974: 93ff.; and chap. 5.1 at n. 56 below.

239. On the emergence of democracies outside Athens in the fifth century: Schuller 1979; Robinson forthcoming.

240. On oligarchs, see the documentation in de Ste. Croix 1954: 4ff. On "democrats," who cannot simply be equated with "lower classes," and on the nature of *dēmos* and *oligoi:* Ruschenbusch 1978: chap. 4, with Detlev Lotze's modifications, *Gnomon* 53 (1981): 249ff.; Lewis 1992: 383–84.

241. Rightly emphasized by de Ste. Croix 1954: 21ff., esp. 29ff.

242. See chap. 6.

243. Thuc. 4.86.3–5 offers a good example.

244. Thuc. 3.69ff., esp. 82.1; Heuss 1965: 82ff., 1973: 17ff., 24ff.; Schuller 1974: 96ff.; Lintott 1981: 90ff., 103ff.; de Ste. Croix 1981: 285ff.; Gehrke 1985; Price 2001. Exporting conflicts: Aesch. *Eum.* 976–87. Smallness of poleis: Ruschenbusch 1978: 3ff.

245. Diodotus in Thuc. 3.47.2 is obviously biased; so is de Ste. Croix 1954: 1, 16.

246. Quinn 1964: 257ff. (quot. 258); accepted in part by de Ste. Croix 1972: 37, 40.

247. E.g., Cook 1961; de Ste. Croix 1972: 37ff.

248. Thuc. 8.48.5 (cf. *HCT* 5 ad loc.; Grayson 1972: 65–73; Hammond 1977), 8.64.3ff. (cf. Pleket 1963: 73ff.; Quinn 1964: 264–65).

249. On this and the following remarks: de Romilly 1966.

250. See chap. 3.1 at nn. 97ff.

251. E.g., Quinn 1964: 259; de Ste. Croix 1972: 36, 40; Davies 1993: 137–39.

5. "Freedom" in Ideology and Propaganda

1. Novelty in the Greek world: Raaflaub 1984a: 47–51, 1994: 114–18.

2. Political thought: Raaflaub 1988a; Rowe and Schofield 2000. Athens as a cultural center: Ostwald 1992; Boedeker and Raaflaub 1998. To what extent Athenian imperial methods and ideology might have been influenced by Near Eastern, especially Persian, antecedents (see, e.g., Larsen 1979; several essays in Raaflaub and Müller-Luckner 1993; Briant 1996: chap. 6) has not been pursued sufficiently so far.

3. Obvious occasions are, apart from other meetings of the league's synod, deliberations about how to proceed against rebellious allies or poleis that resisted incorporation into the alliance, or the decision to move the league's treasury to Athens (chap. 4.1, n. 118, above).

4. E.g., Thuc. 1.73.2 (below at n. 29); 5.89; 6.82–83.

5. Popp 1968; Meiggs 1972: chap. 21; Chambers 1973: 108–9; Forrest 1975. See also Welsh 1983; Henderson 2003; and chap. 4.1 at nn. 63ff. above.

6. On the use of the past in political debate: Chambers 1973; Nouhaud 1982. On freedom as a historical-political argument: "Materialien," sec. 15.3.

7. Strasburger 1958; de Romilly 1963: 58–85, 89ff.; and, more recently, among many, Pouncey 1980; Rengakos 1984; Crane 1998.

8. Meyer 1967: 148–49, 152–54.

9. E.g., de Romilly 1963: 60ff.; Meyer 1967: 147ff.

10. Thuc. 3.36–48; 5.84–113; 6.82–87.

11. Strasburger 1958: 20ff.; Loraux 1973, 1986: esp. chap. 3. At such occasions, of course, there was no room even for veiled criticism.

12. See Kierdorf 1966: 95–110; Robertson 1976: 19; and below at n. 30.

13. See esp. Isocr. 4.74; Strasburger 1958: 20–22.

14. The idea that the strong have a right to dominate the weak, emphasized often especially by Thucydides (e.g., 1.76.2, 77.3; 4.61.5; 5.89, 105), clearly reveals sophistic thought (Kiechle 1963b; more generally, Guthrie 1971: 55ff., esp. 84–88; Kerferd 1981: chap. 10) and thus probably originated in the second half of the fifth century. The view, however, that the strongest member of a group or symmachy is entitled to leadership is very old (e.g., Hdt. 7.160.2, 161.3; and already *Iliad* 2.576–80), but see at n. 17 below. The empirical component can be safely dated to the beginnings of the Delian League (below at n. 33).

15. Aristotle's discussion of the principles of education concerning war and conquests and his criticism of those states that train their citizens primarily "for victory in war and the subjugation of neighboring states" (*Pol.* 1332b12ff., esp. 1333a30–1334a10) reflect the critical debate over the hated rule of Sparta in the first third of the fourth century. Although Athens's rule differed from Sparta's in degree only, not in principle, its defenders (Lysias, Isocrates, and several characters in Thucydides) all attempt to demonstrate that Athens in fact lived up to the very principles that Aristotle later thought acceptable—a sure sign of strong propagandistic influence.

16. Schäfer 1932: 251ff.; Cartledge 1979: 144ff.

17. Thuc. 1.18.1; Bernhardt (1987) sees in this reputation a much later ideological fabrication.

18. Hdt. 1.141.4, 152; 5.38.2, 49.

19. E.g., Plat. *Menex.* 242a–c; see Kierdorf 1966: 92.

20. E.g., Thuc. 1.33–34, esp. 33.1–2. Pericles: Thuc. 2.40.4–5; see n. 88 below.

21. Fleet: Hdt. 7.161.2–3; 8.2–3. *Prostasia:* e.g., in the effective opposition to Sparta's proposals to resettle the Ionians and exclude the "friends of Persia" from the Delphic Amphictyony (Hdt. 9.106.2–4; Plut. *Them.* 20.3). In all this, enhancement and reinterpretation after the events is likely: Frost 1980: 179–80; and already Meyer 1892–99: 2.217 n. 1.

22. E.g., Thuc. 1.73.4–75.1; Lys. 2.24ff. passim.

23. See n. 21 and Hdt. 9.114.

24. See below at n. 33.

25. See esp. Chambers 1973: 42ff. The shift in judgment is especially clear in the case of the battle of Marathon: West 1970; Loraux 1973, 1986: 157ff.; Hölkeskamp 2001. See also the end of this section and Pearson 1936.

26. Lys. 2.47; Isocr. 4.71–72, 95, 99–100; 8.42; also 6.43; 12.52; 14.59; 15.307; Lyc. *Leocr.* 72. On their agendas: Buchner 1958: esp. 1ff., 150ff.; Lévy 1976: 162–63.

27. On the conflation of hegemony and *archē*, see also Thuc. 1.76.2, 95.7; Buchner 1958: 108 n. 2; Winton 1981. Analogies between Thucydides and Lysias-Isocrates: Kierdorf 1966: 103 with n. 3. Generally on the Athenian speech: de Romilly 1963: 244ff.; *CT* 1 ad loc.; Crane 1998: 264–85, with bibliography.

28. Esp. Hdt. 7.139. For widespread ill-will toward Athens: esp. Thuc. 1.75.1 (*epiphthonōs*), 73.2 with Hdt. 7.139.1 (*gnōmēn epiphthonon . . .* on the part of most); in addition, Hdt. 8.140–44 and the second Corinthian speech in Thuc. 1.120ff., esp. 121–22, 124; also, e.g., Thuc. 2.8; 3.63.3. See Strasburger 1955: esp. 7ff., 18ff.; de Romilly 1963: 246–47; further, Pohlenz 1937: 168–69; Kleinknecht 1940: 247–49; Kierdorf 1966: 102–3. On Herodotus and Athens: Ostwald 1991; Moles 2002.

29. Cf. esp. Thuc. 5.89; 6.83.2; Strasburger 1958: 30–33; Kierdorf 1966: 104–5.

30. Kierdorf 1966: 104–10; also Hdt. 9.27, on which Kierdorf 1966: 97ff.

31. Tyrrell 1984: chap. 1; Castriota 1992: 43–58, 76–89, 143–51.

32. Kierdorf (1966: 89ff., esp. 92–94) refers to the despotic treatment of the allies by the Spartan commander Pausanias (Thuc. 1.95.1), a story that is likely itself to be the result of some embellishment (Hdt. 8.3.2; Andrewes 1978b: 91–93 with bibliography in n. 5; Welwei 1999: 77). The threat of imminent Persian retribution must have been equally important.

33. See chap. 3.1 at nn. 126ff. above.

34. See, generally, Pearson 1936, 1962: chap. 5, with examples.

35. Thuc. 3.68.4. The Plataeans: 2.71.3–4; 3.54.1, 3ff., 56.3ff., and passim. Archidamus: 2.72.1. See also 3.68.1 and the speech of the Thebans: 3.61ff., esp. 62.2, 63.1ff., 64.2.

36. Xen. *Hell.* 2.2.10, 14, 19, 20 (quote, tr. R. Warner); cf. Andoc. 1.142; 3.21. For discussion: Lévy 1976: 22–23; Karavites 1982a: 72–73; Kagan 1987: 404–12; Krentz 1989: 187; Andrewes 1992: 495–96.

37. Hermocrates: Thuc. 6.76–80 (quoted below at n. 40). Euphemus: 6.82.3–83.1.

38. Will 1956: 57, 66–67; de Romilly 1963: 83–84, 243–44.

39. Esp. Hdt. 6.11.2–3, 12.1ff. (esp. 3); 8.22, 85.1, and 4.142. See How and Wells 1928 at Hdt. 6.13; *HCT* 1.127; Will 1956: 64–65; Evans 1976; Tozzi 1978: chap. 1; Gillis 1979: chap. 1; and esp. Fornara and Samons 1991: 106–9. Early indications of such prejudices (such as criticism of the Ionians' lavish lifestyle, their softness, and their lack of willingness to fight) are found in many sixth-century sources (compiled in Nestle 1942: 74–75 with nn. 86–87).

40. Thuc. 6.77.1. Hdt. 4.142 reflects a similarly harsh judgment.

41. Isocr. 4.110; cf. Buchner 1958: 122–24.

42. See also Demosthenes' (60.10–12) conspicuous effort not to mention Athens's *archē* in his Funeral Oration; see Kiechle 1963b: 310–11.

43. Lysias: Lateiner 1971. Isocrates: Buchner 1958: 108–48. For Bringmann's different view: n. 53 below. See also in general Mossé 1962: 409ff.; Chambers 1973: 108ff.; Lévy 1976: 57–79. Thucydides writes partly from a similar perspective of Athens after the collapse: de Romilly 1963: esp. pts. 2–3. My purpose here is limited to showing, by focusing on some key examples that are still fairly close to the fifth century, what arguments such efforts at justification were likely to use.

44. Esp. Isocr. 4.110ff., 122, 125ff. with Buchner 1958: 122–26; see also 12.54, 65ff.; and at n. 170 below.

45. Treaties: below at n. 166. Resentments: e.g., Eur. *Iphigenia at Aulis* (esp. 1269ff., 1375ff.); see Diller 1962b: 55; Cavander 1973: 1–15; Aretz 1999: 184–208, esp. 194–95, 206–8. Betrayal: Isocr. 4.122–23; see already Thuc. 8.43.3, 52, 84.5; and below at nn. 166ff.

46. Isocr. 4.123–24.

47. Isocr. 4.115. Catastrophic conditions: Isocr. 4.115–17; cf., e.g., 5.96, 120–21; *ep.* 9.9.

48. See Dem. 23 passim. Deception: e.g., Isocr. 4.114 with Buchner 1958: 126.

49. Lys. 2.56–57, 58ff.; Plat. *Menex.* 241d–e; Isocr. 4.117–18, 119ff.; 12.59–61; cf. Ael. Arist. *Panath.* 208–10. For the limits imposed on the Persian king: also, e.g., Isocr. 7.80; Dem. 19.273; Lyc. *Leocr.* 73. For the "Peace of Callias," invented or attributed much greater historical significance at that time: bibliography cited in chap. 4.1, n. 7, above.

50. See chap. 4.2 at nn. 157–58 (with bibliography).

51. Tribute: Isocr. 12.63, 67–69; cleruchies: Isocr. 4.107–9 (with Buchner 1958: 119–22; Bringmann 1965: 40–41); legal restrictions: Isocr. 12.63, 66; 4.113 (with Buchner 1958: 124–25); mistreatment: Isocr. 4.100ff.; 12.63, 70ff., 92ff.; also Xen. *Hell.* 2.2.3 (with Buchner 1958: 108–42; de Romilly 1963: 92ff., 282ff.; Bringmann 1965: 38).

52. The imposition on the allies of the obligation to face trials in Athens offers a good example: Ps. Xen. *AP* 1.14, 16–18 (with Meder 1938: 172ff., 179ff.; Koch 1991: 148–51). On Aristophanes: Meder 1938: 51ff., 83ff.; Ehrenberg 1951: 156–58; see further Thuc. 1.76.3–77.4 (on 77.1, see esp. de Ste. Croix 1961: 96–100; Schuller 1974: 52–53) and in general the speech of Euphemus in Camarina (6.82–87).

53. Lys. 2.54–57; Isocr. 4.103–6; see Buchner 1958: 112–19. Bringmann (1965: 29, referring to H.-J. Newiger's review of Buchner's book in *Gnomon* 33 [1961]: 764–66) postulates as models for Isocrates above all Gorgias's *Olympic* and *Funeral Orations*. The passages relevant here

are in any case very close to Lysias. See Lévy 1976: 147–69 on the ideological revaluation of old conceptions after 404.

54. Isocr. 4.103–4; 12.61, 69; also Lys. 2.56.

55. Lys. 2.55–56, expanded in Isocr. 4.104–5; cf. Bringmann 1965: 39 with n. 4; Buchner 1958: 113–15.

56. Isocr. 4.106; cf. 12.54; Buchner 1958: 116.

57. Buchner 1958: 118 (my tr.). On Isocrates' argument in general: e.g., Bringmann 1965: 34ff., esp. 37–44. Good *hēgemōn*: Thuc. 1.120.1; Isocr. 4.80; Bringmann 1965: 35.

58. Fifth century: chap. 4.2 above.

59. See, e.g., Thuc. 6.87.4. Encomium: Lys. 2.56–57; Isocr. 4.106.

60. E.g., Hdt. 8.132.1–2; 9.90.1–2; see chap. 3.1 at n. 102 and chap. 3.2 at n. 186 above.

61. Strasburger 1958: 26–27.

62. See esp. Thuc. 1.75–77; see also at nn. 51–52 and below at nn. 68ff.

63. See bibliography cited in chap. 3.2, n. 191, above; Lévy 1976: 157–64.

64. E.g., Nesselhauf 1933: 32–33. "Congress Decree": chap. 4.1, n. 8, above.

65. Documented well, for example, by the reactions to Brasidas's campaign in the Chalcidice: Thuc. 4.85ff., esp. 86.3ff.; see also Diodotus in Thuc. 3.47.2.

66. See also below at nn. 123ff.

67. See esp. Thuc. 2.41.3; Kiechle 1963b: 307–8. On the Athenians' use of the concept of *polis turannos*: Raaflaub 2003: 77–81.

68. Thuc. 1.75.3, 76.2; see *HCT* 1.235; *CT* 1.120; de Romilly 1963: 251ff.; Drexler 1976: 40–45; Raaflaub 1994: 131–36. On the aspect of honor: de Romilly 1973.

69. E.g., Thuc. 6.83.2. Marathon was crucial here precisely because it combined, in an exemplary way, self-defense and protection of others (e.g., Hdt. 9.27.5; Andoc. 1.107; Lys. 2.20ff.; Plat. *Menex.* 240e; see Kiechle 1963b: 309; and the bibliography cited in n. 25 above).

70. Thuc. 1.75.4; 2.63.1; 3.40, esp. 40.5; also 5.90–91.

71. See Kiechle 1963b: 289ff., esp. 298ff.

72. Pericles: Thuc. 1.140.2–141.1; 2.61.1 and esp. 62.3, 64.1; see also Xen. *Hell.* 2.4.20.

73. See chap. 5.2 below.

74. See n. 68.

75. Pearson (1936) illustrates this well.

76. See in detail chap. 4.4 above.

77. See only Thuc. 2.8; a good example of doubts and resistance: 4.84–88.

78. The ideas summarized in this section were first presented (in a broader context) in Raaflaub 1984a.

79. The Greeks did not have a word for "sovereignty"; *autokratōr* (see chap. 6.2, n. 111, below), *autonomos,* and *eleutheros* can each express particular aspects of this concept. What I describe here as "sovereignty" is rendered in Thucydides and Euripides by *eleutheria* and *polis eleuthera.* The context makes clear that the meaning and orientation of *eleutheros* differ in the passages discussed in this section from the formula *eleutherōtatē polis* analyzed below at nn. 119–20.

80. Euphemus in Thuc. 6.82.2 offers a distorted version; see references in n. 21 above.

81. Thuc. 1.89.3–93.2; Diod. 11.39–40; Plut. *Them.* 19. For discussion: Busolt 1905; Meyer 1905; Schäfer 1932: 258–59; Frost 1980: 119–20, 173–74, as well as *HCT* 1.258–60 and *CT* 1.135–38; Fornara and Samons 1991: 118–21 (who expose the flaws in Thucydides' story); Welwei 1999: 77, 370 n. 23 (who again doubts the episode's authenticity). Archaeological evidence (mentioned already in Thuc. 1.93.2 and perhaps the cause of the story's later elaboration): Travlos 1971: 158, 162; Wycherley 1978: 11.

82. Defense: Hdt. 5.74–78 and esp. 91.1. Hellespont: Figueira 1991: chap. 5.

83. Hdt. 5.90–91.

84. Zuntz 1955: 33ff.; on the date, 81ff. On the suppliant theme in the tradition of the funeral orations: Kierdorf 1966: 91–95; Zuntz 1955: 16ff.

85. *Heraclid.* 284ff. (tr. Vellacott); cf. 61–62, 243ff.; see further 111–13, 191–201 (esp. 197–98), 329ff., 954ff. The herald's threats: 19ff., 55ff., 109–10, 158ff., 261ff., 274ff.

86. Date (late 420s): Zuntz 1955: 88ff.; Lesky 1966b: 378; Collard 1975: 1.8–14. See esp. Eur. *Supp.* 467ff. (threats), 518ff. (rejection). In this play, however, the Athenian leader, Theseus, is determined, even before being provoked by the Theban herald, to intervene in Thebes on behalf of the suppliants and their just cause (346ff., 389ff., 571ff.). On this important difference: Fitton 1961: 452. Freedom: *Supp.* 473ff., esp. 477; see Collard 1975: 2.ad loc. On political aspects: Zuntz 1955: 3ff.; Conacher 1956; H. Diller's review of Zuntz 1955 in *Gnomon* 32 (1960): 230–31; Fitton 1961; Collard 1975: 1.23–31.

87. The verb *epitassein* occurs frequently in this speech: Thuc. 1.139.1, 140.2, 5, 141.1; cf. Eur. *Supp.* 518ff.; *HCT* 1.453–54.

88. Cf. esp. Thuc. 2.61.1; 6.82.2–3. A similar thought perhaps underlies 2.40.5: "We alone do good to our neighbors not after a calculation of our own interest, but in the confidence of freedom [*tēs eleutherias tōi pistōi*] and in a frank and fearless spirit" (*CT* 1.307); cf. *HCT* 2.124–25 ("with the confidence that belongs to us as free men"); Diller 1962a: 201–2 (in contrast to Strasburger 1958: 30–31 with n. 1); de Romilly 1963: 139; Flashar 1969: 24–24; Rhodes 1988: 224. Compare here Pericles' characterization in 2.65.8 (*kateiche to plēthos eleutherōs*) with *HCT* ad loc. ("'freely,' i.e., without hesitation, 'as a free man should'"); Diller 1962a: 201; Edmunds and Martin 1977; Parry 1989: 144–48.

89. See chap. 4.1 at n. 147 above. Debates: e.g., Thuc. 1.34.2, 39.1; cf. 42.1, 4; or 5.89, 111.4; cf. Eur. *Phoen.* 535ff.; Schäfer 1932: 160–61.

90. See, e.g., Thuc. 5.95–97, 99, and the accusation of *pleonexia* and *polupragmosunē* raised so often against Athens: Lévy 1976: 119–28; Raaflaub 1994: 107–9 with more bibliography.

91. For the idea of gaining power by exercising power: e.g., Thuc. 1.15.1, 77.3.

92. The exact demarcation of the three generations seems relatively unimportant; their succession presumably corresponds roughly to that of the dominant personalities: Themistocles, Cimon, and Pericles himself. For various interpretations: *HCT* 2.104–5; Kakridis 1961: 11ff.; Flashar 1969: 15 n. 23.

93. Esp. Thuc. 2.38.2, 64.3; Ps. Xen. *AP* 2.7, 11–13; Hermipp. fr. 63 *PCG* = 63 Edm. (from *Phormophoroi*, probably performed in 425); see Braund 1994. Miller (1997) offers a different perspective on these issues.

94. On the philosophical aspects: Wilpert 1950; Widmann 1967: 27–33; Warnach 1971; Gigon 1973: 11ff.; more recent work by Nussbaum 1986; Annas 1993 (in each case, see index, s.v. "self-sufficiency"), as well as Coolsaet 1993 (on which see Hartmut Längin's review in *Gymnasium* 102 [1995]: 157–59). Kraut (1989) and Morpeth (1982, 1993) focus mostly on Aristotle. Wheeler (1955) and Festugière (1987: 67–76) deal with political aspects but not with the emergence and development of *autarkeia* as a political concept. For comparison: Veyne 1979.

95. Aesch. *Cho.* 757 (*nea . . . nēdus autarkēs teknōn;* LSJ: "helping itself, acting instinctively"); Soph. *OC* 1057 (*autarkēi . . . boai;* LSJ: "a self-reliant shout"); Eur. fr. 29N (*autarkē phronein*); Thuc. 2.41.1, 51.3 (n. 98 below) and n. 100 below.

96. Hippoc., *VS*, no. 86 A1; Democr., *VS*, no. 68 B4 (with no. 73 A4); Xen. *Mem.* 1.2.14; 4.7.1, 8.11. On Democritus: Farrar 1988: 230–35. Later developments: bibliography cited in n. 94 and Rich 1956.

97. The tragedians, Herodotus, Thucydides, Xenophon, and the orators use only the adjective; the noun is found only in Democr., *VS*, no. 68 B209, 246, and in the philosophers.

Orators: Isoc. 4.42 (similar to Hdt. 1.32.8); Dem. 3.14 (political); Dem. 19.34; 60.14; 61.13 (non-political). Hdt. 1.32.8 (*anthrōpou sōma hen ouden autarkes esti*, "no single human body is self-sufficient"—nor can a country achieve this in every respect) most likely refutes Pericles' extravagant claim (as reflected in Thuc. 2.36.3, mentioned above), just as Thucydides (next note) seems to refer to Herodotus; see Macleod 1983: 151–52; Loraux 1986: 153–54; Scanlon 1994: 143–64; Moles 1996: 267–69.

98. Thuc. 2.41.1 (*to sōma autarkes parechesthai*, "would provide a self-sufficient individual": Rusten 1989: 159). For paraphrases and discussion of Thucydides' complex formulation of this idea: e.g., *HCT* 2.125–27 ("Each man individually can combine in his own person a wider activity than men elsewhere, and is quicker witted [more flexible], and knows more of the graces of life"); Rusten 1989: 159; *CT* 1.308. In Thuc. 2.51.3 (impact of the plague) the ideal described by Pericles is shown to be an illusion ("no *sōma* appeared *autarkes* against the disease," meaning "clearly no physical constitution was sufficient to resist it": Rusten 1989: 188); the deliberate reference to 41.1 is evident (Flashar 1969: 35), and the formula used here (*sōma autarkes*) makes it likely that Thucydides had Herodotus 1.32.8 in mind (previous note).

99. Flashar 1969: 26; similarly *HCT* 1.127.

100. Thuc. 1.37.2–4 (3: *polis . . . autarkē thesin keimenē*); see *HCT* 1.173.

101. Hdt. and Xen.: see nn. 97–98 and bibliography in nn. 94, 97. Aristot., esp. *EN* 1097a28–b21, 1177a27–b1, also 1169b3ff.; *Pol.* 1253a25ff. On the supreme self-sufficiency of God: Gigon 1973: 11 (with further references).

102. For supporting evidence: Widman 1967: 33–34; Raaflaub 1984a: nn. 69, 71–72.

103. See Widman 1967: 34; Aristot. *Pol.* 1291a8ff.

104. Scanlon (1994: 149–50) cautions, rightly, that even Pericles qualifies his statement in several ways that suggest relative, not absolute, achievement.

105. See, e.g., Hes. *WD* 363–65, 394–95, 399–400, 405–9, 451–54, 475–78; Aymard 1967: 316ff., esp. 328–31; Millett 1984.

106. As indicated early by Solon's law prohibiting the exportation of grain (Plut. *Sol.* 24.1) and by the occupation of strategically important islands on the way to the Hellespont and Black Sea already in the time of the sixth-century tyrants; the problem was a permanent concern in the fifth and fourth centuries: e.g., Aristot. *AP* 43.4; Xen. *Mem.* 3.6.13; Heichelheim 1935: 833ff., esp. 842; de Ste. Croix 1972: 46–47; Garnsey 1988: chaps. 1–3.

107. Lack of practical application: Raaflaub 1984a: 65–66. On the primacy of politics: de Romilly 1963: 71ff.; Will 1972: 629–37, 660–78; Finley 1973a: chap. 6; Austin and Vidal-Naquet 1977: 112–13; Rahe 1994: chap. 1.

108. E.g., Ehrenberg 1965b: 116ff. (= 1969: 95ff.); de Ste. Croix 1972: 47.

109. See also Thuc. 2.64.3. One is tempted to conclude that this specifically Athenian concept originated in the circle of intellectuals grouped around Pericles, to whom one might attribute other theories of power politics current at the time: see Kiechle 1963b. The very existence of such a circle has been cast into doubt: for discussion, see Stadter 1991; Podlecki 1998: chap. 3. Long-term planning: Meier 1980: 435ff., esp. 477ff. (= 1990: chap. 8, esp. 209–10).

110. On the Megarian Decree: chap. 4.1, n. 122, above. Piraeus: e.g., Ps. Xen. *AP* 2.3, 11–12; Garland 1987: chaps. 1–2.

111. Tr. Vellacott. See also Aesch. *Prom.* 926–27. On the prototypes of the figure of Zeus: Groeneboom 1928: ad loc. (the Great King, imagined as a supertyrant); Thomson 1932; Bock 1958: 415 with n. 81; Méautis 1960: 59–72 (the Sicilian tyranny); Podlecki 1966: 107ff., 111ff. (on both). Authorship and date: Méautis 1960; Griffith 1977; Bees 1993.

112. Emphasized often in trials of followers of the Thirty: Lys. 25.32; 28.14; see also 2.62–63; Isocr. 7.62ff., esp. 64–65; Ps. Andoc. 4.1; Dem. 22.68; further, e.g., Thuc. 2.63.2–3 (the perni-

cious influence of the "quiet citizens," *apragmones;* see Carter 1986). Lévy (1976: 147– 48) observes that after 404 *dunamis/dunatos* were avoided. See also Mossé 1962: 409ff.; Chambers 1973: 108ff.

113. Pericles: Thuc. 2.36.3– 4, 63.1–2; also 4.95.2; 5.69.1. Nicias, Alcibiades: below after n. 120.

114. Eur. *Phoen.* 503ff., esp. 506, 519–20, 523–25, 627–28; see also Soph. *Aleadai* fr. 85 Pearson = 85 *TrGF,* and the passages cited by Pearson 1917: ad loc. Hdt. 1.170.2, 210.2 (with 127.1, 129.1– 4); 6.109.3.

115. Hdt. 8.140ff., 143– 44, esp. 144.1: "There is not so much gold in the world nor land so fair that we would take it for pay to join the common enemy and bring Greece into subjection" (tr. de Sélincourt and Marincola).

116. Wealth can replace power or rule throughout this episode; they depend on each other. For Greek lack of understanding of Persian vassalage: chap. 3.2, n. 189, above.

117. On Herodotus's last chapter: Bischoff 1932: 78–83 (= Marg 1965: 681–87); Cobet 1971: 174–76 with n. 704; Lateiner 1989: 48–50; Dewald 1997. On the larger interpretive pattern: Raaflaub 1987, 2002a, 2002b (with bibliography); Moles 1996.

118. See esp. Ps. Xen. *AP* 1.8–9; Eur. *Supp.* 352–53; chap. 6.2 at n. 127 below.

119. Thuc. 8.68.4; cf. 71.1; echoes also in 7.63.3– 4.

120. De Romilly 1963: 80.

121. *HCT* 4.362.

122. Stated explicitly by Nicias (7.69.2: the Athenians "had the liberty to live their own lives in their own way," *anepitaktos pasin es tēn diaitan exousia*) and Pericles (2.37.2, 40.2; see chap. 6.2 at n. 117 below).

123. See, to some extent, Raaflaub 1984a: 68ff., 76 –77, and the partial correction in Raaflaub 2003 (see n. 129 below).

124. See generally de Romilly 1963: esp. 311ff.; Finley 1967: chap. 1.

125. See chap. 3.3 at n. 211 above and the bibliography cited there.

126. Thompson and Wycherley 1972: 100; Wycherley 1978: 36ff.; Camp 1986: 61–87, 2001: 63 –72. The temple of Hephaestus, above the Agora, was constructed in the 450s to early 440s: Travlos 1971: 261–73; Camp 1986: 82– 87.

127. See chap. 3.3 at n. 244 above.

128. Rosivach 1978: 32ff., esp. 41ff.

129. On the ambivalence of tyranny: Connor 1977. In Raaflaub 1984a: 73 –76 (as pointed out correctly by Tuplin 1985: 362), I uncritically accepted Connor's arguments and applied them to the "freedom of the tyrant" in the present context. Reexamination of the evidence has prompted me to revise my interpretation of the Athenians' own use of *polis turannos* (Raaflaub 2003: at nn. 87ff.).

130. A recent debate about the "Greek miracle" is instructive in this context; see, e.g., title and various contributions in Buitron-Oliver 1992 with the critical comments by Wills (1992). For an effort at serious, if not radical, demythologization: Samons forthcoming. For the contribution of slavery to this "miracle": e.g., Osborne 1995; Strauss 1998; and, more generally, de Ste. Croix 1981: 140 – 47; Finley 1982: chap. 6.

131. E.g., Larsen 1962; Aymard 1967: 343ff., esp. 346ff.; Austin and Vidal-Naquet 1977: 125– 26; and esp. Hasebroek 1926: 4–5. "Imperialist impulse": borrowed from Evans 1991: 9.

132. See Ryder 1965: 6. On early Theban efforts to achieve hegemony: chap. 3.1 at n. 77 above. Moreover, around 470 Argos tried to restrain attempts at gaining autonomy on the part of several communities in its territory; such attempts were triggered by Argos's devastating defeat by Sparta at Sepeia; see Gschnitzer 1958: chap. 16; Tomlinson 1972: 93–102; Piérart 1997. As Herodotus shows (1.30.5: Tellus fell in a battle between Eleusinians and Athenians), fights between neighboring communities in Attica were still remembered in his time. Asheri (1988b:

284) interprets this episode as part of the hostilities between Megara and Athens about control of Salamis; Anderson (2000), however, makes a strong case that the unification of Attica was not completed before the end of the sixth century. In the case of Sparta, what matters are less the helots (although throughout the fifth century, they, too, were considered by other Greeks entirely Sparta's own business [Raaflaub forthcoming]) than the *perioikoi*. We know virtually nothing about their sentiments, but it seems symptomatic that only two of their communities (neither in Laconia) participated in the great helot revolt of the 460s (Thuc. 1.101.1–2; Luraghi 2001: 297–301).

133. Syracuse: chap. 3.1, n. 74, above; Lewis 1994: 120–55; Talbert 1997. Mantinea: Thuc. 5.29.1, 33; Amit 1973: 147–63. Sparta: chap. 5.3 below. Thebes after Leuctra: Buckler 1980; Roy 1994; Munn 1997.

134. Given the amount of cultural imitation of things Persian in fifth-century Athens (see Miller 1997), we should expect some impact on the political level as well. See n. 2 above.

135. On some basic aspects: Diller 1962a: esp. 191–95. On Spartan policy in general: de Ste. Croix 1972: 89ff. passim, esp. 151ff.; Lewis 1977; Andrewes 1978b, 1992; Hamilton 1979: pt. 1; Cartledge 1987; and relevant chaps. in *CAH* 6².

136. Thuc. 2.8.4–5; see *HCT* 2.9–10; *CT* 1.246; and chap. 4.4 above. Corinthians: n. 145 below.

137. Plataea: Thuc. 2.72.1; cf. 3.59.4. Mytilene: 3.9–14 (suppression of freedom in the Athenian Empire: esp. 10.2ff., 11.1ff., 12.1; appeal to Sparta: 13.1, see also 13.6–7, 14.1). Brasidas: 4.85–87 (defining this program and explaining the strategic and political significance of its realization: esp. 85.1, 4ff., 86.1, 4–5, 87.2–6; see also 108.2, 114.3–4, 120.3, 121.1; 5.9.9). Melian Dialogue: 5.86, 91.1–2, 92–93, 99–100, 105.2–3, 112.1. Sicily: 4.60.1–2, 61.5, 63.2, 64.1ff., esp. 4–5; 6.20.2, 69.3, 77.1, 88.1; 7.56.2, 66.2 (cf. 6.90.3), 68.2–3, 82.1.

138. On the realization of this prediction (despite the treaties with Persia: Thuc. 8.18, 37): Thuc. 8.52; and below, discussion in next section.

139. Sparta's *prostasia*: so, too, *HCT* 1.228; *CT* 1.113. On *prostasia*: at n. 16 above. Herodotus reminds us carefully of Sparta's own commitment to and achievements for liberty: von Fritz 1965; chap. 3.1 at n. 9 above; chap. 6.2 at n. 147 below. Appeals to Sparta by Thasos: Thuc. 1.101.1–2; by Samos: 1.40.5; by Mytilene: 3.2.1, 13.1.

140. Thuc. 1.68.4, 69.1ff., 71.4, 120.2, 121.1, 122.2ff.

141. Thuc. 1.67.1, 2, 4, 79.2, 82.5–6, 85.2; in addition, 71.4–5, 86.1ff., 87.2–3, 6, 118.3, 119, 121.1.

142. The comments of the Corinthians, protesting against Athens's potential alliance with Corcyra in 433, are especially informative here: Thuc. 1.40.5. Hence, public opinion in Greece turned decisively against Athens only shortly before the war. See n. 132 on Athenian attitudes toward Sparta's helot problem.

143. Nesselhauf 1934: 292–93. On "Hellenic *nomoi*": chap. 6.2, n. 155, below.

144. See the references in n. 141; Nesselhauf 1934. On the other hand, there is no lack of evidence for Sparta's (at least partial) responsibility for the outbreak of the war: Lévy 1976: 49–50. Sparta's doubts: Thuc. 1.85.1–2; 7.18.2. For discussions of the "*Kriegsschuldfrage*": Kagan 1969: chaps. 13–20; de Ste. Croix 1972; Lewis 1977: chap. 3 (from a different perspective), 1992: 370–80.

145. By the Corinthians: Thuc. 1.68.3, 69.1, 123.1, 124.1; by the Thebans: 3.63.1ff., 64.2–3. It is precisely when speaking in the presence of representatives of Sparta that the allies stress the contrast between Athens's initial liberation and later enslavement of Greek poleis; thus, too, the Mytilenians: 3.10ff.

146. Esp. Thuc. 1.76.2; 2.63.2; 3.40.4; 5.89. Rejection of Sparta's authority: e.g., 1.76.2, 144.2.

147. Hdt. 1.5.3, 6.2–3; see also 3.21.2; 7.51.2; tyranny: 5.90–93 with Strasburger 1955; Raaflaub 1987: 223–24. On subjection of Greeks as injustice: Drexler 1976: 28–35. Tyrant city: Thuc. 1.122.3, 124.3. Sparta's reputation: 1.18.1; with chap. 4.1 at n. 26 above.

148. Thuc. 1.80ff. (esp. 82.1, 85.2, 86); so, too, Lévy 1976: 63.

149. Pretext: Thuc. 1.126.1. Megara: 139.1. Autonomy: 139.4.

150. See, e.g., remarks by the Corinthians (Thuc. 1.122.1), Mytilenians (3.13.6–7), and Brasidas (4.85.3ff., 87.2ff.).

151. Again by the Corinthians (Thuc. 1.68ff. passim); also cleverly by the Athenians (1.76.2, with Meiggs 1972: 306); then by the Mytilenians: 3.13.7. See also Brasidas: 4.85.2.

152. For a list of Spartan "sins": de Romilly 1963: 278ff.; Ryder 1965: 10–11; Drexler 1976: 78–85.

153. Thuc. 2.72, 74.2; 3.52ff. (esp. 52.4, 53.1–2, 59.3–4, 63–64, 68); Thucydides' judgment: 68.3–4; see Karavites 1982a: 68–70. Strasburger (1958: 36) labels this a "*Justizmord*"; Diller (1962a: 194–95) sees the Plataean episode as a deliberate analogy to the Athenian treatment of the Mytilenians.

154. See Thuc. 3.92–93, with detailed comm. in *HCT* 2.394–99; *CT* 1.501–8. Other sources: Stählin 1912. Political motives: Andrewes 1978b: 96ff.; see also Malkin 1994: chap. 8.

155. Appeals: Thuc. 4.79.3. Brasidas's speeches: n. 137 above. Sparta's motives: 4.80–81. The outcome (81.2)—that Brasidas's achievements procured for Sparta valuable objects of exchange and increased Athens's willingness to make peace—probably corresponded largely to the intention.

156. Thuc. 4.83.3ff., 84ff., esp. 87.2ff.; Diller 1962a: 195.

157. Fear: Thuc. 4.108.2ff., 120, 123. Force: 4.88, 104ff., 110ff.

158. Thuc. 4.132.3; 5.3.1ff. with the comments in *HCT* and *CT*.

159. Mende: 4.130.6–7. Torone: 5.3.3–4. Scione: 5.32. Exchange of territories: 5.18.5 (with *HCT* 3.668–72; *CT* 2.475–78; and chap. 4.2 at n. 150 above). Clause quoted: 5.18.8 with *HCT* 3.675 ("Sparta withdraws completely . . . from the role of liberator of Hellas."); Lewis 1992: 432 (Sparta bargained "the liberation of Greece for the security of her own system."). Scione suffered Athens's revenge only afterward. Protest: 5.30.2.

160. Thuc. 1.144.2; Hdt. 1.68.6 (see chap. 3.1, n. 65, above). Traditional oligarchies: chap. 4.1 at n. 27. Athens's policy: chap. 4.2 at n. 114.

161. Sicyon, etc.: Thuc. 5.81.2, 82.1ff. with the comments in *HCT* 4 ad loc. Later: e.g., Xen. *Hell.* 5.2.7; Diod. 15.5.12 for Mantinea (385/384); Xen. *Hell.* 5.2.8ff., 3.10ff., 21ff.; Diod. 15.19.3 for Phlius (381–79); see Ryder 1965: 12–14; Cartledge 1987: 258–66.

162. Rejection: Thuc. 5.17.2, 22.1. Clause: 5.18.11, 29.2–3. Reaction of allies: 5.25.1, 27ff. Unrest had been brewing even earlier: 5.14.4, 22.2. Suspicion: 5.27.2, 29.3; cf. already 4.20.4; Arist. *Peace* 1082; Lévy 1976: 64.

163. E.g., Lotze 1964: chap. 4 with references.

164. Thuc. 5.31.1ff.; Xen. *Hell.* 3.2.21ff.; Diod. 14.17.4ff. (Elis); Thuc. 5.29.1, 33.1–2, 81.1 (Mantinea); the principle: 5.79.1. See Hamilton 1979: chap. 1; Cartledge 1987: 51–54.

165. See the preceding discussion. Fears: Thuc. 4.85.6, 86.1–2, 87.2ff. Brasidas's attempt to dispel such fears: 4.86.3ff., esp. 4–5. On Spartan governors: n. 170 below. Further, e.g., the event described in Thuc. 4.130.4: Parke 1930: 42; *CT* 2.405–6.

166. Earlier attempts to ally with Persia: Thuc. 1.82.1; 2.67.1ff. First treaty: 8.18.1, with a supplement in the second treaty, 37.2. Protests: 8.43.3, cf. 8.52 (Lichas), and a close analogy in 5.21 (Clearidas during the Peace of Nicias). New clause: 8.58.2. See Lewis 1977: chap. 4; on Persian claims, also Meister 1982: 39–40.

167. Thuc. 8.84.4–5. Defection of Miletus and other Ionian poleis from Athens: 8.14–17; cf. Gorman 2001: 236–41.

168. War against Persia: Cartledge 1987: chaps. 11, 12, 17. King's Peace: Hampl 1938: 8–12, 85–88; *SV*, no. 242 (with sources); Ryder 1965: chap. 2. On Sparta's position after 411: Lewis 1977: chap. 5; Hamilton 1979: 33ff. See also Seager and Tuplin 1980.

169. Thuc. 8.84.5; Xen. *Hell.* 1.6.8; already Thuc. 4.66.

170. The unconditional obligation to provide military assistance is attested for Athens (Xen. *Hell.* 2.2.20; less specifically, Xen. *An.* 6.1.27; Diod. 13.107.4) and was probably applied to former Athenian subjects as well: Busolt and Swoboda 1926: 1325; Lotze 1964: 62–63; and generally de Ste. Croix 1972: 298ff. Harmosts and garrisons: Parke 1930; Lotze 1964: chap. 4. Decarchies: Xen. *Hell.* 3.5.13; 6.3.8; Plut. *Lys.* 13.3ff.; Nepos *Lys.* 1.4–2.1; Diod. 14.13.1 (more cautious). Their abolition: Xen. *Hell.* 3.4.2, 7. Their reputation: references in Busolt and Swoboda 1926: 1324 n. 3. See also in general Cartledge 1987: chap. 17; Lewis 1994: 29–31.

171. Parke 1930: 76; Lotze 1964: 64–65; Lewis 1977: chap. 6, 1994: 24–29; Andrewes 1978b: 99–102; Hamilton 1979: esp. chap. 1.

172. Esp. Isocr. 4.122–23; 12.103–4. Criticism of Spartan rule: Isocr. 4.110ff., 125ff.; Xen. *Hell.* 6.3.7ff.; see also Plut. *Lys.* 13.8 on Theopomp. com. fr. 65 Edm. = 66 *PCG.*

173. Pol. 6.49.4–5 is especially informative.

174. Thus also Lévy 1976: 63–64.

175. The verb used is *hēgeomai.* Cf. Thuc. 8.2.4; Drexler 1976: 84; Andrewes 1978b.

176. E.g., Pind. *Pyth.* 8.98–99; Thuc. 2.8.4; 8.2.2, 64.5; Xen. *Hell.* 2.2.23; ML, no. 82, lines 8ff. (the revolt of Eretria in 411; cf. Thuc. 8.95). See generally chap. 4.4 above.

177. Esp. Brasidas (Thuc. 4.81) and, to some extent, Lichas and Clearidas (n. 166 above). De Romilly (1963: 45–46) suggests that Thucydides' very positive characterization of Brasidas (see also Andrewes 1978b: 100–101; Connor 1984: 126–40; *CT* 2.268–73) was intended to contrast sharply with that of Lysander.

6. Meaning and Function of Freedom within the Polis

1. See chap. 3.2 above; for the term "isonomic": chap. 3.1 at n. 102; on *isonomia:* chap. 3.2 at nn. 159ff.

2. Ruschenbusch 1979: 30–40; Wolff 1979; Bleicken 1979: 157; Nippel 1980: 64–98. Generally on *stasis* and oligarchy: Gehrke 1985; Ostwald 2000; Price 2001.

3. IG I³ 131, lines 5–7; Isaeus 5.47; Dinarch. 1.101; see Ostwald 1951; Taylor 1991: 1–5.

4. The famous digression on the fall of the Peisistratids (Thuc. 6.54–59); cf. Hdt. 5.55, 62–65; 6.123. See Fornara 1968; *HCT* 4.317–29; Ostwald 1986: 323–33; Munn 2000: 114–18. Fear: Thuc. 6.53.3, 60.1; cf. 27.3.

5. Laws: Ostwald 1955, 1986: 8, 414–15; Rhodes 1981: 220–22; Gagarin 1981b. Fear: Berve 1967: 1.198–99, 2.628; Lévy 1976: 138; see below at nn. 9–10.

6. Berve 1967: 1.194. For analysis of some of the questions involved here: Rosivach 1988; Barceló 1990; McGlew 1993: chap. 6; Raaflaub 2003, where I question (against Adkins 1960: 164–65, 234–35; Lévy 1976: 137–38 with nn. 15–16; Connor 1977, among others) the extent to which traditional aristocratic ambivalences about tyranny came into play here.

7. Meier 1968: 13, 1980: 285–86 (= 1990: 163–64); Schuller 1979: 439–40. Moreover, Athenian democracy, too, assumed elitist traits, for instance, in Pericles' citizenship law of 451/450 (Patterson 1981). A sharp contrast between tyranny and democracy is visible in several tragedies, esp. early on in Aeschylus's *Persians, Suppliants,* and *Prometheus Bound,* as well as in the literary "constitutional debates" (Raaflaub 1989b: 41–46; and at n. 109 below).

8. This was the only way to maintain political continuity, which was not encouraged or, rather, was intentionally obstructed by the institutional setup; see Nippel 1980: 69. That strong leadership needed to be disguised goes without saying; Pericles seems to have mastered this difficult task (Plut. *Per.* 4–8; Meier 1980: 264–65 [= 1990: 149–50]); Alcibiades offended by failing to do so (next n.).

9. See Berve 1967: 1.198, 2.627–28. Pericles: Ehrenberg 1954: 84ff., 104ff.; Schwarze 1971; Klein 1979: 503, 505; Stadter 1989 (index, s.v. "Pericles," "Tyrant"); Schubert 1994: 5–9. Alcibi-

ades: Seager 1967; de Romilly 1995: chap. 5. On both: Vickers 1997 (see index). Cleon and Aristophanic satire: Lévy 1976: 138–39; Ruschenbusch 1979: 37–39; Taylor 1991: 85–92; Giorgini 1993: 239–45; Lenfant 1997; Henderson 2003. Sophists: next n.

10. Lévy 1976: 137–39. Oligarchy and tyranny: Thuc. 6.60.1; further references in Lévy 1976: 139. The doctrine of natural law as the theoretical foundation of oligarchic ambition: Lintott 1981: 168–73.

11. Aeschylus: chap. 3.1, nn. 15–16, 134, 139. Sophocles, Euripides: "Materialien," sec. 9.4.a–b; generally, Berve 1967: 1.194ff.; Seaford 2003. Contemporary glorification of the Tyrannicides is reflected in Soph. *El.* 970ff., esp. 973–85; see also 1256 (restoration of free speech), 1299–1300, 1508–10. Herodotus: "Materialien," sec. 9.4.c–d; Dewald 2003 with bibliography.

12. E.g., Hdt. 1.95.5–96.1; 6.109.3; see also 3.83.2–3 (Otanes' rejection of the throne—a passage clearly influenced by contemporary discussions: Raaflaub 1989b: 61 with n. 50).

13. Cf. Hippoc. *Aer.* 16.3ff., 23.5ff. Date: chap. 4.3, n. 167, above. *Aer.* 16 uses a new term, emerging around that very time, to express this idea: *autokratōr;* see n. 111 below. A similar idea underlies Herodotus's interpretation of Sparta's plan to weaken Athens by reimposing tyranny: 5.90ff., esp. 91.1 (see chap. 4.2 at n. 85). See also chap. 3.2 at n. 191.

14. The term actually used is *isēgoria* (equality of speech), one of the primary characteristics of nontyranny and democracy: see Raaflaub 1980; and below at nn. 87ff.

15. Chap. 3.2 at nn. 189ff. For a good example: Xen. *An.* 3.2.13.

16. See Pind. *Pyth.* 1, discussed immediately below.

17. Pind. *Pyth.* 1.61–62; see chap. 3.2 at n. 136.

18. Earliest evidence: Pind. *Pyth.* 2.86–88. Date: von der Mühll 1958: esp. 218 (275 or early 274); Burton 1962: 111ff., esp. 115 (after 472). Interpretation: esp. Meier 1968: 11–13.

19. *Dēmokratia* is not attested before Herodotus. On the development of the concept of "democracy": Debrunner 1947; Larsen 1948; Ehrenberg 1965a: 264–97; Meier 1968: esp. 18–25, 1970: 44–48, 1972; Sealey 1974; Orsi and Cagnazzi 1980. I have argued in detail (with sources and bibliography) for emergence of *dēmokratia* in the 460s (1995: 46–48); see Raaflaub 1995: 48 nn. 134–35 for arguments against attempts (by Kinzl 1978; Fornara and Samons 1991: 41–42, 48–51, 56; Hansen 1991: 69–71) to date the term to the time of Cleisthenes.

20. Forerunners: Meier 1968: 18–25; *dēmos,* etc.: n. 22 below; *stratos:* n. 41 below.

21. Assembly: esp. Aesch. *Supp.* 365ff., 397ff., 483ff., 517ff., 523, 600–624, 940–49, 963ff. Monarchy: 370ff., 418ff., 423ff. (even if Egypt seems to be imagined almost like another polis: 5ff., 387ff., 852; see Ehrenberg 1965a: 267). Date: Lesky 1966a: 220ff., 1966b: 243–44; Podlecki 1966: 42–45; the debate on this issue is summarized by Stoessl (1979), who himself advocates 475–474; see recently Alan Sommerstein, *OCD* 26 (after 467, exact date unknown); Bernhard Zimmermann, *DNP* 1 (1996): 352 (between 465 and 460, probably 463). Interpretation: esp. Ehrenberg 1965a: 266–74; Raaflaub 1988a: 286–88; Meier 1993b: 84–97.

22. Esp. Aesch. *Supp.* 604: "the ruling hand of the demos" (*dēmou kratousa cheir*); 699: "the demos who rule in the city" (*to dēmion to ptolin kratunei*). Ehrenberg (1965a: 270ff., esp. 272) recognizes *dēmokratia* in such formulations. Contra: Vlastos 1953: 339; Meier 1968: 17 with n. 46; see also Sealey 1974: 263–67.

23. E.g., Eur. *Supp.* 352–53 (quoted below at n. 108), 438–41 (see at n. 110). Aesch. *Supp.* 946ff. refers to free (in the sense of true) speech as an attribute of freemen as opposed to slaves, not as a political right of the citizens; see chap. 3.2 at nn. 170–71 above. Sophocles' *Antigone,* dated to the late 440s, elaborates on Creon's tyranny, pays attention to what the people think (698–700), but does not mention democracy or liberty.

24. Either because it was written early and not significantly altered when incorporated into the main body of the work or, less probably, because it was taken with only minor changes from a somewhat earlier source. For discussion: Apffel 1958 (with earlier bibliography); Asheri

1990: 295–97; in addition, esp. von Fritz 1967: 309ff.; Bringmann 1976; Gschnitzer 1977. Connor (1971: 199–206) and Nippel (1980: 34 n. 17) favor composition relatively late in Herodotus's life.

25. Democracy: Hdt. 3.80.6; see Ostwald 1969: 111ff. Monarchy: Hdt. 3.82.5.

26. See above at n. 13; cf. Thuc. 6.89.3ff., esp. 6 (chap. 5.2 after n. 120); Raaflaub 1989b: 66.

27. On "placing power in the middle" (*es meson tithenai*), see Hdt. 3.80.2; Vlastos 1953: 348 with n. 38; Detienne 1965, 1996: chap. 5.

28. Herodotus's final comment, "The people of Samos, it seems, did not want to be free" (3.143.2), comes close. Assembly: *ekklesiē pantōn tōn astōn* (3.142.2).

29. Because we always have to reckon with late revision and can never be certain about identifying authentic Periclean ideas and formulations (e.g., in the Funeral Oration, Thuc. 2.37); see de Romilly 1963: 110–55. Date of Herodotus's work: chap. 1.3, n. 39, above.

30. Date of Ps. Xen. *AP:* chap. 4.2, n. 63; of Eur. *Supp.:* chap. 5.2, n. 86.

31. See at nn. 107ff. below.

32. Thus Aesch. *Supp.* 604, 699 (see n. 22 above); see also Hdt. 3.80.6. This is illustrated well by the late shift of emphasis (from equality to freedom) in the terminology formulating the right of speech: below at n. 88.

33. Bleicken (1979: 166ff.) emphasizes the importance of this factor.

34. Pride: widely visible in Herodotus (e.g., 7.104–5; 135.2–3 with von Fritz 1965; Thuc. 1.84.1; 5.9.1), and see below at n. 146. Elitist: Plut. *Lyc.* 24–25, 28.11, 30, 31.1. Aristocratic concept: at n. 200 below.

35. At n. 115 below.

36. The limitations and slavery imposed on *perioikoi* and helots, respectively, were generally seen as Sparta's own business throughout the fifth century (Raaflaub forthcoming) and thus did not affect this judgment.

37. Chap. 5.2 at n. 123.

38. Meier 1970: 44–49, 1972: 823ff., esp. 825–26; see also 1990: chap. 7.

39. The earliest testimonia—the name Demokrates (Hansen 1991: 69–71) and circumlocutions of *dēmokratia* in Aeschylus's *Suppliants* (n. 22 above)—reflect a positive assessment, thus weakening the argument of Sealey 1974: 273ff.; see also Nippel 1980: 35 with n. 19; Meier 1990: 161 with n. 14. It is likely, as Lawrence Tritle suggests to me, that other names formed with Demo- (*vel sim.*) became popular around the same time. Sergei Karpiouk is preparing a study on Athenian "democratic" names.

40. Meier 1968: 25ff., 1982: 824.

41. Hence, Pindar (*Pyth.* 2.86–88) uses *stratos* (the armed host, army) for *dēmos;* so, too, *Ol.* 9.95; Aesch. *Pers.* 241 (with intentional ambiguity: Groeneboom 1960: 2, ad loc.; Broadhead 1960: ad loc.); *Eum.* 566, 569, 683, 762; Groeneboom 1928: 244 (at *Prom.* 723) with further references. See Raaflaub 1998b: 41–43, 92–93.

42. Reflected in the role of the Areopagus Council until 462: Arist. *AP* 23.1–2 with Rhodes 1981: ad loc.; Wallace 1989: 77–83. Hence, Meier (1980: 137 = 1990: 77) attributes to the Cleisthenic Council of Five Hundred initially the function of an "opposition": it was intended to be a counterweight, not to lead. See also Martin 1974: 16ff., 28–29.

43. See Raaflaub 1998b: esp. 44–48, 95–97; on the transformation of Athens in this period: Raaflaub 1998c.

44. See n. 21 above.

45. Rhodes 1981: 311ff., 1992: 67–77; Ostwald 1986: 28–83; Meier 1987c; Fornara and Samons 1991: 50–75; Bleicken 1994: 43–46; Raaflaub 1995: 35–46, 1998b: 48–50, 97–101.

46. Eur. *Supp.* 352 (see at n. 108); cf. 406: *dēmos anassei; Cycl.* 119: *dedēmeutai kratos.* Criticism: see n. 9 and Thuc. 2.65.8–9.

47. E.g., Hdt. 3.80.6 ("the many include all," *en tōi pollōi eni ta panta*); 142.2–3; Thuc. 2.37;

4.86.4; 6.39.1; Lys. 34.2–3. Pericles' citizenship law of 451/450 defined this claim for the first time in legal terms but in turn increased exclusiveness (see bibliography in n. 81).

48. This is the ideal of Pericles' Funeral Oration (Thuc. 2.37), which in its essentials probably corresponded to political reality well into the Periclean era; for discussion, see below at n. 115.

49. Early awareness of these principles: Aesch. *Supp.* 604, 699; then Her. 3.80.6; Eur. *Supp.* 406–8, 433–41 (both with important details).

50. See, e.g., *HCT* 1.24–29, 361ff.; Bayer and Heideking 1975.

51. Further discussion of necessary changes below at nn. 75ff.

52. See chap. 5.2 at nn. 111ff.

53. E.g., Bleicken 1979: 156ff.; Wolff 1979; Ruschenbusch 1979: chaps. 3, 5. On the distortion of these issues in late sources (esp. Plutarch): Frost 1964; Andrewes 1978a; Ruschenbusch 1979: chap. 12.

54. Klein (1979), Nippel (1980: 64–75), and Bleicken (1994: 371–79, 571–72, and bibliography on 629) contribute to a more differentiated view; see now also Roberts 1994: pt. 1; Ober 1998a.

55. See esp. Hdt. 3.80.6. On *dēmokratia,* see above at n. 39. On *oligarchia:* Meier 1968: 12 n. 37; Orsi and Cagnazzi 1981; Ostwald 2000: chaps. 1–2. On *aristokratia:* Meier 1972: 2. See also de Romilly 1959.

56. Ps. Xen. *AP* 1.1ff., 3.1, 3.8ff. The possibility of constitutional reorganization is crucial for Herodotus's debate (3.80.1, 83.1ff.).

57. Ps. Xen.: Bowersock 1966, 1968: 463–65, whose dating is accepted, e.g., by Fornara and Samons 1991: 64–65. Herodotus: above at n. 24.

58. See also Andrewes 1978a: 2; Stadter 1989: 135. Such an early date would be all the more likely if the democratic antityranny ideology early on included opposition to narrow oligarchy in the sense of collective tyranny (above at n. 7)—but we have no way of knowing this. Ostwald (2000: 23 n. 43) assumes an earlier date for the polarization between democracy and oligarchy; Hölkeskamp (1998) considers it anachronistic, fitting fourth-century thought patterns.

59. So rightly Eder 1998; cf. Ruschenbusch 1978: chap. 3; Hölkeskamp 1998.

60. Thuc. 1.107.4–5; Arist. *AP* 25.4; Plut. *Cim.* 15–17, *Per.* 10; Prestel 1939: 38ff.; *HCT* ad loc.; Rhodes 1981: 314, 1992: 70. On *Eumenides:* Meier 1990: chap. 5, 1993b: 102–37. On chronology: Bayer and Heideking 1975: 116–22; Fornara and Samons 1991: 127–29; Badian 1993: 89–96; see also Schreiner 1977.

61. The contrast with Cleisthenes' reforms is remarkable. After the initial clash with Isagoras and his faction, no resistance at all survived in the Athenians' collective memory. These reforms thus seem to have served the interests and needs of all major constituencies.

62. This argument is reflected in Aeschylus's *Suppliants:* at nn. 21–23 above; cf. Meier 1987c: 359–64. *Dēmos* in the archaic period: Donlan 1970; Fornara and Samons 1991: 48–49; see also Meier 1968: 25–29 (*plēthos,* a more neutral term, is often preferred to *dēmos*).

63. Indirect evidence includes harsh but unspecific polemics in Old Comedy: Schwarze 1971; Klein 1979.

64. On the date of Thucydides' ostracism: Stadter 1989: 183–84. Conflict: Plut. *Per.* 11–14; for discussion of these problematic chapters: Andrewes 1978a; Ameling 1985; Ostwald 1986: 185–88; Stadter 1989: 130ff.; Hölkeskamp 1998.

65. For the trial of Pericles and connected problems: Raaflaub 2000b with bibliography. For Athenian debates before the outbreak of the war: Kienast 1953: 210ff.; Sealey 1956: 234ff.; Kagan 1969: esp. pt. 3; Klein 1979: 508ff. Critical assessments of Pericles: sources and bibliography in Bayer and Heideking 1975: 161ff.; Lévy 1976: 48ff.; Wick 1977; Schubert 1994: pt. 1; Podlecki 1998: 132–52; of Thucydides: Badian 1993: 125–62.

66. Cleon: n. 9 above. 415 and later: e.g., Ostwald 1986: 312–58; Munn 2000: chaps. 4–5.

67. Thuc. 8.54.4, 65.2, 66.2; see Lehmann 1987. On elite associations (*hetaireiai*): see Calhoun 1913; Sartori 1957; Nippel 1980: 88 n. 11. The Athenians' reaction in 415 to the discovery, shortly before the departure of the fleet for Sicily, of two religious scandals (the mutilation of the Herms and the profanation of the Mysteries) is important in this connection: Thuc. 6.27–29, 53, 60–61, esp. 27, 60; for discussion, *HCT* 4.264–88; Ostwald 1986: 312–58; Furley 1996; Graf 2000; Munn 2000: chaps. 4–5.

68. Ruschenbusch 1979: 100ff. (but see n. 72 below); Nippel 1980: 73ff., 87ff., esp. 89; Lintott 1981: 147ff.

69. On the opponents: Ps. Xen. *AP* 2.20; Will 1972: 367–68; Nippel 1980: 73–74, 84ff. Nippel emphasizes, rightly, that these three divisions exclusively concerned the elite; accordingly, there is no reason to think of factions based on class differences; see also Ruschenbusch 1978: 24ff., 1979: 30ff.

70. On the importance of leadership (on both sides): Nippel 1980: 68ff.

71. Complexity: Connor 1971. Changes: Lévy 1976: pt. 1; Ruschenbusch 1979: 94ff.; Nippel 1980: 64ff.; see also Cartledge 2001.

72. Here I disagree with Ruschenbusch 1979: 100ff. His prosopographic analysis of the Four Hundred is instructive, but we know only twenty-nine of them by name. Our source base is thus very narrow and urges great caution in making generalizations; see also D. Lotze's review in *Gnomon* 53 (1981): 250.

73. De Ste. Croix 1981: 290 with n. 27; Gschnitzer 1981: 134–35; more bibliography in Raaflaub 1994: 133 n. 69.

74. See Donlan 1980: chaps. 4–5; Stein-Hölkeskamp 1989: 224–30: and esp. Ober 1989, 1998a; Bleicken 1994: 371–79, 571–72.

75. See bibliography cited in n. 45.

76. Ruschenbusch 1979: 16–17, 42.

77. See Schuller 1979: 435 (inscriptions), 1984 (connection between empire, increased decision making in foreign policy, and democracy). Organizational modifications: Rhodes 1972: 16–21; Ostwald 1988: 329; Ryan 1994 (introduction of the prytanies); Hignett 1952: 216–18; Wade-Gery 1958: 180–200; Ostwald 1986: 62–77 (multiple *dikastēria* replacing the single *hēliaia*).

78. That later sources exaggerated this controversy for rhetorical and moralistic purposes (Andrewes 1978a; and bibliography cited in chap. 4.2, n. 67, above) is no reason to contest the fact as such.

79. Meier 1972: 825 (my tr.).

80. On the continuing role of the hoplites: Ridley 1979; Hanson 1996. On their political attitudes (in favor of peace but not against democracy): Nippel 1980: 68ff.

81. Humphreys 1974: 93–94; Reinau 1981: 48–49. For summaries of the discussion on the citizenship law: Rhodes 1981: 331–35; Patterson 1981: esp. chap. 4. For more recent explanations: Boegehold 1994; and the summary in Raaflaub 1998c: 35–36. Building program: Plut. *Per.* 12 with bibliography cited in n. 64 above; on the use of league money: Kallet 1998: 48–52 with bibliography.

82. See Meier 1993b: 166–203.

83. Wade-Gery 1932: 205–6; see also Ehrenberg 1954: 84ff.; Frost 1964; Meyer 1967; Will 1972: 268ff.; Andrewes 1978a; Ruschenbusch 1979: 88ff.; Klein 1979; Nippel 1980: 65–66; Stahl 1987: 38–40; Podlecki 1998: chap. 10; and generally Schubert 1994.

84. "Lover": Thuc. 2.43.1, cf. 60.5; Pusey 1940; Connor 1971: chap. 3; Monoson 1994; Wohl 1999. On the citizen's "political identity": Meier 1980: 247ff. (= 1990: chap. 6). On typology: Raaflaub 1994: 104–14. On democratic warfare: Hanson 2001. On Pericles: also de Romilly 1963: 150.

85. See bibliography cited in n. 9 above.

86. Thus Bleicken 1994: 545. Debate of 430s: n. 65 above.

87. For a more detailed discussion (with additional sources and bibliography): Raaflaub 1980. On the right of speech in general: Momigliano 1971, 1974. On *parrhēsia*: Peterson 1929; Schlier 1954; Scarpat 1964. On the intellectual's and comedian's right to free speech: Radin 1927; Herrmann 1964; Dover 1976; Halliwell 1991; Wallace 1994; Henderson 1998. On freedom of speech in democracy: Bonner 1933: 67ff.; Tarkiainen 1966: 296ff., 329ff.; Finley 1976b. On the period when the right of speech was institutionalized in the *ekklēsia*: Griffith 1966; Woodhead 1967; Lewis 1971. Wallace forthcoming is important for all aspects discussed in this section.

88. The evidence is listed in chap. 3.2, n. 170, above. For later evidence: "Materialien," sec. 8.3.b–c (add there in n. 260: Soph. fr. 927a *TrGF*).

89. E.g., Soph. *OT* 408–10.

90. See above, chap. 3.2 at n. 167. On the time and importance of the coining of *isēgoria*: bibliography cited in n. 87; Raaflaub 1980: 23ff. On its significance in Cleisthenes' new order: Woodhead 1967; Raaflaub 1980: 31ff.. On the importance of this development: esp. Meier 1980: 91ff., esp. 113ff., 247ff. (= 1990: chaps. 4, 6); Raaflaub 1980: 28ff., 1998b: 37–44.

91. Hdt. 5.78 (above at n. 13); 6.131.1 (democracy).

92. Ps. Xen. *AP* 1.2, 11–12.

93. For the same characteristic of *parrhēsia*: at n. 99 below.

94. On the word formation: Schlier 1954: 869 n. 1. *Parrhēsia* is first attested in Eur. *Hipp.* 422 (dated to 428); then *El.* 1049, 1056; *Or.* 905; *Ion* 672, 675; *Phoen.* 391; *Ba.* 668; and fr. 737 N; see also Democr., *VS*, no. 68 B226. For the continuing importance of *isēgoria*: Isocr. 6.97; Dem. 15.28; 21.124; 60.28; further references in Scarpat 1964: 22ff.

95. As, e.g., in Eur. *El.* 1049, 1056; *Ba.* 668; fr. 737 N. Additional references in Raaflaub 1980: 50 n. 61.

96. Democr., *VS*, no. 68 B226; Isocr. 6.97; Dem. fr. 21. See also the following n.

97. Eur. *Phoen.* 390–93; *Hipp.* 419–25; *Ion* 670–75 (clearly alluding to the restrictive Athenian citizenship law; cf., e.g., Soph. *Aj.* 1256–63; *OT* 408–10; see further "Materialien," sec. 8.1.d I with nn. 241ff.).

98. Theogn. 173–82, 667–82; also, e.g., 267–70, 419–20, 683–86. Dem. 45.79; [Dem.] 59.28.

99. See, among many, Soph. fr. 201b *TrGF* = 192 Pearson; Aristoph. *Thesm.* 541; Nicostr. com. fr. 30 *PCG* = 29 Edm.; [Demad.] 43, 54; Plat. *Gorg.* 461e; Dem. 18.77; 21.123–24; 60.26. See also Scarpat 1964: 29ff.

100. E.g., Eur. *Or.* 902–5; Isocr. 7.20; Plat. *Rep.* 557b.

101. An alternative explanation might be that *parrhēsia* was primarily a negative term (see previous n.) introduced by opponents to counter the positive value of *isēgoria*. The earliest attestations, though, are positive (Euripides, Democritus, cited in nn. 94–95); so are most of those in the orators. Moreover, as in *isonomia*, in *isēgoria* the scope of equality was not fixed; hence, the term could not be monopolized entirely by democracy. For further discussion, see the chaps. by David Carter and myself in the acts of the conference "Freedom of Speech in Classical Antiquity," organized by Ralph Rosen and Ineke Sluiter in May 2002 at the University of Pennsylvania.

102. See above at n. 86 and bibliography in n. 65.

103. Ps. Xen. *AP* 1.6–9 (partly quoted above at n. 31). This treatise, highly informative, can hardly have been unique. *Stasis* had been prevalent in other Greek poleis and had intensified during the war (Thuc. 3.69ff., esp. 82–84); the events of 411 and 404 merely proved that Athens was not immune; see Heuss 1973: 17–37; Gehrke 1985; Price 2001. On legal restrictions of free speech: e.g., Finley 1976b; Henderson 1998; Wallace forthcoming.

104. See, for similar cases, Thuc. 4.105.2–106.1, 114.3.

105. De Romilly 1963: 7–8; Meier 1980: 304 with n. 72 (= 1990: 172–73 with n. 75). See at nn. 47–49, 62, above.

106. On all this, see, e.g., Whibley 1896: chap. 1, esp. 38ff.; Larsen 1955a; Adkins 1960: chaps. 8ff.; Meier 1972: 2ff.; Arnheim 1977: chaps. 5–6; Donlan 1980: 113ff.; Stein-Hölkeskamp 1989: 205ff.; Starr 1992; Ostwald 2000: chaps. 1–2. On the terms *oligarchia* and *aristokratia*: n. 55 above. On "rule by the best": e.g., Hdt. 3.81.3, 82.3; Ps. Xen. *AP* 1.1–9.

107. Ps. Xen. *AP* 1.2, 6–9; see also 3.11; Ostwald 1969: 82ff.

108. See Collard 1975: 2.198–99. On Theseus as the founder of Athenian democracy: Wade-Gery 1958: 86ff.; Ruschenbusch 1958: 408ff., esp. 415ff.; as *prostatēs dēmou* in Periclean manner: Eur. *Supp.* 393–94 (to be compared with Thuc. 2.65.8–9); *FGrH* 3b supp. 1.311 (on Philochorus 328 F19); Fitton 1961: 432–33. For the use of *isopsēphos* for "equality of vote": Thuc. 1.141.6; 3.11.4 (with *HCT* ad loc.); elsewhere it can describe the tie in a vote: Aesch. *Eum.* 741, 795.

109. For equality of rich and poor, see also fr. 362.7 N and additional references in Collard 1975: vol. 2, ad loc. For the background of the high valuation of rotation in office: Meier 1982: 824 (with bibliography).

110. Cf. esp. Soph. fr. 201b *TrGF* = 192 Pearson. Finley (1976b: 10) calls attention to the boldness of the idea of full equality of justice developed in Eur. *Supp.* 433ff.; see also Ostwald 1969: 47; de Romilly 1971a: 11, 20–21, 148.

111. From about the last third of the century, *autokratōr* provides a new term for "sovereignty"; see esp. Hippoc. *Aer.* 16; Thuc. 3.62.4; 4.63.2; 5.27.2. The word is first attested epigraphically: ML, no. 49, line 9 (dated to 445, referring to the authority of the founder of a colony). ML, no. 58, line 9, *he bole autokrator esto* (*IG* I³ 52, the financial decree of Callias, dated traditionally to 434/433, but to 422/421 by Mattingly 1996 [see index] and even later by others; Samons [2000: 113–33] now argues for 432). The term initially designated the authority of generals or officials, then that of democratic institutions, and finally the sovereignty of the demos in a democracy. A comprehensive examination of the concept's development and meaning is overdue; see, e.g., Soph. *Aj.* 1099 for a forerunner. See Schelle 1932; R. Kuhlen, *HWPh* 1 (1971): 694; *HCT* at Thuc. 1.126.8; 6.8.2 (with bibliography); Meier 1982: 824. P. J. Rhodes in *DNP* 2 (1997): 355 offers little illumination. Thuc. 4.63.2 combines *eleutheros* and *autokratōr*. On *eleutheros* in the sense of "sovereign": chap. 5.2, n. 79, above.

112. On *isokratia*: Ostwald 1973. See above at n. 108 for the paraphrase of *dēmokratia* in *Supp.* 352, and n. 46 for that in *Supp.* 406. On the "power and rule" of the demos: Meier 1982: 824. That *isonomia* contains both components mentioned here (though with varying emphasis) is agreed upon by, e.g., Vlastos 1953: 347ff., esp. 350; Scarpat 1964: 15–16; Ehrenberg 1965a: 157; Borecký 1971: 12ff., 19–20 (on the present passage); Finley 1976b: 10. It is certainly paraphrased in 406–7, and Collard (1975: 2.224 at *Supp.* 429–32) points out that *nomoi koinoi* should be understood in the same sense, since *isonomia* is usable only in prose. The paraphrase of *isēgoria* in 438ff. is obvious.

113. On the play's political themes and the interpretation of the constitutional debate: see Zuntz 1955: 8, 16ff.; de Romilly 1969; Collard 1975: 2.212 (with parallels and bibliography); Bleicken 1979: 158ff.; Burian 1985; Raaflaub 1989b: 45–46, 51–52; Michelini 1994.

114. See generally Kakridis 1961; de Romilly 1963: 130ff.; Flashar 1969 (with Drexler 1976: 239ff.); Loraux 1986; and recently *CT* 1.294–96. On parallels between Euripides and Thucydides: e.g., Finley 1967: chap. 1 (first published in 1938); de Romilly 1963: 133ff.; Collard 1975: 2.212; *HCT* ad loc. That the ideal set up here will soon be dismantled (in the description of the plague and later events) is well known; see, e.g., Connor 1984: 63–65.

115. Specifically on the interpretation of Thuc. 2.37: Kakridis 1961: 22ff.; Vretska 1966;

Flashar 1969: 17ff.; Gaiser 1975 (with a critical postscript by Flashar, 102ff.); *CT* 1.298–99 (with recent bibliography); Harris 1992. Generally on Thucydides' attitude toward democracy: Mc-Gregor 1956; Edelmann 1975: 320–27; Farrar 1988: chap. 5; Pope 1988; Ober 1998a: chap. 2.

116. Free paraphrase; for my interpretation of this difficult sentence, see, apart from the commentaries (*HCT;* Rhodes 1988; Rusten 1989; *CT*), Vretska 1966: 111–12; Grant 1971; Sealey 1974: 281–82; Lévy 1976: 125–26; Nippel 1980: 51 n. 35; Harris 1992.

117. Despite the objections of Vlastos (1964: 15–16) and (Ostwald 1969: 114 n. 3), I see in Thuc. 2.37.1 a paraphrase of *isonomia;* so, too, for various reasons, *HCT* 2.109–10; Vretska 1966: 111; Flashar 1969: 18. The idea probably is that precisely because democracy fully guarantees *isonomia,* it is possible to take *aretē* into account, regardless of wealth and birth.

118. Hence, public and private life are constantly juxtaposed in this chapter. See also Thuc. 2.40.2; de Romilly 1963: 137–38.

119. *HCT* 2.110–11; Diller 1962a: 201–2; Flashar 1969: 44ff., esp. 51, 53–54.

120. *HCT* 2.114–15; and, for the following, *CT* 1.298–303.

121. See esp. Thuc. 4.86.4–5; 8.68.4, 71.1. Ps. Xen. *AP* 1.1ff. of course disagrees.

122. Freedom: see esp. Thuc. 7.69.2; cf. *HCT* 4 ad loc.; Gomme 1962: 143–44; de Romilly 1963: 80; Flashar 1969: 52. Qualities: see, in 2.41.1 (chap. 5.2 at nn. 98–99 above), the reference to the citizen's individual self-sufficiency; furthermore, 2.43.4 (with Kakridis 1961: 93; Flashar 1969: 30–31), 65.8 (the ideal realization of such capabilities in Pericles).

123. Cf. Thuc. 2.40.5 and chap. 5.2, n. 88, above.

124. Fear of *nomoi:* Thuc. 2.37.3 with *HCT* ad loc.; *CT* 1.299–300, 301–3 with recent bibliography. See also Aeschin. 1.4–5. Aristoph. *Eccl.* 938ff. offers a nice parody. Demaratus: Hdt. 7.104.4 (below at n. 144); cf. Thuc. 1.84.3.

125. Aristot. *Pol.* 6.2.1317a40ff., cf. b1off. (tr. T. A. Sinclair); cf. Mulgan 1970: 95ff.; Schütrumpf 1996: 617f.

126. Eur. *Supp.* 406–8 (above at nn. 109–12); cf., importantly, Hdt. 3.83.2.

127. Hansen (1991: 82–83, 1996: 92–93) contests the widespread view that *isonomia* was "the central aspect of democratic equality and of democratic ideology altogether." His evidence is largely influenced by conditions in the fourth century, when *eleutheria* and *parrhēsia* perhaps indeed overshadowed *isonomia.* In most of the fifth century the situation was different. Further arguments against Hansen's view in Raaflaub 1996b: 163 n. 44.

128. Especially since the corresponding criteria for aristocracy and oligarchy are frequently mentioned by authors of the late fifth century (below at nn. 156ff.). The related principle, that freedom is also the purpose and goal of democracy (Aristot. *Rhet.* 1365b21ff., esp. 1366a2ff.), was perhaps already familiar as well. Free status as sole criterion: Aristot. *Pol.* 1282b23–83b20, 1286a36, 1290a30ff., 1294a9ff., 1299b20ff., 1301a28ff.; *EN* 1131a25ff.

129. Ps. Xen. *AP* 1.10–12 (see above at n. 92); see also Dem. 9.3–4.

130. Plat. *Rep.* esp. 557b–558c, 559d–563e; see also 572bff.

131. Aristot. *Pol.* 5.9.1310a25ff. See also 1316b24, 1328b40, 1319b30; Mulgan 1970: 99ff.; Schütrumpf 1996: 541–43.

132. See also Meier 1978: 25. For a more thorough investigation of this topic than can be provided here, and one that transcends the boundaries of Athenian democracy: Barker 1918: 7–8; Gomme 1962: 139–55; Ténékidès 1970; Finley 1976b; Vamvoukos 1979; Hansen 1996; Ostwald 1996; Wallace 1996, forthcoming.

133. "Popularklage": Aristot. *AP* 9.1 (described, typically, as one of Solon's measures that were, not most *eleuthera,* but *dēmotikōtata,* most democratic or most friendly to the people) with Rhodes 1981: ad loc.; Plut. *Sol.* 18.6–7 with Manfredini and Piccirilli 1977: ad loc.; Ruschenbusch 1978: 47–53. *Ephesis:* Wade-Gery 1958: 180ff.; Paoli 1959; Just 1965; MacDowell 1978:

30–31. *Eisangelia:* Hansen 1975, 1980; MacDowell 1978: index, s.v.; Rhodes 1979. On the other issues mentioned: Hansen 1996: 97 with sources.

134. Comparable in late republican Rome to measures that were explicitly called "bulwarks of freedom" (*arces libertatis tuendae,* Livy 3.45.8), such as the *provocatio,* intercession by the tribunes of the plebs, or the secret ballot; see Wirszubski 1950: 62–65; Bleicken 1972: esp. 31ff.; see also below, chap. 7.2 (beginning).

135. Eur. *Supp.* 433ff.; Thuc. 2.37.1–2; Ostwald 1969: 113 n. 1.

136. Dem. 18.132; 22.47–59 (esp. 51–52, 53ff.), 68; 24.160–69; in addition, esp. Ps. Andoc. 4.16ff., esp. 17; Plut. *Alc.* 16.5.

137. Xen. *Symp.* 4.31 (mentioning the freeman's right to travel wherever he wants) falls in a different category.

138. Dem. 21.123–24; see Nicostr. com. fr. 30 *PCG* = 29 Edm.

139. Self-assertion: at n. 78 above; as well as Raaflaub 1980: 20–21, 1994: 138–46. Indivisibility, *politeia:* chap. 7.2 before n. 29 below. See also the next section, on *nomos.*

140. See the beginning of chap. 7.2.

141. "Materialien," sec. 15.7.i–m. Some evidence is listed in n. 198 below; see also above at nn. 129–31. For discussion of such criticism: Mulgan 1970: esp. 105. On democracy and *nomos* in general: Jones 1957: 50ff.; Tarkiainen 1966: 351ff.; Dover 1974: 288ff.; de Romilly 1975: 73ff.; de Ste. Croix 1981: 284–85; Ostwald 1986: 250ff. and index, s.v. *Nomos.*

142. E.g., Heinimann 1945: 59ff.; Ostwald 1969: 20ff., 1986: esp. chap. 2; Quass 1971: 14ff.; Lévy 1976: 90ff., 165ff., 173ff.

143. See esp. Xen. *Cyr.* 8.1.4 (for a contrast, Xen. *Lak. pol.* 8.2); Dem. 24.5, 160ff.; 22.47ff.; Ps. Andoc. 4.19; then esp. Plato. *Rep.* 563d; *Laws* 698–99; Aristot. *Pol.* 1286a36ff., 1310a25ff., 1317b10ff.

144. On this passage, see, among many, Heinimann 1945: 29ff.; Dihle 1962; von Fritz 1965: 7ff., 1967: 254ff.; Cobet 1971: 114ff.; Thomas 2000: chap. 4.

145. Herodotus describes how Sparta (1.65ff.) and Athens (5.66–78) achieved this good order and, consequently, their position of predominance in Greece: Pohlenz 1937: 33ff.; and my comment in von Ungern-Sternberg and Reinau 1988: 213 n. 73. Lycurgus is here seen in analogy with Cleisthenes, Spartan *eunomia* with Athenian *isonomia.* For the analogy, on the level of *eunomia,* between Lycurgus and Solon: Szegedy-Maszak 1978. Imposed law: esp. Hdt. 1.96ff.; Pohlenz 1937: 23; von Fritz 1967: 287ff.; Dewald 2003.

146. Hdt. 7.135.2 (chap. 5.2 at n. 115 above); see also Aesch. *Pers.* 181ff., 241–42; Hippoc. *Aer.* 16, 23. On the Greeks' misunderstanding of Persian vassalage: chap. 3.2, n. 189, above.

147. See esp. von Fritz 1965, 1967: 254ff. (also on Athens). Heinimann (1945: 34) considers the emphasis placed on Sparta less significant. On Spartan pride in freedom: above at n. 34.

148. Herodotus leaves no doubt that Sparta aimed primarily at defending the Peloponnese and was willing to sacrifice the rest of Greece (e.g., 8.56–63, 74; 9.7–11). Thucydides: chap. 5.3 above.

149. On Athens's Panhellenic responsibility: e.g., Hdt. 7.139; 8.140–44; Thuc. 1.73–74; 2.40.5. Suppliant plays: chap. 5.2 at n. 84 above. On the superior goal of communal and individual happiness, see the contrast between Athens (Thuc. 5.9.1, emphasizing the causal chain of bravery-*eleutheria-eudaimonia*) and Sparta (2.43.4, freedom through bravery). See also Plut. *Cleom.* 9.1 on the Spartan sanctuary of Fear ("They honor Phobos ... because they believe that fear is the main bond that holds their *politeia* together"), compared with Thuc. 2.37.3, where Pericles mentions fear of laws and officials (see n. 124) but defensively, almost as an afterthought.

150. E.g., Ps. Xen. *AP* 1.13 and sources listed in n. 143. One need only think of the harm done

to Athens's reputation throughout the centuries by the exceptional case of the Arginusae trial (Xen. *Hell.* 1.7.1ff., esp. 12); see Bleicken 1994: 353–56.

151. See, among others, Jones 1957: 52ff.; Tarkiainen 1966: 353ff. (both with additional references).

152. On the difficulties of realizing this concept: Finley 1976b: 10ff.

153. Bleicken 1994: 325–30, 351–58, with bibliography on 625, 627. See also Ostwald 1986; Sealey 1987; Eder 1998; who all, but variously, see increasing emphasis on law as crucial in the development of democracy in the late fifth and fourth centuries.

154. See below at nn. 169ff.

155. Hdt. 8.144.1–2 and n. 153 above. See also the discussion of Athens's claim to *prostasia* (chap. 5.1 at n. 19). On the problem of "Hellenic *nomoi*": Ostwald 1982: 2–3, 1986: 100–108; Karavites 1982a: esp. chaps. 1 and 4 and pp. 85ff.; cf. *CT* 1.302–3 (with recent bibliography).

156. See Meder 1938; Prestel 1939; Larsen 1954; Jones 1957: 41ff.; de Romilly 1975; Wolff 1979; Roberts 1994; Ober 1996: chap. 10, 1998a..

157. On the author's terminology: Sealey 1974; generally, e.g., Meder 1938: 152ff.; Prestel 1939: 66ff.; Frisch 1942. For more recent discussion of this treatise: Gehrke 1997; Gigante and Maddoli 1997.

158. Ps. Xen. *AP* 1.1–9, 3.11. On self-interest and utilitarianism in fifth-century thought: Spahn 1986.

159. Ps. Xen. *AP* 1.1ff., esp. 5, 9. On *eunomia:* chap. 2.3, n. 164, above; Grossmann 1950: 30ff.

160. Thus esp. Ps. Xen. *AP* 2.20; cf. Thuc. 6.89.3ff. At their core, these are very old views, found already in Pindar and Theognis. See Prestel 1939; Grossmann 1950; then esp. Donlan 1980 (with numerous references); as well as Adkins 1960, 1972; Lintott 1981: 168ff.; Stein-Hölkeskamp 1989.

161. Hdt. 3.80.2ff., esp. 6, 83.2; Eur. *Supp.* 349ff., 404ff., 429ff., 438ff.

162. The corresponding passage in Eur. *Supp.* 410ff. is more differentiated and adds emphasis on economic aspects and the fickleness of popular favor.

163. The latter in Hdt. 3.81.3, 82.3; on the nature of these debates: Bleicken 1979: 159ff.; Raaflaub 1989b: 41–46; and above at n. 113.

164. Thuc. 6.32.3ff. Cleon: *HCT* 4.301, but see Lintott 1981: 192. How much this really had to do with Syracuse is another question; possibly (although there is no way to prove this) the demagogue's name (attested once for a sixth-century tyrant in Ephesus [*Suda*, s.v. "Hipponax"] and more frequently in the Hellenistic period [*RE* 2.2 (1896): 2020]) is intended here to serve as a "pointer" (analogous to Prot-agoras, Arist-agoras, Is-agoras, etc.: "he is Athenian in speaking," "he speaks like an Athenian"), suggesting that his speech is intended to complement preceding Athenian debates. For comments on his speech: *HCT* 4 ad loc.; Larsen 1955a: 43–44; Sealey 1974: 282–83; de Romilly 1975: 150ff.; Nippel 1980: 49–50; Lintott 1981: 191ff.; Connor 1984: 168–76. On the oligarchs' exploitation of the demos: de Ste. Croix 1981: 287–88. On Thucydides' assessment of stasis as a decisive motive for war: Lévy 1976: 37ff.; Price 2001: esp. chap. 6.

165. See, e.g., Isocr. 7.21; Plat. *Rep.* 558c; *Laws* 757b. More below, n. 196.

166. Hdt. 3.80.6: "in the many is all" (*en . . . tōi pollōi eni ta panta*); see Heuss 1965: 81; a different view in Meier 1980: 287 (= 1990: 164). Theory: Aristot. *Pol.* 1281a40ff.; Braun 1959; de Romilly 1975: 66ff.

167. On Athenagoras's phrase (6.39.1: *krinai d'an akousantas arista tous pollous*): *HCT* 4 ad loc.; Meier 1972: 828; Nippel 1980: 50. Pericles in Thuc. 2.37.1; cf. 40.2, 41.1. Protagoras in Plat. *Prot.* 320c ff., esp. 323a (see also 319b–d). The contrary view is expressed, e.g., in Hdt. 3.82.4 (quoted above at n. 162); Thuc. 3.37–38 (esp. 38.4ff.), 42–43; Eur. *Supp.* 412–22.

168. For a partial exception, focusing on the social level: below at n. 200.

169. Preparations: Thuc. 8.45ff. The oligarchic regimes: 8.65ff.; Aristot. *AP* 29ff.; Lys. *Or.* 20. For a detailed analysis of the sources: Busolt 1920: 69ff.; additional bibliography in Bengtson 1969: 245. See esp. Hignett 1952: 356ff.; Hackl 1960: 13ff.; Will 1972: 367ff.; Nippel 1980: 75ff.; Rhodes 1981: 362ff.; Lintott 1981: 135ff., 144ff.; *HCT* 5.93ff., esp. 184ff.; Ostwald 1986: 344ff.; Kagan 1987: chaps. 5–7; Lehmann 1987, 1997; Andrewes 1992: 471–81; Munn 2000: chap. 5. On the Five Thousand: *HCT* 5.323–28 (at Thuc. 8.97.2); Ostwald 1986: 395–411; Kagan 1987: chap. 8; Harris 1990; Bleckmann 1998: 358ff. On the political ideology of oligarchies: e.g., Whibley 1896; Larsen 1955b; Donlan 1980: 113ff.; Ostwald 2000.

170. In Thuc. 8.48.6, however, it is taken for granted that even in a democracy the elite profit most.

171. Power: Thuc. 8.48.1, 66.1, 70.1. Force: 8.48.6, 65.2, 66.2ff., 70.2, 74.2–3. The Five Thousand as mere show, disguising the narrow oligarchy of the Four Hundred: 8.66.1, 72.1; see Nippel 1980: 77–78. *Sōphrosunē*: North 1966; the contrast is with democracy as a "crazy" system: e.g., Ps. Xen. *AP* 1.9; Thuc. 6.89.5–6; and above at n. 159. Bearing arms: Thuc. 8.65.3.

172. Thuc. 8.89.2–3; cf. *HCT* 5.298ff.

173. See esp. Thuc. 8.66.2ff.; and n. 176 below.

174. Thuc. 8.68.4, 71.1; Andoc. 2.27 (written in 409/408).

175. Esp. Thuc. 8.66.2ff., 74.3.

176. See Thuc. 8.47.2, 48.1–2, 53.1, 56. In 48.3 and 54.1 Thucydides asserts that it was only the prospect of this alliance that made the people willing to accept an oligarchy, and only temporarily.

177. Thuc. 8.72.1; cf. 53.3, 86.3. On the significance of the concept of deliverance (*sōtēria*) in this context: Bieler 1951; Lévy 1976: 16ff.; Turato 1979.

178. Thuc. 8.70.2, 71.1, 3; offer of peace turned down in 86.3; cf. 89.2.

179. Democrats: Thuc. 8.75.2; see also 89.1. Oligarchs: 8.89.2, 90.1–2, 3ff., 91.1–2, 92.1–2. Thucydides' own comment: 91.3. See in general Will 1972: 371ff.; Lintott 1981: 145ff. Lévy (1976: 32ff.) documents the prominence of the subject of treason in 411.

180. For discussion of Thucydides' judgment: *HCT* 5 at 8.91.3 (with additional references).

181. References in Berve 1967: 2.632. The "archonless year," caused by the removal of the eponymous archon chosen during the oligarchy from the list of archons (Xen. *Hell.* 2.3.1), is symptomatic. On the Thirty: e.g., Cloché 1915; Lenschau 1937; Hignett 1952: 285ff.; Hackl 1960: 73ff.; Salmon 1969; Lehmann 1972; Will 1972: 393ff.; Lintott 1981: 158ff.; Rhodes 1981: 415ff.; Krentz 1982; Ostwald 1986: chap. 9; Lewis 1994: 32–40; Munn 2000: chaps. 8–10; see also Strauss 1986.

182. Xen. *Hell.* 2.3.12–13, 15, 25; and Theramenes' references to the contradiction between claims and reality in 2.3.19, 22.

183. For various aspects: esp. Lys. 12.5; Xen. *Hell.* 2.3.12 (the persecution of sycophants), 13, 48 (rejection of general participation in politics); Plat. *Ep.* 7.324d.

184. Moderates: Xen. *Hell.* 2.3.48; 4.9. Criticism of the anticipated number of only three thousand full citizens: 2.3.19. For another criterion, also rejected by democrats: Lys. 34.4–5. Radicals: Xen. *Hell.* 2.3.48.

185. Xen. *Hell.* 2.3.13 (see also 23); Lys. 12.51.

186. Terror: Xen. *Hell.* 2.3.12, 14, 17, 19, 21ff. (the murder of metics), 24, 26–27, 39–40, 42; 4.1. Disarming: 2.3.20, 41. Tyranny: 2.3.16; see also 48.

187. Xen. *Hell.* 2.3.13–14. The oligarchs at first paid expenses out of their own pockets; later they confiscated the money (21). See also Lys. 12.39–40, 58ff.

188. The references are numerous and unequivocal, even though the various aspects often

cannot be separated neatly. On tyrants: esp. Xen. *Hell.* 2.4.13, 17. On the few: Xen. *Hell.* 2.3.24; Lys. 12.73; 18.24; 31.26. On foreign rule: Lys. 2.61–62, 63–64; 12.94, 97; 26.2; 28.13; 31.31. See also Lys. 12.39, 67, 78; 13.17; 14.34; 18.5, 27; 31.32; 34.2, 11; *Syll.* 1.186.4ff.

189. See esp. Ps. Xen. *AP* 1.2, 14ff.; Thuc. 6.89.6; Momigliano 1944; de Romilly 1962; chap. 5.2 at n. 119 above.

190. See esp. Lys. 12.70; 25.32 (here in opposition to extreme democrats emulating the oligarchs); conversely 2.63 (concerning the return of the democrats); 28.14. Also Isocr. 7.64–65; 20.10. See in general Ténékidès 1954: 166; Lévy 1976: 34ff.

191. See, e.g., Ps. Xen. *AP* 2.14–15; and, in general, Prestel 1939: 75ff. and passim. See chap. 3.1 at n. 107 above. Fourth century: "Materialien," sec. 15.5.c, 7.e; de Ste. Croix 1981: 298–99.

192. See chap. 5.2 at nn. 111ff above.

193. The silence, in this respect, of Lysias, the "democrat" among the earlier Attic orators, is illuminating.

194. See the beginning of this section (at n. 105) and at nn. 47–49 above; see also Lys. 34.2–3.

195. See at nn. 161ff. above. The comparison between the political systems of Sparta and Athens in Dem. 20.107–8 illustrates this well; see also 15.17–18.

196. See esp. Aristot. *Pol.* 1280a9ff., 1301a25ff., b29ff.; Plat. *Rep.* 558c; *Gorg.* 508a–b; *Laws* 757a–e; Isocr. *Areop.* 21; Harvey 1965; de Romilly 1975: 49ff.

197. See above at n. 62.

198. Lys. 2.19; Isocr. 7.20; 10.32–36, esp. 35; 12.129–31; see n. 141. On *patrios politeia*: Hignett 1952: 268ff., 356ff.; Fuks 1953; Ruschenbusch 1958; Cecchin 1970; Finley 1971; Walters 1976; Nippel 1980: 85 n. 3; Ostwald 1986: index s.v.; Roberts 1994: 60–61, 64ff.

199. Pind. *Pyth.* 2.87; Her. 3.81.1–2.

200. For documentation: "Materialien," secs. 6.3, 8.3, 14.4. The following concepts are particularly important. (1) *Eleutheriotēs* (generosity, liberality) is encountered often in the fifth century (at the latest): "Materialien," secs. 4.2c, 6.3, 8.3d. (2) The concept of *enkuklios* or *eleutherios paideia* ("liberal arts," "liberal education," the Roman *artes liberales*) is not attested before the fourth century but certainly goes back to sophistic ideas in the fifth: "Materialien," sec. 14.5; see bibliography in *DNP* 2 (1997): 64; in addition, Beck 1964: esp. 72ff., 147ff.; and various contributions in Johann 1976. (3) The distinction between "free and unfree occupations" is also attested explicitly in the early fourth century but most likely is considerably older: "Materialien," sec. 14.6. For a more detailed discussion of the significance and origin of all concepts mentioned in this section: Raaflaub 1983: 527ff.

201. For fifth-century allusions to such a typology: above at n. 165.

202. See "Materialien," secs. 4.2, 6.3, 8.3. Aristotle sees *eleutheriotēs*, understood in this sense, as one of the cardinal virtues, and he tries to define the term frequently in his works on ethics; see "Materialien," sec. 14.4, esp. 4.b.

203. Stylow 1972: 3ff. with bibliography. What Gigon (1973: 9) emphasizes is much later and probably secondary.

204. See chap. 1.7, n. 74, above.

205. Details in "Materialien," secs. 14.4–7; and Raaflaub 1983: 527ff., esp. 533.

206. Compare here the saying that in Sparta the free (the Spartiates, because of their special status) were more completely free, the slaves more completely unfree than elsewhere (Critias, *VS*, no. 88 B37; Plut. *Lyc.* 28.11).

207. Esp. Cassola 1964a: 270; Nestle 1967: 16. See chap. 2.1, n. 26, and, generally, chap. 2.2 at nn. 58–60, chap. 3.2 at nn. 141ff.

208. This overlap of social and moral terminology has parallels elsewhere, too; e.g., English "mean," German *gemein,* meaning both "commoner" and "mean."

209. For a nice example: Eur. fr. 413 N.

210. See Meier 1978: 20ff. On the beginnings of this development: chap. 2.3 at nn. 136ff. above.

211. Above at n. 132.

212. See esp. Humphreys 1978: 149, 156; Raaflaub 1980: 38ff., esp. 44ff. Concept of the citizen: Manville 1990.

213. See, e.g., Beck 1964: 80; Heuss 1965: 78ff.; Martin 1974: 6; Meier 1978: 23 with n. 88; and esp. Gschnitzer 1981: 126ff.; Ober 1989: esp. 259–70. A partial countermovement began only toward the end of the Periclean period: Connor 1971: 87ff.

214. See Meier 1980: 257 with n. 23 (= 1990: 145–46), 1984; Raaflaub 1983: 531–32; more generally, Mossé 1969. On the citizens' exclusiveness: Gschnitzer 1981: 120–24; Patterson 1991: chap. 4. On Pericles' citizenship law: n. 81 above.

215. Bleicken 1994: 280–86, 534–38.

216. See esp. Bleicken 1979; Raaflaub 1989b.

7. Summary and Final Considerations

1. See my discussion of Patterson 1991 in the conclusion of chap. 2.2 (at nn. 103ff.).

2. Often, an issue is thematized, and a term coined for it, only when it loses its self-evident and unreflected acceptance. As good examples I mention *isonomia* as a term for aristocratic equality (chap. 3.2 at n. 159) and *aristokratia* as "rule of the best" in contrast to "rule by the masses"; see de Romilly 1959; Donlan 1969; Meier 1970: 42, 1972: 2–3. Generally on challenges to Greek aristocratic predominance: Starr 1977: chap. 6; Donlan 1980: chaps. 3–4; Stein-Hölkeskamp 1989: chap. 3. The terminology of "power" is no less instructive: Meier 1982: 822–23.

3. Which is also suggested, if correct, by the explanation of the word *turannos* as originating in Anatolia and meaning "master": Berve 1967: 1.3, 2.517. For recent discussion: Parker 1998: 145–49.

4. See here Ehrenberg's view of the polis (1965b = 1969, 1965a: 105–38) and that of his critics, including Schäfer 1963: 384–400; Fritz Gschnitzer (rev. in *ZRG* 80 [1963]: 400–404); Nörr 1966; Christian Meier (rev. in *Gnomon* 41 [1969]: 365–79). See also Welwei 1983: esp. pt. 2.

5. See now Patterson 1991: chaps. 1–2. On ancient Near Eastern conceptions of state and society: Jacobsen 1946. In an early phase of emerging Mesopotamian city-states, before the formation of large empires, this may have been different. On the role of councils and assemblies: Schemeil 1999; Fleming forthcoming.

6. O'Neil 1995; Robinson 1997.

7. Meier 1990: chaps. 3–4; Raaflaub 2000c: 39–48.

8. Herman 1987. On narrow oligarchies: Martin 1979a.

9. See Raaflaub 1992: 24–34, 2001b: 106–10. And see chap. 7.2 after n. 25 for freedom as a nonaristocratic value.

10. This is supported by the reflections of Heuss 1981: 18ff.

11. In this respect the Spartan *kosmos* based on *homoioi* did not differ from the isonomic Athenian polis.

12. See chap. 1.1 at n. 17 and 1.7 at n. 78.

13. The important function that the concept of equality assumed in this process, along with that of freedom, has been mentioned only occasionally in the present investigation; it deserves a more thorough analysis.

14. Patterson 1991: 3–4 and chap. 5.

15. As a contrast, see Plut. *Lyc.* 24 on Sparta (the ideal of oligarchy), where "no one was permitted to live as he pleased."

16. Heuss 1965: 82ff., esp. 84; see also Ruschenbusch 1978: chap. 3; Gehrke 1985; Price 2001.

17. On the Roman concept of freedom, see the bibliography cited in chap. 1.1, n. 12, to which I refer for details and documentation. For a comparison between Greek and Roman freedom: Raaflaub 1984b. For a different comparison: Martin 1979b.

18. In the period of the Etruscan kings, Rome was ruled, not by "the Etruscans," but by individual leaders of Etruscan origin, whose families had emigrated to Rome or who had seized power in Rome as leaders of warrior bands; see Cornell 1995: chaps. 5–6.

19. See Cic. *Rep.* 1.31.47; this privilege was of course reserved for the senatorial aristocracy.

20. Several laws introducing the secret ballot (*leges tabellariae*) were hailed as "protectors of freedom" as well; they were, like frequent polemics against the predominance of small factions (*factio paucorum*, denounced as a threat to *libertas populi*), the result of late republican power struggles between populist and conservative politicians (*populares, optimates*).

21. The description in the extant sources of the tyranny and expulsion of Tarquin the Proud (Cornell 1995: chap. 9; cf. 145–50) is strongly influenced by the Greek typology of tyranny and Greek models of the overthrow of tyranny. We cannot know to what extent liberty was an issue in the establishment of the aristocratic republic; the Roman patricians, like their Greek counterparts, may well have been more interested in obtaining a share in power and equality.

22. See bibliography in n. 2 above. Sparta experienced strong and long-lasting pressure, not from outside, but from within, caused by the oppressed helot population. Accordingly, in some respects, Sparta more than any other Greek state is closely comparable to Rome.

23. On the "struggle of the orders": Raaflaub 1986; Cornell 1995: chaps. 10–11, 13.

24. Raaflaub 1986: chap. 7.

25. On the problem of liberty vs. tyranny in Rome: n. 21 above. On the threat of tyranny in early republican Rome, which, as reported in the extant late sources, I consider of doubtful authenticity: Martin 1990; Cornell 1995: index, s.v. "tyrants."

26. Meier 1990: 165ff. (quot. 165, 166) (= 1980: 289ff. [289, 291]).

27. Meier 1990: 169–70 (= 1980: 297–98), also for subsequent quotes. I find Meier's comments here too sweeping. That Greek *eleutheria*, like Roman *libertas*, was initially linked to specific conditions and rights (169 = 297) seems doubtful. In Greece such links can be documented only rarely, and the conditions that prompted the specific evolution of *libertas* in Rome were lacking in Greece (see the comparison at the beginning of this section). The connection with equality (rightly stressed by Meier [169–70 = 297–98]) was established only late. On the basis of the considerations presented in chap. 6.2, I doubt whether freedom in Athens ever was a "simple matter of institutions" (170 = 298).

28. Meier 1990: 170 (= 1980: 298).

29. Bleicken 1994: 371–79; and chap. 6.1 at nn. 56ff. above.

30. Connor 1971; Meier 1972: 8. Betrayal: Ps. Xen. *AP* 2.20.

31. Raaflaub 1994: 138–46. Recognition: Strauss 1996.

32. Raaflaub 1994.

33. See chap. 4.2 at nn. 136ff. above. De Ste. Croix (1972: 16–21) emphasizes the limits of such analogies.

34. See, e.g., Aristot. *AP* 9.1, 10.1; see also Dem. 22.51.

35. For more details: Raaflaub 1980: 39ff., esp. 44–46. On the other hand, the citizenry now showed a marked interest in adopting values, norms, and behavior patterns of the upper class.

36. Ephorus, *FGrH* 70 F149 (Strabo 10.4.16).

37. Though not always as elementary as in the fragment of an anonymous comedian cited by Meier (1975: 427 n. 16): "Corcyra is free: pee where you want!"

Bibliography

Aalders, G. J. D. 1968. *Die Theorie der gemischten Verfassung im Altertum.* Amsterdam.

Accame, Silvio. 1962. *Gli albori della critica.* 2d ed. Naples.

Adkins, Arthur W. H. 1960. *Merit and Responsibility: A Study in Greek Values.* Oxford. Repr., Chicago, 1975.

———. 1971. "Homeric Values and Homeric Society." *JHS* 91: 1–14.

———. 1972. *Moral Values and Political Behaviour in Ancient Greece.* London.

———. 1985. *Poetic Craft in the Early Greek Elegists.* Chicago.

Alföldi, Andreas. 1934. "Die Ausgestaltung des monarchischen Zeremoniells am römischen Kaiserhofe." *RM* 49: 1–118.

———. 1955. "Gewaltherrscher und Theaterkönig." In Kurt Weitzmann, ed., *Late Classical and Medieval Studies in Honor of Albert M. Friend, Jr.,* 15–55. Princeton.

Allison, June W. 1989. *Power and Preparedness in Thucydides.* Baltimore.

Amandry, Pierre. 1971. "Collection Paul Canellopoulos (I)." *BCH* 95: 585–626.

———. 1987. "Trépieds de Delphes et du Péloponnèse." *BCH* 111: 79–131.

Ameling, Walter. 1985. "Plutarch, Perikles 12–14." *Historia* 34: 47–63.

———. 1993. *Karthago: Studien zu Militär, Staat und Gesellschaft.* Vestigia 45. Munich.

Amit, Moshe. 1970. "La date de l'alliance entre Athènes et Platées." *AC* 39: 414–26.

———. 1973. *Great and Small Poleis: A Study in the Relations between the Great Powers and the Small Cities in Ancient Greece.* Collection Latomus 134. Brussels.

Ampolo, Carmine. 1987. "Roma arcaica tra Latini ed Etruschi: Aspetti politici e istituzionali." In Mauro Cristofani, ed., *Etruria e Lazio arcaico,* 75–88. Rome.

Anderson, Greg. 2000. "Alkmeonid 'Homelands,' Political Exile, and the Unification of Attica." *Historia* 49: 387–412.

———. 2003. *The Athenian Experiment: Building an Imagined Political Community in Ancient Attica, 508–490 B.C.* Ann Arbor, Mich.

Ando, Clifford. 1999. "Was Rome a *Polis?*" *CA* 18: 5–34.

Andreae, Bernhard, and Hellmut Flashar. 1977. "Strukturäquivalenzen zwischen den homerischen Epen und der frühgriechischen Vasenkunst." *Poetica* 9: 217–65.

Andreev, Juri V. 1979. "Die politischen Funktionen der Volksversammlung im homerischen Zeitalter." *Klio* 61: 385–405.

Andrewes, Antony. 1938. "Eunomia." *CQ* 32: 89–102.

———. 1952. "Sparta and Arcadia in the Early Fifth Century." *Phoenix* 6: 1–5.

———. 1961. "Phratries in Homer." *Hermes* 89: 129–40.

357

————. 1978a. "The Opposition to Pericles." *JHS* 98: 1–8.

————. 1978b. "Spartan Imperialism?" In Garnsey and Whittaker 1978: 91–102.

————. 1982. "The Growth of the Athenian State," "The Tyranny of Pisistratus." In *CAH* 3.3²: 360–91, 392–416.

————. 1992. "The Spartan Resurgence." In *CAH* 5²: 464–98.

Anhalt, Emily K. 1993. *Solon the Singer: Politics and Poetics*. Lanham Md.

Annas, Julia. 1993. *The Morality of Happiness*. New York.

Apffel, Helmut. 1958. *Die Verfassungsdebatte bei Herodot*. Diss., Univ. of Erlangen. Repr., New York, 1979.

Aretz, Susanne. 1999. *Die Opferung der Iphigeneia in Aulis*. Stuttgart.

Arnheim, M. T. W. 1977. *Aristocracy in Greek Society*. London.

Arthur, Marilyn. 1973. "Early Greece: The Origins of the Western Attitude toward Women." *Arethusa* 6: 7–58. Repr. in John Peradotto and J. P. Sullivan, eds., *Women in the Ancient World: The* Arethusa *Papers*, 7–58. Albany, N.Y.

Asheri, David. 1988a. "Carthaginians and Greeks." *CAH* 4²: 739–80.

————, ed., comm. 1988b. *Erodoto, Le storie libro I: La Lidia e la Persia*. Milan.

————. 1990. *Erodoto, Le storie libro III: La Persia*. Milan.

Assmann, Jan. 1990. *Ma'at: Gerechtigkeit und Unsterblichkeit im Alten Ägypten*. Munich.

Athanassakis, Apostolos N. 1983. *Hesiod,* Theogony, Works and Days, Shield: *Translation, Introduction, Notes*. Baltimore.

Auffahrt, Christoph. 1991. *Der drohende Untergang: "Schöpfung" in Mythos und Ritual im Alten Orient und in Griechenland am Beispiel der* Odyssee *und des Ezechielbuches*. Berlin.

Austin, Michael M. 1990. "Greek Tyrants and the Persians, 546–479 B.C." *CQ* 40: 289–306.

Austin, Michael M., and Pierre Vidal-Naquet. 1977. *Economic and Social History of Ancient Greece: An Introduction*. Tr. and rev. M. M. Austin. Berkeley.

Aymard, André. 1967. *Etudes d'histoire ancienne*. Paris.

Backhaus, Wilhelm. 1976. "Der Hellenen-Barbaren-Gegensatz und die hippokratische Schrift *Peri aerōn hudatōn topōn*." *Historia* 25: 170–85.

Bacon, Helen H. 1961. *Barbarians in Greek Tragedy*. New Haven, Conn.

Badian, Ernst. 1971. "Archons and Strategoi." *Antichthon* 5: 1–34.

————. 1993. *From Plataea to Potidaea: Studies in the History and Historiography of the Pentecontaetia*. Baltimore.

————, ed. 1966. *Ancient Society and Institutions: Studies Presented to Victor Ehrenberg*. Oxford.

Bakker, Egbert. 2002. "The Making of History: Herodotus' *Historiēs Apodexis*." In Bakker et al. 2002: 3–32.

Bakker, Egbert J., Irene J. F. De Jong, and Hans van Wees, eds. 2002. *Brill's Companion to Herodotus*. Leiden.

Balcer, Jack M. 1964. "From Confederate Freedom to Imperial Tyranny: A Study of the Restrictions Imposed by Athens on the Political Self-Determination of the Member States in the Delian Confederacy, 478–431 B.C." Ph.D. diss., Univ. of Michigan.

————. 1974. "Separatism and Anti-Separatism in the Athenian Empire (478–433 B.C.)." *Historia* 23: 21–39.

————. 1976. "Imperial Magistrates in the Athenian Empire." *Historia* 25: 257–87.

————. 1978. *The Athenian Regulations for Chalkis: Studies in Athenian Imperial Law*. Historia Einzelschriften 33. Wiesbaden.

————. 1995. *The Persian Conquest of the Greeks, 545–450 B.C.* Xenia 38. Konstanz.

Balcer, Jack M., Hans-Joachim Gehrke, Kurt A. Raaflaub, and Wolfgang Schuller. 1984. *Studien zum Attischen Seebund*. Xenia 8. Konstanz.

Baldry, H. C. 1962. "The Idea of the Unity of Mankind." In Reverdin 1962: 169–95.

Baltrusch, Ernst. 1994. *Symmachie und Spondai: Untersuchungen zum griechischen Völkerrecht der archaischen und klassischen Zeit (8.–5. Jh. v. Chr.).* Berlin.

———. 1997. "Verträge zur Besserung der Welt, oder: War die *koinē eirēnē* zum Scheitern verurteilt?" *Göttinger Gelehrte Anzeigen* 249: 30–42.

Bannert, Herbert. 1987. "Versammlungsszenen bei Homer." In Jan M. Bremer et al., eds., *Homer: Beyond Oral Poetry: Recent Trends in Homeric Interpretation*, 15–30. Amsterdam.

Barcelò, Pedro. 1990. "Thukydides und die Tyrannis." *Historia* 39: 401–25.

Barker, Ernest. 1918. *Greek Political Theory: Plato and His Predecessors.* London. Repr., New York, 1960.

Barnes, Jonathan. 1992. "Aristotle and Political Liberty." In Günther Patzig, ed., *Aristoteles' Politik: Akten des XI. Symposium Aristotelicum (1987)*, 249–63 (with comments by Richard Sorabji, 264–76). Göttingen.

Barrett, W. S. 1973. "Pindar's Twelfth *Olympian* and the Fall of the Deinomenidai." *JHS* 93: 23–35.

Barron, John P. 1964a. "Religious Propaganda of the Delian League." *JHS* 84: 35–48.

———. 1964b. "The Sixth-Century Tyranny at Samos." *CQ* 14: 210–29.

———. 1990. "All for Salamis." In Craik 1990: 133–41.

Barron, John P., and P. E. Easterling. 1985. "Hesiod." In Easterling and Knox 1985: 92–105.

Bayer, Erich, and Jürgen Heideking. 1975. *Die Chronologie des perikleischen Zeitalters.* Darmstadt.

Beck, F. A. G. 1964. *Greek Education, 450–350 B.C.* New York.

Bees, R. 1993. *Zur Datierung des Prometheus Desmotes.* Stuttgart.

Bekker, Immanuel. 1814. *Anecdota Graeca.* Vol. 1. Berlin.

Bellen, Heinz. 1974. "Der Rachegedanke in der griechisch-persischen Auseinandersetzung." *Chiron* 4: 43–67.

Beloch, Karl Julius. 1893. *Griechische Geschichte.* Vol. 1. Berlin.

———. 1926. *Griechische Geschichte.* Vol. 2.1. 2d ed. Berlin.

Bengtson, Hermann. 1953–54. "Thasos und Themistokles." *Historia* 2: 485–86.

———. 1969. *Griechische Geschichte von den Anfängen bis in die römische Kaiserzeit.* 3d ed. HdAW 3.4. Munich.

———. 1974. *Kleine Schriften zur Alten Geschichte.* Munich.

———. 1975. *Die Staatsverträge des Altertums.* Vol. 2, *Die Verträge der griechisch-römischen Welt von 700–338 v. Chr.* 2d ed. Munich and Berlin.

Bennet, John. 1997. "Homer and the Bronze Age." In Morris and Powell 1997: 511–34.

Benveniste, Emile. 1969. *Le vocabulaire des institutions indo-européennes.* 2 vols. Paris.

Berding, Helmut. 1976. "Begriffsgeschichte und Sozialgeschichte." *HZ* 223: 98–110.

Beringer, Walter. 1961. "Zu den Begriffen für 'Sklaven' und 'Unfreie' bei Homer." *Historia* 10: 259–91.

———. 1964. "Der Standort des *oikeus* in der Gesellschaft des homerischen Epos." *Historia* 13: 1–20.

———. 1982. "'Servile Status' in the Sources for Early Greek History." *Historia* 31: 13–32.

———. 1985. "Freedom, Family, and Citizenship in Early Greece." In Eadie and Ober 1985: 41–56.

Bernhardt, Rainer. 1971. *Imperium und Eleutheria: Die römische Politik gegenüber den freien Städten des griechischen Ostens.* Diss., Univ. of Hamburg.

———. 1987. "Die Entstehung der Legende von der tyrannenfeindlichen Aussenpolitik Spartas im sechsten und fünften Jahrhundert v. Chr." *Historia* 36: 257–89.

Berve, Helmut. 1951–52. *Griechische Geschichte.* 2 vols. 2d ed. Freiburg.

———. 1954. "Wesenszüge der griechischen Tyrannis." *HZ* 177: 1–20. Repr. in Helmut Berve, *Gestaltende Kräfte der Antike,* 208–31. 2d ed. Munich, 1968; Gschnitzer 1969: 161–83.

———. 1967. *Die Tyrannis bei den Griechen.* 2 vols. Munich.

Bickerman, Elias. 1950. "Remarques sur le droit des gens dans la Grèce classique." *RD* 4: 99–127. German tr. in Gschnitzer 1969: 474–502.

———. 1958. "Autonomia: Sur un passage de Thucydide (1,144,2)." *RD,* 3d ser., 5: 313–44.

Bicknell, Peter J. 1969. "Whom Did Kleisthenes Enfranchise?" *PdP* 24: 34–37.

———. 1972. *Studies in Athenian Politics and Genealogy. Historia* Einzelschriften 19. Wiesbaden.

Bieler, Ludwig. 1951. "A Political Slogan in Ancient Athens." *AJP* 72: 181–84.

Bischoff, Heinrich. 1932. *Der Warner bei Herodot.* Diss., Univ. of Marburg. Borna and Leipzig.

Bleckmann, Bruno. 1998. *Athens Weg in die Niederlage: Die letzten Jahre des Peloponnesischen Kriegs.* Beiträge zur Altertumskunde 99. Stuttgart.

Bleicken, Jochen. 1962. "Der Begriff der Freiheit in der letzten Phase der römischen Republik." *HZ* 195: 1–20.

———. 1972. *Staatliche Ordnung und Freiheit in der römischen Republik.* Kallmünz.

———. 1979. "Zur Entstehung der Verfassungstypologie im 5. Jh. v. Chr." *Historia* 28: 148–72.

———. 1994. *Die athenische Demokratie.* 2d ed. Paderborn.

Boardman, John. 1975. "Herakles, Peisistratos and Eleusis." *JHS* 95: 1–12.

Boas, M. 1905. *De epigrammatis Simonideis commentatio critica.* Groningen.

Bock, Martin. 1958. "Aischylos und Akragas." *Gymnasium* 65: 402–50.

Boedeker, Deborah. 1983. "Hecate: A Transfunctional Goddess in the *Theogony?*" *TAPA* 113: 79–93.

———. 1993. "Hero Cult and Politics in Herodotus: The Bones of Orestes." In Dougherty and Kurke 1993: 164–77.

———. 1995. "Simonides on Plataea: Narrative Elegy, Mythodic History." *ZPE* 107: 217–29.

———. 2001. "Paths to Heroization at Plataea." In Boedeker and Sider 2001: 148–63.

Boedeker, Deborah, and John Peradotto, eds. 1987. *Herodotus and the Invention of History. Arethusa* 20.

Boedeker, Deborah, and Kurt Raaflaub, eds. 1998. *Democracy, Empire, and the Arts in Fifth-Century Athens.* Cambridge, Mass.

Boedeker, Deborah, and David Sider, eds. 2001. *The New Simonides: Contexts of Praise and Desire.* Oxford.

Boegehold, Alan L. 1965. "The Salamis Epigram." *GRBS* 6: 179–86.

———. 1994. "Perikles' Citizenship Law of 451/0 B.C." In Boegehold and Scafuro 1994: 57–66.

Boegehold, Alan L., and Adele C. Scafuro, eds. 1994. *Athenian Identity and Civic Ideology.* Baltimore.

Boersma, Johannes S. 1970. *Athenian Building Policy from 561/0 to 404/3 B.C.* Groningen.

Bölte, Felix. 1934. "Ein pylisches Epos." *RhM* 83: 319–47.

Bömer, Franz. 1957–63. *Untersuchungen über die Religion der Sklaven in Griechenland und Rom.* 4 vols. Abh. Akad. Mainz, geistes- und sozialwiss. Kl., 1957, 7; 1960, 1; 1961, 4; 1963, 10. Wiesbaden. 2d enl. ed. prepared by Peter Herz. Wiesbaden, 1981.

Bonner, Robert J. 1933. *Aspects of Athenian Democracy.* Berkeley and Los Angeles.

Bonner, Robert J., and Gertrude Smith. 1930. *The Administration of Justice from Homer to Aristotle.* Vol. 1. Chicago.

Borecký, Borivoj. 1971. "Die politische Isonomie." *Eirene* 9: 5–24.

Bosworth, A. B. 1992. "*Autonomia:* The Use and Abuse of Political Terminology." *SI,* 3d ser., 10: 122–52.

Bovon, A. 1963. "La représentation des guerriers perses et la notion de Barbare dans la première moitié du Vᵉ siècle." *BCH* 87: 579–602.

Bowden, Hugh. 1996. "The Greek Settlement and Sanctuaries at Naukratis: Herodotus and Archaeology." In Hansen and Raaflaub 1996: 17–37.

Bowen, A. J., tr., comm. 1992. *Plutarch: The Malice of Herodotus.* Warminster, England.

Bowersock, Glen W. 1966. "Pseudo-Xenophon." *HSCP* 71: 33–55.

———. 1968. "Constitution of the Athenians." In E. C. Marchant and G. W. Bowersock, eds., trs., *Xenophon,* vol. 7, *Scripta Minora,* 459–507. LCL 183. Cambridge, Mass.

Bowra, Cecil M. 1938. *Early Greek Elegists.* Cambridge, Mass. Repr., Cambridge, England, 1960.

———. 1958. "A Prayer to the Fates." *CQ,* n.s., 8: 231–40.

———. 1961. *Greek Lyric Poetry from Alcman to Simonides.* 2d ed. Oxford.

———. 1963. "Two Lines of Eumelus." *CQ,* n.s., 13: 145–53.

———. 1964. *Pindar.* Oxford.

Bradeen, D. W. 1955. "The Trittyes in Cleisthenes' Reforms." *TAPA* 86: 22–30.

———. 1960. "The Popularity of the Athenian Empire." *Historia* 9: 257–69.

———. 1969. "The Athenian Casualty Lists." *CQ* 19: 149–59.

Braun, E. 1959. "Die Summierungstheorie des Aristoteles." *JÖAI* 44: 157–84.

Braund, David. 1994. "The Luxuries of Athenian Democracy." *G&R* 41: 41–48.

Briant, Pierre. 1996. *Histoire de l'Empire Perse de Cyrus à Alexandre.* Paris.

Bringmann, Klaus. 1965. *Studien zu den politischen Ideen des Isokrates.* Hypomnemata 14. Göttingen.

———. 1976. "Die Verfassungsdebatte bei Herodot und Dareios' Aufstieg zur Königsherrschaft." *Hermes* 104: 266–79.

Broadhead, H. D. 1960. *The Persae of Aeschylus: Edited with Introduction, Critical Notes and Commentary.* Cambridge.

Bruce, I. A. F. 1967. *An Historical Commentary on the "Hellenica Oxyrhynchia."* Cambridge.

Bruck, Eberhard F. 1926. *Totenteil und Seelgerät im griechischen Recht.* Münchener Beiträge zur Papyrusforschung und antiken Rechtsgeschichte 9. Munich.

Brunner, Otto, Werner Conze, and Reinhart Koselleck, eds. 1972–97. *Geschichtliche Grundbegriffe: Historisches Lexikon zur politisch-sozialen Sprache in Deutschland.* 8 vols. Stuttgart.

Brunt, Peter A. 1953. "The Hellenic League against Persia." *Historia* 2: 135–63. Repr. in Brunt 1993: 47–83.

———. 1966. "Athenian Settlements abroad in the Fifth Century." In Badian 1966: 71–92. Repr. with a postscript in Brunt 1993: 112–36.

———. 1988. "*Libertas* in the Republic." In Peter A. Brunt, *The Fall of the Roman Republic and Related Essays,* 281–350. Oxford.

———. 1993. *Studies in Greek History and Thought.* Oxford.

Buchner, Edmund. 1958. *Der Panegyrikos des Isokrates: Eine historisch-philologische Untersuchung.* *Historia* Einzelschriften 2. Wiesbaden.

Buck, Carl Darling, and Walter Petersen. 1945. *A Reverse Index of Greek Nouns and Adjectives.* Chicago. Repr., Hildesheim, 1970.

Buck, Robert J. 1972. "The Formation of the Boeotian League." *CP* 67: 94–101.

———. 1979. *A History of Boeotia.* Edmonton.

Buckler, John. 1980. *The Theban Hegemony, 371–362 B.C.* Cambridge, Mass.

Buitron-Oliver, Diana, ed. 1992. *The Greek Miracle: Classical Sculpture from the Dawn of Democracy, the Fifth Century B.C.* Washington, D.C.

Burckhardt, Leonhard, and Jürgen von Ungern-Sternberg, eds. 2000. *Grosse Prozesse im antiken Athen.* Munich.

Burian, Peter. 1985. *"Logos* and *Pathos:* The Politics of the *Suppliant Women."* In Peter Burian, ed., *Directions in Euripidean Criticism: A Collection of Essays,* 129–55. Durham, N.C.

Burkert, Walter. 1976. "Das hunderttorige Theben und die Datierung der Ilias." *WS* 89: 5–21.

———. 1985. *Greek Religion.* Tr. John Raffan. Cambridge, Mass.

Burn, A. R. 1936. *The World of Hesiod.* London. Repr., New York, 1966.

———. 1962. *Persia and the Greeks: The Defence of the West c. 546–478 B.C.* London.

Burnett, Anne P. 1983. *Three Archaic Poets: Archilochus, Alcaeus, Sappho.* Cambridge, Mass.

Burstein, Stanley M., Ramsay MacMullen, Kurt A. Raaflaub, and Allen M. Ward. 1997. *Ancient History: Recent Work and New Directions.* Claremont, Calif.

Burton, Reginald W. B. 1962. *Pindar's Pythian Odes: Essays in Interpretation.* Oxford.

Busolt, Georg. 1875. "Der Zweite Athenische Bund und die auf der Autonomie beruhende hellenische Politik von der Schlacht bei Knidos bis zum Frieden des Eubulos." *Jahrbücher für classische Philologie* Suppl. 7: 641–866.

———. 1878. *Die Lakedaimonier und ihre Bundesgenossen.* Vol. 1. Leipzig.

———. 1893–1904. *Griechische Geschichte bis zur Schlacht bei Chaeronea.* 4 vols. 2d ed. Gotha. Repr., Hildesheim, 1967.

———. 1905. "Thukydides und der themistokleische Mauerbau: Ein Beitrag zur Sachkritik." *Klio* 5: 255–79.

———. 1920. *Griechische Staatskunde.* Vol. 1. HdAW 4.1.1.1. Munich.

Busolt, Georg, and Heinrich Swoboda. 1926. *Griechische Staatskunde.* Vol. 2. HdAW 4.1.1.2. Munich.

Busse, Dietrich. 1987. *Historische Semantik: Analyse eines Programms.* Stuttgart.

Calabi, Ida. 1953. *Ricerche sui rapporti fra le poleis.* Florence.

Calabi Limentani, Ida, ed., comm. 1964. *Plutarchi* Vita Aristidis: *Introduzione, testo, commento, traduzione e appendice.* Florence.

Calhoun, George. 1913. *Athenian Clubs in Politics and Litigation.* Austin, Tex.

———. 1962. "Polity and Society: The Homeric Picture." In Alan Wace and Frank Stubbings, eds., *A Companion to Homer,* 431–52. London.

Camassa, Giorgio. 1988. "Aux origines de la codification écrite des lois en Grèce." In Marcel Detienne, ed., *Les savoirs de l'écriture en Grèce ancienne,* 130–55. Lille.

———. 1996. "Leggi orali e leggi scritte: I legislatori." In Settis 1996–98: 2.1.561–76.

Camp, John M. 1986. *The Athenian Agora: Excavations in the Heart of Classical Athens.* London.

———. 2001. *The Archaeology of Athens.* New Haven, Conn.

Campbell, David A., ed. and tr. 1982–93. *Greek Lyric.* 5 vols. LCL. Cambridge, Mass.

Cargill, Jack. 1981. *The Second Athenian League: Empire or Free Alliance?* Berkeley.

Carlier, Pierre. 1977. "La vie politique à Sparte sous le règne de Cléomène Ier: Essai d'interprétation." *Ktema* 2: 65–84.

———. 1984. *La royauté en Grèce avant Alexandre.* Strasbourg.

———. 1991. "La procédure de décision politique du monde mycénien à l'époque archaïque." In Domenico Musti et al., eds., *La transizione dal miceneo all'alto arcaismo,* 85–91. Rome.

Carter, L. B. 1986. *The Quiet Athenian.* Oxford.

Cartledge, Paul. 1976. "A New Fifth-Century Spartan Treaty." *LCM* 1: 87–92.

———. 1978. "The New 5th-Century Spartan Treaty Again." *LCM* 3: 189–90.

———. 1979. *Sparta and Lakonia: A Regional History, 1300–362 B.C.* London.

———. 1980. "The Peculiar Position of Sparta in the Development of the Greek City-State." *PRIA* 80: 91–108.

———. 1987. *Agesilaos and the Crisis of Sparta.* London.

———. 1991. "Richard Talbert's Revision of the Spartan-Helot Struggle: A Reply." *Historia* 40: 379–81.

———. 1993. *The Greeks: A Portrait of Self and Others.* Oxford.

———. 1996a. "Comparatively Equal." In Ober and Hedrick 1996: 175–85.

———. 1996b. "La nascita degli opliti e l'organizzazione militare." In Settis 1996–98: 2.1.681–714.

———. 2001. "The Effects of the Peloponnesian (Athenian) War on Athenian and Spartan Societies." In McCann and Strauss 2001: 104–23.

Cartledge, Paul, and F. D. Harvey, eds. 1985. *Crux: Essays Presented to G. E. M. de Ste. Croix.* Exeter.

Cartledge, Paul, Paul Millett, and Stephen Todd, eds. 1990. *Nomos: Essays in Athenian Law, Politics and Society.* Cambridge.

Cassola, Filippo. 1964a. *"Eleutheros-ereutero."* In A. Guarino and L. Labruna, eds., *Synteleia Vincenzo Arangio-Ruiz,* 269–79. Naples.

———. 1964b. "Solone, la terra e gli ectemori." *PdP* 19: 26–68.

———. 1973. "La proprietà del suolo in Attica fino a Pisistrato." *PdP* 28: 75–87.

Castriota, David. 1992. *Myth, Ethos, and Actuality: Official Art in Fifth-Century Athens.* Madison, Wis.

Cataldi, Silvio. 1984. *La democrazia ateniese e gli alleati.* Padua.

Cavander, Kenneth. 1973. *Euripides,* Iphigeneia at Aulis: *A Translation with Commentary.* Englewood Cliffs, N.J.

Cawkwell, George L. 1973. "The Foundation of the Second Athenian Confederacy." *CQ,* n.s., 23: 47–60.

———. 1976. "Agesilaus and Sparta." *CQ,* n.s., 26: 62–84.

———. 1993. "Cleomenes." *Mnemosyne* 46: 506–27.

Cecchin, S. A. 1970. *Patrios politeia.* Turin.

Cerri, G. 1969. *"Isos dasmos* come equivalente di *isonomia* nella silloge teognidea." *QUCC* 8: 97–104.

Chadwick, John. 1976. *The Mycenaean World.* Cambridge.

———. 1988. "The Women of Pylos." In J.-P. Olivier and T. G. Palaima, eds., *Texts, Tablets and Scribes: Studies in Mycenaean Epigraphy and Economy Offered to Emmett L. Bennett, Jr.,* 43–95. *Minos* Suppl. 10. Salamanca.

Chambers, J. T. 1973. "Studies on the Fourth-Century Athenians' View of Their Past." Ph.D. diss., Univ. of Illinois, Urbana.

Chambers, Mortimer. 1990. *Aristoteles, Staat der Athener, übersetzt und erläutert.* Berlin.

———. 1992. "Photographic Enhancement and a Greek Inscription." *CJ* 88: 25–31.

———. 1993. "Aristotle and His Use of Sources." In Piérart 1993: 39–52.

Chambers, Mortimer, R. Gallucci, and P. Spanos. 1990. "Athens' Alliance with Egesta in the Year of Antiphon." *ZPE* 83: 38–63.

Chantraine, Pierre. 1958. *Grammaire homérique.* 2 vols. Paris.

Chrimes, Kathleen M. T. 1949. *Ancient Sparta: A Re-Examination of the Evidence.* Manchester, England.

Christ, Karl. 1967. *Antike Numismatik: Einführung und Bibliographie.* Darmstadt.

Clairmont, Christoph W. 1983. *Patrios Nomos: Public Burial in Athens during the Fifth and Fourth Centuries B.C.* 2 vols. British Archaeological Reports 161. Oxford.

Clerc, M. 1893. *Les métèques Athéniens.* Paris. Repr., New York, 1979.

Cloché, Paul. 1915. *La restauration démocratique à Athènes en 403 av. J.-C.* Paris. Repr., Rome, 1968.

———. 1952. *Thèbes de Béotie, des origines à la conquête romaine.* Namur.

Cobet, Justus. 1971. *Herodots Exkurse und die Frage der Einheit seines Werkes. Historia* Einzelschriften 17. Wiesbaden.

————. 1981. "König, Anführer, Herr; Monarch, Tyrann." In Welskopf 1981–85: 3.11–66.

Collard, Christopher. 1975. *Euripides, Supplices: Edited with Introduction and Commentary.* 2 vols. Groningen.

Conacher, D. J. 1956. "Religious and Ethical Attitudes in Euripides' *Suppliants.*" *TAPA* 87: 8–26.

Connor, W. Robert. 1971. *The New Politicians of Fifth-Century Athens.* Princeton.

————. 1977. "Tyrannis Polis." In John D'Arms and John W. Eadie, eds., *Ancient and Modern: Essays in Honor of Gerald F. Else,* 95–109. Ann Arbor.

————. 1984. *Thucydides.* Princeton.

————. 1988. "Early Greek Land Warfare as Symbolic Expression." *P&P* 119: 3–29.

————. 1994. "The Problem of Athenian Civic Identity." In Boegehold and Scafuro 1994: 34–44.

Constant, Benjamin. 1874. "De la liberté des ancients comparée à celle des modernes." In Benjamin Constant, *Oeuvres politiques,* 258–86. Paris.

Cook, Arthur B. 1914–40. *Zeus: A Study in Ancient Religion.* 3 vols. Cambridge.

Cook, Erwin. 1995. *The Odyssey in Athens: Myths of Cultural Origins.* Ithaca, N.Y.

————. Forthcoming. *Reading the Odyssey.*

Cook, J. M. 1961. "The Problem of Classical Ionia." *PCPhS,* n.s., 7: 9–18.

Coolsaet, W. 1993. *Autarkeia: Rivaliteit en zelfgenoegzaamheid in de Griekse cultuur.* Kampen and Kapelle.

Cornell, Timothy J. 1991. "Rome: The History of an Anachronism." In Molho et al. 1991: 53–69.

————. 1995. *The Beginnings of Rome: Italy and Rome from the Bronze Age to the Punic Wars (c. 1000–264 B.C.).* London.

Corsaro, Mauro. 1997. "I Greci d'Asia." In Settis 1996–98: 2.2.27–59.

Coulson, W. D. E., Olga Palagia, T. Leslie Shear Jr., H. Alan Shapiro, and Frank J. Frost, eds. 1994. *The Archaeology of Athens and Attica under the Democracy.* Oxford.

Cox, Cheryl Anne. 1998. *Household Interests: Property, Marriage Strategies, and Family Dynamics in Ancient Athens.* Princeton.

Craik, Elizabeth M., ed. 1990. *"Owls to Athens": Essays on Classical Subjects Presented to Sir Kenneth Dover.* Oxford.

Crane, Gregory. 1998. *Thucydides and the Ancient Simplicity: The Limits of Political Realism.* Berkeley and Los Angeles.

Crielaard, Jan Paul. 1995. "Homer, History and Archaeology: Some Remarks on the Date of the Homeric World." In Jan Paul Crielaard, ed., *Homeric Questions,* 201–88. Amsterdam.

Croce, Benedetto. 1930. *Constant e Jellinek intorno alla differenza tra la libertà degli antichi e quella dei moderni.* Naples.

Culham, Phyllis. 1978. "The Delian League: Bicameral or Unicameral?" *AJAH* 3: 27–31.

Dahlheim, Werner. 1977. *Gewalt und Herrschaft: Das provinziale Herrschaftssystem der römischen Republik.* Berlin.

Dandamaev (Dandamayev), M. A. 1972. "Politische und wirtschaftliche Geschichte." In Gerold Walser, ed., *Beiträge zur Achämenidengeschichte,* 15–58. Wiesbaden.

————. 1984. *Slavery in Babylonia from Napopolassar to Alexander the Great (626–331 B.C.).* Tr. Victoria A Powell. De Kalb, Ill.

Davies, John K. 1977–78. "Athenian Citizenship: The Descent Group and the Alternatives." *CJ* 73: 105–21.

————. 1992. "Greece after the Persian Wars." *CAH* 5²: 15–33.

————. 1993. *Democracy and Classical Greece.* 2d ed. Cambridge, Mass.

————. 1994. "The Tradition about the First Sacred War." In Simon Hornblower, ed., *Greek Historiography,* 193–212. Oxford.

————. 1996. "Deconstructing Gortyn: When Is a Code a Code?" In Foxhall and Lewis 1996: 33–56.

————. 1997. "The 'Origins of the Greek *Polis*': Where Should We Be Looking?" In Mitchell and Rhodes 1997: 24–38.

Davis, R. W., ed. 1995. *The Origins of Modern Freedom in the West.* Stanford, Calif.

Day, James, and Mortimer Chambers. 1962. *Aristotle's History of Athenian Democracy.* Berkeley. Repr., Amsterdam, 1967.

Debord, Pierre. 1973. "Esclavage mycénien, esclavage homérique." *REA* 75: 225–40.

Debrunner, Otto. 1947. "*Demokratia.*" In *Festschrift für Edouard Tièche,* 11–24. Berne. Repr. in Kinzl 1995: 55–69.

Degani, Enzo, ed. 1983. *Hipponax: Testimonia et Fragmenta.* Leipzig.

Deger-Jalkotzy, Sigrid. 1972. "The Women of PY An 607." *Minos* 13: 137–60.

————. 1988. "Landbesitz und Sozialstruktur im mykenischen Staat von Pylos." In Heltzer and Lipinski 1988: 31–52.

Delcourt, Marie. 1955. *L'oracle de Delphes.* Paris. Repr., 1981.

Detienne, Marcel. 1963. *Crise agraire et attitude religieuse chez Hésiode.* Collection Latomus 68. Brussels.

————. 1965. "En Grèce archaïque: Géométrie, politique et société." *Annales ESC* 20: 425–41.

————. 1996. *The Masters of Truth in Archaic Greece.* Tr. Janet Lloyd. New York.

Deubner, Ludwig. 1932. *Attische Feste.* Berlin.

Develin, Robert, and Martin Kilmer. 1997. "What Kleisthenes Did." *Historia* 46: 3–18.

Dewald, Carolyn. 1997. "Wanton Kings, Pickled Heroes, and Gnomic Founding Fathers: Strategies of Meaning at the End of Herodotus's *Histories.*" In Deborah H. Roberts, Francis M. Dunn, and Don Fowler, eds., *Classical Closure: Reading the End in Greek and Latin Literature,* 62–82. Princeton.

————. 2003. "Form and Content: The Question of Tyranny in Herodotus." In Morgan 2003: 25–58.

Dickinson, O. T. P. K. 1994. *The Aegean Bronze Age.* Cambridge.

Diehl, Ernst, ed. 1925. *Anthologia Lyrica Graeca.* Vol. 2. 2d ed. Leipzig.

————. 1949. *Anthologia Lyrica Graeca.* Vol. 1. 3d ed. Leipzig.

Diels, Hermann, and Walther Kranz, eds., trs. 1961. *Die Fragmente der Vorsokratiker.* Vol. 1. 10th ed. Berlin.

Dihle, Albrecht. 1962. "Herodot und die Sophistik." *Philologus* 106: 207–20.

————. 1970. *Homer-Probleme.* Opladen.

————. 1994. *Die Griechen und die Fremden.* Munich.

Diller, Hans. 1962a. "Freiheit bei Thukydides als Schlagwort und als Wirklichkeit." *Gymnasium* 69: 189–204. Repr. in Herter 1968: 639–60; Diller 1971: 464–81.

————. 1962b. "Die Hellenen-Barbaren-Antithese im Zeitalter der Perserkriege." In Reverdin 1962: 39–68. Repr. in Diller 1971: 419–50.

————. 1971. *Kleine Schriften zur antiken Literatur.* Ed. Hans-Joachim Newiger and Hans Seyffert. Munich.

Dipper, Christof. 2000. "Die 'Geschichtlichen Grundbegriffe': Von der Begriffsgeschichte zur Theorie der historischen Zeiten." *HZ* 270: 281–308.

Dittenberger, Wilhelm, ed. 1915–24. *Sylloge Inscriptionum Graecarum.* 3d ed. 4 vols. Leipzig. Repr., Hildesheim, 1960.

Dobrov, Gregory W., ed. 1997. *The City as Comedy: Society and Representation in Athenian Drama.* Chapel Hill, N.C.

Dodds, E. R. 1960. "Morals and Politics in the 'Oresteia.'" *PCPhS* 186 (n.s., 6): 19–31.

Doherty, Lillian E. 1995. *Siren Songs: Gender, Audiences, and Narrators in the* Odyssey. Ann Arbor, Mich.

Donlan, Walter. 1969. "A Note on Aristos as a Class Term." *Philologus* 113: 268–70.

———. 1970. "Changes and Shifts in the Meaning of *Demos* in the Literature of the Archaic Period." *PdP* 25: 381–95. Repr. in Donlan 1999: 225–36.

———. 1973. "The Tradition of Anti-aristocratic Thought in Early Greek Poetry." *Historia* 22: 145–54. Repr. in Donlan 1999: 237–47.

———. 1980. *The Aristocratic Ideal in Ancient Greece.* Lawrence, Kans. Repr. in Donlan 1999.

———. 1981–82. "Reciprocities in Homer." *CW* 75: 137–75.

———. 1985. "The Social Groups of Dark Age Greece." *CP* 80: 293–308.

———. 1989a. "Homeric *Temenos* and the Land Economy of the Dark Age." *MH* 46: 129–45. Repr. in Donlan 1999: 303–20.

———. 1989b. "The Pre-state Community in Greece." *SO* 64: 5–29. Repr. in Donlan 1999: 283–302.

———. 1999. *The Aristocratic Ideal and Selected Papers.* Wauconda, Ill.

Dornseiff, Franz. 1927. "*Sōtēr.*" *RE* 3A: 1211–21.

Dougherty, Carol, and Leslie Kurke, eds. 1993. *Cultural Poetics in Archaic Greece.* Cambridge.

Dover, Kenneth J. 1974. *Greek Popular Morality in the Time of Plato and Aristotle.* Berkeley and Los Angeles.

———. 1976. "The Freedom of the Intellectual in Greek Society." *Talanta* 7: 24–54. Repr. in Kenneth J. Dover, *The Greeks and Their Legacy: Collected Papers,* 2.135–58. Oxford, 1988.

Dreher, Martin. 1995. *Hegemon und Symmachoi: Untersuchungen zum Zweiten Athenischen Seebund.* Berlin.

———. 2000. "Verbannung ohne Vergehen: Der Ostrakismos (das Scherbengericht)." In Burckhardt and von Ungern-Sternberg 2000: 66–77, 262–64.

Drexler, Hans. 1972. *Herodot-Studien.* Hildesheim.

———. 1976. *Thukydides-Studien.* Hildesheim.

Ducat, Jean. 1973. "La confédération béotienne et l'expansion thébaine à l'époque archaïque." *BCH* 97: 59–73.

———. 1990. *Les hilotes.* Paris.

———. 1994. *Les pénestes de Thessalie.* Paris.

Ducrey, Pierre. 1968a. "Aspects juridiques de la victoire et du traitement des vaincus." In Vernant 1968: 231–43.

———. 1968b. *Le traitement des prisonniers de guerre dans la Grèce antique des origines à la conquête romaine.* Paris.

———. 1977. "L'armée, facteur de profits." In *Armées et fiscalité dans le monde antique,* 421–32. Collection Centre National de Recherche Scientifique 936. Paris.

Duhoux, Yves. 1976. *Aspects du vocabulaire économique mycénien.* Amsterdam.

Dunbabin, Thomas J. 1948. *The Western Greeks.* Oxford.

Dunbar, Nan. 1995. *Aristophanes,* Birds: *Edited with Introduction and Commentary.* Oxford.

Eadie, John W., and Josiah Ober, eds. 1985. *The Craft of the Ancient Historian: Essays in Honor of Chester G. Starr.* Lanham, Md.

Easterling, P. E., and B. M. W. Knox, eds. 1985. *The Cambridge History of Classical Literature.* Vol. 1, *Greek Literature.* Cambridge.

Edelmann, Hannelore. 1975. "Demokratie bei Herodot und Thukydides." *Klio* 57: 313–27.

Eder, Walter. 1986. "The Political Significance of the Codification of Law in Archaic Societies: An Unconventional Hypothesis." In Raaflaub 1986: 262–300.

———. 1988. "Political Self-Confidence and Resistance: The Role of *Demos* and *Plebs* after the Expulsion of the Tyrant in Athens and the King in Rome." In Yuge and Doi 1988: 465–75.

————. 1992. "Polis und Politai: Die Auflösung des Adelsstaates und die Entwicklung des Polisbürgers." In Wolf-Dieter Heilmeyer and Irma Wehgartner, eds., *Euphronios und seine Zeit*, 24–38. Berlin.

————. 1998. "Aristocrats and the Coming of Athenian Democracy." In Morris and Raaflaub 1998: 105–40.

————, ed. 1990. *Staat und Staatlichkeit in der frühen römischen Republik*. Stuttgart.

Eder, Walter, and Karl-Joachim Hölkeskamp, eds. 1997. *Volk und Verfassung im vorhellenistischen Griechenland*. Stuttgart.

Edmonds, John M., ed. 1957–61. *The Fragments of Attic Comedy*. 3 vols. in 4. Leiden.

Edmunds, Lowell, and Richard Martin. 1977. "Thucydides 2.65.8: *Eleutherōs.*" *HSCP* 81: 187–93.

Effenterre, Henri van. 1976. "Clisthène et les mesures de mobilisation." *REG* 89: 1–17.

————. 1985. *La cité grecque: Des origines à la défaite de Marathon*. Paris.

Effenterre, Henri van, and M. van Effenterre. 1969. *Fouilles exécutées à Mallia: Le centre politique*. Vol. 1. Etudes crétoises 17. Paris.

Ehrenberg, Victor. 1921. *Die Rechtsidee im frühen Griechentum*. Leipzig. Repr., Darmstadt, 1966.

————. 1929. "Sparta (Geschichte)." *RE* 3A: 1373–1453.

————. 1940. "Isonomia." *RE* Suppl. 7: 293–301.

————. 1946. *Aspects of the Ancient World: Essays and Reviews*. New York.

————. 1951. *The People of Aristophanes: A Sociology of Old Attic Comedy*. 2d ed. Cambridge, Mass.

————. 1954. *Sophocles and Pericles*. Oxford.

————. 1965a. *Polis und Imperium: Beiträge zur Alten Geschichte*. Zurich.

————. 1965b. *Der Staat der Griechen*. 2d ed. Zurich. English tr., Ehrenberg 1969.

————. 1967. "Freedom—Ideal and Reality." In European Cultural Foundation, ed., *The Living Heritage of Greek Antiquity*, 132–46. The Hague. Repr. in Victor Ehrenberg, *Man, State and Deity*, 19–34. London, 1974.

————. 1968. *From Solon to Socrates: Greek History and Civilization during the Sixth and Fifth Centuries B.C.* London.

————. 1969. *The Greek State*. 2d ed. London.

Ehrhardt, A. 1951. "Rechtsvergleichende Studien zum antiken Sklavenrecht I: Wergeld und Schadenersatz." *ZRG* 68: 74–130.

Ehrhardt, Norbert, and Linda-Marie Günther, eds. 2002. *Widerstand, Anpassung, Integration: Die griechische Staatenwelt und Rom (Festschrift für Jürgen Deininger zum 65. Geburtstag)*. Stuttgart.

Ellinger, Pierre. 1993. *La légende nationale phocidienne: Artémis, les situations extrêmes et les récits de guerre d'anéantissement*. BCH Suppl. 27. Athens.

English, B. R. 1938. *The Problem of Freedom in Greece from Homer to Pindar*. Toronto.

Erasmus, H. J. 1960. "Eunomia." *Acta Classica* 3: 53–64.

Erbse, Hartmut. 1993. "Die Funktion des Rechtsgedankens in Hesiods 'Erga.'" *Hermes* 121: 12–28.

Erler, Michael. 1987. "Das Recht (*Dikē*) als Segensbringerin für die Polis." *SI*, 3d ser., 5: 5–36.

Erxleben, Eberhard. 1975. "Die Kleruchien auf Euböa und Lesbos und die Methoden der attischen Herrschaft im 5. Jh." *Klio* 57: 83–100.

Etienne, Roland, and Piérart, Marcel. 1975. "Un décret du koinon des Hellènes à Platées en l'honneur de Glaucon, fils d'Etéoclès, d'Athènes." *BCH* 99: 51–75.

Evans, J. A. S. 1976. "Herodotus and the Ionian Revolt." *Historia* 25: 31–37.

————. 1979. "Herodotus' Publication Date." *Athenaeum* 57: 145–49.

————. 1991. *Herodotus, Explorer of the Past: Three Essays*. Princeton.

Fadinger, Volker. 1993. "Griechische Tyrannis und Alter Orient." In Raaflaub and Müller-Luckner 1993: 263–316.

Farnell, Lewis R. 1896. *The Cults of the Greek States,* Vol. 1. Oxford. Repr., Chicago, 1971.

———. 1930–32. *The Works of Pindar: Translated with Literary and Critical Commentaries.* 3 vols. London. Repr., Amsterdam, 1961.

Farrar, Cynthia. 1988. *The Origins of Democratic Thinking: The Invention of Politics in Classical Athens.* Cambridge.

Fatouros, Georgios. 1966. *Index verborum zur frühgriechischen Lyrik.* Heidelberg.

Fehr, Burkhard. 1979–81. "Zur religionspolitischen Funktion der Athena Parthenos im Rahmen des Delisch-Attischen Seebundes." 3 parts. *Hephaistos* 1: 71–91; 2: 113–25; 3: 55–93.

Feldman, Thalia P. 1971. "Personification and Structure in Hesiod's *Theogony.*" *SO* 46: 7–41.

Ferrabino, Aldo. 1929. *La dissoluzione della libertà nella Grecia antica.* Padova.

Ferrara, Giovanni. 1964. *La politica di Solone.* Naples.

Ferrill, Arther. 1978. "Herodotus on Tyranny." *Historia* 27: 385–98.

Festugière, A.-J. 1947. *Liberté et civilization chez les Grecs.* Paris. English tr., Festugière 1987.

———. 1987. *Freedom and Civilization among the Greeks.* Tr. P. T. Brannan. Allison Park, Pa.

Figueira, Thomas J. 1985. "Chronological Table: Archaic Megara, 800–500 B.C." In Figueira and Nagy 1985: 261–303.

———. 1990. "*Autonomoi kata tas spondas* (Thucydides 1.67.2)." *BICS* 37: 63–88. Repr. with revisions in Figueira 1993: 255–92.

———. 1991. *Athens and Aigina in the Age of Imperial Colonization.* Baltimore.

———. 1993. *Excursions in Epichoric History: Aiginetan Essays.* Lanham, Md.

———. 1998. *The Power of Money: Coinage and Politics in the Athenian Empire.* Philadelphia.

———. 1999. "The Evolution of Messenian Identity." In Stephen Hodkinson and Anton Powell, eds., *Sparta: New Perspectives,* 211–44. London and Swansea.

Figueira, Thomas J., and Gregory Nagy, eds. 1985. *Theognis of Megara: Poetry and the Polis.* Baltimore.

Fine, John V. A. 1951. *Horoi: Studies in Mortgage, Real Security, and Land Tenure in Ancient Athens.* Athens.

Finley, John H. 1955. *Pindar and Aeschylus.* Cambridge, Mass.

———. 1967. *Three Essays on Thucydides.* Cambridge, Mass.

Finley, M. I. 1971. *The Ancestral Constitution.* Cambridge. Repr. in M. I. Finley, *The Use and Abuse of History,* 34–59. London, 1975.

———. 1973a. *The Ancient Economy.* Berkeley and Los Angeles. Repr., with a foreword by Ian Morris, Berkeley and Los Angeles, 1999.

———, ed. 1973b. *Problèmes de la terre en Grèce ancienne.* Paris and The Hague.

———. 1976a. "Colonies—An Attempt at a Typology." *Transactions of the Royal Historical Society* 26: 167–88.

———. 1976b. "The Freedom of the Citizen in the Greek World." *Talanta* 7: 1–23. Repr. in Finley 1982: 77–94, 261–62.

———. 1977. *The World of Odysseus.* 2d ed. New York.

———. 1978. "The Fifth-Century Athenian Empire: A Balance Sheet." In Garnsey and Whittaker 1978: 103–26, 308–10. Repr. in Finley 1982: 41–61, 255–58.

———. 1980. *Ancient Slavery and Modern Ideology.* New York.

———. 1982. *Economy and Society in Ancient Greece.* New York.

———. 1986. *Ancient History: Evidence and Models.* New York.

Fisher, N. R. E. 1992. Hybris: *A Study in the Values of Honour and Shame in Ancient Greece.* Warminster, England.

Fisher, N. R. E., and Hans van Wees, eds. 1998. *Archaic Greece: New Approaches and New Evidence.* London and Swansea.

Fitton, J. W. 1961. "The Suppliant Women and the Herakleidai of Euripides." *Hermes* 89: 430–61.

Fitzgerald, John T., ed. 1996. *Friendship, Flattery, and Frankness of Speech: Studies on Friendship in the New Testament World.* Leiden.

Flach, Dieter. 1973. "Solons volkswirtschaftliche Reformen." *RSA* 3: 13–27.

Flaig, Egon. 1994. "Das Konsensprinzip im homerischen Olymp: Überlegungen zum göttlichen Entscheidungsprozess Ilias 4, 1–72." *Hermes* 122: 13–31.

———. 1997. "Processus de décision collective et guerre civile: L'exemple de l'*Odyssée* Chant XXIV, vv. 419–470." *Annales HSS* 52: 3–29.

Flashar, Hellmut. 1969. *Der Epitaphios des Perikles: Seine Funktion im Geschichtswerk des Thukydides.* SHAW, 1969, 1. Heidelberg.

Fleming, Daniel. Forthcoming. *Before Democracy: The Town in the Political World of the Mari Archives.*

Flensted-Jensen, Pernille, Thomas Heine Nielsen, and Lene Rubinstein, eds. 2000. *Polis and Politics: Studies in Ancient Greek History Presented to Mogens H. Hansen.* Copenhagen.

Ford, Andrew L. 1985. "The Seal of Theognis: The Politics of Authorship in Archaic Greece." In Figueira and Nagy 1985: 82–95.

Fornara, Charles W. 1968. "The 'Tradition' about the Murder of Hipparchus." *Historia* 17: 400–424.

———. 1970a. "The Cult of Harmodius and Aristogeiton." *Philologus* 114: 155–80.

———. 1970b. "The *Diapsephismos* of Ath. Pol. 13.5." *CP* 65: 243–46.

———. 1971a. "Evidence for the Date of Herodotus' Publication." *JHS* 91: 25–34.

———. 1971b. *Herodotus: An Interpretative Essay.* Oxford.

———. 1977. "*IG* I², 39.52–57 and the 'Popularity' of the Athenian Empire." *CSCA* 10: 39–55.

———. 1981. "Herodotus' Knowledge of the Archidamian War." *Hermes* 109: 149–56.

———, ed., tr. 1983. *Archaic Times to the End of the Peloponnesian War.* Translated Documents of Greece and Rome 1. 2d ed. Cambridge.

Fornara, Charles W., and Loren J. Samons II. 1991. *Athens from Cleisthenes to Pericles.* Berkeley and Los Angeles.

Forrest, W. G. 1960. "Themistokles and Argos." *CQ*, n.s., 10: 221–41.

———. 1963. "Aristophanes' *Acharnians.*" *Phoenix* 17: 1–12.

———. 1966. *The Emergence of Greek Democracy, 800–400 B.C.* New York.

———. 1968. *A History of Sparta, 950–192 B.C.* London.

———. 1975. "Aristophanes and the Athenian Empire." In Barbara Levick, ed., *The Ancient Historian and His Materials (Essays Presented to C. E. Stevens),* 17–29. Farnborough.

———. 1982. "Central Greece and Thessaly [700–500 B.C.]." *CAH* 3.3²: 286–320.

Foxhall, Lin. 1997. "A View from the Top: Evaluating the Solonian Property Classes." In Mitchell and Rhodes 1997: 113–36.

Foxhall, Lin, and Andrew Lewis, eds. 1996. *Greek Law in Its Political Setting: Justifications not Justice.* Oxford.

Fraenkel, Ernst. 1953. "Zur griechischen Wortbildung." *Glotta* 32: 16–33.

Fränkel, Hermann. 1960. *Wege und Formen frühgriechischen Denkens.* 2d ed. Munich.

———. 1962. *Dichtung und Philosophie des frühen Griechentums.* 2d ed. Munich.

———. 1973. *Early Greek Poetry and Philosophy.* Tr. Moses Hadas and James Willis. Oxford.

Fraser, Peter M. 1995. "Citizens, Demesmen and Metics in Athens and Elsewhere." In Mogens H. Hansen, ed., *Sources for the Ancient Greek City-State,* 64–90. Copenhagen.

Frei, Peter. 1981. "*Isonomia:* Politik im Spiegel griechischer Wortbildungslehre." *MH* 38: 205–19.

French, Alfred. 1964. *The Growth of the Athenian Economy.* London.

———. 1972. "Topical Influences on Herodotus' Narrative." *Mnemosyne,* 4th ser., 25: 9–27.

———. 1979. "Athenian Ambitions and the Delian Alliance." *Phoenix* 33: 134–41.

Friedländer, Paul, and Herbert B. Hoffleit. 1948. *Epigrammata: Greek Inscriptions in Verse from the Beginnings to the Persian Wars.* Berkeley and Los Angeles.

Frisch, Hartvig. 1942. *The Constitution of the Athenians: A Philological-Historical Analysis of Pseudo-Xenophon's Treatise* De re publica Atheniensium. Copenhagen.

Frisk, Hjalmar. 1954–72. *Griechisches etymologisches Wörterbuch.* 3 vols. Heidelberg.

Fritz, Kurt von. 1943. "Once more the *Hektēmoroi.*" *AJP* 64: 24–43. Repr. in von Fritz 1976: 117–34.

———. 1965. "Die griechische *eleutheria* bei Herodot." *WS* 78: 5–31.

———. 1967. *Die griechische Geschichtsschreibung.* Vol. 1. Berlin.

———. 1976. *Schriften zur griechischen und römischen Verfassungsgeschichte und Verfassungstheorie.* Berlin.

Frost, Frank J. 1961. "Some Documents in Plutarch's *Lives.*" *C&M* 22: 182–94.

———. 1964. "Pericles, Thucydides, Son of Melesias, and Athenian Politics before the War." *Historia* 13: 385–99.

———. 1968. "Themistocles' Place in Athenian Politics." *CSCA* 1: 105–24.

———. 1976. "Tribal Politics and the Civic State." *AJAH* 1: 66–75.

———. 1980. *Plutarch's* Themistocles: *A Historical Commentary.* Princeton.

———. 1984. "The Athenian Military before Cleisthenes." *Historia* 33: 283–94.

———. 1990. "Peisistratos, the Cults, and the Unification of Attica." *AW* 21: 3–9.

———. 1994. "Aspects of Early Athenian Citizenship." In Boegehold and Scafuro 1994: 45–56.

Fuks, Alexander. 1953. *The Ancestral Constitution.* London.

Furley, William D. 1996. *Andokides and the Herms: A Study of Crisis in Fifth-Century Athenian Religion.* BICS Suppl. 65. London.

Furuyama, Masato. 1988. "The Liberation of *Heilotai:* The Case of *Neodamodeis.*" In Yuge and Doi 1988: 364–68.

Gagarin, Michael. 1973. "*Dike* in the *Works and Days.*" *CP* 68: 81–94.

———. 1974. "Hesiod's Dispute with Perses." *TAPA* 104: 103–11.

———. 1978. "Self-Defense in Athenian Homicide Law." *GRBS* 19: 111–20.

———. 1979. "The Prosecution of Homicide in Athens." *GRBS* 20: 301–23.

———. 1981a. *Drakon and Early Athenian Homicide Law.* New Haven, Conn.

———. 1981b. "The Thesmothetai and the Earliest Athenian Tyranny Law." *TAPA* 111: 71–77.

———. 1982. "The Organization of the Gortyn Law Code." *GRBS* 23: 129–46.

———. 1986. *Early Greek Law.* Berkeley.

———. 1992. "The Poetry of Justice: Hesiod and the Origins of Greek Law." In Apostolos N. Athanassakis, ed., *Essays on Hesiod,* vol. 1. *Ramus* 21: 61–78.

Gaiser, Konrad. 1975. *Das Staatsmodell des Thukydides: Zur Rede des Perikles für die Gefallenen.* Heidelberg.

Gallant, T. W. 1982. "Agricultural Systems, Land Tenure, and the Reforms of Solon." *BSA* 77: 111–24.

Garlan, Yvon. 1988. *Slavery in Ancient Greece.* Tr. Janet Lloyd. Ithaca, N.Y.

———. 1989. *Guerre et économie en Grèce ancienne.* Paris.

Garland, Robert. 1987. *The Piraeus from the Fifth to the First Century B.C.* Ithaca, N.Y.

———. 1992. *Introducing New Gods: The Politics of Athenian Religion.* Ithaca, N.Y.

Garnsey, Peter. 1988. *Famine and Food Supply in the Graeco-Roman World: Responses to Risk and Crisis.* Cambridge.

Garnsey, Peter, and C. R. Whittaker, eds. 1978. *Imperialism in the Ancient World.* Cambridge.

Garvie, A. F. 1986. *Aeschylus,* Choephori, *with Introduction and Commentary.* Oxford.

Gauer, Werner. 1968. *Weihgeschenke aus den Perserkriegen. IM* Beiheft 2. Tübingen.

Gauthier, Philippe. 1960. "Grecs et Phéniciens en Sicile pendant la période archaïque." *RH* 224: 257–74.

———. 1966. Le parallèle Himère-Salamine au Ve et au IVe siècle av. J.-C." *REA* 68: 5–32.

———. 1972. *Symbola: Les étrangers et la justice dans les cités grecques.* Nancy.

———. 1973. "A propos des clérouquies athéniennes du Ve siècle." In Finley 1973: 163–78.

Gawantka, Wilfried. 1975. *Isopolitie.* Vestigia 22. Munich.

Gehrke, Hans-Joachim. 1985. *Stasis: Untersuchungen zu den inneren Kriegen in den griechischen Staaten des 5. und 4. Jahrhunderts v. Chr.* Vestigia 35. Munich.

———. 1987. "Die Griechen und die Rache: Ein Versuch in historischer Psychologie." *Saeculum* 38: 121–49.

———. 1990. *Geschichte des Hellenismus.* Munich.

———. 1993. "Gesetz und Konflikt: Überlegungen zur frühen Polis." In J. Bleicken, ed., *Colloquium aus Anlass des 80. Geburtstages von A. Heuss,* 49–67. Frankfurter althistorische Studien. Kallmünz.

———. 1994. "La storia politica Ateniese arcaica e l'*Athenaion politeia.*" In Maddoli 1994: 191–215.

———. 1997. "Der historische Hintergrund der pseudo-xenophontischen *Athenaion Politeia:* Ein Versuch über griechische Politik." In Gigante and Maddoli 1997: 25–45.

Gelzer, Thomas. 1973. "Die Verteidigung der Freiheit der Griechen gegen die Perser bei Aischylos und Herodot." In A. Mercier, ed., *Freiheit: Begriff und Bedeutung in Geschichte und Gegenwart,* 27–53. Bern.

Gentili, Bruno. 1958. *Bacchilide: Studi.* Urbino.

———. 1968. "Epigramma ed elegia." In O. Reverdin, ed., *L'épigramme grecque,* 37–81. Entretiens sur l'antiquité classique 14. Vandoeuvres and Geneva.

———. 1988. *Poetry and Its Public in Ancient Greece from Homer to the Fifth Century.* Tr. A. T. Cole. Baltimore.

———, ed., comm. 1995. *Pindaro,* Le Pitiche. With the collaboration of Paola Angeli Bernardini, Ettore Cingano, and Pietro Giannini. Milan.

Gentili, Bruno, and Carlo Prato, eds. 1988. *Poetae Elegiaci: Testimonia et Fragmenta.* Leipzig.

Georges, Pericles. 1995. *Barbarian Asia and the Greek Experience from the Archaic Period to the Age of Xenophon.* Baltimore.

———. 2000. "Persian Ionia under Darius: The Revolt Reconsidered." *Historia* 49: 1–39.

Gérard-Rousseau, Monique. 1968. *Les mentions religieuses dans les tablettes mycéniennes.* Rome.

———. 1969. "*Dmōs* et *dmōē* chez Homère." *ZA* 19: 163–73.

Gernet, Louis. 1981. *The Anthropology of Ancient Greece.* Tr. John Hamilton and Blaise Nagy. Baltimore.

Gielow, Hertha E. 1940–41. "Zeus Eleutherios: Ein Stück sizilischer Revolutionsgeschichte im Bilde einer Dankleischen Münze." *Deutsches Jahrbuch für Numismatik, Münzen- und Medaillenkunde sowie Geldgeschichte* 3–4: 103–14.

Gigante, Marcello, and Gianfranco Maddoli, eds. 1997. *L'*Athenaion politeia *dello Pseudo-Senofonte.* Naples.

Gigon, Olof. 1973. "Der Begriff der Freiheit in der Antike." *Gymnasium* 80: 8–56. Repr. in Olof Gigon, *Die antike Philosophie als Maßstab und Realität,* 96–161. Zurich, 1977.

Gill, David W. J. 2001. "The Decision to Build the Temple of Athena Nike (*IG* I^3 35)." *Historia* 50: 257–78.

Gillis, Daniel. 1969. "Marathon and the Alcmaeonids." *GRBS* 10: 133–45.

————. 1971. "The Revolt at Mytilene." *AJP* 92: 38–47.

————. 1979. *Collaboration with the Persians. Historia* Einzelschriften 34. Wiesbaden.

Giorgini, Giovanni. 1993. *La città el il tiranno: Il concetto di tirannide nella Grecia del VII–IV secolo a.C.* Milan.

Giovannini, Adalberto. 1997. "La participation des alliés au financement du Parthénon: *Aparchè* ou tribut?" *Historia* 46: 145–57.

Giovannini, Adalberto, and Gunther Gottlieb. 1980. *Thukydides und die Anfänge der athenischen Arche.* SHAW, 1980, 7. Heidelberg.

Gomme, Arnold W. 1945–56. *A Historical Commentary on Thucydides.* 3 vols. Oxford.

————. 1957. "Interpretations of Some Poems of Alkaios and Sappho." *JHS* 77: 255–66.

————. 1962. *More Essays in Greek History and Literature.* Oxford. Repr., New York, 1987.

Gomme, Arnold W., Antony Andrewes, and K. J. Dover. 1970–81. *A Historical Commentary on Thucydides.* Vols. 4–5. Oxford.

Gorman, Vanessa. 2001. *Miletos, the Ornament of Ionia: A History of the City to 400 B.C.E.* Ann Arbor, Mich.

Gottlieb, Gunther. 1963. *Das Verhältnis der ausserherodoteischen Überlieferung zu Herodot.* Bonn.

Gould, John. 1989. *Herodotus.* New York.

Grace, Emily. 1973. "Status Distinctions in the Draconian Law." *Eirene* 11: 5–30.

Graf, David. 1985. "Greek Tyrants and Achaemenid Politics." In Eadie and Ober 1985: 79–123.

Graf, Fritz. 2000. "Der Mysterienprozess." In Burckhardt and von Ungern-Sternberg 2000: 114–27, 270–73.

Graham, A. John. 1992. "Abdera and Teos." *JHS* 112: 44–73.

Grant, J. R. 1971. "Thucydides 2.37.1." *Phoenix* 25: 104–7.

Grayson, C. H. 1972. "Two Passages in Thucydides." *CQ*, n.s., 22: 62–73.

Greenhalgh, P. A. L. 1972. "Patriotism in the Homeric World." *Historia* 21: 528–37.

Griffith, G. T. 1966. "Isegoria in the Assembly at Athens." In Badian 1966: 115–38.

Griffith, Mark. 1977. *The Authenticity of* Prometheus Bound. Cambridge.

————. 1995. "Brilliant Dynasts: Power and Politics in the *Oresteia.*" *CA* 14: 62–129.

Groeneboom, P. 1928. *Aeschylus' Prometheus met inleiding, critische note en commentaar.* Groningen. Repr., Amsterdam, 1966.

Groningen, Bernard van, ed., comm. 1966. *Théognis: Le premier livre.* Amsterdam.

Grossmann, Gustav. 1950. *Politische Schlagwörter aus der Zeit des Peloponnesischen Krieges.* Zurich. Diss., Univ. of Basel, 1945. Repr., New York, 1973.

Gschnitzer, Fritz. 1954. "Namen und Wesen der thessalischen Tetraden." *Hermes* 82: 451–64. Repr. in Gschnitzer 2001: 269–82.

————. 1955. "Stammes- und Ortsgemeinden im alten Griechenland." *WS* 68: 120–44. Repr. in Gschnitzer 1969: 271–97; 2001: 24–50.

————. 1958. *Abhängige Orte im griechischen Altertum.* Zetemata 17. Munich.

————. 1964. *Studien zur griechischen Terminologie der Sklaverei.* Vol. 1, *Grundzüge des vorhellenistischen Sprachgebrauchs.* Abh. Akad. Mainz, geistes- und sozialwiss. Kl., 1963, 13. Wiesbaden.

————. 1973. "Proxenos." *RE* Suppl. 13: 669–730.

————. 1976a. "Politische Leidenschaft im homerischen Epos." In H. Görgemanns and E. A. Schmidt, eds., *Studien zum antiken Epos,* 1–21. Beitr. zur klass. Philologie 72. Meisenheim. Repr. in Gschnitzer 2001: 212–32.

————. 1976b. *Studien zur griechischen Terminologie der Sklaverei.* Vol. 2, *Untersuchungen zur älteren, insbes. der homerischen Sklaventerminologie.* Forsch. zur antiken Sklaverei 7. Wiesbaden.

————. 1977. *Die sieben Perser und das Königtum des Dareios: Ein Beitrag zur Achaimeniden-geschichte und zur Herodotanalyse.* Sitzungsberichte der Heidelberger Akad. der Wiss., phil.-hist. Kl., 1977, 3. Heidelberg.

————. 1978. *Ein neuer spartanischer Staatsvertrag und die Verfassung des Peloponnesischen Bundes.* Beiträge zur klassischen Philologie 93. Meisenheim.

————. 1979. "Vocabulaire et institutions: La continuité historique du deuxième au premier millénaire." In *Colloquium Mycenaeum 1975:* 109–34. Repr. in Gschnitzer 2001: 106–31.

————. 1981. *Griechische Sozialgeschichte von der mykenischen bis zum Ausgang der klassischen Zeit.* Wiesbaden.

————. 1983. "Der Rat in der Volksversammlung." In Paul Händel and Wolfgang Meid, eds., *Festschrift Robert Muth,* 151–63. Innsbruck. Repr. in Gschnitzer 2001: 199–211.

————. 1991. "Zur homerischen Staats- und Gesellschaftsordnung." In Latacz 1991: 182–204. Repr. in Gschnitzer 2001: 142–64.

————. 2001. *Kleine Schriften zum griechischen und römischen Altertum.* Vol. 1. *Historia* Einzel-schriften 149. Stuttgart.

————, ed. 1969. *Zur griechischen Staatskunde.* Wege der Forschung 96. Darmstadt.

Guarducci, Margareta, ed. 1935–50. *Inscriptiones Creticae.* 4 vols. Rome.

Guazzoni Foà, Virginia. 1974–76. *La libertà nel mondo greco.* 2 vols. Genoa.

Guthrie, W. K. C. 1962. *A History of Greek Philosophy.* Vol. 1, *The Earlier Presocratics and the Pythagoreans.* Cambridge.

————. 1971. *The Sophists.* Cambridge. (Originally published as *A History of Greek Philosophy,* vol. 3.1, *The World of the Sophists* [Cambridge, 1969].)

Habicht, Christian. 1961. "Falsche Urkunden zur Geschichte Athens im Zeitalter der Perser-kriege." *Hermes* 89: 1–35.

Hackl, Ursula. 1960. *Die oligarchische Bewegung in Athen am Ausgang des 5. Jh. v. Chr.* Diss., Univ. of Munich.

Hainsworth, Bryan. 1993. *The Iliad: A Commentary.* Vol. 3, *Books 9–12.* Cambridge.

Hall, Edith. 1989. *Inventing the Barbarian: Greek Self-Definition through Tragedy.* Oxford.

————. 1993. "Asia Unmanned: Images of Victory in Classical Athens." In Rich and Shipley 1993: 108–33.

Hall, Jonathan M. 2000. "Sparta, Lakedaimon and the Nature of Perioikic Dependency." In Pernille Flensted-Jensen, ed., *Further Studies in the Ancient Greek Polis,* 73–89. *Historia* Einzelschriften 138. Stuttgart.

Halliwell, Stephen. 1991. "Comic Satire and Freedom of Speech in Classical Athens." *JHS* 111: 48–70.

Hamilton, Charles D. 1979. *Sparta's Bitter Victories: Politics and Diplomacy in the Corinthian War.* Ithaca, N.Y.

Hammer, Dean. 2002. *The Iliad as Politics: The Performance of Political Thought.* Norman, Okla.

Hammond, N. G. L. 1967a. *A History of Greece to 322 B.C.* 2d ed. Oxford.

————. 1967b. "The Origin and the Nature of the Athenian Alliance of 478/7 B.C." *JHS* 87: 41–61. Repr. as "The Organization of the Athenian Alliance against Persia," in Hammond 1973: 311–45.

————. 1969. "Strategia and Hegemonia in Fifth-Century Athens." *CQ,* n.s., 19: 111–44. Repr. as "Problems of Command in Fifth-Century Athens," in Hammond 1973: 346–94.

————. 1973. *Studies in Greek History.* Oxford.

————. 1977. "The Meaning and Significance of the Reported Speech of Phrynichus in Thucydides 8,48." In Kinzl 1977b: 147–57. Repr. in Hammond, *Collected Studies,* 1.65–75. Amsterdam, 1993.

————. 1982. "The Peloponnese" [8th to 6th centuries]. *CAH* 3.3²: 321–59.

———. 1992. "Plataea's Relations with Thebes, Sparta and Athens." *JHS* 112: 143–50.

Hampl, Franz. 1937. "Die lakedaimonischen Periöken." *Hermes* 72: 1–49.

———. 1938. *Die griechischen Staatsverträge des 4. Jh. v. Chr.* Leipzig. Repr., Rome, 1966.

———. 1939. "Poleis ohne Territorium." *Klio* 32: 1–60. Repr. in Gschnitzer 1969: 403–73.

———. 1975–79. *Geschichte als kritische Wissenschaft.* 3 vols. Darmstadt.

Hans, Linda-Marie. 1983. *Karthago und Sizilien.* Hildesheim.

Hansen, Mogens H. 1975. *Eisangelia.* Odense.

———. 1980. "Eisangelia in Athens: A Reply." *JHS* 100: 89–95.

———. 1989. *Was Athens a Democracy? Popular Rule, Liberty and Equality in Ancient and Modern Political Thought.* Det Kongelige Danske Videnskabernes Selskab, historisk-filosofiske meddelelser 59. Copenhagen.

———. 1991. *The Athenian Democracy in the Age of Demosthenes: Structures, Principles, and Ideology.* Oxford. Repr. (with an addition), Norman, Okla., 1999.

———. 1995. "The 'Autonomous City-State': Ancient Fact or Modern Fiction?" In Hansen and Raaflaub 1995: 21–43.

———. 1996. "The Ancient Athenian and the Modern Liberal View of Liberty as a Democratic Ideal." In Ober and Hedrick 1996: 91–104.

———, ed. 1993. *The Ancient Greek City-State.* Copenhagen.

———. 1997. *The Polis as an Urban Centre and as a Political Community.* Copenhagen.

Hansen, Mogens H., and Kurt Raaflaub, eds. 1995. *Studies in the Ancient Greek* Polis. Historia Einzelschriften 95. Stuttgart.

———. 1996. *More Studies in the Ancient Greek* Polis. Historia Einzelschriften 108. Stuttgart.

Hansen, Peter A., ed. 1983. *Carmina epigraphica Graeca saeculorum, VIII–V a. Chr. n.* Berlin.

Hanson, Victor D. 1989. *The Western Way of War: Infantry Battle in Classical Greece.* New York.

———. 1995. *The Other Greeks: The Family Farm and the Agrarian Roots of Western Civilization.* New York.

———. 1996. "Hoplites into Democrats: The Changing Ideology of Athenian Infantry." In Ober and Hedrick 1996: 289–312.

———. 2001. "Democratic Warfare, Ancient and Modern." In McCann and Strauss 2001: 3–33.

———, ed. 1991. *Hoplites: The Classical Greek Battle Experience.* London.

Harding, Phillip. 1985. *From the End of the Peloponnesian War to the Battle of Ipsus.* Translated Documents of Greece and Rome 2. Cambridge.

Harrell, Sarah. 2002. "King or Private Citizen: Fifth-Century Sicilian Tyrants at Olympia and Delphi." *Mnemosyne* 55: 439–64.

Harris, Edward M. 1990. "The Constitution of the Five Thousand." *HSCP* 93: 243–80.

———. 1992. "Pericles' Praise of Athenian Democracy: Thucydides 2.37.1." *HSCP* 94: 157–67.

———. 1997. "A New Solution to the Riddle of the *Seisachtheia*." In Mitchell and Rhodes 1997: 103–12.

Harrison, A. R. W. 1968. *The Law of Athens.* Vol. 1. Oxford.

Hartog, François. 1988. *The Mirror of Herodotus: The Representation of the Other in the Writing of History.* Tr. Janet Lloyd. Berkeley and Los Angeles.

Harvey, F. David. 1965. "Two Kinds of Equality." *C&M* 26: 101–46.

———. 1984. "The Conspiracy of Agasias and Aischines (Plutarch, Aristeides 13)." *Klio* 66: 58–73.

Hasebroek, Johannes. 1926. *Der imperialistische Gedanke im Altertum.* Stuttgart.

———. 1931. *Griechische Wirtschafts- und Gesellschaftsgeschichte bis zur Perserzeit.* Tübingen.

Haubold, Johannes. 2000. *Homer's People: Epic Poetry and Social Formation.* Cambridge.

Havelock, Eric A. 1972. "War as a Way of Life in Classical Culture." In Etienne Gareau, ed.,

Classical Values and the Modern World, 17–78. The Georges P. Vanier Memorial Lectures. Ottawa.

———. 1978. *The Greek Concept of Justice from Its Shadow in Homer to Its Substance in Plato.* Cambridge, Mass.

Head, Barclay V. 1911. *Historia Numorum.* 2d ed. Oxford. Repr., London, 1963.

Heichelheim, Fritz. 1935. "Sitos." *RE* Suppl. 6: 819–92.

Heidemann, M. L. 1966. *Die Freiheitsparole in der griechisch-römischen Auseinandersetzung (200–188 v. Chr.).* Diss., Univ. of Bonn.

Heinimann, Felix. 1945. Nomos *und* Physis: *Herkunft und Bedeutung einer Antithese im griechischen Denken des 5. Jh.* Basel. Repr., Darmstadt, 1965.

Helly, Bruno. 1995. *L'état Thessalien: Aleuas Le Roux, les tétrades et les "tagoi."* Lyons.

Heltzer, M., and E. Lipinski, eds. 1988. *Society and Economy in the Eastern Mediterranean (c. 1500–1000 B.C.).* Leuven.

Henderson, Jeffrey. 1998. "Attic Old Comedy, Frank Speech, and Democracy." In Boedeker and Raaflaub 1998: 255–73, 405–10.

———. 2003. "Demos, Demagogue, Tyrant in Attic Old Comedy." In Morgan 2003: 155–79.

Hennig, Dieter. 1992. "Herodot 6,108: Athen und Plataiai." *Chiron* 22: 13–24.

Herington, C. J. 1955. *Athena Parthenos and Athena Polias: A Study in the Religion of Periclean Athens.* Manchester.

Herington, John. 1985. *Poetry into Drama: Early Tragedy and the Greek Poetic Tradition.* Berkeley.

Herman, Gabriel. 1987. *Ritualised Friendship and the Greek City.* Cambridge.

Herrmann, Johannes. 1964. "Attische Redefreiheit." In Antonio Guarino and Luigi Labruna, eds., *Synteleia V. Arangio Ruiz*, 2.1142–48. Naples.

Herrmann, Peter. 1968. *Der römische Kaisereid.* Hypomnemata 20. Munich.

Herter, Hans. 1953. "Zur ersten Periklesrede des Thukydides." In George E. Mylonas and Doris Raymond, eds., *Studies Presented to David Moore Robinson*, 2.613–23. St. Louis.

———, ed. 1968. *Thukydides.* Wege der Forschung 98. Darmstadt.

Heubeck, Alfred. 1966. *Aus der Welt der frühgriechischen Lineartafeln.* Göttingen.

———. 1974. *Die homerische Frage.* Darmstadt.

Heuss, Alfred. 1937. *Stadt und Herrscher des Hellenismus in ihren staats- und völkerrechtlichen Beziehungen. Klio* Beiheft 39. Leipzig. Repr., Aalen, 1963.

———. 1946. "Die archaische Zeit Griechenlands als geschichtliche Epoche." *A&A* 2: 26–62. Repr. in Gschnitzer 1969: 36–96.

———. 1962. "Hellas: Die archaische Zeit," "Die klassische Zeit." *Propyläen Weltgeschichte* 3: 69–213, 214–400. Frankfurt am Main.

———. 1965. "Herrschaft und Freiheit im griechisch-römischen Altertum." *Propyläen Weltgeschichte* 11: 65–128. Frankfurt am Main.

———. 1973. "Das Revolutionsproblem im Spiegel der antiken Geschichte." *HZ* 216: 1–72.

———. 1981. "Vom Anfang und Ende 'archaischer' Politik bei den Griechen." In Gebhard Kurz, Dietram Müller, and Walter Nicolai, eds., *Gnomosyne: Menschliches Denken und Handeln in der frühgriechischen Literatur, Festschrift für Walter Marg*, 1–29. Munich.

Highbarger, E. L. 1937. "Theognis and the Persian Wars." *TAPA* 68: 88–111.

Highby, Leo I. 1936. *The Erythrae Decree: Contributions to the Early History of the Delian League and the Peloponnnesian Confederacy. Klio* Beiheft 36. Leipzig.

Hignett, Charles. 1952. *A History of the Athenian Constitution.* Oxford.

———. 1963. *Xerxes' Invasion of Greece.* Oxford.

Hill, G. F., ed. 1951. *Sources for Greek History between the Persian and the Peloponnesian Wars.* New ed. by Russell Meiggs and Antony Andrewes. Oxford.

Hiller, Stefan. 1988. "Dependent Personnel in Mycenaean Texts." In Heltzer and Lipinski 1988: 53–68.

Hiller, Stefan, and Oswald Panagl. 1976. *Die frühgriechischen Texte aus mykenischer Zeit.* Darmstadt.

Hirzel, Rudolf. 1907. *Themis, Dike und Verwandtes.* Leipzig.

Hodkinson, Stephen. 1983. "Social Order and the Conflict of Values in Classical Sparta." *Chiron* 13: 239–81.

———. 1993. "Warfare, Wealth, and the Crisis of Spartiate Society." In Rich and Shipley 1993: 146–76.

———. 1997. "The Development of Spartan Society and Institutions in the Archaic Period." In Mitchell and Rhodes 1997: 83–102.

———. 2000. *Property and Wealth in Classical Sparta.* London.

Hoffmann, Wilhelm. 1956. "Die Polis bei Homer." In *Festschrift für Bruno Snell,* 153–65. Munich. Repr. in Gschnitzer 1969: 123–38.

Hölkeskamp, Karl-Joachim. 1992a (publ. 1995). "Arbitrators, Lawgivers and the 'Codification of Law' in Archaic Greece." *Metis* 7: 49–81.

———.1992b. "Written Law in Archaic Greece." *PCPhS* 38: 87–117.

———. 1997. "Agorai bei Homer." In Eder and Hölkeskamp 1997: 1–19.

———. 1998. "Parteiungen und politische Willensbildung im demokratischen Athen: Perikles und Thukydides, Sohn des Melesias." *HZ* 267: 1–27.

———. 1999. *Schiedsrichter, Gesetzgeber und Gesetzgebung im archaischen Griechenland. Historia* Einzelschriften 131. Stuttgart.

———. 2001. "Marathon—vom Monument zum Mythos." In Papenfuss and Strocka 2001: 329–53.

Holm, Adolf. 1870. *Geschichte Siziliens im Altertum.* Vol. 1. Leipzig.

Hölscher, Uvo. 1989. *Die Odyssee: Epos zwischen Märchen und Roman.* 2d ed. Munich.

Hommel, Hildebrecht. 1932. "Metoikoi." *RE* 15.2: 1413–58.

Hooker, G. T. W., ed. 1963. *Parthenos and Parthenon. G&R* 10, Suppl. Oxford.

Hopper, R. J. 1966. "The Solonian 'Crisis.'" In Badian 1966: 139–46.

Hornblower, Simon. 1991–96. *A Commentary on Thucydides.* 2 vols. Oxford.

———. 1992. "The Religious Dimension to the Peloponnesian War, or, What Thucydides Does Not Tell Us." *HSCP* 94: 169–97.

———. 2000. "The *Old Oligarch* (Pseudo-Xenophon's *Athenaion Politeia*) and Thucydides: A Fourth-Century Date for the *Old Oligarch?* In Flensted-Jensen et al. 2000: 363–84.

How, Walter W., and J. Wells. 1928. *A Commentary on Herodotus.* 2 vols. 2d ed. Oxford. Repr., Oxford, 1964.

Humphreys, S. C. 1974. "The Nothoi of Kynosarges." *JHS* 94: 88–95.

———. 1978. *Anthropology and the Greeks.* London.

———. 1991. "A Historical Approach to Drakon's Law on Homicide." In Michael Gagarin, ed., *Symposion 1990: Papers on Greek and Hellenistic Legal History,* 17–45. Cologne.

———. 1993. "Diffusion, Comparison, Criticism." In Raaflaub and Müller-Luckner 1993: 1–11.

Hunt, Peter. 1998. *Slaves, Warfare, and Ideology in the Greek Historians.* Cambridge.

Hunter, Virginia. 1973/74. "Athens *Tyrannis:* A New Approach to Thucydides." *CJ* 69: 120–26.

Huss, Werner. 1985. *Geschichte der Karthager.* HdAW 3.8. Munich.

Huxley, George. 1967. "The Medism of Caryae." *GRBS* 8: 29–32.

Immerwahr, Henry. 1956–57. "The Samian Stories of Herodotus." *CJ* 52: 312–22.

Jackson, Alastar H. 1969. "The Original Purpose of the Delian League." *Historia* 18: 12–16.

———. 1993. "War and Raids for Booty in the World of Odysseus." In Rich and Shipley 1993: 64–76.

Jacobsen, Thorkild. 1946. "Mesopotamia." In Henri Frankfort et al., *The Intellectual Adventure of Ancient Man*, 125–219. Chicago.

Jacoby, Felix. 1913. "Herodotos (7)." *RE* Suppl. 2: 205–520.

———. 1923–98. *Die Fragmente der griechischen Historiker*. 3 vols. in 14. Berlin, then Leiden.

———. 1944a. "*Chrestous poiein* (Aristotle fr. 592 R.)." *CQ* 38: 15–16.

———. 1944b. "Patrios Nomos: State Burial in Athens and the Public Cemetery in the Kerameikos." *JHS* 64: 37–66.

———. 1945. "Some Athenian Epigrams from the Persian Wars." *Hesperia* 14: 157–211.

Jaeger, Werner. 1926. "Solons Eunomie." *Sitzungsberichte der Preuss. Akad. der Wiss.*, phil.-hist. Kl., 11: 69–85. Repr. in Jaeger 1960: 315–37. English tr. in Jaeger 1966: 75–99.

———. 1937. *Paideia*. Tr. G. Highet. Oxford.

———. 1954–61. *Paideia: The Ideals of Greek Culture*. Tr. Gilbert Highet. 3 vols. Oxford.

———. 1960. *Scripta minora*. Vol. 1. Rome.

———. 1966. *Five Essays*. Montreal.

Jameson, Michael, 1998. "Religion in Athenian Democracy." In Morris and Raaflaub 1998: 171–95.

Janko, Richard. 1982. *Homer, Hesiod and the Hymns*. Cambridge.

Jeffery, Lilian H. 1961. *The Local Scripts of Archaic Greece*. Oxford.

———. 1988. "Greece before the Persian Invasion." *CAH* 4²: 347–67.

Jehne, Martin. 1994. *Koine Eirene: Untersuchungen zu den Befriedungs- und Stabilisierungsbemühungen in der griechischen Poliswelt des 4. Jh. v. Chr.* Stuttgart.

Jenkyns, Richard. 1980. *The Victorians and Ancient Greece*. Cambridge, Mass.

Johann, H.-T., ed. 1976. *Erziehung und Bildung in der heidnischen und christlichen Antike*. Wege der Forschung 377. Darmstadt.

Jones, A. H. M. 1939. "Civitates liberae et immunes in the East." In *Anatolian Studies Presented to W. H. Buckler*, 1.103–17. Manchester.

———. 1957. *Athenian Democracy*. Oxford. Repr., Baltimore, 1986.

Jones, Nicholas. 1999. *The Associations of Classical Athens: The Response to Democracy*. New York.

Jordan, Borimir. 1979. *Servants of the Gods: A Study in the Religion, History and Literature of Sixth-Century Athens*. Hypomnemata 55. Göttingen.

———. 1986. "Religion in Thucydides." *TAPA* 116: 119–47.

Jouanna, Jacques. 1999. *Hippocrates*. Tr. M. B. DeBevoise. Baltimore.

Just, M. 1965. *Die Ephesis in der Geschichte des attischen Prozesses*. Diss., Univ. of Würzburg.

Jüthner, Julius. 1923. *Hellenen und Barbaren: Aus der Geschichte des Nationalbewusstseins*. Leipzig.

Kagan, Donald. 1969. *The Outbreak of the Peloponnesian War*. Ithaca, N.Y.

———. 1974. *The Archidamian War*. Ithaca, N.Y.

———. 1987. *The Fall of the Athenian Empire*. Ithaca, N.Y.

Kahn, Charles H. 1979. *The Art and Thought of Heraclitus*. Cambridge.

Kahrstedt, Ulrich. 1922. *Griechisches Staatsrecht*. Vol. 1, *Sparta und seine Symmachie*. Göttingen.

———. 1934. *Staatsgebiet und Staatsangehörige in Athen*. Göttingen.

Kakridis, J. T. 1961. *Der thukydideische Epitaphios: Ein stilistischer Kommentar*. Zetemata 26. Munich.

Kallet (-Marx), Lisa. 1993. *Money, Expense, and Naval Power in Thucydides' History 1–5.24*. Berkeley and Los Angeles.

————. 1998. "Accounting for Culture in Fifth-Century Athens." In Boedeker and Raaflaub 1998: 43–58, 357–64.

————. 2001. *Money and the Corrosion of Power in Thucydides: The Sicilian Expedition and Its Aftermath.* Berkeley and Los Angeles.

Kapparis, K. 1995. "The Athenian Decree for the Naturalization of the Plataeans." *GRBS* 36: 359–78.

Karavites, Peter (Panayotis). 1977. "Realities and Appearances, 490–480 B.C." *Historia* 26: 129–47.

————. 1982a. *Capitulations and Greek Interstate Relations: The Reflection of Humanistic Ideals in Political Events.* Hypomnemata 71. Göttingen.

————. 1982b. "*Eleutheria* and *Autonomia* in Fifth Century Interstate Relations." *RD* 29: 145–62.

————. 1984. "The Political Use of *Eleutheria* and *Autonomia* in the Fourth Century among the Greek City-States." *RIDA* 31: 167–91.

Kästner, Ursula. 1981. "Bezeichungen für Sklaven." In Welskopf 1981–85: 3.282–318.

Kegel, W. J. H. F. 1962. *Simonides.* Diss., Univ. of Groningen.

Kelly, D. H. 1978. "The New Spartan Treaty." *LCM* 3: 133–41.

Kennedy, George. 1963. *The Art of Persuasion in Greece.* Princeton.

Kennell, Nigel. 1995. *The Gymnasium of Virtue: Education and Culture in Ancient Sparta.* Chapel Hill, N.C.

Kennelly, James J. 1990. "Archaisms in the Troizen Decree." *CQ,* n.s., 40: 539–41.

Kent, Roland G. 1953. *Old Persian: Grammar, Texts, Lexicon.* 2d ed. New Haven, Conn.

Kerferd, G. B. 1981. *The Sophistic Movement.* Cambridge.

Kiechle, Franz. 1958. "Zur Humanität in der Kriegführung der griechischen Staaten." *Historia* 7: 129–56.

————. 1963a. *Lakonien und Sparta.* Vestigia 5. Munich.

————. 1963b. "Ursprung und Wirkung der machtpolitischen Theorien im Geschichtswerk des Thukydides." *Gymnasium* 70: 289–312.

————. 1967. "Athens Politik nach der Abwehr der Perser." *HZ* 204: 265–304.

Kienast, Dietmar. 1953. "Der innenpolitische Kampf in Athen von der Rückkehr des Thukydides bis zu Perikles' Tod." *Gymnasium* 60: 210–29.

————. 1965. "Die innenpolitische Entwicklung Athens im 6. Jahrhundert und die Reformen von 508." *HZ* 200: 265–83.

————. 2002. "Bemerkungen zum Ionischen Aufstand und zur Rolle des Artaphernes." *Historia* 51: 1–31.

Kierdorf, Wilhelm. 1966. *Erlebnis und Darstellung der Perserkriege: Studien zu Simonides, Pindar, Aischylos und den attischen Rednern.* Hypomnemata 16. Göttingen.

Kinzl, Konrad H. 1977a. "Athens: Between Tyranny and Democracy." In Kinzl 1977b: 199–223. Repr. in Kinzl 1995: 213–47.

————. 1978. "*Demokratia:* Studien zur Frühgeschichte des Begriffs." *Gymnasium* 85: 117–27, 312–26.

————. 1979. "Betrachtungen zur älteren Tyrannis." In Konrad H. Kinzl, ed., *Die ältere Tyrannis bis zu den Perserkriegen.* Wege der Forschung 510. Darmstadt.

————, ed. 1977b. *Greece and the Eastern Mediterranean in Ancient History and Prehistory: Studies Presented to Fritz Schachermeyr on the Occasion of His Eightieth Birthday.* Berlin.

————, 1995. Demokratia: *Der Weg zur Demokratie bei den Griechen.* Wege der Forschung 657. Darmstadt.

Kirk, Geoffrey S. 1954. *Heraclitus: The Cosmic Fragments.* Cambridge.

———. 1960. "The Structure and Aim of the *Theogony*." In Geoffrey Kirk et al., *Hésiode et son influence*, 61–95. Entretiens sur l'antiquité classique 7. Vandoeuvres and Geneva.

———. 1985. *The Iliad: A Commentary.* Vol. 1, *Bks. 1–4.* Cambridge.

———. 1990. *The Iliad: A Commentary.* Vol. 2, *Bks. 5–8.* Cambridge.

Kirsten, Ernst. 1941. "Ein politisches Programm in Pindars erstem pythischem Gedicht." *RhM* 90: 58–71.

———. 1950. "Plataiai." *RE* 20.2: 2255–2332.

Klees, Hans. 1975. *Herren und Sklaven: Die Sklaverei im oikonomischen und politischen Schrifttum der Griechen in klassischer Zeit.* Forschungen zur antiken Sklaverei 6. Wiesbaden.

Klein, Richard. 1979. "Die innenpolitische Gegnerschaft gegen Perikles." In Wirth 1979: 494–533.

Kleinknecht, Hermann. 1940. "Herodot und Athen (7,139; 8,140–44)." *Hermes* 75: 241–64. Repr. in Marg 1965: 541–73.

Kloesel, Hans. 1935. *Libertas.* Diss., Univ. of Breslau.

Knox, Bernard M. W. 1954. "Why Is Oedipus Called *Tyrannos?*" *CJ* 50: 97–102.

———. 1957. *Oedipus at Thebes: Sophocles' Tragic Hero and His Time.* New Haven, Conn.

———. 1961. "The *Ajax* of Sophocles." *HSCP* 65: 1–37. Repr. in Knox 1979: 125–60.

———. 1979. *Word and Action: Essays on the Ancient Theater.* Baltimore.

Koch, Christian. 1991. *Volksbeschlüsse in Seebundangelegenheiten: Das Verfahrensrecht Athens im Ersten Attischen Seebund.* Frankfurt am Main.

———. 1993. "Integration unter Vorbehalt—der athenische Volksbeschluss über die Samier von 405/4 v. Chr." *Tyche* 8: 63–75.

Köhnken, Adolf. 1975. "Gods and Descendants of Aiakos in Pindar's Eighth Isthmian Ode." *BICS* 22: 25–36.

Koselleck, Reinhart. 1972a. "Begriffsgeschichte und Sozialgeschichte." *Kölner Zeitschrift für Soziologie und Sozialpsychologie,* special issue, 16: 116–31. Repr. in Reinhart Koselleck, *Vergangene Zukunft: Zur Semantik geschichtlicher Zeiten,* 107–29. Frankfurt am Main, 1979. English tr. in Reinhart Koselleck, *Futures Past,* tr. Keith Tribe, 73–91. Cambridge, Mass., 1979.

———. 1972b. "Einleitung." In Brunner et al. 1972–97: 1.xiii–xxvii.

———. 1987. "Sozialgeschichte und Begriffsgeschichte." In Wolfgang Schieder and Volker Sellin, eds., *Sozialgeschichte in Deutschland,* 1.89–109. Göttingen.

———. 1989. "Linguistic Change and the History of Events." *JMH* 61: 649–66.

———, ed. 1979. *Historische Semantik und Begriffsgeschichte.* Stuttgart.

Kraay, Colin M., and Max Hirmer. 1966. *Greek Coins.* New York.

Kraft, Konrad. 1964. "Bemerkungen zu den Perserkriegen." *Hermes* 92: 144–71.

Kraut, Richard. 1989. *Aristotle on the Human Good.* Princeton.

Krentz, Peter. 1982. *The Thirty at Athens.* Ithaca, N.Y.

———. 1989. *Xenophon, Hellenika I–II.3.10, Edited with an Introduction, Translation and Commentary.* Warminster, England.

———. 2002. "Fighting by the Rules: The Invention of the Hoplite Agōn." *Hesperia* 71: 23–39.

Krumeich, Ralf. 1991. "Zu den goldenen Dreifüssen der Deinomeniden in Delphi." *JDAI* 106: 37–62.

Kuch, Heinrich. 1974. *Kriegsgefangenschaft und Sklaverei bei Euripides.* Berlin.

Kuhrt, Amélie. 1988. "Earth and Water." In Amélie Kuhrt and Heleen Sancisi-Weerdenburg, eds., *Achaemenid History,* vol. 3, *Method and Theory,* 87–99. Leiden.

———. 1995. *The Ancient Near East, c. 3000–330 B.C.* 2 vols. London.

Kunkel, Wolfgang. 1969. "Zum Freiheitsbegriff der späten Republik und des Prinzipats." In Richard Klein, ed., *Prinzipat und Freiheit,* 68–93. Wege der Forschung 135. Darmstadt.

Labarbe, Jules. 1957. *La loi navale de Thémistocle.* Paris.

La Bua, V. 1975. "Sulla conquista persiana di Samo." *MGR* 4: 41–102.

———. 1978. "Logos samio e storia samia in Erodoto." *MGR* 6: 1–88.

Lacey, W. K. 1968. *The Family in Classical Greece.* Ithaca, N.Y.

Laffineur, Robert, and Wolf-Dietrich Niemeier, eds. 1995. *Politeia: Society and State in the Aegean Bronze Age.* Brussels and Austin, Tex.

Laidlaw, William A. 1933. *A History of Delos.* Oxford.

Lambert, Stephen. 1997. "The Attic Genos Salaminioi and the Island of Salamis." *ZPE* 119: 85–106.

Lamberton, Robert. 1988. *Hesiod.* New Haven, Conn.

Lana, Italo. 1955. "La libertà nel mondo antico." *RFIC,* n.s., 33: 1–28.

Lanza, Diego. 1977. *Il tiranno e il suo pubblico.* Turin.

Larsen, Jakob A. O. 1932. "Sparta and the Ionian Revolt: A Study of Spartan Foreign Policy and the Genesis of the Peloponnnesian League." *CP* 27: 136–50.

———. 1933–34. "The Constitution of the Peloponnesian League." 2 parts. *CP* 28: 257–76; *CP* 29: 1–19.

———. 1936. "Perioeci in Crete." *CP* 31: 11–22.

———. 1937. "Perioikoi (1)." *RE* 19: 816–33.

———. 1940. "The Constitution and Original Purpose of the Delian League." *HSCP* 51: 175–213.

———. 1944. "Federation for Peace in Ancient Greece." *CP* 39: 145–62.

———. 1948. "Cleisthenes and the Development of the Theory of Democracy at Athens." In Milton R. Konvitz and Arthur E. Murphy, eds., *Essays in Political Theory, Presented to George H. Sabine,* 1–16. Ithaca, N.Y.

———. 1954. "The Judgment of Antiquity on Democracy." *CP* 49: 1–14.

———. 1955a. "The Boeotian Confederacy and Fifth-Century Oligarchic Theory." *TAPA* 86: 40–50.

———. 1955b. *Representative Government in Greek and Roman History.* Berkeley.

———. 1960. "A New Interpretation of the Thessalian Confederacy." *CP* 55: 229–48.

———. 1962. "Freedom and Its Obstacles in Ancient Greece." *CP* 57: 230–34.

———. 1968. *Greek Federal States: Their Institutions and History.* Oxford.

Larsen, Mogens T., ed. 1979. *Power and Propaganda: A Symposium on Ancient Empires.* Mesopotamia 7. Copenhagen.

Latacz, Joachim. 1977. *Kampfparänese, Kampfdarstellung und Kampfwirklichkeit in der Ilias, bei Kallinos und Tyrtaios.* Munich.

———. 1984. "Das Menschenbild Homers." *Gymnasium* 91: 15–39.

———. 1996. *Homer: His Art and His World.* Tr. James P. Holoka. Ann Arbor, Mich.

———, ed. 1991. *Zweihundert Jahre Homer-Forschung.* Stuttgart.

Lateiner, Donald. 1971. "Lysias and Athenian Politics." Diss., Stanford Univ.

———. 1982. "The Failure of the Ionian Revolt." *Historia* 31: 129–60.

———. 1986. "The Empirical Element in the Methods of Early Greek Medical Writers and Herodotus: A Shared Epistemological Response." *Antichthon* 20: 1–20.

———. 1989. *The Historical Method of Herodotus.* Toronto.

Latte, Kurt. 1968. *Kleine Schriften zu Religion, Recht, Literatur und Sprache der Griechen und Römer.* Munich.

Lattimore, Richmond A. 1942. *Themes in Greek and Latin Epitaphs.* Urbana, Ill. Repr. 1962.

Lauffer, Siegfried. 1960. "Der antike Freiheitsbegriff." In *Atti del XII Congresso Internazionale di Filosofia*, 11.113–16. Florence.

Lauffer, Siegfried, and Dieter Hennig. 1974. "Orchomenos." *RE* Suppl. 14: 290–355.

Lavelle, Brian. 1988. "A Note on the First Three Victims of Ostracism (*Athēnaion Politeia* 22.4)." *CP* 83: 131–35.

———. 1993. *The Sorrow and the Pity: A Prolegomenon to a History of Athens under the Peisistratids, c. 560–510 B.C. Historia* Einzelschriften 80. Stuttgart.

———. 2000. "Herodotos and the 'Parties' of Attika." *C&M* 51: 51–102.

Lazenby, J. F. 1993. *The Defence of Greece, 490–479 B.C.* Warminster, England.

Legon, Ronald P. 1968. "Megara and Mytilene." *Phoenix* 22: 200–25.

Lehmann, Gustav Adolf. 1972. "Die revolutionäre Machtergreifung der 'Dreissig' und die staatliche Teilung Attikas (404–401/0 v. Chr.)." In Stiehl and Lehmann 1972: 201–33.

———. 1980. "Der 'Erste Heilige Krieg'—Eine Fiktion?" *Historia* 29: 242–46.

———. 1981. "Der Ostrakismos-Entscheid in Athen: Von Kleisthenes zur Ära des Themistokles." *ZPE* 41: 85–99.

———. 1987. "Überlegungen zur Krise der attischen Demokratie im Peloponnesischen Krieg: Vom Ostrakismos des Hyperbolos zum Thargelion 411 v. Chr." *ZPE* 69: 33–73.

———. 1997. *Oligarchische Herrschaft im klassischen Athen: Zu den Krisen und Katastrophen der attischen Demokratie im 5. und 4. Jahrhundert v. Chr.* Opladen.

Lehmann, Hartmut, and Melvin Richter, eds. 1996. *The Meaning of Historical Terms and Concepts: New Studies on* Begriffsgeschichte. Washington, D.C.

Lejeune, M. 1958. "Les documents pyliens des séries Na, Ng, Nn." In M. Lejeune, *Mémoires de philologie mycénienne*, 1.127–55. Paris.

———. 1959. "Textes Mycéniens relatifs aux esclaves." *Historia* 8: 129–44.

Lencman, J. A. 1966. *Die Sklaverei im mykenischen und homerischen Griechenland.* Wiesbaden.

Lenfant, Dominique. 1997. "Rois et tyrans dans le théâtre d'Aristophane." *Ktema* 22: 185–200.

Lengauer, Wlodzimierz. 1987. "Die politische Bedeutung der Gleichheitsidee im 5. und 4. Jh. v. Chr.: Einige Bemerkungen über *Isonomia*." In Wolfgang Will and Johannes Heinrichs, eds., *Zu Alexander d. Gr.: Festschrift G. Wirth*, 1.53–87. Amsterdam.

Lenschau, T. 1937. "Triakonta." *RE* 6A.2: 2355–77.

Leppin, Hartmut. 1992. "Die *archontes en tais polesi* des Delisch-Attischen Seebundes." *Historia* 41: 257–71.

Lesky, Albin. 1966a. *Gesammelte Schriften.* Bern and Munich.

———. 1966b. *A History of Greek Literature.* Tr. James Willis and Cornelis de Heer. New York.

———. 1967. "Homeros." *RE* Suppl. 11: 687–846.

Lévêque, Pierre, and Pierre Vidal-Naquet. 1996. *Cleisthenes the Athenian.* Tr. David A. Curtis. Atlantic Highlands, N.J.

Levi, M. A. 1997. "La 'politica estera' di Atene nello Pseudo-Senofonte." In Gigante and Maddoli 1997: 61–68.

Lévy, Edmond. 1973. "Réformes et date de Solon: Réponse à F. Cassola." *PdP* 28: 88–91.

———. 1976. *Athènes devant la défaite de 404: Histoire d'une crise idéologique.* Bibliothèque des Ecoles Françaises d'Athènes et de Rome 225. Athens.

———. 1983. "Autonomia et éleuthéria au Ve siècle." *RPh* 57: 249–70.

———, ed. 1987. *Le système palatial en Orient, en Grèce et à Rome.* Strasbourg.

Lewis, D. M. 1954. "Notes on Attic Inscriptions." *BSA* 49: 17–50.

———. 1977. *Sparta and Persia.* Leiden.

———. 1988. "The Tyranny of the Pisistratidae." *CAH* 4^2: 287–302.

———. 1992. "Mainland Greece, 479–451 B.C.," "The Thirty Years' Peace," "The Archidamian War." *CAH* 5²: 96–120, 121–146, 370–432.

———. 1994. "Sparta as Victor," "Sicily, 413–368 B.C." *CAH* 6²: 24–44, 120–55.

Lewis, D. M., and Ronald Stroud. 1979. "Athens Honors King Euagoras of Salamis." *Hesperia* 48: 180–93.

Lewis, J. D. 1971. "Isegoria at Athens: When Did It Begin?" *Historia* 20: 129–40.

Liddell, H. G., and Robert Scott, eds. 1940. *A Greek-English Lexicon.* Rev. by H. S. Jones. 9th ed. With *A Supplement,* 1968. Oxford.

Lindgren, Margareta. 1973. *The People of Pylos.* 2 vols. Uppsala.

Linforth, Ivan M. 1913. *Solon the Athenian.* Berkeley and Los Angeles.

Link, Stefan. 1991. *Landverteilung und sozialer Frieden im archaischen Griechenland.* Stuttgart.

Lintott, Andrew. 1981. *Violence, Civil Strife and Revolution in the Classical City, 750–330 B.C.* Baltimore.

Lloyd, Alan B. 1988. *Herodotus Book II: Commentary 99–182.* Leiden.

Lloyd, G. E. R. 1996. *Adversaries and Authorities: Investigations into Ancient Greek and Chinese Science.* Cambridge.

Lobel, Edgar, and Denys Page, eds. 1955. *Poetarum Lesbiorum Fragmenta.* Oxford.

Loenen, Dirk. 1930. *Vrijheid en gelijkheid in Athene.* Amsterdam.

Lombardo, Stanley, tr. 1997. *Homer:* Iliad. Indianapolis.

Long, Anthony A. 1970. "Morals and Values in Homer." *JHS* 90: 121–39.

Loraux, Nicole. 1973. "'Marathon' ou l'histoire idéologique." *REA* 75: 13–42.

———. 1986. *The Invention of Athens: The Funeral Oration in the Classical City.* Tr. Alan Sheridan. Cambridge, Mass.

———. 1996. "Clistene e i nuovi caratteri della lotta politica." In Settis 1996–98: 2.1.1083–1110.

Lotze, Detlev. 1959. Metaxy eleutheron kai doulon: *Studien zur Rechtsstellung unfreier Landbevölkerungen in Griechenland bis zum 4. Jh. v. Chr.* Berlin.

———. 1962. "Zu den *woikees* von Gortyn." *Klio* 40: 32–43.

———. 1964. *Lysander und der Peloponnesische Krieg.* Abh. Akad. Leipzig, phil.-hist. Kl., 57.1. Berlin.

———. 1970. "Selbstbewusstsein und Machtpolitik: Bemerkungen zur machtpolitischen Interpretation spartanischen Verhaltens in den Jahren 479–477 v. Chr." *Klio* 52: 255–75.

———. 1993–94. "Bürger zweiter Klasse: Spartas Perioken, ihre Stellung und Funktion im Staat der Lakedaimonier." *Akademie Gemeinnütziger Wissenschaften Erfurt, Sitzungsberichte der geisteswiss. Kl.,* 2: 37–51.

Luke, Joanna. 1994. "The Krater, *Kratos,* and the *Polis." G&R* 41: 23–32.

Luraghi, Nino. 1998. "Il Gran Re e tiranni: Per una valutazione storica della tirannide in Asia Minore durante il regno dei primi Achemenidi." *Klio* 80: 22–46.

———. 2001. "Der Erdbebenaufstand und die Entstehung der messenischen Identität." In Papenfuss and Strocka 2001: 279–301.

———. 2002a. "Becoming Messenian." *JHS* 122: 45–69.

———. 2002b. "Helotic Slavery Reconsidered." In Anton Powell and Stephen Hodkinson, eds., *Sparta: Beyond the Mirage,* 227–48. London.

MacDowell, Douglas M. 1960. "Aegina and the Delian League." *JHS* 80: 118–21.

———. 1963. *Athenian Homicide Law in the Age of the Orators.* Manchester.

———. 1971. *Aristophanes,* Wasps: *Edited with Introduction and Commentary.* Oxford.

———. 1978. *The Law in Classical Athens.* London.

Macleod, Colin. 1983. *Collected Essays.* Oxford.

Mactoux, Marie-Madeleine. 1988. "Lois de Solon sur les esclaves et formation d'une société esclavagiste." In Yuge and Doi 1988: 331–54.

Maddoli, Gianfranco. 1970. *"Damos e basilees:* Contributo allo studio delle origini della *polis."* *SMEA* 12: 7–57.

———, ed. 1994. *L'*Athenaion politeia *di Aristotele, 1891–1991: Per un bilancio di cento anni di studi.* Perugia.

Maidment, K. J., ed. 1941. *Minor Attic Orators.* Vol. 1. LCL 308. Cambridge, Mass.

Malkin, Irad. 1994. *Myth and Territory in the Spartan Mediterranean.* Cambridge.

Manfredini, Mario, and Luigi Piccirilli, comms. 1977. *Plutarco,* La vita di Solone. Milan.

———. 1980. *Plutarco:* Le vite di Licurgo e di Numa. Milan.

Manville, Philip B. 1990. *The Origins of Citizenship in Ancient Athens.* Princeton.

———. 1994. "Toward a New Paradigm of Athenian Citizenship." In Boegehold and Scafuro 1994: 21–33.

Marek, Christian. 1984. *Die Proxenie.* Frankfurt am Main.

Marg, Walter. 1970. *Hesiod: Sämtliche Gedichte.* Zurich.

———, ed. 1965. *Herodot: Eine Auswahl aus der neueren Forschung.* 2d ed. Darmstadt.

Mark, Ira S. 1993. *The Sanctuary of Athena Nike in Athens: Architectural Stages and Chronology. Hesperia* Suppl. 26. Princeton.

Martin, Jochen. 1974. "Von Kleisthenes zu Ephialtes: Zur Entstehung der athenischen Demokratie." *Chiron* 4: 5–42. Repr. in Kinzl 1995: 160–212.

———. 1978. "Monarchie." In Brunner et al. 1972–97: 4.134–40.

———. 1979a. "Dynasteia: Eine begriffs-, verfassungs- und sozialgeschichtliche Skizze." In Koselleck 1979: 228–41.

———. 1979b. "Two Ancient Histories: A Comparative Study of Greece and Rome." *Social History* 4: 285–98.

Martin, Paul M. 1990. "Des tentatives de tyrannies à Rome aux Ve–IVe siècles?" In Eder 1990: 49–73.

Martin, Richard P. 1989. *The Language of Heroes.* Ithaca, N.Y.

Martin, Roland. 1951. *Recherches sur l'agora grecque.* Paris.

Martin, Victor. 1940. *La vie internationale dans la Grèce des cités, VIe–IVe s. av. J-C.* Paris.

Marwitz, H. 1979. "Eine Strigilis." *Antike Kunst* 22: 72–81.

Masaracchia, Agostino. 1958. *Solone.* Florence.

Mastrocinque, Attilio. 1981. "Gli dei protettori della città." In Sordi 1981: 3–21.

Mattingly, Harold B. 1968. "Athenian Finances in the Peloponnesian War." *BCH* 92: 450–85. Repr. in Mattingly 1996: 215–57.

———. 1992. "Epigraphy and the Athenian Empire." *Historia* 41: 129–38.

———. 1996. *The Athenian Empire Restored: Epigraphic and Historical Studies.* Ann Arbor, Mich.

Maurizio, Lisa. 1998. "The Panathenaic Procession: Athens' Participatory Democracy on Display?" In Boedeker and Raaflaub 1998: 297–317.

McCann, David R., and Barry S. Strauss, eds. 2001. *War and Democracy: A Comparative Study of the Korean War and the Peloponnesian War.* Armonk, N.Y., and London.

McCargar, D. J. 1976. "New Evidence for the Kleisthenic *boule." CP* 71: 248–52.

McGlew, James. 1993. *Tyranny and Political Culture in Ancient Greece.* Ithaca, N.Y.

McGregor, M. F. 1956. "The Politics of the Historian Thucydides." *Phoenix* 10: 93–102.

McInerney, Jeremy. 1999. *The Folds of Parnassos: Land and Ethnicity in Ancient Phokis.* Austin, Tex.

Méautis, Georges. 1960. *L'authenticité et la date du* Prométhé Enchaîné *d'Eschyle.* Neuchâtel.

Meder, Anton. 1938. *Der Athenische Demos zur Zeit des Peloponnesischen Krieges im Lichte zeitgenössischer Quellen.* Ph.D. diss., Univ. of Munich.

Meier, Christian. 1968. "Drei Bemerkungen zur Vor- und Frühgeschichte des Begriffs Demokratie." In *Discordia concors: Festgabe für Edgar Bonjour,* 1.3–29. Basel. Repr. in Kinzl 1995: 125–58.

———. 1970. *Entstehung des Begriffs 'Demokratie': Vier Prolegomena zu einer historischen Theorie.* Frankfurt am Main.

———. 1972. "Adel, Aristokratie in der Antike"; "Demokratie: Antike Grundlagen." In Brunner et al. 1972–97: 1.1–11, 821–35.

———. 1973. "Die Entstehung der Historie." In Reinhart Koselleck and Wolf-Dieter Stempel, eds., *Geschichte—Ereignis und Erzählung,* 251–305. Munich.

———. 1975. "Freiheit: Antike Grundlagen." In Brunner et al. 1972–97: 2.426–29.

———. 1977. "Der Wandel der politisch-sozialen Begriffswelt im 5. Jahrhundert v. Chr." *ABG* 21: 7–41. Rev. and expanded in Koselleck 1979: 193–227, and in Meier 1980: 275–325 = 1990: 157–85.

———. 1978. "Entstehung und Besonderheit der griechischen Demokratie." *Zeitschrift für Politik* 25: 1–31. Repr. in Kinzl 1995: 248–301.

———. 1980. *Die Entstehung des Politischen bei den Griechen.* Frankfurt am Main. English tr., Meier 1990.

———. 1982. "Macht, Gewalt: Terminologie und Begrifflichkeit in der Antike." In Brunner et al. 1972–97: 3.820–35.

———. 1984. "Arbeit, Politik, Identität: Neue Fragen im alten Athen?" In V. Schubert, ed., *Der Mensch und seine Arbeit: Eine Ringvorlesung der Universität München,* 47–109. St. Ottilien.

———. 1987a. "Die Entstehung einer autonomen Intelligenz bei den Griechen." In S. N. Eisenstadt, ed., *Kulturen der Achsenzeit,* 1.89–127. Frankfurt am Main. English tr. in S. N. Eisenstadt, ed., *The Origins and Diversity of Axial Age Civilizations,* 65–91. Albany, N.Y., 1986.

———. 1987b. "Historical Answers to Historical Questions: The Origins of History in Ancient Greece." In Boedeker and Peradotto 1987: 41–57.

———. 1987c. "Der Umbruch zur Demokratie in Athen (462/61 v. Chr.)." In R. Herzog and R. Koselleck, eds., *Epochenschwelle und Epochenbewusstsein,* 353–80. Munich.

———. 1988. "Bürger-Identität und Demokratie." In Christian Meier and Paul Veyne, *Kannten die Griechen die Demokratie?* 47–95. Berlin.

———. 1990. *The Greek Discovery of Politics.* Tr. David McLintock. Cambridge, Mass.

———. 1993a. *Athen: Ein Neubeginn der Weltgeschichte.* Berlin. English tr., London, 1999.

———. 1993b. *The Political Art of Greek Tragedy.* Tr. Andrew Webber. Baltimore.

Meiggs, Russell. 1943. "The Growth of Athenian Imperialism." *JHS* 63: 21–34.

———. 1949. "A Note on Athenian Imperialism." *CR* 63: 9–12.

———. 1963. "The Crisis of Athenian Imperialism." *HSCP* 67: 1–36.

———. 1966. "The Dating of Fifth-Century Attic Inscriptions." *JHS* 86: 86–98.

———. 1972. *The Athenian Empire.* Oxford.

Meiggs, Russell, and David Lewis, eds. 1969. *A Selection of Greek Historical Inscriptions to the End of the Fifth Century B.C.* Oxford. Rev. ed., 1988.

Meister, Klaus. 1970. "Das persisch-karthagische Bündnis von 481 v. Chr. (Bengtson, Staatsverträge II nr. 129)." *Historia* 19: 607–12.

———. 1982. *Die Ungeschichtlichkeit des Kalliasfriedens und deren historische Folgen.* Palingenesia 18. Wiesbaden.

Mele, Alfonso. 1968. *Società e lavoro nei poemi omerici.* Naples.

———. 1976. "Eslavage et liberté dans la société mycénienne" (including discussion). In *Actes du Colloque 1973 sur l'esclavage,* 115–55. Paris.

Merante, V. 1972–73. "La Sicilia e Cartagine dal V secolo alla conquista romana." *Kokalos* 18–19: 77–107.

Meritt, Benjamin D. 1952. "Greek Inscriptions." *Hesperia* 21: 340–80.

Meritt, Benjamin D., and H. T. Wade-Gery. 1962–63. "The Dating of Documents to the Mid–Fifth Century." *JHS* 82: 67–74, 83: 100–17.

Meritt, Benjamin D., H. T. Wade-Gery, and Malcolm F. McGregor. 1939–53. *The Athenian Tribute Lists.* 4 vols. Princeton.

Mertens, J. 1947. "Le tétradrachme à la légende *DANKLAION.*" *Revue belge de numismatique et de sigillographie* 93: 19–33.

Meyer, Eduard. 1892–99. *Forschungen zur Alten Geschichte.* 2 vols. Halle.

———. 1905. "Der Mauerbau des Themistokles." *Hermes* 40: 561–69.

Meyer, Hans D. 1963. "Vorgeschichte und Begründung des delisch-attischen Seebundes." *Historia* 12: 405–46.

———. 1967. "Thukydides Melesiou und die oligarchische Opposition gegen Perikles." *Historia* 16: 141–54.

Michelini, Ann. 1994. "Political Themes in Euripides' *Suppliants.*" *AJP* 115: 219–52.

Milani, Celestina. 1981. "Osservazioni sul *wanax* miceneo." In Marta Sordi, ed., *Religione e politica nel mondo antico*, 22–40. Milan.

Miller, M. 1953. "Greek Kinship Terminology." *JHS* 53: 46–52.

Miller, Margaret C. 1997. *Athens and Persia in the Fifth Century B.C.: A Study in Cultural Receptivity.* Cambridge.

Miller, Stephen G. 1995. "Old Metroon and Old Bouleuterion in the Classical Agora of Athens." In Hansen and Raaflaub 1995: 133–56.

Millett, Paul. 1984. "Hesiod and His World." *PCPhS*, n.s., 30: 84–115.

Mills, Sophie. 1997. *Theseus, Tragedy and the Athenian Empire.* Oxford.

Mitchell, B. M. 1975. "Herodotus and Samos." *JHS* 95: 75–91.

Mitchell, Lynette G., and P. J. Rhodes, eds. 1997. *The Development of the Polis in Archaic Greece.* London.

Moles, John. 1996. "Herodotus Warns the Athenians." *Papers of the Leeds International Latin Seminar* 9: 259–84.

———. 2002. "Herodotus and Athens." In Bakker et al. 2002: 33–52.

Molho, Anthony, Kurt Raaflaub, and Julia Emlen, eds. 1991. *Athens and Rome, Florence and Venice: City-States in Classical Antiquity and Medieval Italy.* Stuttgart and Ann Arbor, Mich.

Möller, Astrid. 2000. *Naukratis: Trade in Archaic Greece.* Oxford.

Molyneux, John H. 1992. *Simonides: A Historical Study.* Wauconda, Ill.

Momigliano, Arnaldo. 1944. "Sea-Power in Greek Thought." *CR* 58: 1–7.

———. 1971. "La libertà di parola nel mondo antico." *RSI* 83: 499–524. Repr. in Arnaldo Momigliano, *Sesto contributo alla storia degli studi classici e del mondo antico*, 2.403–36. Rome, 1980.

———. 1974. "Freedom of Speech and Religious Tolerance in the Ancient World." *Annali della Scuola Normale Superiore di Pisa*, 3d ser., 4: 331–49. Repr. in Arnaldo Momigliano, *Sesto contributo*, 459–76, and in Humphreys 1978: 179–93.

———. 1979. "Persian Empire and Greek Freedom." In A. Ryan, ed., *The Idea of Freedom: Essays in Honour of Isaiah Berlin*, 139–51. Oxford. Repr. in Arnaldo Momigliano, *Settimo contributo alla storia degli studi classici e del mondo antico*, 61–75. Rome, 1984.

———. 1996. *Pace e libertà nel mondo antico: Lezioni a Cambridge, gennaio–marzo 1940.* Ed. Riccardo Di Donato. Florence.

Monoson, S. Sara. 1994. "Citizen as Erastes: Erotic Imagery and the Idea of Reciprocity in the Periclean Funeral Oration." *Political Theory* 22: 253–76.

Mørch, Søren. 1970. "Popularité ou impopularité d'Athènes chez Thucydide." *C&M* 31: 49–71.

Morgan, Kathryn, ed. 2003. *Popular Tyranny: Sovereignty and Its Discontents in Classical Athens.* Austin, Tex.

Morpeth, Neil. 1982. "Aristotle, Plato, and Self-Sufficiency: Ancient and Modern Controversy in Economic History and Theory." *Ancient Society: Resources for Teachers* 12: 34–46.

———. 1993. "Autarkeia: Notes on Its Cultural and Historical Context." In Kevin Lee, C. Mackie, and Harold Tarrant, eds., *Multarum Artium Scientia: Festschrift for R. G. Tanner*, 126–30. *Prudentia* Suppl. vol. Auckland, 1993.

Morpurgo-Davies, Anna. 1979. "Terminology of Power and Terminology of Work in Greek and Linear B." In *Colloquium Mycenaeum 1975*, 87–108. Geneva.

Morris, Ian. 1986. "The Use and Abuse of Homer." *CA* 5: 81–138.

———. 1987. *Burial and Ancient Society: The Rise of the Greek City-State.* Cambridge.

———. 1991. "The Early Polis as City and State." In John Rich and Andrew Wallace-Hadrill, eds., *City and Country in the Ancient World*, 27–57. London.

———. 1996. "The Strong Principle of Equality and the Archaic Origins of Greek Democracy." In Ober and Hedrick 1996: 19–48.

Morris, Ian, and Barry Powell, eds. 1997. *A New Companion to Homer.* Leiden.

Morris, Ian, and Kurt Raaflaub, eds. 1998. *Democracy 2500? Questions and Challenges.* Archaeological Institute of America: Colloquia and Conference Papers 2. Dubuque, Iowa.

Morrow, Glenn R. 1937. "The Murder of Slaves in Attic Law." *CP* 32: 210–27.

Mossé, Claude. 1962. *La fin de la démocratie athénienne.* Paris.

———. 1969. *The Ancient World at Work.* Tr. Janet Lloyd. New York.

———. 1979. "Les dépendants paysans dans le monde grec à l'époque archaïque et classique." In *Terres et paysans dépendants dans les sociétés antiques*, 85–150. Paris.

———. 1981. "Die Bezeichnungen besonderer Abhängigkeitsverhältnisse (Sparta, Athen, Kreta)." In Welskopf 1981–85: 3.354–59.

———. 1989. *L'antiquité dans la Révolution française.* Paris.

Mühll, Peter von der. 1958. "Der Anlass zur zweiten Pythie Pindars." *MH* 15: 215–21.

Mulgan, R. G. 1970. "Aristotle and the Democratic Conception of Freedom." In B. F. Harris, ed., *Auckland Classical Essays Presented to E. M. Blaiklock*, 95–111. Auckland and Oxford.

———. 1984. "Liberty in Ancient Greece." In Zbigniew Pelczynski and John Gray, eds., *Conceptions of Liberty in Political Philosophy*, 7–29. New York.

Muller, Herbert J. 1962. *Freedom in the Ancient World.* London.

Munding, Heinz. 1959. *Hesiods Erga in ihrem Verhältnis zur Ilias.* Frankfurt am Main.

Munn, Mark. 1997. "Thebes and Central Greece." In Tritle 1997: 66–106.

———. 2000. *The School of History: Athens in the Age of Socrates.* Berkeley and Los Angeles.

Murdoch, Iris. 1968. *The Nice and the Good.* New York.

Murray, Oswyn. 1988. "The Ionian Revolt." *CAH* 4²: 461–90.

———. 1990. "The Solonian Law of Hybris." In Cartledge et al. 1990: 139–46.

———. 1993. *Early Greece.* 2d ed. Cambridge, Mass.

———. 1995. "Liberty and the Ancient Greeks." In John A. Koumoulides, ed., *The Good Idea: Democracy and Ancient Greece*, 33–55. New Rochelle, N.Y.

Nachtergael, Georges. 1977. *Les Galates en Grèce et les Sôtèria de Delphes.* Brussels.

Nafissi, Massimo. 1991. *La nascita del kosmos: Studi sulla storia e la società di Sparta.* Naples.

Nagy, Gregory. 1979. *The Best of the Achaeans: Concepts of the Hero in Archaic Greek Poetry.* Baltimore.

———. 1983. "Poet and Tyrant: *Theognidea* 39–52, 1081–1082b." *CA* 2: 82–91.

———. 1990. *Greek Mythology and Poetics.* Ithaca, N.Y.

———. 1993. "Images of Justice in Early Greek Poetry." In K. D. Irani and Morris Silver, eds., *Social Justice in the Ancient World*, 61–68. Westport, Conn.

———. 1996. *Homeric Questions*. Austin, Tex.

Nakategawa, Yoshio. 1998. *Liberty and Justice in Ancient Greece* (in Japanese, with English summary, 8–9). Tokyo.

Nauck, Augustus, ed. 1889. *Tragicorum Graecorum Fragmenta*. 2d ed. Leipzig.

Nease, A. S. 1949. "Garrisons in the Athenian Empire." *Phoenix* 3: 102–11.

Nenci, Giuseppe. 1956. *Introduzione alle guerre persiane*. Pisa.

———, ed., tr., comm. 1994. *Erodoto: Le storie V, La rivolta della Ionia*. Milan.

———. 1998. *Erodoto: Le storie VI, La battaglia di Maratona*. Milan.

Nesselhauf, Herbert. 1933. *Untersuchungen zur Geschichte der delisch-attischen Symmachie*. Klio Beiheft 30. Leipzig. Repr., Aalen, 1963.

———. 1934. "Die diplomatischen Verhandlungen vor dem Peloponnesischen Kriege (Thuk. 1.139ff.)." *Hermes* 69: 286–99.

Nestle, Dieter. 1967. *Eleutheria: Studien zum Wesen der Freiheit bei den Griechen und im Neuen Testament*. Vol. 1, *Die Griechen*. Tübingen.

———. 1972. "Freiheit." *RAC* 8: 269–306.

Nestle, Wilhelm. 1942. *Vom Mythos zum Logos*. 2d ed. Stuttgart. Repr., Aalen, 1966.

Nicolai, Walter. 1986. *Versuch über Herodots Geschichtsphilosophie*. Heidelberg.

———. 1993. "Gefolgschaftsverweigerung als politisches Druckmittel in der Ilias." In Raaflaub and Müller-Luckner 1993: 317–41.

Nilsson, Martin P. 1950. *Griechischer Glaube*. Bern.

———. 1951. *Cults, Myths, Oracles, and Politics in Ancient Greece*. Lund. Repr., New York, 1972.

———. 1967. *Geschichte der griechischen Religion*. Vol. 1. 3d ed. HdAW 5.2.1. Munich.

Nippel, Wilfried. 1980. *Mischverfassungstheorie und Verfassungsrealität in Antike und früher Neuzeit*. Stuttgart.

Nisetich, Frank J., tr. 1980. *Pindar's Victory Songs*. Baltimore.

Nolte, Ferdinand. 1923. *Die historisch-politischen Voraussetzungen des Königsfriedens von 386 v. Chr.* Frankfurt am Main.

Nörr, Dieter. 1966. "Vom griechischen Staat." *Der Staat* 3: 353–70.

North, Helen. 1966. *Sophrosyne: Self-Knowledge and Self-Restraint in Greek Literature*. Ithaca, N.Y.

Norwood, Gilbert. 1930. "The Babylonians of Aristophanes." *CP* 25: 1–10.

———. 1932. *Greek Comedy*. Boston. Repr., New York, 1963.

Nouhaud, Michel. 1982. *L'utilisation de l'histoire par les orateurs attiques*. Paris.

Nowag, Werner. 1983. *Raub und Beute in der archaischen Zeit der Griechen*. Frankfurt am Main.

Nussbaum, G. 1960. "Labour and Status in the *Works and Days*." *CQ*, n.s., 10: 213–20.

Nussbaum, Martha. 1986. *The Fragility of Goodness: Luck and Ethics in Greek Tragedy and Philosophy*. Cambridge.

Ober, Josiah. 1989. *Mass and Elite in Democratic Athens: Rhetoric, Ideology, and the Power of the People*. Princeton.

———. 1993. "The Athenian Revolution of 508/7 B.C.E.: Violence, Authority, and the Origins of Democracy." In Dougherty and Kurke 1993: 215–32. Repr. in Ober 1996: chap. 4.

———. 1996. *The Athenian Revolution: Essays on Ancient Greek Democracy and Political Theory*. Princeton.

———. 1998a. *Political Dissent in Democratic Athens: Intellectual Critics of Popular Rule*. Princeton.

———. 1998b. "Revolution Matters: Democracy as Demotic Action." In Morris and Raaflaub 1998: 67–85.

———. 2001. "Thucydides Theoretikos/Thucydides Histor: Realist Theory and the Challenge of History." In McCann and Strauss 2001: 273–306.

Ober, Josiah, and Charles Hedrick, eds. 1996. Dēmokratia: *A Conversation on Democracies, Ancient and Modern.* Princeton.

Oliva, Pavel. 1971. *Sparta and Her Social Problems.* Amsterdam and Prague.

———. 1988. *Solon: Legende und Wirklichkeit.* Konstanx.

Oliver, James H. 1935. "The Athenian Decree concerning Miletus in 450/49 B.C." *TAPA* 66: 177–98.

———. 1960. Demokratia, *the Gods, and the Free World.* Baltimore.

Olivier, Jean-Pierre. 1987. "Des extraits de contrats de vente d'esclaves dans les tablettes de Knossos." In *Studies in Mycenaean and Classical Greek, Presented to John Chadwick. Minos* 20–22: 479–98.

Olson, S. Douglas. 1995. *Blood and Iron: Stories and Storytelling in Homer's* Odyssey. Leiden.

O'Neil, James. 1995. *The Origins and Development of Ancient Greek Democracy.* Lanham, Md.

Orsi, D. P., and Silvana Cagnazzi. 1980. "Lessico politico: *Dēmokratia, dēmos.*" *QS* 11: 267–314.

———. 1981. "Lessico politico: *Oligarchia.*" *QS* 14: 135–50.

Orth, Wolfgang. 1977. *Königlicher Machtanspruch und städtische Freiheit.* Munich.

Osborne, M. J. 1981–83. *Naturalization in Athens.* 4 vols. Brussels.

Osborne, Robin. 1985. *Demos: The Discovery of Classical Attika.* Cambridge.

———. 1994. "Democracy and Imperialism in the Panathenaic Procession: The Parthenon Frieze in Its Context." In Coulson et al. 1994: 143–50.

———. 1995. "The Economics and Politics of Slavery at Athens." In Anton Powell, ed., *The Greek World,* 27–43. London.

———. 1996. *Greece in the Making, 1200–479 B.C.* London.

Ostwald, Martin. 1951. "The Prytaneion Decree Re-examined." *AJP* 72: 24–46.

———. 1955. "The Athenian Legislation against Tyranny and Subversion." *TAPA* 86: 103–28.

———. 1969. Nomos *and the Beginnings of Athenian Democracy.* Oxford.

———. 1973. "Isokratia as a Political Concept (Herodotus, 5.92α.1)." In S. M. Stern, Albert Hourani, and Vivian Brown, eds., *Islamic Philosophy and the Classical Tradition: Essays Presented to Richard Walzer,* 277–91. Oxford.

———. 1982. Autonomia: *Its Genesis and Early History.* American Classical Studies 11. Chico, Calif.

———. 1986. *From Popular Sovereignty to the Sovereignty of Law: Law, Society, and Politics in Fifth-Century Athens.* Berkeley and Los Angeles.

———. 1988. "The Reform of the Athenian State by Cleisthenes." *CAH* 4^2: 303–46.

———. 1991. "Herodotus and Athens." *ICS* 16: 137–48.

———. 1992. "Athens as a Cultural Centre." *CAH* 5^2: 306–69.

———. 1993. "*Stasis* and *autonomia* in Samos: A Comment on an Ideological Fallacy." *SCI* 12: 51–66.

———. 1995. "Freedom and the Greeks." In Davis 1995: 35–63, 326–33.

———. 1996. "Shares and Rights: 'Citizenship' Greek Style and American Style." In Ober and Hedrick 1996: 49–61.

———. 2000. Oligarchia: *The Development of a Constitutional Form in Ancient Greece.* Historia Einzelschriften 144. Stuttgart.

Page, Denys L. 1955. *Sappho and Alcaeus.* Oxford.

———, ed. 1962. *Poetae Melici Graeci.* Oxford.

———. 1981. *Further Greek Epigrams.* Cambridge.

Palmer, L. R. 1963. *The Interpretation of Mycenaean Greek Texts.* Oxford.

Panagl, Oswald, and Stephan Hiller. 1976. "Forschungsbericht Homer." *AAHG* 29: 1–70.

Paoli, U. E. 1959. "Zum attischen Strafrecht und Strafprozessrecht." *ZRG* 76: 97–112.

Papenfuss, Dietrich, and Volker M. Strocka, eds. 2001. *Gab es das griechische Wunder? Griechen-land zwischen dem Ende des 6. und der Mitte des 5. Jahrhunderts v. Chr.* Mainz.

Parke, H. W. 1930. "The Development of the Second Spartan Empire (405–371 B.C.)." *JHS* 50: 37–79.

———. 1977. *Festivals of the Athenians.* Ithaca, N.Y.

Parke, H. W., and D. E. W. Wormell. 1956. *The Delphic Oracle.* 2 vols. Oxford.

Parker, Robert. 1983. *Miasma: Pollution and Purification in Early Greek Religion.* Oxford.

———. 1996. *Athenian Religion: A History.* Oxford.

Parker, Victor. 1997. *Untersuchungen zum Lelantischen Krieg und verwandten Problemen der frühgriechischen Geschichte. Historia* Einzelschriften 109. Stuttgart.

———. 1998. "*Tyrannos*: The Semantics of a Political Concept from Archilochus to Aristotle." *Hermes* 126: 145–72.

Parry, Adam M. 1989. "Classical Philology and Literary Criticism." In Adam M. Parry, *The Language of Achilles and Other Papers,* 141–47. Oxford.

Patterson, Cynthia. 1981. *Pericles' Citizenship Law of 451/0 B.C.* Salem, N.H.

———. 1986. "*Hai Attikai*: The Other Athenians." *Helios* 13: 49–67.

Patterson, Orlando. 1982. *Slavery and Social Death.* Cambridge, Mass.

———. 1991. *Freedom.* Vol. 1, *Freedom in the Making of Western Culture.* New York.

Patzek, Barbara. 1992. *Homer und Mykene: Mündliche Dichtung und Geschichtsschreibung.* Munich.

Pearson, A. C., ed. 1917. *The Fragments of Sophocles.* Cambridge.

Pearson, Lionel I. 1936. "Propaganda in the Archidamian War." *CP* 31: 33–52.

———. 1962. *Popular Ethics in Ancient Greece.* Stanford.

Peek, Werner. 1933. "Ein attisches Skolion." *Hermes* 68: 118–21.

———. 1955. *Griechische Versinschriften.* Vol. 1, *Grabepigramme.* Berlin.

———. 1960. *Griechische Grabgedichte.* Berlin.

———. 1974. *Ein neuer spartanischer Staatsvertrag.* Abh. Sächs. Akad., phil.-hist. Kl., 65.3. Leipzig.

Peremans, Willy. 1972. "Sur l'acquisition du droit de cité à Athènes au VIe s. av. J.C." In Stiehl and Lehmann 1972: 122–30.

Peterson, Erik. 1929. "Zur Bedeutungsgeschichte von *parrhēsia.*" In I. W. Koepp, ed., *Reinhold-Seeberg-Festschrift,* 1.283–97. Leipzig.

Petzold, Karl-Ernst. 1993–94. "Die Gründung des Delisch-Attischen Seebundes: Element einer 'imperialistischen' Politik Athens?" *Historia* 42: 418–43; 43: 1–31. Repr. in Karl-Ernst Pet-zold, *Geschichtsdenken und Geschichtsschreibung: Kleine Schriften zur griechischen und rö-mischen Geschichte,* 300–56. *Historia* Einzelschriften 126. Stuttgart.

Pfeijffer, Ilja Leonard. 1995. "Pindar's Eighth *Pythian*: The Relevance of the Historical Setting." *Hermes* 123: 156–65.

———. 1999. *Three Aeginetan Odes of Pindar: A Commentary on* Nemean V, Nemean III, *and* Pythian VIII. *Mnemosyne* Suppl. 197. Leiden.

Piccirilli, Luigi, ed. 1973. *Gli arbitrati interstatali Greci.* Vol. 1. Pisa.

Piérart, Marcel. 1997. "L'attitude d'Argos à l'égard des autres cités d'Argolide." In Hansen 1997: 321–51.

———, ed. 1993. *Aristote et Athènes.* Fribourg.

Pistorius, Thomas. 1985. *Hegemoniestreben und Autonomiesicherung in der griechischen Ver-tragspolitik klassischer und hellenistischer Zeit.* Frankfurt am Main.

Pleket, Harry W. 1963. "Thasos and the Popularity of the Athenian Empire." *Historia* 12: 70–77.

———. 1972. "*Isonomia* and Cleisthenes: A Note." *Talanta* 4: 63–81.

Podlecki, Anthony J. 1966. *The Political Background of Aeschylean Tragedy.* Ann Arbor, Mich.

———. 1968. "Simonides: 480." *Historia* 17: 257–75.

———. 1973. "Epigraphica Simonidea." *Epigraphica* 35: 24–39.

———. 1984. *The Early Greek Poets and Their Times.* Vancouver.

———. 1998. *Perikles and His Circle.* London.

Pohlenz, Max. 1937. *Herodot: Der erste Geschichtsschreiber des Abendlandes.* Leipzig. Repr., Darmstadt, 1961.

———. 1955. *Griechische Freiheit: Wesen und Werden eines Lebensideals.* Heidelberg. English tr., Pohlenz 1966.

———. 1966. *Freedom in Greek Life and Thought: The History of an Ideal.* Tr. Carl Lofmark. Dordrecht.

Pohlmann, R. 1971. "Autonomie." *HWPh* 1: 701–19. Basel.

Pointner, F. 1969. *Die Verfassungstheorie des Isokrates.* Diss., Univ. of Munich.

Pokorny, Julius. 1959. *Indogermanisches etymologisches Wörterbuch.* Vol. 1. Bern.

Polignac, François de. 1995. *Cults, Territory, and the Origins of the Greek City-State.* Tr. Janet Lloyd. Chicago.

Pope, M. 1988. "Thucydides and Democracy." *Historia* 37: 276–96.

Popp, Harald. 1968. "Zum Verhältnis Athens zu seinen Bündnern im Attisch-Delischen Seebund." *Historia* 17: 425–43.

Pouncey, Peter R. 1980. *The Necessities of War: A Study of Thucydides' Pessimism.* New York.

Powell, Anton. 1988. *Athens and Sparta: Constructing Greek Political and Social History from 478 B.C.* London.

Powell, Barry. 1991. *Homer and the Origin of the Greek Alphabet.* Cambridge.

Prestel, Georg. 1939. *Die antidemokratische Strömung im Athen des 5. Jh.* Breslau. Repr., Aalen, 1974.

Price, Jonathan J. 2001. *Thucydides and Internal War.* Cambridge.

Pritchett, W. Kendrick. 1969. "The Transfer of the Delian Treasury." *Historia* 18: 17–21.

———. 1971–91. *The Greek State at War.* 5 vols. Berkeley.

Privitera, G. Aurelio. 1982. *Pindaro: Le* Istmiche, *Introduction and Commentary.* Milan.

Pusey, Nathan M. 1940. "Alcibiades and *to philopoli.*" *HSCP* 51: 215–31.

Quass, Friedemann. 1971. Nomos *und* Psephisma. Zetemata 55. Munich.

Quinn, T. J. 1964. "Thucydides and the Unpopularity of the Athenian Empire." *Historia* 13: 257–66.

Qviller, Bjørn. 1981. "The Dynamics of Homeric Society." *SO* 56: 109–55.

Raaflaub, Kurt A. 1979a. "Beute, Vergeltung, Freiheit? Zur Zielsetzung des Delisch-Attischen Seebundes." *Chiron* 9: 1–22.

———. 1979b. "Polis Tyrannos: Zur Entstehung einer politischen Metapher." In Glen W. Bowersock, Walter Burkert and Michael C. J. Putnam, eds., Arktouros: *Hellenic Studies Presented to Bernard Knox,* 237–52. Berlin.

———. 1980. "Des freien Bürgers Recht der freien Rede." In Werner Eck et al., eds., *Studien zur antiken Sozialgeschichte: Festschrift Friedrich Vittinghoff,* 7–57. Cologne.

———. 1981. "Zum Freiheitsbegriff der Griechen: Materialien und Untersuchungen zur Bedeutungsentwicklung von *eleutheros/eleutheria* in der archaischen und klassischen Zeit." In Welskopf 1981–85: 4.180–405.

———. 1983. "Democracy, Oligarchy, and the Concept of the 'Free Citizen' in Late Fifth-Century Athens." *Political Theory* 11: 517–44.

———. 1984a. "Athens 'Ideologie der Macht' und die Freiheit des Tyrannen." In Balcer et al. 1984: 45–86.

———. 1984b. "Freiheit in Athen und Rom: Ein Beispiel divergierender politischer Begriffsentwicklung in der Antike." *HZ* 238: 529–67.

———. 1985. *Die Entdeckung der Freiheit.* Vestigia 37. Munich. (1st ed. of present vol.)

———. 1987. "Herodotus, Political Thought, and the Meaning of History." In Boedeker and Peradotto 1987: 221–48.

———. 1988a. "Die Anfänge des politischen Denkens bei den Griechen," "Politisches Denken im Zeitalter Athens." In Iring Fetscher and Herwig Münkler, eds., *Pipers Handbuch der politischen Ideen,* 1.189–271, 273–368. Munich.

———. 1988b. "Homer and the Beginning of Political Thought in Greece." In *Boston Area Colloquium of Ancient Philosophy* 4: 1–25.

———. 1989a. "Die Anfänge des politischen Denkens bei den Griechen." *HZ* 248: 1–32.

———. 1989b. "Contemporary Perceptions of Democracy in Fifth-Century Athens." *C&M* 40: 33–70. Repr. in W. R. Connor et al., *Aspects of Athenian Democracy,* 33–70. Copenhagen.

———. 1990. "Expansion und Machtbildung in frühen Polis-Systemen." In Walter Eder, ed., *Staat und Staatlichkeit in der frühen römischen Republik,* 511–45. Stuttgart.

———. 1991a. "City-State, Territory, and Empire in Classical Antiquity." In Molho et al. 1991: 565–88.

———. 1991b. "Homer und die Geschichte des 8. Jh. v. Chr." In Latacz 1991: 205–56.

———. 1992. "Politisches Denken und Krise der Polis: Athen im Verfassungskonflikt des späten 5. Jh. v. Chr." *HZ* 255: 1–60. Condensed English version in Raaflaub 2001b: 99–117.

———. 1993. "Homer to Solon: The Rise of the Polis (The Written Sources)." In Hansen 1993: 41–105.

———. 1994. "Democracy, Power, and Imperialism in Fifth-Century Athens." In J. Peter Euben, John R. Wallach, and Josiah Ober, eds., *Athenian Political Thought and the Reconstruction of American Democracy,* 103–46. Ithaca, N.Y.

———. 1995. "Einleitung und Bilanz: Kleisthenes, Ephialtes und die Begründung der Demokratie." In Kinzl 1995: 1–54.

———. 1996a. "Born to Be Wolves? Origins of Roman Imperialism." In Robert W. Wallace and Edward M. Harris, eds., *Transitions to Empire: Essays in Greco-Roman History, 360–146 B.C., in Honor of E. Badian,* 273–314. Norman, Okla.

———. 1996b. "Equalities and Inequalities in Athenian Democracy." In Ober and Hedrick 1996: 139–74.

———. 1996c. "Solone, la nuova Atene e l'emergere della politica." In Settis 1996–98: 2.1.1035–81.

———. 1997a. "Homeric Society." In Morris and Powell 1997: 624–49.

———. 1997b. "Legend or Historical Personality? Solon Reconsidered." In J. T. Papademetriou, ed., *Acta: First Panhellenic and International Conference on Ancient Greek Literature,* 97–117. Athens.

———. 1997c. "Politics and Interstate Relations among Early Greek Poleis: Homer and Beyond." *Antichthon* 31: 1–27.

———. 1997d. "Soldiers, Citizens and the Evolution of the Greek Polis." In Mitchell and Rhodes 1997: 49–59.

———. 1998a. "A Historian's Headache: How to Read 'Homeric Society'?" In Fisher and van Wees 1998: 169–93.

———. 1998b. "Power in the Hands of the People: Foundations of Athenian Democracy," "The Thetes and Democracy." In Morris and Raaflaub 1998: 31–66, 87–103.

———. 1998c. "The Transformation of Athens in the Fifth Century." In Boedeker and Raaflaub 1998: 15–41, 348–57.

———. 1999. "Archaic and Classical Greece." In Kurt A. Raaflaub and Nathan Rosenstein, eds., *War and Society in the Ancient and Medieval Worlds,* 129–61. Washington, D.C.

———. 2000a. "Influence, Adaptation, and Interaction: Near Eastern and Early Greek Political Thought." In Sanna Aro and R. M. Whiting, eds., *The Heirs of Assyria*, 51–64. Melammu Symposia 1. Helsinki.

———. 2000b. "Den Olympier herausfordern? Prozesse im Umkreis des Perikles." In Burckhardt and von Ungern-Sternberg 2000: 96–113, 266–70.

———. 2000c. "Poets, Lawgivers, and the Beginnings of Political Reflection in Archaic Greece." In Rowe and Schofield 2000: 23–59.

———. 2000d. "Zeus Eleutherios, Dionysus the Liberator, and the Athenian Tyrannicides: Anachronistic Uses of Fifth-Century Political Concepts." In Flensted-Jensen et al. 2000: 249–75.

———. 2001a. "Father of All, Destroyer of All: War in Late Fifth-Century Athenian Discourse and Ideology." In McCann and Strauss 2001: 307–56.

———. 2001b. "Political Thought, Civic Responsibility, and the Greek Polis." In Johann P. Arnason and Peter Murphy, eds., *Agon, Logos, Polis: The Greek Achievement and Its Aftermath*, 72–117. Stuttgart.

———. 2002a. "Herodot und Thukydides: Persischer Imperialismus im Lichte der athenischen Sizilienpolitik." In Ehrhardt and Günther 2002: 11–40.

———. 2002b. "Philosophy, Science, Politics: Herodotus and the Intellectual Trends of His Time." In Bakker et al. 2002: 149–86.

———. 2003. "Stick and Glue: The Function of Tyranny in Fifth-Century Athenian Democracy." In Morgan 2003: 59–93.

———. Forthcoming. "Freedom for the Messenians? A Note on the Impact of Slavery and Helotage on the Greek Concept of Freedom." In Nino Luraghi and Susan E. Alcock, eds., *Helots and Their Masters: The History and Sociology of a System of Exploitation*.

———, ed. 1986. *Social Struggles in Archaic Rome: New Perspectives on the Conflict of the Orders*. Berkeley and Los Angeles.

Raaflaub, Kurt A., and Elisabeth Müller-Luckner, eds. 1993. *Anfänge politischen Denkens in der Antike: Die nahöstlichen Kulturen und die Griechen*. Munich.

Radin, Max. 1927. "Freedom of Speech in Ancient Athens." *AJP* 48: 215–30.

Rädle, H. 1969. *Untersuchungen zum griechischen Freilassungswesen*. Diss., Univ. of Munich. Bonn.

Radt, Stefan L. 1958. *Pindars zweiter und sechster Paian*. Amsterdam.

Rahe, Paul. 1994. *Republics Ancient and Modern*. Vol. 1, *The Ancien Régime in Classical Greece*. Chapel Hill, N.C.

Ramirez Vidal, Gerardo. 1997. "Ancora sulla data dell'*Athenaion politeia*: L'anonimo e Andocide." In Gigante and Maddoli 1997: 47–60.

Ramming G. 1973. *Die Dienerschaft in der Odyssee*. Diss., Univ. of Erlangen.

Raubitschek, Antony E. 1957. "Das Datislied." In Konrad Schauenburg, ed., *Charites: Studien zur Altertumswissenschaft*, 234–42. Bonn.

———. 1960. "The Covenant of Plataea." *TAPA* 91: 178–83.

Rawlings, Hunter R., III. 1977. "Thucydides on the Purpose of the Delian League." *Phoenix* 31: 1–8.

Redfield, James M. 1975. *Nature and Culture in the* Iliad: *The Tragedy of Hector*. Chicago. Expanded ed., Durham, N.C., 1994.

Rehak, Paul, ed. 1995. *The Role of the Ruler in the Prehistoric Aegean*. 2 vols. Brussels and Austin, Tex.

Reinau, Hansjörg. 1981. *Die Entstehung des Bürgerbegriffs bei den Griechen*. Diss., Univ. of Basel.

Rengakos, Antonios. 1984. *Form und Wandel des Machtdenkens der Athener bei Thukydides*. *Hermes* Einzelschriften 48. Stuttgart.

Rengstorf, Karl H. 1935. "Despotes." In Gerhard Kittel, ed., *Theologisches Wörterbuch zum Neuen Testament*, 2.43–48. Stuttgart.

Reverdin, Olivier, ed. 1962. *Grecs et barbares*. Entretiens sur l'antiquité classique 8. Vandoeuvres and Geneva.

Reverdin, Olivier, and Bernard Grange, ed. 1988. *Hérodote et les peuples non Grecs*. Entretiens sur l'antiquité classique 35. Vandoeuvres and Geneva.

Rhodes, Peter J. 1972. *The Athenian Boule*. Oxford.

———. 1979. "*Eisangelia* in Athens." *JHS* 99: 103–14.

———. 1981. *A Commentary on the Aristotelian* Athenaion Politeia. Oxford.

———, tr. 1984. *Aristotle, The Athenian Constitution*. Harmondsworth.

———. 1985. *The Athenian Empire*. *G&R* New Surveys in the Classics 17. Oxford.

———. 1988. *Thucydides, History II, Edited with Translation and Commentary*. Warminster.

———. 1992. "The Delian League to 449 B.C.," "The Athenian Revolution." In *CAH* 5²: 34–61, 62–95.

———. 1993. "'Alles eitel Gold'? The Sixth and Fifth Centuries in Fourth-Century Athens." In Piérart 1993: 53–64.

Rich, A. N. M. 1956. "The Cynic Conception of *Autarkeia*." *Mnemosyne*, ser. 4.9: 23–29.

Rich, John, and Graham Shipley, eds. 1993. *War and Society in the Greek World*. London.

Richardson, L. J. D. 1952. "The Inner Conflict in the *Persians*: Athenian Dramatist and Persian Characters." In Mary E. White, ed., *Studies in Honour of Gilbert Norwood*, 55–67. Phoenix Suppl. 1. Toronto.

Richardson, N. J. 1974. *The Homeric Hymn to Demeter*. Oxford.

Richter, Melvin. 1986. "Conceptual History (*Begriffsgeschichte*) and Political Theory." *Political Theory* 14: 604–37.

———. 1987. "*Begriffsgeschichte* and the History of Ideas." *JHI* 48: 247–63.

———. 1990. "Pocock, Skinner, and the *Geschichtliche Grundbegriffe*." *History and Theory* 19: 38–70.

———. 1995. *The History of Political and Social Concepts: A Critical Introduction*. New York and Oxford.

———. 1996. "Appreciating a Contemporary Classic: The *Geschichtliche Grundbegriffe* and Future Scholarship." In Lehmann and Richter 1996: 7–19.

Richter, Will. 1968. *Die Landwirtschaft im homerischen Zeitalter*. Archaeologia Homerica, vol. H. Göttingen.

Ridley, R. T. 1979. "The Hoplite as Citizen: Athenian Military Institutions in Their Social Context." *AC* 48: 508–48.

Rihll, T. E. 1991. "*Hektēmoroi*: Partners in Crime?" *JHS* 111: 101–27.

Risch, Ernst. 1972. "Les traits non-homériques chez Homère." In *Mélanges de linguistique et de philologie grecques offerts à Pierre Chantraine*, 191–98. Paris.

Robert, Fernand. 1964. "Sophocle, Périclès, Hérodote et la date d'Ajax." *RPh* 38: 213–27.

Robert, Louis. 1929. "Recherches épigraphiques." *REA* 31: 13–20.

———. 1938. *Etudes épigraphiques et philologiques*. Paris.

Roberts, Jennifer T. 1994. *Athens on Trial: The Antidemocratic Tradition in Western Thought*. Princeton.

———. 1996. "Athenian Equality: A Constant Surrounded by Flux." In Ober and Hedrick 1996: 187–202.

Robertson, Noel. 1976. "False Documents at Athens: Fifth-Century History and Fourth-Century Publicists." *Historical Reflections* 3: 3–25.

———. 1978. "The Myth of the First Sacred War." *CQ*, n.s., 28: 38–73.

———. 1980. "The True Nature of the 'Delian League,' 478–461 B.C." *AJAH* 5: 64–96, 110–33.

———. 1982. "The Decree of Themistocles in Its Contemporary Setting." *Phoenix* 36: 1–44.

———. 1992. *Festivals and Legends: The Formation of Greek Cities in the Light of Public Ritual.* *Phoenix* Suppl. 31. Toronto.

Robinson, E. S. G. 1949. "The Athenian Currency Decree and the Coinages of the Allies." In *Commemorative Studies in Honor of Theodore Leslie Shear,* 324–40. *Hesperia* Suppl. 8. Princeton, N.J.

Robinson, Eric W. 1997. *The First Democracies: Early Popular Government outside Athens.* *Historia* Einzelschriften 107. Stuttgart.

———. 1999. "Thucydidean Sieges, Prosopitis, and the Hellenic Disaster in Egypt." *CA* 18: 132–52.

———. Forthcoming. *Classical Democracy beyond Athens.*

Roisman, Joseph. 1985. "Maiandrios of Samos." *Historia* 34: 257–77.

———. 1988. "On Phrynichos' Sack of Miletos and the Phoinissai." *Eranos* 86: 15–23.

Romilly, Jacqueline de. 1959. "Le classement des constitutions d'Hérodote à Aristote." *REG* 72: 81–99.

———. 1962. "Le Pseudo-Xénophon et Thucydide: Etude sur quelques divergences de vues." *RPh,* 3d ser., 36: 225–41.

———. 1963. *Thucydides and Athenian Imperialism.* Tr. Philip Thody. Oxford.

———. 1966. "Thucydides and the Cities of the Athenian Empire." *BICS* 13: 1–12.

———. 1968. "Guerre et paix entre cités." In Vernant 1968: 207–20.

———. 1969. "Il pensiero di Euripide sulla tirannia." *Dioniso* 43: 175–87.

———. 1971a. *La loi dans la pensée grecque.* Paris.

———. 1971b. "La vengeance comme explication historique dans l'oeuvre d'Hérodote." *REG* 84: 314–37.

———. 1972. "Vocabulaire et propagande ou les premiers emplois du mot *omonoia.*" In Alfred Ernout, ed., *Mélanges de linguistique et de philologie grecques offerts à Pierre Chantraine,* 199–209. Paris.

———. 1973. "Le thème du prestige dans l'oeuvre de Thucydide." *Ancient Society* 4: 39–58.

———. 1975. *Problèmes de la démocratie grecque.* Paris.

———. 1983. "Le thème de la liberté et l'évolution de la tragédie grecque." In *Théâtre et spectacles dans l'antiquité,* 215–26. Leiden.

———. 1989. *La Grèce antique à la découverte de la liberté.* Paris.

———. 1990. "La liberté et les libertés." In Jacqueline de Romilly et al., *Les usages de la liberté,* 13–43 (including discussion). Neuchâtel.

———. 1995. *Alcibiade ou les dangers de l'ambition.* Paris.

Roscher, Wilhelm H. 1924–37. *Ausführliches Lexikon der griechischen und römischen Mythologie.* 7 vols. Leipzig and Berlin. Repr., Hildesheim, 1965.

Rose, Peter, W. 1975. "Class Ambivalence in the Odyssey." *Historia* 24: 129–49.

Rosen, Ralph M. 1997. "The Gendered Polis in Eupolis' *Cities.*" In Dobrov 1997: 149–76.

Rosen, Ralph M., and Joseph Farrell, eds. 1993. Nomodeiktes: *Greek Studies in Honor of Martin Ostwald,* 321–29. Ann Arbor, Mich.

Rosenbloom, David. 1993. "Shouting Fire in a Crowded Theater: Phrynichos's *Capture of Miletos* and the Politics of Fear in Early Attic Tragedy." *Philologus* 137: 159–96.

———. 1996. "Myth, History, and Hegemony in Aeschylus." In Barbara Goff, ed., *History, Tragedy, Theory: Dialogues on Athenian Drama,* 91–130. Austin, Tex.

Rosivach, Vincent J. 1978. "The Altar of Zeus Agoraios in the 'Heracleidae.'" *PdP* 33: 32–47.

———. 1987a. "Autochthony and the Athenians." *CQ,* n.s., 37: 294–305.

———. 1987b. "The Cult of Zeus Eleutherios at Athens." *PdP* 42: 262–85.

———. 1988. "The Tyrant in Athenian Democracy." *QUCC* 59: 43–57.

———. 1992. "Redistribution of Land in Solon, fr. 34 West." *JHS* 112: 153–57.

Rösler, Wolfgang. 1980. *Dichter und Gruppe: Eine Untersuchung zu den Bedingungen und zur historischen Funktion früher griechischer Lyrik am Beispiel Alkaios.* Munich.

Roussel, Pierre. 1924. "La fondation des Sotéria de Delphes." *REA* 26: 97–111.

———. 1933. "L'amende de Chios (Aristophane, *Paix*, v. 169–172)." *REA* 35: 385–86.

Rowe, Christopher, and Malcolm Schofield, eds. 2000. *The Cambridge History of Greek and Roman Political Thought.* Cambridge.

Roy, James. 1994. "Thebes in the 360s B.C." *CAH* 6²: 187–208.

———. 1997. "The *Perioikoi* of Elis." In Hansen 1997. Copenhagen.

Ruck, Carl A. P. 1969. "Marginalia Pindarica III." *Hermes* 96: 661–74.

Ruschenbusch, Eberhard. 1958. "*Patrios Politeia:* Theseus, Drakon, Solon und Kleisthenes in Publizistik und Geschichtsschreibung des 5. und 4. Jh. v. Chr." *Historia* 7: 398–424.

———. 1960. "*Phonos:* Zum Recht Drakons und seiner Bedeutung für das Werden des athenischen Staates." *Historia* 9: 129–54.

———. 1966. Solonos nomoi: *Die Fragmente des solonischen Gesetzeswerkes mit einer Text- und Überlieferungsgeschichte. Historia* Einzelschriften 9. Wiesbaden.

———. 1968. *Untersuchungen zur Geschichte des athenischen Strafrechts.* Cologne.

———. 1978. *Untersuchungen zu Staat und Politik in Griechenland vom 7.–4. Jh. v. Chr.* Bamberg.

———. 1979. *Athenische Innenpolitik im 5. Jh. v. Chr.: Ideologie oder Pragmatismus?* Bamberg.

———. 1983. "Die Polis und das Recht." In Panayotis Dimakis, ed., *Symposion 1979: Beiträge zur griechischen und hellenistischen Rechtsgeschichte,* 305–26. Cologne.

Rusten, J. S., ed. 1989. *Thucydides,* The Peloponnesian War, *Book II.* Cambridge.

Ruzé, Françoise. 1984. "*Plethos:* Aux origines de la majorité politique." In *Aux origines de l'Hellénisme: La Crète et la Grèce: Hommage à Henri van Effenterre,* 247–63. Paris.

———. 1997. *Délibération et pouvoir dans la cité grecque de Nestor à Socrate.* Paris.

Ryan, F. X. 1994. "Areopagite Domination and Prytanies." *AC* 63: 251–52.

Ryder, T. T. B. 1965. Koine Eirene: *General Peace and Local Independence in Ancient Greece.* Oxford.

Sabine, G. H. 1963. *A History of Political Theory.* 3d ed. London.

Saïd, Suzanne. 2002. "Herodotus and Tragedy." In Bakker et al. 2002: 117–47.

Salmon, John B. 1984. *Wealthy Corinth: A History of the City to 338 B.C.* Oxford.

Salmon, Pierre. 1969. "L'établissement des Trente à Athènes." *AC* 38: 497–500.

Salomon, Nicoletta. 1997. *Le cleruchie di Atene: Caratteri e funzione.* Pisa.

Samons, Loren J., II. 1993. "Athenian Finance and the Treasury of Athena." *Historia* 42: 129–38.

———. 1998. "Kimon, Kallias and Peace with Persia." *Historia* 47: 129–40.

———. 2000. *Empire of the Owl: Athenian Imperial Finance. Historia* Einzelschriften 142. Stuttgart.

———. Forthcoming. *The Ignoble Lie.*

Sancisi-Weerdenburg, Heleen. 1987a. "Decadence in the Empire or Decadence in the Sources? From Source to Synthesis: Ctesias." In Heleen Sancisi-Weerdenburg, ed., *Achaemenid History,* vol. 1, *Sources, Structures, and Synthesis,* 33–45. Leiden.

———. 1987b. "The Fifth Oriental Monarchy and Hellenocentrism." In Sancisi-Weerdenburg and Kuhrt 1987: 117–31.

Sancisi-Weerdenburg, Heleen, and Amélie Kuhrt, eds. 1987. *Achaemenid History.* Vol. 2, *The Greek Sources.* Leiden.

Sansone, David, tr., comm. 1989. *Plutarch,* The Lives of Aristeides and Cato. Warminster, England.

Santiago, Rosa A. 1962. "Observaciones sobre algunos usos formularios de ēmar en Homero." *Emerita* 30: 139–50.

Sartori, Franco. 1957. *Le eterie nella vita politica ateniese del VI e V secolo a.C.* Rome.

————. 1968. "Attualità di un libro: La libertà greca di M. Pohlenz." *Paideia* 23: 153–73.

Sasson, Jack M., ed. 1995. *Civilizations of the Ancient Near East.* 4 vols. New York.

Scafuro, Adele C. 1994. "Introduction: Bifurcations and Intersections." In Boegehold and Scafuro 1994: 1–20.

Scala, Rudolf von. 1898. *Die Staatsverträge des Altertums* I. Leipzig. Repr. 1968. Rome.

Scanlon, Thomas F. 1994. "Echoes of Herodotus in Thucydides: Self-Sufficiency, Admiration, and Law." *Historia* 43: 143–76.

Scarpat, G. 1964. *Parrhesia: Storia del termine e delle sue traduzioni in latino.* Brescia.

Schachermeyr, Fritz. 1950. "Pittakos." *RE* 20: 1862–73.

Schachter, Albert. 1994. *Cults of Boeotia.* Vol. 3. *BICS* Suppl. 38.3. London.

Schadewaldt, Wolfgang. 1929. "Sophokles, Aias und Antigone." *Neue Wege zur Antike* 8: 93–117.

————. 1965. *Von Homers Welt und Werk.* 4th ed. Stuttgart.

Schäfer, Hans. 1932. *Staatsform und Politik: Untersuchungen zur griechischen Geschichte des 6. und 5. Jahrhunderts.* Leipzig.

————. 1957. "Politische Ordnung und individuelle Freiheit im Griechentum." *HZ* 183: 5–22. Repr., in Schäfer 1963: 307–22.

————. 1963. *Probleme der Alten Geschichte: Gesammelte Abhandlungen und Vorträge.* Göttingen.

Scheidel, Walter. Forthcoming. "The Demographic Background of the Greek Expansion." In Robert Rollinger and Christoph Ulf, eds., *Griechische Archaik zwischen Ost und West: Interne und externe Impulse.*

Schelle, M. 1932. *Strategos Autokrator.* Ph.D. diss., Univ. of Leipzig.

Schemeil, Yves. 1999. *La politique dans l'ancien Orient.* Paris.

Schlier, E. 1954. "*Parrhēsia* und *parrhēsiazomai* im Griechentum und Hellenismus." In G. Kittel, ed., *Theologisches Wörterbuch zum Neuen Testament,* 5.869–72. Stuttgart.

Schmid, Wilhelm, and Otto Stählin. 1946. *Geschichte der griechischen Literatur.* Vol. 1.4. HdAW 7.1.4. Munich.

Schmitt, Hatto H. 1969. *Die Staatsverträge des Altertums.* Vol. 3, *Die Verträge der griechisch-römischen Welt von 338–200 v. Chr.* Munich.

Schmitz, Winfried. 1988. *Wirtschaftliche Prosperität, soziale Integration und die Seebundpolitik Athens.* Munich.

Schober, F. 1934. "Thebai (Boiotien)." *RE* 5: 1423–92.

————. 1941. "Phokis." *RE* 20.1: 474–96.

Schreiner, Johan H. 1970. "The Origin of Ostracism Again." *C&M* 31: 84–97.

————. 1976. "Anti-Thukydidean Studies in the Pentekontaëtia." *SO* 51: 19–63.

————. 1977. "More Anti-Thukydidean Studies in the Pentekontaëtia." *SO* 52: 19–38.

————. 1997. *Hellanikos, Thukydides and the Era of Kimon.* Aarhus.

Schubert, Charlotte. 1994. *Perikles:* Erträge der Forschung 285. Darmstadt.

Schuller, Wolfgang. 1974. *Die Herrschaft der Athener im Ersten Attischen Seebund.* Berlin.

————. 1978. *Die Stadt als Tyrann: Athens Herrschaft über seine Bundesgenossen.* Konstanzer Universitätsreden 101. Konstanz.

————. 1979. "Zur Entstehung der griechischen Demokratie ausserhalb Athens." In H. Sund and M. Timmermann, eds., *Auf den Weg gebracht: Festschrift K. G. Kiesinger,* 433–47. Konstanz.

———. 1984. "Wirkungen des Ersten Attischen Seebunds auf die Herausbildung der athenischen Demokratie." In Balcer et al. 1984: 87–101.

———. 2002. "Folgen einer Umdatierung des Egesta-Dekrets (IG I³ 11)." In Ehrhardt and Günther 2002: 41–47.

Schultz, Heiner. 1973. "Einige methodische Fragen der Begriffsgeschichte." *ABG* 17: 221–31.

Schütrumpf, Eckart. 1996. *Aristoteles, Politik, Buch IV–VI: Übersetzt und eingeleitet von E. S.; erläutert von E. S. und Hans-Joachim Gehrke.* Berlin.

Schwabl, Hans. 1962. "Das Bild der fremden Welt bei den frühen Griechen." In Reverdin 1962: 3–23.

———. 1972. "Zeus, Pt. 1: Epiklesen." *RE* 10A: 253–376.

———. 1974. "Freiheit in der Sicht der Griechen." *Wiener humanistische Blätter* 16: 1–12.

———. 1978. "Zeus, Pt. 2." *RE* Suppl. 15: 993–1411, with addenda, 1441–81.

Schwahn, Walter. 1932. "Symmachia." *RE* 4A: 1102–34.

Schwarze, Joachim. 1971. *Die Beurteilung des Perikles durch die attische Komödie.* Zetemata 51. Munich.

Schwyzer, Eduard. 1939–53. *Griechische Grammatik.* 3 vols. Munich.

Seaford, Richard. 1994. *Reciprocity and Ritual: Homer and Tragedy in the Developing City-State.* Oxford.

———. 2003. "Tragic Tyranny." In Morgan 2003: 95–115.

Seager, Robin. 1967. "Alcibiades and the Charge of Aiming at Tyranny." *Historia* 16: 6–18.

———. 1969. "The Congress Decree: Some Doubts and a Hypothesis." *Historia* 18: 129–41.

———. 1981. "The Freedom of the Greeks of Asia." *CQ* 31: 106–12.

———. 1994. "The Corinthian War." *CAH* 6²: 97–119.

Seager, Robin, and Christopher Tuplin. 1980. "The Freedom of the Greeks of Asia." *JHS* 100: 141–54.

Sealey, Raphael. 1956. "The Entry of Pericles into History." *Hermes* 84: 234–47.

———. 1960. "Regionalism in Archaic Athens." *Historia* 9: 155–80. Repr. in Raphael Sealey, *Essays in Greek Politics,* 9–38. New York, 1967.

———. 1966. "The Origin of the Delian League." In Badian 1966: 233–55.

———. 1974. "The Origins of *Demokratia.*" *CSCA* 6: 253–95.

———. 1976. "The Pit and the Well: The Persian Heralds of 491 B.C." *CJ* 72: 13–20.

———. 1983. "How Citizenship and the City Began in Athens." *AJAH* 8: 97–129.

———. 1987. *The Athenian Republic: Democracy or the Rule of Law?* University Park, Penn.

Segal, Charles. 1993. *Oedipus Tyrannus: Tragic Heroism and the Limits of Knowledge.* New York.

Seltman, Charles. 1955. *Greek Coins: A History of Metallic Currency and Coinage Down to the Fall of the Hellenistic Kingdoms.* 2d ed. London.

Settis, Salvatore, ed. 1996–98. *I Greci.* Vols. 1–2. Turin.

Shapiro, H. Alan. 1994. "Religion and Politics in Democratic Athens." In Coulson et al. 1994: 123–29.

———. 1996a. "Athena, Apollo, and the Religious Propaganda of the Athenian Empire." In Pontus Hellström and Brita Alroth, eds., *Religion and Power in the Ancient Greek World,* 101–13. Boreas 24. Uppsala.

———. 1996b. "Democracy and Imperialism: The Panathenaia in the Age of Perikles." In Jenifer Neils, ed., *Worshipping Athena: Panathenaia and Parthenon,* 215–25. Madison, Wisc.

———. 1998. "Autochthony and the Visual Arts in Fifth-Century Athens." In Boedeker and Raaflaub 1998: 127–51, 376–84.

Shear, T. Leslie, Jr. 1994. "*Isonomous t'Athēnas epoiēsatēn:* The Agora and the Democracy." In Coulson et al. 1994: 225–48.

———. 1995. "Bouleuterion, Metroon, and the Archives at Athens." In Hansen and Raaflaub 1995: 157–90.

Sherratt, E. S. 1990. "'Reading the Texts': Archaeology and the Homeric Question." *Antiquity* 64: 807–24.

Shimron, Binyamin. 1979. "Ein Wortspiel mit *Homoioi* bei Herodot." *RhM* 122: 131–33.

Shipley, Graham. 1987. *A History of Samos, 800–188 B.C.* Oxford.

———. 1997. "'The Other Lakedaimonians': The Dependent Perioikic *Poleis* of Laconia and Messenia." In Hansen 1997: 189–281.

Shrimpton, Gordon S. 1984. "When Did Plataea Join Athens?" *CP* 79: 295–304.

Siewert, Peter. 1972. *Der Eid von Plataiai.* Vestigia 16. Munich.

———. 1982. *Die Trittyen Attikas und die Heeresreform des Kleisthenes.* Vestigia 33. Munich.

———, ed. 2002. *Ostrakismos-Testimonien: Die Zeugnisse antiker Autoren, der Inschriften und Ostraka über das athenische Scherbengericht aus vorhellenistischer Zeit (487–322 v. Chr.).* Stuttgart.

Simms, Robert M. 1975. "The Eleusinia in the Sixth to Fourth Centuries B.C." *GRBS* 16: 269–79.

Sinclair, T. A. 1967. *A History of Greek Political Thought.* 2d ed. London.

———, ed. 1932. *Hesiod:* Works and Days. London. Repr., Hildesheim, 1966.

Smarczyk, Bernhard. 1990. *Untersuchungen zur Religionspolitik und politischen Propaganda Athens im Delisch-Attischen Seebund.* Munich.

Snell, Bruno. 1965. *Dichtung und Gesellschaft: Studien zum Einfluss der Dichter auf das soziale Denken und Verhalten im alten Griechenland.* Hamburg.

———. 1975. *Die Entdeckung des Geistes.* 4th ed. Göttingen.

Snell, Bruno, and Herwig Maehler, eds. 1970. *Bacchylides.* Leipzig.

———. 1971–75. *Pindarus.* 2 vols. Leipzig.

Snell, Daniel C. 2001. *Flight and Freedom in the Ancient Near East.* Leiden.

Snodgrass, Anthony M. 1974. "An Historical Homeric Society?" *JHS* 94: 114–25.

———. 1980. *Archaic Greece: The Age of Experiment.* Berkeley and Los Angeles.

———. 1993. "The Rise of the Polis: The Archaeological Evidence." In Hansen 1993: 30–40.

Solmsen, Friedrich. 1949. *Hesiod and Aeschylus.* Ithaca, N.Y. Repr., Ithaca, N.Y., 1995.

Solmsen, Lieselotte. 1943. "Speeches in Herodotus' Account of the Ionian Revolt." *AJP* 64: 194–207. German tr. in Marg 1965: 629–44.

———. 1944. "Speeches in Herodotus' Account of the Battle of Plataea." *CP* 39: 241–53. German tr. in Marg 1965: 645–67.

Sommerstein, Alan H. 1980. *Aristophanes,* Acharnians: *Edited with Translation and Notes.* Warminster, England.

———. 1983. *Aristophanes,* Wasps: *Edited with Translation and Notes.* Warminster, England.

Sordi, Marta. 1953a. "La guerra tessalo-focese del V secolo." *RFIC,* n.s., 31: 235–58.

———. 1953b. "Le origini del koinon etolico." *Acme* 6: 419–45.

———. 1958. *La lega tessala fino ad Alessandro Magno.* Rome.

———, ed. 1981. *Religione e politica nel mondo antico.* Milan.

Souza, Philip de. 1998. "Towards Thalassocracy? Archaic Greek Naval Developments." In Fisher and van Wees 1998: 271–93.

Spahn, Peter. 1977. *Mittelschicht und Polisbildung.* Frankfurt am Main.

———. 1980. "Oikos und Polis: Beobachtungen zum Prozess der Polisbildung bei Hesiod, Solon und Aischylos." *HZ* 231: 529–64.

———. 1986. "Das Aufkommen eines politischen Utilitarismus bei den Griechen." *Saeculum* 37: 8–21.

———. 1993. "Individualisierung und politisches Bewusstsein im archaischen Griechenland." In Raaflaub and Müller-Luckner 1993: 343–63.

Squilloni Vignoli, Antonella. Forthcoming. *Libertà "fuori," libertà "dentro": Due categorie del pensiero greco.*

Stadter, Philip A. 1989. *A Commentary on Plutarch's* Pericles. Chapel Hill, N.C.

———. 1991. "Pericles among the Intellectuals." *ICS* 16: 111–24.

———. 1992. "Herodotus and the Athenian *Archē.*" *ASNP,* ser. 3, 22: 781–809.

Stahl, Michael. 1983. "Tyrannis und das Problem der Macht." *Hermes* 111: 202–20.

———. 1987. *Aristokraten und Tyrannen im archaischen Athen.* Stuttgart.

———. 1992. "Solon Fr. 3D: Die Geburtsstunde des demokratischen Gedankens." *Gymnasium* 99: 385–408.

Stählin, Felix. 1912. "Herakleia (4)." *RE* 8: 424–29.

Stallmach, Josef. 1968. *Ate: Zur Frage des Selbst- und Weltverständnisses des frühgriechischen Menschen.* Meisenheim.

Starr, Chester G. 1957. "The Early Greek City State." *PdP* 12: 97–108. Repr. in Starr 1979: 122–33.

———. 1961a. "The Decline of the Early Greek Kings." *Historia* 10: 129–38. Repr. in Starr 1979: 134–43.

———. 1961b. *The Origins of Greek Civilization, 1100–850 B.C.* New York.

———. 1977. *The Economic and Social Growth of Early Greece, 800–500 B.C.* New York.

———. 1979. *Essays on Ancient History.* Ed. Arther Ferrill and Thomas Kelly. Leiden.

———. 1982. "Economic and Social Conditions in the Greek World." *CAH* 3.3²: 417–41.

———. 1986. *Individual and Community: The Rise of the Polis, 800–500 B.C.* New York.

———. 1992. *The Aristocratic Temper of Greek Civilization.* New York.

Ste. Croix, G. E. M. de. 1954. "The Character of the Athenian Empire." *Historia* 3: 1–41.

———. 1961. "Notes on the Jurisdiction in the Athenian Empire I." *CQ,* n.s., 11: 94–112.

———. 1972. *The Origins of the Peloponnesian War.* Ithaca, N.Y.

———. 1981. *The Class Struggle in the Ancient Greek World.* Ithaca, N.Y.

Stegmann von Pritzwald, K. 1930. *Zur Geschichte der Herrscherbezeichnungen von Homer bis Plato.* Forschungen zur Völkerpsychologie und Soziologie 7. Leipzig.

Steinbrecher, Michael. 1985. *Der Delisch-Attische Seebund und die athenisch-spartanischen Beziehungen in der kimonischen Ära (ca. 478/7–462/1).* Palingenesia 21. Stuttgart.

Stein-Hölkeskamp, Elke. 1989. *Adelskultur und Polisgesellschaft.* Stuttgart.

Steuben, Hans von. 1989. "Die Agora des Kleisthenes—Zeugnis eines radikalen Wandels?" In Wolfgang Schuller, Wolfram Hoepfner, and Ernst Ludwig Schwandner, eds., *Demokratie und Architektur: Der hippodamische Städtebau und die Entstehung der Demokratie,* 81–87. Munich.

Stiehl, Ruth, and Gustav-Adolf Lehmann, eds. 1972. *Antike und Universalgeschichte: Festschrift Hans Erich Stier.* Münster.

Stier, H. E. 1928. "Nomos Basileus." *Philologus* 83: 225–58.

Stoessl, F. 1979. *Die Hiketiden des Aischylos als geistesgeschichtliches und theatergeschichtliches Phänomen.* Sitzungsberichte Akad. Wien, phil.-hist. Kl., 356. Vienna.

Storey, Ian. 1994. "The Politics of 'Angry Eupolis.'" *AHB* 8.4: 107–20.

Straaten, M. van. 1972. "What Did the Greeks Mean by Liberty?" *Theta-Pi* 1: 105–27.

Strasburger, Hermann. 1953. "Der soziologische Aspekt der homerischen Epen." *Gymnasium* 60: 97–114. Repr. in Strasburger 1982–90: 1.491–518.

———. 1954. "Der Einzelne und die Gemeinschaft im Denken der Griechen." *HZ* 177: 227–48. Repr. in Strasburger 1982–90: 1.423–48; Gschnitzer 1969: 97–122.

———. 1955. "Herodot und das perikleische Athen." *Historia* 4: 1–25. Repr. in Strasburger 1982–90: 2.592–626; Marg 1965: 574–608.

———. 1958. "Thukydides und die politische Selbstdarstellung der Athener." *Hermes* 86: 17–40. Repr. in Strasburger 1982–90: 2.676–708; Herter 1968: 498–530.

———. 1976. *Zum antiken Gesellschaftsideal.* Abh. Akad. Heidelberg, phil.-hist. Kl., 1976, no. 4. Wiesbaden.

———. 1982–90. *Studien zur Alten Geschichte.* Ed. Walter Schmitthenner and Renate Zoepfel. 3 vols. Hildesheim.

Strauss, Barry S. 1986. *Athens after the Peloponnesian War: Class, Faction, and Policy, 403–386 B.C.* Ithaca, N.Y.

———. 1996. "The Athenian Trireme, School of Democracy." In Ober and Hedrick 1996: 313–25.

———. 1998. "Geneaology, Ideology, and Society in Democratic Athens." In Morris and Raaflaub 1998: 141–54.

Stroud, Ronald. 1968. *Drakon's Law on Homicide.* Berkeley and Los Angeles.

———. 1994. "The Aiakeion and Tholos of Athens in POxy 2087." *ZPE* 103: 1–9.

Stupperich, Reinhard. 1977. *Staatsbegräbnis und Privatgrabmal im klassischen Athen.* Diss., Univ. of Münster.

Stylow, A. U. 1972. *Libertas und Liberalitas: Untersuchungen zur innenpolitischen Propaganda der Römer.* Diss., Univ. of Munich.

Swoboda, Heinrich. 1922. "Konon (3)." *RE* 11: 1319–34.

Szegedy-Maszak, Andrew. 1978. "Legends of the Greek Lawgivers." *GRBS* 19: 199–209.

Szemerényi, O. 1977. "Indo-European Kinship." *Acta Iranica* 16: 1–240.

Talbert, Richard. 1989. "The Role of the Helots in the Class Struggle at Sparta." *Historia* 38: 22–40.

———. 1997. "The Greeks in Sicily and South Italy." In Tritle 1997: 137–65.

Tandy, David W., and Walter C. Neale. 1996. *Hesiod's Works and Days: A Translation and Commentary for the Social Sciences.* Berkeley and Los Angeles.

Taplin, Oliver. 1992. *Homeric Soundings: The Shaping of the Iliad.* Oxford.

Tarkiainen, Tuttu. 1966. *Die athenische Demokratie.* Zurich.

Tausend, Klaus. 1992. *Amphiktyonie und Symmachie: Formen zwischenstaatlicher Beziehungen im archaischen Griechenland. Historia* Einzelschriften 73. Stuttgart.

Taylor, Martha C. 1997. *Salamis and the Salaminioi: The History of an Unofficial Athenian Demos.* Amsterdam.

Taylor, Michael. 1991. *The Tyrant Slayers.* 2d ed. Salem, N.H.

Ténékidès, Georges. 1954. *La notion juridique d'indépendance et la tradition hellénique.* Athens.

———. 1970. "Esquisse d'une théorie des droits internationaux de l'homme dans la Grèce des cités." *Revue des droits de l'homme* 3: 195–246.

Thalmann, William G. 1998a. "Female Slaves in the *Odyssey.*" In Sandra R. Joshel and Sheila Murnaghan, eds., *Women and Slaves in Greco-Roman Culture: Differential Equations,* 22–34. London.

———. 1998b. *The Swineherd and the Bow: Representations of Class in the Odyssey.* Ithaca, N.Y.

Thomas, Carol G. 1966. "Homer and the Polis." *PdP* 21: 5–14.

———. 1976. "The Nature of Mycenaean Kingship." *SMEA* 17: 93–116.

———. 1993. "The Homeric Epics: Strata or Spectrum?" In Hanna M. Roisman and Joseph Roisman, eds., *Essays on Homeric Epic, Colby Quarterly* 29.3: 273–82.

Thomas, Carol G., and Craig Conant. 1999. *Citadel to City-State: The Transformation of Greece, 1200–700 B.C.E.* Bloomington, Ind.

Thomas, Rosalind. 1989. *Oral Tradition and Written Record in Classical Athens.* Cambridge.

———. 2000. *Herodotus in Context: Ethnography, Science and the Art of Persuasion.* Cambridge.

Thommen, Lukas. 1996. *Lakedaimonion politeia: Die Entstehung der spartanischen Verfassung. Historia* Einzelschriften 103. Stuttgart.

Thompson, Homer A. 1937. "Buildings on the West Side of the Agora." *Hesperia* 6: 1–226.

Thompson, Homer A., and R. E. Wycherley. 1972. *The Agora of Athens: The History, Shape and Uses of an Ancient City Center.* Athenian Agora 14. Princeton.

Thomsen, Rudi. 1972. *The Origin of Ostracism.* Gyldenal, Denmark.

Thomson, George. 1929. "*Zeus Tyrannos:* A Note on the *Prometheus Vinctus.*" *CR* 43: 3–5.

———, ed. 1932. *Aeschylus, The* Prometheus Bound. Cambridge. Repr., New York, 1979.

Thummer, Erich. 1968. *Pindar: Die isthmischen Gedichte.* 2 vols. Heidelberg.

Tod, Marcus N., ed. 1946–48. *Greek Historical Inscriptions from the Sixth Century b.c. to the Death of Alexander the Great in 323 b.c.* 2 vols. 2d ed. Oxford. Repr., Chicago, 1985.

Tölle-Kastenbein, Renate. 1976. *Herodot und Samos.* Bochum.

Tomlinson, Richard A. 1972. *Argos and the Argolid.* London.

Tovar, A. 1971. "Indo-European Etymology of *do-e-ro.*" *Minos* 12: 318–25.

Tozzi, Pierluigi. 1978. *La rivolta ionica.* Pisa.

Traill, John S. 1975. *The Political Organization of Attica: A Study of the Demes, Trittyes, and Phylai, and Their Representation in the Athenian Council.* Hesperia Suppl. 14. Princeton.

———. 1986. *Demos and Trittys: Epigraphical and Topographical Studies in the Organization of Attica.* Toronto.

Travlos, John. 1971. *Pictorial Dictionary of Ancient Athens.* London.

Treu, Max. 1967. "Xenophon." *RE* 9A.2: 1567–1982.

Treuil, René, Pascal Darcque, Jean-Claude Poursat, and Gilles Touchais. 1989. *Les civilisations égéennes du Néolithique et de l'Age du Bronze.* Paris.

Triebel-Schubert, Charlotte. 1984. "Der Begriff der Isonomie bei Alkmaion." *Klio* 66: 40–50.

Triepel, Heinrich. 1938. *Die Hegemonie.* Stuttgart. Repr., Aalen, 1961.

Tritle, Lawrence A., ed. 1997. *The Greek World in the Fourth Century.* London.

Tritsch, Franz J. 1958. "The Women of Pylos." In *Minoica: Festschrift zum 80. Geburtstag von Johannes Sundwall,* 406–45. Berlin.

Tulin, Alexander. 1996. *Dike Phonou: The Right of Prosecution and Attic Homicide Procedure.* Beiträge zur Altertumskunde 76. Stuttgart.

Tuplin, Christopher. 1985. "Imperial Tyranny: Some Reflections on a Classical Greek Political Metaphor." In Cartledge and Harvey 1985: 348–75.

Turato, F. 1979. *La crisi della città e l'ideologia del salvaggio nell'Atene del V sec. a.C.* Rome.

Tyrrell, W. Blake. 1984. *Amazons: A Study in Athenian Mythmaking.* Baltimore.

Uchitel, Alexander. 1988. "The Archives of Mycenaean Greece and the Ancient Near East." In Heltzer and Lipinski 1988: 19–30.

Ulf, Christoph. 1990. *Die homerische Gesellschaft: Materialien zur analytischen Beschreibung und historischen Lokalisierung.* Vestigia 43. Munich.

———, ed. 1996. *Wege zur Genese griechischer Identität: Die Bedeutung der frsimcharchaischen Zeit.* Berlin.

Ungern-Sternberg, Jürgen von, and Hansjörg Reinau, eds. 1988. *Vergangenheit in mündlicher Überlieferung.* Coll. Rauricum 1. Stuttgart.

Vamvoukos, Athanassios. 1979. "Fundamental Freedoms in Athens of the Fifth Century." *RIDA,* 3d ser., 26: 89–124.

Vanderpool, Eugene. 1973. "Ostracism at Athens." In C. G. Boulter et al., eds., *Lectures in Memory of Louise Taft Semple,* 2d ser., 217–50. Norman, Okla.

Ventris, Michael, and John Chadwick, eds. 1973. *Documents in Mycenaean Greek.* 2d ed. Cambridge.

Vernant, Jean-Pierre, ed. 1968. *Problèmes de la guerre en Grèce ancienne.* Paris.

Versnel, Henk S. 1995. "Religion and Democracy." In Walter Eder, ed., *Die athenische Demokratie im 4. Jahrhundert v. Chr.: Krise oder Vollendung?* 367–87. Stuttgart.

Veyne, Paul. 1979. "Mythe et réalité de l'autarcie à Rome." *REA* 81: 261–80.

Vickers, Michael. 1997. *Pericles on Stage: Political Comedy in Aristophanes' Early Plays*. Austin, Tex.

Vidal-Naquet, Pierre. 1963. "Homère et le monde mycénien." *Annales ESC* 18: 703–19.

———. 1965. "Economie et société dans la Grèce ancienne: L'oeuvre de Moses I. Finley." *Archives européennes de sociologie* 6: 111–48.

Vlastos, Gregory. 1946. "Solonian Justice." *CP* 41: 65–83. Repr. in Vlastos 1995: 1.32–56.

———. 1947. "Equality and Justice in Early Greek Cosmologies." *CP* 42: 156–78. Repr. in Vlastos 1995: 1.57–88.

———. 1953. "*Isonomia.*" *AJP* 74: 337–66. Repr. in Vlastos 1995: 1.89–111.

———. 1964. "*Isonomia politikē.*" In Jürgen Mau and Ernst Günther Schmidt, eds., Isonomia: *Studien zur Gleichheitsvorstellung im griechischen Denken*, 1–35. Berlin. Repr. in Gregory Vlastos, *Platonic Studies*, 164–203. Princeton, 1981.

———. 1995. *Studies in Greek Philosophy*. Ed. Daniel W. Graham. 2 vols. Princeton.

Volkmann, Hans. 1961. *Die Massenversklavungen der Einwohner eroberter Städte in der hellenistisch-römischen Zeit*. Abh. Akad. Mainz, geistes- und sozialwiss. Kl., 1961, 3. Wiesbaden.

Vretska, Karl. 1966. "Perikles und die Herrschaft des Würdigsten—Thuk. 2.37.1." *RhM* 109: 108–20.

Wachsmuth, Curt. 1890. *Die Stadt Athen im Altertum*. Vol. 2. Leipzig.

Wackernagel, Jacob. 1916. *Sprachliche Untersuchungen zu Homer*. Göttingen.

Wade-Gery, Henry T. 1924. "Jason of Pherae and Aleuas the Red." *JHS* 44: 55–64.

———. 1932. "Thucydides the Son of Melesias: A Study of Periklean Policy." *JHS* 52: 205–27.

———. 1933. "Classical Epigrams and Epitaphs: A Study of the Kimonian Age." *JHS* 53: 71–104.

———. 1949. "Hesiod." *Phoenix* 3: 81–93.

———. 1958. *Essays in Greek History*. Oxford.

Walbank, Frank W. 1951. "The Problem of Greek Nationality." *Phoenix* 5: 41–60.

Walbank, Michael B. 1978. *Athenian Proxenies of the Fifth Century B.C.* Toronto.

Walde, Alois, and J. B. Hofmann. 1965. *Lateinisches etymologisches Wörterbuch*. Vol. 1. 4th ed. Heidelberg.

Walde, Alois, and Julius Pokorny. 1927. *Vergleichendes Wörterbuch der indogermanischen Sprache*. Vol. 1. Berlin.

Wallace, Robert W. 1989. *The Areopagus Council, to 307 B.C.* Baltimore.

———. 1994. "Private Lives and Public Enemies: Freedom of Thought in Classical Athens." In Boegehold and Scafuro 1994: 127–55.

———. 1996. "Law, Freedom, and the Concept of Citizens' Rights in Democratic Athens." In Ober and Hedrick 1996: 105–19.

———. 1998. "Solonian Democracy." In Morris and Raaflaub 1998: 11–29.

———. Forthcoming. *Freedom and Democracy in Ancient Athens*.

Wallinga, H. T. 1993. *Ships and Sea-Power before the Great Persian War*. Leiden.

Walser, Gerold. 1959. "Zur Beurteilung der Perserkriege in der neueren Forschung." *Schweizerische Beiträge zur allgemeinen Geschichte* 17: 219–40.

———. 1975. "Zum griechisch-persischen Verhältnis vor dem Hellenismus." *HZ* 220: 529–42.

———. 1984. *Hellas und Iran: Studien zu den griechisch-persischen Beziehungen vor Alexander*. Darmstadt.

———. 1987. "Persischer Imperialismus und griechische Freiheit." In Sancisi-Weerdenburg and Kuhrt 1987: 155–65.

Walter, Uwe. 1993a. "Herodot und die Ursachen des Ionischen Aufstandes." *Historia* 42: 257–78.

———. 1993b. *An der Polis teilhaben: Bürgerstaat und Zugehörigkeit im archaischen Griechenland*. Historia Einzelschriften 82. Stuttgart.

Walters, K. R. 1976. "The 'Ancestral Constitution' and Fourth-Century Historiography in Athens." *AJAH* 1: 129–44.

Warnach, W. 1971. "Autarkie." *HWPh* 1: 685–90.

Waters, K. H. 1966. "The Purpose of Dramatisation in Herodotus." *Historia* 15: 157–71.

———. 1985. *Herodotos the Historian: His Problems, Methods, and Originality.* Norman, Okla.

Weber, H. 1908. *Aristophanes-Studien.* Leipzig.

Weeber, Karl-Wilhelm. 1973. "Ein vernachlässigtes solonisches Gesetz." *Athenaeum,* n.s., 51: 30–33.

Wees, Hans van. 1992. *Status Warriors: Violence and Society in Homer and History.* Amsterdam.

———. 1994. "The Homeric Way of War: The *Iliad* and the Hoplite Phalanx." *G&R* 41: 1–18, 131–55.

———. 1997. "Homeric Warfare." In Morris and Powell 1997: 668–93.

———. 1998. "Greeks Bearing Arms: The State, the Leisure Class, and the Display of Weapons in Archaic Greece." In Fisher and van Wees 1998: 333–78.

———. 2000. "The Development of the Hoplite Phalanx: Iconography and Reality in the Seventh Century." In Hans van Wees, ed., *War and Violence in Ancient Greece,* 125–66. London and Swansea.

Weiler, Ingomar. 1968. "Greek and Non-Greek World in the Archaic Period." *GRBS* 9: 21–29.

Welles, C. Bradford. 1965. "Greek Liberty." *Journal of Juristic Papyrology* 15: 29–47.

Welsh, D. 1983. "The Chorus of Aristophanes' *Babylonians.*" *GRBS* 24: 137–50.

Welskopf, Elisabeth C. 1964. "Einige Probleme der Sklaverei in der griechisch-römischen Welt." *Acta Antiqua Academiae Scientiarum Hungaricae* 12: 311–58.

———, ed. 1981–85. *Soziale Typenbegriffe im alten Griechenland und ihr Fortleben in den Sprachen der Welt.* 7 vols. Berlin.

Welter, Gabriel. 1938. *Aigina.* Berlin.

Welwei, Karl-Wilhelm. 1967. "Der 'Diapsephismos' nach dem Sturz der Peisistratiden." *Gymnasium* 74: 423–37. Repr. in Welwei 2000: 155–69.

———. 1970. "Die Marathon-Epigramme von der athenischen Agora." *Historia* 19: 295–305. Repr. in Welwei 2000: 180–90.

———. 1974. *Unfreie im antiken Kriegsdienst.* Vol. 1, *Athen und Sparta.* Wiesbaden.

———. 1979. "Das sog. Grab der Plataier im Vranatal bei Marathon." *Historia* 28: 101–6. Repr. in Welwei 2000: 191–96.

———. 1981. "Adel und Demos in der frühen Polis." *Gymnasium* 88: 1–23. Repr. in Welwei 2000: 64–86.

———. 1983. *Die griechische Polis: Verfassung und Gesellschaft in archaischer und klassischer Zeit.* Stuttgart.

———. 1992. *Athen: Vom neolithischen Siedlungsplatz zur archaischen Grosspolis.* Darmstadt.

———. 1996. "Zur 'Herrschaftsterminologie' in der Quadrupelallianz von 420 v. Chr." *ZPE* 111: 88–92. Repr. in Welwei 2000: 229–33.

———. 1999. *Das klassische Athen: Demokratie und Machtpolitik im 5. und 4. Jahrhundert.* Darmstadt.

———. 2000. *Polis und Arché: Kleine Schriften zu Gesellschafts- und Herrschaftsstrukturen in der griechischen Welt.* Ed. Mischa Meier. *Historia* Einzelschriften 146. Stuttgart.

Werner, Robert. 1971. "Probleme der Rechtsbeziehungen zwischen Metropolis und Apoikie." *Chiron* 1: 19–73.

West, Martin L. 1966. *Hesiod,* Theogony: *Edited with Prolegomena and Commentary.* Oxford.

———. 1978. *Hesiod,* Works and Days: *Edited with Prolegomena and Commentary.* Oxford.

———. 1985. *The Hesiodic Catalogue of Women.* Oxford.

———. 1995. "The Date of the Iliad." *MH* 52: 203–19.

————, ed. 1992. *Iambi et Elegi Graeci ante Alexandrum Cantati*, Vol. 2. 2d ed. Oxford.

West, William C. 1970. "Saviors of Greece." *GRBS* 11: 271–82.

————. 1977. "Hellenic *Homonoia* and the New Decree from Plataea." *GRBS* 18: 307–19.

Westermann, William L. 1935. "Sklaverei." *RE* Suppl. 6: 894–1068.

————. 1955. *The Slave-Systems of Greek and Roman Antiquity*. Philadelphia.

Westlake, Henry D. 1936. "The Medism of Thessaly." *JHS* 56: 12–24.

Wheeler, Marcus. 1955. "Self-Sufficiency and the Greek City." *JHI* 16: 416–20.

Whibley, Leonard. 1896. *Greek Oligarchies*. London. Repr., Chicago, 1975.

Whitehead, David. 1977. *The Ideology of the Athenian Metic*. *PCPhS* Suppl. 4. Cambridge.

————. 1984. "Immigrant Communities in the Classical Polis." *AC* 53: 47–59.

————. 1986a. *The Demes of Attica, 508/507–ca. 250 B.C.: A Political and Social Study*. Princeton.

————. 1986b. "The Ideology of the Athenian Metic: Some Pendants and a Reappraisal." *PCPhS*, n.s., 32: 145–58.

————. 1991. "Norms of Citizenship in Ancient Greece." In Molho et al. 1991: 135–54.

————. 1993. "Samian Autonomy." In Rosen and Farrell 1993: 321–29.

Wick, T. E. 1977. "Thucydides and the Megarian Decree." *AC* 46: 74–99.

Wickert, Konrad. 1961. *Der Peloponnesische Bund von seiner Entstehung bis zum Ende des Archidamischen Krieges*. Diss., Univ. of Erlangen-Nürnberg.

Wickert-Micknat, Gisela. 1983. *Unfreiheit im Zeitalter der homerischen Epen*. Forsch. zur ant. Sklaverei 16. Wiesbaden.

Widmann, Günter. 1967. *Autarkie und Philia in den aristotelischen Ethiken*. Diss., Univ. of Tübingen.

Wieacker, Franz. 1967. "Die XII Tafeln in ihrem Jahrhundert." In Olivier Reverdin, ed., *Les origines de la république romaine*, 291–359. Vandoeuvres and Geneva.

Wilamowitz-Möllendorff, Ulrich von. 1884a. "*Eleutherion hydōr*." *Hermes* 19: 463–65.

————. 1884b. *Homerische Untersuchungen*. Berlin.

————. 1913. *Sappho und Simonides: Untersuchungen über griechische Lyriker*. Berlin.

————. 1922. *Pindaros*. Berlin.

Will, Edouard. 1954. "Sur l'évolution des rapports entre colonies et métropoles en Grèce à partir du VIe siècle." *Nouvelle Clio* 6: 413–60.

————. 1955. *Korinthiaka*. Paris.

————. 1956. *Doriens et Ioniens: Essai sur la valeur du critère ethnique appliqué à l'étude de l'histoire et de la civilisation grecques*. Paris.

————. 1957. "Aux origines du régime foncier grec: Homère, Hésiode et l'arrière-plan mycénien." *REA* 59: 5–50.

————. 1965. "La Grèce archaïque." In *Second International Conference of Economic History, Aix-en-Provence, 1962*, vol. 1, *Trade and Politics in the Ancient World*, 41–115. Paris.

————. 1967. "Bulletin historique: Histoire grecque." *RH* 238: 377–452.

————. 1972. *Le monde grec et l'orient*. Vol. 1, *Le Ve siècle (510–403)*. Paris.

Will, Ernest. 1965. "Hésiode: Crise agraire? Ou recul de l'aristocratie?" *REG* 78: 542–56.

Willetts, Ronald F. 1954. "Freedmen at Gortyna." *CQ*, n.s., 4: 216–19.

————. 1955. *Aristocratic Society in Ancient Crete*. London.

————. 1965. *Ancient Crete: A Social History from Early Times until the Roman Occupation*. London.

————. 1967. *The Law Code of Gortyn, Edited with Introduction, Translation and a Commentary*. *Kadmos* Suppl. 1. Berlin.

Williams, G. M. E. 1978. "The Kerameikos Ostraka." *ZPE* 31: 103–13.

———. 1980. "The Image of the Alkmeonidai between 490 B.C. and 487/6 B.C." *Historia* 29: 106–10.

Wills, Gary. 1992. "Athena's Magic." *New York Review of Books,* Dec. 17, 47–50.

Wilpert, P. 1950. "Autarkie." *RAC* 1: 1039–50.

Winton, Richard I. 1981. "Thucydides 1,97,2: The *'arche* of the Athenians' and the Athenian Empire." *MH* 38: 147–52.

Wirszubski, Chaim. 1950. Libertas *as a Political Idea at Rome during the Late Republic and Early Principate.* Cambridge.

Wirth, Gerhard, ed. 1979. *Perikles und seine Zeit.* Wege der Forschung 412. Darmstadt.

Wohl, Victoria. 1999. "The Eros of Alcibiades." *CA* 18: 349–85.

Wolf, Erik. 1950. *Griechisches Rechtsdenken.* Vol. 1, *Vorsokratiker und frühe Dichter.* Frankfurt am Main.

Wolff, Hartmut. 1979. "Die Opposition gegen die radikale Demokratie in Athen bis zum Jahre 411 v. Chr." *ZPE* 36: 279–302.

Wolski, Józef. 1973. "*Mēdismos* et son importance en Grèce à l'époque des Guerres Médiques." *Historia* 22: 3–15.

Woodhead, Arthur Geoffrey. 1967. "*Isēgoria* and the Council of 500." *Historia* 16: 129–40.

———. 1970. *Thucydides on the Nature of Power.* Martin Classical Lectures. Cambridge, Mass.

Woodhouse, William J. 1938. *Solon the Liberator.* Oxford. Repr., New York, 1965.

Wuilleumier, Pierre. 1968. *Tarente des origines à la conquête romaine.* Paris.

Wundsam, Klaus. 1968. *Die politische und soziale Struktur in den mykenischen Residenzen nach den Linear B-Texten.* Vienna.

Wüst, Fritz R. 1954–55. "Amphiktyonie, Eidgenossenschaft, Symmachie." *Historia* 3: 129–53.

Wycherley, R. E. 1957. *Literary and Epigraphical Testimonia.* Athenian Agora 3. Princeton.

———. 1978. *The Stones of Athens.* Princeton.

Yuge, Toro, and Masaoki Doi, eds. 1988. *Forms of Control and Subordination in Antiquity.* Leiden.

Zambelli, M. 1975. "L'origine della Bule dei Cinquecento." *MGR* 4: 103–34.

Zeller, Eduard. 1910. *Kleine Schriften.* Vol. 1. Ed. Otto Leuze. Berlin.

Ziegler, Konrat. 1913. "Himera." *RE* 8: 1613–20.

Zuntz, Günther. 1955. *The Political Plays of Euripides.* Manchester, England.

Index of Terms

aequa libertas, 266
akolasia, 224, 233
anarchia, 233
anax, 32, 42
andrapodismos, andrapodizein, 129, 322n.56
anomia, 55, 94, 252
apeleutheros, 315n.212
apetairoi, 15
aphrētōr, 294n.84
apragmōn, 340n.112
archē, 105, 119, 122, 125, 130, 132–33, 134–43, 179, 198, 207, 259, 319n.6, 335n.27
archesthai, 129
archos, 70
aretē, 26, 64, 233–34, 350n.117
aristokratia, 213, 227, 355n.2
astai, 44
atē, 38
athemistos, 294n.84
Athēnaios, 298n.146
atimētos, 297n.142
atimoi, 51
auctoritas, 265
autarkeia, autarkēs, 8, 119, 147, 184–87, 259, 261, 274, 338nn. 95–97, 339nn. 98–100; *autarkestatē polis*, 184, 187
autetelēs, 259, 328n.151
autodikos, 259, 328n.151
autognōtos, 332n.201
autokratōr, 259, 337n.79, 349n.111
autonomia, autonomos, 8, 119, 147–60, 257, 259, 284n.12, 328nn. 150–51, 332n.201, 337n.79
autopolis, 145

autopolitēs, 145, 259
auxilium, 266

banausoi, 244
bandakā, 313n.189
basileus, 32, 42, 102, 131, 291n.46
beltistoi, 238, 240

cives sine suffragio, 15, 286n.53

dasmos isos, 310n.161
dēmion, 293n.75, 344n.22
dēmokratia, 8, 206–7, 209–10, 213, 220, 222, 228–29, 262–63, 275
dēmos, 206, 208, 214, 220, 226, 237, 242–43, 334n.240, 344n.22; *dēmos anassei*, 345n.46
dēmotikos, 275–76; *dēmotikōtatos*, 350n.133
despoina, 298n.157, 299n.161
despotēs, 42, 54, 57, 61, 129, 176, 234, 252, 260–61, 298nn. 157–58, 299n.161
diapsēphismos, 219, 297n.141
didonai heautous, 76–78
dignitas, 265
dikastēria, 347n.77
dikē, 9, 38–39, 56
dmōs, dmōiē, 22, 287n.69, 288n.85, 289n.11, 291nn. 51, 53, 294n.93
doero, 19–22, 287nn. 70, 74
dōma, 288n.85, 291n.53
doulē, 28, 288n.2
douleia, 73, 79, 128–32, 134–41, 154, 162, 173, 209, 319n.11, 321n.40, 323n.73
douleion eidos, 288n.2

Index of Selected Ancient Sources

General Index

Acanthus, 149–50, 225
accountability, 141
Adeimantus, 63, 308n.122
Aegina, 64, 68, 83, 112, 116, 131–32, 135–36, 145, 148–50, 160, 197, 322n.58, 325n.95, 326nn. 106–7, 332n.206, 333n.220
Aeschylus, 86, 89, 171, 205
Aetna, 61, 90
Agesilaus, 188
Agora, Athenian, 62–63, 113, 191, 312n.182, 315n.217
Alcaeus, 26, 28, 91, 93
Alcibiades, 83, 126, 130, 187, 189, 194, 200, 204, 216, 238–39, 343n.8
Alcidas, 197
Alcmaeonids, 82, 314n.206
Alcmaeon of Croton, 95
Alexander the Great, 103, 117
alliance, 68–69, 72, 74–75, 118–19, 149–50, 152, 253. *See also* Delian League; Peloponnesian League
Amasis of Egypt, 68
Amphictyony, Delphic, 73, 335n.21
Amphipolis, 198
Anacreon, 27, 58
anarchy, 230, 233, 235, 242
Anaximander, 94
Andromache, 44, 293n.73
annual rotation, 227–28, 263
annuity, 266
Apollo, 104, 114–15, 140, 170
arbitration, 183–84
Arcadia, 123
Archidamus, 172, 197, 330n.177

Archilochus, 45
archon, 71–72, 312n.183; archonship, 217
Areopagus Council, 211, 214, 268, 312n.183, 345n.42
Arginusae trial, 352n.150
Argolid, 304n.72
Argos, 69, 83, 125, 145, 192–93, 198, 206, 302n.42, 320nn. 15, 28, 331nn. 188, 195
Aristagoras of Miletus, 80, 81, 169, 308n.125
Aristides, 104, 118, 145
aristocracy, 31–32, 40–41, 44, 47–48, 51, 81, 83, 91–99, 204, 208–12, 214–16, 218, 220, 223, 226–27, 236, 238, 243–47, 251–52, 254–55, 265–71, 273–74, 289n.26, 291nn. 46, 48–49
Aristophanes (comic poet), 131, 133–34, 141, 167, 175
Aristophanes of Boeotia, 303n.58
Aristotle, 10–11, 185, 230–31, 247–48
Artemis Elaphebolia, 71; Soteira, 314n.210
Artemisium, 62, 64
Asia, 308n.117
Asopus river, 76
assembly, 34–35, 40, 99, 124, 206, 217–18, 254, 268, 293n.75, 344n.21; Athenian, 139–40, 210–11, 222, 228, 262, 269, 306n.105
Astyanax, 33, 293n.67
Athena, 33, 102, 107, 109, 115, 314n.206; Hellania, 112; Mistress of Athens (*Athenōn medeousa*), 139, 331n.192; Nike, 115–16, 191; Polias, 115, 318n.240; Promachos, 115; protectress of Athenian empire, 140, 191, 262; Soteira, 113, 316n.222; Syllania, 112
Athenagoras, 237, 352n.164

413